MznLnx

Missing Links Exam Preps

Exam Prep for

Physical Geology

Plummer & McGeary & Carlson, 10th Edition

The MznLnx Exam Prep is your link from the texbook and lecture to your exams.
The MznLnx Exam Preps are unauthorized and comprehensive reviews of your textbooks.

All material provided by MznLnx and Rico Publications (c) 2010
Textbook publishers and textbook authors do not particpate in or contribute to these reviews.

MznLnx

Rico
Publications

Exam Prep for Physical Geology
10th Edition
Plummer & McGeary & Carlson

Publisher: Raymond Houge
Assistant Editor: Michael Rouger
Text and Cover Designer: Lisa Buckner
Marketing Manager: Sara Swagger
Project Manager, Editorial Production: Jerry Emerson
Art Director: Vernon Lowerui

Product Manager: Dave Mason
Editorial Assitant: Rachel Guzmanji
Pedagogy: Debra Long
Cover Image: Jim Reed/Getty Images
Text and Cover Printer: City Printing, Inc.
Compositor: Media Mix, Inc.

(c) 2010 Rico Publications
ALL RIGHTS RESERVED. No part of this work
covered by the copyright may be reproduced or
used in any form or by an means--graphic, electronic,
or mechanical, including photocopying, recording,
taping, Web distribution, information storage, and
retrieval systems, or in any other manner--without the
written permission of the publisher.

Printed in the United States
ISBN:

For more information about our products, contact us at:
Dave.Mason@RicoPublications.com

For permission to use material from this text or
product, submit a request online to:
Dave.Mason@RicoPublications.com

Contents

CHAPTER 1
Introducing Geology and an Overview of Important Concepts   1

CHAPTER 2
Atoms, Elements, and Minerals   12

CHAPTER 3
Igneous Rocks, Intrusive Activity, and the Origin of Igneous Rocks   30

CHAPTER 4
Volcanism and Extrusive Rocks   48

CHAPTER 5
Weathering and Soil   72

CHAPTER 6
Sediment and Sedimentary Rocks   95

CHAPTER 7
Metamorphism, Metamorphic Rocks, and Hydrothermal Rocks   121

CHAPTER 8
Time and Geology   143

CHAPTER 9
Mass Wasting   164

CHAPTER 10
Streams and Floods   178

CHAPTER 11
Ground Water   198

CHAPTER 12
Glaciers and Glaciation   216

CHAPTER 13
Deserts and Wind Action   239

CHAPTER 14
Waves, Beaches, and Coasts   257

CHAPTER 15
Geologic Structures   270

CHAPTER 16
Earthquakes   286

CHAPTER 17
Earth's Interior and Geophysical Properties   303

CHAPTER 18
The Sea Floor   326

CHAPTER 19
Plate Tectonics   350

CHAPTER 20
Mountain Belts and the Continental Crust   375

Contents (Cont.)

CHAPTER 21
  Geologic Resources   393
CHAPTER 22
  The Earth`s Companions   419
ANSWER KEY   433

TO THE STUDENT

COMPREHENSIVE

The *MznLnx* Exam Prep series is designed to help you pass your exams. Editors at MznLnx review your textbooks and then prepare these practice exams to help you master the textbook material. Unlike study guides, workbooks, and practice tests provided by the texbook publisher and textbook authors, *MznLnx* gives you **all** of the material in each chapter in exam form, not just samples, so you can be sure to nail your exam.

MECHANICAL

The MznLnx Exam Prep series creates exams that will help you learn the subject matter as well as test you on your understanding. Each question is designed to help you master the concept. Just working through the exams, you gain an understanding of the subject--its a simple mechanical process that produces success.

INTEGRATED STUDY GUIDE AND REVIEW

MznLnx is not just a set of exams designed to test you, its also a comprehensive review of the subject content. Each exam question is also a review of the concept, making sure that you will get the answer correct without having to go to other sources of material. You learn as you go! Its the easiest way to pass an exam.

HUMOR

Studying can be tedious and dry. MznLnx's instructional design includes moderate humor within the exam questions on occassion, to break the tedium and revitalize the brain

Chapter 1. Introducing Geology and an Overview of Important Concepts 1

1. The _____ is chemically divided into layers. The Earth has an outer silicate solid crust, a highly viscous mantle, a liquid outer core that is much less viscous than the mantle, and a solid inner core. Many of the rocks now making up the Earth's crust formed less than 100 million ago.
   a. Earth's interior0
   b. Thing
   c. Undefined
   d. Undefined

2. An _____ is the result from the sudden release of stored energy in the Earth's crust that creates seismic waves. At the Earth's surface, earthquakes may manifest themselves by a shaking or displacement of the ground. An _____ is caused by tectonic plates getting stuck and putting a strain on the ground. The strain becomes so great that rocks give way by breaking and sliding along fault planes.
   a. Thing
   b. Earthquake0
   c. Undefined
   d. Undefined

3. _____ is Solar Radiation emitted from our sun. It has been used in many traditional technologies for centuries, and has come into widespread use where other power supplies are absent, such as in remote locations and in space.
   a. Thing
   b. Solar power0
   c. Undefined
   d. Undefined

4. An _____ is a layer of gases that may surround a material body of sufficient mass. The gases are attracted by the gravity of the body, and are retained for a longer duration if gravity is high and the _____'s temperature is low. Some planets consist mainly of various gases, and thus have very deep atmospheres.
   a. Atmosphere0
   b. Place
   c. Undefined
   d. Undefined

5. A _____ is a body of water with a current, confined within a bed and banks. Streams are important as conduits in the water cycle, instruments in aquifer recharge, and corridors for fish and wildlife migration.
   a. Thing
   b. Stream0
   c. Undefined
   d. Undefined

6. _____ is a small island located in the middle of San Francisco Bay in California, United States. It served as a lighthouse, then a military fortification, then a military prison followed by a federal prison until 1963, when it became a national recreation area.
   a. Place
   b. Alcatraz Island0
   c. Undefined
   d. Undefined

7. A _____ is a section of a river of relatively steep gradient causing an increase in water flow and turbulence. A _____ is a hydrological feature between a run and a cascade. It is characterized by the river becoming shallower and having some rocks exposed above the flow surface.
   a. Rapid0
   b. Thing
   c. Undefined
   d. Undefined

8. In geology, a _____ is the outermost layer of a planet, part of its lithosphere. They are generally composed of a less dense material than its deeper layers. Earths' is composed mainly of basalt and granite. It is cooler and more rigid than the deeper layers of the mantle and core.
   a. Thing
   b. Crust0
   c. Undefined
   d. Undefined

Chapter 1. Introducing Geology and an Overview of Important Concepts

9. Earth's _____ is a ~2,900 km thick rocky shell comprizing approximately 70% of Earth's volume. It is predominantly solid and overlies the Earth's iron-rich core, which occupies about 30% of Earth's volume. Past episodes of melting and volcanism at the shallower levels of the _____ have produced a very thin crust of crystallized melt products near the surface, upon which we live.
   a. Mantle0
   b. Thing
   c. Undefined
   d. Undefined

10. _____ is the part of Earth's lithosphere that surfaces in the ocean basins. _____ is primarily composed of mafic rocks, or sima. It is thinner than continental crust, or sial, generally less than 10 kilometers thick, however it is more dense, having a mean density of about 3.3 grams per cubic centimeter.
    a. Thing
    b. Oceanic crust0
    c. Undefined
    d. Undefined

11. The _____ is the layer of granitic, sedimentary, and metamorphic rocks which form the continents and the areas of shallow seabed close to their shores, known as continental shelves. It is less dense than the material of the Earth's mantle and thus "floats" on top of it. _____ is also less dense than oceanic crust, though it is considerably thicker. About 40% of the Earth's surface is now underlain by _____.
    a. Thing
    b. Continental crust0
    c. Undefined
    d. Undefined

12. A _____ is one of several large landmasses on Earth. They are generally identified by convention rather than any strict criteria, but seven areas are commonly reckoned as continents – they are: Asia, Africa, North America, South America, Antarctica, Europe, and Australia.
    a. Thing
    b. Continent0
    c. Undefined
    d. Undefined

13. An _____ is a term for any perforation through the Earth's surface designed to find and release both petroleum oil and gas hydrocarbons.
    a. Oil well0
    b. Thing
    c. Undefined
    d. Undefined

14. The _____ is the region of the Earth between 100-200 km below the surface that is the weak or "soft" zone in the upper mantle. It lies just below the lithosphere, which is involved in plate movements and isostatic adjustments. In spite of its heat, pressures keep it plastic, and it has a relatively low density. Seismic waves pass relatively slowly through the _____.
    a. Thing
    b. Asthenosphere0
    c. Undefined
    d. Undefined

15. The _____ is the solid outermost shell of a rocky planet. On the Earth, the _____ includes the crust and the uppermost mantle which is joined to the crust across the Mohorovièiæ discontinuity. _____ is underlain by asthenosphere, the weaker, hotter, and deeper part of the upper mantle.
    a. Lithosphere0
    b. Thing
    c. Undefined
    d. Undefined

Chapter 1. Introducing Geology and an Overview of Important Concepts 3

16. A _____ is a natural depression or hole in the surface topography caused by the removal of soil or bedrock, often both, by water. They may vary in size from less than a meter to several hundred meters both in diameter and depth, and vary in form from soil-lined bowls to bedrock-edged chasms.
   a. Sinkhole0
   b. Thing
   c. Undefined
   d. Undefined

17. _____ is the science and study of the solid matter that constitute the Earth. Encompassing such things as rocks, soil, and gemstones, _____ studies the composition, structure, physical properties, history, and the processes that shape Earth's components.
   a. Geology0
   b. Thing
   c. Undefined
   d. Undefined

18. _____ is a field of study within geology concerned generally with the structures within the crust of the Earth, or other planets, and particularly with the forces and movements that have operated in a region to create these structures.
   a. Tectonics0
   b. Thing
   c. Undefined
   d. Undefined

19. A _____ is a landform that extends above the surrounding terrain in a limited area. A _____ is generally steeper than a hill, but there is no universally accepted standard definition for the height of a _____ or a hill although a _____ usually has an identifiable summit.
   a. Mountain0
   b. Place
   c. Undefined
   d. Undefined

20. A _____ is a group of mountains bordered by lowlands or separated from other mountain ranges by passes or rivers. Individual mountains within the same _____ do not necessarily have the same geology; they may be a mix of different orogeny, for example volcanoes, uplifted mountains or fold mountains and may, therefore, be of different rock.
   a. Mountain range0
   b. Thing
   c. Undefined
   d. Undefined

21. _____ is a theory of geology that has been developed to explain the observed evidence for large scale motions of the Earth's lithosphere. The theory encompassed and superseded the older theory of continental drift.
   a. Plate tectonics0
   b. Thing
   c. Undefined
   d. Undefined

22. In plate tectonics, a _____ a linear feature that exists between two tectonic plates that are moving away from each other. These areas can form in the middle of continents but eventually form ocean basins.
   a. Thing
   b. Divergent plate boundary0
   c. Undefined
   d. Undefined

23. In plate tectonics, a _____ is an actively deforming region where two tectonic plates or fragments of lithosphere move towards one another. When two plates move toward one another, they form either a subduction zone or a continental collision.
   a. Thing
   b. Convergent boundary0
   c. Undefined
   d. Undefined

Chapter 1. Introducing Geology and an Overview of Important Concepts

24. A _____ is a type of excavation or depression in the ground. They are generally defined by being deeper than they are wide, and by being narrow compared to their length.
    a. Thing
    b. Trench0
    c. Undefined
    d. Undefined

25. A _____ is a geological feature that is also known as a Rip in the earth causing magma to flow out and forming an undersea volcano, it also has geological features, a continuous elevational crest for some distance. Ridges are usually termed hills or mountains as well, depending on size.
    a. Ridge0
    b. Thing
    c. Undefined
    d. Undefined

26. _____ refers to the movement of the Earth's continents relative to each other. _____ is a concept that said the shapes of continents on either side of the Atlantic Ocean seem to fit together and the similarity of southern continent fossil faunae could mean that all the continents had once been joined into a supercontinent. It was suggested that the continents had been pulled apart by the centrifugal pseudoforce of the Earth's rotation.
    a. Continental drift0
    b. Thing
    c. Undefined
    d. Undefined

27. _____ is a 16-ton, manned deep-ocean research submersible owned by the United States Navy and operated by the Woods Hole Oceanographic Institution in Woods Hole, Massachusetts. The three-person vessel allows for two scientists and one pilot to dive for up to nine hours at 4500 metersor 15,000 feet.
    a. Alvin0
    b. Thing
    c. Undefined
    d. Undefined

28. In geology, a _____ is a place where the Earth's crust and lithosphere are being pulled apart.
    a. Thing
    b. Rift0
    c. Undefined
    d. Undefined

29. A _____ in geology is a valley created by the formation of a rift.
    a. Rift valley0
    b. Thing
    c. Undefined
    d. Undefined

30. In geology, a _____ is a depression with predominant extent in one direction. The terms U-shaped and V-shaped are descriptive terms of geography to characterize the form of valleys. Most valleys belong to one of these two main types or a mixture of them, at least with respect of the cross section of the slopes or hillsides.
    a. Thing
    b. Valley0
    c. Undefined
    d. Undefined

31. _____ is molten rock located beneath the surface of the Earth, and which often collects in a _____ chamber. _____ is a complex high-temperature fluid substance. Most are silicate solutions. It is capable of intrusion into adjacent rocks or of extrusion onto the surface as lava or ejected explosively as tephra to form pyroclastic rock. Environments of _____ formation include subduction zones, continental rift zones, mid-oceanic ridges, and hotspots, some of which are interpreted as mantle plumes.
    a. Magma0
    b. Thing
    c. Undefined
    d. Undefined

Chapter 1. Introducing Geology and an Overview of Important Concepts 5

32. _____ is the process of heating a solid substance to a point where it turns into a liquid. An object that has melted is molten.
   a. Melting0
   b. Thing
   c. Undefined
   d. Undefined

33. A _____ is a large underground pool of molten rock lying under the surface of the earth's crust. The molten rock in such a chamber is under great pressure, and given enough time and pressure can gradually fracture the rock around it creating outlets for the magma.
   a. Thing
   b. Magma chamber0
   c. Undefined
   d. Undefined

34. The _____ is the second-largest of the world's oceanic divisions; with a total area of about 106.4 million square kilometres , it covers approximately one-fifth of the Earth's surface. The _____ occupies an elongated, S-shaped basin extending longitudinally between the Americas to the west, and Eurasia and Africa to the east.
   a. Place
   b. Atlantic Ocean0
   c. Undefined
   d. Undefined

35. In plate tectonics, a _____ is said to occur when tectonic plates slide and grind against each other along a transform fault. The relative motion of such plates is horizontal in either sinistral or dextral direction. Many transform boundaries are locked in tension before suddenly releasing, and causing earthquakes.
   a. Thing
   b. Transform boundary0
   c. Undefined
   d. Undefined

36. The _____ is a geological fault that runs a length of roughly 800 miles through western and southern California in the United States. The fault, a right-lateral strike-slip fault, marks a transform boundary between the Pacific Plate and the North American Plate.
   a. Thing
   b. San Andreas fault0
   c. Undefined
   d. Undefined

37. Faults are planar rock fractures, which show evidence of relative movement. Large faults within the Earth's crust are the result of shear motion and active _____ zones are the causal locations of most earthquakes. Earthquakes are caused by energy release during rapid slippage along faults. The largest examples are at tectonic plate boundaries but many faults occur far from active plate boundaries. Since faults do not usually consist of a single, clean fracture, the term _____ zone is used when referring to the zone of complex deformation that is associated with the _____ plane.
   a. Fault0
   b. Thing
   c. Undefined
   d. Undefined

38. In geology, a _____ zone is an area on Earth where two tectonic plates meet and move towards one another, with one sliding underneath the other and moving down into the mantle, at rates typically measured in centimeters per year. An oceanic plate ordinarily slides underneath a continental plate; this often creates an orogenic zone with many volcanoes and earthquakes.
   a. Subduction0
   b. Thing
   c. Undefined
   d. Undefined

6 *Chapter 1. Introducing Geology and an Overview of Important Concepts*

39. A _____ is an area on Earth where two tectonic plates meet and move towards one another, with one sliding underneath the other and moving down into the mantle, at rates typically measured in centimeters per year. In a sense, subduction zones are the opposite of divergent boundaries, areas where material rises up from the mantle and plates are moving apart.
- a. Subduction zone0
- b. Thing
- c. Undefined
- d. Undefined

40. The _____ are hemispheric-scale long but narrow topographic depressions of the sea floor. They are also the deepest parts of the ocean floor. Trenches define one of the most important natural boundaries on the Earth's solid surface, that between two lithospheric plates. There are three types of lithospheric plate boundaries: divergent, convergent, and transform. Trenches are the spectacular and distinctive morphological features of convergent plate boundaries.
- a. Thing
- b. Oceanic trenches0
- c. Undefined
- d. Undefined

41. _____ is the result of the transformation of a pre-existing rock type, the protolith, in a process called metamorphism, which means "change in form". The protolith is subjected to heat and extreme pressure causing profound physical and/or chemical change. The protolith may be sedimentary rock, igneous rock or another older rock.
- a. Metamorphic rock0
- b. Thing
- c. Undefined
- d. Undefined

42. Metamorphic rock is the result of the transformation of a pre-existing rock type, the protolith, in a process called metamorphism. The protolith is subjected to heat and extreme pressure causing profound physical and/or chemical change. _____ make up a large part of the Earth's crust. They are formed deep beneath the Earth's surface by great stresses from rocks above and high pressures and temperatures.
- a. Thing
- b. Metamorphic rocks0
- c. Undefined
- d. Undefined

43. _____ can be defined as the solid state recrystallisation of pre-existing rocks due to changes in heat and/or pressure and/or introduction of fluids. There will be mineralogical, chemical and crystallographic changes. _____ produced with increasing pressure and temperature conditions is known as prograde _____. Conversely, decreasing temperatures and pressure characterize retrograde _____.
- a. Metamorphism0
- b. Thing
- c. Undefined
- d. Undefined

44. Mean _____ is the average height of the sea, with reference to a suitable reference surface.
- a. Thing
- b. Sea level0
- c. Undefined
- d. Undefined

45. _____ rock is one of the three main rock groups. Rock formed from these covers 75% of the Earth's land area, and includes common types such as chalk, limestone, dolomite, sandstone, and shale.
- a. Thing
- b. Sedimentary0
- c. Undefined
- d. Undefined

Chapter 1. Introducing Geology and an Overview of Important Concepts

46. _____ is one of the three main rock groups. _____ covers 75% of the Earth's land area. Four basic processes are involved in the formation of a clastic _____: weathering caused mainly by friction of waves, transportation where the sediment is carried along by a current, deposition and compaction where the sediment is squashed together to form a rock of this kind.
   a. Sedimentary rock0
   b. Thing
   c. Undefined
   d. Undefined

47. _____ rocks form when molten rock, magma, cools and solidifies, with or without crystallization, either below the surface as intrusive, plutonic rocks or on the surface as extrusive, volcanic, rocks.
   a. Thing
   b. Igneous0
   c. Undefined
   d. Undefined

48. _____ is a body of techniques for investigating phenomena and acquiring new knowledge, as well as for correcting and integrating previous knowledge. It is based on gathering observable, empirical and measurable evidence subject to specific principles of reasoning,
   a. Thing
   b. Scientific method0
   c. Undefined
   d. Undefined

49. _____ is the rise of land masses that were depressed by the huge weight of ice sheets during the last ice age, through a process known as isostatic depression. It affects northern Europe, especially Scotland and Scandinavia, Siberia, Canada, and the Great Lakes of Canada and the United States.
   a. Post glacial rebound0
   b. Thing
   c. Undefined
   d. Undefined

50. _____ is the rise of land masses that were depressed by the huge weight of ice sheets during the last ice age, through a process known as isostatic depression.
   a. Post-glacial rebound0
   b. Thing
   c. Undefined
   d. Undefined

51. A _____ in physical geography describes the collective mass of water found on, under, and over the surface of a planet.
   a. Thing
   b. Hydrosphere0
   c. Undefined
   d. Undefined

52. A _____ is a disturbance that propagates through space or spacetime, transferring energy and momentum and sometimes angular momentum.
   a. Thing
   b. Wave0
   c. Undefined
   d. Undefined

53. _____, in everyday life, is most familiar as the agency that endows objects with weight. _____ is responsible for keeping the Earth and the other planets in their orbits around the Sun; for the formation of tides; and for various other phenomena that we observe. _____ is also the reason for the very existence of the Earth, the Sun, and most macroscopic objects in the universe; without it, matter would not have coalesced into these large masses, and life, as we know it, would not exist.

Chapter 1. Introducing Geology and an Overview of Important Concepts

a. Gravitation0
b. Thing
c. Undefined
d. Undefined

54. A _____ is a large, slow moving river of ice, formed from compacted layers of snow, that slowly deforms and flows in response to gravity. _____ ice is the largest reservoir of fresh water on Earth, and second only to oceans as the largest reservoir of total water. Glaciers cover vast areas of polar regions but are restricted to the highest mountains in the tropics.
   a. Glacier0
   b. Thing
   c. Undefined
   d. Undefined

55. _____ is displacement of solids by the agents of ocean currents, wind, water, or ice by downward or down-slope movement in response to gravity or by living organisms.
   a. Thing
   b. Erosion0
   c. Undefined
   d. Undefined

56. _____ is a term used in Geology to refer to the state of gravitational equilibrium between the Earth's lithosphere and asthenosphere such that the tectonic plates "float" at an elevation which depends on their thickness and density. It is invoked to explain how different topographic heights can exist at the Earth's surface.
   a. Thing
   b. Isostasy0
   c. Undefined
   d. Undefined

57. An _____ is a large piece of freshwater ice that has broken off from a snow-formed glacier or ice shelf and is floating in open water. Typically, only one ninth of the volume of an _____ is above water. The shape of the remainder under the water can be difficult to surmise from looking at what is visible above the surface.
   a. Thing
   b. Iceberg0
   c. Undefined
   d. Undefined

58. _____ is the condition of a system in which competing influences are balanced.
   a. Equilibrium0
   b. Thing
   c. Undefined
   d. Undefined

59. _____ is a term used to describe a group of hydrous aluminium phyllosilicate minerals, that are typically less than 2 micrometres in diameter. _____ consists of a variety of phyllosilicate minerals rich in silicon and aluminium oxides and hydroxides which include variable amounts of structural water. Clays are generally formed by the chemical weathering of silicate-bearing rocks by carbonic acid but some are formed by hydrothermal activity.
   a. Clay0
   b. Thing
   c. Undefined
   d. Undefined

60. _____ is any particulate matter that can be transported by fluid flow and which eventually is deposited as a layer of solid particles on the bed or bottom of a body of water or other liquid.
   a. Thing
   b. Sediment0
   c. Undefined
   d. Undefined

61. _____ is the process of deposition of dissolved mineral components in the interstices of sediments. It is an important factor in the consolidation of coarse-grained clastic sedimentary rocks such as sandstones, conglomerates, or breccias during diagenesis or lithification. Cementing materials may include silica, carbonates, iron oxides, or clay minerals.

Chapter 1. Introducing Geology and an Overview of Important Concepts

a. Cementation0   b. Thing
c. Undefined   d. Undefined

62. The _____ is used by geologists and other scientists to describe the timing and relationships between events that have occurred during the history of Earth.
a. Thing   b. Geological time scale0
c. Undefined   d. Undefined

63. _____ is the geological process whereby material is added to a landform. This is the process by which wind and water create a sediment deposit, through the laying down of granular material that has been eroded and transported from another geographical location.
a. Thing   b. Deposition0
c. Undefined   d. Undefined

64. _____ forms when rock cools and solidifies either below the surface as intrusive rocks or on the surface as extrusive rocks. This magma can be derived from partial melts of pre-existing rocks in either the Earth's mantle or crust. Typically, the melting is caused by one or more of the following processes -- an increase in temperature, a decrease in pressure, or a change in composition.
a. Thing   b. Igneous rock0
c. Undefined   d. Undefined

65. A _____ is a geological phenomenon which includes a wide range of ground movement, such as rock falls, deep failure of slopes and shallow debris flows. Although gravity's action on an over-steepened slope is the primary reason for a _____, there are other contributing factors affecting the original slope stability.
a. Thing   b. Landslide0
c. Undefined   d. Undefined

66. The _____ is defined as the summation of all particles and energy that exist and the space-time in which all events occur.
a. Universe0   b. Place
c. Undefined   d. Undefined

67. _____ was a German interdisciplinary scientist and meteorologist, who became famous for his theory of continental drift.
a. Alfred Wegener0   b. Thing
c. Undefined   d. Undefined

68. _____ is the supercontinent that existed during the Paleozoic and Mesozoic eras before each of the component continents were separated into their current configuration.
a. Pangaea0   b. Event
c. Undefined   d. Undefined

69. In geology, a _____ is a land mass comprizing more than one continental core, or craton.
a. Thing   b. Supercontinent0
c. Undefined   d. Undefined

Chapter 1. Introducing Geology and an Overview of Important Concepts

70. Fossils are the mineralized or otherwise preserved remains or traces of animals, plants, and other organisms. The totality of fossils, both discovered and undiscovered, and their placement in fossiliferous rock formations and sedimentary layers is known as the _____ record.
    a. Fossil0
    b. Thing
    c. Undefined
    d. Undefined

71. _____ is an ecological concept referring to the relative representation of a species in a particular ecosystem. It is usually measured as the mean number of individuals found per sample.
    a. Abundance0
    b. Thing
    c. Undefined
    d. Undefined

72. _____ are tetrapods and amniotes, animals whose embryos are surrounded by an amniotic membrane, and members of the class Sauropsida. They rely on gathering and losing heat from the environment to regulate their internal temperature, e.g, by moving between sun and shade, or by preferential circulation — moving warmed blood into the body core, while pushing cool blood to the periphery.
    a. Reptiles0
    b. Thing
    c. Undefined
    d. Undefined

73. A _____ is a process that results in the interconversion of chemical substances. The substance or substances initially involved in a _____ are called reactants. Chemical reactions are characterized by a chemical change, and they yield one or more products which are, in general, different from the reactants.
    a. Thing
    b. Chemical reaction0
    c. Undefined
    d. Undefined

74. The _____ consists of the Sun and the other celestial objects gravitationally bound to it: the eight planets, their 165 known moons, three currently identified dwarf planets and their four known moons, and billions of small bodies.
    a. Thing
    b. Solar system0
    c. Undefined
    d. Undefined

75. The _____ is the part of the earth, including air, land, surface rocks, and water, within which life occurs, and which biotic processes in turn alter or transform. From the broadest biophysiological point of view, the _____ is the global ecological system integrating all living beings and their relationships, including their interaction with the elements of the lithosphere, hydrosphere, and atmosphere. This _____ is postulated to have evolved, beginning through a process of biogenesis or biopoesis, at least some 3.5 billion years ago.
    a. Thing
    b. Biosphere0
    c. Undefined
    d. Undefined

76. _____ is the region of space that is dominated by "geogenic" matter, that is, originating from and bound to the Earth.
    a. Geosphere0
    b. Thing
    c. Undefined
    d. Undefined

77. _____ is the native consolidated rock underlying the Earth's surface. Above the _____ is usually an area of broken and weathered unconsolidated rock in the basal subsoil.

Chapter 1. Introducing Geology and an Overview of Important Concepts

a. Bedrock0
b. Thing
c. Undefined
d. Undefined

78. _____ is a general term that includes rocks and materials that are not by definition rocks but are commonly regarded as rocks.
   a. Earth materials0
   b. Thing
   c. Undefined
   d. Undefined

79. The _____ is a primarily solid sphere about 1220 km in radius situated at Earth's center. The existence of an _____ that is different from the liquid outer core was discovered in 1936 by seismologist Inge Lehman using observations of earthquake-generated seismic waves that partly reflect from its boundary and can be detected by sensitive instruments at Earth's surface called seismographs.
   a. Inner core0
   b. Thing
   c. Undefined
   d. Undefined

80. The _____ in Mahican, is a river that runs through the eastern portion of New York State and, along its southern terminus, demarcates the border between the states of New York and New Jersey. It is named for Henry Hudson, an Englishman sailing for the Netherlands, who explored it in 1609.
   a. Place
   b. Hudson River0
   c. Undefined
   d. Undefined

Chapter 2. Atoms, Elements, and Minerals

1. A _____ is any aspect of an object or substance that can be measured or perceived without changing its identity. Physical properties can be intensive or extensive. An intensive property does not depend on the size or amount of matter in the object, while an extensive property does.
   a. Thing
   b. Physical property0
   c. Undefined
   d. Undefined

2. A _____ is a naturally occurring substance formed through geological processes that has a characteristic chemical composition, a highly ordered atomic structure and specific physical properties. A rock, by comparison, is an aggregate of minerals and need not have a specific chemical composition. Minerals range in composition from pure elements and simple salts to very complex silicates with thousands of known forms.
   a. Mineral0
   b. Thing
   c. Undefined
   d. Undefined

3. The carbonate mineral _____ is a chemical or biochemical calcium carbonate and is one of the most widely distributed minerals on the Earth's surface. It is a common constituent of sedimentary rocks, limestone in particular. It is also the primary mineral in metamorphic marble
   a. Thing
   b. Calcite0
   c. Undefined
   d. Undefined

4. The _____ is the part of the earth, including air, land, surface rocks, and water, within which life occurs, and which biotic processes in turn alter or transform. From the broadest biophysiological point of view, the _____ is the global ecological system integrating all living beings and their relationships, including their interaction with the elements of the lithosphere, hydrosphere, and atmosphere. This _____ is postulated to have evolved, beginning through a process of biogenesis or biopoesis, at least some 3.5 billion years ago.
   a. Biosphere0
   b. Thing
   c. Undefined
   d. Undefined

5. A _____ in physical geography describes the collective mass of water found on, under, and over the surface of a planet.
   a. Hydrosphere0
   b. Thing
   c. Undefined
   d. Undefined

6. An _____ is a layer of gases that may surround a material body of sufficient mass. The gases are attracted by the gravity of the body, and are retained for a longer duration if gravity is high and the _____'s temperature is low. Some planets consist mainly of various gases, and thus have very deep atmospheres.
   a. Atmosphere0
   b. Place
   c. Undefined
   d. Undefined

7. _____ is the mineral form of sodium chloride. _____ forms isometric crystals. It commonly occurs with other evaporite deposit minerals such as several of the sulfates, halides and borates. _____ occurs in vast lakes of sedimentary evaporite minerals that result from the drying up of enclosed beds, playas, and seas.
   a. Thing
   b. Halite0
   c. Undefined
   d. Undefined

8. _____ contains low concentrations of dissolved salts and other total dissolved solids. It is an important renewable resource, necessary for the survival of most terrestrial organisms, and required by humans for drinking and agriculture, among many other uses.

Chapter 2. Atoms, Elements, and Minerals

a. Thing
c. Undefined
b. Fresh water0
d. Undefined

9. _____ is a layer of gases surrounding the planet Earth and retained by the Earth's gravity. This mixture of gases is commonly known as air.
   a. Thing
   c. Undefined
   b. Earths atmosphere0
   d. Undefined

10. _____ is a term used to describe a group of hydrous aluminium phyllosilicate minerals, that are typically less than 2 micrometres in diameter. _____ consists of a variety of phyllosilicate minerals rich in silicon and aluminium oxides and hydroxides which include variable amounts of structural water. Clays are generally formed by the chemical weathering of silicate-bearing rocks by carbonic acid but some are formed by hydrothermal activity.
    a. Thing
    c. Undefined
    b. Clay0
    d. Undefined

11. _____ are hydrous aluminium phyllosilicates, sometimes with variable amounts of iron, magnesium, alkali metals, alkaline earths and other cations. Clays have structures similar to the micas and therefore form flat hexagonal sheets. _____ are common weathering products and low temperature hydrothermal alteration products.
    a. Clay minerals0
    c. Undefined
    b. Thing
    d. Undefined

12. A _____ is a solid in which the constituent atoms, molecules, or ions are packed in a regularly ordered, repeating pattern extending in all three spatial dimensions. Most metals encountered in everyday life are polycrystals. Crystals are often symmetrically intergrown to form _____ twins.
    a. Crystal0
    c. Undefined
    b. Thing
    d. Undefined

13. A _____ is a unique arrangement of atoms in a crystal. It is composed of a unit cell, a set of atoms arranged in a particular way, which is periodically repeated in three dimensions on a lattice. The spacing between unit cells in various directions is called its lattice parameters. The symmetry properties of the crystal are embodied in its space group.
    a. Crystal structure0
    c. Undefined
    b. Thing
    d. Undefined

14. _____ is a chemical element metal. It is a lustrous, silvery soft metal. It and nickel are notable for being the final elements produced by stellar nucleosynthesis, and thus are the heaviest elements which do not require a supernova or similarly cataclysmic event for formation.
    a. Iron0
    c. Undefined
    b. Thing
    d. Undefined

15. _____ is a common and widely occurring type of intrusive, felsic, igneous rock. Granites are usually medium to coarsely crystalline, occasionally with some individual crystals larger than the groundmass forming a rock known as porphyry. Granites can be pink to dark gray or even black, depending on their chemistry and mineralogy.
    a. Granite0
    c. Undefined
    b. Thing
    d. Undefined

Chapter 2. Atoms, Elements, and Minerals

16. _____ is molten rock located beneath the surface of the Earth, and which often collects in a _____ chamber. _____ is a complex high-temperature fluid substance. Most are silicate solutions. It is capable of intrusion into adjacent rocks or of extrusion onto the surface as lava or ejected explosively as tephra to form pyroclastic rock. Environments of _____ formation include subduction zones, continental rift zones, mid-oceanic ridges, and hotspots, some of which are interpreted as mantle plumes.
   a. Thing
   b. Magma0
   c. Undefined
   d. Undefined

17. In geology, a _____ is the outermost layer of a planet, part of its lithosphere. They are generally composed of a less dense material than its deeper layers. Earths' is composed mainly of basalt and granite. It is cooler and more rigid than the deeper layers of the mantle and core.
   a. Thing
   b. Crust0
   c. Undefined
   d. Undefined

18. _____ is the second most common mineral in the Earth's continental crust. It is made up of a lattice of silica tetrahedra. _____ belongs to the rhombohedral crystal system. In nature _____ crystals are often twinned, distorted, or so intergrown with adjacent crystals of _____ or other minerals as to only show part of this shape, or to lack obvious crystal faces altogether and appear massive.
   a. Thing
   b. Quartz0
   c. Undefined
   d. Undefined

19. _____ is the name of a group of rock-forming minerals which make up as much as sixty percent of the Earth's crust. Feldspars crystallize from magma in both intrusive and extrusive rocks, and they can also occur as compact minerals, as veins, and are also present in many types of metamorphic rock.
   a. Feldspar0
   b. Thing
   c. Undefined
   d. Undefined

20. _____ are the fundamental building blocks of chemistry, and are conserved in chemical reactions.
   a. Thing
   b. Atoms0
   c. Undefined
   d. Undefined

21. An _____ is a type of atom that is defined by its atomic number; that is, by the number of protons in its nucleus.
   a. Thing
   b. Element0
   c. Undefined
   d. Undefined

22. In chemistry, a _____ is defined as a sufficiently stable electrically neutral group of at least two atoms in a definite arrangement held together by strong chemical bonds.
   a. Molecule0
   b. Thing
   c. Undefined
   d. Undefined

23. _____ is a chemical element represented by the symbol H and an atomic number of 1. At standard temperature and pressure it is a colorless, odorless, nonmetallic, tasteless, highly flammable diatomic gas . With an atomic mass of 1.00794 g/mol, _____ is the lightest element. _____ is the most abundant of the chemical elements, constituting roughly 75% of the universe's elemental mass.

a. Hydrogen0
b. Thing
c. Undefined
d. Undefined

24. In physics, the _____ is a subatomic particle with no net electric charge.
a. Thing
b. Neutron0
c. Undefined
d. Undefined

25. The _____ is a fundamental subatomic particle that carries a negative electric charge.
a. Electron0
b. Thing
c. Undefined
d. Undefined

26. In physics, the _____ is a subatomic particle with an electric charge of one positive fundamental unit a diameter of about 1.5×10^{-15} m, and a mass of 938.27231(28) MeV/c2 (1.6726×10^{-27} kg), 1.007 276 466 88(13) u or about 1836 times the mass of an electron.
a. Proton0
b. Thing
c. Undefined
d. Undefined

27. _____ is a fundamental conserved property of some subatomic particles, which determines their electromagnetic interaction. Electrically charged matter is influenced by, and produces, electromagnetic fields. The interaction between a moving charge and an electromagnetic field is the source of the electromagnetic force, which is one of the four fundamental forces.
a. Thing
b. Electric charge0
c. Undefined
d. Undefined

28. In chemistry and physics, the _____ is the number of protons found in the nucleus of an atom. It is traditionally represented by the symbol Z.
a. Thing
b. Atomic number0
c. Undefined
d. Undefined

29. _____ is a highly sought-after precious metal which, for many centuries, has been used as money, a store of value and in jewelery. The metal occurs as nuggets or grains in rocks, underground "veins" and in alluvial deposits. It is one of the coinage metals. Itis dense, soft, shiny and the most malleable and ductile of the known metals.
a. Thing
b. Gold0
c. Undefined
d. Undefined

30. The _____ A, also called atomic _____ or nucleon number, is the number of nucleons in an atomic nucleus. The _____ is unique for each isotope of an element and is written either after the element name or as a superscript to the left of an element's symbol. For example, carbon-12 has 6 protons and 6 neutrons.
a. Thing
b. Mass number0
c. Undefined
d. Undefined

31. The _____ is the mass of an atom at rest, most often expressed in unified _____ units.[
a. Atomic mass0
b. Thing
c. Undefined
d. Undefined

Chapter 2. Atoms, Elements, and Minerals

32. A _____, as defined by the International Astronomical Union, is a celestial body orbiting a star or stellar remnant that is massive enough to be rounded by its own gravity, not massive enough to cause thermonuclear fusion in its core, and has cleared its neighboring region of planetesimals.
    a. Planet0
    b. Thing
    c. Undefined
    d. Undefined

33. _____ are any of the several different forms of an element each having different atomic mass. _____ of an element have nuclei with the same number of protons but different numbers of neutrons.
    a. Thing
    b. Isotopes0
    c. Undefined
    d. Undefined

34. A _____ is a body of water or other liquid of considerable size contained on a body of land. A vast majority are fresh water, and lie in the Northern Hemisphere at higher latitudes. Most have a natural outflow in the form of a river or stream, but some do not, and lose water solely by evaporation and/or underground seepage.
    a. Thing
    b. Lake0
    c. Undefined
    d. Undefined

35. _____ is one of the four seasons of temperate zones. Almost all English-language calendars, going by astronomy, state that _____ begins on the _____ solstice, and ends on the spring equinox. Calculated more by the weather, it begins and ends earlier and is the season with the shortest days and the lowest temperatures.
    a. Thing
    b. Winter0
    c. Undefined
    d. Undefined

36. The _____ is the region around the Earth's North Pole, opposite the Antarctic region around the South Pole. In the northern hemisphere, the _____ includes the _____ Ocean and parts of Canada, Greenland, Russia, the United States, Iceland, Norway, Sweden and Finland. The word _____ comes from the Greek word arktos, which means bear. This is due to the location of the constellation Ursa Major, the "Great Bear", above the _____ region.
    a. Arctic0
    b. Place
    c. Undefined
    d. Undefined

37. The _____, located in the northern hemisphere and mostly in the Arctic north polar region, is the smallest of the world's five major oceanic divisions and the shallowest.
    a. Place
    b. Arctic Ocean0
    c. Undefined
    d. Undefined

38. A _____ is a natural depression or hole in the surface topography caused by the removal of soil or bedrock, often both, by water. They may vary in size from less than a meter to several hundred meters both in diameter and depth, and vary in form from soil-lined bowls to bedrock-edged chasms.
    a. Sinkhole0
    b. Thing
    c. Undefined
    d. Undefined

39. A _____, also called a Geiger-Müller counter, is a type of particle detector that measures ionizing radiation. Geiger counters are used to detect ionizing radiation, usually alpha and beta radiation, but also other types of radiation as well.
    a. Geiger counter0
    b. Thing
    c. Undefined
    d. Undefined

Chapter 2. Atoms, Elements, and Minerals

40. _____ is approximately 70% more dense than lead and is weakly radioactive. It occurs naturally in low concentrations in soil, rock and water.
   a. Thing
   b. Uranium0
   c. Undefined
   d. Undefined

41. _____ is the science and study of the solid matter that constitute the Earth. Encompassing such things as rocks, soil, and gemstones, _____ studies the composition, structure, physical properties, history, and the processes that shape Earth's components.
   a. Geology0
   b. Thing
   c. Undefined
   d. Undefined

42. _____ is a chemical element. An abundant nonmetallic, tetravalent element, _____ has several allotropic forms. This element is the basis of the chemistry of all known life.
   a. Thing
   b. Carbon0
   c. Undefined
   d. Undefined

43. _____ or sulphur is the chemical element that has the symbol S and atomic number 16. It is an abundant, tasteless, multivalent non-metal. _____, in its native form, is a yellow crystalline solid. In nature, it can be found as the pure element or as sulfide and sulfate minerals. It is an essential element for life and is found in two amino acids, cysteine and methionine.
   a. Sulfur0
   b. Thing
   c. Undefined
   d. Undefined

44. A _____ is an optical instrument used to measure properties of light over a specific portion of the electromagnetic spectrum. The variable measured is most often the light's intensity but could also, for instance, be the polarization state.
   a. Spectrometer0
   b. Thing
   c. Undefined
   d. Undefined

45. Mass spectrometry or informally is an analytical technique used to measure the mass-to-charge ratio of ions. It is most generally used to find the composition of a physical sample by generating a mass spectrum representing the masses of sample components. The mass spectrum is measured by a _____.
   a. Thing
   b. Mass spectrometer0
   c. Undefined
   d. Undefined

46. _____ is an ecological concept referring to the relative representation of a species in a particular ecosystem. It is usually measured as the mean number of individuals found per sample.
   a. Abundance0
   b. Thing
   c. Undefined
   d. Undefined

47. The _____ is used by geologists and other scientists to describe the timing and relationships between events that have occurred during the history of Earth.
   a. Thing
   b. Geological time scale0
   c. Undefined
   d. Undefined

48. _____ is the average and variations of weather over long periods of time. _____ zones can be defined using parameters such as temperature and rainfall.

Chapter 2. Atoms, Elements, and Minerals

a. Thing
c. Undefined
b. Climate0
d. Undefined

49. _____ refers to the variation in the Earth's global climate or in regional climates over time. It describes changes in the variability or average state of the atmosphere over time scales ranging from decades to millions of years. These changes can be caused by processes internal to the Earth, external forces or, more recently, human activities.
a. Thing
c. Undefined
b. Climate change0
d. Undefined

50. The _____ are a large group of amoeboid protists with reticulating pseudopods, fine strands of cytoplasm that branch and merge to form a dynamic net. They typically produce a test, or shell, which can have either one or multiple chambers, some becoming quite elaborate in structure.[
a. Foraminifera0
c. Undefined
b. Thing
d. Undefined

51. _____ is water from a sea or ocean. On average, _____ in the world's oceans has a salinity of ~3.5%, or 35 parts per thousand. This means that every 1 kg of _____ has approximately 35 grams of dissolved salts.
a. Seawater0
c. Undefined
b. Thing
d. Undefined

52. _____ is any particulate matter that can be transported by fluid flow and which eventually is deposited as a layer of solid particles on the bed or bottom of a body of water or other liquid.
a. Thing
c. Undefined
b. Sediment0
d. Undefined

53. Water collecting on the ground or in a stream, river, lake, or wetland is called _____; as opposed to groundwater. _____ is naturally replenished by precipitation and naturally lost through discharge to the oceans, evaporation, and sub-surface seepage into the groundwater. _____ is the largest source of fresh water.
a. Thing
c. Undefined
b. Surface water0
d. Undefined

54. An _____ is a geological interval of warmer global average temperature that separates glacials, or ice ages. The current Holocene _____ has persisted since the Pleistocene, about 11,400 years ago.
a. Interglacial0
c. Undefined
b. Thing
d. Undefined

55. _____ is the gas phase of water. _____ is one state of the water cycle within the hydrosphere. _____ can be produced from the evaporation of liquid water or from the sublimation of ice. Under normal atmospheric conditions, _____ is continuously evaporating and condensing.
a. Thing
c. Undefined
b. Water vapor0
d. Undefined

56. _____ is the gas phase component of a another state of matter which does not completely fill its container. It is distinguished from the pure gas phase by the presence of the same substance in another state of matter. Hence when a liquid has completely evaporated, it is said that the system has been completely transformed to the gas phase.

Chapter 2. Atoms, Elements, and Minerals

a. Vapor0
b. Thing
c. Undefined
d. Undefined

57. A _____ is a process that results in the interconversion of chemical substances. The substance or substances initially involved in a _____ are called reactants. Chemical reactions are characterized by a chemical change, and they yield one or more products which are, in general, different from the reactants.
a. Thing
b. Chemical reaction0
c. Undefined
d. Undefined

58. _____ is the process of breaking down rocks, soils and their minerals through direct contact with the atmosphere. _____ occurs without movement. Two main classifications of _____ processes exist. Mechanical or physical _____ involves the breakdown of rocks and soils through direct contact with atmospheric conditions. The second classification, chemical _____, involves the direct effect of atmospheric chemicals in the breakdown of rocks, soils and minerals.
a. Weathering0
b. Thing
c. Undefined
d. Undefined

59. An _____ is an atom or group of atoms which have lost or gained one or more electrons, making them negatively or positively charged.
a. Ion0
b. Thing
c. Undefined
d. Undefined

60. _____ is a form of chemical bonding that is characterized by the sharing of pairs of electrons between atoms.
a. Covalent bonding0
b. Thing
c. Undefined
d. Undefined

61. _____ are the hardest natural material known to man and the third-hardest known material. Its hardness and high dispersion of light make it useful for industrial applications and jewelry.
a. Thing
b. Diamonds0
c. Undefined
d. Undefined

62. _____ is the bonding between atoms within metals. It involves the delocalized sharing of free electrons among a lattice of metal atoms. Thus, they may be compared to molten salts.
a. Metallic bonding0
b. Thing
c. Undefined
d. Undefined

63. _____ or specific conductivity is a measure of a material's ability to conduct an electric current. When an electrical potential difference is placed across a conductor, its movable charges flow, giving rise to an electric current.
a. Electrical conductivity0
b. Thing
c. Undefined
d. Undefined

64. _____ is one of the allotropes of carbon. It holds the distinction of being the most stable form of solid carbon ever discovered. It may be considered to be the highest grade of coal, just above anthracite, although it is not normally used as fuel because it is hard to ignite.

Chapter 2. Atoms, Elements, and Minerals

    a. Graphite0
    b. Thing
    c. Undefined
    d. Undefined

65. A _____ is a rodent that belongs to one of numerous species of small mammals. Due to its ability to live commensally with humans, it is regarded to be the third most successful mammalian species living on Earth today, after humans and the rat.
    a. Mouse0
    b. Thing
    c. Undefined
    d. Undefined

66. A _____ is a movement of an object in a circular motion. A two-dimensional object rotates around a center of _____. A three-dimensional object rotates around a line called an axis. A circular motion about an external point, e.g. the Earth about the Sun, is called an orbit or more properly an orbital revolution.
    a. Rotation0
    b. Thing
    c. Undefined
    d. Undefined

67. _____ is the oxide of silicon, chemical formula SiO_2, and is known for its hardness as early as the 16th century. It is a principle component in most types of glass and substances such as concrete.
    a. Silica0
    b. Thing
    c. Undefined
    d. Undefined

68. In geology and astronomy, the term _____ is used to denote types of rock that consist predominantly of _____ minerals. Such rocks include a wide range of igneous, metamorphic and sedimentary types. Most of the Earth's mantle and crust are made up of _____ rocks. The same is true of the Moon and the other rocky planets.
    a. Silicate0
    b. Thing
    c. Undefined
    d. Undefined

69. A _____ is a concise way of expressing information about the atoms that constitute a particular chemical compound. A _____ is also a short way of showing how a chemical reaction occurs. For molecular compounds, it identifies each constituent element by its chemical symbol and indicates the number of atoms of each element found in each discrete molecule of that compound.
    a. Chemical formula0
    b. Thing
    c. Undefined
    d. Undefined

70. _____ is a silvery and ductile member of the poor metal group of chemical elements. It has the symbol Al and atomic number 13.
    a. Aluminum0
    b. Thing
    c. Undefined
    d. Undefined

71. A _____ is a chemical substance of two or more different chemically bonded chemical elements, with a fixed ratio determining the composition. The ratio of each element is usually expressed by chemical formula.
    a. Thing
    b. Chemical compound0
    c. Undefined
    d. Undefined

72. _____ is a ductile metal with excellent electrical conductivity, and finds extensive use as an electrical conductor, heat conductor, as a building material, and as a component of various alloys.

Chapter 2. Atoms, Elements, and Minerals

a. Thing
b. Copper0
c. Undefined
d. Undefined

73. A _____ is one of several large landmasses on Earth. They are generally identified by convention rather than any strict criteria, but seven areas are commonly reckoned as continents – they are: Asia, Africa, North America, South America, Antarctica, Europe, and Australia.
a. Thing
b. Continent0
c. Undefined
d. Undefined

74. _____ in meteorology are large scale patterns in the atmospheric pressure field that are nearly stationary, effectively "blocking" or redirecting migratory cyclones. These _____ can remain in place for several days or even weeks, causing the areas affected by them to have the same kind of weather for an extended period of time.
a. Blocks0
b. Thing
c. Undefined
d. Undefined

75. _____ has the symbol Mg. It is the ninth most abundant element in the universe by mass. It constitutes about 2% of the Earth's crust by mass, and it is the third most abundant element dissolved in seawater. It is essential to all living cells, and is the 11th most abundant element by mass in the human body.
a. Thing
b. Magnesium0
c. Undefined
d. Undefined

76. The mineral _____ is a magnesium iron silicate. It is one of the most common minerals on Earth, and has also been identified on the Moon, Mars, and comet Wild 2.
a. Thing
b. Olivine0
c. Undefined
d. Undefined

77. _____ defines an important group of generally dark-colored rock-forming inosilicate minerals linked at the vertices and generally containing ions of iron and/or magnesium in their structures. Amphiboles crystallize into two crystal systems, monoclinic and orthorhombic.
a. Thing
b. Amphibole0
c. Undefined
d. Undefined

78. The _____ group of sheet silicate minerals includes several closely related materials having highly perfect basal cleavage. All are monoclinic with a tendency towards pseudo-hexagonal crystals and are similar in chemical composition. The highly perfect cleavage, which is the most prominent characteristic of _____, is explained by the hexagonal sheet-like arrangement of its atoms.
a. Mica0
b. Thing
c. Undefined
d. Undefined

79. _____ describes any of a group of minerals that can be fibrous, many of which are metamorphic and are hydrous magnesium silicates.
a. Asbestos0
b. Thing
c. Undefined
d. Undefined

80. An _____ is a chemical compound containing an oxygen atom and other elements. Most of the earth's crust consists of them. They result when elements are oxidized by air.

a. Thing
b. Oxide0
c. Undefined
d. Undefined

81. In inorganic chemistry, a _____ is a salt of sulfuric acid
   a. Sulfate0
   b. Thing
   c. Undefined
   d. Undefined

82. The term _____ refers to several types of chemical compounds containing sulfur in its lowest oxidation number of −2.
   a. Sulfide0
   b. Thing
   c. Undefined
   d. Undefined

83. _____ is a very soft mineral composed of calcium sulfate dihydrate, with the chemical formula $CaSO_4 \cdot 2H_2O$. _____ occurs in nature as flattened and often twinned crystals and transparent cleavable masses. It may also occur silky and fibrous. Finally it may also be granular or quite compact.
   a. Gypsum0
   b. Thing
   c. Undefined
   d. Undefined

84. The mineral _____ is iron disulfide, FeS_2. It has isometric crystals that usually appear as cubes. Its metallic luster and pale-to-normal, brass-yellow hue have earned it a nickname due to many miners mistaking it for the real thing.
   a. Pyrite0
   b. Thing
   c. Undefined
   d. Undefined

85. _____ is a very common mineral, colored black to steel or silver-gray, brown to reddish brown, or red. It is mined as the main ore of iron. Varieties include kidney ore, martite iron rose and specularite. While the forms of it vary, they all have a rust-red streak. it is harder than pure iron, but much more brittle.
   a. Hematite0
   b. Thing
   c. Undefined
   d. Undefined

86. _____ is the substance of which physical objects are composed. _____ can be solid, liquid, plasma or gas. It constitutes the observable universe.
   a. Thing
   b. Matter0
   c. Undefined
   d. Undefined

87. _____ is a group of common rock-forming hydrous magnesium iron phyllosilicate $|Mg, Fe|_3Si_2O_5|OH|_4$ minerals; it may contain minor amounts of other elements including chromium, manganese, cobalt and nickel. There are three important mineral polymorphs of _____: antigorite, chrysotile and lizardite.
   a. Serpentine0
   b. Thing
   c. Undefined
   d. Undefined

88. _____ is an asbestiform sub-group within the serpentine group of minerals. There are three known species and they form the fibrous members of the this group and have been extensively mined as asbestos.
   a. Chrysotile0
   b. Thing
   c. Undefined
   d. Undefined

Chapter 2. Atoms, Elements, and Minerals

89. The _____ is an agency of the federal government of the United States charged with protecting human health and with safeguarding the natural environment: air, water, and land.
   a. Environmental Protection Agency0
   b. Person
   c. Undefined
   d. Undefined

90. The _____ was enacted by the United States Congress in response to the Love Canal disaster. The Act was created to protect people, families, communities and others from heavily contaminated toxic waste sites that have been abandoned. It paid for toxic waste cleanups at sites where no other responsible parties could pay for a cleanup by assessing a tax on petroleum and chemical industries.
   a. Comprehensive Environmental Response, Compensation, and Liability Act0
   b. Thing
   c. Undefined
   d. Undefined

91. _____ is the extraction of valuable minerals or other geological materials from the earth, usually from an ore body, vein, or seam. Any material that cannot be grown from agricultural processes, or created artificially in a laboratory or factory, is usually extracted from the earth by this method.
   a. Mining0
   b. Thing
   c. Undefined
   d. Undefined

92. _____ is an Earth Science focused around the chemistry, crystal structure, and physical properties of minerals. Specific studies within _____ include the processes of mineral origin and formation, classification of minerals, their geographical distribution, as well as their utilization.
   a. Mineralogy0
   b. Thing
   c. Undefined
   d. Undefined

93. _____ is a very important series of tectosilicate minerals within the feldspar family. Rather than referring to a particular mineral with a specific chemical composition, it is a solid solution series.
   a. Thing
   b. Plagioclase0
   c. Undefined
   d. Undefined

94. _____: a _____ is an ion with a positive charge. It is the inverse anion.
   a. Thing
   b. Cation0
   c. Undefined
   d. Undefined

95. An _____ is a negetive ion.
   a. Thing
   b. Anion0
   c. Undefined
   d. Undefined

96. _____ is an important tectosilicate mineral, which forms igneous rock. _____ is named based on the Greek for "straight fracture," because its two cleavages are at right angles to each other. _____ crystallizes in the monoclinic crystal system. It has a hardness of 6, a specific gravity of 2.56-2.58, and a vitreous to pearly luster. It can be colored white, gray, yellow, pink, or red; rarely green.
   a. Orthoclase0
   b. Thing
   c. Undefined
   d. Undefined

Chapter 2. Atoms, Elements, and Minerals

97. _____ is an important igneous rock forming tectosilicate mineral. It is common in granite and pegmatites. _____ forms during slow cooling of orthoclase; it is stable at lower temperatures than orthoclase.
   a. Microcline0
   b. Thing
   c. Undefined
   d. Undefined

98. _____ is a chemical element. It is a soft silvery-white metallic alkali metal that occurs naturally bound to other elements in seawater and many minerals. It oxidizes rapidly in air and is very reactive, especially towards water. In many respects, it and sodium are chemically similar, although organisms in general, and animal cells in particular, treat them very differently.
   a. Potassium0
   b. Thing
   c. Undefined
   d. Undefined

99. The _____ are a group of important rock-forming silicate minerals found in many igneous and metamorphic rocks. They share a common structure comprised of single chains of silica tetrahedra and they crystalise in the monoclinic and orthorhombic system.
   a. Pyroxenes0
   b. Thing
   c. Undefined
   d. Undefined

100. _____ is a complex inosilicate series of minerals. _____ is not a recognized mineral, in its own right but the name is used as a general or field term, to refer to a dark amphibole. It is an isomorphous mixture of three molecules; a calcium-iron-magnesium silicate, an aluminium-iron-magnesium silicate and an iron-magnesium silicate.
   a. Thing
   b. Hornblende0
   c. Undefined
   d. Undefined

101. _____ is a single chain inosilicate mineral described chemically as $|Ca,Mg,Fe|SiO_3$ or calcium magnesium iron silicate. The crystals are monoclinic and prismatic. _____ has two prominent prismatic cleavages, meeting at angles near 90°.
   a. Thing
   b. Augite0
   c. Undefined
   d. Undefined

102. _____ is a clay mineral with the chemical composition $Al_2Si_2O_5|OH|_4$. It is a layered silicate mineral, with one tetrahedral sheet linked through oxygen atoms to one octahedral sheet of alumina octahedra. Rocks that are rich in _____ are known as china clay or kaolin
   a. Kaolinite0
   b. Thing
   c. Undefined
   d. Undefined

103. _____ is a very soft phyllosilicate mineral that typically forms in microscopic crystals, forming a clay. It is the main constituent of the volcanic ash weathering product, bentonite.
   a. Montmorillonite0
   b. Thing
   c. Undefined
   d. Undefined

104. An _____ is the result from the sudden release of stored energy in the Earth's crust that creates seismic waves. At the Earth's surface, earthquakes may manifest themselves by a shaking or displacement of the ground. An _____ is caused by tectonic plates getting stuck and putting a strain on the ground. The strain becomes so great that rocks give way by breaking and sliding along fault planes.

a. Earthquake0
b. Thing
c. Undefined
d. Undefined

105. _____ is the native consolidated rock underlying the Earth's surface. Above the _____ is usually an area of broken and weathered unconsolidated rock in the basal subsoil.
   a. Bedrock0
   b. Thing
   c. Undefined
   d. Undefined

106. A _____ is a barrier across flowing water that obstructs, directs or slows down the flow, often creating a reservoir, lake or impoundment.
   a. Dam0
   b. Thing
   c. Undefined
   d. Undefined

107. Most often, a _____ refers to an artificial lake, used to store water for various uses. Reservoirs are created first by building a sturdy dam, usually out of cement, earth, rock, or a mixture. Once the dam is completed, a stream is allowed to flow behind it and eventually fill it to capacity.
   a. Thing
   b. Reservoir0
   c. Undefined
   d. Undefined

108. _____ is a phyllosilicate mineral of aluminium and potassium. It has a highly perfect basal cleavage yielding remarkably thin laminae , which are often highly elastic. Sheets of _____ 5 metres by 3 metres have been found in Nellore, India.
   a. Muscovite0
   b. Thing
   c. Undefined
   d. Undefined

109. _____ is a common phyllosilicate mineral within the mica group. Primarily a solid-solution series between the iron-endmember annite, and the magnesium-endmember phlogopite; more aluminous endmembers include siderophyllite.
   a. Thing
   b. Biotite0
   c. Undefined
   d. Undefined

110. _____ rock is one of the three main rock groups. Rock formed from these covers 75% of the Earth's land area, and includes common types such as chalk, limestone, dolomite, sandstone, and shale.
   a. Sedimentary0
   b. Thing
   c. Undefined
   d. Undefined

111. _____ is one of the three main rock groups. _____ covers 75% of the Earth's land area. Four basic processes are involved in the formation of a clastic _____: weathering caused mainly by friction of waves, transportation where the sediment is carried along by a current, deposition and compaction where the sediment is squashed together to form a rock of this kind.
   a. Sedimentary rock0
   b. Thing
   c. Undefined
   d. Undefined

112. In organic chemistry, a _____ is a salt of carbonic acid.
   a. Thing
   b. Carbonate0
   c. Undefined
   d. Undefined

113. _____ is a metamorphic rock resulting from the metamorphism of limestone, composed mostly of calcite. It is extensively used for sculpture, as a building material, and in many other applications. The word '_____' is colloquially used to refer to many other stones that are capable of taking a high polish.
   a. Marble0
   b. Thing
   c. Undefined
   d. Undefined

114. _____ is a sedimentary rock composed largely of the mineral calcite. _____ often contains variable amounts of silica in the form of chert or flint, as well as varying amounts of clay, silt and sand as disseminations, nodules, or layers within the rock. The primary source of the calcite in _____ is most commonly marine organisms. These organisms secrete shells that settle out of the water column and are deposited on ocean floors as pelagic ooze or alternatively is conglomerated in a coral reef.
   a. Thing
   b. Limestone0
   c. Undefined
   d. Undefined

115. Earth's _____ is a ~2,900 km thick rocky shell comprizing approximately 70% of Earth's volume. It is predominantly solid and overlies the Earth's iron-rich core, which occupies about 30% of Earth's volume. Past episodes of melting and volcanism at the shallower levels of the _____ have produced a very thin crust of crystallized melt products near the surface, upon which we live.
   a. Thing
   b. Mantle0
   c. Undefined
   d. Undefined

116. An _____ is a volume of rock containing components or minerals in a mode of occurrence that renders it valuable for mining.
   a. Thing
   b. Ore0
   c. Undefined
   d. Undefined

117. _____ is a ferrimagnetic mineral one of several iron oxides and a member of the spinel group. The chemical IUPAC name is iron oxide and the common chemical name ferrous-ferric oxide.
   a. Thing
   b. Magnetite0
   c. Undefined
   d. Undefined

118. _____ is a copper iron sulfide mineral that crystallizes in the tetragonal system. It has the chemical composition $CuFeS_2$.
   a. Chalcopyrite0
   b. Thing
   c. Undefined
   d. Undefined

119. A _____ is one which contains both magnesium and iron.
   a. Thing
   b. Ferromagnesian mineral0
   c. Undefined
   d. Undefined

120. _____ are substances inside a confined amount of liquid, gas, or solid, which differ from the chemical composition of the material or compound.
   a. Impurities0
   b. Thing
   c. Undefined
   d. Undefined

Chapter 2. Atoms, Elements, and Minerals

121. _____ is a description of the way light interacts with the surface of a crystal, rock, or mineral. For example, a diamond is said to have an adamantine _____ and pyrite is said to have a metallic _____.
   a. Luster0
   b. Thing
   c. Undefined
   d. Undefined

122. _____ is the characteristic of a solid material expressing its resistance to permanent deformation.
   a. Thing
   b. Hardness0
   c. Undefined
   d. Undefined

123. An _____ is a homogeneous mixture of two or more elements, at least one of which is a metal, and where the resulting material has metallic properties. The resulting metallic substance usually has different properties from those of its components.
   a. Thing
   b. Alloy0
   c. Undefined
   d. Undefined

124. _____ are flat faces on geometric shapes. They reflect the underlying symmetry of the crystal structure. Gemstones commonly have them cut into them in order to improve their appearance.
   a. Facets0
   b. Thing
   c. Undefined
   d. Undefined

125. A _____ is a highly attractive and valuable piece of mineral, which, when cut and polished, is used in jewelry or other adornments.
   a. Thing
   b. Gemstone0
   c. Undefined
   d. Undefined

126. _____ is the single-crystal form of aluminium oxide, a mineral known as corundum. It can be found naturally as gemstones or manufactured in large crystal boules for varied applications, including infrared optical components, watch faces, high-durability windows, and wafers for the deposition of semiconductors such as GaN nanorods.
   a. Sapphire0
   b. Thing
   c. Undefined
   d. Undefined

127. _____ is the state of being colored, distinguishing a species due to color arrangement.
   a. Coloration0
   b. Thing
   c. Undefined
   d. Undefined

128. _____ is a crystalline form of aluminium oxide and one of the rock-forming minerals. It is naturally clear, but can have different colors when impurities are present. Transparent specimens are used as gems, called ruby if red, while all other colors are called sapphire.
   a. Corundum0
   b. Thing
   c. Undefined
   d. Undefined

129. _____ is a steel-gray, lustrous, hard metal that takes a high polish and has a high melting point. It is also odourless, tasteless, and malleable
   a. Chromium0
   b. Thing
   c. Undefined
   d. Undefined

Chapter 2. Atoms, Elements, and Minerals

130. The mineral _____ is a beryllium aluminium cyclosilicate with the chemical formula Be_3Al_26. The hexagonal crystals of _____ may be very small or range to several meters in size. Terminated crystals are relatively rare. _____ exhibits conchoidal fracture, has a hardness of 7.5–8, a specific gravity of 2.63–2.80. It has a vitreous luster and can be transparent or translucent.
   a. Beryl0
   b. Thing
   c. Undefined
   d. Undefined

131. _____ is a mineral composed of calcium fluoride, CaF_2. It is an isometric mineral with a cubic habit, though octahedral and more complex isometric forms are not uncommon.
   a. Fluorite0
   b. Thing
   c. Undefined
   d. Undefined

132. _____, in mineralogy, is the tendency of crystalline materials to split along definite planes, creating smooth surfaces.
   a. Cleavage0
   b. Thing
   c. Undefined
   d. Undefined

133. _____ is a mineral that is the chief ore of zinc. It consists largely of zinc sulfide in crystalline form but almost always contains variable iron.
   a. Thing
   b. Sphalerite0
   c. Undefined
   d. Undefined

134. _____ is a chemical element in the periodic table that has the symbol Zn and atomic number 30. In some historical and sculptural contexts, it is known as spelter.
   a. Thing
   b. Zinc0
   c. Undefined
   d. Undefined

135. _____ describes the way that brittle materials break when they do not follow any natural planes of separation. Materials that break in this way include flint and other fine-grained minerals, as well as most amorphous solids, such as obsidian and other types of glass.
   a. Conchoidal fracture0
   b. Thing
   c. Undefined
   d. Undefined

136. _____, in everyday life, is most familiar as the agency that endows objects with weight. _____ is responsible for keeping the Earth and the other planets in their orbits around the Sun; for the formation of tides; and for various other phenomena that we observe. _____ is also the reason for the very existence of the Earth, the Sun, and most macroscopic objects in the universe; without it, matter would not have coalesced into these large masses, and life, as we know it, would not exist.
   a. Gravitation0
   b. Thing
   c. Undefined
   d. Undefined

137. _____ is the natural mineral form of lead sulfide. It is the most important lead ore mineral. It is one of the most abundant and widely distributed sulfide minerals. It crystallizes in the cubic crystal system often showing octahedral forms. It is often associated with the minerals sphalerite, calcite and fluorite.

Chapter 2. Atoms, Elements, and Minerals

   a. Galena0
   b. Thing
   c. Undefined
   d. Undefined

138. _____ is soil or rock derived granular material of a specific grain size. _____ may occur as a soil or alternatively as suspended sediment in a water column of any surface water body. It may also exist as deposition soil at the bottom of a water body.
   a. Thing
   b. Silt0
   c. Undefined
   d. Undefined

139. The Earth's _____ is the wandering point on the Earth's surface at which the Earth's magnetic field points vertically downwards i.e. the "dip" is 90°. It should not be confused with the lesser known North Geomagnetic Pole.
   a. Thing
   b. Magnetic north0
   c. Undefined
   d. Undefined

140. _____ is one of the phenomena by which materials exert attractive or repulsive forces on other materials. Some well known materials that exhibit easily detectable magnetic properties are nickel, iron, some steels, and the mineral magnetite; however, all materials are influenced to greater or lesser degree by the presence of a magnetic field.
   a. Thing
   b. Magnetism0
   c. Undefined
   d. Undefined

141. A _____ is a scientific instrument used to measure the strength and/or direction of the magnetic field in the vicinity of the instrument.
   a. Magnetometer0
   b. Thing
   c. Undefined
   d. Undefined

142. _____ is the change in direction of a wave due to a change in its speed. This is most commonly seen when a wave passes from one medium to another.
   a. Refraction0
   b. Thing
   c. Undefined
   d. Undefined

143. In physics, _____ is defined as the rate of change of displacement or the rate of displacement. Simply put, it is distance per units of time.
   a. Velocity0
   b. Thing
   c. Undefined
   d. Undefined

144. _____ is a chemical compound, normally in a gaseous state, and is composed of one carbon and two oxygen atoms. It is often referred to by its formula CO_2. It is present in the Earth's atmosphere at a concentration of approximately .000383 by volume and is an important greenhouse gas due to its ability to absorb many infrared wavelengths of sunlight, and due to the length of time it stays in the atmosphere.
   a. Carbon dioxide0
   b. Thing
   c. Undefined
   d. Undefined

145. _____ are those minerals containing the carbonate ion: CO_3^{2-}.
   a. Thing
   b. Carbonate minerals0
   c. Undefined
   d. Undefined

Chapter 3. Igneous Rocks, Intrusive Activity, and the Origin of Igneous Rocks

1. An _____ is a body of igneous rock that has crystallized from a molten magma below the surface of the Earth.
   a. Thing
   b. Intrusion0
   c. Undefined
   d. Undefined

2. _____ is a field of study within geology concerned generally with the structures within the crust of the Earth, or other planets, and particularly with the forces and movements that have operated in a region to create these structures.
   a. Thing
   b. Tectonics0
   c. Undefined
   d. Undefined

3. The _____ is a fundamental concept in geology that describes the dynamic transitions through geologic time among the three main rock types: sedimentary, metamorphic, and igneous.
   a. Rock cycle0
   b. Thing
   c. Undefined
   d. Undefined

4. _____ is a small island located in the middle of San Francisco Bay in California, United States. It served as a lighthouse, then a military fortification, then a military prison followed by a federal prison until 1963, when it became a national recreation area.
   a. Alcatraz Island0
   b. Place
   c. Undefined
   d. Undefined

5. A _____ in physical geography describes the collective mass of water found on, under, and over the surface of a planet.
   a. Hydrosphere0
   b. Thing
   c. Undefined
   d. Undefined

6. _____ rocks form when molten rock, magma, cools and solidifies, with or without crystallization, either below the surface as intrusive, plutonic rocks or on the surface as extrusive, volcanic, rocks.
   a. Thing
   b. Igneous0
   c. Undefined
   d. Undefined

7. An _____ is a layer of gases that may surround a material body of sufficient mass. The gases are attracted by the gravity of the body, and are retained for a longer duration if gravity is high and the _____'s temperature is low. Some planets consist mainly of various gases, and thus have very deep atmospheres.
   a. Place
   b. Atmosphere0
   c. Undefined
   d. Undefined

8. _____ is molten rock located beneath the surface of the Earth, and which often collects in a _____ chamber. _____ is a complex high-temperature fluid substance. Most are silicate solutions. It is capable of intrusion into adjacent rocks or of extrusion onto the surface as lava or ejected explosively as tephra to form pyroclastic rock. Environments of _____ formation include subduction zones, continental rift zones, mid-oceanic ridges, and hotspots, some of which are interpreted as mantle plumes.
   a. Magma0
   b. Thing
   c. Undefined
   d. Undefined

Chapter 3. Igneous Rocks, Intrusive Activity, and the Origin of Igneous Rocks

9. Earth's _____ is a ~2,900 km thick rocky shell comprizing approximately 70% of Earth's volume. It is predominantly solid and overlies the Earth's iron-rich core, which occupies about 30% of Earth's volume. Past episodes of melting and volcanism at the shallower levels of the _____ have produced a very thin crust of crystallized melt products near the surface, upon which we live.
   a. Mantle0
   b. Thing
   c. Undefined
   d. Undefined

10. A _____, as defined by the International Astronomical Union, is a celestial body orbiting a star or stellar remnant that is massive enough to be rounded by its own gravity, not massive enough to cause thermonuclear fusion in its core, and has cleared its neighboring region of planetesimals.
   a. Thing
   b. Planet0
   c. Undefined
   d. Undefined

11. A _____ is a naturally occurring substance formed through geological processes that has a characteristic chemical composition, a highly ordered atomic structure and specific physical properties. A rock, by comparison, is an aggregate of minerals and need not have a specific chemical composition. Minerals range in composition from pure elements and simple salts to very complex silicates with thousands of known forms.
   a. Mineral0
   b. Thing
   c. Undefined
   d. Undefined

12. An _____ is a type of atom that is defined by its atomic number; that is, by the number of protons in its nucleus.
   a. Thing
   b. Element0
   c. Undefined
   d. Undefined

13. _____ is a highly sought-after precious metal which, for many centuries, has been used as money, a store of value and in jewelery. The metal occurs as nuggets or grains in rocks, underground "veins" and in alluvial deposits. It is one of the coinage metals. Itis dense, soft, shiny and the most malleable and ductile of the known metals.
   a. Thing
   b. Gold0
   c. Undefined
   d. Undefined

14. An _____ is a volume of rock containing components or minerals in a mode of occurrence that renders it valuable for mining.
   a. Ore0
   b. Thing
   c. Undefined
   d. Undefined

15. _____ is a ductile metal with excellent electrical conductivity, and finds extensive use as an electrical conductor, heat conductor, as a building material, and as a component of various alloys.
   a. Copper0
   b. Thing
   c. Undefined
   d. Undefined

16. _____ is water from a sea or ocean. On average, _____ in the world's oceans has a salinity of ~3.5%, or 35 parts per thousand. This means that every 1 kg of _____ has approximately 35 grams of dissolved salts.
   a. Thing
   b. Seawater0
   c. Undefined
   d. Undefined

32 *Chapter 3. Igneous Rocks, Intrusive Activity, and the Origin of Igneous Rocks*

17. The _____ is the part of the earth, including air, land, surface rocks, and water, within which life occurs, and which biotic processes in turn alter or transform. From the broadest biophysiological point of view, the _____ is the global ecological system integrating all living beings and their relationships, including their interaction with the elements of the lithosphere, hydrosphere, and atmosphere. This _____ is postulated to have evolved, beginning through a process of biogenesis or biopoesis, at least some 3.5 billion years ago.
    a. Biosphere0
    b. Thing
    c. Undefined
    d. Undefined

18. A _____ is a spring that is produced by the emergence of geothermally-heated groundwater from the earth's crust. They are all over the earth, on every continent and even under the oceans and seas.
    a. Thing
    b. Hot spring0
    c. Undefined
    d. Undefined

19. _____, in everyday life, is most familiar as the agency that endows objects with weight. _____ is responsible for keeping the Earth and the other planets in their orbits around the Sun; for the formation of tides; and for various other phenomena that we observe. _____ is also the reason for the very existence of the Earth, the Sun, and most macroscopic objects in the universe; without it, matter would not have coalesced into these large masses, and life, as we know it, would not exist.
    a. Thing
    b. Gravitation0
    c. Undefined
    d. Undefined

20. _____ is any particulate matter that can be transported by fluid flow and which eventually is deposited as a layer of solid particles on the bed or bottom of a body of water or other liquid.
    a. Thing
    b. Sediment0
    c. Undefined
    d. Undefined

21. A _____ is one of several large landmasses on Earth. They are generally identified by convention rather than any strict criteria, but seven areas are commonly reckoned as continents – they are: Asia, Africa, North America, South America, Antarctica, Europe, and Australia.
    a. Continent0
    b. Thing
    c. Undefined
    d. Undefined

22. _____ is the condition of a system in which competing influences are balanced.
    a. Thing
    b. Equilibrium0
    c. Undefined
    d. Undefined

23. _____ is the science and study of the solid matter that constitute the Earth. Encompassing such things as rocks, soil, and gemstones, _____ studies the composition, structure, physical properties, history, and the processes that shape Earth's components.
    a. Geology0
    b. Thing
    c. Undefined
    d. Undefined

24. _____ can be defined as the solid state recrystallisation of pre-existing rocks due to changes in heat and/or pressure and/or introduction of fluids. There will be mineralogical, chemical and crystallographic changes. _____ produced with increasing pressure and temperature conditions is known as prograde _____. Conversely, decreasing temperatures and pressure characterize retrograde _____.

Chapter 3. Igneous Rocks, Intrusive Activity, and the Origin of Igneous Rocks   33

    a. Metamorphism0
    c. Undefined
    b. Thing
    d. Undefined

25. _____ rock is one of the three main rock groups. Rock formed from these covers 75% of the Earth's land area, and includes common types such as chalk, limestone, dolomite, sandstone, and shale.
    a. Thing
    c. Undefined
    b. Sedimentary0
    d. Undefined

26. _____ refers to the mode of igneous volcanic rock formation in which hot magma from inside the Earth flows out onto the surface as lava or explodes violently into the atmosphere to fall back as pyroclastics or tuff.
    a. Extrusive0
    c. Undefined
    b. Thing
    d. Undefined

27. _____ forms when rock cools and solidifies either below the surface as intrusive rocks or on the surface as extrusive rocks. This magma can be derived from partial melts of pre-existing rocks in either the Earth's mantle or crust. Typically, the melting is caused by one or more of the following processes -- an increase in temperature, a decrease in pressure, or a change in composition.
    a. Igneous rock0
    c. Undefined
    b. Thing
    d. Undefined

28. _____ is the process of breaking down rocks, soils and their minerals through direct contact with the atmosphere. _____ occurs without movement. Two main classifications of _____ processes exist. Mechanical or physical _____ involves the breakdown of rocks and soils through direct contact with atmospheric conditions. The second classification, chemical _____, involves the direct effect of atmospheric chemicals in the breakdown of rocks, soils and minerals.
    a. Weathering0
    c. Undefined
    b. Thing
    d. Undefined

29. _____ is one of the three main rock groups. _____ covers 75% of the Earth's land area. Four basic processes are involved in the formation of a clastic _____: weathering caused mainly by friction of waves, transportation where the sediment is carried along by a current, deposition and compaction where the sediment is squashed together to form a rock of this kind.
    a. Thing
    c. Undefined
    b. Sedimentary rock0
    d. Undefined

30. A _____ is an opening, or rupture, in the Earth's surface or crust, which allows hot, molten rock, ash and gases to escape from deep below the surface.
    a. Thing
    c. Undefined
    b. Volcano0
    d. Undefined

31. _____ is the result of the transformation of a pre-existing rock type, the protolith, in a process called metamorphism, which means "change in form". The protolith is subjected to heat and extreme pressure causing profound physical and/or chemical change. The protolith may be sedimentary rock, igneous rock or another older rock.
    a. Thing
    c. Undefined
    b. Metamorphic rock0
    d. Undefined

Chapter 3. Igneous Rocks, Intrusive Activity, and the Origin of Igneous Rocks

32. Metamorphic rock is the result of the transformation of a pre-existing rock type, the protolith, in a process called metamorphism. The protolith is subjected to heat and extreme pressure causing profound physical and/or chemical change. _____ make up a large part of the Earth's crust. They are formed deep beneath the Earth's surface by great stresses from rocks above and high pressures and temperatures.
- a. Thing
- b. Metamorphic rocks0
- c. Undefined
- d. Undefined

33. In geology, a _____ zone is an area on Earth where two tectonic plates meet and move towards one another, with one sliding underneath the other and moving down into the mantle, at rates typically measured in centimeters per year. An oceanic plate ordinarily slides underneath a continental plate; this often creates an orogenic zone with many volcanoes and earthquakes.
- a. Thing
- b. Subduction0
- c. Undefined
- d. Undefined

34. A _____ is an area on Earth where two tectonic plates meet and move towards one another, with one sliding underneath the other and moving down into the mantle, at rates typically measured in centimeters per year. In a sense, subduction zones are the opposite of divergent boundaries, areas where material rises up from the mantle and plates are moving apart.
- a. Subduction zone0
- b. Thing
- c. Undefined
- d. Undefined

35. _____ is a theory of geology that has been developed to explain the observed evidence for large scale motions of the Earth's lithosphere. The theory encompassed and superseded the older theory of continental drift.
- a. Plate tectonics0
- b. Thing
- c. Undefined
- d. Undefined

36. _____ is the process of heating a solid substance to a point where it turns into a liquid. An object that has melted is molten.
- a. Melting0
- b. Thing
- c. Undefined
- d. Undefined

37. In plate tectonics, a _____ is an actively deforming region where two tectonic plates or fragments of lithosphere move towards one another. When two plates move toward one another, they form either a subduction zone or a continental collision.
- a. Thing
- b. Convergent boundary0
- c. Undefined
- d. Undefined

38. _____ is displacement of solids by the agents of ocean currents, wind, water, or ice by downward or down-slope movement in response to gravity or by living organisms.
- a. Erosion0
- b. Thing
- c. Undefined
- d. Undefined

39. _____ is a fine-grained sedimentary rock whose original constituents were clays or muds. It is characterized by thin laminae breaking with an irregular curving fracture, often splintery and usually parallel to the often-indistinguishable bedding plane.

Chapter 3. Igneous Rocks, Intrusive Activity, and the Origin of Igneous Rocks   35

a. Shale0	b. Thing
c. Undefined	d. Undefined

40. _____ is a common gray to black extrusive volcanic rock. It is usually fine-grained due to rapid cooling of lava on the Earth's surface. It may be porphyritic containing larger crystals in a fine matrix, or vesicular, or frothy scoria.
a. Thing	b. Basalt0
c. Undefined	d. Undefined

41. _____ is the oxide of silicon, chemical formula SiO_2, and is known for its hardness as early as the 16th century. It is a principle component in most types of glass and substances such as concrete.
a. Thing	b. Silica0
c. Undefined	d. Undefined

42. _____ is a common and widely occurring type of intrusive, felsic, igneous rock. Granites are usually medium to coarsely crystalline, occasionally with some individual crystals larger than the groundmass forming a rock known as porphyry. Granites can be pink to dark gray or even black, depending on their chemistry and mineralogy.
a. Thing	b. Granite0
c. Undefined	d. Undefined

43. _____ is the second most common mineral in the Earth's continental crust. It is made up of a lattice of silica tetrahedra. _____ belongs to the rhombohedral crystal system. In nature _____ crystals are often twinned, distorted, or so intergrown with adjacent crystals of _____ or other minerals as to only show part of this shape, or to lack obvious crystal faces altogether and appear massive.
a. Thing	b. Quartz0
c. Undefined	d. Undefined

44. _____ is the name of a group of rock-forming minerals which make up as much as sixty percent of the Earth's crust. Feldspars crystallize from magma in both intrusive and extrusive rocks, and they can also occur as compact minerals, as veins, and are also present in many types of metamorphic rock.
a. Thing	b. Feldspar0
c. Undefined	d. Undefined

45. _____ is an igneous rock of volcanic origin. They often have a vesicular texture, which is the result voids left by volatiles escaping from the molten lava. Pumice is a rock, which is an example of explosive volcanic eruption. It is so vesicular that it floats in water.
a. Thing	b. Volcanic rock0
c. Undefined	d. Undefined

46. A _____ is a section of a river of relatively steep gradient causing an increase in water flow and turbulence. A _____ is a hydrological feature between a run and a cascade. It is characterized by the river becoming shallower and having some rocks exposed above the flow surface.
a. Thing	b. Rapid0
c. Undefined	d. Undefined

Chapter 3. Igneous Rocks, Intrusive Activity, and the Origin of Igneous Rocks

47. In geology and astronomy, the term _____ is used to denote types of rock that consist predominantly of _____ minerals. Such rocks include a wide range of igneous, metamorphic and sedimentary types. Most of the Earth's mantle and crust are made up of _____ rocks. The same is true of the Moon and the other rocky planets.
    a. Thing
    b. Silicate0
    c. Undefined
    d. Undefined

48. _____ is the gas phase of water. _____ is one state of the water cycle within the hydrosphere. _____ can be produced from the evaporation of liquid water or from the sublimation of ice. Under normal atmospheric conditions, _____ is continuously evaporating and condensing.
    a. Water vapor0
    b. Thing
    c. Undefined
    d. Undefined

49. _____ is the gas phase component of a another state of matter which does not completely fill its container. It is distinguished from the pure gas phase by the presence of the same substance in another state of matter. Hence when a liquid has completely evaporated, it is said that the system has been completely transformed to the gas phase.
    a. Thing
    b. Vapor0
    c. Undefined
    d. Undefined

50. _____ is the process of formation of solid crystals from a uniform solution. It is also a chemical solid-liquid separation technique, in which mass transfer of a solute from the liquid solution to a pure solid crystalline phase occurs.
    a. Crystallization0
    b. Thing
    c. Undefined
    d. Undefined

51. _____ refers to the diameter of individual grains of sediment, or the lithified particles in clastic rocks. The term may also be applied to other granular materials. This is different from the crystallite size, which is the size of a single crystal inside the particles or grains.
    a. Particle size0
    b. Thing
    c. Undefined
    d. Undefined

52. _____ is an igneous, volcanic rock, of felsic composition. It may have any texture from aphanitic to porphyritic. The mineral assemblage is usually quartz, alkali feldspar and plagioclase. Biotite and pyroxene are common accessory minerals.
    a. Thing
    b. Rhyolite0
    c. Undefined
    d. Undefined

53. _____ is an igneous, volcanic rock, of intermediate composition, with aphanitic to porphyritic texture.
    a. Thing
    b. Andesite0
    c. Undefined
    d. Undefined

54. _____, also designated 134340 _____, is the second-largest known dwarf planet in the Solar System and the tenth-largest body observed directly orbiting the Sun. It is primarily composed of rock and ice and is relatively small; approximately a fifth the mass of the Earth's Moon and a third its volume.
    a. Pluto0
    b. Place
    c. Undefined
    d. Undefined

Chapter 3. Igneous Rocks, Intrusive Activity, and the Origin of Igneous Rocks

55. _____ is a very coarse-grained igneous rock that has a grain size of 20 mm or more; such rocks are referred to as pegmatitic.
 a. Pegmatite0
 b. Thing
 c. Undefined
 d. Undefined

56. A _____ is a solid in which the constituent atoms, molecules, or ions are packed in a regularly ordered, repeating pattern extending in all three spatial dimensions. Most metals encountered in everyday life are polycrystals. Crystals are often symmetrically intergrown to form _____ twins.
 a. Crystal0
 b. Thing
 c. Undefined
 d. Undefined

57. _____ is a very important series of tectosilicate minerals within the feldspar family. Rather than referring to a particular mineral with a specific chemical composition, it is a solid solution series.
 a. Thing
 b. Plagioclase0
 c. Undefined
 d. Undefined

58. _____ is a chemical element. It is a soft silvery-white metallic alkali metal that occurs naturally bound to other elements in seawater and many minerals. It oxidizes rapidly in air and is very reactive, especially towards water. In many respects, it and sodium are chemically similar, although organisms in general, and animal cells in particular, treat them very differently.
 a. Thing
 b. Potassium0
 c. Undefined
 d. Undefined

59. _____ is a grey to dark grey intermediate intrusive igneous rock composed principally of plagioclase feldspar, biotite, hornblende, and/or pyroxene. It may contain small amounts of quartz, microcline and olivine.
 a. Diorite0
 b. Thing
 c. Undefined
 d. Undefined

60. _____ is a dark, coarse-grained, intrusive igneous rock chemically equivalent to basalt. It is a plutonic rock, formed when molten magma is trapped beneath the Earth's surface and cools into a crystalline mass.
 a. Thing
 b. Gabbro0
 c. Undefined
 d. Undefined

61. _____ is a measure of the resistance of a fluid to deform under shear stress. It is commonly perceived as "thickness", or resistance to flow. _____ describes a fluid's internal resistance to flow and may be thought of as a measure of fluid friction.
 a. Thing
 b. Viscosity0
 c. Undefined
 d. Undefined

62. An _____ is an atom or group of atoms which have lost or gained one or more electrons, making them negatively or positively charged.
 a. Ion0
 b. Thing
 c. Undefined
 d. Undefined

63. In chemistry, a _____ is defined as a sufficiently stable electrically neutral group of at least two atoms in a definite arrangement held together by strong chemical bonds.

Chapter 3. Igneous Rocks, Intrusive Activity, and the Origin of Igneous Rocks

a. Thing
b. Molecule
c. Undefined
d. Undefined

64. A _____ in geology is an intrusive igneous rock body that crystallized from a magma below the surface of the Earth. Plutons include batholiths, dikes, sills, laccoliths, lopoliths, and other igneous bodies. In practice, "_____" usually refers to a distinctive mass of igneous rock, typically kilometers in dimension, without a tabular shape like those of dikes and sills.
   a. Pluton
   b. Thing
   c. Undefined
   d. Undefined

65. _____ are the fundamental building blocks of chemistry, and are conserved in chemical reactions.
   a. Atoms
   b. Thing
   c. Undefined
   d. Undefined

66. A _____ is an intrusion into a cross-cutting fissure, meaning a _____ cuts across other pre-existing layers or bodies of rock, this means that a _____ is always younger than the rocks that contain it. The thickness is usually much smaller than the other two dimensions. Thickness can vary from sub-centimeter scale to many meters in thickness and the lateral dimensions can extend over many kilometers.
   a. Dike
   b. Thing
   c. Undefined
   d. Undefined

67. The _____ group of sheet silicate minerals includes several closely related materials having highly perfect basal cleavage. All are monoclinic with a tendency towards pseudo-hexagonal crystals and are similar in chemical composition. The highly perfect cleavage, which is the most prominent characteristic of _____, is explained by the hexagonal sheet-like arrangement of its atoms.
   a. Thing
   b. Mica
   c. Undefined
   d. Undefined

68. _____ is a phyllosilicate mineral of aluminium and potassium. It has a highly perfect basal cleavage yielding remarkably thin laminae, which are often highly elastic. Sheets of _____ 5 metres by 3 metres have been found in Nellore, India.
   a. Thing
   b. Muscovite
   c. Undefined
   d. Undefined

69. _____, in mineralogy, is the tendency of crystalline materials to split along definite planes, creating smooth surfaces.
   a. Cleavage
   b. Thing
   c. Undefined
   d. Undefined

70. _____ is approximately 70% more dense than lead and is weakly radioactive. It occurs naturally in low concentrations in soil, rock and water.
   a. Thing
   b. Uranium
   c. Undefined
   d. Undefined

Chapter 3. Igneous Rocks, Intrusive Activity, and the Origin of Igneous Rocks

71. The mineral _____ is a beryllium aluminium cyclosilicate with the chemical formula $Be_3Al_2_6$. The hexagonal crystals of _____ may be very small or range to several meters in size. Terminated crystals are relatively rare. _____ exhibits conchoidal fracture, has a hardness of 7.5–8, a specific gravity of 2.63–2.80. It has a vitreous luster and can be transparent or translucent.
   a. Thing
   b. Beryl0
   c. Undefined
   d. Undefined

72. _____ is the chemical element that has the symbol Be and atomic number 4. A bivalent element, elemental _____ is a steel grey, strong, light-weight yet brittle, alkaline earth metal
   a. Thing
   b. Beryllium0
   c. Undefined
   d. Undefined

73. _____ is a soft white lustrous transition metal, it has the highest electrical and thermal conductivity for a metal.
   a. Thing
   b. Silver0
   c. Undefined
   d. Undefined

74. _____ is a chemical element in the periodic table that has the symbol Zn and atomic number 30. In some historical and sculptural contexts, it is known as spelter.
   a. Zinc0
   b. Thing
   c. Undefined
   d. Undefined

75. A _____ is any aspect of an object or substance that can be measured or perceived without changing its identity. Physical properties can be intensive or extensive. An intensive property does not depend on the size or amount of matter in the object, while an extensive property does.
   a. Physical property0
   b. Thing
   c. Undefined
   d. Undefined

76. A _____ is one which contains both magnesium and iron.
   a. Ferromagnesian mineral0
   b. Thing
   c. Undefined
   d. Undefined

77. _____ is a term used in geology to refer to silicate minerals, magmas, and rocks which are enriched in the lighter elements such as silica, oxygen, aluminium, sodium, and potassium. _____ minerals are usually light in color and have specific gravities less than 3. Common _____ minerals include quartz, muscovite, orthoclase, and the sodium rich plagioclase feldspars.
   a. Thing
   b. Felsic0
   c. Undefined
   d. Undefined

78. In geology, _____ minerals and rocks are silicate minerals, magmas, and volcanic and intrusive igneous rocks that have relatively high concentrations of the heavier elements. The term is a combination of "magnesium" and ferrum.
   a. Mafic0
   b. Thing
   c. Undefined
   d. Undefined

79. _____ is an intrusive igneous rock similar to granite, but contains more plagioclase than potassium feldspar. It usually contains abundant biotite mica and hornblende, giving it a darker appearance than true granite.

Chapter 3. Igneous Rocks, Intrusive Activity, and the Origin of Igneous Rocks

    a. Granodiorite0   b. Thing
    c. Undefined   d. Undefined

80. An _____ is a chemical compound containing an oxygen atom and other elements. Most of the earth's crust consists of them. They result when elements are oxidized by air.
    a. Oxide0   b. Thing
    c. Undefined   d. Undefined

81. _____ has the symbol Mg. It is the ninth most abundant element in the universe by mass. It constitutes about 2% of the Earth's crust by mass, and it is the third most abundant element dissolved in seawater. It is essential to all living cells, and is the 11th most abundant element by mass in the human body.
    a. Magnesium0   b. Thing
    c. Undefined   d. Undefined

82. _____ is a chemical element metal. It is a lustrous, silvery soft metal. It and nickel are notable for being the final elements produced by stellar nucleosynthesis, and thus are the heaviest elements which do not require a supernova or similarly cataclysmic event for formation.
    a. Iron0   b. Thing
    c. Undefined   d. Undefined

83. _____ is a silvery and ductile member of the poor metal group of chemical elements. It has the symbol Al and atomic number 13.
    a. Thing   b. Aluminum0
    c. Undefined   d. Undefined

84. _____ is a dense, coarse-grained igneous rock, consisting mostly of the minerals olivine and pyroxene. _____ is ultramafic and ultrabasic, as the rock contains less than 45% silica. This type of rock is derived from the Earth's mantle, either as solid blocks and fragments, or as crystals accumulated from magmas that formed in the mantle.
    a. Peridotite0   b. Thing
    c. Undefined   d. Undefined

85. The mineral _____ is a magnesium iron silicate. It is one of the most common minerals on Earth, and has also been identified on the Moon, Mars, and comet Wild 2.
    a. Olivine0   b. Thing
    c. Undefined   d. Undefined

86. The _____ are a group of important rock-forming silicate minerals found in many igneous and metamorphic rocks. They share a common structure comprised of single chains of silica tetrahedra and they crystalise in the monoclinic and orthorhombic system.
    a. Thing   b. Pyroxenes0
    c. Undefined   d. Undefined

87. In geology, a _____ is the outermost layer of a planet, part of its lithosphere. They are generally composed of a less dense material than its deeper layers.Earths' is composed mainly of basalt and granite. It is cooler and more rigid than the deeper layers of the mantle and core.

Chapter 3. Igneous Rocks, Intrusive Activity, and the Origin of Igneous Rocks   41

a. Thing
b. Crust0
c. Undefined
d. Undefined

88. _____ is molten rock expelled by a volcano during an eruption. When first extruded from a volcanic vent, it is a liquid at temperatures from 700 °C to 1,200 °C.
a. Lava0
b. Thing
c. Undefined
d. Undefined

89. In geography, a _____ is a landscape form or region that receives very little precipitation. They are defined as areas that receive an average annual precipitation of less than 250 mm. A _____ where vegetation cover is exceedingly sparse correspond to the 'hyperarid' regions of the earth, where rainfall is exceedingly rare and infrequent.
a. Place
b. Desert0
c. Undefined
d. Undefined

90. _____ is a rock formation rizing nearly 1,800 feet above the high-desert plain on the Navajo reservation, about 20 kilometers southwest of the northern New Mexico town of _____, which is named for the peak.
a. Place
b. Shiprock0
c. Undefined
d. Undefined

91. In geology, a _____ is a tabular pluton that has intruded between older layers of sedimentary rock, beds of volcanic lava or tuff, or even along the direction of foliation in metamorphic rock. The term _____ is synonymous with concordant intrusive sheet. This means that the _____ does not cut across preexisting rocks. Contrast this with dikes.
a. Sill0
b. Thing
c. Undefined
d. Undefined

92. A _____ coastline occurs where bands of differing rock type run perpendicular to the coast.
a. Thing
b. Discordant0
c. Undefined
d. Undefined

93. A _____ coastline occurs where the bands of differing rock types run parallel to the coast. The outer hard rock provides a protective barrier to erosion of the softer rocks further inland.
a. Thing
b. Concordant0
c. Undefined
d. Undefined

94. A _____ is a volcanic landform created when lava hardens within a vent on an active volcano. When forming, a plug can cause an extreme build-up of pressure if volatile-charged magma is trapped beneath it, and this can sometimes lead to an explosive eruption.
a. Thing
b. Volcanic neck0
c. Undefined
d. Undefined

95. A _____ is a geological feature that is also known as a Rip in the earth causing magma to flow out and forming an undersea volcano, it also has geological features, a continuous elevational crest for some distance. Ridges are usually termed hills or mountains as well, depending on size.
a. Thing
b. Ridge0
c. Undefined
d. Undefined

42 *Chapter 3. Igneous Rocks, Intrusive Activity, and the Origin of Igneous Rocks*

96. A _____ is a large emplacement of igneous intrusive rock that forms from cooled magma deep in the Earth's crust. They are almost always made mostly of felsic or intermediate rock-types, such as granite, quartz monzonite, or diorite.
    a. Thing
    b. Batholith0
    c. Undefined
    d. Undefined

97. _____ are large emplacements of igneous intrusive rock that forms from cooled magma deep in the Earth's crust. They are almost always made mostly of felsic or intermediate rock-types, such as granite, quartz monzonite, or diorite.
    a. Batholiths0
    b. Thing
    c. Undefined
    d. Undefined

98. A _____ is an intrusion caused by buoyancy and pressure differentials. A _____ is any relatively mobile mass that intrudes into preexisting strata. Diapirs commonly intrude vertically upward along fractures or zones of structural weakness through more dense overlying rocks because of density contrast between a less dense, lower rock mass and overlying denser rocks. The density contrast manifests as a force of buoyancy.
    a. Thing
    b. Diapir0
    c. Undefined
    d. Undefined

99. A _____ is a landform that extends above the surrounding terrain in a limited area. A _____ is generally steeper than a hill, but there is no universally accepted standard definition for the height of a _____ or a hill although a _____ usually has an identifiable summit.
    a. Mountain0
    b. Place
    c. Undefined
    d. Undefined

100. The _____ is a mountain range that is almost entirely in the eastern portion of the U.S. state of California. The _____ stretches 400 miles , from Fredonyer Pass in the north to Tehachapi Pass in the south. It is bounded on the west by California's Central Valley, and on the east by the Great Basin.
    a. Sierra Nevada0
    b. Place
    c. Undefined
    d. Undefined

101. The _____ is defined as the part of the land adjoining or near the ocean. A coastline is properly a line on a map indicating the disposition of a _____, but the word is often used to refer to the _____ itself. The adjective coastal describes something as being on, near to, or associated with a _____.
    a. Coast0
    b. Place
    c. Undefined
    d. Undefined

102. A _____ is a group of mountains bordered by lowlands or separated from other mountain ranges by passes or rivers. Individual mountains within the same _____ do not necessarily have the same geology; they may be a mix of different orogeny, for example volcanoes, uplifted mountains or fold mountains and may, therefore, be of different rock.
    a. Mountain range0
    b. Thing
    c. Undefined
    d. Undefined

103. The _____ are a vast system of mountains in eastern North America.
    a. Place
    b. Appalachian Mountains0
    c. Undefined
    d. Undefined

Chapter 3. Igneous Rocks, Intrusive Activity, and the Origin of Igneous Rocks

104. _____ is an ecological concept referring to the relative representation of a species in a particular ecosystem. It is usually measured as the mean number of individuals found per sample.
- a. Thing
- b. Abundance0
- c. Undefined
- d. Undefined

105. The _____ are the broad expanse of prairie and steppe which lie east of the Rocky Mountains in the United States and Canada.
- a. Great Plains0
- b. Place
- c. Undefined
- d. Undefined

106. A _____ is a deep valley between cliffs often carved from the landscape by a river. Most were formed by a process of long-time erosion from a plateau level. The cliffs form because harder rock strata that are resistant to erosion and weathering remain exposed on the valley walls.
- a. Thing
- b. Canyon0
- c. Undefined
- d. Undefined

107. The _____ is a river in the southwestern United States and northwestern Mexico, approximately 1,450 mi long, draining a part of the arid regions on the western slope of the Rocky Mountains. The natural course of the river flows into the Gulf of California, but the heavy use of the river as an irrigation source for the Imperial Valley has desiccated the lower course of the river in Mexico such that it no longer consistently reaches the sea.
- a. Colorado River0
- b. Place
- c. Undefined
- d. Undefined

108. The _____ is a very colorful, steep-sided gorge, carved by the Colorado River in the U.S. state of Arizona. It is one of the first national parks in the United States.
- a. Grand Canyon0
- b. Place
- c. Undefined
- d. Undefined

109. The _____ are a small, isolated mountain range rizing from the Great Plains of North America in western South Dakota and extending into Wyoming, USA. Set off from the main body of the Rocky Mountains, the region is somewhat of a geological anomaly—accurately described as an "island of trees in a sea of grass.
- a. Black Hills0
- b. Place
- c. Undefined
- d. Undefined

110. In geology, _____ refers to heat sources within the planet. The planet's internal heat was originally generated during its accretion, due to gravitational binding energy, and since then additional heat has continued to be generated by the radioactive decay of elements such as uranium, thorium, and potassium.
- a. Geothermal0
- b. Thing
- c. Undefined
- d. Undefined

111. The _____ is the rate of increase in temperature per unit depth in the Earth. It varies with location and is typically measured by determining the bottom open-hole temperature after the drilling of a borehole.
- a. Thing
- b. Geothermal gradient0
- c. Undefined
- d. Undefined

Chapter 3. Igneous Rocks, Intrusive Activity, and the Origin of Igneous Rocks

112. A _____ is an upwelling of abnormally hot rock within the Earth's mantle. As the heads of mantle plumes can partly melt when they reach shallow depths, they are thought to be the cause of volcanic centers known as hotspots and probably also to have caused flood basalts.
   a. Event
   b. Mantle plume0
   c. Undefined
   d. Undefined

113. _____ in the most general terms refers to the movement of currents within fluids. _____ is one of the major modes of Heat and mass transfer. In fluids, convective heat and mass transfer take place through both diffusion and by advection, in which matter or heat is transported by the larger-scale motion of currents in the fluid.
   a. Thing
   b. Convection0
   c. Undefined
   d. Undefined

114. _____ is an oceanographic phenomenon that involves wind-driven motion of dense, cooler, and usually nutrient-rich water towards the ocean surface, replacing the warmer, usually nutrient-deplete surface water.
   a. Thing
   b. Upwelling0
   c. Undefined
   d. Undefined

115. _____ is a location on the Earth's surface that has experienced active volcanism for a long period of time. J. Tuzo Wilson came up with the idea in 1963 that volcanic chains like the Hawaiian Islands result from the slow movement of a tectonic plate across a "fixed" hot spot deep beneath the surface of the planet.
   a. Thing
   b. Hot spots0
   c. Undefined
   d. Undefined

116. An _____ is any piece of land that is completely surrounded by water, above high tide. There are two main types of islands: continental islands and oceanic islands. There are also artificial islands. A grouping of geographically and/or geologically related islands is called an archipelago.
   a. Thing
   b. Island0
   c. Undefined
   d. Undefined

117. The _____ form an archipelago of nineteen islands and atolls, numerous smaller islets, and undersea seamounts trending northwest by southeast in the North Pacific Ocean between latitudes 19° N and 29° N. The archipelago takes its name from the largest island in the group and extends some 1500 miles from the Island of Hawai'i in the south to northernmost Kure Atoll.
   a. Place
   b. Hawaiian Islands0
   c. Undefined
   d. Undefined

118. The _____ of a crystalline solid is the temperature range at which it changes state from solid to liquid. Although the phrase would suggest a specific temperature, most crystalline compounds actually melt over a range of a few degrees or less. At the _____ the solid and liquid phase exist in equilibrium.
   a. Melting point0
   b. Thing
   c. Undefined
   d. Undefined

119. _____ involves the study of the interaction of humans with the geologic environment including the biosphere, the lithosphere, the hydrosphere, and to some extent the atmosphere.

Chapter 3. Igneous Rocks, Intrusive Activity, and the Origin of Igneous Rocks

a. Environmental geology0
b. Thing
c. Undefined
d. Undefined

120. A _____ is a large underground pool of molten rock lying under the surface of the earth's crust. The molten rock in such a chamber is under great pressure, and given enough time and pressure can gradually fracture the rock around it creating outlets for the magma.
a. Magma chamber0
b. Thing
c. Undefined
d. Undefined

121. _____ is a general term for a variety of phenomena resulting from the presence and flow of charge. This includes many well-known physical phenomena such as lightning, electromagnetic fields and electric currents, and is put to use in industrial applications such as electronics and electric power.
a. Thing
b. Electricity0
c. Undefined
d. Undefined

122. A _____ is a body of water or other liquid of considerable size contained on a body of land. A vast majority are fresh water, and lie in the Northern Hemisphere at higher latitudes. Most have a natural outflow in the form of a river or stream, but some do not, and lose water solely by evaporation and/or underground seepage.
a. Lake0
b. Thing
c. Undefined
d. Undefined

123. _____ is a chemical element in the periodic table that has the symbol Sn. This silvery, malleable poor metal that is not easily oxidized in air and resists corrosion is found in many alloys and is used to coat other metals to prevent corrosion. It is obtained chiefly from the mineral cassiterite, where it occurs as an oxide. It is the classic alloying metal to make bronze.
a. Thing
b. Tin0
c. Undefined
d. Undefined

124. _____ defines an important group of generally dark-colored rock-forming inosilicate minerals linked at the vertices and generally containing ions of iron and/or magnesium in their structures. Amphiboles crystallize into two crystal systems, monoclinic and orthorhombic.
a. Amphibole0
b. Thing
c. Undefined
d. Undefined

125. A _____ is a unique arrangement of atoms in a crystal. It is composed of a unit cell, a set of atoms arranged in a particular way, which is periodically repeated in three dimensions on a lattice. The spacing between unit cells in various directions is called its lattice parameters. The symmetry properties of the crystal are embodied in its space group.
a. Thing
b. Crystal structure0
c. Undefined
d. Undefined

126. _____ is a common phyllosilicate mineral within the mica group. Primarily a solid-solution series between the iron-endmember annite, and the magnesium-endmember phlogopite; more aluminous endmembers include siderophyllite.
a. Thing
b. Biotite0
c. Undefined
d. Undefined

Chapter 3. Igneous Rocks, Intrusive Activity, and the Origin of Igneous Rocks

127. _____ is a chemical element. A heavy, malleable, ductile, precious, grey-white transition metal, it is resistant to corrosion and occurs in some nickel and copper ores along with some native deposits. It is used in jewelry, laboratory equipment, electrical contacts, dentistry, and automobile emissions control devices.
   a. Platinum0
   b. Thing
   c. Undefined
   d. Undefined

128. _____ is a steel-gray, lustrous, hard metal that takes a high polish and has a high melting point. It is also odourless, tasteless, and malleable
   a. Thing
   b. Chromium0
   c. Undefined
   d. Undefined

129. A _____ is a natural depression or hole in the surface topography caused by the removal of soil or bedrock, often both, by water. They may vary in size from less than a meter to several hundred meters both in diameter and depth, and vary in form from soil-lined bowls to bedrock-edged chasms.
   a. Thing
   b. Sinkhole0
   c. Undefined
   d. Undefined

130. _____ in meteorology are large scale patterns in the atmospheric pressure field that are nearly stationary, effectively "blocking" or redirecting migratory cyclones. These _____ can remain in place for several days or even weeks, causing the areas affected by them to have the same kind of weather for an extended period of time.
   a. Thing
   b. Blocks0
   c. Undefined
   d. Undefined

131. The _____ is the layer of granitic, sedimentary, and metamorphic rocks which form the continents and the areas of shallow seabed close to their shores, known as continental shelves. It is less dense than the material of the Earth's mantle and thus "floats" on top of it. _____ is also less dense than oceanic crust, though it is considerably thicker. About 40% of the Earth's surface is now underlain by _____.
   a. Thing
   b. Continental crust0
   c. Undefined
   d. Undefined

132. _____ is the part of Earth's lithosphere that surfaces in the ocean basins. _____ is primarily composed of mafic rocks, or sima. It is thinner than continental crust, or sial, generally less than 10 kilometers thick, however it is more dense, having a mean density of about 3.3 grams per cubic centimeter.
   a. Oceanic crust0
   b. Thing
   c. Undefined
   d. Undefined

133. In plate tectonics, a _____ a linear feature that exists between two tectonic plates that are moving away from each other. These areas can form in the middle of continents but eventually form ocean basins.
   a. Divergent plate boundary0
   b. Thing
   c. Undefined
   d. Undefined

134. The _____ is the region of the Earth between 100-200 km below the surface that is the weak or "soft" zone in the upper mantle. It lies just below the lithosphere, which is involved in plate movements and isostatic adjustments. In spite of its heat, pressures keep it plastic, and it has a relatively low density. Seismic waves pass relatively slowly through the _____.

Chapter 3. Igneous Rocks, Intrusive Activity, and the Origin of Igneous Rocks

a. Thing
b. Asthenosphere0
c. Undefined
d. Undefined

135. A _____, is a tall, conical volcano composed of many layers of hardened lava, tephra, and volcanic ash. These volcanoes are characterized by a steep profile and periodic, explosive eruptions. The lava that flows from them is viscous, and cools and hardens before spreading very far.
a. Stratovolcano0
b. Thing
c. Undefined
d. Undefined

136. The _____ is the solid outermost shell of a rocky planet. On the Earth, the _____ includes the crust and the uppermost mantle which is joined to the crust across the Mohorovièiæ discontinuity. _____ is underlain by asthenosphere, the weaker, hotter, and deeper part of the upper mantle.
a. Thing
b. Lithosphere0
c. Undefined
d. Undefined

137. A _____ is a type of excavation or depression in the ground. They are generally defined by being deeper than they are wide, and by being narrow compared to their length.
a. Trench0
b. Thing
c. Undefined
d. Undefined

138. _____ is a granite dome located in _____, Georgia, a suburb of Atlanta. It is the world's largest exposed mass of granite. At its summit, the elevation is 1,683 feet above the surrounding plateau.
a. Stone Mountain0
b. Place
c. Undefined
d. Undefined

Chapter 4. Volcanism and Extrusive Rocks

1. _____ is the average and variations of weather over long periods of time. _____ zones can be defined using parameters such as temperature and rainfall.
   a. Climate0
   b. Thing
   c. Undefined
   d. Undefined

2. _____ is the gas phase of water. _____ is one state of the water cycle within the hydrosphere. _____ can be produced from the evaporation of liquid water or from the sublimation of ice. Under normal atmospheric conditions, _____ is continuously evaporating and condensing.
   a. Thing
   b. Water vapor0
   c. Undefined
   d. Undefined

3. _____ is the gas phase component of a another state of matter which does not completely fill its container. It is distinguished from the pure gas phase by the presence of the same substance in another state of matter. Hence when a liquid has completely evaporated, it is said that the system has been completely transformed to the gas phase.
   a. Thing
   b. Vapor0
   c. Undefined
   d. Undefined

4. _____ is the change in matter of a substance to a denser phase, such as a gas to a liquid. _____ commonly occurs when a vapor is cooled to a liquid, but can also occur if a vapor is compressed into a liquid, or undergoes a combination of cooling and compression.
   a. Thing
   b. Condensation0
   c. Undefined
   d. Undefined

5. A _____ in physical geography describes the collective mass of water found on, under, and over the surface of a planet.
   a. Thing
   b. Hydrosphere0
   c. Undefined
   d. Undefined

6. A _____ is a disturbance that propagates through space or spacetime, transferring energy and momentum and sometimes angular momentum.
   a. Wave0
   b. Thing
   c. Undefined
   d. Undefined

7. A _____ is a series of waves created when a body of water, such as an ocean, is rapidly displaced on a massive scale. Earthquakes, mass movements above or below water, volcanic eruptions and other underwater explosions, landslides, large meteorite impacts and testing with nuclear weapons at sea all have the potential to generate a _____. The effects of a _____ can range from unnoticeable to devastating.
   a. Thing
   b. Tsunami0
   c. Undefined
   d. Undefined

8. An _____ is any piece of land that is completely surrounded by water, above high tide. There are two main types of islands: continental islands and oceanic islands. There are also artificial islands. A grouping of geographically and/or geologically related islands is called an archipelago.
   a. Thing
   b. Island0
   c. Undefined
   d. Undefined

Chapter 4. Volcanism and Extrusive Rocks

9. _____ is the process of heating a solid substance to a point where it turns into a liquid. An object that has melted is molten.
   a. Melting0
   b. Thing
   c. Undefined
   d. Undefined

10. A _____ is a large, slow moving river of ice, formed from compacted layers of snow, that slowly deforms and flows in response to gravity. _____ ice is the largest reservoir of fresh water on Earth, and second only to oceans as the largest reservoir of total water. Glaciers cover vast areas of polar regions but are restricted to the highest mountains in the tropics.
    a. Glacier0
    b. Thing
    c. Undefined
    d. Undefined

11. The _____ is the part of the earth, including air, land, surface rocks, and water, within which life occurs, and which biotic processes in turn alter or transform. From the broadest biophysiological point of view, the _____ is the global ecological system integrating all living beings and their relationships, including their interaction with the elements of the lithosphere, hydrosphere, and atmosphere. This _____ is postulated to have evolved, beginning through a process of biogenesis or biopoesis, at least some 3.5 billion years ago.
    a. Biosphere0
    b. Thing
    c. Undefined
    d. Undefined

12. _____ is the theory that Earth has been affected by sudden, short-lived, violent events that were sometimes worldwide in scope. The dominant paradigm of geology has been uniformitarianism, but recently a more inclusive and integrated view of geologic events has developed resulting in a gradual change in the scientific consensus, reflecting acceptance of some catastrophic events.
    a. Thing
    b. Catastrophism0
    c. Undefined
    d. Undefined

13. _____ is a general term for the plant life of a region; it refers to the ground cover provided by plants, and is, by far, the most abundant biotic element of the biosphere. Primeval redwood forests, coastal mangrove stands, sphagnum bogs, desert soil crusts, roadside weed patches, wheat fields, cultivated gardens and lawns; are all encompassed by the term _____.
    a. Vegetation0
    b. Place
    c. Undefined
    d. Undefined

14. _____ is a layer of gases surrounding the planet Earth and retained by the Earth's gravity. This mixture of gases is commonly known as air.
    a. Thing
    b. Earths atmosphere0
    c. Undefined
    d. Undefined

15. _____ consists of very fine rock and mineral particles less than 2 mm in diameter that are ejected from a volcanic vent. The very fine particles may be carried for many miles, settling out as a dust-like layer across the landscape
    a. Thing
    b. Ash fall0
    c. Undefined
    d. Undefined

16. In biology and ecology, _____ is the cessation of existence of a species or group of taxa, reducing biodiversity. The moment of _____ is generally considered to be the death of the last individual of that species.

Chapter 4. Volcanism and Extrusive Rocks

    a. Thing
    b. Extinction0
    c. Undefined
    d. Undefined

17. A _____ is an area with a high density of trees, historically, a wooded area set aside for hunting. These plant communities cover large areas of the globe and function as animal habitats, hydrologic flow modulators, and soil conservers, constituting one of the most important aspects of the Earth's biosphere.
    a. Forest0
    b. Thing
    c. Undefined
    d. Undefined

18. The _____ consists of the Sun and the other celestial objects gravitationally bound to it: the eight planets, their 165 known moons, three currently identified dwarf planets and their four known moons, and billions of small bodies.
    a. Thing
    b. Solar system0
    c. Undefined
    d. Undefined

19. _____ is the fifth planet from the Sun and the largest planet within the solar system. It is two and a half times as massive as all of the other planets in our solar system combined. _____, along with Saturn, Uranus and Neptune, is classified as a gas giant.
    a. Place
    b. Jupiter0
    c. Undefined
    d. Undefined

20. The _____ is Earth's only natural satellite. It makes a complete orbit around the Earth every 27.3 days, and the periodic variations in the geometry of the Earth–_____–Sun system are responsible for the lunar phases that repeat every 29.5 days.
    a. Moon0
    b. Thing
    c. Undefined
    d. Undefined

21. _____ is molten rock located beneath the surface of the Earth, and which often collects in a _____ chamber. _____ is a complex high-temperature fluid substance. Most are silicate solutions. It is capable of intrusion into adjacent rocks or of extrusion onto the surface as lava or ejected explosively as tephra to form pyroclastic rock. Environments of _____ formation include subduction zones, continental rift zones, mid-oceanic ridges, and hotspots, some of which are interpreted as mantle plumes.
    a. Magma0
    b. Thing
    c. Undefined
    d. Undefined

22. A _____ is any aspect of an object or substance that can be measured or perceived without changing its identity. Physical properties can be intensive or extensive. An intensive property does not depend on the size or amount of matter in the object, while an extensive property does.
    a. Thing
    b. Physical property0
    c. Undefined
    d. Undefined

23. _____ is molten rock expelled by a volcano during an eruption. When first extruded from a volcanic vent, it is a liquid at temperatures from 700 °C to 1,200 °C.
    a. Thing
    b. Lava0
    c. Undefined
    d. Undefined

Chapter 4. Volcanism and Extrusive Rocks

24. A _____ is a landform that extends above the surrounding terrain in a limited area. A _____ is generally steeper than a hill, but there is no universally accepted standard definition for the height of a _____ or a hill although a _____ usually has an identifiable summit.
   a. Place
   b. Mountain0
   c. Undefined
   d. Undefined

25. A _____ is an opening, or rupture, in the Earth's surface or crust, which allows hot, molten rock, ash and gases to escape from deep below the surface.
   a. Thing
   b. Volcano0
   c. Undefined
   d. Undefined

26. _____ is the part of Earth's lithosphere that surfaces in the ocean basins. _____ is primarily composed of mafic rocks, or sima. It is thinner than continental crust, or sial, generally less than 10 kilometers thick, however it is more dense, having a mean density of about 3.3 grams per cubic centimeter.
   a. Oceanic crust0
   b. Thing
   c. Undefined
   d. Undefined

27. _____ is the process of building mountains, and may be studied as a tectonic structural event, as a geographical event and a chronological event, in that orogenic events cause distinctive structural phenomena and related tectonic activity, affect certain regions of rocks and crust and happen within a time frame.
   a. Orogeny0
   b. Thing
   c. Undefined
   d. Undefined

28. In geology, a _____ is the outermost layer of a planet, part of its lithosphere. They are generally composed of a less dense material than its deeper layers. Earths' is composed mainly of basalt and granite. It is cooler and more rigid than the deeper layers of the mantle and core.
   a. Crust0
   b. Thing
   c. Undefined
   d. Undefined

29. The _____ is the largest of the Earth's oceanic divisions. It extends from the Arctic in the north to the Antarctic in the south, bounded by Asia and Australia on the west and the Americas on the east. At 169.2 million square kilometres in area, this largest division of the World Ocean – and, in turn, the hydrosphere – covers about 46% of the Earth's water surface and about 32% of its total surface area, making it larger than all of the Earth's land area combined.
   a. Pacific Ocean0
   b. Place
   c. Undefined
   d. Undefined

30. _____ is the oxide of silicon, chemical formula SiO_2, and is known for its hardness as early as the 16th century. It is a principle component in most types of glass and substances such as concrete.
   a. Silica0
   b. Thing
   c. Undefined
   d. Undefined

31. _____ is air-fall material produced by a volcanic eruption regardless of composition or fragment size. It is typically rhyolitic in composition as most explosive volcanoes are the product of the more viscous felsic or high silica magmas.
   a. Tephra0
   b. Thing
   c. Undefined
   d. Undefined

Chapter 4. Volcanism and Extrusive Rocks

32. _____ are clastic rocks composed solely or primarily of volcanic materials.
    a. Thing
    b. Pyroclastics0
    c. Undefined
    d. Undefined

33. _____ refers to the mode of igneous volcanic rock formation in which hot magma from inside the Earth flows out onto the surface as lava or explodes violently into the atmosphere to fall back as pyroclastics or tuff.
    a. Thing
    b. Extrusive0
    c. Undefined
    d. Undefined

34. A _____ comprises a geomorphological unit, and is largely defined by its surface form and location in the landscape, as part of the terrain, and as such, is typically an element of topography. They are categorised by features such as elevation, slope, orientation, stratification, rock exposure, and soil type. They include berms, mounds, hills, cliffs, valleys, rivers and numerous other elements.
    a. Thing
    b. Landform0
    c. Undefined
    d. Undefined

35. A _____ is a significant vertical, or near vertical, rock exposure. Cliffs are categorized as erosion landforms due to the processes of erosion and weathering that produce them. Cliffs are common on coasts, in mountainous areas, escarpments and along rivers. Cliffs are usually formed by rock that is resistant to erosion and weathering.
    a. Thing
    b. Cliff0
    c. Undefined
    d. Undefined

36. A _____ is any of a number of an extinct genus of proboscidean, often with long curved tusks and, in northern species, a covering of long hair. They lived from the Pliocene epoch from to around 4,000 years ago.
    a. Thing
    b. Mammoth0
    c. Undefined
    d. Undefined

37. A _____ is a geological phenomenon which includes a wide range of ground movement, such as rock falls, deep failure of slopes and shallow debris flows. Although gravity's action on an over-steepened slope is the primary reason for a _____, there are other contributing factors affecting the original slope stability.
    a. Landslide0
    b. Thing
    c. Undefined
    d. Undefined

38. A _____ is a section of a river of relatively steep gradient causing an increase in water flow and turbulence. A _____ is a hydrological feature between a run and a cascade. It is characterized by the river becoming shallower and having some rocks exposed above the flow surface.
    a. Rapid0
    b. Thing
    c. Undefined
    d. Undefined

39. An _____ is the result from the sudden release of stored energy in the Earth's crust that creates seismic waves. At the Earth's surface, earthquakes may manifest themselves by a shaking or displacement of the ground. An _____ is caused by tectonic plates getting stuck and putting a strain on the ground. The strain becomes so great that rocks give way by breaking and sliding along fault planes.
    a. Thing
    b. Earthquake0
    c. Undefined
    d. Undefined

Chapter 4. Volcanism and Extrusive Rocks

40. _____ are very large slides of snow or rock down a mountainside, caused when a buildup of snow is released down a slope, and is one of the major dangers faced in the mountains.
    a. Thing
    b. Avalanches0
    c. Undefined
    d. Undefined

41. A _____ is a large underground pool of molten rock lying under the surface of the earth's crust. The molten rock in such a chamber is under great pressure, and given enough time and pressure can gradually fracture the rock around it creating outlets for the magma.
    a. Magma chamber0
    b. Thing
    c. Undefined
    d. Undefined

42. _____ is an igneous rock of volcanic origin. They often have a vesicular texture, which is the result voids left by volatiles escaping from the molten lava. Pumice is a rock, which is an example of explosive volcanic eruption. It is so vesicular that it floats in water.
    a. Thing
    b. Volcanic rock0
    c. Undefined
    d. Undefined

43. A _____ is the most rapid up to 80 km/h and fluid type of downhill mass wasting.
    a. Mudflow0
    b. Thing
    c. Undefined
    d. Undefined

44. _____ is a stratovolcano in the Cascade Volcanic Arc in northern Oregon, in the Pacific Northwest region of the United States. It is located about 50 miles east-southeast of the city of Portland, on the border between Clackamas and Hood River counties.
    a. Mount Hood0
    b. Place
    c. Undefined
    d. Undefined

45. _____ is a dormant stratovolcano in the southernmost Coast Mountains of British Columbia. This heavily eroded dome complex is located within Garibaldi Provincial Park overlooking the town of Squamish, about 65 km north of Vancouver. The volcano is part of the Garibaldi Volcanic Belt which is a segment of the Cascade Volcanic Arc, but it is not within the geographic boundary of the Cascade Range.
    a. Mount Garibaldi0
    b. Place
    c. Undefined
    d. Undefined

46. _____ is a glaciated andesitic stratovolcano in the Cascade Volcanic Arc and the Cascades of Washington State in the United States about 30 miles due east of the city of Bellingham, Whatcom County. It is also easily visible from much of Greater Victoria, Greater Vancouver and the Fraser Valley just across the Canadian border to the north.
    a. Mount Baker0
    b. Place
    c. Undefined
    d. Undefined

47. A _____ is an area of highland, usually consisting of relatively flat rural area.
    a. Plateau0
    b. Place
    c. Undefined
    d. Undefined

48. A _____ is a flat, wide surface that is formed when lava comes out of the ground and spreads out very quickly.

Chapter 4. Volcanism and Extrusive Rocks

    a. Lava plateau0
    b. Thing
    c. Undefined
    d. Undefined

49. _____ is the science and study of the solid matter that constitute the Earth. Encompassing such things as rocks, soil, and gemstones, _____ studies the composition, structure, physical properties, history, and the processes that shape Earth's components.
    a. Geology0
    b. Thing
    c. Undefined
    d. Undefined

50. Earth's _____ is a ~2,900 km thick rocky shell comprizing approximately 70% of Earth's volume. It is predominantly solid and overlies the Earth's iron-rich core, which occupies about 30% of Earth's volume. Past episodes of melting and volcanism at the shallower levels of the _____ have produced a very thin crust of crystallized melt products near the surface, upon which we live.
    a. Thing
    b. Mantle0
    c. Undefined
    d. Undefined

51. The _____ is a region in the northwest of North America. The _____, broadly defined, extends from the ocean to the continental divide and includes all of Washington, most of Oregon, Idaho and British Columbia, and adjoining parts of Alaska, Yukon Territory and California. Both the name "_____" and the name "Cascadia", which is derived from the Cascade Range, are commonly used without a definition, although the term "_____" is considerably older, having its origins in the early 19th Century.
    a. Pacific Northwest0
    b. Place
    c. Undefined
    d. Undefined

52. The _____ are a volcanic arc which stretches from northern California to southwestern British Columbia, a distance of well over 700 mi. The arc has formed due to subduction along the Cascadia Subduction Zone and is part of the Pacific Ring of Fire.
    a. Cascade Volcanoes0
    b. Thing
    c. Undefined
    d. Undefined

53. In geology, _____ are rock s with a grain size of usually no less than 256 mm diameter.
    a. Thing
    b. Boulders0
    c. Undefined
    d. Undefined

54. _____ is an active volcano in the Hawaiian Islands, one of five shield volcanoes that together form the Island of Hawai'i. In Hawaiian, the word _____ means "spewing" or "much spreading", in reference to the mountain's frequent outpouring of lava. It is presently the most active volcano and one of the most visited active volcanoes on the planet.
    a. Kilauea0
    b. Thing
    c. Undefined
    d. Undefined

55. _____ is the highest mountain on Earth, as measured by the height of its summit above sea level. The mountain, which is part of the Himalaya range in High Asia, is located on the border between Nepal and Tibet, China.
    a. Place
    b. Mount Everest0
    c. Undefined
    d. Undefined

Chapter 4. Volcanism and Extrusive Rocks

56. _____ is an active shield volcano in the Hawaiian Islands, one of five volcanoes that form the Island of Hawai'i. _____ is Earth's largest volcano, with a volume estimated at approximately 18,000 cubic miles, although its peak is about 36 m lower than that of its neighbor, Mauna Kea.
    a. Place
    b. Mauna Loa0
    c. Undefined
    d. Undefined

57. Mean _____ is the average height of the sea, with reference to a suitable reference surface.
    a. Sea level0
    b. Thing
    c. Undefined
    d. Undefined

58. _____ rocks form when molten rock, magma, cools and solidifies, with or without crystallization, either below the surface as intrusive, plutonic rocks or on the surface as extrusive, volcanic, rocks.
    a. Igneous0
    b. Thing
    c. Undefined
    d. Undefined

59. In geology, _____ refers to heat sources within the planet. The planet's internal heat was originally generated during its accretion, due to gravitational binding energy, and since then additional heat has continued to be generated by the radioactive decay of elements such as uranium, thorium, and potassium.
    a. Geothermal0
    b. Thing
    c. Undefined
    d. Undefined

60. _____ is the use of geothermal heat to generate electricity.
    a. Geothermal power0
    b. Thing
    c. Undefined
    d. Undefined

61. _____ is a general term for a variety of phenomena resulting from the presence and flow of charge. This includes many well-known physical phenomena such as lightning, electromagnetic fields and electric currents, and is put to use in industrial applications such as electronics and electric power.
    a. Electricity0
    b. Thing
    c. Undefined
    d. Undefined

62. An _____ is a layer of gases that may surround a material body of sufficient mass. The gases are attracted by the gravity of the body, and are retained for a longer duration if gravity is high and the _____'s temperature is low. Some planets consist mainly of various gases, and thus have very deep atmospheres.
    a. Atmosphere0
    b. Place
    c. Undefined
    d. Undefined

63. _____ is an active stratovolcano located on the island of Luzon in the Philippines, at the intersection of the borders of the provinces of Zambales, Tarlac, and Pampanga.
    a. Mount Pinatubo0
    b. Thing
    c. Undefined
    d. Undefined

64. _____ is radiant energy emitted by the sun from a nuclear fusion reaction that creates electromagnetic energy. The spectrum of _____ is close to that of a black body with a temperature of about 5800 K. About half of the radiation is in the visible short-wave part of the electromagnetic spectrum. The other half is mostly in the near-infrared part, with some in the ultraviolet part of the spectrum.

Chapter 4. Volcanism and Extrusive Rocks

a. Solar radiation0
b. Thing
c. Undefined
d. Undefined

65. _____ as used in physics, is energy in the form of waves or moving subatomic particles.
    a. Radiation0
    b. Thing
    c. Undefined
    d. Undefined

66. _____ is the increase in the average temperature of the Earth's near-surface air and oceans in recent decades and its projected continuation. An increase in global temperatures can in turn cause other changes, including sea level rise, and changes in the amount and pattern of precipitation resulting in floods and drought. There may also be changes in the frequency and intensity of extreme weather events.
    a. Global warming0
    b. Thing
    c. Undefined
    d. Undefined

67. _____ is a solid deposition of water vapor from saturated air. If solid surfaces in contact with the air are chilled below the deposition point, then spicules of ice grow out from the solid surface. _____ is often observed around cracks in wooden sidewalks due to the moist air escaping from the ground below. Other objects on which _____ develops are those with low specific heat and high thermal emissivity, such as blackened metals.
    a. Frost0
    b. Thing
    c. Undefined
    d. Undefined

68. The _____ is the set of all extant phenomena in a given atmosphere at a given time. The term usually refers to the activity of these phenomena over short periods, as opposed to the term climate, which refers to the average atmospheric conditions over longer periods of time.
    a. Thing
    b. Weather0
    c. Undefined
    d. Undefined

69. _____ is the production of food, feed, fiber, fuel and other goods by the systematic raizing of plants and animals.
    a. Agriculture0
    b. Thing
    c. Undefined
    d. Undefined

70. _____ is a ruined Roman city near modern Naples in the Italian region of Campania. It, along with Herculaneum, was destroyed, and completely buried, during a catastrophic eruption of the volcano Mount Vesuvius spanning 2 days on 24 August 79 AD.
    a. Place
    b. Pompeii0
    c. Undefined
    d. Undefined

71. _____ is the most commonly used technique within the science of archaeology. It is the exposure, processing and recording of archaeological remains.
    a. Excavation0
    b. Thing
    c. Undefined
    d. Undefined

72. _____ refers to all species of microscopic fungi that grow in the form of multicellular filaments, called hyphae.
    a. Thing
    b. Mold0
    c. Undefined
    d. Undefined

Chapter 4. Volcanism and Extrusive Rocks

73. _____ is a chemical element represented by the symbol H and an atomic number of 1. At standard temperature and pressure it is a colorless, odorless, nonmetallic, tasteless, highly flammable diatomic gas . With an atomic mass of 1.00794 g/mol, _____ is the lightest element._____ is the most abundant of the chemical elements, constituting roughly 75% of the universe's elemental mass.
   a. Hydrogen0
   b. Thing
   c. Undefined
   d. Undefined

74. A _____ is a body of water or other liquid of considerable size contained on a body of land. A vast majority are fresh water, and lie in the Northern Hemisphere at higher latitudes. Most have a natural outflow in the form of a river or stream, but some do not, and lose water solely by evaporation and/or underground seepage.
   a. Lake0
   b. Thing
   c. Undefined
   d. Undefined

75. A _____ is an approximately circular depression in the surface of a planet, moon or other solid body in the Solar System, formed by the hyper-velocity impact of a smaller body with the surface. Impact craters typically have raised rims, and they range from small, simple, bowl-shaped depressions to large, complex, multi-ringed, impact basins.
   a. Thing
   b. Crater0
   c. Undefined
   d. Undefined

76. _____ is a caldera lake in the U.S. state of Oregon. It is the main feature of _____ National Park and famous for its deep blue color and water clarity. The lake partly fills a nearly 4,000 feet deep caldera that was formed around 5,677 by the collapse of the volcano Mount Mazama.
   a. Place
   b. Crater Lake0
   c. Undefined
   d. Undefined

77. _____ is a destroyed stratovolcano in the Oregon part of the Cascade Volcanic Belt and the Cascade Range. The volcano's collapsed caldera holds Crater Lake, and the entire mountain is located in Crater Lake National Park.
   a. Place
   b. Mount Mazama0
   c. Undefined
   d. Undefined

78. A _____ is a section of land devoted to the production and management of food, either produce or livestock. It is the basic unit in agricultural production.
   a. Farm0
   b. Thing
   c. Undefined
   d. Undefined

79. _____ is a measure of the resistance of a fluid to deform under shear stress. It is commonly perceived as "thickness", or resistance to flow. _____ describes a fluid's internal resistance to flow and may be thought of as a measure of fluid friction.
   a. Viscosity0
   b. Thing
   c. Undefined
   d. Undefined

80. In geology, _____ minerals and rocks are silicate minerals, magmas, and volcanic and intrusive igneous rocks that have relatively high concentrations of the heavier elements. The term is a combination of "magnesium" and ferrum.
   a. Thing
   b. Mafic0
   c. Undefined
   d. Undefined

81. _____ is a term used in geology to refer to silicate minerals, magmas, and rocks which are enriched in the lighter elements such as silica, oxygen, aluminium, sodium, and potassium. _____ minerals are usually light in color and have specific gravities less than 3. Common _____ minerals include quartz, muscovite, orthoclase, and the sodium rich plagioclase feldspars.
   a. Felsic0
   b. Thing
   c. Undefined
   d. Undefined

82. _____ is a volcanic fissure situated in the south of Iceland, not far from the canyon of Eldgjá and the small town Kirkjubæjarklaustur, in Skaftafell National Park. _____ is part of a volcanic system, centering on the Grímsvötn volcano and including the Eldgjá canyon and Katla volcano, and lies between the glaciers of Mýrdalsjökull and Vatnajökull, in an area of fissures which run in a south-west to north-east direction.
   a. Place
   b. Laki0
   c. Undefined
   d. Undefined

83. _____ is an atmospheric discharge of electricity, which usually, but not always, occurs during rain storms, and frequently during volcanic eruptions or dust storms.
   a. Thing
   b. Lightning0
   c. Undefined
   d. Undefined

84. _____ is an active volcano and is the highest peak in the Aleutian Range on the Alaska Peninsula in Alaska. It is located in the Chigmit Mountains southwest of Anchorage, Alaska.
   a. Place
   b. Mount Redoubt0
   c. Undefined
   d. Undefined

85. _____ is the elevation of an object from a known level or datum. Common datums are mean sea level and the surface of the World Geodetic System geoid, used by Global Positioning System. In aviation, _____ is measured in feet. For non-aviation uses, _____ may be measured in other units such as metres or miles.
   a. Altitude0
   b. Thing
   c. Undefined
   d. Undefined

86. _____ is a reaction force applied by a stretched string, rope or a similar object on the objects which stretch it. The direction of the force of it is parallel to the string, towards the string.
   a. Tension0
   b. Thing
   c. Undefined
   d. Undefined

87. The _____ of a crystalline solid is the temperature range at which it changes state from solid to liquid. Although the phrase would suggest a specific temperature, most crystalline compounds actually melt over a range of a few degrees or less. At the _____ the solid and liquid phase exist in equilibrium.
   a. Thing
   b. Melting point0
   c. Undefined
   d. Undefined

88. _____ technically refers to airborne solid particles or liquid droplets.
   a. Aerosol0
   b. Thing
   c. Undefined
   d. Undefined

Chapter 4. Volcanism and Extrusive Rocks

89. _____ is a strong mineral acid. It is soluble in water at all concentrations. _____ has many applications, and is one of the top products of the chemical industry. Principal uses include ore processing, fertilizer manufacturing, oil refining, wastewater processing, and chemical synthesis.
- a. Sulfuric acid0
- b. Thing
- c. Undefined
- d. Undefined

90. A _____ is a naturally occurring substance formed through geological processes that has a characteristic chemical composition, a highly ordered atomic structure and specific physical properties. A rock, by comparison, is an aggregate of minerals and need not have a specific chemical composition. Minerals range in composition from pure elements and simple salts to very complex silicates with thousands of known forms.
- a. Mineral0
- b. Thing
- c. Undefined
- d. Undefined

91. _____ is the process of formation of solid crystals from a uniform solution. It is also a chemical solid-liquid separation technique, in which mass transfer of a solute from the liquid solution to a pure solid crystalline phase occurs.
- a. Thing
- b. Crystallization0
- c. Undefined
- d. Undefined

92. In geology and astronomy, the term _____ is used to denote types of rock that consist predominantly of _____ minerals. Such rocks include a wide range of igneous, metamorphic and sedimentary types. Most of the Earth's mantle and crust are made up of _____ rocks. The same is true of the Moon and the other rocky planets.
- a. Thing
- b. Silicate0
- c. Undefined
- d. Undefined

93. _____ are the fundamental building blocks of chemistry, and are conserved in chemical reactions.
- a. Atoms0
- b. Thing
- c. Undefined
- d. Undefined

94. A _____ is a solid in which the constituent atoms, molecules, or ions are packed in a regularly ordered, repeating pattern extending in all three spatial dimensions. Most metals encountered in everyday life are polycrystals. Crystals are often symmetrically intergrown to form _____ twins.
- a. Crystal0
- b. Thing
- c. Undefined
- d. Undefined

95. _____, in everyday life, is most familiar as the agency that endows objects with weight. _____ is responsible for keeping the Earth and the other planets in their orbits around the Sun; for the formation of tides; and for various other phenomena that we observe. _____ is also the reason for the very existence of the Earth, the Sun, and most macroscopic objects in the universe; without it, matter would not have coalesced into these large masses, and life, as we know it, would not exist.
- a. Gravitation0
- b. Thing
- c. Undefined
- d. Undefined

96. _____ is a highly vesicular pyroclastic extrusive igneous rock of intermediate to siliceous magmas including rhyolite, trachyte and phonolite. _____ is usually light in color ranging from white, yellowish, gray, gray brown, and a dull red. Most of the time, it is white. As an extrusive rock it was made from a volcanic eruption.

Chapter 4. Volcanism and Extrusive Rocks

    a. Thing
    b. Pumice0
    c. Undefined
    d. Undefined

97. A _____ is a common and devastating result of some volcanic eruptions. The flows are fast-moving fluidized bodies of hot gas, ash and rock. The flows normally hug the ground and travel downhill under gravity, their speed depending upon the gradient of the slope and the size of the flow.
    a. Thing
    b. Pyroclastic flow0
    c. Undefined
    d. Undefined

98. _____ is an active volcano on the northern tip of the French overseas department of Martinique in the Caribbean. It is a stratovolcano, its volcanic cone composed of layers of volcanic ash and hardened lava.
    a. Mount Pelee0
    b. Thing
    c. Undefined
    d. Undefined

99. _____ forms when rock cools and solidifies either below the surface as intrusive rocks or on the surface as extrusive rocks. This magma can be derived from partial melts of pre-existing rocks in either the Earth's mantle or crust. Typically, the melting is caused by one or more of the following processes -- an increase in temperature, a decrease in pressure, or a change in composition.
    a. Igneous rock0
    b. Thing
    c. Undefined
    d. Undefined

100. _____ has the symbol Mg. It is the ninth most abundant element in the universe by mass. It constitutes about 2% of the Earth's crust by mass, and it is the third most abundant element dissolved in seawater. It is essential to all living cells, and is the 11th most abundant element by mass in the human body.
    a. Thing
    b. Magnesium0
    c. Undefined
    d. Undefined

101. _____ is a chemical element metal. It is a lustrous, silvery soft metal. It and nickel are notable for being the final elements produced by stellar nucleosynthesis, and thus are the heaviest elements which do not require a supernova or similarly cataclysmic event for formation.
    a. Thing
    b. Iron0
    c. Undefined
    d. Undefined

102. _____ is the second most common mineral in the Earth's continental crust. It is made up of a lattice of silica tetrahedra. _____ belongs to the rhombohedral crystal system. In nature _____ crystals are often twinned, distorted, or so intergrown with adjacent crystals of _____ or other minerals as to only show part of this shape, or to lack obvious crystal faces altogether and appear massive.
    a. Thing
    b. Quartz0
    c. Undefined
    d. Undefined

103. _____ is the name of a group of rock-forming minerals which make up as much as sixty percent of the Earth's crust. Feldspars crystallize from magma in both intrusive and extrusive rocks, and they can also occur as compact minerals, as veins, and are also present in many types of metamorphic rock.
    a. Thing
    b. Feldspar0
    c. Undefined
    d. Undefined

Chapter 4. Volcanism and Extrusive Rocks

104. A _____ is one which contains both magnesium and iron.
 a. Thing
 b. Ferromagnesian mineral0
 c. Undefined
 d. Undefined

105. _____ is an ecological concept referring to the relative representation of a species in a particular ecosystem. It is usually measured as the mean number of individuals found per sample.
 a. Thing
 b. Abundance0
 c. Undefined
 d. Undefined

106. _____ is an igneous, volcanic rock, of felsic composition. It may have any texture from aphanitic to porphyritic. The mineral assemblage is usually quartz, alkali feldspar and plagioclase. Biotite and pyroxene are common accessory minerals.
 a. Thing
 b. Rhyolite0
 c. Undefined
 d. Undefined

107. _____ is a high-silica igneous, volcanic rock. It is intermediate in compositions between andesite and rhyolite, and, like andesite, it consists mostly of plagioclase feldspar with biotite, hornblende, and pyroxene.
 a. Dacite0
 b. Thing
 c. Undefined
 d. Undefined

108. The mineral _____ is a magnesium iron silicate. It is one of the most common minerals on Earth, and has also been identified on the Moon, Mars, and comet Wild 2.
 a. Olivine0
 b. Thing
 c. Undefined
 d. Undefined

109. _____ is a common gray to black extrusive volcanic rock. It is usually fine-grained due to rapid cooling of lava on the Earth's surface. It may be porphyritic containing larger crystals in a fine matrix, or vesicular, or frothy scoria.
 a. Thing
 b. Basalt0
 c. Undefined
 d. Undefined

110. _____ is a very important series of tectosilicate minerals within the feldspar family. Rather than referring to a particular mineral with a specific chemical composition, it is a solid solution series.
 a. Plagioclase0
 b. Thing
 c. Undefined
 d. Undefined

111. _____ is a chemical element. It is a soft silvery-white metallic alkali metal that occurs naturally bound to other elements in seawater and many minerals. It oxidizes rapidly in air and is very reactive, especially towards water. In many respects, it and sodium are chemically similar, although organisms in general, and animal cells in particular, treat them very differently.
 a. Thing
 b. Potassium0
 c. Undefined
 d. Undefined

112. _____ is a silvery and ductile member of the poor metal group of chemical elements. It has the symbol Al and atomic number 13.

a. Thing
b. Aluminum0
c. Undefined
d. Undefined

113. _____ is an igneous, volcanic rock, of intermediate composition, with aphanitic to porphyritic texture.
   a. Andesite0
   b. Thing
   c. Undefined
   d. Undefined

114. The _____ are a group of important rock-forming silicate minerals found in many igneous and metamorphic rocks. They share a common structure comprised of single chains of silica tetrahedra and they crystalise in the monoclinic and orthorhombic system.
   a. Thing
   b. Pyroxenes0
   c. Undefined
   d. Undefined

115. _____ is a small island located in the middle of San Francisco Bay in California, United States. It served as a lighthouse, then a military fortification, then a military prison followed by a federal prison until 1963, when it became a national recreation area.
   a. Alcatraz Island0
   b. Place
   c. Undefined
   d. Undefined

116. _____ defines an important group of generally dark-colored rock-forming inosilicate minerals linked at the vertices and generally containing ions of iron and/or magnesium in their structures. Amphiboles crystallize into two crystal systems, monoclinic and orthorhombic.
   a. Thing
   b. Amphibole0
   c. Undefined
   d. Undefined

117. A _____ is a relatively large and usually conspicuous crystal distinctly larger than the grains of the rock groundmass of a porphyritic igneous rock. They often have euhedral forms either due to early growth within a magma or by post-emplacement recrystallization.
   a. Phenocryst0
   b. Thing
   c. Undefined
   d. Undefined

118. _____ is a type of naturally-occurring glass formed as an extrusive igneous rock. It is produced when felsic lava erupted from a volcano cools rapidly through the glass transition temperature and freezes without sufficient time for crystal growth. _____ is commonly found within the margins of rhyolitic lava flows known as _____ flows, where cooling of the lava is rapid.
   a. Obsidian0
   b. Thing
   c. Undefined
   d. Undefined

119. _____ in meteorology are large scale patterns in the atmospheric pressure field that are nearly stationary, effectively "blocking" or redirecting migratory cyclones. These _____ can remain in place for several days or even weeks, causing the areas affected by them to have the same kind of weather for an extended period of time.
   a. Thing
   b. Blocks0
   c. Undefined
   d. Undefined

Chapter 4. Volcanism and Extrusive Rocks

120. _____ refers to the diameter of individual grains of sediment, or the lithified particles in clastic rocks. The term may also be applied to other granular materials. This is different from the crystallite size, which is the size of a single crystal inside the particles or grains.
 a. Thing
 b. Particle size0
 c. Undefined
 d. Undefined

121. An _____ is a body of igneous rock that has crystallized from a molten magma below the surface of the Earth.
 a. Thing
 b. Intrusion0
 c. Undefined
 d. Undefined

122. _____ rock is the fine-grained mass of material in which larger grains or crystals are embedded. The _____ of an igneous rock consists of fine-grained, often microscopic, crystals in which larger crystals are embedded. This porphyritic texture is indicative of multi-stage cooling of magma.
 a. Thing
 b. Groundmass0
 c. Undefined
 d. Undefined

123. _____ is a chemical element. An abundant nonmetallic, tetravalent element, _____ has several allotropic forms. This element is the basis of the chemistry of all known life.
 a. Carbon0
 b. Thing
 c. Undefined
 d. Undefined

124. _____ is a chemical compound, normally in a gaseous state, and is composed of one carbon and two oxygen atoms. It is often referred to by its formula CO_2. It is present in the Earth's atmosphere at a concentration of approximately .000383 by volume and is an important greenhouse gas due to its ability to absorb many infrared wavelengths of sunlight, and due to the length of time it stays in the atmosphere.
 a. Carbon dioxide0
 b. Thing
 c. Undefined
 d. Undefined

125. In cell biology, a _____ is a relatively small and enclosed compartment, separated from the cytosol by at least one lipid bilayer.
 a. Vesicle0
 b. Thing
 c. Undefined
 d. Undefined

126. _____ is the vesicular ejecta of basaltic and andesitic magmas. Generally a dark brownish black or red, _____ is generally thought of as the mafic version of pumice, forming when magma rich in dissolved gases is vented. _____ is composed of volcanic glass fragments, and has few mineral crystals.
 a. Scoria0
 b. Thing
 c. Undefined
 d. Undefined

127. _____ is a type of rock consisting of consolidated volcanic ash ejected from vents during a volcanic eruption.
 a. Tuff0
 b. Thing
 c. Undefined
 d. Undefined

128. _____ are pyroclastic rocks formed by explosive eruption of lava and any rocks which are entrained within the eruptive column. This may include rocks plucked off the wall of the magma conduit, or physically picked up by the ensuing pyroclastic surge.

a. Thing
b. Volcanic breccia0
c. Undefined
d. Undefined

129. _____ is a rock composed of angular fragments of rocks or minerals in a matrix, that is a cementing material, that may be similar or different in composition to the fragments.
a. Thing
b. Breccia0
c. Undefined
d. Undefined

130. A _____ is a globe of molten rock larger than 65 mm in diameter, formed when a volcano ejects viscous fragments of lava during an eruption. They cool into solid fragments before they reach the ground. Lava bombs can be thrown many kilometres from an erupting vent, and often acquire aerodynamic shapes during their flight.
a. Thing
b. Volcanic bomb0
c. Undefined
d. Undefined

131. _____ are globes of molten rock larger than 65 mm in diameter, formed when a volcano ejects viscous fragments of lava during an eruption. They cool into solid fragments before they reach the ground.
a. Thing
b. Volcanic Bombs0
c. Undefined
d. Undefined

132. A _____ is a fragment of cooled pyroclastic material, lava or magma.
a. Cinder0
b. Thing
c. Undefined
d. Undefined

133. A _____ is a large volcano with shallowly-sloping sides. A _____ is formed by lava flows of low viscosity — lava that flows easily. Consequently, a volcanic mountain having a broad profile is built up over time by flow after flow of relatively fluid basaltic lava issuing from vents or fissures on the surface of the volcano.
a. Thing
b. Shield volcano0
c. Undefined
d. Undefined

134. The _____ form an archipelago of nineteen islands and atolls, numerous smaller islets, and undersea seamounts trending northwest by southeast in the North Pacific Ocean between latitudes 19° N and 29° N. The archipelago takes its name from the largest island in the group and extends some 1500 miles from the Island of Hawai'i in the south to northernmost Kure Atoll.
a. Place
b. Hawaiian Islands0
c. Undefined
d. Undefined

135. In geology, a _____ is a deformational feature consisting of symmetrically-dipping anticlines; their general outline on a geologic map is circular or oval.
a. Dome0
b. Thing
c. Undefined
d. Undefined

136. A _____ flow typically advances as a series of small lobes and toes that continually break out from a cooled crust. Also forms lava tubes where the minimal heat loss maintains low viscosity.
a. Thing
b. Pāhoehoe0
c. Undefined
d. Undefined

Chapter 4. Volcanism and Extrusive Rocks

137. A _____ is formed of molten lava ejected from a vent somewhat like taffy. Expanding gases in the lava fountains tear the liquid rock into irregular gobs that fall back to earth, forming a heap around the vent.
  a. Spatter cone0
  b. Thing
  c. Undefined
  d. Undefined

138. A _____ is a natural underground void large enough for a human to enter. Some people suggest that the term '_____' should only apply to cavities that have some part which does not receive daylight; however, in popular usage, the term includes smaller spaces like a sea _____, rock shelters, and grottos.
  a. Cave0
  b. Place
  c. Undefined
  d. Undefined

139. _____ is a measure of solar radiation energy incident on a surface. It is the amount of solar energy received on a given area; and may be expressed in W/m2 or over time measured in kilowatt-hours per square meter.
  a. Insolation0
  b. Thing
  c. Undefined
  d. Undefined

140. A _____ is a body of water with a current, confined within a bed and banks. Streams are important as conduits in the water cycle, instruments in aquifer recharge, and corridors for fish and wildlife migration.
  a. Thing
  b. Stream0
  c. Undefined
  d. Undefined

141. _____, located in Siskiyou and Modoc Counties, California, is the site of the largest concentration of lava tube caves in the United States. It was established as a United States National Monument on November 21, 1925..
  a. Place
  b. Lava Beds National Monument0
  c. Undefined
  d. Undefined

142. _____ are steep, conical hills of volcanic fragments that accumulate around and downwind from a volcanic vent. The rock fragments, often called cinders are glassy and contain numerous gas bubbles "frozen" into place as magma exploded into the air and then cooled quickly.
  a. Thing
  b. Cinder cones0
  c. Undefined
  d. Undefined

143. A _____ is a natural object originating in outer space that survives an impact with the Earth's surface without being destroyed. While in space it is called a meteoroid. When it enters the atmosphere, air resistance causes the body to heat up and emit light, thus forming a fireball.
  a. Thing
  b. Meteorite0
  c. Undefined
  d. Undefined

144. A _____ is a type of excavation or depression in the ground. They are generally defined by being deeper than they are wide, and by being narrow compared to their length.
  a. Trench0
  b. Thing
  c. Undefined
  d. Undefined

Chapter 4. Volcanism and Extrusive Rocks

145. _____ is typically used to describe any of the long, narrow depressions in the lunar surface that resemble channels. Typically a _____ can be up to several kilometers wide and hundreds of kilometers in length. However, the term has also been used loosely to describe similar structures on a number of planets in the solar system, including Mars, Venus, and on a number of moons.
- a. Thing
- b. Rille0
- c. Undefined
- d. Undefined

146. A _____, as defined by the International Astronomical Union, is a celestial body orbiting a star or stellar remnant that is massive enough to be rounded by its own gravity, not massive enough to cause thermonuclear fusion in its core, and has cleared its neighboring region of planetesimals.
- a. Thing
- b. Planet0
- c. Undefined
- d. Undefined

147. _____ is a chemical element in the periodic table that has the symbol Hg and atomic number 80. A heavy, silvery transition metal, _____ is one of five elements that are liquid at or near room temperature and pressure.
- a. Mercury0
- b. Thing
- c. Undefined
- d. Undefined

148. _____ is the second-closest planet to the Sun, orbiting it every 224.7 Earth days. It is the brightest natural object in the night sky, except for the Moon, reaching an apparent magnitude of −4.6. Because _____ is an inferior planet, from Earth it never appears to venture far from the Sun: its elongation reaches a maximum of 47.8°.
- a. Venus0
- b. Thing
- c. Undefined
- d. Undefined

149. Faults are planar rock fractures, which show evidence of relative movement. Large faults within the Earth's crust are the result of shear motion and active _____ zones are the causal locations of most earthquakes. Earthquakes are caused by energy release during rapid slippage along faults. The largest examples are at tectonic plate boundaries but many faults occur far from active plate boundaries. Since faults do not usually consist of a single, clean fracture, the term _____ zone is used when referring to the zone of complex deformation that is associated with the _____ plane.
- a. Fault0
- b. Thing
- c. Undefined
- d. Undefined

150. _____ or sulphur is the chemical element that has the symbol S and atomic number 16. It is an abundant, tasteless, multivalent non-metal. _____, in its native form, is a yellow crystalline solid. In nature, it can be found as the pure element or as sulfide and sulfate minerals. It is an essential element for life and is found in two amino acids, cysteine and methionine.
- a. Sulfur0
- b. Thing
- c. Undefined
- d. Undefined

151. _____ the fourth planet from the Sun in the Solar System. The planet is named after _____, the Roman god of war. It is also referred to as the "Red Planet" because of its reddish appearance as seen from Earth.
- a. Thing
- b. Mars0
- c. Undefined
- d. Undefined

Chapter 4. Volcanism and Extrusive Rocks

152. _____ is the tallest known volcano and mountain in our solar system, located on the planet Mars. _____ is located in the Tharsis bulge, a huge swelling in the Martian surface that bears numerous other large volcanic features. Among them are a chain of lesser shield volcanoes including Arsia Mons, Pavonis Mons and Ascraeus Mons, which are small only in comparison to _____ itself.
   a. Olympus Mons0
   b. Place
   c. Undefined
   d. Undefined

153. A _____ is a chemical substance of two or more different chemically bonded chemical elements, with a fixed ratio determining the composition. The ratio of each element is usually expressed by chemical formula.
   a. Thing
   b. Chemical compound0
   c. Undefined
   d. Undefined

154. _____ are volcanic features formed by the collapse of land following a volcanic eruption. They are often confused with volcanic craters.
   a. Calderas0
   b. Thing
   c. Undefined
   d. Undefined

155. _____ is the planet Neptune's largest moon and the seventh largest moon in the Solar System. _____ has a complex geological history and it is believed to have a relatively young surface.
   a. Triton0
   b. Thing
   c. Undefined
   d. Undefined

156. _____ is the eighth and farthest known planet from the Sun in the Solar System. It is the fourth largest planet by diameter, and the third largest by mass.
   a. Neptune0
   b. Place
   c. Undefined
   d. Undefined

157. _____ is a chemical element which has the symbol N and atomic number 7. Elemental _____ is a colorless, odourless, tasteless and mostly inert diatomic gas at standard conditions, constituting 78.1% by volume of Earth's atmosphere.
   a. Nitrogen0
   b. Thing
   c. Undefined
   d. Undefined

158. _____ is displacement of solids by the agents of ocean currents, wind, water, or ice by downward or down-slope movement in response to gravity or by living organisms.
   a. Thing
   b. Erosion0
   c. Undefined
   d. Undefined

159. A _____, is a tall, conical volcano composed of many layers of hardened lava, tephra, and volcanic ash. These volcanoes are characterized by a steep profile and periodic, explosive eruptions. The lava that flows from them is viscous, and cools and hardens before spreading very far.
   a. Thing
   b. Stratovolcano0
   c. Undefined
   d. Undefined

Chapter 4. Volcanism and Extrusive Rocks

160. A glacier is a large, slow moving river of ice, formed from compacted layers of snow, that slowly deforms and flows in response to gravity. Glacier ice is the largest reservoir of fresh water on Earth, and second only to oceans as the largest reservoir of total water. _____ cover vast areas of polar regions but are restricted to the highest mountains in the tropics.
   a. Thing
   b. Glaciers0
   c. Undefined
   d. Undefined

161. _____ are a type of extrusive land form. Many of the larger, classically shaped volcanos result from altering types of eruption where first ash, and then lava are ejected.
   a. Thing
   b. Composite cones0
   c. Undefined
   d. Undefined

162. _____ is the second-highest peak in the Cascade Range and the fifth highest peak in California. It is a member in the Cascade Volcanic Arc and is located in Siskiyou County, and has an estimated volume of 108 cubic miles, making it the most voluminous stratovolcano of the Cascades.
   a. Mount Shasta0
   b. Place
   c. Undefined
   d. Undefined

163. _____ is an Andean stratovolcano in Caldas Department, Colombia. It is the northernmost and highest Colombian volcano with historical activity. Its 1985 eruption produced a lahar which completely buried Armero and caused an estimated 23,000 deaths.
   a. Nevado del Ruiz0
   b. Thing
   c. Undefined
   d. Undefined

164. _____ in Antarctica is the southernmost active volcano on Earth. 3,794 metres high, it is located on Ross Island, which is also home to three inactive volcanoes, notably Mt. Terror. _____ is part of the Pacific Ring of Fire, which includes over 160 active volcanoes.
   a. Place
   b. Mount Erebus0
   c. Undefined
   d. Undefined

165. The _____ are a chain of more than 300 small volcanic islands forming an island arc in the Northern Pacific Ocean, occupying an area of 6,821 sq mi westward from the Alaska Peninsula toward the Kamchatka Peninsula.
   a. Place
   b. Aleutian Islands0
   c. Undefined
   d. Undefined

166. _____ is a small, circular archipelago of volcanic islands located in southern Aegean Sea, about 200 km south-east from Greece's mainland. It is the southernmost member of the Cyclades group of islands, with an area of approximately 73 km², and in 2001 had an estimated population of 13,600. _____ is essentially what has been left from an enormous volcanic explosion which destroyed the settlements thereon and led to the creation of the current geological caldera.
   a. Santorini0
   b. Place
   c. Undefined
   d. Undefined

167. _____ is an active volcano on the east coast of Sicily, close to Messina and Catania. It is the largest active volcano in Europe, currently standing about 3,326 m high, though it should be noted that this varies with summit eruptions; the mountain is 21.6 m lower now than it was in 1865. It is the highest mountain in Italy south of the Alps.

Chapter 4. Volcanism and Extrusive Rocks

a. Mount Etna0
c. Undefined
b. Place
d. Undefined

168. A _____ is a barrier across flowing water that obstructs, directs or slows down the flow, often creating a reservoir, lake or impoundment.
   a. Thing
   b. Dam0
   c. Undefined
   d. Undefined

169. A _____ is a roughy circular mound-shaped protrusion resulting from the slow eruption of felsic lava from a volcano. The viscosity, or stickiness, of the lava does not allow for the lava to flow very far from its vent before solidifying. Domes may reach heights of several hundred meters, and can grow slowly and steadily for months or years. The sides of these structures are composed of unstable rock debris.
   a. Lava dome0
   b. Thing
   c. Undefined
   d. Undefined

170. In geology, a _____ is a depression with predominant extent in one direction. The terms U-shaped and V-shaped are descriptive terms of geography to characterize the form of valleys. Most valleys belong to one of these two main types or a mixture of them, at least with respect of the cross section of the slopes or hillsides.
   a. Valley0
   b. Thing
   c. Undefined
   d. Undefined

171. A _____ is any disturbed state of an astronomical body's atmosphere, especially affecting its surface, and strongly implying severe weather. It may be marked by strong wind, thunder and lightning, heavy precipitation, such as ice, or wind transporting some substance through the atmosphere.
   a. Storm0
   b. Thing
   c. Undefined
   d. Undefined

172. The _____ is an active complex stratovolcano with many lava domes forming its summit on the Caribbean island of Montserrat. After a long period of dormancy it became active in 1995, and has continued to erupt ever since. Its eruptions have rendered much of Montserrat uninhabitable, destroying the capital, Plymouth, and causing widespread evacuations and about two thirds of the population to leave the island.
   a. Place
   b. Soufriere Hills0
   c. Undefined
   d. Undefined

173. _____ is a mountain near Barcelona, in Catalonia, in Spain. It is the site of a Benedictine abbey, Santa María de _____, which hosts the Virgin of _____ sanctuary and which is identified by some with the location of the Holy Grail in Arthurian myth.
   a. Place
   b. Montserrat0
   c. Undefined
   d. Undefined

174. A _____ is used by seismologists to measure and record the size and force of seismic waves.
   a. Thing
   b. Seismograph0
   c. Undefined
   d. Undefined

175. A _____ is an instrument designed to measure very small changes from the horizontal level, either on the ground or in structures. A similar term, in less common usage, is the inclinometer.

a. Tiltmeter0
b. Thing
c. Undefined
d. Undefined

176. Ocean _____ are any more or less continuous, directed movement of ocean water that flows in one of the Earth's oceans. They are rivers of hot or cold water within the ocean. They are generated from the forces acting upon the water like the earth's rotation, the wind, the temperature and salinity differences and the gravitation of the moon.
    a. Thing
    b. Currents0
    c. Undefined
    d. Undefined

177. The _____ lies across parts of the U.S. states of Washington, Oregon, and Idaho. During late Miocene and early Pliocene times, one of the largest flood basalts ever to appear on the earth's surface engulfed about 63,000 square miles of the Pacific Northwest, forming a large igneous province.
    a. Place
    b. Columbia Plateau0
    c. Undefined
    d. Undefined

178. A _____ is an upwelling of abnormally hot rock within the Earth's mantle. As the heads of mantle plumes can partly melt when they reach shallow depths, they are thought to be the cause of volcanic centers known as hotspots and probably also to have caused flood basalts.
    a. Event
    b. Mantle plume0
    c. Undefined
    d. Undefined

179. The _____ is the solid outermost shell of a rocky planet. On the Earth, the _____ includes the crust and the uppermost mantle which is joined to the crust across the Mohorovièiæ discontinuity. _____ is underlain by asthenosphere, the weaker, hotter, and deeper part of the upper mantle.
    a. Lithosphere0
    b. Thing
    c. Undefined
    d. Undefined

180. _____ were vertebrate animals that dominated terrestrial ecosystems for over 160 million years, first appearing approximately 230 million years ago. At the end of the Cretaceous Period, approximately 65 million years ago, a catastrophic extinction event ended _____' dominance on land.
    a. Dinosaurs0
    b. Thing
    c. Undefined
    d. Undefined

181. _____ are a class of astronomical objects. The term is generally used to indicate a diverse group of small celestial bodies that drift in the solar system in orbit around the Sun.
    a. Asteroids0
    b. Thing
    c. Undefined
    d. Undefined

182. _____ is a 16-ton, manned deep-ocean research submersible owned by the United States Navy and operated by the Woods Hole Oceanographic Institution in Woods Hole, Massachusetts. The three-person vessel allows for two scientists and one pilot to dive for up to nine hours at 4500 metersor 15,000 feet.
    a. Alvin0
    b. Thing
    c. Undefined
    d. Undefined

Chapter 4. Volcanism and Extrusive Rocks

183. A _____ is a geological feature that is also known as a Rip in the earth causing magma to flow out and forming an undersea volcano, it also has geological features, a continuous elevational crest for some distance. Ridges are usually termed hills or mountains as well, depending on size.
    a. Thing
    b. Ridge0
    c. Undefined
    d. Undefined

184. _____ is the largest island in the Vestmannaeyjar cluster, approximately 4 nautical miles off the south coast of Iceland. It is the only island in Vestmannaeyjar that is populated, and currently there are around 4,500 inhabitants.
    a. Heimaey0
    b. Place
    c. Undefined
    d. Undefined

185. A _____ is a group of mountains bordered by lowlands or separated from other mountain ranges by passes or rivers. Individual mountains within the same _____ do not necessarily have the same geology; they may be a mix of different orogeny, for example volcanoes, uplifted mountains or fold mountains and may, therefore, be of different rock.
    a. Thing
    b. Mountain range0
    c. Undefined
    d. Undefined

186. A _____ is an intrusion into a cross-cutting fissure, meaning a _____ cuts across other pre-existing layers or bodies of rock, this means that a _____ is always younger than the rocks that contain it. The thickness is usually much smaller than the other two dimensions. Thickness can vary from sub-centimeter scale to many meters in thickness and the lateral dimensions can extend over many kilometers.
    a. Dike0
    b. Thing
    c. Undefined
    d. Undefined

187. An _____ is a type of atom that is defined by its atomic number; that is, by the number of protons in its nucleus.
    a. Thing
    b. Element0
    c. Undefined
    d. Undefined

188. _____ is when long fractures form vertically in rock as it cools and contracts.
    a. Thing
    b. Columnar jointing0
    c. Undefined
    d. Undefined

189. _____ is a volcano east of Naples, Italy. It is the only volcano on the European mainland to have erupted within the last hundred years, although it is not currently erupting.
    a. Mount Vesuvius0
    b. Place
    c. Undefined
    d. Undefined

190. _____ is the study of volcanoes, lava, magma, and related geological phenomena.
    a. Volcanology0
    b. Thing
    c. Undefined
    d. Undefined

Chapter 5. Weathering and Soil

1. _____ is the process of breaking down rocks, soils and their minerals through direct contact with the atmosphere. _____ occurs without movement. Two main classifications of _____ processes exist. Mechanical or physical _____ involves the breakdown of rocks and soils through direct contact with atmospheric conditions. The second classification, chemical _____, involves the direct effect of atmospheric chemicals in the breakdown of rocks, soils and minerals.
    a. Weathering0
    b. Thing
    c. Undefined
    d. Undefined

2. A _____, as defined by the International Astronomical Union, is a celestial body orbiting a star or stellar remnant that is massive enough to be rounded by its own gravity, not massive enough to cause thermonuclear fusion in its core, and has cleared its neighboring region of planetesimals.
    a. Planet0
    b. Thing
    c. Undefined
    d. Undefined

3. A _____ is a naturally occurring substance formed through geological processes that has a characteristic chemical composition, a highly ordered atomic structure and specific physical properties. A rock, by comparison, is an aggregate of minerals and need not have a specific chemical composition. Minerals range in composition from pure elements and simple salts to very complex silicates with thousands of known forms.
    a. Mineral0
    b. Thing
    c. Undefined
    d. Undefined

4. _____ refers to the reduction of the body of a formerly living organism into simpler forms of matter.
    a. Decomposition0
    b. Thing
    c. Undefined
    d. Undefined

5. A _____ is an organism that is microscopic. They can be bacteria, fungi, archaea or protists, but not viruses and prions, which are generally classified as non-living. Micro-organisms are generally single-celled, or unicellular organisms.
    a. Thing
    b. Microorganism0
    c. Undefined
    d. Undefined

6. _____ involves the change in the composition of rock, often leading to a 'break down' in its form.
    a. Thing
    b. Chemical weathering0
    c. Undefined
    d. Undefined

7. The _____ is a fundamental concept in geology that describes the dynamic transitions through geologic time among the three main rock types: sedimentary, metamorphic, and igneous.
    a. Thing
    b. Rock cycle0
    c. Undefined
    d. Undefined

8. The _____ is the part of the earth, including air, land, surface rocks, and water, within which life occurs, and which biotic processes in turn alter or transform. From the broadest biophysiological point of view, the _____ is the global ecological system integrating all living beings and their relationships, including their interaction with the elements of the lithosphere, hydrosphere, and atmosphere. This _____ is postulated to have evolved, beginning through a process of biogenesis or biopoesis, at least some 3.5 billion years ago.
    a. Biosphere0
    b. Thing
    c. Undefined
    d. Undefined

Chapter 5. Weathering and Soil

9. _____ is a small island located in the middle of San Francisco Bay in California, United States. It served as a lighthouse, then a military fortification, then a military prison followed by a federal prison until 1963, when it became a national recreation area.
   a. Place
   b. Alcatraz Island0
   c. Undefined
   d. Undefined

10. An _____ is a layer of gases that may surround a material body of sufficient mass. The gases are attracted by the gravity of the body, and are retained for a longer duration if gravity is high and the _____'s temperature is low. Some planets consist mainly of various gases, and thus have very deep atmospheres.
    a. Place
    b. Atmosphere0
    c. Undefined
    d. Undefined

11. _____ is displacement of solids by the agents of ocean currents, wind, water, or ice by downward or down-slope movement in response to gravity or by living organisms.
    a. Thing
    b. Erosion0
    c. Undefined
    d. Undefined

12. _____ is a common and widely occurring type of intrusive, felsic, igneous rock. Granites are usually medium to coarsely crystalline, occasionally with some individual crystals larger than the groundmass forming a rock known as porphyry. Granites can be pink to dark gray or even black, depending on their chemistry and mineralogy.
    a. Granite0
    b. Thing
    c. Undefined
    d. Undefined

13. A _____ is a large, slow moving river of ice, formed from compacted layers of snow, that slowly deforms and flows in response to gravity. _____ ice is the largest reservoir of fresh water on Earth, and second only to oceans as the largest reservoir of total water. Glaciers cover vast areas of polar regions but are restricted to the highest mountains in the tropics.
    a. Glacier0
    b. Thing
    c. Undefined
    d. Undefined

14. A _____ is a significant vertical, or near vertical, rock exposure. Cliffs are categorized as erosion landforms due to the processes of erosion and weathering that produce them. Cliffs are common on coasts, in mountainous areas, escarpments and along rivers. Cliffs are usually formed by rock that is resistant to erosion and weathering.
    a. Cliff0
    b. Thing
    c. Undefined
    d. Undefined

15. A _____ is a disturbance that propagates through space or spacetime, transferring energy and momentum and sometimes angular momentum.
    a. Wave0
    b. Thing
    c. Undefined
    d. Undefined

16. A _____ is a body of water with a current, confined within a bed and banks. Streams are important as conduits in the water cycle, instruments in aquifer recharge, and corridors for fish and wildlife migration.
    a. Thing
    b. Stream0
    c. Undefined
    d. Undefined

17. _____ is the oxide that is formed by open-air oxidation of iron.
   a. Rust0
   b. Thing
   c. Undefined
   d. Undefined

18. The _____ consists of the Sun and the other celestial objects gravitationally bound to it: the eight planets, their 165 known moons, three currently identified dwarf planets and their four known moons, and billions of small bodies.
   a. Solar system0
   b. Thing
   c. Undefined
   d. Undefined

19. _____ is a chemical element. An abundant nonmetallic, tetravalent element, _____ has several allotropic forms. This element is the basis of the chemistry of all known life.
   a. Carbon0
   b. Thing
   c. Undefined
   d. Undefined

20. _____ is a chemical compound, normally in a gaseous state, and is composed of one carbon and two oxygen atoms. It is often referred to by its formula CO_2. It is present in the Earth's atmosphere at a concentration of approximately .000383 by volume and is an important greenhouse gas due to its ability to absorb many infrared wavelengths of sunlight, and due to the length of time it stays in the atmosphere.
   a. Carbon dioxide0
   b. Thing
   c. Undefined
   d. Undefined

21. _____ is an ecological concept referring to the relative representation of a species in a particular ecosystem. It is usually measured as the mean number of individuals found per sample.
   a. Thing
   b. Abundance0
   c. Undefined
   d. Undefined

22. Water collecting on the ground or in a stream, river, lake, or wetland is called _____; as opposed to groundwater. _____ is naturally replenished by precipitation and naturally lost through discharge to the oceans, evaporation, and sub-surface seepage into the groundwater. _____ is the largest source of fresh water.
   a. Thing
   b. Surface water0
   c. Undefined
   d. Undefined

23. _____ the fourth planet from the Sun in the Solar System. The planet is named after _____, the Roman god of war. It is also referred to as the "Red Planet" because of its reddish appearance as seen from Earth.
   a. Thing
   b. Mars0
   c. Undefined
   d. Undefined

24. A _____ in physical geography describes the collective mass of water found on, under, and over the surface of a planet.
   a. Hydrosphere0
   b. Thing
   c. Undefined
   d. Undefined

25. _____ is a chemical element metal. It is a lustrous, silvery soft metal. It and nickel are notable for being the final elements produced by stellar nucleosynthesis, and thus are the heaviest elements which do not require a supernova or similarly cataclysmic event for formation.

Chapter 5. Weathering and Soil

a. Iron0
b. Thing
c. Undefined
d. Undefined

26. _____ is the native consolidated rock underlying the Earth's surface. Above the _____ is usually an area of broken and weathered unconsolidated rock in the basal subsoil.
   a. Thing
   b. Bedrock0
   c. Undefined
   d. Undefined

27. _____ is the substance of which physical objects are composed. _____ can be solid, liquid, plasma or gas. It constitutes the observable universe.
   a. Matter0
   b. Thing
   c. Undefined
   d. Undefined

28. _____ is matter that has come from a recently living organism; is capable of decay, or the product of decay; or is composed of organic compounds. The definition of _____ varies upon the subject it is being used for.
   a. Thing
   b. Organic matter0
   c. Undefined
   d. Undefined

29. In biology and ecology, an _____ is a living complex adaptive system of organs that influence each other in such a way that they function in some way as a stable whole.
   a. Organism0
   b. Thing
   c. Undefined
   d. Undefined

30. _____ is the gas phase of water. _____ is one state of the water cycle within the hydrosphere. _____ can be produced from the evaporation of liquid water or from the sublimation of ice. Under normal atmospheric conditions, _____ is continuously evaporating and condensing.
   a. Water vapor0
   b. Thing
   c. Undefined
   d. Undefined

31. _____ is the gas phase component of a another state of matter which does not completely fill its container. It is distinguished from the pure gas phase by the presence of the same substance in another state of matter. Hence when a liquid has completely evaporated, it is said that the system has been completely transformed to the gas phase.
   a. Thing
   b. Vapor0
   c. Undefined
   d. Undefined

32. _____ is a layer of gases surrounding the planet Earth and retained by the Earth's gravity. This mixture of gases is commonly known as air.
   a. Earths atmosphere0
   b. Thing
   c. Undefined
   d. Undefined

33. A _____ is a chemical substance of two or more different chemically bonded chemical elements, with a fixed ratio determining the composition. The ratio of each element is usually expressed by chemical formula.
   a. Thing
   b. Chemical compound0
   c. Undefined
   d. Undefined

34. _____ is the second most common mineral in the Earth's continental crust. It is made up of a lattice of silica tetrahedra. _____ belongs to the rhombohedral crystal system. In nature _____ crystals are often twinned, distorted, or so intergrown with adjacent crystals of _____ or other minerals as to only show part of this shape, or to lack obvious crystal faces altogether and appear massive.
   a. Thing
   b. Quartz0
   c. Undefined
   d. Undefined

35. _____ is the name of a group of rock-forming minerals which make up as much as sixty percent of the Earth's crust. Feldspars crystallize from magma in both intrusive and extrusive rocks, and they can also occur as compact minerals, as veins, and are also present in many types of metamorphic rock.
   a. Thing
   b. Feldspar0
   c. Undefined
   d. Undefined

36. A _____ is one which contains both magnesium and iron.
   a. Ferromagnesian mineral0
   b. Thing
   c. Undefined
   d. Undefined

37. _____ is a solid deposition of water vapor from saturated air. If solid surfaces in contact with the air are chilled below the deposition point, then spicules of ice grow out from the solid surface. _____ is often observed around cracks in wooden sidewalks due to the moist air escaping from the ground below. Other objects on which _____ develops are those with low specific heat and high thermal emissivity, such as blackened metals.
   a. Thing
   b. Frost0
   c. Undefined
   d. Undefined

38. A _____ is a solid in which the constituent atoms, molecules, or ions are packed in a regularly ordered, repeating pattern extending in all three spatial dimensions. Most metals encountered in everyday life are polycrystals. Crystals are often symmetrically intergrown to form _____ twins.
   a. Thing
   b. Crystal0
   c. Undefined
   d. Undefined

39. The _____ group of sheet silicate minerals includes several closely related materials having highly perfect basal cleavage. All are monoclinic with a tendency towards pseudo-hexagonal crystals and are similar in chemical composition. The highly perfect cleavage, which is the most prominent characteristic of _____, is explained by the hexagonal sheet-like arrangement of its atoms.
   a. Thing
   b. Mica0
   c. Undefined
   d. Undefined

40. A _____ is a unique arrangement of atoms in a crystal. It is composed of a unit cell, a set of atoms arranged in a particular way, which is periodically repeated in three dimensions on a lattice. The spacing between unit cells in various directions is called its lattice parameters. The symmetry properties of the crystal are embodied in its space group.
   a. Crystal structure0
   b. Thing
   c. Undefined
   d. Undefined

Chapter 5. Weathering and Soil

41. _____ is a term used to describe a group of hydrous aluminium phyllosilicate minerals, that are typically less than 2 micrometres in diameter. _____ consists of a variety of phyllosilicate minerals rich in silicon and aluminium oxides and hydroxides which include variable amounts of structural water. Clays are generally formed by the chemical weathering of silicate-bearing rocks by carbonic acid but some are formed by hydrothermal activity.
   a. Clay0
   b. Thing
   c. Undefined
   d. Undefined

42. _____ is a metamorphic rock resulting from the metamorphism of limestone, composed mostly of calcite. It is extensively used for sculpture, as a building material, and in many other applications. The word '_____' is colloquially used to refer to many other stones that are capable of taking a high polish.
   a. Thing
   b. Marble0
   c. Undefined
   d. Undefined

43. _____ is a sedimentary rock composed largely of the mineral calcite. _____ often contains variable amounts of silica in the form of chert or flint, as well as varying amounts of clay, silt and sand as disseminations, nodules, or layers within the rock. The primary source of the calcite in _____ is most commonly marine organisms. These organisms secrete shells that settle out of the water column and are deposited on ocean floors as pelagic ooze or alternatively is conglomerated in a coral reef.
   a. Thing
   b. Limestone0
   c. Undefined
   d. Undefined

44. _____ in meteorology are large scale patterns in the atmospheric pressure field that are nearly stationary, effectively "blocking" or redirecting migratory cyclones. These _____ can remain in place for several days or even weeks, causing the areas affected by them to have the same kind of weather for an extended period of time.
   a. Thing
   b. Blocks0
   c. Undefined
   d. Undefined

45. In geology and astronomy, the term _____ is used to denote types of rock that consist predominantly of _____ minerals. Such rocks include a wide range of igneous, metamorphic and sedimentary types. Most of the Earth's mantle and crust are made up of _____ rocks. The same is true of the Moon and the other rocky planets.
   a. Thing
   b. Silicate0
   c. Undefined
   d. Undefined

46. _____ is a fine-grained, homogeneous, metamorphic rock derived from an original shale-type sedimentary rock composed of clay or volcanic ash through low grade regional metamorphism. The result is a foliated rock in which the foliation may not correspond to the original sedimentary layering.
   a. Thing
   b. Slate0
   c. Undefined
   d. Undefined

47. _____ is the production of food, feed, fiber, fuel and other goods by the systematic raizing of plants and animals.
   a. Thing
   b. Agriculture0
   c. Undefined
   d. Undefined

48. _____ is water from a sea or ocean. On average, _____ in the world's oceans has a salinity of ~3.5%, or 35 parts per thousand. This means that every 1 kg of _____ has approximately 35 grams of dissolved salts.

Chapter 5. Weathering and Soil

    a. Thing
    c. Undefined
    b. Seawater0
    d. Undefined

49. An _____ is a volume of rock containing components or minerals in a mode of occurrence that renders it valuable for mining.
    a. Ore0
    c. Undefined
    b. Thing
    d. Undefined

50. _____ is a ductile metal with excellent electrical conductivity, and finds extensive use as an electrical conductor, heat conductor, as a building material, and as a component of various alloys.
    a. Copper0
    c. Undefined
    b. Thing
    d. Undefined

51. _____ is a silvery and ductile member of the poor metal group of chemical elements. It has the symbol Al and atomic number 13.
    a. Thing
    c. Undefined
    b. Aluminum0
    d. Undefined

52. _____ is a type of chemical weathering that creates rounded boulders and helps to create domed monoliths. This should not be confused with stream abrasion, a physical process which also creates rounded rocks on a much smaller scale.
    a. Spheroidal weathering0
    c. Undefined
    b. Thing
    d. Undefined

53. _____ rocks form when molten rock, magma, cools and solidifies, with or without crystallization, either below the surface as intrusive, plutonic rocks or on the surface as extrusive, volcanic, rocks.
    a. Thing
    c. Undefined
    b. Igneous0
    d. Undefined

54. _____ forms when rock cools and solidifies either below the surface as intrusive rocks or on the surface as extrusive rocks. This magma can be derived from partial melts of pre-existing rocks in either the Earth's mantle or crust. Typically, the melting is caused by one or more of the following processes -- an increase in temperature, a decrease in pressure, or a change in composition.
    a. Thing
    c. Undefined
    b. Igneous rock0
    d. Undefined

55. A _____ is a deep valley between cliffs often carved from the landscape by a river. Most were formed by a process of long-time erosion from a plateau level. The cliffs form because harder rock strata that are resistant to erosion and weathering remain exposed on the valley walls.
    a. Thing
    c. Undefined
    b. Canyon0
    d. Undefined

56. _____ is a fine-grained sedimentary rock whose original constituents were clays or muds. It is characterized by thin laminae breaking with an irregular curving fracture, often splintery and usually parallel to the often-indistinguishable bedding plane.

Chapter 5. Weathering and Soil

a. Thing
b. Shale0
c. Undefined
d. Undefined

57. _____ is a sedimentary rock composed mainly of sand-size mineral or rock grains. Most _____ is composed of quartz and/or feldspar because these are the most common minerals in the Earth's crust. Like sand, _____ may be any color, but the most common colors are tan, brown, yellow, red, gray and white.
  a. Sandstone0
  b. Thing
  c. Undefined
  d. Undefined

58. The _____ is a very colorful, steep-sided gorge, carved by the Colorado River in the U.S. state of Arizona. It is one of the first national parks in the United States.
  a. Place
  b. Grand Canyon0
  c. Undefined
  d. Undefined

59. _____ rock is one of the three main rock groups. Rock formed from these covers 75% of the Earth's land area, and includes common types such as chalk, limestone, dolomite, sandstone, and shale.
  a. Thing
  b. Sedimentary0
  c. Undefined
  d. Undefined

60. _____ is one of the three main rock groups. _____ covers 75% of the Earth's land area. Four basic processes are involved in the formation of a clastic _____: weathering caused mainly by friction of waves, transportation where the sediment is carried along by a current, deposition and compaction where the sediment is squashed together to form a rock of this kind.
  a. Thing
  b. Sedimentary rock0
  c. Undefined
  d. Undefined

61. The _____ is the set of all extant phenomena in a given atmosphere at a given time. The term usually refers to the activity of these phenomena over short periods, as opposed to the term climate, which refers to the average atmospheric conditions over longer periods of time.
  a. Thing
  b. Weather0
  c. Undefined
  d. Undefined

62. A _____ comprises a geomorphological unit, and is largely defined by its surface form and location in the landscape, as part of the terrain, and as such, is typically an element of topography. They are categorised by features such as elevation, slope, orientation, stratification, rock exposure, and soil type. They include berms, mounds, hills, cliffs, valleys, rivers and numerous other elements.
  a. Landform0
  b. Thing
  c. Undefined
  d. Undefined

63. A _____ is one of the major divisions of the year, generally based on yearly periodic changes in weather. They are recognized as: spring, summer, autumn, and winter.
  a. Season0
  b. Thing
  c. Undefined
  d. Undefined

Chapter 5. Weathering and Soil

64. An _____ is a narrow mass of ice that can be 3 or 4 meters wide at ground surface and extend up to 10 meters downwards. During winter the ground gets very cold and the water in the ground freezes and expands. Then, as the temperature falls further, the soil and frozen ice acts as a solid and contracts as it gets colder, forming cracks.
    a. Ice wedge0
    b. Thing
    c. Undefined
    d. Undefined

65. _____ is one of the four seasons of temperate zones. Almost all English-language calendars, going by astronomy, state that _____ begins on the _____ solstice, and ends on the spring equinox. Calculated more by the weather, it begins and ends earlier and is the season with the shortest days and the lowest temperatures.
    a. Winter0
    b. Thing
    c. Undefined
    d. Undefined

66. In geology, _____ are rock s with a grain size of usually no less than 256 mm diameter.
    a. Thing
    b. Boulders0
    c. Undefined
    d. Undefined

67. A _____ is a large emplacement of igneous intrusive rock that forms from cooled magma deep in the Earth's crust. They are almost always made mostly of felsic or intermediate rock-types, such as granite, quartz monzonite, or diorite.
    a. Batholith0
    b. Thing
    c. Undefined
    d. Undefined

68. _____, in everyday life, is most familiar as the agency that endows objects with weight. _____ is responsible for keeping the Earth and the other planets in their orbits around the Sun; for the formation of tides; and for various other phenomena that we observe. _____ is also the reason for the very existence of the Earth, the Sun, and most macroscopic objects in the universe; without it, matter would not have coalesced into these large masses, and life, as we know it, would not exist.
    a. Thing
    b. Gravitation0
    c. Undefined
    d. Undefined

69. A _____ is a landform that extends above the surrounding terrain in a limited area. A _____ is generally steeper than a hill, but there is no universally accepted standard definition for the height of a _____ or a hill although a _____ usually has an identifiable summit.
    a. Mountain0
    b. Place
    c. Undefined
    d. Undefined

70. _____ is Canada's oldest national park, established in 1885, in the Canadian Rockies. _____ has been shaped by tension between conservation and development interests. The park was established in 1885, in response to conflicting claims over who discovered hot springs there, and who had the right to develop the hot springs for commercial interests.
    a. Place
    b. Banff National Park0
    c. Undefined
    d. Undefined

71. _____ is a term given to broken rock that appears at the bottom of crags, mountain cliffs or valley shoulders, forming a _____ slope. The maximum inclination of such deposits corresponds to the angle of repose of the mean debris size.

Chapter 5. Weathering and Soil

    a. Thing
    b. Scree0
    c. Undefined
    d. Undefined

72. In geology, a _____ is a deformational feature consisting of symmetrically-dipping anticlines; their general outline on a geologic map is circular or oval.
    a. Dome0
    b. Thing
    c. Undefined
    d. Undefined

73. _____ in geology is a weathering process, mainly caused in arid areas by differential heating and cooling of rock surfaces. There needs to be a high diurnal temperature range.
    a. Exfoliation0
    b. Thing
    c. Undefined
    d. Undefined

74. The _____ is a mountain range that is almost entirely in the eastern portion of the U.S. state of California. The _____ stretches 400 miles, from Fredonyer Pass in the north to Tehachapi Pass in the south. It is bounded on the west by California's Central Valley, and on the east by the Great Basin.
    a. Sierra Nevada0
    b. Place
    c. Undefined
    d. Undefined

75. In geography, a _____ is a landscape form or region that receives very little precipitation. They are defined as areas that receive an average annual precipitation of less than 250 mm. A _____ where vegetation cover is exceedingly sparse correspond to the 'hyperarid' regions of the earth, where rainfall is exceedingly rare and infrequent.
    a. Place
    b. Desert0
    c. Undefined
    d. Undefined

76. A _____ is an area with a high density of trees, historically, a wooded area set aside for hunting. These plant communities cover large areas of the globe and function as animal habitats, hydrologic flow modulators, and soil conservers, constituting one of the most important aspects of the Earth's biosphere.
    a. Thing
    b. Forest0
    c. Undefined
    d. Undefined

77. A _____ is an uncontrolled fire that pops up fire often occurring in wildland areas, but which can also consume houses or agricultural resources. Common causes include lightning, human carelessness, arson, volcano eruption, and pyroclastic cloud from active volcano. Heat waves, droughts, and cyclical climate changes such as El Niño can also have a dramatic effect on the risk of wildfires.
    a. Forest fire0
    b. Thing
    c. Undefined
    d. Undefined

78. A _____ is a dome of granite, formed by exfoliation. Granite forms plutons of igneous rock several kilometers below the surface as magma slowly cools and crystallizes. The granite is under great overhead pressure. Then, granite is uplifted to the surface during a mountain-building event.
    a. Granite dome0
    b. Thing
    c. Undefined
    d. Undefined

Chapter 5. Weathering and Soil

79. _____ is a national park located largely in Mariposa and Tuolumne Counties, California, United States. It is one of the largest and least fragmented habitat blocks in the Sierra Nevada, and the park supports a diversity of plants and animals. The park has an elevation range from 2,000 to 13,114 feet.
    a. Yosemite National Park0
    b. Place
    c. Undefined
    d. Undefined

80. _____ is molten rock located beneath the surface of the Earth, and which often collects in a _____ chamber. _____ is a complex high-temperature fluid substance. Most are silicate solutions. It is capable of intrusion into adjacent rocks or of extrusion onto the surface as lava or ejected explosively as tephra to form pyroclastic rock. Environments of _____ formation include subduction zones, continental rift zones, mid-oceanic ridges, and hotspots, some of which are interpreted as mantle plumes.
    a. Thing
    b. Magma0
    c. Undefined
    d. Undefined

81. _____ are the fundamental building blocks of chemistry, and are conserved in chemical reactions.
    a. Thing
    b. Atoms0
    c. Undefined
    d. Undefined

82. _____ is the condition of a system in which competing influences are balanced.
    a. Equilibrium0
    b. Thing
    c. Undefined
    d. Undefined

83. _____ is a valley in the U.S. state of California, and is the location of the lowest elevation in North America at –282 feet. Located southeast of the Sierra Nevada range in the Great Basin and the Mojave Desert, it constitutes much of _____ National Park. It runs north-south between the Amargosa Range to the east and the Panamint Range to the west; the Sylvania Mountains and the Owlshead Mountains form its northern and southern boundaries, respectively.
    a. Death Valley0
    b. Place
    c. Undefined
    d. Undefined

84. In geology, a _____ is a depression with predominant extent in one direction. The terms U-shaped and V-shaped are descriptive terms of geography to characterize the form of valleys. Most valleys belong to one of these two main types or a mixture of them, at least with respect of the cross section of the slopes or hillsides.
    a. Thing
    b. Valley0
    c. Undefined
    d. Undefined

85. An _____ is a type of atom that is defined by its atomic number; that is, by the number of protons in its nucleus.
    a. Element0
    b. Thing
    c. Undefined
    d. Undefined

86. An _____ is a chemical compound containing an oxygen atom and other elements. Most of the earth's crust consists of them. They result when elements are oxidized by air.
    a. Thing
    b. Oxide0
    c. Undefined
    d. Undefined

87. _____ is the oxide of silicon, chemical formula SiO_2, and is known for its hardness as early as the 16th century. It is a principle component in most types of glass and substances such as concrete.

Chapter 5. Weathering and Soil

a. Silica0	b. Thing
c. Undefined	d. Undefined

88. The mineral _____ is a magnesium iron silicate. It is one of the most common minerals on Earth, and has also been identified on the Moon, Mars, and comet Wild 2.

a. Thing	b. Olivine0
c. Undefined	d. Undefined

89. The _____ are a group of important rock-forming silicate minerals found in many igneous and metamorphic rocks. They share a common structure comprised of single chains of silica tetrahedra and they crystalise in the monoclinic and orthorhombic system.

a. Thing	b. Pyroxenes0
c. Undefined	d. Undefined

90. _____ is a common phyllosilicate mineral within the mica group. Primarily a solid-solution series between the iron-endmember annite, and the magnesium-endmember phlogopite; more aluminous endmembers include siderophyllite.

a. Thing	b. Biotite0
c. Undefined	d. Undefined

91. _____ defines an important group of generally dark-colored rock-forming inosilicate minerals linked at the vertices and generally containing ions of iron and/or magnesium in their structures. Amphiboles crystallize into two crystal systems, monoclinic and orthorhombic.

a. Amphibole0	b. Thing
c. Undefined	d. Undefined

92. _____ is a very common mineral, colored black to steel or silver-gray, brown to reddish brown, or red. It is mined as the main ore of iron. Varieties include kidney ore, martite iron rose and specularite. While the forms of it vary, they all have a rust-red streak. it is harder than pure iron, but much more brittle.

a. Hematite0	b. Thing
c. Undefined	d. Undefined

93. _____ is an ore consisting in a mixture of hydrated iron oxide-hydroxide of varying composition. It often contains a varying amount of oxide compared to hydroxide.

a. Thing	b. Limonite0
c. Undefined	d. Undefined

94. An _____ solid is a solid in which there is no long-range order of the positions of the atoms. These materials are often prepared by rapidly cooling molten material, such as glass. The cooling reduces the mobility of the material's molecules before they can pack into a more thermodynamically favorable crystalline state.

a. Thing	b. Amorphous0
c. Undefined	d. Undefined

95. An _____ is an atom or group of atoms which have lost or gained one or more electrons, making them negatively or positively charged.

Chapter 5. Weathering and Soil

a. Thing
b. Ion0
c. Undefined
d. Undefined

96. _____ is a chemical element represented by the symbol H and an atomic number of 1. At standard temperature and pressure it is a colorless, odorless, nonmetallic, tasteless, highly flammable diatomic gas . With an atomic mass of 1.00794 g/mol, _____ is the lightest element. _____ is the most abundant of the chemical elements, constituting roughly 75% of the universe's elemental mass.
   a. Hydrogen0
   b. Thing
   c. Undefined
   d. Undefined

97. _____ is a strong mineral acid. It is soluble in water at all concentrations. _____ has many applications, and is one of the top products of the chemical industry. Principal uses include ore processing, fertilizer manufacturing, oil refining, wastewater processing, and chemical synthesis.
   a. Thing
   b. Sulfuric acid0
   c. Undefined
   d. Undefined

98. A _____ is a sort of hot spring or fumarole consisting of a pool of usually bubbling mud. They form in high-temperature geothermal areas where water is in short supply. The little water that is available rises to the surface at a spot where the soil is rich in volcanic ash, clay and other fine particulates.
   a. Mudpot0
   b. Thing
   c. Undefined
   d. Undefined

99. A _____ is a section of a river of relatively steep gradient causing an increase in water flow and turbulence. A _____ is a hydrological feature between a run and a cascade. It is characterized by the river becoming shallower and having some rocks exposed above the flow surface.
   a. Rapid0
   b. Thing
   c. Undefined
   d. Undefined

100. The _____ is the centerpiece of the Greater Yellowstone Ecosystem, the largest intact ecosystem in the Earth's northern temperate zone. Located mostly in the U.S. state of Wyoming, the park extends into Montana and Idaho. The park is known for its wildlife and geothermal features; Old Faithful Geyser is one of the most popular features in the park.
   a. Place
   b. Yellowstone National Park0
   c. Undefined
   d. Undefined

101. _____ or sulphur is the chemical element that has the symbol S and atomic number 16. It is an abundant, tasteless, multivalent non-metal. _____, in its native form, is a yellow crystalline solid. In nature, it can be found as the pure element or as sulfide and sulfate minerals. It is an essential element for life and is found in two amino acids, cysteine and methionine.
   a. Sulfur0
   b. Thing
   c. Undefined
   d. Undefined

102. A _____ is a spring that is produced by the emergence of geothermally-heated groundwater from the earth's crust. They are all over the earth, on every continent and even under the oceans and seas.
   a. Hot spring0
   b. Thing
   c. Undefined
   d. Undefined

Chapter 5. Weathering and Soil

103. The mineral _____ is iron disulfide, FeS2. It has isometric crystals that usually appear as cubes. Its metallic luster and pale-to-normal, brass-yellow hue have earned it a nickname due to many miners mistaking it for the real thing.
   a. Pyrite0
   b. Thing
   c. Undefined
   d. Undefined

104. _____ is the natural or artificial removal of surface and sub-surface water from a given area. Many agricultural soils need _____ to improve production or to manage water supplies.
   a. Drainage0
   b. Thing
   c. Undefined
   d. Undefined

105. _____ is a chemical element which has the symbol N and atomic number 7. Elemental _____ is a colorless, odourless, tasteless and mostly inert diatomic gas at standard conditions, constituting 78.1% by volume of Earth's atmosphere.
   a. Thing
   b. Nitrogen0
   c. Undefined
   d. Undefined

106. The carbonate mineral _____ is a chemical or biochemical calcium carbonate and is one of the most widely distributed minerals on the Earth's surface. It is a common constituent of sedimentary rocks, limestone in particular. It is also the primary mineral in metamorphic marble
   a. Thing
   b. Calcite0
   c. Undefined
   d. Undefined

107. A _____ is a natural underground void large enough for a human to enter. Some people suggest that the term '_____' should only apply to cavities that have some part which does not receive daylight; however, in popular usage, the term includes smaller spaces like a sea _____, rock shelters, and grottos.
   a. Place
   b. Cave0
   c. Undefined
   d. Undefined

108. The _____ was enacted by the United States Congress in response to the Love Canal disaster. The Act was created to protect people, families, communities and others from heavily contaminated toxic waste sites that have been abandoned. It paid for toxic waste cleanups at sites where no other responsible parties could pay for a cleanup by assessing a tax on petroleum and chemical industries.
   a. Comprehensive Environmental Response, Compensation, and Liability Act0
   b. Thing
   c. Undefined
   d. Undefined

109. _____ is the result of the transformation of a pre-existing rock type, the protolith, in a process called metamorphism, which means "change in form". The protolith is subjected to heat and extreme pressure causing profound physical and/or chemical change. The protolith may be sedimentary rock, igneous rock or another older rock.
   a. Metamorphic rock0
   b. Thing
   c. Undefined
   d. Undefined

110. _____ can be defined as the solid state recrystallisation of pre-existing rocks due to changes in heat and/or pressure and/or introduction of fluids. There will be mineralogical, chemical and crystallographic changes. _____ produced with increasing pressure and temperature conditions is known as prograde _____. Conversely, decreasing temperatures and pressure characterize retrograde _____.

Chapter 5. Weathering and Soil

a. Metamorphism0
b. Thing
c. Undefined
d. Undefined

111. _____ refers to the outflow of acidic water from abandoned metal mines. However, other areas where the earth has been disturbed may also contribute _____ to the environment
a. Thing
b. Acid mine drainage0
c. Undefined
d. Undefined

112. A _____ is a barrier across flowing water that obstructs, directs or slows down the flow, often creating a reservoir, lake or impoundment.
a. Dam0
b. Thing
c. Undefined
d. Undefined

113. _____ are hydrous aluminium phyllosilicates, sometimes with variable amounts of iron, magnesium, alkali metals, alkaline earths and other cations. Clays have structures similar to the micas and therefore form flat hexagonal sheets. _____ are common weathering products and low temperature hydrothermal alteration products.
a. Thing
b. Clay minerals0
c. Undefined
d. Undefined

114. _____ is a chemical element. It is a soft silvery-white metallic alkali metal that occurs naturally bound to other elements in seawater and many minerals. It oxidizes rapidly in air and is very reactive, especially towards water. In many respects, it and sodium are chemically similar, although organisms in general, and animal cells in particular, treat them very differently.
a. Potassium0
b. Thing
c. Undefined
d. Undefined

115. _____ is a very important series of tectosilicate minerals within the feldspar family. Rather than referring to a particular mineral with a specific chemical composition, it is a solid solution series.
a. Plagioclase0
b. Thing
c. Undefined
d. Undefined

116. The chemical compound _____ is an aqueous solution of hydrogen nitrate. It is a highly corrosive and toxic acid that can cause severe burns. Colorless when pure, older samples tend to acquire a yellow cast due to the accumulation of oxides of nitrogen.
a. Thing
b. Nitric acid0
c. Undefined
d. Undefined

117. _____ is a fossil fuel formed in swamp ecosystems where plant remains were saved by water and mud from oxidization and biodegradation. It is a sedimentary rock, but the harder forms, such as anthracite _____, can be regarded as metamorphic rocks because of later exposure to elevated temperature and pressure. It is composed primarily of carbon along with assorted other elements, including sulfur.
a. Thing
b. Coal0
c. Undefined
d. Undefined

118. The _____ is a measure of the acidity or alkalinity of a solution. Solutions with less than seven are considered acidic, while those with a number greater than seven are considered basic

Chapter 5. Weathering and Soil

a. PH scale0
b. Thing
c. Undefined
d. Undefined

119. _____ is a chemical compound with the formula SO2. This important gas is the main product from the combustion of sulfur compounds and is of significant environmental concern. Sulphur dioxide is produced by volcanoes and in various industrial processes.
a. Thing
b. Sulfur dioxide0
c. Undefined
d. Undefined

120. Fossils are the mineralized or otherwise preserved remains or traces of animals, plants, and other organisms. The totality of fossils, both discovered and undiscovered, and their placement in fossiliferous rock formations and sedimentary layers is known as the _____ record.
a. Fossil0
b. Thing
c. Undefined
d. Undefined

121. Fossil fuels are hydrocarbons, primarily coal and petroleum, formed from the fossilized remains of dead plants and animals. In common parlance, the term _____ also includes hydrocarbon-containing natural resources that are not derived from animal or plant sources. Fossil fuels have made large-scale industrial development possible and have largely supplanted water-driven mills, as well as the combustion of wood or peat for heat.
a. Thing
b. Fossil fuel0
c. Undefined
d. Undefined

122. _____ are hydrocarbons, primarily coal and petroleum, formed from the fossilized remains of dead plants and animals by exposure to heat and pressure in the Earth's crust over hundreds of millions of years. The burning of _____ by humans is the largest source of emissions of carbon dioxide, which is one of the greenhouse gases that enhances radiative forcing and contributes to global warming.
a. Thing
b. Fossil fuels0
c. Undefined
d. Undefined

123. The term _____ is commonly used to mean the deposition of acidic components in rain, snow, dew, or dry particles. _____ occurs when sulfur dioxide and nitrogen oxides are emitted into the atmosphere, undergo chemical transformations and are absorbed by water droplets in clouds. The droplets then fall to earth as rain, snow, mist, dry dust, hail, or sleet. This increases the acidity of the soil, and affects the chemical balance of lakes and streams.
a. Thing
b. Acid precipitation0
c. Undefined
d. Undefined

124. In geography, a _____ is a type of wetland which is subject to almost continuous inundation. Typically it features grasses, rushes, reeds, typhas, sedges, and other herbaceous plants in a context of shallow water. It is different from a swamp, which has a greater proportion of open water surface, and is generally deeper than a it.
a. Marsh0
b. Thing
c. Undefined
d. Undefined

125. A _____ is a body of water or other liquid of considerable size contained on a body of land. A vast majority are fresh water, and lie in the Northern Hemisphere at higher latitudes. Most have a natural outflow in the form of a river or stream, but some do not, and lose water solely by evaporation and/or underground seepage.

a. Thing
b. Lake0
c. Undefined
d. Undefined

126. _____ is the physical process responsible for the attractive interactions between atoms and molecules, and that which confers stability to diatomic and polyatomic chemical compounds.
   a. Chemical Bonding0
   b. Thing
   c. Undefined
   d. Undefined

127. _____ are the hardest natural material known to man and the third-hardest known material. Its hardness and high dispersion of light make it useful for industrial applications and jewelry.
   a. Diamonds0
   b. Thing
   c. Undefined
   d. Undefined

128. _____ is a type of rock best known for sometimes containing diamonds. It is an ultrapotassic, ultramafic, igneous rock composed of olivine, phlogopite, pyroxene and garnet, with a variety of chemically anomalous trace minerals.
   a. Thing
   b. Kimberlite0
   c. Undefined
   d. Undefined

129. _____ is the average and variations of weather over long periods of time. _____ zones can be defined using parameters such as temperature and rainfall.
   a. Thing
   b. Climate0
   c. Undefined
   d. Undefined

130. A _____ is a geological feature that is also known as a Rip in the earth causing magma to flow out and forming an undersea volcano, it also has geological features, a continuous elevational crest for some distance. Ridges are usually termed hills or mountains as well, depending on size.
   a. Ridge0
   b. Thing
   c. Undefined
   d. Undefined

131. The _____ are a vast system of mountains in eastern North America.
   a. Place
   b. Appalachian Mountains0
   c. Undefined
   d. Undefined

132. _____ is the region of space that is dominated by "geogenic" matter, that is, originating from and bound to the Earth.
   a. Geosphere0
   b. Thing
   c. Undefined
   d. Undefined

133. _____ is soil or rock derived granular material of a specific grain size. _____ may occur as a soil or alternatively as suspended sediment in a water column of any surface water body. It may also exist as deposition soil at the bottom of a water body.
   a. Thing
   b. Silt0
   c. Undefined
   d. Undefined

134. _____ is soil composed of sand, silt, and clay in relatively even concentration. Loams are gritty, plastic when moist, and retain water easily. They generally contain more nutrients than sandy soils.

Chapter 5. Weathering and Soil

    a. Thing
    b. Loam0
    c. Undefined
    d. Undefined

135. _____ is the uppermost layer of soil, usually the top 2 to 6 inches. It has the highest concentration of organic matter and microorganisms, and is where most of the Earth's biological soil activity occurs. Plants generally concentrate their roots in, and obtain most of their nutrients from this layer. The actual depth of the _____ layer can be measured as the depth from the surface to the first densely packed soil layer known as hardpan.
    a. Topsoil0
    b. Thing
    c. Undefined
    d. Undefined

136. _____ is the layer of soil under the topsoil on the surface of the ground. The _____ may include substances such as clay and has only been partially broken down by air, sunlight, water, etc., to produce true soil.
    a. Subsoil0
    b. Thing
    c. Undefined
    d. Undefined

137. In chemistry, a _____ is defined as a sufficiently stable electrically neutral group of at least two atoms in a definite arrangement held together by strong chemical bonds.
    a. Molecule0
    b. Thing
    c. Undefined
    d. Undefined

138. A _____ is a specific layer in the soil which parallels the land surface and possesses physical characteristics which differ from the layers above and beneath.
    a. Soil horizon0
    b. Thing
    c. Undefined
    d. Undefined

139. In soil science, cation exchange capacity is the _____ capacity of soil for positively charged ions. Soils can be considered as natural weak cation exchangers.
    a. Thing
    b. Ion exchange0
    c. Undefined
    d. Undefined

140. The _____ is a soil layer being dominated by the presence of large amounts of organic material in varying stages of decomposition.
    a. Thing
    b. O horizon0
    c. Undefined
    d. Undefined

141. _____ is a general term for the plant life of a region; it refers to the ground cover provided by plants, and is, by far, the most abundant biotic element of the biosphere. Primeval redwood forests, coastal mangrove stands, sphagnum bogs, desert soil crusts, roadside weed patches, wheat fields, cultivated gardens and lawns; are all encompassed by the term _____.
    a. Vegetation0
    b. Place
    c. Undefined
    d. Undefined

142. The _____ is the top layer of the soil horizon. The technical definition of it may vary, but it is most commonly described in terms relative to deeper layers.

Chapter 5. Weathering and Soil

   a. Thing
   b. A horizon0
   c. Undefined
   d. Undefined

143. The _____ has been significantly leached of its mineral and/or organic content, leaving a pale layer largely composed of silicates.
   a. Thing
   b. E horizon0
   c. Undefined
   d. Undefined

144. _____ is the process of extracting a substance from a solid by dissolving it in a liquid.
   a. Thing
   b. Leaching0
   c. Undefined
   d. Undefined

145. On a glacier, the _____ is the area above the firn line, where snowfall accumulates and exceeds the losses from ablation.
   a. Thing
   b. Accumulation zone0
   c. Undefined
   d. Undefined

146. _____ consist of mineral layers which may contain concentrations of clay or minerals such as iron or aluminium, or organic material. In addition, they are defined by having a distinctly different structure or consistence to the A horizon above and the horizons below.
   a. B horizon0
   b. Thing
   c. Undefined
   d. Undefined

147. _____ is simply named so because they come 'after' A and B within the soil profile. These layers are little affected by soil forming processes, and their lack of pedological development is one of their defining attributes
   a. C horizon0
   b. Thing
   c. Undefined
   d. Undefined

148. _____, in soil science, means the underlying geological material in which soil horizons form. Soils typically get a great deal of structure and minerals from their _____.
   a. Thing
   b. Parent material0
   c. Undefined
   d. Undefined

149. _____ is a dynamic subject, from the structure of the system itself, to the definitions of classes, and finally in the application in the field. It can be approached from both the pespective of pedogenesis and from soil morphology.
   a. Thing
   b. Soil classification0
   c. Undefined
   d. Undefined

150. _____ is a set of management strategies for prevention of soil being eroded from the earth's surface or becoming chemically altered by overuse, salinization, acidification, or other chemical soil contamination.
   a. Thing
   b. Soil conservation0
   c. Undefined
   d. Undefined

Chapter 5. Weathering and Soil

151. _____ is a term used to describe two different types of organic material in soil. In the earth sciences, _____ refers to any organic matter which has reached a point of stability, where it will break down no further and might, if conditions do not change, remain essentially as it is for centuries, or millennia. In agriculture, _____ is often used simply to mean mature compost, or natural compost extracted from a forest or other spontaneous source for use to amend soil.
- a. Humus0
- b. Thing
- c. Undefined
- d. Undefined

152. _____ is a layer of loose, heterogeneous material covering solid rock. _____ is present on Earth, the Moon, some asteroids, and other planets.
- a. Regolith0
- b. Thing
- c. Undefined
- d. Undefined

153. _____ is any particulate matter that can be transported by fluid flow and which eventually is deposited as a layer of solid particles on the bed or bottom of a body of water or other liquid.
- a. Thing
- b. Sediment0
- c. Undefined
- d. Undefined

154. _____ occurs when snow falls on a glacier, is compressed, and becomes part of a glacier that winds its way toward a body of water.
- a. Thing
- b. Blue ice0
- c. Undefined
- d. Undefined

155. Among the classifications of soil types, _____, is a fine, silty, windblown type of unconsolidated deposit. It is derived from glacial deposits, where glacial activity has ground rocks very fine. After drying, these deposits are highly susceptible to wind erosion, and downwind deposits may become very deep. _____ deposits are geologically unstable by nature, and will erode even without being disturbed by humans.
- a. Thing
- b. Loess0
- c. Undefined
- d. Undefined

156. The _____ is a region in the northwest of North America. The _____, broadly defined, extends from the ocean to the continental divide and includes all of Washington, most of Oregon, Idaho and British Columbia, and adjoining parts of Alaska, Yukon Territory and California. Both the name "_____" and the name "Cascadia", which is derived from the Cascade Range, are commonly used without a definition, although the term "_____" is considerably older, having its origins in the early 19th Century.
- a. Place
- b. Pacific Northwest0
- c. Undefined
- d. Undefined

157. _____ is a common gray to black extrusive volcanic rock. It is usually fine-grained due to rapid cooling of lava on the Earth's surface. It may be porphyritic containing larger crystals in a fine matrix, or vesicular, or frothy scoria.
- a. Basalt0
- b. Thing
- c. Undefined
- d. Undefined

158. _____ is molten rock expelled by a volcano during an eruption. When first extruded from a volcanic vent, it is a liquid at temperatures from 700 °C to 1,200 °C.

Chapter 5. Weathering and Soil

    a. Lava0
    b. Thing
    c. Undefined
    d. Undefined

159. An _____ is a mass of glacier ice that covers surrounding terrain and is greater than 19,305 mile². The only current ice sheets are in Antarctica and Greenland. Ice sheets are bigger than ice shelves or glaciers. Masses of ice covering less than 50,000 km² are termed an ice cap. An ice cap will typically feed a series of glaciers around its periphery. Although the surface is cold, the base of an _____ is generally warmer. This process produces fast-flowing channels in the _____.
    a. Thing
    b. Ice sheet0
    c. Undefined
    d. Undefined

160. _____ is a general term that includes rocks and materials that are not by definition rocks but are commonly regarded as rocks.
    a. Earth materials0
    b. Thing
    c. Undefined
    d. Undefined

161. In organic chemistry, a _____ is a salt of carbonic acid.
    a. Carbonate0
    b. Thing
    c. Undefined
    d. Undefined

162. A _____ in petrology or mineralogy is an irregular rounded to spherical concretion. They are typically solid replacement bodies of chert or iron oxides formed during diagenesis of a sedimentary rock.
    a. Thing
    b. Nodule0
    c. Undefined
    d. Undefined

163. The _____ is a United States Federal Executive Department. Its purpose is to develop and execute policy on farming, agriculture, and food. It aims to meet the needs of farmers and ranchers, promote agricultural trade and production, work to assure food safety, protect natural resources, foster rural communities and end hunger, in America and abroad. Former Nebraska governor Mike Johanns is the department's current secretary.
    a. US Department of Agriculture0
    b. Person
    c. Undefined
    d. Undefined

164. _____ is the ability of a substance to draw another substance into it. The standard reference is to a tube in plants but can be seen readily with porous paper. It occurs when the adhesive intermolecular forces between the liquid and a substance are stronger than the cohesive intermolecular forces inside the liquid. The effect causes a concave meniscus to form where the substance is touching a vertical surface. The same effect is what causes porous materials to soak up liquids.
    a. Thing
    b. Capillary action0
    c. Undefined
    d. Undefined

165. _____ is the process by which molecules in a liquid state become a gas.
    a. Thing
    b. Evaporation0
    c. Undefined
    d. Undefined

Chapter 5. Weathering and Soil

166. _____ is any product of the condensation of atmospheric water vapor that is deposited on the earth's surface. It occurs when the atmosphere becomes saturated with water vapour and the water condenses and falls out of solution. Air becomes saturated via two processes, cooling and adding moisture.
- a. Precipitation0
- b. Thing
- c. Undefined
- d. Undefined

167. _____ is a hardened deposit of calcium carbonate. This calcium carbonate cements together other materials, including gravel, sand, clay, and silt. It is found in aridisol and mollisol soil orders. _____ occurs worldwide, generally in arid or semi-arid regions.
- a. Thing
- b. Caliche0
- c. Undefined
- d. Undefined

168. _____ is the most commonly used technique within the science of archaeology. It is the exposure, processing and recording of archaeological remains.
- a. Excavation0
- b. Thing
- c. Undefined
- d. Undefined

169. _____ are an order in USA soil taxonomy, best known for their occurrence in tropical rain forest, 15-25 degrees north and south of the Equator. They are defined as soils containing at all depths no more than 10 percent weatherable minerals, and less than 10 percent base saturation. _____ are always a red or yellowish color, due to the high concentration of iron III and aluminium oxides and hydroxides.
- a. Oxisols0
- b. Thing
- c. Undefined
- d. Undefined

170. _____ is a surface formation in hot and wet tropical areas which is enriched in iron and aluminium and develops by intensive and long lasting weathering of the underlying parent rock. Nearly all kinds of rocks can be deeply decomposed by the action of high rainfall and elevated temperatures. This gives rise to a residual concentration of more insoluble elements.
- a. Thing
- b. Laterite0
- c. Undefined
- d. Undefined

171. _____ are rocks and minerals from which metallic iron can be extracted. The ores are usually rich in iron oxides and vary in color from dark grey to rusty red. The iron itself is usually found in the form of magnetite, hematite, limonite or siderite.
- a. Iron ores0
- b. Thing
- c. Undefined
- d. Undefined

172. _____ is an aluminium ore. It consists largely of the Al minerals gibbsite, boehmite and diaspore, together with the iron oxides goethite and hematite, the clay mineral kaolinite and small amounts of anatase.
- a. Bauxite0
- b. Thing
- c. Undefined
- d. Undefined

173. _____ is a type of rock consisting of consolidated volcanic ash ejected from vents during a volcanic eruption.
- a. Thing
- b. Tuff0
- c. Undefined
- d. Undefined

Chapter 5. Weathering and Soil

174. _____ is the reprocessing of materials into new products. It prevents useful material resources being wasted, reduces the consumption of raw materials and reduces energy usage, and hence greenhouse gas emissions, compared to virgin production.

a. Thing
b. Recycling0
c. Undefined
d. Undefined

175. _____ is the increase in the average temperature of the Earth's near-surface air and oceans in recent decades and its projected continuation. An increase in global temperatures can in turn cause other changes, including sea level rise, and changes in the amount and pattern of precipitation resulting in floods and drought. There may also be changes in the frequency and intensity of extreme weather events.

a. Thing
b. Global warming0
c. Undefined
d. Undefined

176. _____ is the science and study of the solid matter that constitute the Earth. Encompassing such things as rocks, soil, and gemstones, _____ studies the composition, structure, physical properties, history, and the processes that shape Earth's components.

a. Geology0
b. Thing
c. Undefined
d. Undefined

Chapter 6. Sediment and Sedimentary Rocks

1. _____ is the process of breaking down rocks, soils and their minerals through direct contact with the atmosphere. _____ occurs without movement. Two main classifications of _____ processes exist. Mechanical or physical _____ involves the breakdown of rocks and soils through direct contact with atmospheric conditions. The second classification, chemical _____, involves the direct effect of atmospheric chemicals in the breakdown of rocks, soils and minerals.
   a. Weathering0
   b. Thing
   c. Undefined
   d. Undefined

2. _____ is the result of the transformation of a pre-existing rock type, the protolith, in a process called metamorphism, which means "change in form". The protolith is subjected to heat and extreme pressure causing profound physical and/or chemical change. The protolith may be sedimentary rock, igneous rock or another older rock.
   a. Thing
   b. Metamorphic rock0
   c. Undefined
   d. Undefined

3. Metamorphic rock is the result of the transformation of a pre-existing rock type, the protolith, in a process called metamorphism. The protolith is subjected to heat and extreme pressure causing profound physical and/or chemical change. _____ make up a large part of the Earth's crust. They are formed deep beneath the Earth's surface by great stresses from rocks above and high pressures and temperatures.
   a. Thing
   b. Metamorphic rocks0
   c. Undefined
   d. Undefined

4. _____ can be defined as the solid state recrystallisation of pre-existing rocks due to changes in heat and/or pressure and/or introduction of fluids. There will be mineralogical, chemical and crystallographic changes. _____ produced with increasing pressure and temperature conditions is known as prograde _____. Conversely, decreasing temperatures and pressure characterize retrograde _____.
   a. Thing
   b. Metamorphism0
   c. Undefined
   d. Undefined

5. _____ is any particulate matter that can be transported by fluid flow and which eventually is deposited as a layer of solid particles on the bed or bottom of a body of water or other liquid.
   a. Sediment0
   b. Thing
   c. Undefined
   d. Undefined

6. _____ rock is one of the three main rock groups. Rock formed from these covers 75% of the Earth's land area, and includes common types such as chalk, limestone, dolomite, sandstone, and shale.
   a. Sedimentary0
   b. Thing
   c. Undefined
   d. Undefined

7. _____ is one of the three main rock groups. _____ covers 75% of the Earth's land area. Four basic processes are involved in the formation of a clastic _____: weathering caused mainly by friction of waves, transportation where the sediment is carried along by a current, deposition and compaction where the sediment is squashed together to form a rock of this kind.
   a. Thing
   b. Sedimentary rock0
   c. Undefined
   d. Undefined

8. In geology, _____ are sedimentary structures that indicate agitation by or wind.

Chapter 6. Sediment and Sedimentary Rocks

    a. Thing
    b. Ripple marks0
    c. Undefined
    d. Undefined

9. Fossils are the mineralized or otherwise preserved remains or traces of animals, plants, and other organisms. The totality of fossils, both discovered and undiscovered, and their placement in fossiliferous rock formations and sedimentary layers is known as the _____ record.
    a. Fossil0
    b. Thing
    c. Undefined
    d. Undefined

10. _____ is a small island located in the middle of San Francisco Bay in California, United States. It served as a lighthouse, then a military fortification, then a military prison followed by a federal prison until 1963, when it became a national recreation area.
    a. Alcatraz Island0
    b. Place
    c. Undefined
    d. Undefined

11. _____ is a fossil fuel formed in swamp ecosystems where plant remains were saved by water and mud from oxidization and biodegradation. It is a sedimentary rock, but the harder forms, such as anthracite _____, can be regarded as metamorphic rocks because of later exposure to elevated temperature and pressure. It is composed primarily of carbon along with assorted other elements, including sulfur.
    a. Coal0
    b. Thing
    c. Undefined
    d. Undefined

12. _____ is a sedimentary rock composed largely of the mineral calcite. _____ often contains variable amounts of silica in the form of chert or flint, as well as varying amounts of clay, silt and sand as disseminations, nodules, or layers within the rock. The primary source of the calcite in _____ is most commonly marine organisms. These organisms secrete shells that settle out of the water column and are deposited on ocean floors as pelagic ooze or alternatively is conglomerated in a coral reef.
    a. Limestone0
    b. Thing
    c. Undefined
    d. Undefined

13. A _____ is one of several large landmasses on Earth. They are generally identified by convention rather than any strict criteria, but seven areas are commonly reckoned as continents – they are: Asia, Africa, North America, South America, Antarctica, Europe, and Australia.
    a. Continent0
    b. Thing
    c. Undefined
    d. Undefined

14. _____ is a chemical element metal. It is a lustrous, silvery soft metal. It and nickel are notable for being the final elements produced by stellar nucleosynthesis, and thus are the heaviest elements which do not require a supernova or similarly cataclysmic event for formation.
    a. Iron0
    b. Thing
    c. Undefined
    d. Undefined

15. _____ is a gaseous fossil fuel consisting primarily of methane but including significant quantities of ethane, butane, propane, carbon dioxide, nitrogen, helium and hydrogen sulfide.

Chapter 6. Sediment and Sedimentary Rocks

a. Natural gas0
b. Thing
c. Undefined
d. Undefined

16. _____ is a naturally occurring liquid found in formations in the Earth consisting of a complex mixture of hydrocarbons of various lengths.
a. Petroleum0
b. Thing
c. Undefined
d. Undefined

17. _____ is approximately 70% more dense than lead and is weakly radioactive. It occurs naturally in low concentrations in soil, rock and water.
a. Thing
b. Uranium0
c. Undefined
d. Undefined

18. _____ are rocks and minerals from which metallic iron can be extracted. The ores are usually rich in iron oxides and vary in color from dark grey to rusty red. The iron itself is usually found in the form of magnetite, hematite, limonite or siderite.
a. Iron ores0
b. Thing
c. Undefined
d. Undefined

19. _____ is a very soft mineral composed of calcium sulfate dihydrate, with the chemical formula $CaSO_4 \cdot 2H_2O$. _____ occurs in nature as flattened and often twinned crystals and transparent cleavable masses. It may also occur silky and fibrous. Finally it may also be granular or quite compact.
a. Gypsum0
b. Thing
c. Undefined
d. Undefined

20. An _____ is a volume of rock containing components or minerals in a mode of occurrence that renders it valuable for mining.
a. Ore0
b. Thing
c. Undefined
d. Undefined

21. An _____ is a layer of gases that may surround a material body of sufficient mass. The gases are attracted by the gravity of the body, and are retained for a longer duration if gravity is high and the _____'s temperature is low. Some planets consist mainly of various gases, and thus have very deep atmospheres.
a. Place
b. Atmosphere0
c. Undefined
d. Undefined

22. A _____ is a hill of sand built by eolian processes. Dunes are subject to different forms and sizes based on their interaction with the wind. Most kinds of _____ are longer on the windward side where the sand is pushed up the _____, and a shorter in the lee of the wind. The trough between dunes is called a slack. A "_____ field" is an area covered by extensive sand dunes. Large _____ fields are known as ergs.
a. Dune0
b. Thing
c. Undefined
d. Undefined

23. A _____ in physical geography describes the collective mass of water found on, under, and over the surface of a planet.

Chapter 6. Sediment and Sedimentary Rocks

    a. Hydrosphere0   b. Thing
    c. Undefined   d. Undefined

24. A _____ is a body of water with a current, confined within a bed and banks. Streams are important as conduits in the water cycle, instruments in aquifer recharge, and corridors for fish and wildlife migration.
    a. Stream0   b. Thing
    c. Undefined   d. Undefined

25. An _____ is any more or less continuous, directed movement of ocean water that flows in one of the Earth's oceans. Ocean Currents are rivers of hot or cold water within the ocean. The currents are generated from the forces acting upon the water like the earth's rotation, the wind, the temperature and salinity differences and the gravitation of the moon. The depth contours, the shoreline and other currents influence the current's direction and strength.
    a. Thing   b. Ocean current0
    c. Undefined   d. Undefined

26. Ocean _____ are any more or less continuous, directed movement of ocean water that flows in one of the Earth's oceans. They are rivers of hot or cold water within the ocean. They are generated from the forces acting upon the water like the earth's rotation, the wind, the temperature and salinity differences and the gravitation of the moon.
    a. Thing   b. Currents0
    c. Undefined   d. Undefined

27. A _____ is a large, slow moving river of ice, formed from compacted layers of snow, that slowly deforms and flows in response to gravity. _____ ice is the largest reservoir of fresh water on Earth, and second only to oceans as the largest reservoir of total water. Glaciers cover vast areas of polar regions but are restricted to the highest mountains in the tropics.
    a. Glacier0   b. Thing
    c. Undefined   d. Undefined

28. _____ is any product of the condensation of atmospheric water vapor that is deposited on the earth's surface. It occurs when the atmosphere becomes saturated with water vapour and the water condenses and falls out of solution. Air becomes saturated via two processes, cooling and adding moisture.
    a. Thing   b. Precipitation0
    c. Undefined   d. Undefined

29. The _____ is the part of the earth, including air, land, surface rocks, and water, within which life occurs, and which biotic processes in turn alter or transform. From the broadest biophysiological point of view, the _____ is the global ecological system integrating all living beings and their relationships, including their interaction with the elements of the lithosphere, hydrosphere, and atmosphere. This _____ is postulated to have evolved, beginning through a process of biogenesis or biopoesis, at least some 3.5 billion years ago.
    a. Thing   b. Biosphere0
    c. Undefined   d. Undefined

30. _____ is the substance of which physical objects are composed. _____ can be solid, liquid, plasma or gas. It constitutes the observable universe.

Chapter 6. Sediment and Sedimentary Rocks

a. Matter0
b. Thing
c. Undefined
d. Undefined

31. _____ is matter that has come from a recently living organism; is capable of decay, or the product of decay; or is composed of organic compounds. The definition of _____ varies upon the subject it is being used for.
   a. Organic matter0
   b. Thing
   c. Undefined
   d. Undefined

32. In biology and ecology, an _____ is a living complex adaptive system of organs that influence each other in such a way that they function in some way as a stable whole.
   a. Organism0
   b. Thing
   c. Undefined
   d. Undefined

33. A _____ is a body of water or other liquid of considerable size contained on a body of land. A vast majority are fresh water, and lie in the Northern Hemisphere at higher latitudes. Most have a natural outflow in the form of a river or stream, but some do not, and lose water solely by evaporation and/or underground seepage.
   a. Lake0
   b. Thing
   c. Undefined
   d. Undefined

34. In geology, _____ are rock s with a grain size of usually no less than 256 mm diameter.
   a. Boulders0
   b. Thing
   c. Undefined
   d. Undefined

35. A _____ is a rock, sandbar, or other feature lying beneath the surface of the water yet shallow enough to be a hazard to ships. They result from abiotic processes—deposition of sand, wave erosion planning down rock outcrops, and other natural processes.
   a. Thing
   b. Reef0
   c. Undefined
   d. Undefined

36. A _____ is a disturbance that propagates through space or spacetime, transferring energy and momentum and sometimes angular momentum.
   a. Thing
   b. Wave0
   c. Undefined
   d. Undefined

37. A _____ is any disturbed state of an astronomical body's atmosphere, especially affecting its surface, and strongly implying severe weather. It may be marked by strong wind, thunder and lightning, heavy precipitation, such as ice, or wind transporting some substance through the atmosphere.
   a. Thing
   b. Storm0
   c. Undefined
   d. Undefined

38. _____ refer to marine animals from the class Anthozoa and exist as small sea anemone-like polyps, typically in colonies of many identical individuals. The group includes the important reef builders that are found in tropical oceans, which secrete calcium carbonate to form a hard skeleton.
   a. Thing
   b. Coral0
   c. Undefined
   d. Undefined

Chapter 6. Sediment and Sedimentary Rocks

39. _____ is displacement of solids by the agents of ocean currents, wind, water, or ice by downward or down-slope movement in response to gravity or by living organisms.
   a. Erosion0
   b. Thing
   c. Undefined
   d. Undefined

40. _____ is rock that is of a certain particle size range. In geology, _____ is any loose rock that is at least two millimeters in its largest dimension and no more than 75 millimeters.
   a. Gravel0
   b. Thing
   c. Undefined
   d. Undefined

41. _____ is a silvery white metal that takes on a high polish. It belongs to the transition metals, and is hard and ductile. It occurs most usually in combination with sulfur and iron in pentlandite, with sulfur in millerite, with arsenic in the mineral niccolite, and with arsenic and sulfur.
   a. Nickel0
   b. Thing
   c. Undefined
   d. Undefined

42. _____ is soil or rock derived granular material of a specific grain size. _____ may occur as a soil or alternatively as suspended sediment in a water column of any surface water body. It may also exist as deposition soil at the bottom of a water body.
   a. Silt0
   b. Thing
   c. Undefined
   d. Undefined

43. _____ refers to the diameter of individual grains of sediment, or the lithified particles in clastic rocks. The term may also be applied to other granular materials. This is different from the crystallite size, which is the size of a single crystal inside the particles or grains.
   a. Thing
   b. Particle size0
   c. Undefined
   d. Undefined

44. _____ is a term used to describe a group of hydrous aluminium phyllosilicate minerals, that are typically less than 2 micrometres in diameter. _____ consists of a variety of phyllosilicate minerals rich in silicon and aluminium oxides and hydroxides which include variable amounts of structural water. Clays are generally formed by the chemical weathering of silicate-bearing rocks by carbonic acid but some are formed by hydrothermal activity.
   a. Clay0
   b. Thing
   c. Undefined
   d. Undefined

45. _____ is a fine-grained sedimentary rock whose original constituents were clays or muds. It is characterized by thin laminae breaking with an irregular curving fracture, often splintery and usually parallel to the often-indistinguishable bedding plane.
   a. Thing
   b. Shale0
   c. Undefined
   d. Undefined

46. _____ is a sedimentary rock which has a composition intermediate in grain size between the coarser sandstones and the finer mudstones and shales.
   a. Siltstone0
   b. Thing
   c. Undefined
   d. Undefined

Chapter 6. Sediment and Sedimentary Rocks 101

47. _____ is a sedimentary rock composed mainly of sand-size mineral or rock grains. Most _____ is composed of quartz and/or feldspar because these are the most common minerals in the Earth's crust. Like sand, _____ may be any color, but the most common colors are tan, brown, yellow, red, gray and white.
   a. Sandstone0
   b. Thing
   c. Undefined
   d. Undefined

48. A _____ is a rock consisting of individual stones that have become cemented together. Conglomerates are sedimentary rocks consisting of rounded fragements and are thus differentiated from breccias, which consist of angular clasts. Both conglomerates and breccias are characterized by clasts larger than sand.
   a. Thing
   b. Conglomerate0
   c. Undefined
   d. Undefined

49. A _____ is a naturally occurring substance formed through geological processes that has a characteristic chemical composition, a highly ordered atomic structure and specific physical properties. A rock, by comparison, is an aggregate of minerals and need not have a specific chemical composition. Minerals range in composition from pure elements and simple salts to very complex silicates with thousands of known forms.
   a. Thing
   b. Mineral0
   c. Undefined
   d. Undefined

50. In geology and astronomy, the term _____ is used to denote types of rock that consist predominantly of _____ minerals. Such rocks include a wide range of igneous, metamorphic and sedimentary types. Most of the Earth's mantle and crust are made up of _____ rocks. The same is true of the Moon and the other rocky planets.
   a. Silicate0
   b. Thing
   c. Undefined
   d. Undefined

51. _____ are hydrous aluminium phyllosilicates, sometimes with variable amounts of iron, magnesium, alkali metals, alkaline earths and other cations. Clays have structures similar to the micas and therefore form flat hexagonal sheets. _____ are common weathering products and low temperature hydrothermal alteration products.
   a. Clay minerals0
   b. Thing
   c. Undefined
   d. Undefined

52. _____ is the second most common mineral in the Earth's continental crust. It is made up of a lattice of silica tetrahedra. _____ belongs to the rhombohedral crystal system. In nature _____ crystals are often twinned, distorted, or so intergrown with adjacent crystals of _____ or other minerals as to only show part of this shape, or to lack obvious crystal faces altogether and appear massive.
   a. Quartz0
   b. Thing
   c. Undefined
   d. Undefined

53. _____ involves the change in the composition of rock, often leading to a 'break down' in its form.
   a. Chemical weathering0
   b. Thing
   c. Undefined
   d. Undefined

54. _____ consists of clay-sized particles of rock, generated by glacial erosion or by artificial grinding to a similar size. Because the material is very small, it is suspended in river water making the water appear cloudy. If the river flows into a glacial lake, the lake may appear turquoise in color as a result.

a. Rock flour0 b. Thing
c. Undefined d. Undefined

55. _____ is the water released by the melting of snow or ice, including glacial ice. _____ provides drinking water for a large proportion of the world's population, as well as providing water for irrigation and hydroelectric plants.
   a. Meltwater0 b. Thing
   c. Undefined d. Undefined

56. _____ is the geological process whereby material is added to a landform. This is the process by which wind and water create a sediment deposit, through the laying down of granular material that has been eroded and transported from another geographical location.
   a. Thing b. Deposition0
   c. Undefined d. Undefined

57. _____, in everyday life, is most familiar as the agency that endows objects with weight. _____ is responsible for keeping the Earth and the other planets in their orbits around the Sun; for the formation of tides; and for various other phenomena that we observe. _____ is also the reason for the very existence of the Earth, the Sun, and most macroscopic objects in the universe; without it, matter would not have coalesced into these large masses, and life, as we know it, would not exist.
   a. Thing b. Gravitation0
   c. Undefined d. Undefined

58. _____ is a measure of the resistance of a fluid to deform under shear stress. It is commonly perceived as "thickness", or resistance to flow. _____ describes a fluid's internal resistance to flow and may be thought of as a measure of fluid friction.
   a. Thing b. Viscosity0
   c. Undefined d. Undefined

59. _____ occurs when snow falls on a glacier, is compressed, and becomes part of a glacier that winds its way toward a body of water.
   a. Blue ice0 b. Thing
   c. Undefined d. Undefined

60. A _____ is a wetland that features temporary or permanent inundation of large areas of land by shallow bodies of water, generally with a substantial number of hummocks, or dry-land protrusions, and covered by aquatic vegetation, or vegetation that tolerates periodical inundation.
   a. Swamp0 b. Thing
   c. Undefined d. Undefined

61. _____ is water from a sea or ocean. On average, _____ in the world's oceans has a salinity of ~3.5%, or 35 parts per thousand. This means that every 1 kg of _____ has approximately 35 grams of dissolved salts.
   a. Seawater0 b. Thing
   c. Undefined d. Undefined

Chapter 6. Sediment and Sedimentary Rocks

62. A _____ is a solid in which the constituent atoms, molecules, or ions are packed in a regularly ordered, repeating pattern extending in all three spatial dimensions. Most metals encountered in everyday life are polycrystals. Crystals are often symmetrically intergrown to form _____ twins.
   a. Crystal0
   b. Thing
   c. Undefined
   d. Undefined

63. The carbonate mineral _____ is a chemical or biochemical calcium carbonate and is one of the most widely distributed minerals on the Earth's surface. It is a common constituent of sedimentary rocks, limestone in particular. It is also the primary mineral in metamorphic marble
   a. Thing
   b. Calcite0
   c. Undefined
   d. Undefined

64. _____ is the oxide of silicon, chemical formula SiO_2, and is known for its hardness as early as the 16th century. It is a principle component in most types of glass and substances such as concrete.
   a. Silica0
   b. Thing
   c. Undefined
   d. Undefined

65. A _____ is a landform that extends above the surrounding terrain in a limited area. A _____ is generally steeper than a hill, but there is no universally accepted standard definition for the height of a _____ or a hill although a _____ usually has an identifiable summit.
   a. Place
   b. Mountain0
   c. Undefined
   d. Undefined

66. Mean _____ is the average height of the sea, with reference to a suitable reference surface.
   a. Sea level0
   b. Thing
   c. Undefined
   d. Undefined

67. _____ rocks are rocks formed from fragments of pre-existing rock.
   a. Clastic0
   b. Thing
   c. Undefined
   d. Undefined

68. _____ is the process in which sediments compact under pressure, expel connate fluids, and gradually become solid rock.
   a. Thing
   b. Lithification0
   c. Undefined
   d. Undefined

69. _____ is the process of a material being more closely packed together.
   a. Compaction0
   b. Thing
   c. Undefined
   d. Undefined

70. _____ is the process of deposition of dissolved mineral components in the interstices of sediments. It is an important factor in the consolidation of coarse-grained clastic sedimentary rocks such as sandstones, conglomerates, or breccias during diagenesis or lithification. Cementing materials may include silica, carbonates, iron oxides, or clay minerals.
   a. Cementation0
   b. Thing
   c. Undefined
   d. Undefined

Chapter 6. Sediment and Sedimentary Rocks

71. _____ is the process of formation of solid crystals from a uniform solution. It is also a chemical solid-liquid separation technique, in which mass transfer of a solute from the liquid solution to a pure solid crystalline phase occurs.
    a. Thing
    b. Crystallization0
    c. Undefined
    d. Undefined

72. _____ is a term used in geology to denote the pressure imposed on a stratigraphic layer by the weight of overlying layers of material.
    a. Lithostatic pressure0
    b. Event
    c. Undefined
    d. Undefined

73. In organic chemistry, a _____ is a salt of carbonic acid.
    a. Thing
    b. Carbonate0
    c. Undefined
    d. Undefined

74. _____ are those minerals containing the carbonate ion: CO_3^{2-}.
    a. Carbonate minerals0
    b. Thing
    c. Undefined
    d. Undefined

75. An _____ is an atom or group of atoms which have lost or gained one or more electrons, making them negatively or positively charged.
    a. Ion0
    b. Thing
    c. Undefined
    d. Undefined

76. An _____ is a chemical compound containing an oxygen atom and other elements. Most of the earth's crust consists of them. They result when elements are oxidized by air.
    a. Thing
    b. Oxide0
    c. Undefined
    d. Undefined

77. _____ is the name of a group of rock-forming minerals which make up as much as sixty percent of the Earth's crust. Feldspars crystallize from magma in both intrusive and extrusive rocks, and they can also occur as compact minerals, as veins, and are also present in many types of metamorphic rock.
    a. Feldspar0
    b. Thing
    c. Undefined
    d. Undefined

78. _____ rocks form when molten rock, magma, cools and solidifies, with or without crystallization, either below the surface as intrusive, plutonic rocks or on the surface as extrusive, volcanic, rocks.
    a. Igneous0
    b. Thing
    c. Undefined
    d. Undefined

79. _____ forms when rock cools and solidifies either below the surface as intrusive rocks or on the surface as extrusive rocks. This magma can be derived from partial melts of pre-existing rocks in either the Earth's mantle or crust. Typically, the melting is caused by one or more of the following processes -- an increase in temperature, a decrease in pressure, or a change in composition.
    a. Igneous rock0
    b. Thing
    c. Undefined
    d. Undefined

Chapter 6. Sediment and Sedimentary Rocks

80. _____ is an essentially physical process that has meanings in chemistry, metallurgy and geology. In geology, solid-state _____ is a metamorphic process that occurs under situations of intense temperature and pressure where grains, atoms or molecules of a rock or mineral are packed closer together, creating a new crystal structure.
   a. Recrystallization0
   b. Thing
   c. Undefined
   d. Undefined

81. In materials science, _____ is the distribution of crystallographic orientations of a sample.
   a. Thing
   b. Crystalline texture0
   c. Undefined
   d. Undefined

82. _____ is a common and widely occurring type of intrusive, felsic, igneous rock. Granites are usually medium to coarsely crystalline, occasionally with some individual crystals larger than the groundmass forming a rock known as porphyry. Granites can be pink to dark gray or even black, depending on their chemistry and mineralogy.
   a. Thing
   b. Granite0
   c. Undefined
   d. Undefined

83. A _____ is an aragonite structure produced by living organisms, found in shallow, tropical marine waters with little to no nutrients in the water.
   a. Coral reef0
   b. Thing
   c. Undefined
   d. Undefined

84. _____ encompass several groups of relatively simple living aquatic organisms that capture light energy through photosynthesis, using it to convert inorganic substances into organic matter.
   a. Thing
   b. Algae0
   c. Undefined
   d. Undefined

85. _____ is the mineral form of sodium chloride. _____ forms isometric crystals. It commonly occurs with other evaporite deposit minerals such as several of the sulfates, halides and borates. _____ occurs in vast lakes of sedimentary evaporite minerals that result from the drying up of enclosed beds, playas, and seas.
   a. Halite0
   b. Thing
   c. Undefined
   d. Undefined

86. In geology the term _____ refers to the system of forces that tend to decrease the volume of or shorten rocks. Compressive strength refers to the maximum compressive stress that can be applied to a material before failure occurs.
   a. Compression0
   b. Thing
   c. Undefined
   d. Undefined

87. _____ refers to small, soft plants that are typically 1–10 cm tall, though some species are much larger. They commonly grow close together in clumps or mats in damp or shady locations. They do not have flowers or seeds, and their simple leaves cover the thin wiry stems.
   a. Thing
   b. Moss0
   c. Undefined
   d. Undefined

88. _____ is a rock composed of angular fragments of rocks or minerals in a matrix, that is a cementing material, that may be similar or different in composition to the fragments.

Chapter 6. Sediment and Sedimentary Rocks

    a. Thing
    c. Undefined
    b. Breccia0
    d. Undefined

89. _____ is rock formed from fragments of pre-existing rock. The most common usage is for clastic or detrital sedimentary rocks. However, the usage is not restricted to sediments.
    a. Clastic rock0
    c. Undefined
    b. Thing
    d. Undefined

90. A _____ is a geological phenomenon which includes a wide range of ground movement, such as rock falls, deep failure of slopes and shallow debris flows. Although gravity's action on an over-steepened slope is the primary reason for a _____, there are other contributing factors affecting the original slope stability.
    a. Landslide0
    c. Undefined
    b. Thing
    d. Undefined

91. A _____ is a significant vertical, or near vertical, rock exposure. Cliffs are categorized as erosion landforms due to the processes of erosion and weathering that produce them. Cliffs are common on coasts, in mountainous areas, escarpments and along rivers. Cliffs are usually formed by rock that is resistant to erosion and weathering.
    a. Cliff0
    c. Undefined
    b. Thing
    d. Undefined

92. _____ is a detrital sedimentary rock, specifically a type of sandstone containing at least 25% feldspar. Arkosic sand is sand that is similarly rich in feldspar, and thus the potential precursor of _____. The other mineral components may vary, but quartz is commonly dominant, and minor mica is often present. Apart from the mineral content, rock fragments may also be a significant component.
    a. Arkose0
    c. Undefined
    b. Thing
    d. Undefined

93. _____ is the third or vertical dimension of land surface. When _____ is described underwater, the term bathymetry is used.
    a. Terrain0
    c. Undefined
    b. Thing
    d. Undefined

94. A _____ is a deep valley between cliffs often carved from the landscape by a river. Most were formed by a process of long-time erosion from a plateau level. The cliffs form because harder rock strata that are resistant to erosion and weathering remain exposed on the valley walls.
    a. Thing
    c. Undefined
    b. Canyon0
    d. Undefined

95. A _____ is a steep-sided valley on the sea floor of the continental slope. They are formed by powerful turbidity currents, volcanic and earthquake activity. Many continue as submarine channels across continental rise areas and may extend for hundreds of kilometers.
    a. Thing
    c. Undefined
    b. Submarine canyon0
    d. Undefined

Chapter 6. Sediment and Sedimentary Rocks

96. _____ is a 16-ton, manned deep-ocean research submersible owned by the United States Navy and operated by the Woods Hole Oceanographic Institution in Woods Hole, Massachusetts. The three-person vessel allows for two scientists and one pilot to dive for up to nine hours at 4500 metersor 15,000 feet.
 a. Thing
 b. Alvin0
 c. Undefined
 d. Undefined

97. In geography, a _____ is a landscape form or region that receives very little precipitation. They are defined as areas that receive an average annual precipitation of less than 250 mm. A _____ where vegetation cover is exceedingly sparse correspond to the 'hyperarid' regions of the earth, where rainfall is exceedingly rare and infrequent.
 a. Place
 b. Desert0
 c. Undefined
 d. Undefined

98. A _____ is a section of a river of relatively steep gradient causing an increase in water flow and turbulence. A _____ is a hydrological feature between a run and a cascade. It is characterized by the river becoming shallower and having some rocks exposed above the flow surface.
 a. Thing
 b. Rapid0
 c. Undefined
 d. Undefined

99. _____ is the average and variations of weather over long periods of time. _____ zones can be defined using parameters such as temperature and rainfall.
 a. Climate0
 b. Thing
 c. Undefined
 d. Undefined

100. _____ is a variety of sandstone generally characterized by its hardness, dark color, and poorly-sorted, angular grains of quartz, feldspar, and small rock fragments set in a compact, clay-fine matrix. It is a texturally-immature sedimentary rock generally found in Palaeozoic strata. The larger grains can be sand-to-gravel-sized, and matrix materials generally constitute more than 15% of the rock by volume.
 a. Thing
 b. Greywacke0
 c. Undefined
 d. Undefined

101. _____ is a cloudiness or haziness of water caused by individual particles that are generally invisible to the naked eye, thus being much like smoke in air. _____ is generally caused by phytoplankton. Measurement of _____ is a key test of water quality.
 a. Thing
 b. Turbidity0
 c. Undefined
 d. Undefined

102. A _____ is a current of rapidly moving, sediment-laden water moving down a slope through air, water, or another fluid. The current moves because it has a higher density and turbidity than the fluid through which it flows.
 a. Thing
 b. Turbidity current0
 c. Undefined
 d. Undefined

103. _____ is a fine-grained sedimentary rock whose original constituents were clays or muds. Grain size is up to 0.0625 mm with individual grains too small to be distinguished without a microscope.
 a. Thing
 b. Mudstone0
 c. Undefined
 d. Undefined

Chapter 6. Sediment and Sedimentary Rocks

104. A _____ is a landform where the mouth of a river flows into an ocean, sea, desert, estuary or lake. It builds up sediment outwards into the flat area which the river's flow encounters transported by the water and set down as the currents slow.
   a. Delta0
   b. Thing
   c. Undefined
   d. Undefined

105. A _____ is flat or nearly flat land adjacent to a stream or river that experiences occasional or periodic flooding. It includes the floodway, which consists of the stream channel and adjacent areas that carry flood flows, and the flood fringe, which are areas covered by the flood, but which do not experience a strong current.
   a. Thing
   b. Floodplain0
   c. Undefined
   d. Undefined

106. _____ is a geological term used to describe a sedimentary rock that is composed primarily of clay-sized particles.
   a. Claystone0
   b. Thing
   c. Undefined
   d. Undefined

107. In geology, a _____ is a depression with predominant extent in one direction. The terms U-shaped and V-shaped are descriptive terms of geography to characterize the form of valleys. Most valleys belong to one of these two main types or a mixture of them, at least with respect of the cross section of the slopes or hillsides.
   a. Thing
   b. Valley0
   c. Undefined
   d. Undefined

108. _____ is a fine-grained silica-rich cryptocrystalline sedimentary rock that may contain small fossils. It varies greatly in color from white to black, but most often manifests as gray, brown, grayish brown and light green to rusty red; its color is an expression of trace elements present in the rock, and both red and green are most often related to traces of iron.
   a. Chert0
   b. Thing
   c. Undefined
   d. Undefined

109. _____ are a class of sedimentary rocks composed primarily of carbonate minerals. The two major types are limestone and dolomite, composed of calcite and the mineral dolomite respectively. Chalk and tufa are also minor sedimentary carbonates.
   a. Carbonate rocks0
   b. Thing
   c. Undefined
   d. Undefined

110. _____ is the name of a sedimentary carbonate rock and a mineral, both composed of calcium magnesium carbonate found in crystals. _____ rock is composed predominantly of the mineral _____. Limestone that is partially replaced by _____ is referred to as dolomitic limestone.
   a. Dolomite0
   b. Thing
   c. Undefined
   d. Undefined

111. The _____ is the extended perimeter of each continent and associated coastal plain, which is covered during interglacial periods such as the current epoch by relatively shallow seas and gulfs. The shelf usually ends at a point of increasing slope.

Chapter 6. Sediment and Sedimentary Rocks

a. Thing
c. Undefined
b. Continental shelf0
d. Undefined

112. An _____ is any piece of land that is completely surrounded by water, above high tide. There are two main types of islands: continental islands and oceanic islands. There are also artificial islands. A grouping of geographically and/or geologically related islands is called an archipelago.
a. Thing
c. Undefined
b. Island0
d. Undefined

113. The Commonwealth of The _____ is an English-speaking nation consisting of two thousand cays and seven hundred islands that form an archipelago. It is located in the Atlantic Ocean, east of Florida and the United States, north of Cuba and the Caribbean, and northwest of the British overseas territory of the Turks and Caicos Islands.
a. Place
c. Undefined
b. Bahamas0
d. Undefined

114. _____ is an incompletely consolidated sedimentary rock of biochemical origin, mainly composed of mineral calcite, often including some phosphate, in the form of seashells or coral. It is created in association with marine reefs. While not usually referred to as such, it is actually a subset of limestone.
a. Thing
c. Undefined
b. Coquina0
d. Undefined

115. A _____ is the fringe of land at the edge of a large body of water, such as an ocean, sea, or lake. A strict definition is the strip of land along a water body that is alternately exposed and covered by waves and tides.
a. Thing
c. Undefined
b. Shoreline0
d. Undefined

116. _____ is a soft, white, porous sedimentary rock, a form of limestone composed of the mineral calcite. It forms under relatively deep marine conditions from the gradual accumulation of minute calcite plates shed from micro-organisms called coccolithophores. It is common to find flint nodules embedded in it.
a. Thing
c. Undefined
b. Chalk0
d. Undefined

117. _____ refers to small spheroidal "coated" grains, usually composed of calcium carbonate, but sometimes made up of iron or phosphate minerals. They usually form on the sea floor, most commonly in shallow tropical seas. After being buried under additional sediment, these _____ grains can be cemented together to form a sedimentary rock called an oolite.
a. Ooid0
c. Undefined
b. Thing
d. Undefined

118. An _____ is a sedimentary rock formed from ooids, spherical grains composed of concentric layers.
a. Oolite0
c. Undefined
b. Thing
d. Undefined

119. _____ is a sedimentary rock. _____ is a natural chemical precipitate of carbonate minerals; typically aragonite, but often recrystallized to or primarily calcite; which is deposited from the water of mineral springs or streams saturated with calcium carbonate.

Chapter 6. Sediment and Sedimentary Rocks

a. Travertine0	b. Thing
c. Undefined	d. Undefined

120. _____ is the name for an unusual geological form of calcite rock. _____ is a rough, thick, rock-like calcium carbonate deposit that forms by precipitation from bodies of water with a high dissolved calcium content.

a. Thing	b. Tufa0
c. Undefined	d. Undefined

121. _____ contains low concentrations of dissolved salts and other total dissolved solids. It is an important renewable resource, necessary for the survival of most terrestrial organisms, and required by humans for drinking and agriculture, among many other uses.

a. Thing	b. Fresh water0
c. Undefined	d. Undefined

122. A _____ is a natural underground void large enough for a human to enter. Some people suggest that the term '_____' should only apply to cavities that have some part which does not receive daylight; however, in popular usage, the term includes smaller spaces like a sea _____, rock shelters, and grottos.

a. Cave0	b. Place
c. Undefined	d. Undefined

123. _____ has the symbol Mg. It is the ninth most abundant element in the universe by mass. It constitutes about 2% of the Earth's crust by mass, and it is the third most abundant element dissolved in seawater. It is essential to all living cells, and is the 11th most abundant element by mass in the human body.

a. Thing	b. Magnesium0
c. Undefined	d. Undefined

124. _____ involves the study of the interaction of humans with the geologic environment including the biosphere, the lithosphere, the hydrosphere, and to some extent the atmosphere.

a. Environmental geology0	b. Thing
c. Undefined	d. Undefined

125. _____ is the science and study of the solid matter that constitute the Earth. Encompassing such things as rocks, soil, and gemstones, _____ studies the composition, structure, physical properties, history, and the processes that shape Earth's components.

a. Thing	b. Geology0
c. Undefined	d. Undefined

126. _____ is a naturally occurring, soft, chalk-like sedimentary rock that is easily crumbled into a fine white to off-white powder. This powder has an abrasive feel, similar to pumice powder, and is very light, due to its high porosity.

a. Thing	b. Diatomaceous earth0
c. Undefined	d. Undefined

127. _____ are a major group of eukaryotic algae, and are one of the most common types of phytoplankton. Most _____ are unicellular, although some form chains or simple colonies. A characteristic feature of diatom cells is that they are encased within a unique cell wall made of silica called a frustule.

Chapter 6. Sediment and Sedimentary Rocks 111

a. Diatoms0
b. Thing
c. Undefined
d. Undefined

128. A _____, in inorganic chemistry, is a salt of phosphoric acid. In organic chemistry it is an ester of phosphoric acid.
a. Thing
b. Phosphate0
c. Undefined
d. Undefined

129. _____ refers to water-soluble, mineral sediments that result from the evaporation of bodies of surficial water.
a. Evaporite0
b. Thing
c. Undefined
d. Undefined

130. _____ or sulphur is the chemical element that has the symbol S and atomic number 16. It is an abundant, tasteless, multivalent non-metal. _____, in its native form, is a yellow crystalline solid. In nature, it can be found as the pure element or as sulfide and sulfate minerals. It is an essential element for life and is found in two amino acids, cysteine and methionine.
a. Thing
b. Sulfur0
c. Undefined
d. Undefined

131. _____ is a strong mineral acid. It is soluble in water at all concentrations. _____ has many applications, and is one of the top products of the chemical industry. Principal uses include ore processing, fertilizer manufacturing, oil refining, wastewater processing, and chemical synthesis.
a. Thing
b. Sulfuric acid0
c. Undefined
d. Undefined

132. _____ is a chemical element. It is a soft silvery-white metallic alkali metal that occurs naturally bound to other elements in seawater and many minerals. It oxidizes rapidly in air and is very reactive, especially towards water. In many respects, it and sodium are chemically similar, although organisms in general, and animal cells in particular, treat them very differently.
a. Potassium0
b. Thing
c. Undefined
d. Undefined

133. Most often, a _____ refers to an artificial lake, used to store water for various uses. Reservoirs are created first by building a sturdy dam, usually out of cement, earth, rock, or a mixture. Once the dam is completed, a stream is allowed to flow behind it and eventually fill it to capacity.
a. Thing
b. Reservoir0
c. Undefined
d. Undefined

134. The _____ is defined as the part of the land adjoining or near the ocean. A coastline is properly a line on a map indicating the disposition of a _____, but the word is often used to refer to the _____ itself. The adjective coastal describes something as being on, near to, or associated with a _____.
a. Coast0
b. Place
c. Undefined
d. Undefined

135. _____ is the process by which molecules in a liquid state become a gas.

Chapter 6. Sediment and Sedimentary Rocks

a. Thing
b. Evaporation0
c. Undefined
d. Undefined

136. _____ is water saturated or nearly saturated with salt and is a common fluid used in the transport of heat from place to place. It is used because the addition of salt to water lowers the freezing temperature of the solution and a relatively great efficiency in the transport can be obtained for the low cost of the material.
a. Brine0
b. Thing
c. Undefined
d. Undefined

137. _____ is an increase in sea level. Multiple complex factors may influence such changes.
a. Sea level rise0
b. Thing
c. Undefined
d. Undefined

138. A _____ is a process that results in the interconversion of chemical substances. The substance or substances initially involved in a _____ are called reactants. Chemical reactions are characterized by a chemical change, and they yield one or more products which are, in general, different from the reactants.
a. Thing
b. Chemical reaction0
c. Undefined
d. Undefined

139. _____, located in the northern part of the U.S. state of Utah, is the largest salt lake in the Western Hemisphere, the fourth-largest terminal lake in the world, and the 33rd largest lake on Earth.
a. Place
b. Great Salt Lake0
c. Undefined
d. Undefined

140. A _____ in petrology or mineralogy is an irregular rounded to spherical concretion. They are typically solid replacement bodies of chert or iron oxides formed during diagenesis of a sedimentary rock.
a. Thing
b. Nodule0
c. Undefined
d. Undefined

141. In geography, _____ latitudes of the globe lie between the tropics and the polar circles. The changes in these regions between summer and winter are generally subtle: warm or cool, rather than extreme hot or cold.
a. Temperate0
b. Thing
c. Undefined
d. Undefined

142. _____ are wetland types that accumulate acidic peat, a deposit of dead plant material.
a. Bogs0
b. Thing
c. Undefined
d. Undefined

143. A _____ is one of two main structural axes of a vascular plant. It is normally divided into nodes and internodes, the nodes hold buds which grow into one or more leaves, inflorescence, cones etc.
a. Stem0
b. Thing
c. Undefined
d. Undefined

144. _____ is an accumulation of partially decayed vegetation matter. It forms in wetlands.

Chapter 6. Sediment and Sedimentary Rocks 113

   a. Thing
   b. Peat0
   c. Undefined
   d. Undefined

145. A _____ is a chemical substance of two or more different chemically bonded chemical elements, with a fixed ratio determining the composition. The ratio of each element is usually expressed by chemical formula.
   a. Chemical compound0
   b. Thing
   c. Undefined
   d. Undefined

146. _____ is a chemical element. An abundant nonmetallic, tetravalent element, _____ has several allotropic forms. This element is the basis of the chemistry of all known life.
   a. Thing
   b. Carbon0
   c. Undefined
   d. Undefined

147. _____ is an accumulate in the abyssal plain of the deep ocean, far away from terrestrial sources that provide terrigenous sediments; the latter are primarily limited to the continental shelf, and deposited by rivers.
   a. Pelagic sediment0
   b. Thing
   c. Undefined
   d. Undefined

148. _____ is a part of mathematics concerned with questions of size, shape, and relative position of figures and with properties of space. _____ is one of the oldest sciences. Initially a body of practical knowledge concerning lengths, areas, and volumes, in the third century B.C. _____ was put into an axiomatic form by Euclid, whose treatment set a standard for many centuries to follow.
   a. Thing
   b. Geometry0
   c. Undefined
   d. Undefined

149. The principle or _____ states that sediments are deposited under the influence of gravity as nearly horizontal beds. Observations in a wide variety of sedimentary environments support this principle. If we find folded or faulted strata, we know that the layers were deformed by tectonic forces after the sediments were deposited. This principle can be combined with the principle of superposition.
   a. Thing
   b. Original horizontality0
   c. Undefined
   d. Undefined

150. _____ are where one sedimetary deposit ends and another one begins. The rock is prone to breakage at these points because of the weakness between the layers.
   a. Thing
   b. Bedding planes0
   c. Undefined
   d. Undefined

151. _____ is a United States National Park located in the Southwestern United States, near Springdale, Utah. Located at the junction of the Colorado Plateau, Great Basin, and Mojave Desert regions, this unique geography and variety of life zones allow for unusual plant and animal diversity.
   a. Place
   b. Zion National Park0
   c. Undefined
   d. Undefined

152. A _____, as defined by the International Astronomical Union, is a celestial body orbiting a star or stellar remnant that is massive enough to be rounded by its own gravity, not massive enough to cause thermonuclear fusion in its core, and has cleared its neighboring region of planetesimals.

Chapter 6. Sediment and Sedimentary Rocks

   a. Thing
   b. Planet0
   c. Undefined
   d. Undefined

153. _____ the fourth planet from the Sun in the Solar System. The planet is named after _____, the Roman god of war. It is also referred to as the "Red Planet" because of its reddish appearance as seen from Earth.
   a. Mars0
   b. Thing
   c. Undefined
   d. Undefined

154. A _____ is an approximately circular depression in the surface of a planet, moon or other solid body in the Solar System, formed by the hyper-velocity impact of a smaller body with the surface. Impact craters typically have raised rims, and they range from small, simple, bowl-shaped depressions to large, complex, multi-ringed, impact basins.
   a. Crater0
   b. Thing
   c. Undefined
   d. Undefined

155. The _____ is the lowest layer in the ocean, existing below the thermocline. Little or no light penetrates this area of the ocean, and most of its organisms rely on falling organic matter produced in the photic zone for subsistence. For this reason life is much more sparse, becoming rarer still with increasing depth. The other essential ingredient in for life is oxygen, which is brought to the ocean's depths via the thermohaline circulation.
   a. Deep sea0
   b. Thing
   c. Undefined
   d. Undefined

156. A _____ is a meteorological phenomenon common in arid and semi-arid regions. Such a storm may result from the passage of a gust front or simply a substantial increase in wind velocity over a wider region. In all instances, the ground must be very dry and loosely consolidated.
   a. Dust storm0
   b. Thing
   c. Undefined
   d. Undefined

157. A _____ is an opening, or rupture, in the Earth's surface or crust, which allows hot, molten rock, ash and gases to escape from deep below the surface.
   a. Thing
   b. Volcano0
   c. Undefined
   d. Undefined

158. _____ are clastic rocks composed solely or primarily of volcanic materials.
   a. Thing
   b. Pyroclastics0
   c. Undefined
   d. Undefined

159. A _____ is a geological feature that is also known as a Rip in the earth causing magma to flow out and forming an undersea volcano, it also has geological features, a continuous elevational crest for some distance. Ridges are usually termed hills or mountains as well, depending on size.
   a. Thing
   b. Ridge0
   c. Undefined
   d. Undefined

160. In geology, a _____ is one characterized by coarse sediments at its base, which grade upward into progressively finer ones. They are perhaps best represented in turbidite strata, where they indicate a sudden strong current that deposits heavy, coarse sediments first, with finer ones following as the current weakens.

Chapter 6. Sediment and Sedimentary Rocks

a. Graded bed0
b. Thing
c. Undefined
d. Undefined

161. _____ refers to the cyclic rizing and falling of Earth's ocean surface caused by the tidal forces of the Moon and the sun acting on the oceans. They cause changes in the depth of the marine and estuarine water bodies and produce oscillating currents known as tidal streams, making prediction of tides important for coastal navigation.
a. Thing
b. Tide0
c. Undefined
d. Undefined

162. _____ is a measure of the void spaces in a material, and is measured as a fraction, between 0–1, or as a percentage between 0–100%.
a. Porosity0
b. Thing
c. Undefined
d. Undefined

163. _____ refers to all species of microscopic fungi that grow in the form of multicellular filaments, called hyphae.
a. Thing
b. Mold0
c. Undefined
d. Undefined

164. Fossil fuels are hydrocarbons, primarily coal and petroleum, formed from the fossilized remains of dead plants and animals. In common parlance, the term _____ also includes hydrocarbon-containing natural resources that are not derived from animal or plant sources. Fossil fuels have made large-scale industrial development possible and have largely supplanted water-driven mills, as well as the combustion of wood or peat for heat.
a. Thing
b. Fossil fuel0
c. Undefined
d. Undefined

165. _____ are hydrocarbons, primarily coal and petroleum, formed from the fossilized remains of dead plants and animals by exposure to heat and pressure in the Earth's crust over hundreds of millions of years. The burning of _____ by humans is the largest source of emissions of carbon dioxide, which is one of the greenhouse gases that enhances radiative forcing and contributes to global warming.
a. Thing
b. Fossil fuels0
c. Undefined
d. Undefined

166. _____ is a common gray to black extrusive volcanic rock. It is usually fine-grained due to rapid cooling of lava on the Earth's surface. It may be porphyritic containing larger crystals in a fine matrix, or vesicular, or frothy scoria.
a. Basalt0
b. Thing
c. Undefined
d. Undefined

167. _____ is a common and widely distributed type of rock formed by high-grade regional metamorphic processes from preexisting formations that were originally either igneous or sedimentary rocks. Gneissic rocks are usually medium to coarse foliated and largely recrystallized but do not carry large quantities of micas, chlorite or other platy minerals.
a. Thing
b. Gneiss0
c. Undefined
d. Undefined

168. _____ is a geologic formation in the Glen Canyon Group that is spread across the U.S. states of northern Arizona, northwest Colorado, Nevada, and Utah. It is located in the Colorado Plateau province of the United States.

116   *Chapter 6. Sediment and Sedimentary Rocks*

    a. Navajo Sandstone0
    b. Place
    c. Undefined
    d. Undefined

169. The _____ is a distinctive sequence of Late Jurassic sedimentary rock that is found in the western United States and Canada, which has been the most fertile source of dinosaur fossils in North America. It is composed of mudstone, sandstone, siltstone and limestone and is light grey, greenish gray, or red. Most of the fossils occur in the green siltstone beds and lower sandstones, relics of the rivers and floodplains of the Jurassic period.
    a. Morrison Formation0
    b. Thing
    c. Undefined
    d. Undefined

170. The _____ is a very colorful, steep-sided gorge, carved by the Colorado River in the U.S. state of Arizona. It is one of the first national parks in the United States.
    a. Grand Canyon0
    b. Place
    c. Undefined
    d. Undefined

171. The _____ one of the United States' oldest national parks and is located in Arizona. Within the park lies the Grand Canyon, a gorge of the Colorado River, considered to be one of the major natural wonders of the world. The park covers 1,902 mi².
    a. Place
    b. Grand Canyon National Park0
    c. Undefined
    d. Undefined

172. _____ is a common phyllosilicate mineral within the mica group. Primarily a solid-solution series between the iron-endmember annite, and the magnesium-endmember phlogopite; more aluminous endmembers include siderophyllite.
    a. Thing
    b. Biotite0
    c. Undefined
    d. Undefined

173. _____ were vertebrate animals that dominated terrestrial ecosystems for over 160 million years, first appearing approximately 230 million years ago. At the end of the Cretaceous Period, approximately 65 million years ago, a catastrophic extinction event ended _____' dominance on land.
    a. Dinosaurs0
    b. Thing
    c. Undefined
    d. Undefined

174. _____ is mechanical scraping of a rock surface by friction between rocks and moving particles during their transport in wind, glacier, waves, gravity or running water.
    a. Abrasion0
    b. Thing
    c. Undefined
    d. Undefined

175. A _____ shows elevation. A _____ for a function of two variables is a curve connecting points where the function has a same particular value. A contour map is a map illustrated with contour lines, for example a topographic map.
    a. Thing
    b. Contour line0
    c. Undefined
    d. Undefined

176. An _____ plain is a relatively flat and gently sloping landform found at the base of a range of hills or mountains, formed by the deposition of _____ soil over a long period of time by one or more rivers coming from the mountains.

Chapter 6. Sediment and Sedimentary Rocks

a. Alluvial0
b. Thing
c. Undefined
d. Undefined

177. An alluvial fan is a fan-shaped deposit formed where a fast flowing stream flattens, slows, and spreads typically at the exit of a canyon onto a flatter plain. A convergence of neighboring _____ into a single apron of deposits against a slope is called a bajada, or compound alluvial fan.
   a. Thing
   b. Alluvial fans0
   c. Undefined
   d. Undefined

178. A _____ is a body of comparatively shallow salt or brackish water separated from the deeper sea by a shallow or exposed sandbank, coral reef, or similar feature. Thus, the enclosed body of water behind a barrier reef or barrier islands or enclosed by an atoll reef is called a _____.
   a. Place
   b. Lagoon0
   c. Undefined
   d. Undefined

179. _____ is a detrital sedimentary rock, specifically a type of containing at least 25% feldspar.
   a. Arkosic sandstone0
   b. Thing
   c. Undefined
   d. Undefined

180. At times when larger waves attack the beach berm, some of the beach material is redistributed offshore to become a _____ possibly visible at low tide.
   a. Thing
   b. Longshore bar0
   c. Undefined
   d. Undefined

181. _____ are reptiles of the order Squamata, normally possessing four legs, external ear openings and movable eyelids. The adult length of species within the order range from a few centimeters to nearly three meters.
   a. Lizards0
   b. Thing
   c. Undefined
   d. Undefined

182. A _____ is a geologic event during which sea level rises relative to the land and the shoreline moves toward higher ground, resulting in flooding. Transgressions can be caused either by the land sinking or the ocean basins filling with water.
   a. Transgression0
   b. Thing
   c. Undefined
   d. Undefined

183. The name _____ applies to most members of the molluscan class Gastropoda that have coiled shells. They are found in freshwater, marine, and terrestrial environments. Most are of herbivorous nature, though a few land species and many marine species may be omnivores or carnivores.
   a. Snail0
   b. Thing
   c. Undefined
   d. Undefined

184. _____ are coastal wetlands that form when mud is deposited by the tides or rivers, sea and oceans. They are found in sheltered areas such as bays, bayous, lagoons, and estuaries. _____ may be viewed geologically as exposed layers of bay mud, resulting from deposition of estuarine silts, clays and marine animal detritus.

Chapter 6. Sediment and Sedimentary Rocks

   a. Thing
   b. Mudflats0
   c. Undefined
   d. Undefined

185. _____ are the cyclic rizing and falling of Earth's ocean surface caused by the tidal forces of the Moon and the sun acting on the oceans. _____ cause changes in the depth of the marine and estuarine water bodies and produce oscillating currents known as tidal streams, making prediction of _____ important for coastal navigation.
   a. Tides0
   b. Thing
   c. Undefined
   d. Undefined

186. _____ is a field of study within geology concerned generally with the structures within the crust of the Earth, or other planets, and particularly with the forces and movements that have operated in a region to create these structures.
   a. Tectonics0
   b. Thing
   c. Undefined
   d. Undefined

187. _____ is a theory of geology that has been developed to explain the observed evidence for large scale motions of the Earth's lithosphere. The theory encompassed and superseded the older theory of continental drift.
   a. Thing
   b. Plate tectonics0
   c. Undefined
   d. Undefined

188. A _____ is a group of mountains bordered by lowlands or separated from other mountain ranges by passes or rivers. Individual mountains within the same _____ do not necessarily have the same geology; they may be a mix of different orogeny, for example volcanoes, uplifted mountains or fold mountains and may, therefore, be of different rock.
   a. Thing
   b. Mountain range0
   c. Undefined
   d. Undefined

189. The _____ is a mountain range that is almost entirely in the eastern portion of the U.S. state of California. The _____ stretches 400 miles , from Fredonyer Pass in the north to Tehachapi Pass in the south. It is bounded on the west by California's Central Valley, and on the east by the Great Basin.
   a. Place
   b. Sierra Nevada0
   c. Undefined
   d. Undefined

190. _____ geological formations have their origins in turbidity current deposits, deposits from a form of underwater avalanche that are responsible for distributing vast amounts of clastic sediment into the deep ocean.
   a. Turbidite0
   b. Thing
   c. Undefined
   d. Undefined

191. Clastic sedimentary rocks are rocks composed predominantly of broken pieces or _____ of older weathered and eroded rocks.
   a. Clasts0
   b. Thing
   c. Undefined
   d. Undefined

192. The _____ are a broad mountain range in western North America. The _____ stretch more than 4,800 kilometers from northernmost British Columbia, in Canada, to New Mexico, in the United States.
   a. Rocky Mountains0
   b. Place
   c. Undefined
   d. Undefined

Chapter 6. Sediment and Sedimentary Rocks

193. The _____ are a mountain range in Asia, separating the Indian subcontinent from the Tibetan Plateau. By extension, it is also the name of the massive mountain system which includes the Himalaya proper, the Karakoram, the Hindu Kush, and a host of minor ranges extending from the Pamir Knot.
   a. Place
   b. Himalayas0
   c. Undefined
   d. Undefined

194. The _____ is the name for one of the great mountain range systems of Europe, stretching from Austria and Slovenia in the east, through Italy, Switzerland, Liechtenstein and Germany to France in the west.
   a. Alps0
   b. Place
   c. Undefined
   d. Undefined

195. _____ is the process of building mountains, and may be studied as a tectonic structural event, as a geographical event and a chronological event, in that orogenic events cause distinctive structural phenomena and related tectonic activity, affect certain regions of rocks and crust and happen within a time frame.
   a. Orogeny0
   b. Thing
   c. Undefined
   d. Undefined

196. Faults are planar rock fractures, which show evidence of relative movement. Large faults within the Earth's crust are the result of shear motion and active _____ zones are the causal locations of most earthquakes. Earthquakes are caused by energy release during rapid slippage along faults. The largest examples are at tectonic plate boundaries but many faults occur far from active plate boundaries. Since faults do not usually consist of a single, clean fracture, the term _____ zone is used when referring to the zone of complex deformation that is associated with the _____ plane.
   a. Thing
   b. Fault0
   c. Undefined
   d. Undefined

197. A _____ is a geological fault that is a special case of strike-slip faulting which terminates abruptly, at both ends, at a major transverse geological feature. Also known as a conservative plate boundary.
   a. Transform fault0
   b. Thing
   c. Undefined
   d. Undefined

198. A _____ is an old and stable part of the continental crust that has survived the merging and splitting of continents and supercontinents. Cratons are generally found in the interiors of continents and are characteristically composed of ancient crystalline basement crust of lightweight felsic igneous rock such as granite. They have a thick crust and deep roots that extend into the mantle beneath to depths of 200 km.
   a. Thing
   b. Craton0
   c. Undefined
   d. Undefined

199. In geology, a _____ is a place where the Earth's crust and lithosphere are being pulled apart.
   a. Rift0
   b. Thing
   c. Undefined
   d. Undefined

200. A _____ in geology is a valley created by the formation of a rift.
   a. Thing
   b. Rift valley0
   c. Undefined
   d. Undefined

Chapter 6. Sediment and Sedimentary Rocks

201. In plate tectonics, a _____ a linear feature that exists between two tectonic plates that are moving away from each other. These areas can form in the middle of continents but eventually form ocean basins.
   a. Divergent plate boundary0
   b. Thing
   c. Undefined
   d. Undefined

202. In physics, _____ is defined as the rate of change of displacement or the rate of displacement. Simply put, it is distance per units of time.
   a. Thing
   b. Velocity0
   c. Undefined
   d. Undefined

203. The _____ is the set of all extant phenomena in a given atmosphere at a given time. The term usually refers to the activity of these phenomena over short periods, as opposed to the term climate, which refers to the average atmospheric conditions over longer periods of time.
   a. Thing
   b. Weather0
   c. Undefined
   d. Undefined

204. An _____ is a type of atom that is defined by its atomic number; that is, by the number of protons in its nucleus.
   a. Thing
   b. Element0
   c. Undefined
   d. Undefined

205. In plate tectonics, a _____ is said to occur when tectonic plates slide and grind against each other along a transform fault. The relative motion of such plates is horizontal in either sinistral or dextral direction. Many transform boundaries are locked in tension before suddenly releasing, and causing earthquakes.
   a. Thing
   b. Transform boundary0
   c. Undefined
   d. Undefined

206. The _____ is a fundamental concept in geology that describes the dynamic transitions through geologic time among the three main rock types: sedimentary, metamorphic, and igneous.
   a. Thing
   b. Rock cycle0
   c. Undefined
   d. Undefined

207. An _____ is a natural unit consisting of all plants, animals and micro organisms in an area functioning together with all the non living physical factors of the environment.
   a. Thing
   b. Ecosystem0
   c. Undefined
   d. Undefined

Chapter 7. Metamorphism, Metamorphic Rocks, and Hydrothermal Rocks

1. _____ can be defined as the solid state recrystallisation of pre-existing rocks due to changes in heat and/or pressure and/or introduction of fluids. There will be mineralogical, chemical and crystallographic changes. _____ produced with increasing pressure and temperature conditions is known as prograde _____. Conversely, decreasing temperatures and pressure characterize retrograde _____.
   a. Thing
   b. Metamorphism0
   c. Undefined
   d. Undefined

2. The _____ group of sheet silicate minerals includes several closely related materials having highly perfect basal cleavage. All are monoclinic with a tendency towards pseudo-hexagonal crystals and are similar in chemical composition. The highly perfect cleavage, which is the most prominent characteristic of _____, is explained by the hexagonal sheet-like arrangement of its atoms.
   a. Mica0
   b. Thing
   c. Undefined
   d. Undefined

3. _____ is a small island located in the middle of San Francisco Bay in California, United States. It served as a lighthouse, then a military fortification, then a military prison followed by a federal prison until 1963, when it became a national recreation area.
   a. Alcatraz Island0
   b. Place
   c. Undefined
   d. Undefined

4. A _____ is a solid in which the constituent atoms, molecules, or ions are packed in a regularly ordered, repeating pattern extending in all three spatial dimensions. Most metals encountered in everyday life are polycrystals. Crystals are often symmetrically intergrown to form _____ twins.
   a. Thing
   b. Crystal0
   c. Undefined
   d. Undefined

5. _____ is a field of study within geology concerned generally with the structures within the crust of the Earth, or other planets, and particularly with the forces and movements that have operated in a region to create these structures.
   a. Thing
   b. Tectonics0
   c. Undefined
   d. Undefined

6. An _____ is a volume of rock containing components or minerals in a mode of occurrence that renders it valuable for mining.
   a. Thing
   b. Ore0
   c. Undefined
   d. Undefined

7. _____ is the result of the transformation of a pre-existing rock type, the protolith, in a process called metamorphism, which means "change in form". The protolith is subjected to heat and extreme pressure causing profound physical and/or chemical change. The protolith may be sedimentary rock, igneous rock or another older rock.
   a. Metamorphic rock0
   b. Thing
   c. Undefined
   d. Undefined

8. Metamorphic rock is the result of the transformation of a pre-existing rock type, the protolith, in a process called metamorphism. The protolith is subjected to heat and extreme pressure causing profound physical and/or chemical change. _____ make up a large part of the Earth's crust. They are formed deep beneath the Earth's surface by great stresses from rocks above and high pressures and temperatures.

a. Thing   b. Metamorphic rocks0
c. Undefined   d. Undefined

9. In geology, a _____ is the outermost layer of a planet, part of its lithosphere. They are generally composed of a less dense material than its deeper layers.Earths' is composed mainly of basalt and granite. It is cooler and more rigid than the deeper layers of the mantle and core.
   a. Thing   b. Crust0
   c. Undefined   d. Undefined

10. A _____ is a landform that extends above the surrounding terrain in a limited area. A _____ is generally steeper than a hill, but there is no universally accepted standard definition for the height of a _____ or a hill although a _____ usually has an identifiable summit.
    a. Place   b. Mountain0
    c. Undefined   d. Undefined

11. A _____ is one of several large landmasses on Earth. They are generally identified by convention rather than any strict criteria, but seven areas are commonly reckoned as continents – they are: Asia, Africa, North America, South America, Antarctica, Europe, and Australia.
    a. Continent0   b. Thing
    c. Undefined   d. Undefined

12. A _____ is a wet place where a liquid, usually groundwater, has oozed from the ground to the surface. They are usually not flowing, with the liquid sourced only from underground. The term may also refer to the movement of liquid hydrocarbons to the surface through fractures and fissures in the rock and between geological layers. It may be a significant source of pollution.
    a. Seep0   b. Thing
    c. Undefined   d. Undefined

13. A _____ in physical geography describes the collective mass of water found on, under, and over the surface of a planet.
    a. Hydrosphere0   b. Thing
    c. Undefined   d. Undefined

14. A _____ is a naturally occurring substance formed through geological processes that has a characteristic chemical composition, a highly ordered atomic structure and specific physical properties. A rock, by comparison, is an aggregate of minerals and need not have a specific chemical composition. Minerals range in composition from pure elements and simple salts to very complex silicates with thousands of known forms.
    a. Thing   b. Mineral0
    c. Undefined   d. Undefined

15. _____ rocks form when molten rock, magma, cools and solidifies, with or without crystallization, either below the surface as intrusive, plutonic rocks or on the surface as extrusive, volcanic, rocks.
    a. Thing   b. Igneous0
    c. Undefined   d. Undefined

Chapter 7. Metamorphism, Metamorphic Rocks, and Hydrothermal Rocks

16. _____ is a highly sought-after precious metal which, for many centuries, has been used as money, a store of value and in jewelery. The metal occurs as nuggets or grains in rocks, underground "veins" and in alluvial deposits. It is one of the coinage metals. Itis dense, soft, shiny and the most malleable and ductile of the known metals.
    a. Thing
    b. Gold0
    c. Undefined
    d. Undefined

17. _____ is a ductile metal with excellent electrical conductivity, and finds extensive use as an electrical conductor, heat conductor, as a building material, and as a component of various alloys.
    a. Copper0
    b. Thing
    c. Undefined
    d. Undefined

18. An _____ is a layer of gases that may surround a material body of sufficient mass. The gases are attracted by the gravity of the body, and are retained for a longer duration if gravity is high and the _____'s temperature is low. Some planets consist mainly of various gases, and thus have very deep atmospheres.
    a. Atmosphere0
    b. Place
    c. Undefined
    d. Undefined

19. _____ is a chemical element. An abundant nonmetallic, tetravalent element, _____ has several allotropic forms. This element is the basis of the chemistry of all known life.
    a. Carbon0
    b. Thing
    c. Undefined
    d. Undefined

20. _____ is a chemical compound, normally in a gaseous state, and is composed of one carbon and two oxygen atoms. It is often referred to by its formula CO2. It is present in the Earth's atmosphere at a concentration of approximately .000383 by volume and is an important greenhouse gas due to its ability to absorb many infrared wavelengths of sunlight, and due to the length of time it stays in the atmosphere.
    a. Carbon dioxide0
    b. Thing
    c. Undefined
    d. Undefined

21. _____ rock is one of the three main rock groups. Rock formed from these covers 75% of the Earth's land area, and includes common types such as chalk, limestone, dolomite, sandstone, and shale.
    a. Thing
    b. Sedimentary0
    c. Undefined
    d. Undefined

22. The carbonate mineral _____ is a chemical or biochemical calcium carbonate and is one of the most widely distributed minerals on the Earth's surface. It is a common constituent of sedimentary rocks, limestone in particular. It is also the primary mineral in metamorphic marble
    a. Calcite0
    b. Thing
    c. Undefined
    d. Undefined

23. In geology and astronomy, the term _____ is used to denote types of rock that consist predominantly of _____ minerals. Such rocks include a wide range of igneous, metamorphic and sedimentary types. Most of the Earth's mantle and crust are made up of _____ rocks. The same is true of the Moon and the other rocky planets.
    a. Thing
    b. Silicate0
    c. Undefined
    d. Undefined

124 *Chapter 7. Metamorphism, Metamorphic Rocks, and Hydrothermal Rocks*

24. _____ is the second most common mineral in the Earth's continental crust. It is made up of a lattice of silica tetrahedra. _____ belongs to the rhombohedral crystal system. In nature _____ crystals are often twinned, distorted, or so intergrown with adjacent crystals of _____ or other minerals as to only show part of this shape, or to lack obvious crystal faces altogether and appear massive.
  a. Thing
  b. Quartz0
  c. Undefined
  d. Undefined

25. A _____ is a building where plants are cultivated.
  a. Thing
  b. Greenhouse0
  c. Undefined
  d. Undefined

26. The _____, discovered by Joseph Fourier in 1829 and first investigated quantitatively by Svante Arrhenius in 1896, is the process in which the emission of infrared radiation by the atmosphere warms a planet's surface.
  a. Greenhouse effect0
  b. Thing
  c. Undefined
  d. Undefined

27. _____ is the average and variations of weather over long periods of time. _____ zones can be defined using parameters such as temperature and rainfall.
  a. Climate0
  b. Thing
  c. Undefined
  d. Undefined

28. The _____, is a term that comprises all living and non-living things that occur naturally on Earth or some part of it.
  a. Natural environment0
  b. Thing
  c. Undefined
  d. Undefined

29. The _____ is a fundamental concept in geology that describes the dynamic transitions through geologic time among the three main rock types: sedimentary, metamorphic, and igneous.
  a. Rock cycle0
  b. Thing
  c. Undefined
  d. Undefined

30. _____ is a general term that includes rocks and materials that are not by definition rocks but are commonly regarded as rocks.
  a. Earth materials0
  b. Thing
  c. Undefined
  d. Undefined

31. _____ is molten rock located beneath the surface of the Earth, and which often collects in a _____ chamber. _____ is a complex high-temperature fluid substance. Most are silicate solutions. It is capable of intrusion into adjacent rocks or of extrusion onto the surface as lava or ejected explosively as tephra to form pyroclastic rock. Environments of _____ formation include subduction zones, continental rift zones, mid-oceanic ridges, and hotspots, some of which are interpreted as mantle plumes.
  a. Magma0
  b. Thing
  c. Undefined
  d. Undefined

32. _____, in soil science, means the underlying geological material in which soil horizons form. Soils typically get a great deal of structure and minerals from their _____.

a. Parent material0
b. Thing
c. Undefined
d. Undefined

33. _____ is one of the three main rock groups. _____ covers 75% of the Earth's land area. Four basic processes are involved in the formation of a clastic _____: weathering caused mainly by friction of waves, transportation where the sediment is carried along by a current, deposition and compaction where the sediment is squashed together to form a rock of this kind.
   a. Sedimentary rock0
   b. Thing
   c. Undefined
   d. Undefined

34. The _____ is a large shield covered by a thin layer of soil that forms the nucleus of the North American craton. It has a deep, common, joined bedrock region in eastern and central Canada and stretches North from the Great Lakes to the Arctic Ocean, covering half the country.
   a. Canadian Shield0
   b. Thing
   c. Undefined
   d. Undefined

35. An _____ is a body of igneous rock that has crystallized from a molten magma below the surface of the Earth.
   a. Intrusion0
   b. Thing
   c. Undefined
   d. Undefined

36. The _____ is an informal name for the eons of the geologic timescale that came before the current Phanerozoic eon. It spans from the formation of Earth around 4500 Ma to the evolution of abundant macroscopic hard-shelled animals, which marked the beginning of the Cambrian, the first period of the first era of the Phanerozoic eon, some 542 Ma.
   a. Thing
   b. Precambrian0
   c. Undefined
   d. Undefined

37. _____ forms when rock cools and solidifies either below the surface as intrusive rocks or on the surface as extrusive rocks. This magma can be derived from partial melts of pre-existing rocks in either the Earth's mantle or crust. Typically, the melting is caused by one or more of the following processes -- an increase in temperature, a decrease in pressure, or a change in composition.
   a. Thing
   b. Igneous rock0
   c. Undefined
   d. Undefined

38. _____ is a metamorphic rock resulting from the metamorphism of limestone, composed mostly of calcite. It is extensively used for sculpture, as a building material, and in many other applications. The word '_____' is colloquially used to refer to many other stones that are capable of taking a high polish.
   a. Marble0
   b. Thing
   c. Undefined
   d. Undefined

39. _____ is a sedimentary rock composed largely of the mineral calcite. _____ often contains variable amounts of silica in the form of chert or flint, as well as varying amounts of clay, silt and sand as disseminations, nodules, or layers within the rock. The primary source of the calcite in _____ is most commonly marine organisms. These organisms secrete shells that settle out of the water column and are deposited on ocean floors as pelagic ooze or alternatively is conglomerated in a coral reef.

Chapter 7. Metamorphism, Metamorphic Rocks, and Hydrothermal Rocks

    a. Limestone0   b. Thing
    c. Undefined   d. Undefined

40. An _____ is a type of atom that is defined by its atomic number; that is, by the number of protons in its nucleus.
    a. Element0   b. Thing
    c. Undefined   d. Undefined

41. _____ is the condition of a system in which competing influences are balanced.
    a. Thing   b. Equilibrium0
    c. Undefined   d. Undefined

42. _____ is a fine-grained sedimentary rock whose original constituents were clays or muds. It is characterized by thin laminae breaking with an irregular curving fracture, often splintery and usually parallel to the often-indistinguishable bedding plane.
    a. Shale0   b. Thing
    c. Undefined   d. Undefined

43. _____ is a term used to describe a group of hydrous aluminium phyllosilicate minerals, that are typically less than 2 micrometres in diameter. _____ consists of a variety of phyllosilicate minerals rich in silicon and aluminium oxides and hydroxides which include variable amounts of structural water. Clays are generally formed by the chemical weathering of silicate-bearing rocks by carbonic acid but some are formed by hydrothermal activity.
    a. Thing   b. Clay0
    c. Undefined   d. Undefined

44. _____ are hydrous aluminium phyllosilicates, sometimes with variable amounts of iron, magnesium, alkali metals, alkaline earths and other cations. Clays have structures similar to the micas and therefore form flat hexagonal sheets. _____ are common weathering products and low temperature hydrothermal alteration products.
    a. Clay minerals0   b. Thing
    c. Undefined   d. Undefined

45. _____ is a common and widely occurring type of intrusive, felsic, igneous rock. Granites are usually medium to coarsely crystalline, occasionally with some individual crystals larger than the groundmass forming a rock known as porphyry. Granites can be pink to dark gray or even black, depending on their chemistry and mineralogy.
    a. Thing   b. Granite0
    c. Undefined   d. Undefined

46. A _____ in geology is an intrusive igneous rock body that crystallized from a magma below the surface of the Earth. Plutons include batholiths, dikes, sills, laccoliths, lopoliths, and other igneous bodies. In practice, "_____" usually refers to a distinctive mass of igneous rock, typically kilometers in dimension, without a tabular shape like those of dikes and sills.
    a. Thing   b. Pluton0
    c. Undefined   d. Undefined

47. _____ is a sedimentary rock composed mainly of sand-size mineral or rock grains. Most _____ is composed of quartz and/or feldspar because these are the most common minerals in the Earth's crust. Like sand, _____ may be any color, but the most common colors are tan, brown, yellow, red, gray and white.

Chapter 7. Metamorphism, Metamorphic Rocks, and Hydrothermal Rocks

a. Sandstone0
b. Thing
c. Undefined
d. Undefined

48. _____ is a self-governed Danish territory lying between the Arctic and Atlantic Oceans. Though geographically and ethnically an Arctic island nation associated with the continent of North America, politically and historically _____ is closely tied to Europe. It is the largest island in the world that is not also considered a continent.
a. Greenland0
b. Place
c. Undefined
d. Undefined

49. A _____ is a chemical substance of two or more different chemically bonded chemical elements, with a fixed ratio determining the composition. The ratio of each element is usually expressed by chemical formula.
a. Chemical compound0
b. Thing
c. Undefined
d. Undefined

50. In geology, _____ refers to heat sources within the planet. The planet's internal heat was originally generated during its accretion, due to gravitational binding energy, and since then additional heat has continued to be generated by the radioactive decay of elements such as uranium, thorium, and potassium.
a. Thing
b. Geothermal0
c. Undefined
d. Undefined

51. _____ is the use of geothermal heat to generate electricity.
a. Geothermal power0
b. Thing
c. Undefined
d. Undefined

52. _____ is the numerical difference between the minimum and maximum values of temperature observed in a system, such as atmospheric temperature in a given location. A _____ may refer to a period of time or to an average.
a. Thing
b. Temperature range0
c. Undefined
d. Undefined

53. _____ is a layer of gases surrounding the planet Earth and retained by the Earth's gravity. This mixture of gases is commonly known as air.
a. Thing
b. Earths atmosphere0
c. Undefined
d. Undefined

54. _____ is the pressure at any point in the Earth's atmosphere.
a. Thing
b. Atmospheric pressure0
c. Undefined
d. Undefined

55. _____, in everyday life, is most familiar as the agency that endows objects with weight. _____ is responsible for keeping the Earth and the other planets in their orbits around the Sun; for the formation of tides; and for various other phenomena that we observe. _____ is also the reason for the very existence of the Earth, the Sun, and most macroscopic objects in the universe; without it, matter would not have coalesced into these large masses, and life, as we know it, would not exist.
a. Gravitation0
b. Thing
c. Undefined
d. Undefined

128   *Chapter 7. Metamorphism, Metamorphic Rocks, and Hydrothermal Rocks*

56. _____ are the fundamental building blocks of chemistry, and are conserved in chemical reactions.
   a. Atoms0
   b. Thing
   c. Undefined
   d. Undefined

57. A _____ is a unique arrangement of atoms in a crystal. It is composed of a unit cell, a set of atoms arranged in a particular way, which is periodically repeated in three dimensions on a lattice. The spacing between unit cells in various directions is called its lattice parameters. The symmetry properties of the crystal are embodied in its space group.
   a. Crystal structure0
   b. Thing
   c. Undefined
   d. Undefined

58. _____ is the process of heating a solid substance to a point where it turns into a liquid. An object that has melted is molten.
   a. Thing
   b. Melting0
   c. Undefined
   d. Undefined

59. Mean _____ is the average height of the sea, with reference to a suitable reference surface.
   a. Thing
   b. Sea level0
   c. Undefined
   d. Undefined

60. The _____ is a physical quantity that describes in which direction and at what rate the pressure changes the most rapidly around a particular location. The _____ is a dimensional quantity expressed in units of pressure per unit length.
   a. Thing
   b. Pressure gradient0
   c. Undefined
   d. Undefined

61. Overburden, or _____ pressure, is a term used in geology to denote the pressure imposed on a stratigraphic layer by the weight of overlying layers of material.
   a. Lithostatic0
   b. Thing
   c. Undefined
   d. Undefined

62. _____ is a term used in geology to denote the pressure imposed on a stratigraphic layer by the weight of overlying layers of material.
   a. Event
   b. Lithostatic pressure0
   c. Undefined
   d. Undefined

63. _____ is the stress applied to materials resulting in their compaction, decrease of volume.
   a. Thing
   b. Compression stress0
   c. Undefined
   d. Undefined

64. Faults are planar rock fractures, which show evidence of relative movement. Large faults within the Earth's crust are the result of shear motion and active _____ zones are the causal locations of most earthquakes. Earthquakes are caused by energy release during rapid slippage along faults. The largest examples are at tectonic plate boundaries but many faults occur far from active plate boundaries. Since faults do not usually consist of a single, clean fracture, the term _____ zone is used when referring to the zone of complex deformation that is associated with the _____ plane.

a. Fault0
b. Thing
c. Undefined
d. Undefined

65. _____ is a fine-grained, compact rock produced by dynamic crystallization of the constituent minerals resulting in a reduction of the grain size of the rock. It is classified as a metamorphic rock. They can have many different mineralogical compositions, it is a classification based on the textural appearance of the rock.
   a. Thing
   b. Mylonite0
   c. Undefined
   d. Undefined

66. _____ has penetrative planar fabric present within it. It is common to rocks affected by regional metamorphic compression typical of orogenic belts.
   a. Thing
   b. Foliated metamorphic rock0
   c. Undefined
   d. Undefined

67. _____ is a complex inosilicate series of minerals. _____ is not a recognized mineral, in its own right but the name is used as a general or field term, to refer to a dark amphibole. It is an isomorphous mixture of three molecules; a calcium-iron-magnesium silicate, an aluminium-iron-magnesium silicate and an iron-magnesium silicate.
   a. Hornblende0
   b. Thing
   c. Undefined
   d. Undefined

68. _____ is the gas phase component of a another state of matter which does not completely fill its container. It is distinguished from the pure gas phase by the presence of the same substance in another state of matter. Hence when a liquid has completely evaporated, it is said that the system has been completely transformed to the gas phase.
   a. Vapor0
   b. Thing
   c. Undefined
   d. Undefined

69. An _____ is an atom or group of atoms which have lost or gained one or more electrons, making them negatively or positively charged.
   a. Ion0
   b. Thing
   c. Undefined
   d. Undefined

70. A _____ is a section of a river of relatively steep gradient causing an increase in water flow and turbulence. A _____ is a hydrological feature between a run and a cascade. It is characterized by the river becoming shallower and having some rocks exposed above the flow surface.
   a. Rapid0
   b. Thing
   c. Undefined
   d. Undefined

71. A _____ is a process that results in the interconversion of chemical substances. The substance or substances initially involved in a _____ are called reactants. Chemical reactions are characterized by a chemical change, and they yield one or more products which are, in general, different from the reactants.
   a. Thing
   b. Chemical reaction0
   c. Undefined
   d. Undefined

72. _____ defines an important group of generally dark-colored rock-forming inosilicate minerals linked at the vertices and generally containing ions of iron and/or magnesium in their structures. Amphiboles crystallize into two crystal systems, monoclinic and orthorhombic.

a. Amphibole0 b. Thing
c. Undefined d. Undefined

73. _____ are a group of minerals that have been used since the Bronze Age as gemstones and abrasives. _____ are most often seen in red, but are available in a wide variety of colors spanning the entire spectrum.
    a. Garnets0 b. Thing
    c. Undefined d. Undefined

74. A _____ column is a column of rizing air in the lower altitudes of the Earth's atmosphere. Thermals are created by the uneven heating of the Earth's surface from solar radiation, and are an example of convection. The Sun warms the ground, which in turn warms the air directly above it.
    a. Thing b. Thermal0
    c. Undefined d. Undefined

75. _____ is a description of the way light interacts with the surface of a crystal, rock, or mineral. For example, a diamond is said to have an adamantine _____ and pyrite is said to have a metallic _____.
    a. Luster0 b. Thing
    c. Undefined d. Undefined

76. _____ is a very important series of tectosilicate minerals within the feldspar family. Rather than referring to a particular mineral with a specific chemical composition, it is a solid solution series.
    a. Thing b. Plagioclase0
    c. Undefined d. Undefined

77. A _____ is one which contains both magnesium and iron.
    a. Thing b. Ferromagnesian mineral0
    c. Undefined d. Undefined

78. The _____ refers to a group of medium-grade metamorphic rocks, chiefly notable for the preponderance of lamellar minerals such as micas, chlorite, talc, hornblende, graphite, and others. Quartz often occurs in drawn-out grains to such an extent that a particular form called quartz _____ is produced.
    a. Schist0 b. Thing
    c. Undefined d. Undefined

79. _____ is a common phyllosilicate mineral within the mica group. Primarily a solid-solution series between the iron-endmember annite, and the magnesium-endmember phlogopite; more aluminous endmembers include siderophyllite.
    a. Thing b. Biotite0
    c. Undefined d. Undefined

80. _____ is the name of a group of rock-forming minerals which make up as much as sixty percent of the Earth's crust. Feldspars crystallize from magma in both intrusive and extrusive rocks, and they can also occur as compact minerals, as veins, and are also present in many types of metamorphic rock.
    a. Feldspar0 b. Thing
    c. Undefined d. Undefined

Chapter 7. Metamorphism, Metamorphic Rocks, and Hydrothermal Rocks   131

81. _____ is the group designation for a series of contact metamorphic rocks that have been baked and indurated by the heat of intrusive igneous masses and have been rendered massive, hard, splintery, and in some cases exceedingly tough and durable. Most _____ are fine-grained.
   a. Thing
   b. Hornfels0
   c. Undefined
   d. Undefined

82. _____ is a common gray to black extrusive volcanic rock. It is usually fine-grained due to rapid cooling of lava on the Earth's surface. It may be porphyritic containing larger crystals in a fine matrix, or vesicular, or frothy scoria.
   a. Basalt0
   b. Thing
   c. Undefined
   d. Undefined

83. _____ is the name of a sedimentary carbonate rock and a mineral, both composed of calcium magnesium carbonate found in crystals. _____ rock is composed predominantly of the mineral _____. Limestone that is partially replaced by _____ is referred to as dolomitic limestone.
   a. Thing
   b. Dolomite0
   c. Undefined
   d. Undefined

84. _____ are small bodies in the solar system that orbit the Sun and occasionally exhibit a coma or atmosphere and/or a tail — both primarily from the effects of solar radiation upon its nucleus, which itself is a minor body composed of rock, dust, and ice.
   a. Comets0
   b. Thing
   c. Undefined
   d. Undefined

85. A _____, as defined by the International Astronomical Union, is a celestial body orbiting a star or stellar remnant that is massive enough to be rounded by its own gravity, not massive enough to cause thermonuclear fusion in its core, and has cleared its neighboring region of planetesimals.
   a. Thing
   b. Planet0
   c. Undefined
   d. Undefined

86. _____ is the fifth planet from the Sun and the largest planet within the solar system. It is two and a half times as massive as all of the other planets in our solar system combined. _____, along with Saturn, Uranus and Neptune, is classified as a gas giant.
   a. Place
   b. Jupiter0
   c. Undefined
   d. Undefined

87. A _____ is an approximately circular depression in the surface of a planet, moon or other solid body in the Solar System, formed by the hyper-velocity impact of a smaller body with the surface. Impact craters typically have raised rims, and they range from small, simple, bowl-shaped depressions to large, complex, multi-ringed, impact basins.
   a. Thing
   b. Crater0
   c. Undefined
   d. Undefined

88. _____ are a class of astronomical objects. The term is generally used to indicate a diverse group of small celestial bodies that drift in the solar system in orbit around the Sun.
   a. Asteroids0
   b. Thing
   c. Undefined
   d. Undefined

Chapter 7. Metamorphism, Metamorphic Rocks, and Hydrothermal Rocks

89. _____ is the science and study of the solid matter that constitute the Earth. Encompassing such things as rocks, soil, and gemstones, _____ studies the composition, structure, physical properties, history, and the processes that shape Earth's components.
- a. Thing
- b. Geology0
- c. Undefined
- d. Undefined

90. A _____ is a natural object originating in outer space that survives an impact with the Earth's surface without being destroyed. While in space it is called a meteoroid. When it enters the atmosphere, air resistance causes the body to heat up and emit light, thus forming a fireball.
- a. Thing
- b. Meteorite0
- c. Undefined
- d. Undefined

91. A _____ is a large sand to boulder-sized particle of debris in the Solar system. Its visible path when it enters the Earth's atmosphere is commonly called a shooting star or falling star.
- a. Thing
- b. Meteoroid0
- c. Undefined
- d. Undefined

92. _____ is a form of silicon dioxide that is formed when very high pressure (2–3 gigapascals) and moderately high temperature (700 °C) are applied to quartz. The presence of it in unmetamorphosed rocks may be evidence of a meteorite impact event or of an atomic bomb explosion.
- a. Coesite0
- b. Thing
- c. Undefined
- d. Undefined

93. Tektites are natural glass objects, up to a few centimeters in size, which have been formed by the impact of large meteorites on Earth's surface. A _____ is among the "driest" rocks, with an average water content of 0.005%. This is very unusual, as most if not all of the craters where tektites may have formed were underwater before impact.
- a. Tektite0
- b. Thing
- c. Undefined
- d. Undefined

94. _____ were vertebrate animals that dominated terrestrial ecosystems for over 160 million years, first appearing approximately 230 million years ago. At the end of the Cretaceous Period, approximately 65 million years ago, a catastrophic extinction event ended _____' dominance on land.
- a. Thing
- b. Dinosaurs0
- c. Undefined
- d. Undefined

95. In biology and ecology, _____ is the cessation of existence of a species or group of taxa, reducing biodiversity. The moment of _____ is generally considered to be the death of the last individual of that species.
- a. Thing
- b. Extinction0
- c. Undefined
- d. Undefined

96. The _____ is Earth's only natural satellite. It makes a complete orbit around the Earth every 27.3 days, and the periodic variations in the geometry of the Earth–_____–Sun system are responsible for the lunar phases that repeat every 29.5 days.
- a. Moon0
- b. Thing
- c. Undefined
- d. Undefined

Chapter 7. Metamorphism, Metamorphic Rocks, and Hydrothermal Rocks

97. _____ is a chemical element in the periodic table that has the symbol Hg and atomic number 80. A heavy, silvery transition metal, _____ is one of five elements that are liquid at or near room temperature and pressure.
a. Thing
b. Mercury0
c. Undefined
d. Undefined

98. _____ is the second-closest planet to the Sun, orbiting it every 224.7 Earth days. It is the brightest natural object in the night sky, except for the Moon, reaching an apparent magnitude of −4.6. Because _____ is an inferior planet, from Earth it never appears to venture far from the Sun: its elongation reaches a maximum of 47.8°.
a. Venus0
b. Thing
c. Undefined
d. Undefined

99. _____ the fourth planet from the Sun in the Solar System. The planet is named after _____, the Roman god of war. It is also referred to as the "Red Planet" because of its reddish appearance as seen from Earth.
a. Thing
b. Mars0
c. Undefined
d. Undefined

100. _____ is displacement of solids by the agents of ocean currents, wind, water, or ice by downward or down-slope movement in response to gravity or by living organisms.
a. Thing
b. Erosion0
c. Undefined
d. Undefined

101. _____ is the process of breaking down rocks, soils and their minerals through direct contact with the atmosphere. _____ occurs without movement. Two main classifications of _____ processes exist. Mechanical or physical _____ involves the breakdown of rocks and soils through direct contact with atmospheric conditions. The second classification, chemical _____, involves the direct effect of atmospheric chemicals in the breakdown of rocks, soils and minerals.
a. Thing
b. Weathering0
c. Undefined
d. Undefined

102. _____ is a hard, metamorphic rock which was originally sandstone. Sandstone is converted into _____ through heating and pressure usually related to tectonic compression within orogenic belts.
a. Thing
b. Quartzite0
c. Undefined
d. Undefined

103. _____ involves the change in the composition of rock, often leading to a 'break down' in its form.
a. Thing
b. Chemical weathering0
c. Undefined
d. Undefined

104. _____ is the characteristic of a solid material expressing its resistance to permanent deformation.
a. Hardness0
b. Thing
c. Undefined
d. Undefined

105. The _____ is the rate of increase in temperature per unit depth in the Earth. It varies with location and is typically measured by determining the bottom open-hole temperature after the drilling of a borehole.

Chapter 7. Metamorphism, Metamorphic Rocks, and Hydrothermal Rocks

a. Geothermal gradient0   b. Thing
c. Undefined   d. Undefined

106. _____ is a general field petrologic term applied to metamorphic and/or altered mafic volcanic rock. The green is due to abundant green chlorite, actinolite and epidote minerals that dominate the rock.
a. Greenschist0   b. Thing
c. Undefined   d. Undefined

107. _____ is the name given to a rock consisting mainly of hornblende amphibole, the use of the term being restricted, however, to metamorphic rocks. The modern terminology for a holocrystalline plutonic igneous rocks rock composed primarily of hornblende amphibole is a hornblendite, which are usually crystal cumulates.
a. Amphibolite0   b. Thing
c. Undefined   d. Undefined

108. A _____ is an intrusion caused by buoyancy and pressure differentials. A _____ is any relatively mobile mass that intrudes into preexisting strata. Diapirs commonly intrude vertically upward along fractures or zones of structural weakness through more dense overlying rocks because of density contrast between a less dense, lower rock mass and overlying denser rocks. The density contrast manifests as a force of buoyancy.
a. Thing   b. Diapir0
c. Undefined   d. Undefined

109. _____, in mineralogy, is the tendency of crystalline materials to split along definite planes, creating smooth surfaces.
a. Cleavage0   b. Thing
c. Undefined   d. Undefined

110. _____ is a fine-grained, homogeneous, metamorphic rock derived from an original shale-type sedimentary rock composed of clay or volcanic ash through low grade regional metamorphism. The result is a foliated rock in which the foliation may not correspond to the original sedimentary layering.
a. Slate0   b. Thing
c. Undefined   d. Undefined

111. _____ is a type of foliated metamorphic rock primarily composed of quartz, sericite mica, and chlorite; the rock represents a gradiation in the degree of metamorphism between slate and mica schist. Minute crystals of graphite, sericite, or chlorite impart a silky, sometimes golden sheen to the surfaces of cleavage.
a. Phyllite0   b. Thing
c. Undefined   d. Undefined

112. _____ is an essentially physical process that has meanings in chemistry, metallurgy and geology. In geology, solid-state _____ is a metamorphic process that occurs under situations of intense temperature and pressure where grains, atoms or molecules of a rock or mineral are packed closer together, creating a new crystal structure.
a. Thing   b. Recrystallization0
c. Undefined   d. Undefined

Chapter 7. Metamorphism, Metamorphic Rocks, and Hydrothermal Rocks

113. _____ is a common and widely distributed type of rock formed by high-grade regional metamorphic processes from preexisting formations that were originally either igneous or sedimentary rocks. Gneissic rocks are usually medium to coarse foliated and largely recrystallized but do not carry large quantities of micas, chlorite or other platy minerals.
- a. Thing
- b. Gneiss0
- c. Undefined
- d. Undefined

114. _____ is a grey to dark grey intermediate intrusive igneous rock composed principally of plagioclase feldspar, biotite, hornblende, and/or pyroxene. It may contain small amounts of quartz, microcline and olivine.
- a. Thing
- b. Diorite0
- c. Undefined
- d. Undefined

115. _____ also called Bucholzite is an alumino-silicate mineral with the chemical formula Al_2SiO_5.
- a. Thing
- b. Sillimanite0
- c. Undefined
- d. Undefined

116. _____, whose name derives from the Greek word kyanos, meaning blue, is a typically blue silicate mineral, commonly found in aluminium-rich metamorphic pegmatites and/or sedimentary rock. _____ is a diagnostic mineral of the Blueschist Facies of metamorphic rocks.
- a. Kyanite0
- b. Thing
- c. Undefined
- d. Undefined

117. _____ is an aluminium nesosilicate mineral with the chemical formula Al_2SiO_5.
- a. Thing
- b. Andalusite0
- c. Undefined
- d. Undefined

118. _____ is an ecological concept referring to the relative representation of a species in a particular ecosystem. It is usually measured as the mean number of individuals found per sample.
- a. Thing
- b. Abundance0
- c. Undefined
- d. Undefined

119. _____ is a silvery and ductile member of the poor metal group of chemical elements. It has the symbol Al and atomic number 13.
- a. Aluminum0
- b. Thing
- c. Undefined
- d. Undefined

120. _____ is a rock at the frontier between igneous and metamorphic rocks. They can also be known as diatexite.
- a. Migmatite0
- b. Thing
- c. Undefined
- d. Undefined

121. _____ is the rise of land masses that were depressed by the huge weight of ice sheets during the last ice age, through a process known as isostatic depression. It affects northern Europe, especially Scotland and Scandinavia, Siberia, Canada, and the Great Lakes of Canada and the United States.
- a. Post glacial rebound0
- b. Thing
- c. Undefined
- d. Undefined

136   Chapter 7. Metamorphism, Metamorphic Rocks, and Hydrothermal Rocks

122. _____ is the rise of land masses that were depressed by the huge weight of ice sheets during the last ice age, through a process known as isostatic depression.
   a. Thing
   b. Post-glacial rebound0
   c. Undefined
   d. Undefined

123. _____ in meteorology are large scale patterns in the atmospheric pressure field that are nearly stationary, effectively "blocking" or redirecting migratory cyclones. These _____ can remain in place for several days or even weeks, causing the areas affected by them to have the same kind of weather for an extended period of time.
   a. Thing
   b. Blocks0
   c. Undefined
   d. Undefined

124. _____ is a theory of geology that has been developed to explain the observed evidence for large scale motions of the Earth's lithosphere. The theory encompassed and superseded the older theory of continental drift.
   a. Plate tectonics0
   b. Thing
   c. Undefined
   d. Undefined

125. Earth's _____ is a ~2,900 km thick rocky shell comprizing approximately 70% of Earth's volume. It is predominantly solid and overlies the Earth's iron-rich core, which occupies about 30% of Earth's volume. Past episodes of melting and volcanism at the shallower levels of the _____ have produced a very thin crust of crystallized melt products near the surface, upon which we live.
   a. Mantle0
   b. Thing
   c. Undefined
   d. Undefined

126. In geology, a _____ zone is an area on Earth where two tectonic plates meet and move towards one another, with one sliding underneath the other and moving down into the mantle, at rates typically measured in centimeters per year. An oceanic plate ordinarily slides underneath a continental plate; this often creates an orogenic zone with many volcanoes and earthquakes.
   a. Subduction0
   b. Thing
   c. Undefined
   d. Undefined

127. A _____ is an area on Earth where two tectonic plates meet and move towards one another, with one sliding underneath the other and moving down into the mantle, at rates typically measured in centimeters per year. In a sense, subduction zones are the opposite of divergent boundaries, areas where material rises up from the mantle and plates are moving apart.
   a. Subduction zone0
   b. Thing
   c. Undefined
   d. Undefined

128. _____ is the part of Earth's lithosphere that surfaces in the ocean basins. _____ is primarily composed of mafic rocks, or sima. It is thinner than continental crust, or sial, generally less than 10 kilometers thick, however it is more dense, having a mean density of about 3.3 grams per cubic centimeter.
   a. Oceanic crust0
   b. Thing
   c. Undefined
   d. Undefined

129. The _____ is the solid outermost shell of a rocky planet. On the Earth, the _____ includes the crust and the uppermost mantle which is joined to the crust across the Mohorovièiæ discontinuity. _____ is underlain by asthenosphere, the weaker, hotter, and deeper part of the upper mantle.

Chapter 7. Metamorphism, Metamorphic Rocks, and Hydrothermal Rocks

    a. Thing
    b. Lithosphere0
    c. Undefined
    d. Undefined

130. The _____ are the broad expanse of prairie and steppe which lie east of the Rocky Mountains in the United States and Canada.
    a. Great Plains0
    b. Place
    c. Undefined
    d. Undefined

131. The _____ is the region of the Earth between 100-200 km below the surface that is the weak or "soft" zone in the upper mantle. It lies just below the lithosphere, which is involved in plate movements and isostatic adjustments. In spite of its heat, pressures keep it plastic, and it has a relatively low density. Seismic waves pass relatively slowly through the _____.
    a. Thing
    b. Asthenosphere0
    c. Undefined
    d. Undefined

132. _____ is a historical and geographical region centered on the Scandinavian Peninsula in Northern Europe and includes the three kingdoms of Denmark, Norway and Sweden. The other Nordic countries, Finland, Iceland and the Faroe Islands, are also sometimes included because of their close historic and cultural relations to Norway, Sweden, and Denmark.
    a. Place
    b. Scandinavia0
    c. Undefined
    d. Undefined

133. A _____ should ideally be a distinctive rock that forms under certain conditions of sedimentation, reflecting a particular process or environment.
    a. Facies0
    b. Thing
    c. Undefined
    d. Undefined

134. A vine is any plant of genus Vitis or by extension, any similar _____ or trailing plant.
    a. Thing
    b. Climbing plant0
    c. Undefined
    d. Undefined

135. _____ refers to metamorphic rocks that have experienced high temperatures of metamorphism. Many granulites represent samples of the deep continental crust.
    a. Granulite0
    b. Thing
    c. Undefined
    d. Undefined

136. _____ is a phyllosilicate of calcium and aluminium with the formula: $Ca_2Al|AlSi_3O_{10}||OH|_2$. Limited Fe_3+ substitutes for aluminium in the structure. _____ crystallizes in the orthorhombic crystal system.
    a. Thing
    b. Prehnite0
    c. Undefined
    d. Undefined

137. _____ is a rock that forms by the metamorphism of basalt and rocks with similar composition at high pressures and low temperatures, approximately corresponding to a depth of 15 to 30 kilometers and 200 to ~500 degrees Celsius. The blue color of the rock comes from the presence of the mineral glaucophane.

Chapter 7. Metamorphism, Metamorphic Rocks, and Hydrothermal Rocks

a. Blueschist0
b. Thing
c. Undefined
d. Undefined

138. In plate tectonics, a _____ is an actively deforming region where two tectonic plates or fragments of lithosphere move towards one another. When two plates move toward one another, they form either a subduction zone or a continental collision.
a. Thing
b. Convergent boundary0
c. Undefined
d. Undefined

139. _____ is the chemical alteration of a rock by hydrothermal and other fluids. _____ can occur via the action of hydrothermal fluids from an igneous or metamorphic source. In the metamorphic environment, _____ is created by mass transfer from a volume of metamorphic rock at higher stress and temperature into a zone with lower stress and temperature, with metamorphic hydrothermal solutions acting as a solvent.
a. Metasomatism0
b. Thing
c. Undefined
d. Undefined

140. A _____ is a geological feature that is also known as a Rip in the earth causing magma to flow out and forming an undersea volcano, it also has geological features, a continuous elevational crest for some distance. Ridges are usually termed hills or mountains as well, depending on size.
a. Thing
b. Ridge0
c. Undefined
d. Undefined

141. In plate tectonics, a _____ a linear feature that exists between two tectonic plates that are moving away from each other. These areas can form in the middle of continents but eventually form ocean basins.
a. Divergent plate boundary0
b. Thing
c. Undefined
d. Undefined

142. _____ is a dark, coarse-grained, intrusive igneous rock chemically equivalent to basalt. It is a plutonic rock, formed when molten magma is trapped beneath the Earth's surface and cools into a crystalline mass.
a. Gabbro0
b. Thing
c. Undefined
d. Undefined

143. A _____ is a spring that is produced by the emergence of geothermally-heated groundwater from the earth's crust. They are all over the earth, on every continent and even under the oceans and seas.
a. Thing
b. Hot spring0
c. Undefined
d. Undefined

144. A _____, is a fissure in a planet's surface from which geothermally heated water issues. Hydrothermal vents are commonly found near volcanically active places, tectonic plates that are moving apart, ocean basins, and hotspots.
a. Thing
b. Hydrothermal vent0
c. Undefined
d. Undefined

145. _____ is a 16-ton, manned deep-ocean research submersible owned by the United States Navy and operated by the Woods Hole Oceanographic Institution in Woods Hole, Massachusetts. The three-person vessel allows for two scientists and one pilot to dive for up to nine hours at 4500 metersor 15,000 feet.

Chapter 7. Metamorphism, Metamorphic Rocks, and Hydrothermal Rocks

    a. Alvin0
    b. Thing
    c. Undefined
    d. Undefined

146. The mineral _____ is a magnesium iron silicate. It is one of the most common minerals on Earth, and has also been identified on the Moon, Mars, and comet Wild 2.
    a. Olivine0
    b. Thing
    c. Undefined
    d. Undefined

147. The _____ are a group of important rock-forming silicate minerals found in many igneous and metamorphic rocks. They share a common structure comprised of single chains of silica tetrahedra and they crystalise in the monoclinic and orthorhombic system.
    a. Thing
    b. Pyroxenes0
    c. Undefined
    d. Undefined

148. The term _____ refers to several types of chemical compounds containing sulfur in its lowest oxidation number of −2.
    a. Thing
    b. Sulfide0
    c. Undefined
    d. Undefined

149. _____ is water from a sea or ocean. On average, _____ in the world's oceans has a salinity of ~3.5%, or 35 parts per thousand. This means that every 1 kg of _____ has approximately 35 grams of dissolved salts.
    a. Thing
    b. Seawater0
    c. Undefined
    d. Undefined

150. A _____ is a mineral containing sulfide as the major anion. Closely related and often included within the sulfide class are selenide and telluride minerals.
    a. Thing
    b. Sulfide mineral0
    c. Undefined
    d. Undefined

151. _____ is the extraction of valuable minerals or other geological materials from the earth, usually from an ore body, vein, or seam. Any material that cannot be grown from agricultural processes, or created artificially in a laboratory or factory, is usually extracted from the earth by this method.
    a. Mining0
    b. Thing
    c. Undefined
    d. Undefined

152. _____ is any particulate matter that can be transported by fluid flow and which eventually is deposited as a layer of solid particles on the bed or bottom of a body of water or other liquid.
    a. Sediment0
    b. Thing
    c. Undefined
    d. Undefined

153. _____ is the gas phase of water. _____ is one state of the water cycle within the hydrosphere. _____ can be produced from the evaporation of liquid water or from the sublimation of ice. Under normal atmospheric conditions, _____ is continuously evaporating and condensing.
    a. Water vapor0
    b. Thing
    c. Undefined
    d. Undefined

Chapter 7. Metamorphism, Metamorphic Rocks, and Hydrothermal Rocks

154. _____ is a chemical element. It is a soft silvery-white metallic alkali metal that occurs naturally bound to other elements in seawater and many minerals. It oxidizes rapidly in air and is very reactive, especially towards water. In many respects, it and sodium are chemically similar, although organisms in general, and animal cells in particular, treat them very differently.
   a. Potassium0
   b. Thing
   c. Undefined
   d. Undefined

155. _____ is a chemical element metal. It is a lustrous, silvery soft metal. It and nickel are notable for being the final elements produced by stellar nucleosynthesis, and thus are the heaviest elements which do not require a supernova or similarly cataclysmic event for formation.
   a. Iron0
   b. Thing
   c. Undefined
   d. Undefined

156. _____ is a soft white lustrous transition metal, it has the highest electrical and thermal conductivity for a metal.
   a. Silver0
   b. Thing
   c. Undefined
   d. Undefined

157. _____ is a very hard, heavy, steel-gray to white transition metal, it is found in several ores including wolframite and scheelite and is remarkable for its robust physical properties, especially the fact that it has the highest melting point of all the non-alloyed metals and the second highest of all the elements after carbon. The pure form is used mainly in electrical applications.
   a. Thing
   b. Tungsten0
   c. Undefined
   d. Undefined

158. _____ is a chemical element in the periodic table that has the symbol Zn and atomic number 30. In some historical and sculptural contexts, it is known as spelter.
   a. Zinc0
   b. Thing
   c. Undefined
   d. Undefined

159. _____ is a ferrimagnetic mineral one of several iron oxides and a member of the spinel group. The chemical IUPAC name is iron oxide and the common chemical name ferrous-ferric oxide.
   a. Magnetite0
   b. Thing
   c. Undefined
   d. Undefined

160. _____ is the oxide of silicon, chemical formula SiO_2, and is known for its hardness as early as the 16th century. It is a principle component in most types of glass and substances such as concrete.
   a. Silica0
   b. Thing
   c. Undefined
   d. Undefined

161. _____ is a chemical element in the periodic table that has the symbol Sn. This silvery, malleable poor metal that is not easily oxidized in air and resists corrosion is found in many alloys and is used to coat other metals to prevent corrosion. It is obtained chiefly from the mineral cassiterite, where it occurs as an oxide. It is the classic alloying metal to make bronze.
   a. Tin0
   b. Thing
   c. Undefined
   d. Undefined

Chapter 7. Metamorphism, Metamorphic Rocks, and Hydrothermal Rocks

162. A _____ is a deep valley between cliffs often carved from the landscape by a river. Most were formed by a process of long-time erosion from a plateau level. The cliffs form because harder rock strata that are resistant to erosion and weathering remain exposed on the valley walls.
    a. Canyon0
    b. Thing
    c. Undefined
    d. Undefined

163. A _____ is a body of water or other liquid of considerable size contained on a body of land. A vast majority are fresh water, and lie in the Northern Hemisphere at higher latitudes. Most have a natural outflow in the form of a river or stream, but some do not, and lose water solely by evaporation and/or underground seepage.
    a. Lake0
    b. Thing
    c. Undefined
    d. Undefined

164. _____ is a copper iron sulfide mineral that crystallizes in the tetragonal system. It has the chemical composition $CuFeS_2$.
    a. Thing
    b. Chalcopyrite0
    c. Undefined
    d. Undefined

165. A _____ is any disturbed state of an astronomical body's atmosphere, especially affecting its surface, and strongly implying severe weather. It may be marked by strong wind, thunder and lightning, heavy precipitation, such as ice, or wind transporting some substance through the atmosphere.
    a. Thing
    b. Storm0
    c. Undefined
    d. Undefined

166. A _____ is a meteorological phenomenon common in arid and semi-arid regions. Such a storm may result from the passage of a gust front or simply a substantial increase in wind velocity over a wider region. In all instances, the ground must be very dry and loosely consolidated.
    a. Dust storm0
    b. Thing
    c. Undefined
    d. Undefined

167. _____ is a strong mineral acid. It is soluble in water at all concentrations. _____ has many applications, and is one of the top products of the chemical industry. Principal uses include ore processing, fertilizer manufacturing, oil refining, wastewater processing, and chemical synthesis.
    a. Thing
    b. Sulfuric acid0
    c. Undefined
    d. Undefined

168. _____ or sulphur is the chemical element that has the symbol S and atomic number 16. It is an abundant, tasteless, multivalent non-metal. _____, in its native form, is a yellow crystalline solid. In nature, it can be found as the pure element or as sulfide and sulfate minerals. It is an essential element for life and is found in two amino acids, cysteine and methionine.
    a. Thing
    b. Sulfur0
    c. Undefined
    d. Undefined

169. _____ is the process of formation of solid crystals from a uniform solution. It is also a chemical solid-liquid separation technique, in which mass transfer of a solute from the liquid solution to a pure solid crystalline phase occurs.

a. Crystallization0
b. Thing
c. Undefined
d. Undefined

170. _____ is a variety of igneous rock consisting of large-grained crystals, such as feldspar or quartz, dispersed in a fine-grained feldspathic matrix or groundmass. The larger crystals are called phenocrysts.

a. Porphyry0
b. Thing
c. Undefined
d. Undefined

Chapter 8. Time and Geology

1. The _____ is used by geologists and other scientists to describe the timing and relationships between events that have occurred during the history of Earth.
   a. Thing
   b. Geological time scale0
   c. Undefined
   d. Undefined

2. A _____ is a deep valley between cliffs often carved from the landscape by a river. Most were formed by a process of long-time erosion from a plateau level. The cliffs form because harder rock strata that are resistant to erosion and weathering remain exposed on the valley walls.
   a. Thing
   b. Canyon0
   c. Undefined
   d. Undefined

3. The _____ is a very colorful, steep-sided gorge, carved by the Colorado River in the U.S. state of Arizona. It is one of the first national parks in the United States.
   a. Grand Canyon0
   b. Place
   c. Undefined
   d. Undefined

4. A _____ is one of several large landmasses on Earth. They are generally identified by convention rather than any strict criteria, but seven areas are commonly reckoned as continents – they are: Asia, Africa, North America, South America, Antarctica, Europe, and Australia.
   a. Thing
   b. Continent0
   c. Undefined
   d. Undefined

5. Fossils are the mineralized or otherwise preserved remains or traces of animals, plants, and other organisms. The totality of fossils, both discovered and undiscovered, and their placement in fossiliferous rock formations and sedimentary layers is known as the _____ record.
   a. Fossil0
   b. Thing
   c. Undefined
   d. Undefined

6. An _____ is any piece of land that is completely surrounded by water, above high tide. There are two main types of islands: continental islands and oceanic islands. There are also artificial islands. A grouping of geographically and/or geologically related islands is called an archipelago.
   a. Island0
   b. Thing
   c. Undefined
   d. Undefined

7. A _____ is a landform that extends above the surrounding terrain in a limited area. A _____ is generally steeper than a hill, but there is no universally accepted standard definition for the height of a _____ or a hill although a _____ usually has an identifiable summit.
   a. Place
   b. Mountain0
   c. Undefined
   d. Undefined

8. _____ is the substance of which physical objects are composed. _____ can be solid, liquid, plasma or gas. It constitutes the observable universe.
   a. Matter0
   b. Thing
   c. Undefined
   d. Undefined

9. Mean _____ is the average height of the sea, with reference to a suitable reference surface.

a. Sea level0   b. Thing
c. Undefined   d. Undefined

10. _____ rock is one of the three main rock groups. Rock formed from these covers 75% of the Earth's land area, and includes common types such as chalk, limestone, dolomite, sandstone, and shale.
a. Sedimentary0   b. Thing
c. Undefined   d. Undefined

11. _____ is one of the three main rock groups. _____ covers 75% of the Earth's land area. Four basic processes are involved in the formation of a clastic _____: weathering caused mainly by friction of waves, transportation where the sediment is carried along by a current, deposition and compaction where the sediment is squashed together to form a rock of this kind.
a. Sedimentary rock0   b. Thing
c. Undefined   d. Undefined

12. _____ is the science and study of the solid matter that constitute the Earth. Encompassing such things as rocks, soil, and gemstones, _____ studies the composition, structure, physical properties, history, and the processes that shape Earth's components.
a. Geology0   b. Thing
c. Undefined   d. Undefined

13. _____ was a Scottish lawyer, geologist, and populariser of uniformitarianism. Principles of Geology, his first book, was also his most famous, most influential, and most important. First published in three volumes in 1830-33, it established his credentials as an important geological theorist and introduced the doctrine of uniformitarianism.
a. Charles Lyell0   b. Person
c. Undefined   d. Undefined

14. _____ generally denotes the integration of Charles Darwin's theory of the evolution of species by natural selection, Gregor Mendel's theory of genetics as the basis for biological inheritance, random genetic mutation as the source of variation, and mathematical population genetics.
a. Thing   b. Modern evolutionary synthesis0
c. Undefined   d. Undefined

15. _____ was already eminent as an English naturalist when he proposed and provided evidence for the theory that all species have evolved over time from one or a few common ancestors through the process of natural selection. The fact that evolution occurs became accepted by the scientific community and the general public in his lifetime, while his theory of natural selection came to be widely seen as the primary explanation of the process of evolution in the 1930s, and now forms the basis of modern evolutionary theory. In modified form, Darwin's theory remains a cornerstone of biology, as it provides a unifying explanation for the diversity of life.
a. Charles Darwin0   b. Person
c. Undefined   d. Undefined

16. _____ is a phrase which is a shorthand for a concept relating to competition for survival or predominance.
a. Survival of the fittest0   b. Thing
c. Undefined   d. Undefined

Chapter 8. Time and Geology

17. _____ refers to the principle that the same processes that shape the universe occurred in the past as they do now, and that the same laws of physics apply in all parts of the knowable universe.
   a. Thing
   b. Uniformitarianism0
   c. Undefined
   d. Undefined

18. _____ in meteorology are large scale patterns in the atmospheric pressure field that are nearly stationary, effectively "blocking" or redirecting migratory cyclones. These _____ can remain in place for several days or even weeks, causing the areas affected by them to have the same kind of weather for an extended period of time.
   a. Thing
   b. Blocks0
   c. Undefined
   d. Undefined

19. _____ is the native consolidated rock underlying the Earth's surface. Above the _____ is usually an area of broken and weathered unconsolidated rock in the basal subsoil.
   a. Bedrock0
   b. Thing
   c. Undefined
   d. Undefined

20. The principle or _____ states that sediments are deposited under the influence of gravity as nearly horizontal beds. Observations in a wide variety of sedimentary environments support this principle. If we find folded or faulted strata, we know that the layers were deformed by tectonic forces after the sediments were deposited. This principle can be combined with the principle of superposition.
   a. Original horizontality0
   b. Thing
   c. Undefined
   d. Undefined

21. The basic idea of this is that an object, event or entity can be spanned across multiple realities or universes. When combined, these multiple, unique, pan-dimensional segments of the object, consciousness or event, make up parts or constituents of its _____.
   a. Thing
   b. Superposition0
   c. Undefined
   d. Undefined

22. _____ is an igneous rock of volcanic origin. They often have a vesicular texture, which is the result voids left by volatiles escaping from the molten lava. Pumice is a rock, which is an example of explosive volcanic eruption. It is so vesicular that it floats in water.
   a. Thing
   b. Volcanic rock0
   c. Undefined
   d. Undefined

23. The _____ is an axiom that forms one of the bases of the sciences of geology, archaeology, and other fields dealing with stratigraphy. In its plainest form, that is: layers are arranged in a time sequence, with the oldest on the bottom and the youngest on the top, unless later processes disturb this arrangement.
   a. Thing
   b. Law of Superposition0
   c. Undefined
   d. Undefined

24. _____ is any particulate matter that can be transported by fluid flow and which eventually is deposited as a layer of solid particles on the bed or bottom of a body of water or other liquid.
   a. Sediment0
   b. Thing
   c. Undefined
   d. Undefined

Chapter 8. Time and Geology

25. _____ is molten rock expelled by a volcano during an eruption. When first extruded from a volcanic vent, it is a liquid at temperatures from 700 °C to 1,200 °C.
    a. Lava0
    b. Thing
    c. Undefined
    d. Undefined

26. A _____ is a deep V-shaped valley formed by erosion. It may contain a small stream or dry creek bed and is usually larger in size than a gully. Occasionally, sudden intense rainfall may produce flash floods in the area of the _____.
    a. Gulch0
    b. Thing
    c. Undefined
    d. Undefined

27. _____ is a sedimentary rock composed largely of the mineral calcite. _____ often contains variable amounts of silica in the form of chert or flint, as well as varying amounts of clay, silt and sand as disseminations, nodules, or layers within the rock. The primary source of the calcite in _____ is most commonly marine organisms. These organisms secrete shells that settle out of the water column and are deposited on ocean floors as pelagic ooze or alternatively is conglomerated in a coral reef.
    a. Limestone0
    b. Thing
    c. Undefined
    d. Undefined

28. The _____ states that layers of sediment initially extend laterally in all directions; in other words, they are laterally continuous. As a result, rocks that are otherwise similar, but are now separated by a valley or other erosional feature, can be assumed to be originally continuous.
    a. Thing
    b. Principle of lateral continuity0
    c. Undefined
    d. Undefined

29. In geology, a _____ is a depression with predominant extent in one direction. The terms U-shaped and V-shaped are descriptive terms of geography to characterize the form of valleys. Most valleys belong to one of these two main types or a mixture of them, at least with respect of the cross section of the slopes or hillsides.
    a. Valley0
    b. Thing
    c. Undefined
    d. Undefined

30. _____ is the geological process whereby material is added to a landform. This is the process by which wind and water create a sediment deposit, through the laying down of granular material that has been eroded and transported from another geographical location.
    a. Thing
    b. Deposition0
    c. Undefined
    d. Undefined

31. _____ is a common and widely occurring type of intrusive, felsic, igneous rock. Granites are usually medium to coarsely crystalline, occasionally with some individual crystals larger than the groundmass forming a rock known as porphyry. Granites can be pink to dark gray or even black, depending on their chemistry and mineralogy.
    a. Granite0
    b. Thing
    c. Undefined
    d. Undefined

32. An _____ is a body of igneous rock that has crystallized from a molten magma below the surface of the Earth.

Chapter 8. Time and Geology

a. Thing
b. Intrusion0
c. Undefined
d. Undefined

33. _____ is displacement of solids by the agents of ocean currents, wind, water, or ice by downward or down-slope movement in response to gravity or by living organisms.
   a. Erosion0
   b. Thing
   c. Undefined
   d. Undefined

34. A _____ is an intrusion into a cross-cutting fissure, meaning a _____ cuts across other pre-existing layers or bodies of rock, this means that a _____ is always younger than the rocks that contain it. The thickness is usually much smaller than the other two dimensions. Thickness can vary from sub-centimeter scale to many meters in thickness and the lateral dimensions can extend over many kilometers.
   a. Dike0
   b. Thing
   c. Undefined
   d. Undefined

35. A _____ is a body of water with a current, confined within a bed and banks. Streams are important as conduits in the water cycle, instruments in aquifer recharge, and corridors for fish and wildlife migration.
   a. Stream0
   b. Thing
   c. Undefined
   d. Undefined

36. _____ can be defined as the solid state recrystallisation of pre-existing rocks due to changes in heat and/or pressure and/or introduction of fluids. There will be mineralogical, chemical and crystallographic changes. _____ produced with increasing pressure and temperature conditions is known as prograde _____. Conversely, decreasing temperatures and pressure characterize retrograde _____.
   a. Thing
   b. Metamorphism0
   c. Undefined
   d. Undefined

37. The _____ refers to a group of medium-grade metamorphic rocks, chiefly notable for the preponderance of lamellar minerals such as micas, chlorite, talc, hornblende, graphite, and others. Quartz often occurs in drawn-out grains to such an extent that a particular form called quartz _____ is produced.
   a. Thing
   b. Schist0
   c. Undefined
   d. Undefined

38. _____ is a small island located in the middle of San Francisco Bay in California, United States. It served as a lighthouse, then a military fortification, then a military prison followed by a federal prison until 1963, when it became a national recreation area.
   a. Place
   b. Alcatraz Island0
   c. Undefined
   d. Undefined

39. An _____ is a buried erosion surface separating two rock masses or strata of different ages, indicating that sediment deposition was not continuous. In general, the older layer was exposed to erosion for an interval of time before deposition of the younger, but the term is used to describe any break in the sedimentary geologic record.
   a. Thing
   b. Unconformity0
   c. Undefined
   d. Undefined

Chapter 8. Time and Geology

40. A _____ is an unconformity between parallel layers of sedimentary rocks which represents a period of erosion or non-deposition.
   a. Thing
   b. Disconformity0
   c. Undefined
   d. Undefined

41. _____ is an unconformity where horizontally parallel strata of sedimentary rock are deposited on tilted and eroded layers that may be either vertical or at an angle to the overlying horizontal layers
   a. Angular unconformity0
   b. Thing
   c. Undefined
   d. Undefined

42. _____ is the result of the transformation of a pre-existing rock type, the protolith, in a process called metamorphism, which means "change in form". The protolith is subjected to heat and extreme pressure causing profound physical and/or chemical change. The protolith may be sedimentary rock, igneous rock or another older rock.
   a. Thing
   b. Metamorphic rock0
   c. Undefined
   d. Undefined

43. In geology, a _____ is the outermost layer of a planet, part of its lithosphere. They are generally composed of a less dense material than its deeper layers. Earths' is composed mainly of basalt and granite. It is cooler and more rigid than the deeper layers of the mantle and core.
   a. Thing
   b. Crust0
   c. Undefined
   d. Undefined

44. _____ rocks form when molten rock, magma, cools and solidifies, with or without crystallization, either below the surface as intrusive, plutonic rocks or on the surface as extrusive, volcanic, rocks.
   a. Thing
   b. Igneous0
   c. Undefined
   d. Undefined

45. _____ is the process of formation of solid crystals from a uniform solution. It is also a chemical solid-liquid separation technique, in which mass transfer of a solute from the liquid solution to a pure solid crystalline phase occurs.
   a. Thing
   b. Crystallization0
   c. Undefined
   d. Undefined

46. A _____ in geology is an intrusive igneous rock body that crystallized from a magma below the surface of the Earth. Plutons include batholiths, dikes, sills, laccoliths, lopoliths, and other igneous bodies. In practice, "_____" usually refers to a distinctive mass of igneous rock, typically kilometers in dimension, without a tabular shape like those of dikes and sills.
   a. Pluton0
   b. Thing
   c. Undefined
   d. Undefined

47. _____, a branch of geology, studies rock layers and layering. It is primarily used in the study of sedimentary and layered volcanic rocks. _____ includes two related subfields: lithologic or lithostratigraphy and biologic _____ or biostratigraphy.
   a. Thing
   b. Stratigraphy0
   c. Undefined
   d. Undefined

Chapter 8. Time and Geology

48. _____ is a sedimentary rock composed mainly of sand-size mineral or rock grains. Most _____ is composed of quartz and/or feldspar because these are the most common minerals in the Earth's crust. Like sand, _____ may be any color, but the most common colors are tan, brown, yellow, red, gray and white.
   a. Thing
   b. Sandstone0
   c. Undefined
   d. Undefined

49. A _____ is a significant vertical, or near vertical, rock exposure. Cliffs are categorized as erosion landforms due to the processes of erosion and weathering that produce them. Cliffs are common on coasts, in mountainous areas, escarpments and along rivers. Cliffs are usually formed by rock that is resistant to erosion and weathering.
   a. Thing
   b. Cliff0
   c. Undefined
   d. Undefined

50. The _____ is the earliest of three geologic eras of the Phanerozoic eon. The _____ is subdivided into six geologic periods; from oldest to youngest they are: the Cambrian, Ordovician, Silurian, Devonian, Carboniferous, and Permian.
   a. Paleozoic0
   b. Thing
   c. Undefined
   d. Undefined

51. Metamorphic rock is the result of the transformation of a pre-existing rock type, the protolith, in a process called metamorphism. The protolith is subjected to heat and extreme pressure causing profound physical and/or chemical change. _____ make up a large part of the Earth's crust. They are formed deep beneath the Earth's surface by great stresses from rocks above and high pressures and temperatures.
   a. Metamorphic rocks0
   b. Thing
   c. Undefined
   d. Undefined

52. The _____ is an informal name for the eons of the geologic timescale that came before the current Phanerozoic eon. It spans from the formation of Earth around 4500 Ma to the evolution of abundant macroscopic hard-shelled animals, which marked the beginning of the Cambrian, the first period of the first era of the Phanerozoic eon, some 542 Ma.
   a. Precambrian0
   b. Thing
   c. Undefined
   d. Undefined

53. _____ has penetrative planar fabric present within it. It is common to rocks affected by regional metamorphic compression typical of orogenic belts.
   a. Thing
   b. Foliated metamorphic rock0
   c. Undefined
   d. Undefined

54. _____ is a United States National Park located in the Southwestern United States, near Springdale, Utah. Located at the junction of the Colorado Plateau, Great Basin, and Mojave Desert regions, this unique geography and variety of life zones allow for unusual plant and animal diversity.
   a. Place
   b. Zion National Park0
   c. Undefined
   d. Undefined

55. A _____ is a hill of sand built by eolian processes. Dunes are subject to different forms and sizes based on their interaction with the wind. Most kinds of _____ are longer on the windward side where the sand is pushed up the _____, and a shorter in the lee of the wind. The trough between dunes is called a slack. A "_____ field" is an area covered by extensive sand dunes. Large _____ fields are known as ergs.

Chapter 8. Time and Geology

a. Thing
b. Dune0
c. Undefined
d. Undefined

56. _____ is a fine-grained sedimentary rock whose original constituents were clays or muds. It is characterized by thin laminae breaking with an irregular curving fracture, often splintery and usually parallel to the often-indistinguishable bedding plane.
   a. Shale0
   b. Thing
   c. Undefined
   d. Undefined

57. _____ is a common gray to black extrusive volcanic rock. It is usually fine-grained due to rapid cooling of lava on the Earth's surface. It may be porphyritic containing larger crystals in a fine matrix, or vesicular, or frothy scoria.
   a. Basalt0
   b. Thing
   c. Undefined
   d. Undefined

58. The _____ is one of three geologic eras of the Phanerozoic eon. The _____ was a time of tectonic, climatic and evolutionary activity, shifting from a state of connectedness into their present configuration. The climate was exceptionally warm throughout the period, also playing an important role in the evolution and diversification of new animal species. By the end of the era, the basis of modern life was in place.
   a. Thing
   b. Mesozoic0
   c. Undefined
   d. Undefined

59. _____ is a fossil fuel formed in swamp ecosystems where plant remains were saved by water and mud from oxidization and biodegradation. It is a sedimentary rock, but the harder forms, such as anthracite _____, can be regarded as metamorphic rocks because of later exposure to elevated temperature and pressure. It is composed primarily of carbon along with assorted other elements, including sulfur.
   a. Thing
   b. Coal0
   c. Undefined
   d. Undefined

60. _____ was an English geologist, credited with creating the first nationwide geologic map. He is known as the "Father of English Geology", however recognition was slow in coming. His work was plagiarised, he was financially ruined, and he spent time in debtors' prison. It was only much later in his life that Smith received recognition for his accomplishments.
   a. Person
   b. William Smith0
   c. Undefined
   d. Undefined

61. The _____ holds that sedimentary rock strata are observed to contain fossilised flora and fauna, and that these fossil forms succeed each other in a specific, reliable order that can be identified over wide distances.
   a. Faunal succession0
   b. Thing
   c. Undefined
   d. Undefined

62. In biology and ecology, _____ is the cessation of existence of a species or group of taxa, reducing biodiversity. The moment of _____ is generally considered to be the death of the last individual of that species.
   a. Extinction0
   b. Thing
   c. Undefined
   d. Undefined

Chapter 8. Time and Geology

63. The _____ is the part of the earth, including air, land, surface rocks, and water, within which life occurs, and which biotic processes in turn alter or transform. From the broadest biophysiological point of view, the _____ is the global ecological system integrating all living beings and their relationships, including their interaction with the elements of the lithosphere, hydrosphere, and atmosphere. This _____ is postulated to have evolved, beginning through a process of biogenesis or biopoesis, at least some 3.5 billion years ago.
   a. Thing
   b. Biosphere0
   c. Undefined
   d. Undefined

64. _____ are organisms without a cell nucleus or any other membrane-bound organelles. Most are unicellular, but some are multicellular.
   a. Thing
   b. Prokaryotes0
   c. Undefined
   d. Undefined

65. Animals, plants, fungi, and protists are _____, organisms with a complex cell or cells, where the genetic material is organized into a membrane-bound nucleus or nuclei.
   a. Eukaryotes0
   b. Thing
   c. Undefined
   d. Undefined

66. _____ encompass several groups of relatively simple living aquatic organisms that capture light energy through photosynthesis, using it to convert inorganic substances into organic matter.
   a. Thing
   b. Algae0
   c. Undefined
   d. Undefined

67. An _____ is a long period of time with different technical and colloquial meanings, and usages in language. It begins with some beginning event known as an epoch, epochal date, epochal event or epochal moment.
   a. Era0
   b. Thing
   c. Undefined
   d. Undefined

68. The _____ Era meaning "new life", is the most recent of the three classic geological eras. It covers the 65.5 million years since the Cretaceous-Tertiary extinction event at the end of the Cretaceous that marked the demise of the last non-avian dinosaurs and the end of the Mesozoic Era. The _____ era is ongoing.
   a. Cenozoic0
   b. Thing
   c. Undefined
   d. Undefined

69. The _____ is the most recent of the three classic geological eras. It covers the 65.5 million years since the Cretaceous-Tertiary extinction event at the end of the Cretaceous that marked the demise of the last non-avian dinosaurs and the end of the Mesozoic Era.
   a. Cenozoic era0
   b. Thing
   c. Undefined
   d. Undefined

70. The _____ is a major division of the geologic timescale. The _____ is the earliest period in whose rocks are found numerous large, distinctly fossilizable multicellular organisms that are more complex than sponges or medusoids. During this time, roughly fifty separate major groups of organisms or "phyla" emerged suddenly, in most cases without evident precursors. This radiation of animal phyla is referred to as the _____ explosion.

a. Cambrian0 b. Event
c. Undefined d. Undefined

71. _____ are extinct arthropods. They appeared in the second Epoch of the Cambrian period and flourished throughout the lower Paleozoic era before beginning a drawn-out decline to extinction when all _____, with the sole exception of Proetida, died out. The last of the _____ disappeared in the mass extinction at the end of the Permian.
a. Trilobites0 b. Thing
c. Undefined d. Undefined

72. _____ are fish with a full cartilaginous skeleton and a streamlined body. They respire with the use of five to seven gill slits.
a. Thing b. Sharks0
c. Undefined d. Undefined

73. The _____ is a geologic period of the Paleozoic era. During the _____ the first fish evolved legs and started to walk on land as tetrapods and the first insects and spiders also started to colonize terrestrial habitats. The first seed-bearing plants spread across dry land, forming huge forests. In the oceans, Primitive sharks became more numerous. The first ammonite mollusks appeared, and trilobites as well as great coral reefs were still common.
a. Devonian0 b. Thing
c. Undefined d. Undefined

74. _____ are a taxon of animals that include all living tetrapods or four-legged vertebrates, that do not have amniotic eggs, are ectothermic, term for the animals whose body heat is regulated by the external environment; previously known as cold-blooded, and generally spend part of their time on land.
a. Thing b. Amphibians0
c. Undefined d. Undefined

75. _____ are tetrapods and amniotes, animals whose embryos are surrounded by an amniotic membrane, and members of the class Sauropsida.They rely on gathering and losing heat from the environment to regulate their internal temperature, e.g, by moving between sun and shade, or by preferential circulation — moving warmed blood into the body core, while pushing cool blood to the periphery.
a. Reptiles0 b. Thing
c. Undefined d. Undefined

76. The _____ is an epoch of the Carboniferous period lasting from roughly 325 Ma to 299 Ma. As with most other geologic periods, the rock beds that define the period are well identified, but the exact date of the start and end are uncertain by a few million years.
a. Thing b. Pennsylvanian0
c. Undefined d. Undefined

77. _____ is the scientific study of the distribution and abundance of living organisms and how the distribution and abundance are affected by interactions between the organisms and their environment.
a. Ecology0 b. Thing
c. Undefined d. Undefined

Chapter 8. Time and Geology

78. _____ were vertebrate animals that dominated terrestrial ecosystems for over 160 million years, first appearing approximately 230 million years ago. At the end of the Cretaceous Period, approximately 65 million years ago, a catastrophic extinction event ended _____' dominance on land.
   a. Dinosaurs0
   b. Thing
   c. Undefined
   d. Undefined

79. The _____ is the longest geological period and constitutes nearly half of the Mesozoic. The end of the Cretaceous defines the boundary between the Mesozoic and Cenozoic eras. The Cretaceous as a separate period was first defined using strata in the Paris Basin and named for the extensive beds of chalk.
   a. Cretaceous Period0
   b. Thing
   c. Undefined
   d. Undefined

80. The term _____ is ambiguous: it can refer to all cetaceans, to just the larger ones, or only to members of particular families within the order Cetacea.
   a. Whales0
   b. Thing
   c. Undefined
   d. Undefined

81. _____ are a major group of arthropods and the most diverse group of animals on the Earth, with over a million described species—more than all other animal groups combined. They may be found in nearly all environments on the planet, although only a small number of species occur in the oceans where crustaceans tend to predominate instead.
   a. Insects0
   b. Thing
   c. Undefined
   d. Undefined

82. _____, palaeontology or palæontology is the study of prehistoric life forms on Earth through the examination of plant and animal fossils. This includes the study of body fossils, tracks, burrows, cast-off parts, fossilised faeces, palynomorphs and chemical residues. See also paleoanthropology.
   a. Paleontology0
   b. Thing
   c. Undefined
   d. Undefined

83. _____ are people who study prehistoric life forms on Earth through the examination of plant and animal fossils. This includes the study of body fossils, tracks, burrows, cast-off parts, fossilised faeces, palynomorphs and chemical residues.
   a. Paleontologists0
   b. Person
   c. Undefined
   d. Undefined

84. In science, the term _____ refers to a rational approach to the study of the universe, which is understood as obeying rules or laws of natural origin.
   a. Thing
   b. Natural science0
   c. Undefined
   d. Undefined

85. The _____ is the first epoch of the Palaeogene Period in the modern Cenozoic era. The _____ immediately followed the mass extinction event at the end of the Cretaceous, which marks the demise of the dinosaurs. The die-off of the dinosaurs left unfilled ecological niches worldwide, and the name _____ refers to the older, new fauna that arose during the epoch, prior to the emergence of modern mammalian orders in the Eocene.

Chapter 8. Time and Geology

a. Thing
b. Paleocene0
c. Undefined
d. Undefined

86. The _____ is a major division of the geologic timescale that extends from the end of the Ordovician period to the beginning of the Devonian period. The base of the _____ is set at a major extinction event when 60% of marine species were wiped out.
   a. Silurian0
   b. Thing
   c. Undefined
   d. Undefined

87. _____ is the first period of the Mesozoic Era. Both the start and end of the _____ are marked by major extinction events. During the _____, both marine and continental life show an adaptive radiation beginning from the starkly impoverished biosphere that followed the Permian-_____ extinction. Corals of the hexacorallia group made their first appearance. The first flowering plants may have evolved during the _____, as did the first flying vertebrates, the pterosaurs.
   a. Triassic0
   b. Event
   c. Undefined
   d. Undefined

88. The _____ is the last period of the Palaeozoic Era. As the _____ opened, the Earth was still in the grip of an ice age, so the polar regions were covered with deep layers of ice. During the _____, all the Earth's major land masses except portions of East Asia were collected into a single supercontinent known as Pangaea. The _____ ended with the most extensive extinction event recorded in paleontology: the _____-Triassic extinction event.
   a. Thing
   b. Permian0
   c. Undefined
   d. Undefined

89. The _____ Epoch is a period of time that extends from about 23.03 to 5.332 million years before the present. As with other older geologic periods, the rock beds that define the start and end are well identified but the exact dates of the start and end of the period are uncertain.
   a. Miocene0
   b. Thing
   c. Undefined
   d. Undefined

90. The _____ was an epoch of the Carboniferous period lasting from roughly 360 to 325 Ma. As with most other geologic periods, the rock beds that define the period are well identified, but the exact start and end dates are uncertain by a few million years.
   a. Thing
   b. Mississippian0
   c. Undefined
   d. Undefined

91. The _____ is a major division of the geologic timescale that extends from the end of the Devonian period to the beginning of the Permian period. As with most older geologic periods, the rock beds that define the period's start and end are well identified, but the exact dates are uncertain. The first third of the _____ is called the Mississippian epoch, and the remainder is called the Pennsylvanian.
   a. Thing
   b. Carboniferous0
   c. Undefined
   d. Undefined

92. The _____ is the second of the six periods of the Paleozoic era. It follows the Cambrian period and is followed by the Silurian period. The _____ started at a major extinction called the Cambrian-_____ extinction and lasted for about 44.6 million years. It ended with another major extinction event that wiped out 60% of marine genera.

Chapter 8. Time and Geology

    a. Thing
    c. Undefined
    b. Ordovician0
    d. Undefined

93. The _____ is part of the Neogene and Quaternary periods. Human civilization dates entirely within the _____. The _____ was preceded by the Younger Dryas cold period, the final part of the Pleistocene epoch. The _____ starts late in the retreat of the Pleistocene glaciers. It can be considered an interglacial in the current ice age.
    a. Thing
    c. Undefined
    b. Holocene0
    d. Undefined

94. The _____ consists of the Sun and the other celestial objects gravitationally bound to it: the eight planets, their 165 known moons, three currently identified dwarf planets and their four known moons, and billions of small bodies.
    a. Thing
    c. Undefined
    b. Solar system0
    d. Undefined

95. An _____ is a natural unit consisting of all plants, animals and micro organisms in an area functioning together with all the non living physical factors of the environment.
    a. Thing
    c. Undefined
    b. Ecosystem0
    d. Undefined

96. A _____ in physical geography describes the collective mass of water found on, under, and over the surface of a planet.
    a. Hydrosphere0
    c. Undefined
    b. Thing
    d. Undefined

97. An _____ is a layer of gases that may surround a material body of sufficient mass. The gases are attracted by the gravity of the body, and are retained for a longer duration if gravity is high and the _____'s temperature is low. Some planets consist mainly of various gases, and thus have very deep atmospheres.
    a. Place
    c. Undefined
    b. Atmosphere0
    d. Undefined

98. _____ is the average and variations of weather over long periods of time. _____ zones can be defined using parameters such as temperature and rainfall.
    a. Thing
    c. Undefined
    b. Climate0
    d. Undefined

99. _____ refers to the variation in the Earth's global climate or in regional climates over time. It describes changes in the variability or average state of the atmosphere over time scales ranging from decades to millions of years. These changes can be caused by processes internal to the Earth, external forces or, more recently, human activities.
    a. Thing
    c. Undefined
    b. Climate change0
    d. Undefined

100. _____ was a famed Nobel Prize-winning physicist who won the 1968 Nobel Prize in Physics for "the discovery of a large number of resonance states, made possible through his development of the technique of using hydrogen bubble chamber and data analysis". Specifically, his research made it possible to record and study the short lived particles created in particle accelerators..

a. Luis Alvarez0   b. Person
c. Undefined   d. Undefined

101. _____ was the son of Nobel Prize winning physicist Luis Alvarez. Alvarez and his father are most widely known for their discovery boundary was highly enriched in the element iridium. Since iridium enrichment is common in asteroids, but very uncommon on the Earth, they further postulated that the layer had been created by the impact of a large asteroid with the Earth and that this impact event was the likely cause of the Cretaceous-Tertiary extinction event.
     a. Walter Alvarez0   b. Person
     c. Undefined   d. Undefined

102. _____ are a class of astronomical objects. The term is generally used to indicate a diverse group of small celestial bodies that drift in the solar system in orbit around the Sun.
     a. Thing   b. Asteroids0
     c. Undefined   d. Undefined

103. _____ are small bodies in the solar system that orbit the Sun and occasionally exhibit a coma or atmosphere and/or a tail — both primarily from the effects of solar radiation upon its nucleus, which itself is a minor body composed of rock, dust, and ice.
     a. Comets0   b. Thing
     c. Undefined   d. Undefined

104. _____ is a chemical element. A dense, very hard, brittle, silvery-white transition metal of the platinum family, it is used in high strength alloys that can withstand high temperatures and occurs in natural alloys with platinum or osmium. It is notable for being the most corrosion resistant element known and for its significance in the determination of the probable cause of the demise, by a meteorite strike, of the dinosaurs. It is used in high temperature apparatus, electrical contacts, and as a hardening agent for platinum.
     a. Thing   b. Iridium0
     c. Undefined   d. Undefined

105. A _____ is a natural object originating in outer space that survives an impact with the Earth's surface without being destroyed. While in space it is called a meteoroid. When it enters the atmosphere, air resistance causes the body to heat up and emit light, thus forming a fireball.
     a. Meteorite0   b. Thing
     c. Undefined   d. Undefined

106. A _____ is an approximately circular depression in the surface of a planet, moon or other solid body in the Solar System, formed by the hyper-velocity impact of a smaller body with the surface. Impact craters typically have raised rims, and they range from small, simple, bowl-shaped depressions to large, complex, multi-ringed, impact basins.
     a. Thing   b. Crater0
     c. Undefined   d. Undefined

107. A _____ is the fringe of land at the edge of a large body of water, such as an ocean, sea, or lake. A strict definition is the strip of land along a water body that is alternately exposed and covered by waves and tides.
     a. Thing   b. Shoreline0
     c. Undefined   d. Undefined

108. A _____ is a disturbance that propagates through space or spacetime, transferring energy and momentum and sometimes angular momentum.
   a. Thing
   b. Wave0
   c. Undefined
   d. Undefined

109. _____ in the broad sense is the total spectrum of the electromagnetic radiation given off by the Sun. On Earth, it is filtered through the atmosphere, and the solar radiation is obvious as daylight when the Sun is above the horizon.
   a. Thing
   b. Sunlight0
   c. Undefined
   d. Undefined

110. _____ is the second most common mineral in the Earth's continental crust. It is made up of a lattice of silica tetrahedra. _____ belongs to the rhombohedral crystal system. In nature _____ crystals are often twinned, distorted, or so intergrown with adjacent crystals of _____ or other minerals as to only show part of this shape, or to lack obvious crystal faces altogether and appear massive.
   a. Thing
   b. Quartz0
   c. Undefined
   d. Undefined

111. The _____ is defined as the part of the land adjoining or near the ocean. A coastline is properly a line on a map indicating the disposition of a _____, but the word is often used to refer to the _____ itself. The adjective coastal describes something as being on, near to, or associated with a _____.
   a. Coast0
   b. Place
   c. Undefined
   d. Undefined

112. The _____ separates the Caribbean Sea from the Gulf of Mexico. The peninsula lies east of the Isthmus of Tehuantepec, a northwestern geographic partition separating the region of Central America from the rest of North America.
   a. Yucatan peninsula0
   b. Place
   c. Undefined
   d. Undefined

113. _____ is a rock composed of angular fragments of rocks or minerals in a matrix, that is a cementing material, that may be similar or different in composition to the fragments.
   a. Breccia0
   b. Thing
   c. Undefined
   d. Undefined

114. _____ is a common and widely distributed type of rock formed by high-grade regional metamorphic processes from preexisting formations that were originally either igneous or sedimentary rocks. Gneissic rocks are usually medium to coarse foliated and largely recrystallized but do not carry large quantities of micas, chlorite or other platy minerals.
   a. Thing
   b. Gneiss0
   c. Undefined
   d. Undefined

115. A _____ is a naturally occurring substance formed through geological processes that has a characteristic chemical composition, a highly ordered atomic structure and specific physical properties. A rock, by comparison, is an aggregate of minerals and need not have a specific chemical composition. Minerals range in composition from pure elements and simple salts to very complex silicates with thousands of known forms.
   a. Mineral0
   b. Thing
   c. Undefined
   d. Undefined

Chapter 8. Time and Geology

116. _____ is a mineral belonging to the group of nesosilicates. Its chemical name is zirconium silicate and its corresponding chemical formula is ZrSiO4.
- a. Zircon0
- b. Thing
- c. Undefined
- d. Undefined

117. A _____ is a solid in which the constituent atoms, molecules, or ions are packed in a regularly ordered, repeating pattern extending in all three spatial dimensions. Most metals encountered in everyday life are polycrystals. Crystals are often symmetrically intergrown to form _____ twins.
- a. Crystal0
- b. Thing
- c. Undefined
- d. Undefined

118. _____ is molten rock located beneath the surface of the Earth, and which often collects in a _____ chamber. _____ is a complex high-temperature fluid substance. Most are silicate solutions. It is capable of intrusion into adjacent rocks or of extrusion onto the surface as lava or ejected explosively as tephra to form pyroclastic rock. Environments of _____ formation include subduction zones, continental rift zones, mid-oceanic ridges, and hotspots, some of which are interpreted as mantle plumes.
- a. Thing
- b. Magma0
- c. Undefined
- d. Undefined

119. _____ is the process in which an unstable atomic nucleus loses energy by emitting radiation in the form of particles or electromagnetic waves.
- a. Thing
- b. Radioactive decay0
- c. Undefined
- d. Undefined

120. An _____ is a type of atom that is defined by its atomic number; that is, by the number of protons in its nucleus.
- a. Element0
- b. Thing
- c. Undefined
- d. Undefined

121. _____ is a technique used to date materials based on a knowledge of the decay rates of naturally occurring isotopes, and the current abundances. It is the principal source of information about the age of the Earth and a significant source of information about rates of evolutionary change.
- a. Thing
- b. Radiometric dating0
- c. Undefined
- d. Undefined

122. In optics, _____ is the field that studies the measurement of electromagnetic radiation, including visible light. Note that light is also measured using the techniques of photometry, which deal with brightness as perceived by the human eye, rather than absolute power.
- a. Thing
- b. Radiometry0
- c. Undefined
- d. Undefined

123. In physics, the _____ is a subatomic particle with no net electric charge.
- a. Neutron0
- b. Thing
- c. Undefined
- d. Undefined

124. _____ are the fundamental building blocks of chemistry, and are conserved in chemical reactions.

Chapter 8. Time and Geology

a. Thing
b. Atoms0
c. Undefined
d. Undefined

125. _____ are any of the several different forms of an element each having different atomic mass. _____ of an element have nuclei with the same number of protons but different numbers of neutrons.
   a. Thing
   b. Isotopes0
   c. Undefined
   d. Undefined

126. In physics, the _____ is a subatomic particle with an electric charge of one positive fundamental unit a diameter of about 1.5×10^{-15} m, and a mass of 938.27231(28) MeV/c2 (1.6726×10^{-27} kg), 1.007 276 466 88(13) u or about 1836 times the mass of an electron.
   a. Thing
   b. Proton0
   c. Undefined
   d. Undefined

127. _____ is approximately 70% more dense than lead and is weakly radioactive. It occurs naturally in low concentrations in soil, rock and water.
   a. Uranium0
   b. Thing
   c. Undefined
   d. Undefined

128. A _____, also called a Geiger-Müller counter, is a type of particle detector that measures ionizing radiation. Geiger counters are used to detect ionizing radiation, usually alpha and beta radiation, but also other types of radiation as well.
   a. Thing
   b. Geiger counter0
   c. Undefined
   d. Undefined

129. The _____ A, also called atomic _____ or nucleon number, is the number of nucleons in an atomic nucleus. The _____ is unique for each isotope of an element and is written either after the element name or as a superscript to the left of an element's symbol. For example, carbon-12 has 6 protons and 6 neutrons.
   a. Thing
   b. Mass number0
   c. Undefined
   d. Undefined

130. _____ is a type of radioactive decay in which an atomic nucleus emits an alpha particle and transforms into an atom with a mass number 4 less and atomic number 2 less.
   a. Alpha decay0
   b. Thing
   c. Undefined
   d. Undefined

131. In chemistry and physics, the _____ is the number of protons found in the nucleus of an atom. It is traditionally represented by the symbol Z.
   a. Atomic number0
   b. Thing
   c. Undefined
   d. Undefined

132. The _____ is a fundamental subatomic particle that carries a negative electric charge.
   a. Electron0
   b. Thing
   c. Undefined
   d. Undefined

133. In nuclear physics, _____ is a type of radioactive decay in which a beta particle, an electron or a positron, is emitted.
   a. Thing
   b. Beta decay0
   c. Undefined
   d. Undefined

134. In nuclear physics, a decay product, also known as a _____, daughter isotope or daughter nuclide, is a nuclide resulting from the radioactive decay of a parent isotope or precursor nuclide. The _____ may be stable or it may decay to form a _____ of its own. The daughter of a _____ is sometimes called a granddaughter product.
   a. Thing
   b. Daughter product0
   c. Undefined
   d. Undefined

135. A _____, in inorganic chemistry, is a salt of phosphoric acid. In organic chemistry it is an ester of phosphoric acid.
   a. Phosphate0
   b. Thing
   c. Undefined
   d. Undefined

136. The _____ is an agency of the federal government of the United States charged with protecting human health and with safeguarding the natural environment: air, water, and land.
   a. Environmental Protection Agency0
   b. Person
   c. Undefined
   d. Undefined

137. A _____ is a wet place where a liquid, usually groundwater, has oozed from the ground to the surface. They are usually not flowing, with the liquid sourced only from underground. The term may also refer to the movement of liquid hydrocarbons to the surface through fractures and fissures in the rock and between geological layers. It may be a significant source of pollution.
   a. Thing
   b. Seep0
   c. Undefined
   d. Undefined

138. _____ is one of the four seasons of temperate zones. Almost all English-language calendars, going by astronomy, state that _____ begins on the _____ solstice, and ends on the spring equinox. Calculated more by the weather, it begins and ends earlier and is the season with the shortest days and the lowest temperatures.
   a. Thing
   b. Winter0
   c. Undefined
   d. Undefined

139. _____ is a chemical element. It is a soft silvery-white metallic alkali metal that occurs naturally bound to other elements in seawater and many minerals. It oxidizes rapidly in air and is very reactive, especially towards water. In many respects, it and sodium are chemically similar, although organisms in general, and animal cells in particular, treat them very differently.
   a. Potassium0
   b. Thing
   c. Undefined
   d. Undefined

140. A _____ is a process that results in the interconversion of chemical substances. The substance or substances initially involved in a _____ are called reactants. Chemical reactions are characterized by a chemical change, and they yield one or more products which are, in general, different from the reactants.

Chapter 8. Time and Geology

    a. Thing
    b. Chemical reaction0
    c. Undefined
    d. Undefined

141. _____, is a radioactive isotope of carbon discovered on February 27, 1940, by Martin Kamen and Sam Ruben. Its nucleus contains 6 protons and 8 neutrons. Its presence in organic materials is used extensively as basis of the _____ dating method to date archaeological, geological, and hydrogeological samples.
    a. Radiocarbon0
    b. Thing
    c. Undefined
    d. Undefined

142. _____ is a chemical element. An abundant nonmetallic, tetravalent element, _____ has several allotropic forms. This element is the basis of the chemistry of all known life.
    a. Carbon0
    b. Thing
    c. Undefined
    d. Undefined

143. _____ is a chemical element which has the symbol N and atomic number 7. Elemental _____ is a colorless, odourless, tasteless and mostly inert diatomic gas at standard conditions, constituting 78.1% by volume of Earth's atmosphere.
    a. Thing
    b. Nitrogen0
    c. Undefined
    d. Undefined

144. _____ as used in physics, is energy in the form of waves or moving subatomic particles.
    a. Radiation0
    b. Thing
    c. Undefined
    d. Undefined

145. In biology and ecology, an _____ is a living complex adaptive system of organs that influence each other in such a way that they function in some way as a stable whole.
    a. Thing
    b. Organism0
    c. Undefined
    d. Undefined

146. An _____ is a period of long-term reduction in the temperature of Earth's climate, resulting in an expansion of the continental ice sheets, polar ice sheets and mountain glaciers .
    a. Thing
    b. Ice Age0
    c. Undefined
    d. Undefined

147. A _____ is a large, slow moving river of ice, formed from compacted layers of snow, that slowly deforms and flows in response to gravity. _____ ice is the largest reservoir of fresh water on Earth, and second only to oceans as the largest reservoir of total water. Glaciers cover vast areas of polar regions but are restricted to the highest mountains in the tropics.
    a. Glacier0
    b. Thing
    c. Undefined
    d. Undefined

148. In geology, _____ are rock s with a grain size of usually no less than 256 mm diameter.
    a. Thing
    b. Boulders0
    c. Undefined
    d. Undefined

Chapter 8. Time and Geology

149. _____ literally translates to equal tension. An _____ cellular environment occurs when an equal solute concentration exists inside and outside the cell.
   a. Thing
   b. Isotonic0
   c. Undefined
   d. Undefined

150. In thermodynamics, a _____ can exchange heat and work, but not matter, with its surroundings.
   a. Thing
   b. Closed system0
   c. Undefined
   d. Undefined

151. _____ forms when rock cools and solidifies either below the surface as intrusive rocks or on the surface as extrusive rocks. This magma can be derived from partial melts of pre-existing rocks in either the Earth's mantle or crust. Typically, the melting is caused by one or more of the following processes -- an increase in temperature, a decrease in pressure, or a change in composition.
   a. Igneous rock0
   b. Thing
   c. Undefined
   d. Undefined

152. _____ is the process of breaking down rocks, soils and their minerals through direct contact with the atmosphere. _____ occurs without movement. Two main classifications of _____ processes exist. Mechanical or physical _____ involves the breakdown of rocks and soils through direct contact with atmospheric conditions. The second classification, chemical _____, involves the direct effect of atmospheric chemicals in the breakdown of rocks, soils and minerals.
   a. Weathering0
   b. Thing
   c. Undefined
   d. Undefined

153. _____ consists of very fine rock and mineral particles less than 2 mm in diameter that are ejected from a volcanic vent. The very fine particles may be carried for many miles, settling out as a dust-like layer across the landscape
   a. Thing
   b. Ash fall0
   c. Undefined
   d. Undefined

154. The _____ is the geologic eon before the Archean. It extends back to the Earth's formation, and ended roughly 3.8 billion years ago, though the date varies according to different sources.
   a. Thing
   b. Hadean0
   c. Undefined
   d. Undefined

155. The _____ is a geologic eon before the Proterozoic. Instead of being based on stratigraphy, this date is defined chronometrically. The lower boundary has not been officially recognized by the International Commission on Stratigraphy, but it is usually set at the end of the Hadean eon.
   a. Archean0
   b. Thing
   c. Undefined
   d. Undefined

156. The _____ is a geological eon representing a period before the first abundant complex life on Earth. The _____ Eon extended from 2500 million years ago to 542.0 ± 1.0 million years ago. The _____ is the most recent part of the old informal Precambrian time.
   a. Thing
   b. Proterozoic0
   c. Undefined
   d. Undefined

Chapter 8. Time and Geology

157. _____ was a predatory synapsid genus that flourished during the Permian Period. It was more closely related to mammals than to true reptiles, like dinosaurs, lizards and birds. _____ is not a dinosaur, rather, it is classified as a pelycosaur.
    a. Thing
    b. Dimetrodon0
    c. Undefined
    d. Undefined

158. A _____, as defined by the International Astronomical Union, is a celestial body orbiting a star or stellar remnant that is massive enough to be rounded by its own gravity, not massive enough to cause thermonuclear fusion in its core, and has cleared its neighboring region of planetesimals.
    a. Thing
    b. Planet0
    c. Undefined
    d. Undefined

159. The _____ of a quantity, subject to exponential decay, is the time required for the quantity to decay to half of its initial value. The concept originated in the study of radioactive decay, but applies to many other fields as well, including phenomena which are described by non-exponential decays.
    a. Thing
    b. Half-life0
    c. Undefined
    d. Undefined

160. _____ is the name of a group of rock-forming minerals which make up as much as sixty percent of the Earth's crust. Feldspars crystallize from magma in both intrusive and extrusive rocks, and they can also occur as compact minerals, as veins, and are also present in many types of metamorphic rock.
    a. Thing
    b. Feldspar0
    c. Undefined
    d. Undefined

Chapter 9. Mass Wasting

1. A _____ comprises a geomorphological unit, and is largely defined by its surface form and location in the landscape, as part of the terrain, and as such, is typically an element of topography. They are categorised by features such as elevation, slope, orientation, stratification, rock exposure, and soil type. They include berms, mounds, hills, cliffs, valleys, rivers and numerous other elements.
    a. Thing
    b. Landform0
    c. Undefined
    d. Undefined

2. A _____ is a natural underground void large enough for a human to enter. Some people suggest that the term '_____' should only apply to cavities that have some part which does not receive daylight; however, in popular usage, the term includes smaller spaces like a sea _____, rock shelters, and grottos.
    a. Place
    b. Cave0
    c. Undefined
    d. Undefined

3. A _____ is a hill of sand built by eolian processes. Dunes are subject to different forms and sizes based on their interaction with the wind. Most kinds of _____ are longer on the windward side where the sand is pushed up the _____, and a shorter in the lee of the wind. The trough between dunes is called a slack. A "_____ field" is an area covered by extensive sand dunes. Large _____ fields are known as ergs.
    a. Thing
    b. Dune0
    c. Undefined
    d. Undefined

4. A _____ is a significant vertical, or near vertical, rock exposure. Cliffs are categorized as erosion landforms due to the processes of erosion and weathering that produce them. Cliffs are common on coasts, in mountainous areas, escarpments and along rivers. Cliffs are usually formed by rock that is resistant to erosion and weathering.
    a. Cliff0
    b. Thing
    c. Undefined
    d. Undefined

5. _____ is the geological process whereby material is added to a landform. This is the process by which wind and water create a sediment deposit, through the laying down of granular material that has been eroded and transported from another geographical location.
    a. Deposition0
    b. Thing
    c. Undefined
    d. Undefined

6. _____ is the process of breaking down rocks, soils and their minerals through direct contact with the atmosphere. _____ occurs without movement. Two main classifications of _____ processes exist. Mechanical or physical _____ involves the breakdown of rocks and soils through direct contact with atmospheric conditions. The second classification, chemical _____, involves the direct effect of atmospheric chemicals in the breakdown of rocks, soils and minerals.
    a. Thing
    b. Weathering0
    c. Undefined
    d. Undefined

7. _____ is displacement of solids by the agents of ocean currents, wind, water, or ice by downward or down-slope movement in response to gravity or by living organisms.
    a. Thing
    b. Erosion0
    c. Undefined
    d. Undefined

Chapter 9. Mass Wasting

8. An _____ is the result from the sudden release of stored energy in the Earth's crust that creates seismic waves. At the Earth's surface, earthquakes may manifest themselves by a shaking or displacement of the ground. An _____ is caused by tectonic plates getting stuck and putting a strain on the ground. The strain becomes so great that rocks give way by breaking and sliding along fault planes.
   a. Earthquake0
   b. Thing
   c. Undefined
   d. Undefined

9. _____ is the geomorphic process by which soil, regolith, and rock move downslope under the force of gravity. Types of _____ include creep, slides, flows, topples, and falls, each with their own characteristic features, and take place over timescales from seconds to years. _____ occurs on both terrestrial and submarine slopes, and has been observed on Earth, Mars, and Venus.
   a. Thing
   b. Mass wasting0
   c. Undefined
   d. Undefined

10. A _____ is a geological phenomenon which includes a wide range of ground movement, such as rock falls, deep failure of slopes and shallow debris flows. Although gravity's action on an over-steepened slope is the primary reason for a _____, there are other contributing factors affecting the original slope stability.
    a. Landslide0
    b. Thing
    c. Undefined
    d. Undefined

11. In meteorology, a _____ is an area of low atmospheric pressure characterized by inward spiraling winds that rotate counter clockwise in the northern hemisphere and clockwise in the southern hemisphere of the Earth.
    a. Cyclone0
    b. Thing
    c. Undefined
    d. Undefined

12. _____ is the region of space that is dominated by "geogenic" matter, that is, originating from and bound to the Earth.
    a. Thing
    b. Geosphere0
    c. Undefined
    d. Undefined

13. A _____ in physical geography describes the collective mass of water found on, under, and over the surface of a planet.
    a. Thing
    b. Hydrosphere0
    c. Undefined
    d. Undefined

14. In geography, a _____ is a landscape form or region that receives very little precipitation. They are defined as areas that receive an average annual precipitation of less than 250 mm. A _____ where vegetation cover is exceedingly sparse correspond to the 'hyperarid' regions of the earth, where rainfall is exceedingly rare and infrequent.
    a. Place
    b. Desert0
    c. Undefined
    d. Undefined

15. _____ is the average and variations of weather over long periods of time. _____ zones can be defined using parameters such as temperature and rainfall.
    a. Thing
    b. Climate0
    c. Undefined
    d. Undefined

16. _____ is a sedimentary rock composed largely of the mineral calcite. _____ often contains variable amounts of silica in the form of chert or flint, as well as varying amounts of clay, silt and sand as disseminations, nodules, or layers within the rock. The primary source of the calcite in _____ is most commonly marine organisms. These organisms secrete shells that settle out of the water column and are deposited on ocean floors as pelagic ooze or alternatively is conglomerated in a coral reef.
- a. Limestone0
- b. Thing
- c. Undefined
- d. Undefined

17. The _____ is defined as the part of the land adjoining or near the ocean. A coastline is properly a line on a map indicating the disposition of a _____, but the word is often used to refer to the _____ itself. The adjective coastal describes something as being on, near to, or associated with a _____.
- a. Coast0
- b. Place
- c. Undefined
- d. Undefined

18. A _____ is a disturbance that propagates through space or spacetime, transferring energy and momentum and sometimes angular momentum.
- a. Thing
- b. Wave0
- c. Undefined
- d. Undefined

19. An _____ is a layer of gases that may surround a material body of sufficient mass. The gases are attracted by the gravity of the body, and are retained for a longer duration if gravity is high and the _____'s temperature is low. Some planets consist mainly of various gases, and thus have very deep atmospheres.
- a. Atmosphere0
- b. Place
- c. Undefined
- d. Undefined

20. A _____ is any disturbed state of an astronomical body's atmosphere, especially affecting its surface, and strongly implying severe weather. It may be marked by strong wind, thunder and lightning, heavy precipitation, such as ice, or wind transporting some substance through the atmosphere.
- a. Storm0
- b. Thing
- c. Undefined
- d. Undefined

21. A _____ is a meteorological phenomenon common in arid and semi-arid regions. Such a storm may result from the passage of a gust front or simply a substantial increase in wind velocity over a wider region. In all instances, the ground must be very dry and loosely consolidated.
- a. Dust storm0
- b. Thing
- c. Undefined
- d. Undefined

22. _____ is a chemical element. An abundant nonmetallic, tetravalent element, _____ has several allotropic forms. This element is the basis of the chemistry of all known life.
- a. Carbon0
- b. Thing
- c. Undefined
- d. Undefined

23. _____ is a chemical compound, normally in a gaseous state, and is composed of one carbon and two oxygen atoms. It is often referred to by its formula CO_2. It is present in the Earth's atmosphere at a concentration of approximately .000383 by volume and is an important greenhouse gas due to its ability to absorb many infrared wavelengths of sunlight, and due to the length of time it stays in the atmosphere.

Chapter 9. Mass Wasting

a. Thing
c. Undefined
b. Carbon dioxide0
d. Undefined

24. _____ involves the change in the composition of rock, often leading to a 'break down' in its form.
   a. Thing
   b. Chemical weathering0
   c. Undefined
   d. Undefined

25. The _____ is the part of the earth, including air, land, surface rocks, and water, within which life occurs, and which biotic processes in turn alter or transform. From the broadest biophysiological point of view, the _____ is the global ecological system integrating all living beings and their relationships, including their interaction with the elements of the lithosphere, hydrosphere, and atmosphere. This _____ is postulated to have evolved, beginning through a process of biogenesis or biopoesis, at least some 3.5 billion years ago.
   a. Thing
   b. Biosphere0
   c. Undefined
   d. Undefined

26. A _____ is one of several types of adverse geologic conditions capable of causing damage or loss of property and life. These can consist of sudden or slow phenomena.
   a. Geologic hazard0
   b. Thing
   c. Undefined
   d. Undefined

27. A _____ is a violently rotating column of air which is in contact with both a cumulonimbus cloud base and the surface of the earth. They come in many sizes, but are typically in the form of a visible condensation funnel, with the narrow end touching the earth. Often, a cloud of debris encircles the lower portion of the funnel.
   a. Tornado0
   b. Thing
   c. Undefined
   d. Undefined

28. _____ is the science and study of the solid matter that constitute the Earth. Encompassing such things as rocks, soil, and gemstones, _____ studies the composition, structure, physical properties, history, and the processes that shape Earth's components.
   a. Geology0
   b. Thing
   c. Undefined
   d. Undefined

29. A _____ is a landform that extends above the surrounding terrain in a limited area. A _____ is generally steeper than a hill, but there is no universally accepted standard definition for the height of a _____ or a hill although a _____ usually has an identifiable summit.
   a. Place
   b. Mountain0
   c. Undefined
   d. Undefined

30. A _____ is one of several large landmasses on Earth. They are generally identified by convention rather than any strict criteria, but seven areas are commonly reckoned as continents – they are: Asia, Africa, North America, South America, Antarctica, Europe, and Australia.
   a. Thing
   b. Continent0
   c. Undefined
   d. Undefined

31. _____, in everyday life, is most familiar as the agency that endows objects with weight. _____ is responsible for keeping the Earth and the other planets in their orbits around the Sun; for the formation of tides; and for various other phenomena that we observe. _____ is also the reason for the very existence of the Earth, the Sun, and most macroscopic objects in the universe; without it, matter would not have coalesced into these large masses, and life, as we know it, would not exist.
- a. Gravitation0
- b. Thing
- c. Undefined
- d. Undefined

32. _____ is the native consolidated rock underlying the Earth's surface. Above the _____ is usually an area of broken and weathered unconsolidated rock in the basal subsoil.
- a. Bedrock0
- b. Thing
- c. Undefined
- d. Undefined

33. A _____ is a section of a river of relatively steep gradient causing an increase in water flow and turbulence. A _____ is a hydrological feature between a run and a cascade. It is characterized by the river becoming shallower and having some rocks exposed above the flow surface.
- a. Thing
- b. Rapid0
- c. Undefined
- d. Undefined

34. _____, is the slow downward progression of rock and soil down a low grade slope; it can also refer to slow deformation of such materials as a result of prolonged pressure and stress.
- a. Creep0
- b. Thing
- c. Undefined
- d. Undefined

35. _____ are downslope, viscous flows of saturated, fine-grained materials, that move at any speed from slow to fast. Typically, they can move at speeds from .17 to 20 km/h. Though these are a lot like mudflows, overall they are slower moving and are covered with solid material carried along by flow from within.
- a. Earthflows0
- b. Thing
- c. Undefined
- d. Undefined

36. _____ are very large slides of snow or rock down a mountainside, caused when a buildup of snow is released down a slope, and is one of the major dangers faced in the mountains.
- a. Avalanches0
- b. Thing
- c. Undefined
- d. Undefined

37. In physics, _____ is defined as the rate of change of displacement or the rate of displacement. Simply put, it is distance per units of time.
- a. Thing
- b. Velocity0
- c. Undefined
- d. Undefined

38. _____ often refers to mudslides, mudflows, jökulhlaups, or debris avalanches. They consist primarily of geological material mixed with water. They may be generated when hillside colluvium or landslide material becomes rapidly saturated with water and flows into a channel.
- a. Debris flow0
- b. Thing
- c. Undefined
- d. Undefined

Chapter 9. Mass Wasting

39. _____ is a form of mass wasting event that occurs when loosely consolidated materials or rock layers move a short distance down a slope. When the movement occurs in soil, there is often a distinctive rotational movement to the mass, that cuts vertically through bedding planes.
   a. Thing
   b. Slump0
   c. Undefined
   d. Undefined

40. In geology, a _____ is a depression with predominant extent in one direction. The terms U-shaped and V-shaped are descriptive terms of geography to characterize the form of valleys. Most valleys belong to one of these two main types or a mixture of them, at least with respect of the cross section of the slopes or hillsides.
   a. Thing
   b. Valley0
   c. Undefined
   d. Undefined

41. Mean _____ is the average height of the sea, with reference to a suitable reference surface.
   a. Sea level0
   b. Thing
   c. Undefined
   d. Undefined

42. _____ refers to quantities of rock falling freely from a cliff face.
   a. Thing
   b. Rockfall0
   c. Undefined
   d. Undefined

43. A _____ is a large, slow moving river of ice, formed from compacted layers of snow, that slowly deforms and flows in response to gravity. _____ ice is the largest reservoir of fresh water on Earth, and second only to oceans as the largest reservoir of total water. Glaciers cover vast areas of polar regions but are restricted to the highest mountains in the tropics.
   a. Glacier0
   b. Thing
   c. Undefined
   d. Undefined

44. A _____ is a body of water or other liquid of considerable size contained on a body of land. A vast majority are fresh water, and lie in the Northern Hemisphere at higher latitudes. Most have a natural outflow in the form of a river or stream, but some do not, and lose water solely by evaporation and/or underground seepage.
   a. Lake0
   b. Thing
   c. Undefined
   d. Undefined

45. A _____ is a geological feature that is also known as a Rip in the earth causing magma to flow out and forming an undersea volcano, it also has geological features, a continuous elevational crest for some distance. Ridges are usually termed hills or mountains as well, depending on size.
   a. Ridge0
   b. Thing
   c. Undefined
   d. Undefined

46. A _____ is a body of water with a current, confined within a bed and banks. Streams are important as conduits in the water cycle, instruments in aquifer recharge, and corridors for fish and wildlife migration.
   a. Thing
   b. Stream0
   c. Undefined
   d. Undefined

47. _____ is the third or vertical dimension of land surface. When _____ is described underwater, the term bathymetry is used.

a. Terrain0 b. Thing
c. Undefined d. Undefined

48. _____ are where one sedimetary deposit ends and another one begins. The rock is prone to breakage at these points because of the weakness between the layers.
   a. Bedding planes0 b. Thing
   c. Undefined d. Undefined

49. _____ has penetrative planar fabric present within it. It is common to rocks affected by regional metamorphic compression typical of orogenic belts.
   a. Thing b. Foliated metamorphic rock0
   c. Undefined d. Undefined

50. _____ is a general term for the plant life of a region; it refers to the ground cover provided by plants, and is, by far, the most abundant biotic element of the biosphere. Primeval redwood forests, coastal mangrove stands, sphagnum bogs, desert soil crusts, roadside weed patches, wheat fields, cultivated gardens and lawns; are all encompassed by the term _____.
   a. Place b. Vegetation0
   c. Undefined d. Undefined

51. _____ in meteorology are large scale patterns in the atmospheric pressure field that are nearly stationary, effectively "blocking" or redirecting migratory cyclones. These _____ can remain in place for several days or even weeks, causing the areas affected by them to have the same kind of weather for an extended period of time.
   a. Thing b. Blocks0
   c. Undefined d. Undefined

52. _____ is the process of heating a solid substance to a point where it turns into a liquid. An object that has melted is molten.
   a. Thing b. Melting0
   c. Undefined d. Undefined

53. _____ is an effect within the surface layer of a liquid that causes that layer to behave as an elastic sheet. This effect allows insects to walk on water. It allows small metal objects such as needles, razor blades, or foil fragments to float on the surface of water, and causes capillary action.
   a. Surface tension0 b. Thing
   c. Undefined d. Undefined

54. _____ is a reaction force applied by a stretched string, rope or a similar object on the objects which stretch it. The direction of the force of it is parallel to the string, towards the string.
   a. Thing b. Tension0
   c. Undefined d. Undefined

55. _____ refers to the cyclic rizing and falling of Earth's ocean surface caused by the tidal forces of the Moon and the sun acting on the oceans. They cause changes in the depth of the marine and estuarine water bodies and produce oscillating currents known as tidal streams, making prediction of tides important for coastal navigation.

Chapter 9. Mass Wasting

a. Thing
c. Undefined
b. Tide0
d. Undefined

56. A _____ is the most rapid up to 80 km/h and fluid type of downhill mass wasting.
a. Thing
c. Undefined
b. Mudflow0
d. Undefined

57. _____ is a Northern California mountain with elevation 3,786 feet and located at approximately 37.114° N, 121.846 W in the Santa Cruz Mountains. The peak is located on private property, about 11 miles west of Morgan Hill and within the boundaries of Santa Clara County.
a. Place
c. Undefined
b. Loma Prieta0
d. Undefined

58. The _____ was a major earthquake affecting the greater San Francisco Bay Area of California. It occurred on Tuesday October 17, 1989 at 5:04 p.m. and measured 6.9 on the Moment magnitude scale. It lasted approximately 15 seconds and its epicenter was at located in Forest of Nisene Marks State Park, in the Santa Cruz Mountains.
a. Thing
c. Undefined
b. Loma Prieta earthquake0
d. Undefined

59. _____ is a type of mass wasting where waterlogged sediment slowly moves downslope over impermeable material. It can occur in any climate where the ground is saturated by water, though it is most often found in periglacial environments where the ground is permanently frozen.
a. Thing
c. Undefined
b. Soil creep0
d. Undefined

60. _____ rock is one of the three main rock groups. Rock formed from these covers 75% of the Earth's land area, and includes common types such as chalk, limestone, dolomite, sandstone, and shale.
a. Thing
c. Undefined
b. Sedimentary0
d. Undefined

61. A _____, in the context of an ocean, is a formation of long wavelength ocean surface waves on the sea. They are far more stable in their directions and frequency than normal oceanic waves since they are formed by tropical storms and by stable wind systems.
a. Swell0
c. Undefined
b. Thing
d. Undefined

62. _____ is one of the four seasons of temperate zones. Almost all English-language calendars, going by astronomy, state that _____ begins on the _____ solstice, and ends on the spring equinox. Calculated more by the weather, it begins and ends earlier and is the season with the shortest days and the lowest temperatures.
a. Winter0
c. Undefined
b. Thing
d. Undefined

63. An _____ is a transition zone between different physiogeographic provinces that involves an elevation differential, often involving high cliffs. Most commonly, an _____, is a transition from one series of sedimentary rocks to another series of a different age and composition. In such cases, the _____ usually represents the line of erosional loss of the newer rock over the older.

Chapter 9. Mass Wasting

 a. Thing
 b. Escarpment0
 c. Undefined
 d. Undefined

64. _____ is a small unincorporated community in western Ventura County, California, on U.S. Route 101 just southeast of the Santa Barbara county line. The entire town consists of two streets parallel to the shore, with ten short perpendicular streets, ending at the base of Rincon Mountain.
 a. La Conchita0
 b. Place
 c. Undefined
 d. Undefined

65. A _____, the key component of a septic system, is a small scale sewage treatment system common in areas with no connection to main sewerage pipes provided by private corporations or local governments.
 a. Thing
 b. Septic tank0
 c. Undefined
 d. Undefined

66. A _____ is the fringe of land at the edge of a large body of water, such as an ocean, sea, or lake. A strict definition is the strip of land along a water body that is alternately exposed and covered by waves and tides.
 a. Shoreline0
 b. Thing
 c. Undefined
 d. Undefined

67. In geology, _____, is a type of mass wasting where waterlogged sediment slowly moves downslope over impermeable material. It can occur in any climate where the ground is saturated by water, though it is most often found in periglacial environments where the ground is permanently frozen.
 a. Solifluction0
 b. Thing
 c. Undefined
 d. Undefined

68. In geology, _____ is soil at or below the freezing point of water for two or more years. Ice is not always present, as may be in the case of nonporous bedrock, but it frequently occurs and it may be in amounts exceeding the potential hydraulic saturation of the ground material. Most _____ is located in high latitudes, but alpine _____ exists at high altitudes.
 a. Permafrost0
 b. Thing
 c. Undefined
 d. Undefined

69. The _____ is a region in the Northern Hemisphere immediately south of the true Arctic and covering much of Canada and Siberia, the north of Scandinavia, northern Mongolia and the Chinese province of Heilongjiang. Generally, _____ regions fall between 50°N and 70°N latitude, depending on local climates.
 a. Subarctic0
 b. Thing
 c. Undefined
 d. Undefined

70. The _____ is the region around the Earth's North Pole, opposite the Antarctic region around the South Pole. In the northern hemisphere, the _____ includes the _____ Ocean and parts of Canada, Greenland, Russia, the United States, Iceland, Norway, Sweden and Finland. The word _____ comes from the Greek word arktos, which means bear. This is due to the location of the constellation Ursa Major, the "Great Bear", above the _____ region.
 a. Arctic0
 b. Place
 c. Undefined
 d. Undefined

71. _____ transport is a transportation of goods through a pipe. Most commonly, liquid and gases are sent, but pneumatic tubes that transport solid capsules using compressed air have also been used..

a. Pipeline0
b. Thing
c. Undefined
d. Undefined

72. The _____ is a major U.S. oil pipeline connecting oil fields in northern Alaska to a sea port where the oil can be shipped to the Lower 48 states for refining. Construction of the pipeline presented significant challenges due to the remoteness of the terrain and the harshness of the environment it had to pass through.
    a. Thing
    b. Alaska Pipeline0
    c. Undefined
    d. Undefined

73. _____ is a small island located in the middle of San Francisco Bay in California, United States. It served as a lighthouse, then a military fortification, then a military prison followed by a federal prison until 1963, when it became a national recreation area.
    a. Place
    b. Alcatraz Island0
    c. Undefined
    d. Undefined

74. _____ is soil or rock derived granular material of a specific grain size. _____ may occur as a soil or alternatively as suspended sediment in a water column of any surface water body. It may also exist as deposition soil at the bottom of a water body.
    a. Thing
    b. Silt0
    c. Undefined
    d. Undefined

75. _____ is any particulate matter that can be transported by fluid flow and which eventually is deposited as a layer of solid particles on the bed or bottom of a body of water or other liquid.
    a. Sediment0
    b. Thing
    c. Undefined
    d. Undefined

76. _____ is a term used to describe a group of hydrous aluminium phyllosilicate minerals, that are typically less than 2 micrometres in diameter. _____ consists of a variety of phyllosilicate minerals rich in silicon and aluminium oxides and hydroxides which include variable amounts of structural water. Clays are generally formed by the chemical weathering of silicate-bearing rocks by carbonic acid but some are formed by hydrothermal activity.
    a. Clay0
    b. Thing
    c. Undefined
    d. Undefined

77. _____ are forests characterized by high rainfall, with definitions setting minimum normal annual rainfall.
    a. Rainforests0
    b. Thing
    c. Undefined
    d. Undefined

78. A _____ is an area with a high density of trees, historically, a wooded area set aside for hunting. These plant communities cover large areas of the globe and function as animal habitats, hydrologic flow modulators, and soil conservers, constituting one of the most important aspects of the Earth's biosphere.
    a. Thing
    b. Forest0
    c. Undefined
    d. Undefined

79. In geology, _____ are rock s with a grain size of usually no less than 256 mm diameter.

a. Thing
b. Boulders0
c. Undefined
d. Undefined

80. _____ is the result of the transformation of a pre-existing rock type, the protolith, in a process called metamorphism, which means "change in form". The protolith is subjected to heat and extreme pressure causing profound physical and/or chemical change. The protolith may be sedimentary rock, igneous rock or another older rock.
   a. Metamorphic rock0
   b. Thing
   c. Undefined
   d. Undefined

81. Metamorphic rock is the result of the transformation of a pre-existing rock type, the protolith, in a process called metamorphism. The protolith is subjected to heat and extreme pressure causing profound physical and/or chemical change. _____ make up a large part of the Earth's crust. They are formed deep beneath the Earth's surface by great stresses from rocks above and high pressures and temperatures.
   a. Thing
   b. Metamorphic rocks0
   c. Undefined
   d. Undefined

82. _____ can be defined as the solid state recrystallisation of pre-existing rocks due to changes in heat and/or pressure and/or introduction of fluids. There will be mineralogical, chemical and crystallographic changes. _____ produced with increasing pressure and temperature conditions is known as prograde _____. Conversely, decreasing temperatures and pressure characterize retrograde _____.
   a. Thing
   b. Metamorphism0
   c. Undefined
   d. Undefined

83. _____ is a national park located largely in Mariposa and Tuolumne Counties, California, United States. It is one of the largest and least fragmented habitat blocks in the Sierra Nevada, and the park supports a diversity of plants and animals. The park has an elevation range from 2,000 to 13,114 feet.
   a. Yosemite National Park0
   b. Place
   c. Undefined
   d. Undefined

84. _____ in geology is a weathering process, mainly caused in arid areas by differential heating and cooling of rock surfaces. There needs to be a high diurnal temperature range.
   a. Exfoliation0
   b. Thing
   c. Undefined
   d. Undefined

85. An _____ is a fold that is convex up or to the youngest beds. Anticlines are usually recognized by a sequence of rock layers that are progressively older toward the center of the fold because the uplifted core of the fold is preferentially eroded to a deeper stratigraphic level relative to the topographically lower flanks. If an _____ plunges, the surface strata will form Vs that point in the direction of the plunge.
   a. Anticline0
   b. Thing
   c. Undefined
   d. Undefined

86. _____ is a term given to broken rock that appears at the bottom of crags, mountain cliffs or valley shoulders, forming a _____ slope. The maximum inclination of such deposits corresponds to the angle of repose of the mean debris size.

Chapter 9. Mass Wasting

  a. Scree0   b. Thing
  c. Undefined   d. Undefined

87. _____ involves the study of the interaction of humans with the geologic environment including the biosphere, the lithosphere, the hydrosphere, and to some extent the atmosphere.
  a. Thing   b. Environmental geology0
  c. Undefined   d. Undefined

88. A _____ is a barrier across flowing water that obstructs, directs or slows down the flow, often creating a reservoir, lake or impoundment.
  a. Thing   b. Dam0
  c. Undefined   d. Undefined

89. The _____ is a river in the southwestern United States and northwestern Mexico, approximately 1,450 mi long, draining a part of the arid regions on the western slope of the Rocky Mountains. The natural course of the river flows into the Gulf of California, but the heavy use of the river as an irrigation source for the Imperial Valley has desiccated the lower course of the river in Mexico such that it no longer consistently reaches the sea.
  a. Place   b. Colorado River0
  c. Undefined   d. Undefined

90. Faults are planar rock fractures, which show evidence of relative movement. Large faults within the Earth's crust are the result of shear motion and active _____ zones are the causal locations of most earthquakes. Earthquakes are caused by energy release during rapid slippage along faults. The largest examples are at tectonic plate boundaries but many faults occur far from active plate boundaries. Since faults do not usually consist of a single, clean fracture, the term _____ zone is used when referring to the zone of complex deformation that is associated with the _____ plane.
  a. Thing   b. Fault0
  c. Undefined   d. Undefined

91. Most often, a _____ refers to an artificial lake, used to store water for various uses. Reservoirs are created first by building a sturdy dam, usually out of cement, earth, rock, or a mixture. Once the dam is completed, a stream is allowed to flow behind it and eventually fill it to capacity.
  a. Reservoir0   b. Thing
  c. Undefined   d. Undefined

92. A _____ is a wet place where a liquid, usually groundwater, has oozed from the ground to the surface. They are usually not flowing, with the liquid sourced only from underground. The term may also refer to the movement of liquid hydrocarbons to the surface through fractures and fissures in the rock and between geological layers. It may be a significant source of pollution.
  a. Thing   b. Seep0
  c. Undefined   d. Undefined

93. _____ is a fine-grained sedimentary rock whose original constituents were clays or muds. It is characterized by thin laminae breaking with an irregular curving fracture, often splintery and usually parallel to the often-indistinguishable bedding plane.

a. Thing
b. Shale0
c. Undefined
d. Undefined

94. _____ is a sedimentary rock composed mainly of sand-size mineral or rock grains. Most _____ is composed of quartz and/or feldspar because these are the most common minerals in the Earth's crust. Like sand, _____ may be any color, but the most common colors are tan, brown, yellow, red, gray and white.
a. Sandstone0
b. Thing
c. Undefined
d. Undefined

95. _____ is one of the three main rock groups. _____ covers 75% of the Earth's land area. Four basic processes are involved in the formation of a clastic _____: weathering caused mainly by friction of waves, transportation where the sediment is carried along by a current, deposition and compaction where the sediment is squashed together to form a rock of this kind.
a. Thing
b. Sedimentary rock0
c. Undefined
d. Undefined

96. An _____ is any piece of land that is completely surrounded by water, above high tide. There are two main types of islands: continental islands and oceanic islands. There are also artificial islands. A grouping of geographically and/or geologically related islands is called an archipelago.
a. Thing
b. Island0
c. Undefined
d. Undefined

97. The _____ form an archipelago of nineteen islands and atolls, numerous smaller islets, and undersea seamounts trending northwest by southeast in the North Pacific Ocean between latitudes 19° N and 29° N. The archipelago takes its name from the largest island in the group and extends some 1500 miles from the Island of Hawai'i in the south to northernmost Kure Atoll.
a. Place
b. Hawaiian Islands0
c. Undefined
d. Undefined

98. The _____ is the point on the Earth's surface that is directly above the point where an earthquake or other underground explosion originates or focus. It is directly above the hypocenter the actual location of the energy released inside the earth and usually suffers the maximum destruction.
a. Thing
b. Epicenter0
c. Undefined
d. Undefined

99. _____ is a cloudiness or haziness of water caused by individual particles that are generally invisible to the naked eye, thus being much like smoke in air. _____ is generally caused by phytoplankton. Measurement of _____ is a key test of water quality.
a. Thing
b. Turbidity0
c. Undefined
d. Undefined

100. A _____ is a current of rapidly moving, sediment-laden water moving down a slope through air, water, or another fluid. The current moves because it has a higher density and turbidity than the fluid through which it flows.
a. Turbidity current0
b. Thing
c. Undefined
d. Undefined

Chapter 9. Mass Wasting

101. Ocean _____ are any more or less continuous, directed movement of ocean water that flows in one of the Earth's oceans.They are rivers of hot or cold water within the ocean. They are generated from the forces acting upon the water like the earth's rotation, the wind, the temperature and salinity differences and the gravitation of the moon.
    a. Currents0
    b. Thing
    c. Undefined
    d. Undefined

102. _____ is a 16-ton, manned deep-ocean research submersible owned by the United States Navy and operated by the Woods Hole Oceanographic Institution in Woods Hole, Massachusetts. The three-person vessel allows for two scientists and one pilot to dive for up to nine hours at 4500 metersor 15,000 feet.
    a. Thing
    b. Alvin0
    c. Undefined
    d. Undefined

103. The _____, is a term that comprises all living and non-living things that occur naturally on Earth or some part of it.
    a. Thing
    b. Natural environment0
    c. Undefined
    d. Undefined

104. In agriculture, a _____ is a leveled section of a hilly cultivated area, designed as a method of soil conservation to slow or prevent the rapid surface runoff of irrigation water
    a. Thing
    b. Terrace0
    c. Undefined
    d. Undefined

105. The _____ is a mountain range that is almost entirely in the eastern portion of the U.S. state of California. The _____ stretches 400 miles , from Fredonyer Pass in the north to Tehachapi Pass in the south. It is bounded on the west by California's Central Valley, and on the east by the Great Basin.
    a. Sierra Nevada0
    b. Place
    c. Undefined
    d. Undefined

Chapter 10. Streams and Floods

1. Any accumulation of material, by mechanical settling from water or air, chemical precipitation, evaporation from solution, etc is referred to as _____.
   a. 1509 Istanbul earthquake
   b. Deposition10
   c. Undefined
   d. Undefined

2. _____ is the displacement of solids (soil, mud, rock, and other particles) by the agents of wind, water, ice, movement in response to gravity, or living organisms.
   a. Erosion10
   b. Thing
   c. Undefined
   d. Undefined

3. _____ refers to a body of water found on the Earth's surface and confined to a narrow topographic depression, down which it flows and transports rock particles, sediment, and dissolved particles. Rivers, creeks, brooks, and runs are all streams.
   a. 1509 Istanbul earthquake
   b. Stream10
   c. Undefined
   d. Undefined

4. _____ refers to the water that lies beneath the ground surface, filling the cracks, crevices, and pore space of rocks.
   a. 1509 Istanbul earthquake
   b. Ground water10
   c. Undefined
   d. Undefined

5. _____ is the geomorphic process by which soil, regolith, and rock move downslope under the force of gravity. Types of _____ include creep, slides, flows, topples, and falls, each with their own characteristic features, and take place over timescales from seconds to years.
   a. Mass wasting10
   b. Thing
   c. Undefined
   d. Undefined

6. A moving body of ice that forms on land from the accumulation and compaction of snow, and that flows downslope or outward due to gravity and the pressure of its own weight is a _____.
   a. Glacier10
   b. 1509 Istanbul earthquake
   c. Undefined
   d. Undefined

7. _____ is the continuous circulation of water within the Earth's hydrosphere, and is driven by solar energy. This includes the atmosphere, land, surface water and groundwater. As water moves through the cycle, it changes state between liquid, solid, and gas phases.
   a. Thing
   b. Hydrologic cycle10
   c. Undefined
   d. Undefined

8. _____ refers to any condensed water falling from the atmosphere to the surface of the earth. Common types include rain, snow, sleet, and hail.
   a. 1509 Istanbul earthquake
   b. Precipitation10
   c. Undefined
   d. Undefined

9. _____ refers to water molecules in the gaseous state. Also is one state of the water cycle.
   a. Water vapor10
   b. Thing
   c. Undefined
   d. Undefined

10. _____ refers to water in the gaseous state.

a. Vapor10
b. 1509 Istanbul earthquake
c. Undefined
d. Undefined

11. The situation in mass wasting that occurs when material free-falls or bounces down a cliff is called a _____.
a. 1509 Istanbul earthquake
b. Fall10
c. Undefined
d. Undefined

12. Distinct crystals of ice are called _____. Commonly accumulates with a density of 50 - 200 kg·m, although wind-abraded and packed _____ may have a higher initial density.
a. Snow10
b. 1509 Istanbul earthquake
c. Undefined
d. Undefined

13. The percentage of moisture in the air compared with how much the air can hold at the given temperature is called _____.
a. Relative humidity10
b. Thing
c. Undefined
d. Undefined

14. Earth's _____ is a layer of gases surrounding the planet Earth and retained by the Earth's gravity. It contains roughly 78% nitrogen and 21% oxygen, with trace amounts of other gases.
a. Thing
b. Atmosphere10
c. Undefined
d. Undefined

15. _____ is the concentration of water vapor in the air. The concentration can be expressed as absolute _____, specific _____, or relative _____.
a. Humidity10
b. Thing
c. Undefined
d. Undefined

16. _____ refers to the release of water vapor to the atmosphere by plants.
a. Transpiration10
b. 1509 Istanbul earthquake
c. Undefined
d. Undefined

17. _____ refers to the change of state of water from the liquid to vapor phase. Requires the addition of 80 calories per cubic centimeter.
a. Evaporation10
b. AASHTO Soil Classification System
c. Undefined
d. Undefined

18. The movement of surface water into rock or soil through cracks and pore spaces is called _____.
a. Infiltration10
b. AASHTO Soil Classification System
c. Undefined
d. Undefined

19. Water entering rivers, lakes, reservoirs, or the ocean from land surfaces is _____.
a. Thing
b. Runoff10
c. Undefined
d. Undefined

20. Weather condition of an area including especially prevailing temperature and average daily/yearly rainfall over a long period of time is called _____.

Chapter 10. Streams and Floods

a. Climate10
b. Thing
c. Undefined
d. Undefined

21. A major branch of a stream system is referred to as a _____.
a. 1509 Istanbul earthquake
b. River10
c. Undefined
d. Undefined

22. _____ refers to a naturally formed aggregate of usually inorganic materials from within the Earth.
a. 1509 Istanbul earthquake
b. Rock10
c. Undefined
d. Undefined

23. _____ refers to the top few meters of regolith, generally including some organic matter derived from plants.
a. Soil10
b. 1509 Istanbul earthquake
c. Undefined
d. Undefined

24. _____ is a chemical element in the periodic table that has the symbol Pb and atomic number 82. A soft, heavy, toxic and malleable poor metal, _____ is bluish white when freshly cut but tarnishes to dull gray when exposed to air. _____ is used in building construction, _____-acid batteries, bullets and shot, and is part of solder, pewter, and fusible alloys.
a. Thing
b. Lead10
c. Undefined
d. Undefined

25. Runoff moving in unconfined thin sheets is called _____.
a. 1509 Istanbul earthquake
b. Sheet flow10
c. Undefined
d. Undefined

26. The force of attraction exerted by one body in the universe on another is _____. _____ is directly proportional to the product of the masses of the two attracted bodies. The force of attraction exerted by the Earth on bodies on or near its surface, tending to pull them toward the Earth's center.
a. Gravity10
b. 1509 Istanbul earthquake
c. Undefined
d. Undefined

27. _____ refers to a feature on the surface of the planet Mars that very closely resembles certain types of stream channels on Earth.
a. 1509 Istanbul earthquake
b. Channel10
c. Undefined
d. Undefined

28. A cross-section of a stream channel along its descending course from the head to the mouth is called the _____.
a. Longitudinal profile10
b. 1509 Istanbul earthquake
c. Undefined
d. Undefined

29. The place where the stream enters the sea, a large lake, or a larger stream is a _____.
a. Stream mouth10
b. 1509 Istanbul earthquake
c. Undefined
d. Undefined

30. A large mass of rock projecting above surrounding terrain is called a _____.

Chapter 10. Streams and Floods

a. 1509 Istanbul earthquake
b. Mountain10
c. Undefined
d. Undefined

31. The point downstream where a river empties into another stream or water body is called _____.
a. Mouth10
b. 1509 Istanbul earthquake
c. Undefined
d. Undefined

32. The nearly level plain that borders a stream and is subject to inundation under flood stage conditions unless protected artificially is called _____.
a. 1509 Istanbul earthquake
b. Flood plain10
c. Undefined
d. Undefined

33. _____ is any particulate matter that can be transported by fluid flow and which eventually is deposited as a layer of solid particles on the bed or bottom of a body of water or other liquid.
a. Sediment10
b. Thing
c. Undefined
d. Undefined

34. The quantity of water in a stream that passes a given point in a period of time is referred to as _____.
a. 1509 Istanbul earthquake
b. Discharge10
c. Undefined
d. Undefined

35. The entire area between the tops of the slopes on both sides of a stream is a _____.
a. Valley10
b. 1509 Istanbul earthquake
c. Undefined
d. Undefined

36. _____ refers to the height of floodwaters in feet or meters above an established datum plane.
a. 1509 Istanbul earthquake
b. Stage10
c. Undefined
d. Undefined

37. A long, narrow depression, shaped and more or less filled by a stream is referred to as a _____.
a. Stream channel10
b. 1509 Istanbul earthquake
c. Undefined
d. Undefined

38. Any relatively sunken part of the Earth's surface, especially a low-lying area surrounded by higher ground is called a _____.
a. 1509 Istanbul earthquake
b. Depression10
c. Undefined
d. Undefined

39. Water flowing down a slope in a layer is called _____.
a. Sheetwash10
b. 1509 Istanbul earthquake
c. Undefined
d. Undefined

40. A _____ is a landscape form or region that receives little precipitation - less than 250 mm (10 in) per year. It is a biome characterized by organisms adapted to sparse rainfall and rapid evaporation.

Chapter 10. Streams and Floods

   a. Thing
   b. Desert10
   c. Undefined
   d. Undefined

41. _____ refers to the removal of a thin layer of surface material, usually topsoil, by a flowing sheet of water.
   a. 1509 Istanbul earthquake
   b. Sheet erosion10
   c. Undefined
   d. Undefined

42. _____ is the uppermost layer of soil, usually the top 15-20 cm. It has the highest concentration of organic matter and microorganisms, and is where most of the Earth's biological soil activity occurs.
   a. Thing
   b. Topsoil10
   c. Undefined
   d. Undefined

43. _____ refer to tiny channels that develop as unconfined flow begins producing threads of current.
   a. Rills10
   b. 1509 Istanbul earthquake
   c. Undefined
   d. Undefined

44. _____ refers to a drainage divide that separates streams flowing toward opposite sides of a continent.
   a. 1509 Istanbul earthquake
   b. Continental divide10
   c. Undefined
   d. Undefined

45. _____ refers to the area of land drained by a river system.
   a. 1509 Istanbul earthquake
   b. Drainage basin10
   c. Undefined
   d. Undefined

46. In ethology, sociobiology and behavioral ecology, the term _____ refers to any geographical area that an animal of a particular species consistently defends against conspecifics (and, occasionally, animals of other species).
   a. Thing
   b. Territory10
   c. Undefined
   d. Undefined

47. An imaginary line that separates the drainage of two streams, often found along a ridge is referred to as the _____.
   a. 1509 Istanbul earthquake
   b. Divide10
   c. Undefined
   d. Undefined

48. A round or oval depression in the Earth's surface, containing the youngest section of rock in its lowest, central part is a _____.
   a. 1509 Istanbul earthquake
   b. Basin10
   c. Undefined
   d. Undefined

49. The arrangement in which a stream erodes the channels of its network of tributaries is a _____.
   a. Drainage pattern10
   b. 1509 Istanbul earthquake
   c. Undefined
   d. Undefined

50. Aggregates of minerals or rock fragments are called _____.

a. 1509 Istanbul earthquake
b. Rocks10
c. Undefined
d. Undefined

51. An irregular stream drainage network that resembles the limbs of a branching tree is a _____.
a. Dendritic drainage10
b. 1509 Istanbul earthquake
c. Undefined
d. Undefined

52. The layer of rock and mineral fragments that nearly everywhere covers Earth's land surface is referred to as _____.
a. 1509 Istanbul earthquake
b. Regolith10
c. Undefined
d. Undefined

53. A drainage pattern characterized by numerous right angle bends that develops on jointed or fractured bedrock is called a _____.
a. 1509 Istanbul earthquake
b. Rectangular pattern10
c. Undefined
d. Undefined

54. A system of streams running in all directions away from a central elevated structure, such as a volcano is referred to as a _____.
a. 1509 Istanbul earthquake
b. Radial pattern10
c. Undefined
d. Undefined

55. _____ refers to a crack or break in a rock. To break in random places instead of cleaving.
a. 1509 Istanbul earthquake
b. Fracture10
c. Undefined
d. Undefined

56. _____ refers to a round or oval bulge on the Earth's surface, containing the oldest section of rock in its raised, central part.
a. Dome10
b. 1509 Istanbul earthquake
c. Undefined
d. Undefined

57. _____ refers to a drainage pattern consisting of parallel main streams with short tributaries meeting them at right angles.
a. 1509 Istanbul earthquake
b. Trellis pattern10
c. Undefined
d. Undefined

58. _____ refers to a clastic rock composed of particles that range in diameter from 1/16 millimeter to 2 millimeters in diameter. Sandstones make up about 25% of all sedimentary rocks.
a. Sandstone10
b. 1509 Istanbul earthquake
c. Undefined
d. Undefined

59. _____ refers to a sedimentary rock composed of detrital sediment particles less than 0.004 millimeters in diameter. _____ tends to be red, brown, black, or gray, and usually originate in relatively still waters.
a. 1509 Istanbul earthquake
b. Shale10
c. Undefined
d. Undefined

Chapter 10. Streams and Floods

60. _____ refers to the set of physical features, such as mountains, valleys, and the shapes of landforms, that characterizes a given landscape.
   a. 1509 Istanbul earthquake
   b. Topography10
   c. Undefined
   d. Undefined

61. Downhill slope of a stream's bed or the water surface, if the stream is very large is a _____.
   a. Stream gradient10
   b. 1509 Istanbul earthquake
   c. Undefined
   d. Undefined

62. The vertical drop in a stream's elevation over a given horizontal distance, expressed as an angle is referred to as a _____.
   a. Gradient10
   b. 1509 Istanbul earthquake
   c. Undefined
   d. Undefined

63. A stream system that resembles the pattern of a branching tree is a _____.
   a. Dendritic pattern10
   b. 1509 Istanbul earthquake
   c. Undefined
   d. Undefined

64. _____ refers to the speed at which water in a stream travels.
   a. 1509 Istanbul earthquake
   b. Stream velocity10
   c. Undefined
   d. Undefined

65. _____ refers to objects at rest tend to remain at rest, and objects in motion tend to stay in motion unless either is acted upon by an outside force.
   a. Inertia10
   b. AASHTO Soil Classification System
   c. Undefined
   d. Undefined

66. The movement of eroded particles by agents such as rivers, waves, glaciers, or wind is referred to as _____.
   a. Transportation10
   b. 1509 Istanbul earthquake
   c. Undefined
   d. Undefined

67. Ability to do work is referred to as _____. Most evident in glacial systems as radiant _____ from the sun and as latent _____ required to melt ice to water.
   a. Energy10
   b. AASHTO Soil Classification System
   c. Undefined
   d. Undefined

68. _____ refers to soil particles between the size of sand particles and clay particles, namely particles 0.002-0.2 mm in diameter.
   a. Silt10
   b. Thing
   c. Undefined
   d. Undefined

69. A body of fine, solid particles, typically of sand, clay, and silt, that travels with stream water without coming in contact with the stream bed is referred to as a _____.
   a. 1509 Istanbul earthquake
   b. Suspended load10
   c. Undefined
   d. Undefined

Chapter 10. Streams and Floods

70. A part of a stream channel in which the water suddenly begins flowing more swiftly and turbulently because of an abrupt steepening of the gradient is referred to as _____.
    a. 1509 Istanbul earthquake
    b. Rapids10
    c. Undefined
    d. Undefined

71. Any unconsolidated material at Earth's surface is _____.
    a. Debris10
    b. 1509 Istanbul earthquake
    c. Undefined
    d. Undefined

72. The mass movement of a single, intact mass of rock, soil, or unconsolidated material along a weak plane, such as a fault, fracture, or bedding plane is a _____. A _____ may involve as little as a minor displacement of soil or as much as the displacement of an entire mountainside.
    a. 1509 Istanbul earthquake
    b. Slide10
    c. Undefined
    d. Undefined

73. Angular chunk of solid rock ejected during an eruption is referred to as a _____.
    a. Block10
    b. 1509 Istanbul earthquake
    c. Undefined
    d. Undefined

74. _____ refer to unit of water flow or stream discharge. One cubic foot per second is 7.48 gallons passing a given point in one second.
    a. Cubic feet per second10
    b. 1509 Istanbul earthquake
    c. Undefined
    d. Undefined

75. _____ refers to a stream that supplies water to a larger stream.
    a. 1509 Istanbul earthquake
    b. Tributary10
    c. Undefined
    d. Undefined

76. A pink-colored, felsic, plutonic rock that contains potassium and usually sodium feldspars, and has quartz content of about 10% is _____. _____ is commonly found on continents but virtually absent from the ocean basins.
    a. 1509 Istanbul earthquake
    b. Granite10
    c. Undefined
    d. Undefined

77. A climate in which yearly precipitation is less than the potential loss of water by evaporation is a _____.
    a. 1509 Istanbul earthquake
    b. Dry climate10
    c. Undefined
    d. Undefined

78. _____ refers to a basic unit of the geologic time scale that is a subdivision of an era. Periods may be divided into smaller units called epochs.
    a. Period10
    b. 1509 Istanbul earthquake
    c. Undefined
    d. Undefined

79. The ability of water to pick up and move rock and sediment is _____.
    a. Hydraulic action10
    b. 1509 Istanbul earthquake
    c. Undefined
    d. Undefined

Chapter 10. Streams and Floods

80. A form of mechanical weathering that occurs when loose fragments or particles of rocks and minerals that are being transported, as by water or air, collide with each other or scrape the surfaces of stationary rocks is referred to as _____.
   a. AASHTO Soil Classification System
   b. Abrasion10
   c. Undefined
   d. Undefined

81. Usually slow but effective process of weathering and erosion in which rocks are dissolved by water is a _____.
   a. Solution10
   b. 1509 Istanbul earthquake
   c. Undefined
   d. Undefined

82. The process by which exposure to atmospheric agents, such as air or moisture, causes rocks and minerals to break down is called _____. This process takes place at or near the Earth's surface. _____ entails little or no movement of the material that it loosens from the rocks and minerals.
   a. Weathering10
   b. 1509 Istanbul earthquake
   c. Undefined
   d. Undefined

83. _____ is a sedimentary rock composed largely of the mineral calcite (calcium carbonate: $CaCO_3$). _____ often contains variable amounts of silica in the form of chert or flint, as well as varying amounts of clay, silt and sand as disseminations, nodules, or layers within the rock.
   a. Limestone10
   b. Thing
   c. Undefined
   d. Undefined

84. Rocks formed by solidification of sediments formed and transported at the Earth's surface are referred to as _____.
   a. 1509 Istanbul earthquake
   b. Sedimentary rocks10
   c. Undefined
   d. Undefined

85. _____ is one of the three main rock groups and is formed in three main ways—by the deposition of the weathered remains of other rocks; by the deposition of the results of biogenic activity; and by precipitation from solution.
   a. Event
   b. Sedimentary rock10
   c. Undefined
   d. Undefined

86. The solid material that precipitates in the pore space of sediments, binding the grains together to form solid rock is referred to as _____.
   a. 1509 Istanbul earthquake
   b. Cement10
   c. Undefined
   d. Undefined

87. Rounded particles coarser than 2 mm in diameter are called _____.
   a. 1509 Istanbul earthquake
   b. Gravel10
   c. Undefined
   d. Undefined

88. The direction or trend of a bedding plane or fault, as it intersects the horizontal is referred to as a _____.
   a. Strike10
   b. 1509 Istanbul earthquake
   c. Undefined
   d. Undefined

89. A depression formed in a stream channel by the abrasive action of the water's sediment load is a _____.

Chapter 10. Streams and Floods

a. 1509 Istanbul earthquake
b. Pothole10
c. Undefined
d. Undefined

90. A rock particle 2 to 64 mm in diameter is referred to as the _____.
a. 1509 Istanbul earthquake
b. Pebble10
c. Undefined
d. Undefined

91. A body of sediment carried by a stream in the form of ions that have dissolved in the water is a _____.
a. Dissolved load10
b. 1509 Istanbul earthquake
c. Undefined
d. Undefined

92. _____ refers to a body of coarse particles that move along the bottom of a stream.
a. Bed load10
b. 1509 Istanbul earthquake
c. Undefined
d. Undefined

93. A mode of sediment transport in which the upward currents in eddies of turbulent flow are capable of supporting the weight of sediment particles and keeping them held indefinitely in the surrounding fluid is called _____.
a. Suspension10
b. 1509 Istanbul earthquake
c. Undefined
d. Undefined

94. The process of bouncing of grains along a surface by flowing air or water is referred to as _____.
a. Saltation10
b. 1509 Istanbul earthquake
c. Undefined
d. Undefined

95. Dragging or rolling of particles on a surface is _____.
a. 1509 Istanbul earthquake
b. Traction10
c. Undefined
d. Undefined

96. _____ refers to the process by which chemical reactions alter the chemical composition of rocks and minerals that are unstable at the Earth's surface and convert them into more stable substances; weathering that changes the chemical makeup of a rock or mineral.
a. Chemical weathering10
b. 1509 Istanbul earthquake
c. Undefined
d. Undefined

97. _____ is a chemical element in the periodic table. It has the symbol K (L. kalium) and atomic number 19. _____ is a soft silvery-white metallic alkali metal that occurs naturally bound to other elements in seawater and many minerals.
a. Thing
b. Potassium10
c. Undefined
d. Undefined

98. One of several minerals containing positive sulfur ions bonded to negative oxygen ions is _____.
a. 1509 Istanbul earthquake
b. Sulfate10
c. Undefined
d. Undefined

Chapter 10. Streams and Floods

99. _____ is the chemical element in the periodic table that has the symbol Ca and atomic number 20. _____ is a soft grey alkaline earth metal that is used as a reducing agent in the extraction of thorium, zirconium and uranium. _____ is also the fifth most abundant element in the Earth's crust.
- a. Calcium10
- b. Thing
- c. Undefined
- d. Undefined

100. _____ is the chemical element in the periodic table that has the symbol Na (Natrium in Latin) and atomic number 11. _____ is a soft, waxy, silvery reactive metal belonging to the alkali metals that is abundant in natural compounds (especially halite). It is highly reactive.
- a. Sodium10
- b. Thing
- c. Undefined
- d. Undefined

101. _____ refers to an atom or molecule that has gained or lost one or more electrons, thus acquiring an electrical charge.
- a. Thing
- b. Ion10
- c. Undefined
- d. Undefined

102. _____ refers to drop out of a saturated solution as crystals. The crystals that drop out of a saturated solution.
- a. 1509 Istanbul earthquake
- b. Precipitate10
- c. Undefined
- d. Undefined

103. Inorganic chemical sediment that precipitates when the salty water in which it had dissolved evaporates is called _____.
- a. Evaporite10
- b. AASHTO Soil Classification System
- c. Undefined
- d. Undefined

104. A naturally occurring, usually inorganic, solid consisting of either a single element or a compound, and having a definite chemical composition and a systematic internal arrangement of atoms is referred to as a _____.
- a. Mineral10
- b. 1509 Istanbul earthquake
- c. Undefined
- d. Undefined

105. _____ is a solid in which the constituent atoms, molecules, or ions are packed in a regularly ordered, repeating pattern extending in all three spatial dimensions.
- a. Crystal10
- b. Thing
- c. Undefined
- d. Undefined

106. A triangular deposit of sediment left by a stream that has lost velocity upon entering a broad, relatively flat valley is referred to as an _____.
- a. AASHTO Soil Classification System
- b. Alluvial fan10
- c. Undefined
- d. Undefined

107. _____ refers to pertaining to material or processes associated with transportation and or subaerial deposition by concentrated running water.
- a. AASHTO Soil Classification System
- b. Alluvial10
- c. Undefined
- d. Undefined

Chapter 10. Streams and Floods

108. An alluvial fan having its apex at the mouth of a stream is a _____.
   a. Delta10
   b. 1509 Istanbul earthquake
   c. Undefined
   d. Undefined

109. _____ is a chemical element in the periodic table that has the symbol Au and atomic number 79. A soft, shiny, yellow, dense, malleable, ductile (trivalent and univalent) transition metal, _____ does not react with most chemicals but is attacked by chlorine, fluorine and aqua regia.
   a. Gold10
   b. Thing
   c. Undefined
   d. Undefined

110. A deposit of heavy or durable minerals, such as gold or diamonds, typically found where the flow of water abruptly slows is called a _____.
   a. Placer deposit10
   b. 1509 Istanbul earthquake
   c. Undefined
   d. Undefined

111. _____ refers to a deposit formed when heavy minerals are mechanically concentrated by currents, most commonly streams and waves. Placers are sources of gold, tin, platinum, diamonds, and other valuable minerals.
   a. 1509 Istanbul earthquake
   b. Placer10
   c. Undefined
   d. Undefined

112. _____ refers to a major division on the geologic time scale; eras are divided into shorter units called periods.
   a. AASHTO Soil Classification System
   b. Era10
   c. Undefined
   d. Undefined

113. _____ is a common gray to black volcanic rock. It is usually fine-grained due to rapid cooling of lava on the Earth's surface.
   a. Thing
   b. Basalt10
   c. Undefined
   d. Undefined

114. _____ refers to the rapid, downward mass movement of particles coarser than sand, often including boulders one meter or more in diameter, at a rate ranging from 2 to 40 kilometers per hour. Debris flows occur along fairly steep slopes.
   a. Debris flow10
   b. 1509 Istanbul earthquake
   c. Undefined
   d. Undefined

115. Magma that comes to the Earth's surface through a volcano or fissure is referred to as _____.
   a. Lava10
   b. 1509 Istanbul earthquake
   c. Undefined
   d. Undefined

116. A network of converging and diverging streams separated from each other by narrow strips of sand and gravel are referred to as a _____.
   a. Braided stream10
   b. 1509 Istanbul earthquake
   c. Undefined
   d. Undefined

117. _____ refers to the process of water seeping down through cracks and pores in soil or rock.

a. Percolation10   b. Thing
c. Undefined   d. Undefined

118. A stream that traverses relatively flat land in fairly evenly spaced loops and separated from each other by narrow strips of floodplain is referred to as a _____.
   a. 1509 Istanbul earthquake   b. Meandering stream10
   c. Undefined   d. Undefined

119. A low ridge of sediment that forms along the inner bank of a meandering stream is referred to as a _____.
   a. 1509 Istanbul earthquake   b. Point bar10
   c. Undefined   d. Undefined

120. A _____ is a bend in a river, also known as an oxbow loop. A stream or river flowing through a wide valley or flat plain will tend to form a meandering stream course as it alternatively erodes and deposites sediments along its course.
   a. Meander10   b. Thing
   c. Undefined   d. Undefined

121. A new, shorter channel across the narrow neck of a meander is a _____.
   a. 1509 Istanbul earthquake   b. Meander cutoff10
   c. Undefined   d. Undefined

122. A short channel segment created when a river erodes through the narrow neck of land between meanders is referred to as _____.
   a. 1509 Istanbul earthquake   b. Cutoff10
   c. Undefined   d. Undefined

123. A crescent-shaped body of standing water formed from a single loop that was cut off from a meandering stream, typically by a flood that allowed the stream to flow through its floodplain and bypass the loop, is called the _____.
   a. AASHTO Soil Classification System   b. Oxbow lake10
   c. Undefined   d. Undefined

124. The accumulation of precipitation into surface and underground areas, including lakes, rivers, and aquifers is a _____.
   a. Collection10   b. 1509 Istanbul earthquake
   c. Undefined   d. Undefined

125. _____ refers to a long, broad low ridge or embankment of sand and coarse silt, built by a stream on its flood plain and along both sides of its channel, especially in time of flood when water overflowing the normal banks is forced to deposit the coarsest part of its load.
   a. Natural levee10   b. 1509 Istanbul earthquake
   c. Undefined   d. Undefined

126. _____ refer to embankments of sand or silt built by a stream along both banks of its channel. They are deposited during floods, when waters overflowing the stream banks are forced to deposit sediment.

Chapter 10. Streams and Floods 191

a. Levees10
b. 1509 Istanbul earthquake
c. Undefined
d. Undefined

127.   A protective barrier built along the banks of a stream to prevent flooding is a _____.
a. 1509 Istanbul earthquake
b. Levee10
c. Undefined
d. Undefined

128.   _____ refers to the section of a floodplain where deposits of fine silts and clays settle after a flood. Backswamps usually lie behind a stream's natural levees.
a. Backswamp10
b. 1509 Istanbul earthquake
c. Undefined
d. Undefined

129.   One of a network of small streams carrying water and sediment from a trunk stream into an ocean is called a _____.
a. Distributary10
b. 1509 Istanbul earthquake
c. Undefined
d. Undefined

130.   A delta formed by the reworking of sand by wave action is referred to as a _____.
a. Wave-dominated delta10
b. 1509 Istanbul earthquake
c. Undefined
d. Undefined

131.   A long and narrow island that is built by waves along the coast is called _____.
a. Barrier island10
b. Thing
c. Undefined
d. Undefined

132.   _____ refers to a delta formed by the reworking of sand by strong tides.
a. 1509 Istanbul earthquake
b. Tide-dominated delta10
c. Undefined
d. Undefined

133.   The alternating horizontal movement of water associated with the rise and fall of the tide is _____.
a. 1509 Istanbul earthquake
b. Tidal current10
c. Undefined
d. Undefined

134.   _____ refers to the area of dry land that borders on a body of water.
a. Coast10
b. 1509 Istanbul earthquake
c. Undefined
d. Undefined

135.   The periodic, rhythmic rise and fall of the sea surface caused by changes in gravitational forces external to the Earth is referred to as the _____.
a. Tide10
b. Thing
c. Undefined
d. Undefined

136.   The excavation of earth material from the bottom of a body of water by a floating barge or raft equipped to scoop up, discharge by conveyors, and process or transport materials is called _____.

Chapter 10. Streams and Floods

a. Dredging10
b. 1509 Istanbul earthquake
c. Undefined
d. Undefined

137. _____ refers to an inclined bed deposited along the front of a delta.
a. Foreset bed10
b. 1509 Istanbul earthquake
c. Undefined
d. Undefined

138. _____ refers to an essentially horizontal sedimentary layer deposited on top of a delta during floodstage.
a. 1509 Istanbul earthquake
b. Topset bed10
c. Undefined
d. Undefined

139. A layer of fine sediment deposited beyond the advancing edge of a delta and then buried by continued delta growth is referred to as _____.
a. Bottomset bed10
b. 1509 Istanbul earthquake
c. Undefined
d. Undefined

140. The diagenetic process by which the volume or thickness of sediment is reduced due to pressure from overlying layers of sediment is called _____.
a. 1509 Istanbul earthquake
b. Compaction10
c. Undefined
d. Undefined

141. _____ is a term used in geology, engineering and surveying to denote the motion of a surface (usually, the earth's surface) downwards relative to a datum such as sea-level.
a. Subsidence10
b. Thing
c. Undefined
d. Undefined

142. _____ refers to a delta with fingerlike distributaries formed by the dominance of stream sedimentation.
a. 1509 Istanbul earthquake
b. Stream-dominated delta10
c. Undefined
d. Undefined

143. _____ refers to a portion of a rock unit that possesses a distinctive set of characteristics that distinguishes it from other parts of the same unit.
a. Facies10
b. 1509 Istanbul earthquake
c. Undefined
d. Undefined

144. _____ is a term used for ionic compounds composed of positively charged cations and negatively charged anions, so that the product is neutral and without a net charge.
a. Thing
b. Salt10
c. Undefined
d. Undefined

145. The top of the ocean, where the water meets the atmosphere is called _____.
a. Sea level10
b. 1509 Istanbul earthquake
c. Undefined
d. Undefined

146. The time between winter and summer is _____.

Chapter 10. Streams and Floods

a. Spring10
c. Undefined

b. 1509 Istanbul earthquake
d. Undefined

147. _____ refers to the return period of an event, such as a flood or earthquake, of a given magnitude. For flooding, it is the average interval of time within which a given flood will be equaled or exceeded by the annual maximum discharge.
   a. 1509 Istanbul earthquake
   c. Undefined
   b. Recurrence interval10
   d. Undefined

148. _____ or capillarity is the ability of a narrow tube to draw a liquid upwards against the force of gravity. It occurs when the adhesive intermolecular forces between the liquid and a solid are stronger than the cohesive intermolecular forces within the liquid.
   a. Thing
   c. Undefined
   b. Capillary action10
   d. Undefined

149. _____ refers to flood of very high discharge and short duration; sudden and local in extent.
   a. 1509 Istanbul earthquake
   c. Undefined
   b. Flash flood10
   d. Undefined

150. _____ refers to the altitude, or vertical distance, above or below sea level.
   a. Elevation10
   c. Undefined
   b. AASHTO Soil Classification System
   d. Undefined

151. The average time interval between floods that is equal to or greater than a specified discharge is referred to as _____.
   a. Flood frequency10
   c. Undefined
   b. 1509 Istanbul earthquake
   d. Undefined

152. A mineral or fuel deposit, known or not yet discovered, that may be or become available for human exploitation is called a _____.
   a. 1509 Istanbul earthquake
   c. Undefined
   b. Resource10
   d. Undefined

153. _____ refers to an embankment constructed to contain a stream at flood stage.
   a. Artificial levee10
   c. Undefined
   b. AASHTO Soil Classification System
   d. Undefined

154. A pile of large, angular boulders built seaward of the shoreline to prevent erosion by waves or current is referred to as a _____.
   a. 1509 Istanbul earthquake
   c. Undefined
   b. Riprap10
   d. Undefined

155. A heavily reinforced wall designed to contain a stream at flood stage is referred to as a _____.
   a. Floodwall10
   c. Undefined
   b. 1509 Istanbul earthquake
   d. Undefined

Chapter 10. Streams and Floods

156. _____ refers to any physical, recognizable form or feature on the earth's surface, having a characteristic shape and range in composition, and produced by natural causes.
    a. 1509 Istanbul earthquake
    b. Landform10
    c. Undefined
    d. Undefined

157. A valley-deepening process caused by erosion of a stream bed is called _____.
    a. Downcutting10
    b. 1509 Istanbul earthquake
    c. Undefined
    d. Undefined

158. The lowest level to which a stream can erode the channel through which it flows, generally equal to the prevailing global sea level is referred to as the _____.
    a. 1509 Istanbul earthquake
    b. Base level10
    c. Undefined
    d. Undefined

159. _____ refers to the beginning or source area for a stream. Also called the headwaters.
    a. Head10
    b. 1509 Istanbul earthquake
    c. Undefined
    d. Undefined

160. The first epoch of the Quaternary Period, beginning 2 to 3 million years ago and ending approximately 10,000 years ago is referred to as the _____.
    a. Pleistocene epoch10
    b. 1509 Istanbul earthquake
    c. Undefined
    d. Undefined

161. A geologic epoch, characterized by alternating glacial and interglacial stages, that ended about 10,000 years ago, that lasted for 2 million years is called the _____ epoch.
    a. Thing
    b. Pleistocene10
    c. Undefined
    d. Undefined

162. A unit of the geologic time scale that is a subdivision of a period is referred to as an _____.
    a. AASHTO Soil Classification System
    b. Epoch10
    c. Undefined
    d. Undefined

163. _____ refers to a place in which water is stored, including the oceans, glaciers and polar ice, groundwater, lakes and rivers, the atmosphere, and the biosphere. A source or place of residence for elements in a chemical cycle or hydrologic cycle.
    a. Reservoir10
    b. 1509 Istanbul earthquake
    c. Undefined
    d. Undefined

164. A fracture dividing a rock into two sections that have visibly moved relative to each other is a _____.
    a. Fault10
    b. 1509 Istanbul earthquake
    c. Undefined
    d. Undefined

165. The level of a lake, resistant rock layer, or any other base level that stands above sea level is a _____.
    a. Temporary base level10
    b. 1509 Istanbul earthquake
    c. Undefined
    d. Undefined

Chapter 10. Streams and Floods

166. A stream maintaining an equilibrium between the processes of erosion and deposition, and therefore between aggradation and degradation is called _____.
 a. 1509 Istanbul earthquake
 b. Graded stream10
 c. Undefined
 d. Undefined

167. The ability of a given stream to carry sediment, measured as the maximum quantity it can transport past a given point on the channel bank in a given amount of time is called _____.
 a. 1509 Istanbul earthquake
 b. Capacity10
 c. Undefined
 d. Undefined

168. _____ refers to erosion and undercutting of stream banks caused by a stream swinging from side to side across its valley floor.
 a. Lateral erosion10
 b. 1509 Istanbul earthquake
 c. Undefined
 d. Undefined

169. The extension upslope of the head of a valley due to erosion is _____.
 a. 1509 Istanbul earthquake
 b. Headward erosion10
 c. Undefined
 d. Undefined

170. _____ refers to the cutting of channels into the landscape by running water. When extreme, it renders farmland useless.
 a. Gullying10
 b. 1509 Istanbul earthquake
 c. Undefined
 d. Undefined

171. A level plain lying above and running parallel to a streambed is a _____. A _____ is formed when a stream's bed erodes to a substantially lower level, leaving its floodplain high above it.
 a. 1509 Istanbul earthquake
 b. Stream terrace10
 c. Undefined
 d. Undefined

172. A flat, steplike surface that lines a stream above the floodplain, often paired one on each side of the stream, marking a former floodplain that existed at a higher level before regional uplift or an increase in discharge caused the stream to erode into it is called the _____.
 a. 1509 Istanbul earthquake
 b. Terrace10
 c. Undefined
 d. Undefined

173. The unstable, newly-formed front of a lava delta is a _____.
 a. Bench10
 b. 1509 Istanbul earthquake
 c. Undefined
 d. Undefined

174. _____ refers to deposits of stratified sand, gravel, and silt that have been removed from a glacier by meltwater streams.
 a. 1509 Istanbul earthquake
 b. Glacial outwash10
 c. Undefined
 d. Undefined

175. A load of sediment, consisting of sand and gravel that is deposited by meltwater in front of a glacier is called _____.

Chapter 10. Streams and Floods

a. Outwash10
b. AASHTO Soil Classification System
c. Undefined
d. Undefined

176. _____ refers to general term referring to the rock underlying other unconsolidated material, i.e. soil.
a. 1509 Istanbul earthquake
b. Bedrock10
c. Undefined
d. Undefined

177. _____ refers to a meandering channel that flows in a steep, narrow valley. These features form either when an area is uplifted or when base level drops.
a. AASHTO Soil Classification System
b. Incised meander10
c. Undefined
d. Undefined

178. A body of rock identified by lithic characteristics and stratigraphic position and is mappable at the earth's surface or traceable in the subsurface is a _____.
a. 1509 Istanbul earthquake
b. Formation10
c. Undefined
d. Undefined

179. _____ refers to a stream that cuts through a ridge lying across its path. The stream established its course on uniform layers at a higher level without regard to underlying structures.
a. Superposed stream10
b. 1509 Istanbul earthquake
c. Undefined
d. Undefined

180. _____ refers to a group of closely spaced mountains or parallel ridges.
a. 1509 Istanbul earthquake
b. Mountain range10
c. Undefined
d. Undefined

181. The scientific study of the Earth, its origins and evolution, the materials that make it up, and the processes that act on it is called _____.
a. 1509 Istanbul earthquake
b. Geology10
c. Undefined
d. Undefined

182. The _____ is one of three geologic eras of the Phanerozoic eon. The division of time into eras dates back to Giovanni Arduino in the 18th century, although his original name for the era now called the _____ was "Secondary".
a. Mesozoic10
b. Thing
c. Undefined
d. Undefined

183. Parallel layers of sedimentary rock are called _____.
a. 1509 Istanbul earthquake
b. Strata10
c. Undefined
d. Undefined

184. _____ refers to a term loosely used for an igneous or metamorphic rock, as distinguished from a sedimentary rock. In mining, a rock that requires drilling and blasting for economical removal.
a. Hard rock10
b. 1509 Istanbul earthquake
c. Undefined
d. Undefined

185. Temporary base level is referred to as _____.

Chapter 10. Streams and Floods

a. Local base level10
c. Undefined
b. 1509 Istanbul earthquake
d. Undefined

186. A numerical expression of the amount of energy released by an earthquake, determined by measuring earthquake waves on standardized recording instruments is called a _____. The number scale for magnitudes is logarithmic rather than arithmetic. Therefore, deflections on a seismograph for a _____ 5 earthquake, for example, are 10 times greater than those for a _____ 4 earthquake, 100 times greater than for a _____ 3 earthquake, and so on.

a. Magnitude10
c. Undefined
b. 1509 Istanbul earthquake
d. Undefined

Chapter 11. Ground Water

1. _____ refers to the water that lies beneath the ground surface, filling the cracks, crevices, and pore space of rocks.
   a. Ground water11
   b. 1509 Istanbul earthquake
   c. Undefined
   d. Undefined

2. A major branch of a stream system is referred to as a _____.
   a. 1509 Istanbul earthquake
   b. River11
   c. Undefined
   d. Undefined

3. A mineral or fuel deposit, known or not yet discovered, that may be or become available for human exploitation is called a _____.
   a. Resource11
   b. 1509 Istanbul earthquake
   c. Undefined
   d. Undefined

4. Weather condition of an area including especially prevailing temperature and average daily/yearly rainfall over a long period of time is called _____.
   a. Climate11
   b. Thing
   c. Undefined
   d. Undefined

5. Any environmental change that adversely affects the lives and health of living things is referred to as _____.
   a. Pollution11
   b. Thing
   c. Undefined
   d. Undefined

6. Group of organisms of the same species occupying a certain area and sharing a common gene pool is referred to as _____.
   a. Population11
   b. Thing
   c. Undefined
   d. Undefined

7. A material that forms as the organic matter of buried wood is either filled in or replaced by inorganic silica carried in by ground water is called _____.
   a. Petrified wood11
   b. 1509 Istanbul earthquake
   c. Undefined
   d. Undefined

8. A large hole resulting from the collapse of an underground cavern is called _____.
   a. Sinkhole11
   b. Thing
   c. Undefined
   d. Undefined

9. _____ refers to a naturally formed opening beneath the surface of the Earth, generally formed by dissolution of carbonate bedrock. Caves may also form by erosion of coastal bedrock, partial melting of glaciers, or solidification of lava into hollow tubes.
   a. 1509 Istanbul earthquake
   b. Cave11
   c. Undefined
   d. Undefined

10. _____ refers to useful energy derived from the naturally hot interior of Earth.
    a. Thing
    b. Geothermal energy11
    c. Undefined
    d. Undefined

Chapter 11. Ground Water

11. _____ is the naturally hot interior of Earth. The heat is maintained by naturally occurring nuclear reactions in Earth's interior.
    a. Geothermal11
    b. Thing
    c. Undefined
    d. Undefined

12. Ability to do work is referred to as _____. Most evident in glacial systems as radiant _____ from the sun and as latent _____ required to melt ice to water.
    a. Energy11
    b. AASHTO Soil Classification System
    c. Undefined
    d. Undefined

13. _____ in physical geography, describes the collective mass of water found on, under, and over the surface of a planet.
    a. Thing
    b. Hydrosphere11
    c. Undefined
    d. Undefined

14. Earth's _____ is a layer of gases surrounding the planet Earth and retained by the Earth's gravity. It contains roughly 78% nitrogen and 21% oxygen, with trace amounts of other gases.
    a. Atmosphere11
    b. Thing
    c. Undefined
    d. Undefined

15. _____ refers to a place in which water is stored, including the oceans, glaciers and polar ice, groundwater, lakes and rivers, the atmosphere, and the biosphere. A source or place of residence for elements in a chemical cycle or hydrologic cycle.
    a. 1509 Istanbul earthquake
    b. Reservoir11
    c. Undefined
    d. Undefined

16. A moving body of ice that forms on land from the accumulation and compaction of snow, and that flows downslope or outward due to gravity and the pressure of its own weight is a _____.
    a. 1509 Istanbul earthquake
    b. Glacier11
    c. Undefined
    d. Undefined

17. _____ refers to the top few meters of regolith, generally including some organic matter derived from plants.
    a. 1509 Istanbul earthquake
    b. Soil11
    c. Undefined
    d. Undefined

18. Includes all bodies of water, lakes, rivers, ponds, and so on that are on the surface of the earth, in contrast to groundwater, which lies below the surface is _____.
    a. Surface water11
    b. Thing
    c. Undefined
    d. Undefined

19. _____ refers to any condensed water falling from the atmosphere to the surface of the earth. Common types include rain, snow, sleet, and hail.
    a. 1509 Istanbul earthquake
    b. Precipitation11
    c. Undefined
    d. Undefined

20. _____ refers to a naturally formed aggregate of usually inorganic materials from within the Earth.

a. Rock11
b. 1509 Istanbul earthquake
c. Undefined
d. Undefined

21. The capability of a given substance to allow the passage of a fluid is called _____. _____ depends on the size of and the degree of connection among a substance's pores.
   a. 1509 Istanbul earthquake
   b. Permeability11
   c. Undefined
   d. Undefined

22. The percentage of a soil, rock, or sediment's volume that is made up of pores is _____.
   a. 1509 Istanbul earthquake
   b. Porosity11
   c. Undefined
   d. Undefined

23. _____ is any particulate matter that can be transported by fluid flow and which eventually is deposited as a layer of solid particles on the bed or bottom of a body of water or other liquid.
   a. Sediment11
   b. Thing
   c. Undefined
   d. Undefined

24. Describing a substance in which the atoms are arranged in a regular, repeating, orderly pattern is called _____.
   a. 1509 Istanbul earthquake
   b. Crystalline11
   c. Undefined
   d. Undefined

25. _____ is a sedimentary rock composed largely of the mineral calcite (calcium carbonate: $CaCO_3$). _____ often contains variable amounts of silica in the form of chert or flint, as well as varying amounts of clay, silt and sand as disseminations, nodules, or layers within the rock.
   a. Thing
   b. Limestone11
   c. Undefined
   d. Undefined

26. A pink-colored, felsic, plutonic rock that contains potassium and usually sodium feldspars, and has quartz content of about 10% is _____. _____ is commonly found on continents but virtually absent from the ocean basins.
   a. 1509 Istanbul earthquake
   b. Granite11
   c. Undefined
   d. Undefined

27. A coarse-grained, strongly foliated metamorphic rock that develops from phyllite and splits easily into flat, parallel slabs is _____.
   a. Schist11
   b. 1509 Istanbul earthquake
   c. Undefined
   d. Undefined

28. Aggregates of minerals or rock fragments are called _____.
   a. 1509 Istanbul earthquake
   b. Rocks11
   c. Undefined
   d. Undefined

29. _____ refers to any of a group of naturally occurring substances made up of hydrocarbons. These substances may be gaseous, liquid, or semi-solid.
   a. Petroleum11
   b. 1509 Istanbul earthquake
   c. Undefined
   d. Undefined

Chapter 11. Ground Water

30. The ability of a given stream to carry sediment, measured as the maximum quantity it can transport past a given point on the channel bank in a given amount of time is called _____.
   a. Capacity11
   b. 1509 Istanbul earthquake
   c. Undefined
   d. Undefined

31. _____ refers to a crack or break in a rock. To break in random places instead of cleaving.
   a. 1509 Istanbul earthquake
   b. Fracture11
   c. Undefined
   d. Undefined

32. _____ refers to a clastic rock composed of particles more than 2 millimeters in diameter and marked by the roundness of its component grains and rock fragments.
   a. Conglomerate11
   b. 1509 Istanbul earthquake
   c. Undefined
   d. Undefined

33. _____ refers to a clastic rock composed of particles that range in diameter from 1/16 millimeter to 2 millimeters in diameter. Sandstones make up about 25% of all sedimentary rocks.
   a. Sandstone11
   b. 1509 Istanbul earthquake
   c. Undefined
   d. Undefined

34. _____ refers to a sedimentary rock composed of detrital sediment particles less than 0.004 millimeters in diameter. _____ tends to be red, brown, black, or gray, and usually originate in relatively still waters.
   a. 1509 Istanbul earthquake
   b. Shale11
   c. Undefined
   d. Undefined

35. _____ refers to the process of water seeping down through cracks and pores in soil or rock.
   a. Thing
   b. Percolation11
   c. Undefined
   d. Undefined

36. A _____ is the outer layer of a planet, part of its lithosphere. Planetary _____ is generally composed of a less dense material than that of its deeper layers. The _____ of the Earth is composed mainly of basalt and granite.
   a. Crust11
   b. Thing
   c. Undefined
   d. Undefined

37. _____ is one of the three main rock groups and is formed in three main ways—by the deposition of the weathered remains of other rocks; by the deposition of the results of biogenic activity; and by precipitation from solution.
   a. Sedimentary rock11
   b. Event
   c. Undefined
   d. Undefined

38. The solid material that precipitates in the pore space of sediments, binding the grains together to form solid rock is referred to as _____.
   a. 1509 Istanbul earthquake
   b. Cement11
   c. Undefined
   d. Undefined

39. _____ refers to the area of dry land that borders on a body of water.

202   Chapter 11. Ground Water

    a. Coast11
    c. Undefined
    b. 1509 Istanbul earthquake
    d. Undefined

40. _____ refers to the zone below the water table.
    a. 1509 Istanbul earthquake
    b. Saturated zone11
    c. Undefined
    d. Undefined

41. Any relatively sunken part of the Earth's surface, especially a low-lying area surrounded by higher ground is called a _____.
    a. Depression11
    b. 1509 Istanbul earthquake
    c. Undefined
    d. Undefined

42. _____ refers to the beginning or source area for a stream. Also called the headwaters.
    a. 1509 Istanbul earthquake
    b. Head11
    c. Undefined
    d. Undefined

43. _____ refers to the altitude, or vertical distance, above or below sea level.
    a. AASHTO Soil Classification System
    b. Elevation11
    c. Undefined
    d. Undefined

44. _____ refers to a zone in which water is held as a film on the surface of soil particles and may be used by plants or withdrawn by evaporation. The uppermost subdivision of the zone of aeration.
    a. Belt of soil moisture11
    b. 1509 Istanbul earthquake
    c. Undefined
    d. Undefined

45. _____ refer to hydrous aluminum silicates that have a layered atomic structure. They are very fine grained and become plastic when wet. Most belong to one of three clay groups: kaolinite, illite, and smectite.
    a. 1509 Istanbul earthquake
    b. Clay minerals11
    c. Undefined
    d. Undefined

46. A hydrous aluminum-silicate that occurs as a platy grain of microscopic size with a sheet silicate structure is _____.
    a. 1509 Istanbul earthquake
    b. Clay mineral11
    c. Undefined
    d. Undefined

47. The _____, also termed the unsaturated zone, is the portion of Earth between the land surface and the water table, and is thus not considered groundwater. It comprises the unsaturated portion of the soil, regolith or bedrock, as well as the unsaturated portion of the capillary fringe above the water table.
    a. Vadose zone11
    b. Thing
    c. Undefined
    d. Undefined

48. A naturally occurring, usually inorganic, solid consisting of either a single element or a compound, and having a definite chemical composition and a systematic internal arrangement of atoms is referred to as a _____.
    a. 1509 Istanbul earthquake
    b. Mineral11
    c. Undefined
    d. Undefined

Chapter 11. Ground Water

49. _____ refers to a body of water found on the Earth's surface and confined to a narrow topographic depression, down which it flows and transports rock particles, sediment, and dissolved particles. Rivers, creeks, brooks, and runs are all streams.
   a. Stream11
   b. 1509 Istanbul earthquake
   c. Undefined
   d. Undefined

50. The time between winter and summer is _____.
   a. Spring11
   b. 1509 Istanbul earthquake
   c. Undefined
   d. Undefined

51. _____ refers to the difference in potential between two points, divided by the lateral distance between the points.
   a. 1509 Istanbul earthquake
   b. Hydraulic gradient11
   c. Undefined
   d. Undefined

52. Water stored beneath the surface in open pore spaces and fractures in rock is called _____.
   a. 1509 Istanbul earthquake
   b. Groundwater11
   c. Undefined
   d. Undefined

53. The vertical drop in a stream's elevation over a given horizontal distance, expressed as an angle is referred to as a _____.
   a. Gradient11
   b. 1509 Istanbul earthquake
   c. Undefined
   d. Undefined

54. The extent to which a given substance allows water to flow through it, determined by such factors as sorting and grain size and shape is called _____.
   a. 1509 Istanbul earthquake
   b. Hydraulic conductivity11
   c. Undefined
   d. Undefined

55. An _____ is an underground layer of water-bearing permeable rock, or unconsolidated materials (gravel, sand, silt, or clay) from which groundwater can be usefully extracted using a water well.
   a. Thing
   b. Aquifer11
   c. Undefined
   d. Undefined

56. The force of attraction exerted by one body in the universe on another is _____. _____ is directly proportional to the product of the masses of the two attracted bodies. The force of attraction exerted by the Earth on bodies on or near its surface, tending to pull them toward the Earth's center.
   a. Gravity11
   b. 1509 Istanbul earthquake
   c. Undefined
   d. Undefined

57. _____ in referring to sediment grains, loose, separate, or unattached to one another.
   a. Unconsolidated11
   b. AASHTO Soil Classification System
   c. Undefined
   d. Undefined

58. Rounded particles coarser than 2 mm in diameter are called _____.

a. 1509 Istanbul earthquake
b. Gravel11
c. Undefined
d. Undefined

59. _____ refers to the smallest possible unit of a substance that has the properties of that substance.
a. 1509 Istanbul earthquake
b. Molecule11
c. Undefined
d. Undefined

60. _____ refers to a coarse-grained, foliated metamorphic rock marked by bands of light-colored minerals such as quartz and feldspar that alternate with bands of dark-colored minerals. This alternation develops through metamorphic differentiation.
a. Gneiss11
b. 1509 Istanbul earthquake
c. Undefined
d. Undefined

61. _____ refers to any of a group of dark, dense, phaneritic, intrusive rocks that are the plutonic equivalent to basalt.
a. 1509 Istanbul earthquake
b. Gabbro11
c. Undefined
d. Undefined

62. An aquifer overlain by a non-permeable layer or layers, in which pressure will force water to rise above the aquifer, is called _____.
a. 1509 Istanbul earthquake
b. Confined aquifer11
c. Undefined
d. Undefined

63. With reference to groundwater, the area over which infiltration and resupply of a given aquifer occurs is a _____.
a. Recharge area11
b. Thing
c. Undefined
d. Undefined

64. The quantity of water in a stream that passes a given point in a period of time is referred to as _____.
a. Discharge11
b. 1509 Istanbul earthquake
c. Undefined
d. Undefined

65. _____ refers to the addition of new water to an aquifer or to the zone of saturation.
a. Recharge11
b. 1509 Istanbul earthquake
c. Undefined
d. Undefined

66. _____ refers to a cone-shaped depression in the water table immediately surrounding a well.
a. 1509 Istanbul earthquake
b. Cone of depression11
c. Undefined
d. Undefined

67. _____ refers to the difference in height between the bottom of a cone of depression and the original height of the water table.
a. Drawdown11
b. 1509 Istanbul earthquake
c. Undefined
d. Undefined

68. A well in an aquifer where the groundwater is confined under pressure and the water level will rise above the top of the confined aquifer is an _____.

a. AASHTO Soil Classification System
b. Artesian well11
c. Undefined
d. Undefined

69. The relationship between humans and their geological environment is called _____.
a. Environmental geology11
b. AASHTO Soil Classification System
c. Undefined
d. Undefined

70. The scientific study of the Earth, its origins and evolution, the materials that make it up, and the processes that act on it is called _____.
a. 1509 Istanbul earthquake
b. Geology11
c. Undefined
d. Undefined

71. _____ refers to a person who studies the geology and management of underground and related aspects of surface waters.
a. 1509 Istanbul earthquake
b. Hydrogeologist11
c. Undefined
d. Undefined

72. A naturally formed underground chamber or series of chambers most commonly produced by solution activity in limestone is called a _____.
a. Cavern11
b. 1509 Istanbul earthquake
c. Undefined
d. Undefined

73. A fracture dividing a rock into two sections that have visibly moved relative to each other is a _____.
a. Fault11
b. 1509 Istanbul earthquake
c. Undefined
d. Undefined

74. Streams that lose water to the groundwater system by outflow through the streambed are called a _____.
a. 1509 Istanbul earthquake
b. Losing stream11
c. Undefined
d. Undefined

75. _____ refers to a chemical substance that kills plants.
a. Thing
b. Herbicide11
c. Undefined
d. Undefined

76. To dissolve from a rock is called _____.
a. Leach11
b. 1509 Istanbul earthquake
c. Undefined
d. Undefined

77. _____ refers to a salt of nitric acid; a compound containing the radical NO_3; biologically, the final form of nitrogen from the oxidation of organic nitrogen compounds.
a. Thing
b. Nitrate11
c. Undefined
d. Undefined

78. _____ is a chemical element in the periodic table that has the symbol Hg and atomic number 80. A heavy, silvery, transition metal, _____ is one of five elements that are liquid at or near standard room temperature (the others are the metals caesium, francium, and gallium, and the nonmetal bromine).

a. Mercury11
b. Thing
c. Undefined
d. Undefined

79. _____ is a class of organic compounds with 1 to 10 chlorine atoms attached to biphenyl and a general structure of $C_{12}H_{10-x}Cl_x$.
   a. Polychlorinated biphenyl11
   b. Thing
   c. Undefined
   d. Undefined

80. The _____ are a group of elements between copper and lead on the periodic table of the elements—having atomic weights between 63.546 and 200.590 and specific gravities greater than 4.0.
   a. Heavy metals11
   b. Thing
   c. Undefined
   d. Undefined

81. An electrically neutral substance that consists of two or more elements combined in specific, constant proportions is a _____. A _____ typically has physical characteristics different from those of its constituent elements.
   a. Compound11
   b. 1509 Istanbul earthquake
   c. Undefined
   d. Undefined

82. _____ is a chemical element in the periodic table that has the symbol Cr and atomic number 24. _____ (0) is unstable in oxygen, immediately producing a thin oxide layer that is impermeable to oxygen and protects the metal below.
   a. Thing
   b. Chromium11
   c. Undefined
   d. Undefined

83. A _____ is an organism that spends a significant portion of its life in or on the living tissue of a host organism and which causes harm to the host without immediately killing it. They also commonly show highly specialized adaptations allowing them to exploit host resources.
   a. Parasite11
   b. Thing
   c. Undefined
   d. Undefined

84. _____ is a chemical element in the periodic table that has the symbol Cd and atomic number 48. A relatively rare, soft, bluish-white, toxic transition metal, _____ occurs with zinc ores and is used largely in batteries.
   a. Thing
   b. Cadmium11
   c. Undefined
   d. Undefined

85. _____ is a chemical element in the periodic table that has the symbol Cu (L.: Cuprum) and atomic number 29. It is a ductile metal with excellent electrical conductivity, and finds extensive use as a building material, as an electrical conductor, and as a component of various alloys.
   a. Thing
   b. Copper11
   c. Undefined
   d. Undefined

86. _____ is a chemical element in the periodic table that has the symbol Pb and atomic number 82. A soft, heavy, toxic and malleable poor metal, _____ is bluish white when freshly cut but tarnishes to dull gray when exposed to air. _____ is used in building construction, _____-acid batteries, bullets and shot, and is part of solder, pewter, and fusible alloys.

Chapter 11. Ground Water

    a. Thing   b. Lead11
    c. Undefined   d. Undefined

87. _____ refers to the outflow of acidic water from abandoned metal mines. In many localities the liquor that drains from coal stocks, coal handling facilities, coal washeries, and even coal waste tips can be highly acidic, and in such cases it is treated as _____.
    a. Acid mine drainage11   b. Thing
    c. Undefined   d. Undefined

88. An _____ is a water-soluble, sour-tasting chemical compound that when dissolved in water, gives a solution with a pH of less than 7.
    a. Thing   b. Acid11
    c. Undefined   d. Undefined

89. A member of a group of easily combustible, organic sedimentary rocks composed mostly of plant remains and containing a high proportion of carbon is called _____.
    a. 1509 Istanbul earthquake   b. Coal11
    c. Undefined   d. Undefined

90. _____ refers to the major constituent of acid precipitation. Formed as a result of sulfur dioxide emissions reacting with water vapor in the atmosphere.
    a. Thing   b. Sulfuric acid11
    c. Undefined   d. Undefined

91. _____ refers to the loss of electrons from a substance involved in a redox reaction; always accompanies reduction.
    a. Thing   b. Oxidation11
    c. Undefined   d. Undefined

92. One of the minerals that is abundant in the hot water that seeps through hydrothermal vents is _____.
    a. Thing   b. Sulfide11
    c. Undefined   d. Undefined

93. _____ is the chemical element in the periodic table that has the symbol S and atomic number 16. It is an abundant, tasteless, odorless, multivalent non-metal. _____, in its native form, is a yellow crystaline solid. In nature, it can be found as the pure element or as sulfide and sulfate minerals.
    a. Thing   b. Sulfur11
    c. Undefined   d. Undefined

94. A term used to describe the property of releasing energy or particles from an unstable atom is called _____.
    a. Radioactive11   b. Thing
    c. Undefined   d. Undefined

95. A large mass of rock projecting above surrounding terrain is called a _____.

a. Mountain11
b. 1509 Istanbul earthquake
c. Undefined
d. Undefined

96. _____ refers to any natural or artificial substance that enters the ecosystem in such quantities that it does harm to the ecosystem; any introduced substance that makes a resource unfit for a specific purpose.
a. Pollutant11
b. Thing
c. Undefined
d. Undefined

97. A chemical _____, often called simply _____, is a chemical substance that cannot be divided or changed into other chemical substances by any ordinary chemical technique. An _____ is a class of substances that contain the same number of protons in all its atoms.
a. Element11
b. Thing
c. Undefined
d. Undefined

98. A _____ is a landscape form or region that receives little precipitation - less than 250 mm (10 in) per year. It is a biome characterized by organisms adapted to sparse rainfall and rapid evaporation.
a. Thing
b. Desert11
c. Undefined
d. Undefined

99. _____ is the chemical element in the periodic table that has the symbol Na (Natrium in Latin) and atomic number 11. _____ is a soft, waxy, silvery reactive metal belonging to the alkali metals that is abundant in natural compounds (especially halite). It is highly reactive.
a. Sodium11
b. Thing
c. Undefined
d. Undefined

100. _____ is a term used for ionic compounds composed of positively charged cations and negatively charged anions, so that the product is neutral and without a net charge.
a. Thing
b. Salt11
c. Undefined
d. Undefined

101. Iron/magnesium bearing mineral, such as augite, hornblende, olivine, or biotite is a _____.
a. 1509 Istanbul earthquake
b. Ferromagnesian mineral11
c. Undefined
d. Undefined

102. _____ refers to the process by which chemical reactions alter the chemical composition of rocks and minerals that are unstable at the Earth's surface and convert them into more stable substances; weathering that changes the chemical makeup of a rock or mineral.
a. Chemical weathering11
b. 1509 Istanbul earthquake
c. Undefined
d. Undefined

103. _____ refers to minerals or rocks that are rich in iron and magnesium, such as olivine and pyroxene.
a. 1509 Istanbul earthquake
b. Ferromagnesian11
c. Undefined
d. Undefined

Chapter 11. Ground Water

104. The process by which exposure to atmospheric agents, such as air or moisture, causes rocks and minerals to break down is called _____. This process takes place at or near the Earth's surface. _____ entails little or no movement of the material that it loosens from the rocks and minerals.
   a. Weathering11
   b. 1509 Istanbul earthquake
   c. Undefined
   d. Undefined

105. _____ is the chemical element in the periodic table that has the symbol Mg and atomic number 12 and an atomic mass of 24.31.
   a. Thing
   b. Magnesium11
   c. Undefined
   d. Undefined

106. _____ is the chemical element in the periodic table that has the symbol Ca and atomic number 20. _____ is a soft grey alkaline earth metal that is used as a reducing agent in the extraction of thorium, zirconium and uranium. _____ is also the fifth most abundant element in the Earth's crust.
   a. Calcium11
   b. Thing
   c. Undefined
   d. Undefined

107. _____ is soil composed of a relatively even mixture of three mineral particle size groups: sand, silt, and clay.
   a. Thing
   b. Loam11
   c. Undefined
   d. Undefined

108. _____ refers to an atom or molecule that has gained or lost one or more electrons, thus acquiring an electrical charge.
   a. Thing
   b. Ion11
   c. Undefined
   d. Undefined

109. _____ refers to drop out of a saturated solution as crystals. The crystals that drop out of a saturated solution.
   a. 1509 Istanbul earthquake
   b. Precipitate11
   c. Undefined
   d. Undefined

110. _____ refers to subsurface erosion in sandy materials caused by the percolation of water under pressure.
   a. Piping11
   b. 1509 Istanbul earthquake
   c. Undefined
   d. Undefined

111. _____ refers to a vertical conduit through the Earth's crust below a volcano, through which magmatic materials have passed. Commonly filled with volcanic breccia and fragments of older rock.
   a. Pipe11
   b. 1509 Istanbul earthquake
   c. Undefined
   d. Undefined

112. Usually slow but effective process of weathering and erosion in which rocks are dissolved by water is a _____.
   a. Solution11
   b. 1509 Istanbul earthquake
   c. Undefined
   d. Undefined

113. The relationship between distance on a map and the distance on the terrain being represented by that map is a _____.

Chapter 11. Ground Water

a. 1509 Istanbul earthquake b. Scale11
c. Undefined d. Undefined

114. _____ refers to the reduction of the body of a formerly living organism into simpler forms of matter.
a. Thing b. Decomposition11
c. Undefined d. Undefined

115. _____ is a physical or chemical phenomenon or a process in which atoms, molecules, or ions enter some bulk phase - gas, liquid or solid material. In nutrition, amino acids are broken down through digestion, which begins in the stomach.
a. Thing b. Absorption11
c. Undefined d. Undefined

116. _____ involved in passive transport is the movement of water and solute molecules across the cell membrane due to hydrostatic pressure by the cardiovascular system.
a. Thing b. Filtration11
c. Undefined d. Undefined

117. The _____ is that part of a planet's outer shell — including air, land, surface rocks and water — within which life occurs, and which biotic processes in turn alter or transform.
a. Thing b. Biosphere11
c. Undefined d. Undefined

118. _____ is a complex organic substance resulting from the breakdown of plant material in a process called humification. This process can occur naturally in soil, or in the production of compost.
a. Humus11 b. Thing
c. Undefined d. Undefined

119. _____ refers to capable of being molded into any form, which is retained.
a. 1509 Istanbul earthquake b. Plastic11
c. Undefined d. Undefined

120. Water entering rivers, lakes, reservoirs, or the ocean from land surfaces is _____.
a. Thing b. Runoff11
c. Undefined d. Undefined

121. _____ refers to a discordant pluton that is substantially wider than it is thick. Dikes are often steeply inclined or nearly vertical.
a. 1509 Istanbul earthquake b. Dike11
c. Undefined d. Undefined

122. _____ refers to a method of burying waste where each day's dumping is covered with soil to protect the surrounding area. This is also monitored to ensure protection of local underground water.
a. 1509 Istanbul earthquake b. Sanitary landfill11
c. Undefined d. Undefined

Chapter 11. Ground Water

123. _____ is a term used in geology, engineering and surveying to denote the motion of a surface (usually, the earth's surface) downwards relative to a datum such as sea-level.
   a. Thing
   b. Subsidence11
   c. Undefined
   d. Undefined

124. The entire area between the tops of the slopes on both sides of a stream is a _____.
   a. 1509 Istanbul earthquake
   b. Valley11
   c. Undefined
   d. Undefined

125. The diagenetic process by which the volume or thickness of sediment is reduced due to pressure from overlying layers of sediment is called _____.
   a. Compaction11
   b. 1509 Istanbul earthquake
   c. Undefined
   d. Undefined

126. _____ refers to the unnatural addition of surface waters to groundwater. Recharge could result from reservoirs, storage basins, leaky canals, direct injection of water into an aquifer, or by spreading water over a large land surface.
   a. Artificial recharge11
   b. AASHTO Soil Classification System
   c. Undefined
   d. Undefined

127. _____ refers to the upper surface of groundwater. It rises and falls with the amount of groundwater.
   a. Thing
   b. Water table11
   c. Undefined
   d. Undefined

128. The movement of surface water into rock or soil through cracks and pore spaces is called _____.
   a. AASHTO Soil Classification System
   b. Infiltration11
   c. Undefined
   d. Undefined

129. A topography characterized by caves, sinkholes, disappearing streams, and underground drainage is referred to as _____. _____ forms when groundwater dissolves pockets of limestone, dolomite, or gypsum in bedrock.
   a. Karst11
   b. 1509 Istanbul earthquake
   c. Undefined
   d. Undefined

130. _____ is an atmospheric gas comprized of one carbon and two oxygen atoms. A very widely known chemical compound, it is frequently called by its formula CO_2. In its solid state, it is commonly known as dry ice.
   a. Carbon dioxide11
   b. Thing
   c. Undefined
   d. Undefined

131. _____ is a chemical element in the periodic table that has the symbol C and atomic number 6. An abundant nonmetallic, tetravalent element, _____ has several allotropic forms.
   a. Carbon11
   b. Thing
   c. Undefined
   d. Undefined

132. The situation in mass wasting that occurs when material free-falls or bounces down a cliff is called a _____.
   a. 1509 Istanbul earthquake
   b. Fall11
   c. Undefined
   d. Undefined

Chapter 11. Ground Water

133. A mineral deposit of calcium carbonate that precipitates from solution in a cave is referred to as _____.
    a. 1509 Istanbul earthquake
    b. Speleothem11
    c. Undefined
    d. Undefined

134. _____ refers to deposits of calcite built up by dripping water in caves.
    a. 1509 Istanbul earthquake
    b. Dripstone11
    c. Undefined
    d. Undefined

135. _____ refers to an icicle-like mineral formation that hangs from the ceiling of a cave and is usually made up of travertine, which precipitates as water rich in dissolved limestone drips down from the cave's ceiling.
    a. Stalactite11
    b. 1509 Istanbul earthquake
    c. Undefined
    d. Undefined

136. _____ refers to a passage followed by magma in a volcano.
    a. Conduit11
    b. 1509 Istanbul earthquake
    c. Undefined
    d. Undefined

137. A cone-shaped mineral deposit that forms on the floor of a cave and is usually made up of travertine, which precipitates as water rich in dissolved limestone drips down from the cave's ceiling is called a _____.
    a. Stalagmite11
    b. 1509 Istanbul earthquake
    c. Undefined
    d. Undefined

138. A feature found in caves that is formed when a stalactite and stalagmite join is referred to as a _____.
    a. Column11
    b. 1509 Istanbul earthquake
    c. Undefined
    d. Undefined

139. _____ refers to calcite precipitated by flowing water on cave walls and floors.
    a. 1509 Istanbul earthquake
    b. Flowstone11
    c. Undefined
    d. Undefined

140. An evaporite composed of halite is referred to as _____.
    a. Rock salt11
    b. 1509 Istanbul earthquake
    c. Undefined
    d. Undefined

141. _____ is a landscape of distinctive dissolution patterns often marked by underground drainages. These are areas where the bedrock has a soluble layer or layers, usually, but not always, of carbonate rock such as limestone or dolomite. In such places there may be little or no surface drainage.
    a. Thing
    b. Karst topography11
    c. Undefined
    d. Undefined

142. _____ refers to the set of physical features, such as mountains, valleys, and the shapes of landforms, that characterizes a given landscape.
    a. Topography11
    b. 1509 Istanbul earthquake
    c. Undefined
    d. Undefined

143. _____ refers to a chemical combination of silicon and oxygen.

Chapter 11. Ground Water

  a. 1509 Istanbul earthquake
  c. Undefined
  b. Silica11
  d. Undefined

144. _____ is essential to all organisms, except for a few bacteria. It is mostly stably incorporated in the inside of metalloproteins, because in exposed or in free form it causes production of free radicals that are generally toxic to cells.
  a. Thing
  c. Undefined
  b. Iron11
  d. Undefined

145. Hard, rounded mass that develops when a considerable amount of cementing material precipitates locally in a rock, often around an organic nucleus is called _____.
  a. 1509 Istanbul earthquake
  c. Undefined
  b. Concretion11
  d. Undefined

146. _____ refers to the central part of an atom, containing most of the atom's mass and having a positive charge due to the presence of protons.
  a. Nucleus11
  c. Undefined
  b. 1509 Istanbul earthquake
  d. Undefined

147. A preserved remnant or impression of an organism that lived in the past is referred to as _____.
  a. Thing
  c. Undefined
  b. Fossil11
  d. Undefined

148. _____ refers to partly hollow, globelike body found in limestone or other cavernous rock.
  a. 1509 Istanbul earthquake
  c. Undefined
  b. Geode11
  d. Undefined

149. _____ refers to non-crystalline; lacking a crystal structure; a solid such as glass, opal, wood, coal, that lacks an ordered atomic arrangement.
  a. AASHTO Soil Classification System
  c. Undefined
  b. Amorphous11
  d. Undefined

150. _____ is a solid in which the constituent atoms, molecules, or ions are packed in a regularly ordered, repeating pattern extending in all three spatial dimensions.
  a. Thing
  c. Undefined
  b. Crystal11
  d. Undefined

151. A hole or opening, as at the bed of a glacier is a _____. When the rate of deformation into a space behind an obstacle is less the rate of movement past the obstacle, a _____ will form.
  a. Cavity11
  c. Undefined
  b. 1509 Istanbul earthquake
  d. Undefined

152. Mineral with the formula SiO is referred to as _____.
  a. Quartz11
  c. Undefined
  b. 1509 Istanbul earthquake
  d. Undefined

Chapter 11. Ground Water

153. Soil containing such a great quantity of sodium salts precipitated by evaporating ground water that it is generally unfit for plant growth is an _____.
   a. AASHTO Soil Classification System
   b. Alkali soil11
   c. Undefined
   d. Undefined

154. A spring in which the water is 6-9°C warmer than the mean annual air temperature of its locality is called _____.
   a. Hot spring11
   b. 1509 Istanbul earthquake
   c. Undefined
   d. Undefined

155. The set of geological processes that result in the expulsion of lava, pyroclastics, and gases at the Earth's surface is referred to as _____.
   a. 1509 Istanbul earthquake
   b. Volcanism11
   c. Undefined
   d. Undefined

156. _____ refers to a natural spring marked by the intermittent escape of hot water and steam.
   a. Geyser11
   b. 1509 Istanbul earthquake
   c. Undefined
   d. Undefined

157. _____ refers to the process by which solid, liquid, and gaseous materials are ejected into the earth's atmosphere and onto the earth's surface by volcanic activity. Eruptions range from the quiet overflow of liquid rock to the tremendously violent expulsion of pyroclastics.
   a. Eruption11
   b. AASHTO Soil Classification System
   c. Undefined
   d. Undefined

158. _____ refers to water molecules in the gaseous state. Also is one state of the water cycle.
   a. Thing
   b. Water vapor11
   c. Undefined
   d. Undefined

159. _____ refers to water in the gaseous state.
   a. 1509 Istanbul earthquake
   b. Vapor11
   c. Undefined
   d. Undefined

160. A deposit of silica that forms around many geysers and hot springs is referred to as the _____.
   a. Geyserite11
   b. 1509 Istanbul earthquake
   c. Undefined
   d. Undefined

161. An opening in the Earth's surface through which lava, gases, and hot particles are expelled is a _____. Also called volcanic _____ and volcano.
   a. 1509 Istanbul earthquake
   b. Vent11
   c. Undefined
   d. Undefined

162. Power generated by using the heat energy of the earth is called _____.
   a. Geothermal power11
   b. 1509 Istanbul earthquake
   c. Undefined
   d. Undefined

163. A gaseous mixture of naturally occurring hydrocarbons is _____.

Chapter 11. Ground Water

a. 1509 Istanbul earthquake
b. Natural gas11
c. Undefined
d. Undefined

164. The gas that is produced in anoxic sediments is referred to as _____.
a. Hydrogen sulfide11
b. Thing
c. Undefined
d. Undefined

165. _____ is a chemical element in the periodic table that has the symbol H and atomic number 1. At standard temperature and pressure it is a colorless, odorless, nonmetallic, univalent, tasteless, highly flammable diatomic gas.
a. Thing
b. Hydrogen11
c. Undefined
d. Undefined

166. _____ refers to a million watts; 1,000 kilowatts.
a. 1509 Istanbul earthquake
b. Megawatt11
c. Undefined
d. Undefined

167. A mineral deposit that can be mined for a profit is called _____.
a. Ore11
b. AASHTO Soil Classification System
c. Undefined
d. Undefined

Chapter 12. Glaciers and Glaciation

1. The movement of eroded particles by agents such as rivers, waves, glaciers, or wind is referred to as _____.
   a. 1509 Istanbul earthquake
   b. Transportation12
   c. Undefined
   d. Undefined

2. Any accumulation of material, by mechanical settling from water or air, chemical precipitation, evaporation from solution, etc is referred to as _____.
   a. Deposition12
   b. 1509 Istanbul earthquake
   c. Undefined
   d. Undefined

3. _____ is the displacement of solids (soil, mud, rock, and other particles) by the agents of wind, water, ice, movement in response to gravity, or living organisms.
   a. Thing
   b. Erosion12
   c. Undefined
   d. Undefined

4. A moving body of ice that forms on land from the accumulation and compaction of snow, and that flows downslope or outward due to gravity and the pressure of its own weight is a _____.
   a. 1509 Istanbul earthquake
   b. Glacier12
   c. Undefined
   d. Undefined

5. _____ is a chemical element in the periodic table that has the symbol Pb and atomic number 82. A soft, heavy, toxic and malleable poor metal, _____ is bluish white when freshly cut but tarnishes to dull gray when exposed to air. _____ is used in building construction, _____-acid batteries, bullets and shot, and is part of solder, pewter, and fusible alloys.
   a. Lead12
   b. Thing
   c. Undefined
   d. Undefined

6. A _____, often called an ice age, is a geological phenomenon in which massive ice sheets form in the Arctic and Antarctic and advance toward the equator.
   a. Glaciation12
   b. Thing
   c. Undefined
   d. Undefined

7. _____ refers to a naturally formed aggregate of usually inorganic materials from within the Earth.
   a. Rock12
   b. 1509 Istanbul earthquake
   c. Undefined
   d. Undefined

8. _____ state that earth is made up of four basic systems: the lithosphere, the hydrosphere, the atmosphere, and the biosphere. These systems interact to produce most of the geological processes that occur on Earth. An event involving one of these systems may affect some or all of the others.
   a. Earth systems12
   b. AASHTO Soil Classification System
   c. Undefined
   d. Undefined

9. All the parts of our planet and all their interactions, taken together is an _____.
   a. AASHTO Soil Classification System
   b. Earth system12
   c. Undefined
   d. Undefined

10. _____ in physical geography, describes the collective mass of water found on, under, and over the surface of a planet.

a. Thing
b. Hydrosphere12
c. Undefined
d. Undefined

11. A major branch of a stream system is referred to as a _____.
   a. River12
   b. 1509 Istanbul earthquake
   c. Undefined
   d. Undefined

12. _____ refers to the ice component of the climate system, comprising the polar ice caps, glaciers, and other surface ice.
   a. 1509 Istanbul earthquake
   b. Cryosphere12
   c. Undefined
   d. Undefined

13. _____ refers to ice, which covers an ocean or sea; includes mostly continuous pack ice, broken only by narrow open water 'leads' or wider 'polynas', and discrete ice floes.
   a. 1509 Istanbul earthquake
   b. Sea ice12
   c. Undefined
   d. Undefined

14. _____ refers to a climate typical of the mid-latitudes, with neither exceptionally high nor low temperatures and precipitation.
   a. 1509 Istanbul earthquake
   b. Temperate climate12
   c. Undefined
   d. Undefined

15. An area surrounding one of the two magnetic poles of a planet is a _____.
   a. Polar region12
   b. Thing
   c. Undefined
   d. Undefined

16. Weather condition of an area including especially prevailing temperature and average daily/yearly rainfall over a long period of time is called _____.
   a. Thing
   b. Climate12
   c. Undefined
   d. Undefined

17. _____ is a term denoting the solid body of the Earth (i.e. the hydrosphere, lithosphere [including pedosphere] and in some definitions also the internal part of the Earth) and the atmosphere of the Earth.
   a. Thing
   b. Geosphere12
   c. Undefined
   d. Undefined

18. Earth's _____ is a layer of gases surrounding the planet Earth and retained by the Earth's gravity. It contains roughly 78% nitrogen and 21% oxygen, with trace amounts of other gases.
   a. Thing
   b. Atmosphere12
   c. Undefined
   d. Undefined

19. The top of the ocean, where the water meets the atmosphere is called _____.
   a. Sea level12
   b. 1509 Istanbul earthquake
   c. Undefined
   d. Undefined

20. The liquid portion of magma excluding the solid crystals is called _____.

Chapter 12. Glaciers and Glaciation

a. 1509 Istanbul earthquake
b. Melt12
c. Undefined
d. Undefined

21. An _____ is a period of long-term downturn in the temperature of Earth's climate, resulting in an expansion of the continental ice sheets, polar ice sheets and mountain glaciers ("glaciation"). Glaciologically, _____ is often used to mean a period of ice sheets in the northern and southern hemispheres; by this definition we are still in an _____ (because the Greenland and Antarctic ice sheets still exist).
   a. Thing
   b. Ice age12
   c. Undefined
   d. Undefined

22. A slow but steady rise in Earth's surface temperature, caused by increasing concentrations of greenhouse gases in the atmosphere is referred to as _____.
   a. Thing
   b. Global warming12
   c. Undefined
   d. Undefined

23. _____ refers to the area of dry land that borders on a body of water.
   a. 1509 Istanbul earthquake
   b. Coast12
   c. Undefined
   d. Undefined

24. At times in the past, colder climates prevailed during which significantly more of the land surface of Earth was glaciated than at present is the _____.
   a. 1509 Istanbul earthquake
   b. Theory of glacial ages12
   c. Undefined
   d. Undefined

25. Distinct crystals of ice are called _____. Commonly accumulates with a density of 50 - 200 kg·m, although wind-abraded and packed _____ may have a higher initial density.
   a. 1509 Istanbul earthquake
   b. Snow12
   c. Undefined
   d. Undefined

26. _____ refers to a basic unit of the geologic time scale that is a subdivision of an era. Periods may be divided into smaller units called epochs.
   a. Period12
   b. 1509 Istanbul earthquake
   c. Undefined
   d. Undefined

27. The covering of a large region of a continent by a sheet of glacial ice is referred to as _____.
   a. Continental glaciation12
   b. 1509 Istanbul earthquake
   c. Undefined
   d. Undefined

28. _____ refers to glaciation of a mountainous area.
   a. AASHTO Soil Classification System
   b. Alpine glaciation12
   c. Undefined
   d. Undefined

29. Compacted and intergrown mass of crystalline ice with a density is _____.
   a. 1509 Istanbul earthquake
   b. Glacial ice12
   c. Undefined
   d. Undefined

Chapter 12. Glaciers and Glaciation

30. _____ refers to a tentative explanation of a given set of data that is expected to remain valid after future observation and experimentation.
    a. Hypothesis12
    b. 1509 Istanbul earthquake
    c. Undefined
    d. Undefined

31. A mountain glacier that is confined by highlands is called an _____.
    a. Alpine glacier12
    b. AASHTO Soil Classification System
    c. Undefined
    d. Undefined

32. _____ refers to the scientific law stating that the geological processes taking place in the present operated similarly in the past and can therefore be used to explain past geologic events.
    a. Principle of uniformitarianism12
    b. 1509 Istanbul earthquake
    c. Undefined
    d. Undefined

33. The hypothesis that Earth developed gradually through natural processes, similar to those at work today, that occur over long periods of time is referred to as _____.
    a. Uniformitarianism12
    b. Thing
    c. Undefined
    d. Undefined

34. An _____ is a volcanic event that is distinguished by its duration or style.
    a. Episode12
    b. AASHTO Soil Classification System
    c. Undefined
    d. Undefined

35. _____ refers to the water that lies beneath the ground surface, filling the cracks, crevices, and pore space of rocks.
    a. 1509 Istanbul earthquake
    b. Ground water12
    c. Undefined
    d. Undefined

36. _____ is any particulate matter that can be transported by fluid flow and which eventually is deposited as a layer of solid particles on the bed or bottom of a body of water or other liquid.
    a. Sediment12
    b. Thing
    c. Undefined
    d. Undefined

37. An extremely slow moving, thick sheet of ice that covers a large part of a continent is a _____.
    a. Continental glacier12
    b. 1509 Istanbul earthquake
    c. Undefined
    d. Undefined

38. The entire area between the tops of the slopes on both sides of a stream is a _____.
    a. 1509 Istanbul earthquake
    b. Valley12
    c. Undefined
    d. Undefined

39. _____ refers to the top few meters of regolith, generally including some organic matter derived from plants.
    a. 1509 Istanbul earthquake
    b. Soil12
    c. Undefined
    d. Undefined

40. A large mass of rock projecting above surrounding terrain is called a _____.

a. Mountain12
b. 1509 Istanbul earthquake
c. Undefined
d. Undefined

41. _____ refers to any condensed water falling from the atmosphere to the surface of the earth. Common types include rain, snow, sleet, and hail.
   a. Precipitation12
   b. 1509 Istanbul earthquake
   c. Undefined
   d. Undefined

42. _____ refers to the altitude, or vertical distance, above or below sea level.
   a. AASHTO Soil Classification System
   b. Elevation12
   c. Undefined
   d. Undefined

43. _____ refers to the mosaic of interlocking ice crystals that form a glacier.
   a. Glacier ice12
   b. 1509 Istanbul earthquake
   c. Undefined
   d. Undefined

44. A climate in which yearly precipitation is less than the potential loss of water by evaporation is a _____.
   a. 1509 Istanbul earthquake
   b. Dry climate12
   c. Undefined
   d. Undefined

45. Block of glacier-derived ice floating in water is called an _____.
   a. AASHTO Soil Classification System
   b. Iceberg12
   c. Undefined
   d. Undefined

46. _____ refers to an alpine glacier that flows through a preexisting stream valley.
   a. Valley glacier12
   b. 1509 Istanbul earthquake
   c. Undefined
   d. Undefined

47. _____ refers to a body of water found on the Earth's surface and confined to a narrow topographic depression, down which it flows and transports rock particles, sediment, and dissolved particles. Rivers, creeks, brooks, and runs are all streams.
   a. 1509 Istanbul earthquake
   b. Stream12
   c. Undefined
   d. Undefined

48. The relationship between humans and their geological environment is called _____.
   a. Environmental geology12
   b. AASHTO Soil Classification System
   c. Undefined
   d. Undefined

49. Electricity generated by falling water that is used to drive turbines is called _____.
   a. Hydroelectric power12
   b. 1509 Istanbul earthquake
   c. Undefined
   d. Undefined

50. _____ refers to a place in which water is stored, including the oceans, glaciers and polar ice, groundwater, lakes and rivers, the atmosphere, and the biosphere. A source or place of residence for elements in a chemical cycle or hydrologic cycle.

Chapter 12. Glaciers and Glaciation

a. Reservoir12
b. 1509 Istanbul earthquake
c. Undefined
d. Undefined

51. The scientific study of the Earth, its origins and evolution, the materials that make it up, and the processes that act on it is called _____.
   a. 1509 Istanbul earthquake
   b. Geology12
   c. Undefined
   d. Undefined

52. The situation in mass wasting that occurs when material free-falls or bounces down a cliff is called a _____.
   a. Fall12
   b. 1509 Istanbul earthquake
   c. Undefined
   d. Undefined

53. A mineral or fuel deposit, known or not yet discovered, that may be or become available for human exploitation is called a _____.
   a. Resource12
   b. 1509 Istanbul earthquake
   c. Undefined
   d. Undefined

54. A member of a group of easily combustible, organic sedimentary rocks composed mostly of plant remains and containing a high proportion of carbon is called _____.
   a. Coal12
   b. 1509 Istanbul earthquake
   c. Undefined
   d. Undefined

55. _____ refers to a glacier of considerable thickness and more than 50,000 square kilometers in area, forming a continuous cover of snow and ice over a land surface, spreading outward in all directions and not confined by the underlying topography. Ice sheets are now confined to Polar Regions, but during the Pleistocene Epoch they covered large parts of North America and northern Europe.
   a. AASHTO Soil Classification System
   b. Ice sheet12
   c. Undefined
   d. Undefined

56. _____ refers to a rugged region of the lunar surface representing an early period in lunar history when intense meteorite bombardment formed craters.
   a. 1509 Istanbul earthquake
   b. Highland12
   c. Undefined
   d. Undefined

57. An alpine glacier that covers the peak of a mountain is referred to as an _____.
   a. AASHTO Soil Classification System
   b. Ice cap12
   c. Undefined
   d. Undefined

58. Runoff moving in unconfined thin sheets is called _____.
   a. Sheet flow12
   b. 1509 Istanbul earthquake
   c. Undefined
   d. Undefined

59. _____ is the result of the transformation of a pre-existing rock type, the protolith, in a process called metamorphism, which means "change in form". The protolith is subjected to heat (greater than 150 degrees Celsius) and extreme pressure causing profound physical and/or chemical change.

222 Chapter 12. Glaciers and Glaciation

    a. Metamorphic rock12   b. Thing
    c. Undefined   d. Undefined

60. _____ is one of the three main rock groups and is formed in three main ways—by the deposition of the weathered remains of other rocks; by the deposition of the results of biogenic activity; and by precipitation from solution.
    a. Sedimentary rock12   b. Event
    c. Undefined   d. Undefined

61. _____ refers to the term from the Greek 'meta' and 'morph', commonly occurs to rocks which are subjected to increased heat and/or pressure. Also applies to the conversion of snow into glacial ice.
    a. Metamorphic12   b. 1509 Istanbul earthquake
    c. Undefined   d. Undefined

62. A body of rock identified by lithic characteristics and stratigraphic position and is mappable at the earth's surface or traceable in the subsurface is a _____.
    a. Formation12   b. 1509 Istanbul earthquake
    c. Undefined   d. Undefined

63. The diagenetic process by which the volume or thickness of sediment is reduced due to pressure from overlying layers of sediment is called _____.
    a. Compaction12   b. 1509 Istanbul earthquake
    c. Undefined   d. Undefined

64. The time between winter and summer is _____.
    a. Spring12   b. 1509 Istanbul earthquake
    c. Undefined   d. Undefined

65. Firmly packed snow that has survived a summer melting season. _____ has a density of about 0.4 gram per cubic centimeter. Ultimately, _____ turns into glacial ice.
    a. 1509 Istanbul earthquake   b. Firn12
    c. Undefined   d. Undefined

66. _____ refers to a clastic rock composed of particles that range in diameter from 1/16 millimeter to 2 millimeters in diameter. Sandstones make up about 25% of all sedimentary rocks.
    a. 1509 Istanbul earthquake   b. Sandstone12
    c. Undefined   d. Undefined

67. _____ refers to the diagenetic process by which unstable minerals in buried sediment are transformed into stable ones.
    a. 1509 Istanbul earthquake   b. Recrystallization12
    c. Undefined   d. Undefined

68. The process by which conditions within the Earth, below the zone of diagenesis, alter the mineral content, chemical composition, and structure of solid rock without melting it is called _____. Igneous, sedimentary, and metamorphic rocks may all undergo _____.

Chapter 12. Glaciers and Glaciation

a. 1509 Istanbul earthquake
b. Metamorphism12
c. Undefined
d. Undefined

69. _____ refers to an extremely durable, nonfoliated metamorphic rock derived from pure sandstone and consisting primarily of quartz.
a. 1509 Istanbul earthquake
b. Quartzite12
c. Undefined
d. Undefined

70. The force of attraction exerted by one body in the universe on another is _____. _____ is directly proportional to the product of the masses of the two attracted bodies. The force of attraction exerted by the Earth on bodies on or near its surface, tending to pull them toward the Earth's center.
a. 1509 Istanbul earthquake
b. Gravity12
c. Undefined
d. Undefined

71. _____ refers to the change of state of water from the liquid to vapor phase. Requires the addition of 80 calories per cubic centimeter.
a. AASHTO Soil Classification System
b. Evaporation12
c. Undefined
d. Undefined

72. _____ refers to all processes by which snow and ice are lost from a glacier, floating ice, or snow cover; or the amount which is melted. These processes include melting, evaporation, wind erosion, and calving.
a. Ablation12
b. AASHTO Soil Classification System
c. Undefined
d. Undefined

73. Breaking off and floating away as icebergs of either a tidewater glacier or an ice shelf is called _____. _____ is a very efficient form of ablation, thus helps stabilize the extent of ice sheets which might otherwise expand continuously from a positive mass budget.
a. 1509 Istanbul earthquake
b. Calving12
c. Undefined
d. Undefined

74. Angular chunk of solid rock ejected during an eruption is referred to as a _____.
a. Block12
b. 1509 Istanbul earthquake
c. Undefined
d. Undefined

75. The balance, or lack of balance, between ice formation at the upper end of a glacier, and ice loss in the zone of wastage is a _____.
a. 1509 Istanbul earthquake
b. Glacial budget12
c. Undefined
d. Undefined

76. Glacier with a positive budget, so that accumulation results in the lower edges being pushed outward and downward is called an _____.
a. AASHTO Soil Classification System
b. Advancing glacier12
c. Undefined
d. Undefined

77. A glacier with a negative budget, which causes the glacier to grow smaller as its edges melt back, is referred to as _____.

a. 1509 Istanbul earthquake
b. Receding glacier12
c. Undefined
d. Undefined

78. The part of a glacier in which there is greater overall gain than loss in volume is the _____. A _____ can be identified by a blanket of snow that survives summer melting.
   a. Zone of accumulation12
   b. 1509 Istanbul earthquake
   c. Undefined
   d. Undefined

79. The part of a glacier in which there is greater overall loss than gain in volume is the _____. A _____ can be identified in the summer by an expanse of bare ice.
   a. Zone of ablation12
   b. 1509 Istanbul earthquake
   c. Undefined
   d. Undefined

80. All processes that adds snow or ice to a glacier or to floating ice or snow cove are referred to as _____.
   a. AASHTO Soil Classification System
   b. Accumulation12
   c. Undefined
   d. Undefined

81. The point in a glacier where overall gain in volume equals overall loss, so that the net volume remains stable is the _____. The _____ marks the border between the zone of accumulation and the zone of ablation.
   a. Equilibrium line12
   b. AASHTO Soil Classification System
   c. Undefined
   d. Undefined

82. Material is in _____ if it is adjusted to the physical and chemical conditions of its environment so that it does not change or alter with time.
   a. AASHTO Soil Classification System
   b. Equilibrium12
   c. Undefined
   d. Undefined

83. The outer margin of a glacier is called _____.
   a. 1509 Istanbul earthquake
   b. Terminus12
   c. Undefined
   d. Undefined

84. _____ occurs when living things move from one biome to another. In most cases organisms migrate to avoid local shortages of food, usually caused by winter. Animals may also migrate to a certain location to breed, as is the case with some fish.
   a. Migration12
   b. Thing
   c. Undefined
   d. Undefined

85. _____ refers to a vertical conduit through the Earth's crust below a volcano, through which magmatic materials have passed. Commonly filled with volcanic breccia and fragments of older rock.
   a. Pipe12
   b. 1509 Istanbul earthquake
   c. Undefined
   d. Undefined

86. A type of glacial movement that occurs within the glacier, below a depth of approximately 50 meters, in which the ice is not fractured, is referred to as _____.

a. 1509 Istanbul earthquake   b. Plastic flow12
c. Undefined   d. Undefined

87. _____ refers to a crack in a glacier caused by rapid extension. Crevasses over 10 m deep would be healed by internal flow, but much deeper crevasses can be maintained by continued tension.
a. 1509 Istanbul earthquake   b. Crevasse12
c. Undefined   d. Undefined

88. _____ refers to capable of being molded into any form, which is retained.
a. 1509 Istanbul earthquake   b. Plastic12
c. Undefined   d. Undefined

89. _____ refers to general term referring to the rock underlying other unconsolidated material, i.e. soil.
a. 1509 Istanbul earthquake   b. Bedrock12
c. Undefined   d. Undefined

90. The solid structure created when lava, gases, and hot particles escape to the Earth's surface through vents is called a _____. Volcanoes are usually conical. A _____ is 'active' when it is erupting or has erupted recently. Volcanoes that have not erupted recently but are considered likely to erupt in the future are said to be 'dormant.' A _____ that has not erupted for a long time and is not expected to erupt in the future is 'extinct'.
a. 1509 Istanbul earthquake   b. Volcano12
c. Undefined   d. Undefined

91. _____ refers to the process by which solid, liquid, and gaseous materials are ejected into the earth's atmosphere and onto the earth's surface by volcanic activity. Eruptions range from the quiet overflow of liquid rock to the tremendously violent expulsion of pyroclastics.
a. AASHTO Soil Classification System   b. Eruption12
c. Undefined   d. Undefined

92. The innermost layer of the Earth, consisting primarily of pure metals such as iron and nickel is the _____. The _____ is the densest layer of the Earth, and is divided into the outer _____, which is believed to be liquid, and the inner _____, which is believed to be solid.
a. 1509 Istanbul earthquake   b. Core12
c. Undefined   d. Undefined

93. In general terms an _____ can be thought of as an assemblage of organisms (plant, animal and other living organisms living together with their environment, functioning as a loose unit. That is, a dynamic and complex whole, interacting as an "ecological unit".
a. Ecosystem12   b. Thing
c. Undefined   d. Undefined

94. Any unconsolidated material at Earth's surface is _____.
a. 1509 Istanbul earthquake   b. Debris12
c. Undefined   d. Undefined

Chapter 12. Glaciers and Glaciation

95. The mass movement of a single, intact mass of rock, soil, or unconsolidated material along a weak plane, such as a fault, fracture, or bedding plane is a _____. A _____ may involve as little as a minor displacement of soil or as much as the displacement of an entire mountainside.
   a. 1509 Istanbul earthquake
   b. Slide12
   c. Undefined
   d. Undefined

96. Upper part of a glacier in which there is no plastic flow is the _____.
   a. 1509 Istanbul earthquake
   b. Rigid zone12
   c. Undefined
   d. Undefined

97. The process by which a glacier undergoes thawing at its base, producing a film of water along which the glacier then flows is called _____. _____ primarily affects glaciers in warm climates or mid-latitude mountain ranges.
   a. Basal sliding12
   b. 1509 Istanbul earthquake
   c. Undefined
   d. Undefined

98. A force that stretches a body and tends to pull it apart is called _____.
   a. Tensional force12
   b. 1509 Istanbul earthquake
   c. Undefined
   d. Undefined

99. A force that squeezes together or shortens a body is referred to as _____.
   a. 1509 Istanbul earthquake
   b. Compressive force12
   c. Undefined
   d. Undefined

100. _____ refers to a group of closely spaced mountains or parallel ridges.
   a. 1509 Istanbul earthquake
   b. Mountain range12
   c. Undefined
   d. Undefined

101. _____ is an atmospheric gas comprized of one carbon and two oxygen atoms. A very widely known chemical compound, it is frequently called by its formula CO_2. In its solid state, it is commonly known as dry ice.
   a. Thing
   b. Carbon dioxide12
   c. Undefined
   d. Undefined

102. _____ refers to extremely small fragments, usually of glass, that forms when escaping gases force a fine spray of magma from a volcano.
   a. 1509 Istanbul earthquake
   b. Volcanic ash12
   c. Undefined
   d. Undefined

103. _____ is a chemical element in the periodic table that has the symbol C and atomic number 6. An abundant nonmetallic, tetravalent element, _____ has several allotropic forms.
   a. Thing
   b. Carbon12
   c. Undefined
   d. Undefined

104. Fine particles of pulverized rock blown from an explosion vent are called _____. Measuring less than 1/10 inch in diameter, _____ may be either solid or molten when first erupted.

Chapter 12. Glaciers and Glaciation

a. AASHTO Soil Classification System
c. Undefined
b. Ash12
d. Undefined

105. A term used to describe the property of releasing energy or particles from an unstable atom is called _____.
a. Radioactive12
c. Undefined
b. Thing
d. Undefined

106. _____ refer to varieties of the same element that have different mass numbers; their nuclei contain the same number of protons but different numbers of neutrons.
a. AASHTO Soil Classification System
c. Undefined
b. Isotopes12
d. Undefined

107. An _____ is a form of an element whose nuclei have the same atomic number - the number of protons in the nucleus - but different mass numbers because they contain different numbers of neutrons.
a. Thing
c. Undefined
b. Isotope12
d. Undefined

108. Describing a mineral that will not react with or convert to a new mineral or substance, given enough time is referred to as _____.
a. Stable12
c. Undefined
b. 1509 Istanbul earthquake
d. Undefined

109. _____ refers to the microscopic shells and other remains of marine organisms that make up biogenous sediments.
a. Microfossils12
c. Undefined
b. Thing
d. Undefined

110. _____ is a chemical element in the periodic table. It has the symbol O and atomic number 8. _____ is the second most common element on Earth, composing around 46% of the mass of Earth's crust and 28% of the mass of Earth as a whole, and is the third most common element in the universe.
a. Oxygen12
c. Undefined
b. Thing
d. Undefined

111. _____ refers to a volcano that is erupting. Also, a volcano that is not presently erupting, but that has erupted within historical time and is considered likely to do so in the future.
a. Active volcano12
c. Undefined
b. AASHTO Soil Classification System
d. Undefined

112. Any relatively sunken part of the Earth's surface, especially a low-lying area surrounded by higher ground is called a _____.
a. Depression12
c. Undefined
b. 1509 Istanbul earthquake
d. Undefined

113. Aggregates of minerals or rock fragments are called _____.

Chapter 12. Glaciers and Glaciation

a. 1509 Istanbul earthquake
b. Rocks12
c. Undefined
d. Undefined

114. _____ refers to a process of glacial erosion by which blocks of rock are loosened, detached, and borne away from bedrock by the freezing of water in fissures.
   a. Plucking12
   b. 1509 Istanbul earthquake
   c. Undefined
   d. Undefined

115. A form of mechanical weathering that occurs when loose fragments or particles of rocks and minerals that are being transported, as by water or air, collide with each other or scrape the surfaces of stationary rocks is referred to as _____.
   a. AASHTO Soil Classification System
   b. Abrasion12
   c. Undefined
   d. Undefined

116. A rock fragment with one or more flat surfaces caused by erosive action is called _____.
   a. 1509 Istanbul earthquake
   b. Faceted12
   c. Undefined
   d. Undefined

117. A rock particle 2 to 64 mm in diameter is referred to as the _____.
   a. 1509 Istanbul earthquake
   b. Pebble12
   c. Undefined
   d. Undefined

118. _____ refer to multiple scratches or minute lines, generally parallel but occasionally cross-cutting, inscribed on a rock surface by a geologic agent. Common indicators of direction of glacier flow.
   a. Striations12
   b. 1509 Istanbul earthquake
   c. Undefined
   d. Undefined

119. One of a group of usually parallel scratches engraved in bedrock by a glacier or other geological agent is _____.
   a. Striation12
   b. 1509 Istanbul earthquake
   c. Undefined
   d. Undefined

120. The _____ Era is a major division of the geologic timescale, one of four geologic eras. The division of time into eras, the largest division of geologic time, dates back to Giovanni Arduino in the 18th century, although his original name for the era now called the _____ was "Primitive".
   a. Paleozoic12
   b. Thing
   c. Undefined
   d. Undefined

121. _____ refers to finely ground rock material, usually associated with glaciers. Can be mixed with water and formed into loaves which, when baked for 45 minutes at 350 deg., are totally inedible.
   a. Rock flour12
   b. 1509 Istanbul earthquake
   c. Undefined
   d. Undefined

122. A naturally occurring, usually inorganic, solid consisting of either a single element or a compound, and having a definite chemical composition and a systematic internal arrangement of atoms is referred to as a _____.
   a. 1509 Istanbul earthquake
   b. Mineral12
   c. Undefined
   d. Undefined

Chapter 12. Glaciers and Glaciation

123. _____ refers to soil particles between the size of sand particles and clay particles, namely particles 0.002-0.2 mm in diameter.
   a. Silt12
   b. Thing
   c. Undefined
   d. Undefined

124. _____ is the geomorphic process by which soil, regolith, and rock move downslope under the force of gravity. Types of _____ include creep, slides, flows, topples, and falls, each with their own characteristic features, and take place over timescales from seconds to years.
   a. Thing
   b. Mass wasting12
   c. Undefined
   d. Undefined

125. A valley-deepening process caused by erosion of a stream bed is called _____.
   a. 1509 Istanbul earthquake
   b. Downcutting12
   c. Undefined
   d. Undefined

126. A form of mechanical weathering caused by the freezing of water that has entered a pore or crack in a rock is _____. The water expands as it freezes, widening the cracks or pores and often loosening or dislodging rock fragments. As the ice forms, it attracts more water, increasing the effects of _____.
   a. Frost wedging12
   b. 1509 Istanbul earthquake
   c. Undefined
   d. Undefined

127. A large mass of material or mixtures of material falling or sliding rapidly under the force of gravity is an _____. Avalanches often are classified by their content, such as snow, ice, soil, or rock avalanches. A mixture of these materials is a debris _____.
   a. Avalanche12
   b. AASHTO Soil Classification System
   c. Undefined
   d. Undefined

128. Characteristic cross-profile of a valley carved by glacial erosion is a _____.
   a. U-shaped valley12
   b. AASHTO Soil Classification System
   c. Undefined
   d. Undefined

129. _____ refer to triangular-shaped cliffs produced when spurs of land that extend into a valley are removed by the great erosional force of a valley glacier.
   a. Truncated spurs12
   b. 1509 Istanbul earthquake
   c. Undefined
   d. Undefined

130. _____ refers to a triangular facet where the lower end of a ridge has been eroded by glacial ice.
   a. Truncated spur12
   b. 1509 Istanbul earthquake
   c. Undefined
   d. Undefined

131. A round or oval depression in the Earth's surface, containing the youngest section of rock in its lowest, central part is a _____.
   a. 1509 Istanbul earthquake
   b. Basin12
   c. Undefined
   d. Undefined

132. A high mountain peak that forms when the walls of three or more cirques intersect is called a _____.

Chapter 12. Glaciers and Glaciation

    a. Horn12
    b. 1509 Istanbul earthquake
    c. Undefined
    d. Undefined

133. Bedrock that is more resistant to glacial erosion, stands out as _____, usually elongated parallel to the direction of glacier flow are _____.
    a. Rounded knobs12
    b. 1509 Istanbul earthquake
    c. Undefined
    d. Undefined

134. _____ refers to a crack or break in a rock. To break in random places instead of cleaving.
    a. Fracture12
    b. 1509 Istanbul earthquake
    c. Undefined
    d. Undefined

135. A lake occupying a depression caused by glacial erosion of bedrock is a _____.
    a. Rock-basin lake12
    b. 1509 Istanbul earthquake
    c. Undefined
    d. Undefined

136. A tributary valley that enters a glacial trough at a considerable height above the floor of the trough is referred to as a _____.
    a. 1509 Istanbul earthquake
    b. Hanging valley12
    c. Undefined
    d. Undefined

137. A deep, typically circular lake that forms when a cirque glacier melts is a _____.
    a. 1509 Istanbul earthquake
    b. Tarn12
    c. Undefined
    d. Undefined

138. A series of rock-basin lakes carved by glacial erosion are _____.
    a. Paternoster lakes12
    b. 1509 Istanbul earthquake
    c. Undefined
    d. Undefined

139. A deep, semi-circular basin eroded out of a mountain by an alpine glacier is referred to as a _____.
    a. Cirque12
    b. 1509 Istanbul earthquake
    c. Undefined
    d. Undefined

140. A narrow ridge separating two cirque valleys is called the _____.
    a. Arete12
    b. AASHTO Soil Classification System
    c. Undefined
    d. Undefined

141. _____ refers to the beginning or source area for a stream. Also called the headwaters.
    a. Head12
    b. 1509 Istanbul earthquake
    c. Undefined
    d. Undefined

142. The process by which exposure to atmospheric agents, such as air or moisture, causes rocks and minerals to break down is called _____. This process takes place at or near the Earth's surface. _____ entails little or no movement of the material that it loosens from the rocks and minerals.

Chapter 12. Glaciers and Glaciation

a. Weathering12
b. 1509 Istanbul earthquake
c. Undefined
d. Undefined

143. _____ refers to the set of physical features, such as mountains, valleys, and the shapes of landforms, that characterizes a given landscape.
   a. Topography12
   b. 1509 Istanbul earthquake
   c. Undefined
   d. Undefined

144. _____ refers to a feature on the surface of the planet Mars that very closely resembles certain types of stream channels on Earth.
   a. 1509 Istanbul earthquake
   b. Channel12
   c. Undefined
   d. Undefined

145. In ethology, sociobiology and behavioral ecology, the term _____ refers to any geographical area that an animal of a particular species consistently defends against conspecifics (and, occasionally, animals of other species).
   a. Territory12
   b. Thing
   c. Undefined
   d. Undefined

146. The grinding away of sharp edges and corners of rock fragments during transportation is called _____.
   a. Rounding12
   b. 1509 Istanbul earthquake
   c. Undefined
   d. Undefined

147. The topographically highest hillslope position of a hillslope profile and exhibiting a nearly level surface is referred to as the _____.
   a. 1509 Istanbul earthquake
   b. Summit12
   c. Undefined
   d. Undefined

148. Dominantly unsorted and unstratified drift, generally unconsolidated deposited directly by and underneath a glacier without subsequent reworking by meltwater, and consisting of a hetergeneous mixture of clay, silt, sand, gravel, stones, and boulders is called _____.
   a. 1509 Istanbul earthquake
   b. Till12
   c. Undefined
   d. Undefined

149. _____ refers to a rock fragment carried by glacial ice, or by floating ice, and subsequently deposited at some distance from the outcrop of which it was derived.
   a. AASHTO Soil Classification System
   b. Erratic12
   c. Undefined
   d. Undefined

150. A geologic epoch, characterized by alternating glacial and interglacial stages, that ended about 10,000 years ago, that lasted for 2 million years is called the _____ epoch.
   a. Thing
   b. Pleistocene12
   c. Undefined
   d. Undefined

151. _____ is the general term for debris of all sorts originally transported by glaciers or ice sheets that have since melted away. Till is another word used to describe the sediments left by glaciers.

a. Moraine12   b. Thing
c. Undefined   d. Undefined

152. A ridge-like moraine carried on and deposited at the side margin of a valley glacier is the _____.
a. 1509 Istanbul earthquake   b. Lateral moraine12
c. Undefined   d. Undefined

153. Of either earth or stone pebbles, generally covering a burial chamber or deposit is called _____.
a. 1509 Istanbul earthquake   b. Mound12
c. Undefined   d. Undefined

154. A ridge of till formed when lateral moraines from two coalescing alpine glaciers join is the _____.
a. Medial moraine12   b. 1509 Istanbul earthquake
c. Undefined   d. Undefined

155. _____ refers to a stream that supplies water to a larger stream.
a. Tributary12   b. 1509 Istanbul earthquake
c. Undefined   d. Undefined

156. A ridge-like accumulation that is being or was produced at the outer margin of an actively flowing glacier at any given time is referred to as the _____.
a. AASHTO Soil Classification System   b. End moraine12
c. Undefined   d. Undefined

157. An end or lateral moraine, built during a temporary but significant halt in the final retreat of a glacier is called the _____.
a. 1509 Istanbul earthquake   b. Recessional moraine12
c. Undefined   d. Undefined

158. _____ refers to a steep-sided, bowl-shaped depression commonly without surface drainage; usually formed by a large detached block of stagnant ice that had been partially or wholly buried in the drift.
a. Kettle12   b. 1509 Istanbul earthquake
c. Undefined   d. Undefined

159. An end moraine that marks the farthest advance of a glacier and usually has the form of a massive concentric ridge or complex of ridges, underlain by till and other types of drift is a _____.
a. Terminal moraine12   b. 1509 Istanbul earthquake
c. Undefined   d. Undefined

160. _____ refers to an extensive, fairly even layer of till, having an uneven or undulating surface; a deposit of rock and mineral debris dragged along, in, on, or beneath a glacier and emplaced by process including basal lodgement.
a. Ground moraine12   b. 1509 Istanbul earthquake
c. Undefined   d. Undefined

161. _____ refers to a long, spoon-shaped hill that develops when pressure from an overriding glacier reshapes a moraine. Drumlins range in height from 5 to 50 meters and in length from 400 to 2000 meters. They slope down in the direction of the ice flow.
  a. 1509 Istanbul earthquake
  b. Drumlin12
  c. Undefined
  d. Undefined

162. A load of sediment, consisting of sand and gravel that is deposited by meltwater in front of a glacier is called _____.
  a. AASHTO Soil Classification System
  b. Outwash12
  c. Undefined
  d. Undefined

163. _____ refers to the process by which a given transport medium separates out certain particles, as on the basis of size, shape, or density.
  a. Sorting12
  b. 1509 Istanbul earthquake
  c. Undefined
  d. Undefined

164. A ridge of sediment that forms under a glacier's zone of ablation, made up of sand and gravel deposited by melt water is an _____. An _____ may be less than 100 meters or more than 500 kilometers long, and may be anywhere from 3 to over 300 meters high.
  a. Esker12
  b. AASHTO Soil Classification System
  c. Undefined
  d. Undefined

165. _____ refers to lake formed when a block of ice melted and left a depression in the surrounding clays.
  a. Thing
  b. Kettle lake12
  c. Undefined
  d. Undefined

166. _____ refers to a low mound, knob, hummock, or short irregular ridge, composed of stratified sand and gravel deposited by a subglacial stream as a fan or delta at the margin of a melting glacier; or as a ponded deposit on the surface or at the margin of stagnant ice; or by a supraglacial stream in a low place or hole on the surface of the glacier.
  a. Kame12
  b. 1509 Istanbul earthquake
  c. Undefined
  d. Undefined

167. A mode of sediment transport in which the upward currents in eddies of turbulent flow are capable of supporting the weight of sediment particles and keeping them held indefinitely in the surrounding fluid is called _____.
  a. 1509 Istanbul earthquake
  b. Suspension12
  c. Undefined
  d. Undefined

168. A lake that derives much or all of its water from the melting of glacier ice, fed by meltwater, and lying outside the glaciers margin is called the _____.
  a. 1509 Istanbul earthquake
  b. Glacial lake12
  c. Undefined
  d. Undefined

169. _____ refers to a pair of sediment beds deposited by a lake on its floor, typically consisting of a thick, coarse, light-colored bed deposited in the summer and a thin, fine-grained, dark-colored bed deposited in the winter. Varves are most often found in lakes that freeze in the winter. The number and nature of varves on the bottom of a lake provide information about the lake's age and geologic events that affected the lake's development.

Chapter 12. Glaciers and Glaciation

    a. Varve12
    b. 1509 Istanbul earthquake
    c. Undefined
    d. Undefined

170. The accumulation of precipitation into surface and underground areas, including lakes, rivers, and aquifers is a _____.
    a. Collection12
    b. 1509 Istanbul earthquake
    c. Undefined
    d. Undefined

171. Any portion of a meteoroid that survives its traverse through Earth's atmosphere and strikes the surface is referred to as a _____.
    a. Meteorite12
    b. 1509 Istanbul earthquake
    c. Undefined
    d. Undefined

172. _____ refers to the smallest possible unit of a substance that has the properties of that substance.
    a. Molecule12
    b. 1509 Istanbul earthquake
    c. Undefined
    d. Undefined

173. A preserved remnant or impression of an organism that lived in the past is referred to as _____.
    a. Fossil12
    b. Thing
    c. Undefined
    d. Undefined

174. Bright streaks that appear to radiate from certain craters on the lunar surface are _____. The _____ consist of fine debris ejected from the primary crater.
    a. Rays12
    b. 1509 Istanbul earthquake
    c. Undefined
    d. Undefined

175. The term _____, such as the current era, is used to denote the absence of large-scale glaciation on a global scale — i.e., a non-Ice Age. They are, in general, shorter than glacial epochs.
    a. Interglacial12
    b. Thing
    c. Undefined
    d. Undefined

176. _____ refers to a volume of space in which a given electron occurs 90% of the time. It is the quantum state of the individual electrons in the electron cloud around a single atom.
    a. Thing
    b. Orbital12
    c. Undefined
    d. Undefined

177. _____ refers to a timeline based on a stratigraphic succession that provides a chronological record of the history of a region. The entire span of time since the Earth formed.
    a. Geologic time12
    b. 1509 Istanbul earthquake
    c. Undefined
    d. Undefined

178. The warming of the atmosphere caused by COD CH4, and other gases that absorb infrared radiation and slow its escape from Earth's surface is called _____.
    a. Greenhouse effect12
    b. Thing
    c. Undefined
    d. Undefined

Chapter 12. Glaciers and Glaciation

179. _____ refers to rigid parts of the Earth's crust and part of the Earth's upper mantle that moves and adjoins each other along zones of seismic activity.
   a. Plate12
   b. 1509 Istanbul earthquake
   c. Undefined
   d. Undefined

180. A geological period between ice ages when, as at present, the earth's climate is relatively warm is referred to as the _____.
   a. Thing
   b. Interglacial period12
   c. Undefined
   d. Undefined

181. Describing a substance in which the atoms are arranged in a regular, repeating, orderly pattern is called _____.
   a. Crystalline12
   b. 1509 Istanbul earthquake
   c. Undefined
   d. Undefined

182. An area with sparse vegetation owing to some physical or chemical property of the soil is referred to as _____.
   a. Barren12
   b. Thing
   c. Undefined
   d. Undefined

183. A load of silt that is produced by the erosion of outwash and transported by wind is _____. Much _____ found in the Mississippi Valley, China, and Europe is believed to have been deposited during the Pleistocene Epoch.
   a. 1509 Istanbul earthquake
   b. Loess12
   c. Undefined
   d. Undefined

184. _____ refers to the boundary between a body of water and dry land.
   a. 1509 Istanbul earthquake
   b. Shoreline12
   c. Undefined
   d. Undefined

185. A long, narrow depression, shaped and more or less filled by a stream is referred to as a _____.
   a. 1509 Istanbul earthquake
   b. Stream channel12
   c. Undefined
   d. Undefined

186. _____ refer to lakes formed in closed basins as a result of climates, which also encouraged glaciation.
   a. Pluvial lakes12
   b. 1509 Istanbul earthquake
   c. Undefined
   d. Undefined

187. A lake that formed from rainwater falling into a landlocked basin during a glacial period marked by greater precipitation than is found in the region in prior or subsequent periods is a _____.
   a. 1509 Istanbul earthquake
   b. Pluvial lake12
   c. Undefined
   d. Undefined

188. _____ is a term used for ionic compounds composed of positively charged cations and negatively charged anions, so that the product is neutral and without a net charge.
   a. Thing
   b. Salt12
   c. Undefined
   d. Undefined

189. _____ refers to a level surface formed by wave erosion of coastal bedrock beneath the surf zone. May be visible at low tide.
   a. Wave-cut terrace12
   b. 1509 Istanbul earthquake
   c. Undefined
   d. Undefined

190. A flat, steplike surface that lines a stream above the floodplain, often paired one on each side of the stream, marking a former floodplain that existed at a higher level before regional uplift or an increase in discharge caused the stream to erode into it is called the _____.
   a. 1509 Istanbul earthquake
   b. Terrace12
   c. Undefined
   d. Undefined

191. _____ is a chemical element in the periodic table that has the symbol B and atomic number 5. A trivalent metalloid element, _____ occurs abundantly in the ore borax.
   a. Boron12
   b. Thing
   c. Undefined
   d. Undefined

192. The shallow part of the seafloor immediately adjacent to a continent is called the _____.
   a. Continental shelf12
   b. Thing
   c. Undefined
   d. Undefined

193. A _____ is a narrow inlet of the sea between cliffs or steep slopes, which results from marine inundation of a glaciated valley. Typical characteristics of a _____ include: a narrow inlet, a bottom glacially eroded significantly below sea level, steep-sided walls which continue to descend below the sea surface, greater depths in the upper and middle reaches than on the seaward side, and communication with the open sea.
   a. Fjord12
   b. Thing
   c. Undefined
   d. Undefined

194. A steep-sided inlet of the sea formed when a glacial trough was partially submerged is a _____.
   a. Fiord12
   b. 1509 Istanbul earthquake
   c. Undefined
   d. Undefined

195. The rise of Earth's crust after the removal of glacial ice is referred to as _____.
   a. Crustal rebound12
   b. 1509 Istanbul earthquake
   c. Undefined
   d. Undefined

196. A _____ is the outer layer of a planet, part of its lithosphere. Planetary _____ is generally composed of a less dense material than that of its deeper layers. The _____ of the Earth is composed mainly of basalt and granite.
   a. Thing
   b. Crust12
   c. Undefined
   d. Undefined

197. An unconfined glacier that covers much or all of a continent is referred to as _____.
   a. Continental ice sheet12
   b. 1509 Istanbul earthquake
   c. Undefined
   d. Undefined

Chapter 12. Glaciers and Glaciation

198. The _____ is an informal name for the eons of the geologic timescale that came before the current Phanerozoic eon. It spans from the formation of Earth around 4500 Ma (million years ago) to the evolution of abundant macroscopic hard-shelled fossils, which marked the beginning of the Cambrian.
   a. Thing
   b. Precambrian12
   c. Undefined
   d. Undefined

199. The hypothesis that glaciers covered the planet's land masses from pole to pole 750 to 570 million years ago is called _____.
   a. Snowball earth12
   b. Thing
   c. Undefined
   d. Undefined

200. A spherical accumulation of water in the crystalline form is referred to as a _____.
   a. Snowball12
   b. 1509 Istanbul earthquake
   c. Undefined
   d. Undefined

201. _____ refers to a gas, such as carbon dioxide or methane, that traps sunlight energy in a planet's atmosphere as heat; a gas that participates in the greenhouse effect.
   a. Greenhouse gas12
   b. Thing
   c. Undefined
   d. Undefined

202. _____ refers to the study of the global-scale movements of Earth's crust that have resulted in.
   a. Thing
   b. Plate tectonics12
   c. Undefined
   d. Undefined

203. _____ refers to the study of the large-scale processes that collectively deform Earth's crust.
   a. 1509 Istanbul earthquake
   b. Tectonics12
   c. Undefined
   d. Undefined

204. An elevated area with relatively little internal relief is called a _____.
   a. Plateau12
   b. 1509 Istanbul earthquake
   c. Undefined
   d. Undefined

205. Magma that comes to the Earth's surface through a volcano or fissure is referred to as _____.
   a. 1509 Istanbul earthquake
   b. Lava12
   c. Undefined
   d. Undefined

206. _____ is a common gray to black volcanic rock. It is usually fine-grained due to rapid cooling of lava on the Earth's surface.
   a. Thing
   b. Basalt12
   c. Undefined
   d. Undefined

207. A network of converging and diverging streams separated from each other by narrow strips of sand and gravel are referred to as a _____.
   a. Braided stream12
   b. 1509 Istanbul earthquake
   c. Undefined
   d. Undefined

208. Rounded particles coarser than 2 mm in diameter are called _____.
   a. Gravel12
   b. 1509 Istanbul earthquake
   c. Undefined
   d. Undefined

209. A sedimentary structure consisting of a very small dune of sand or silt whose long dimension is at right angles to the current is a _____.
   a. 1509 Istanbul earthquake
   b. Ripple12
   c. Undefined
   d. Undefined

210. _____ refers to a glacial lake in northwest Montana during Pleistocene times, which was formed by an ice dam of the Cordilleran ice sheet; this dam broke periodically, flooding a portion of current-day northern Idaho and Washington.
   a. 1509 Istanbul earthquake
   b. Lake Missoula12
   c. Undefined
   d. Undefined

211. _____ refers to deposits of stratified sand, gravel, and silt that have been removed from a glacier by meltwater streams.
   a. 1509 Istanbul earthquake
   b. Glacial outwash12
   c. Undefined
   d. Undefined

212. The _____ meaning "new life" is the most recent of the three classic geological eras. It covers the 65.5 million years since the Cretaceous-Tertiary extinction event at the end of the Cretaceous that marked the demise of the last dinosaurs and the end of the Mesozoic Era. The _____ is ongoing.
   a. Cenozoic Era12
   b. Thing
   c. Undefined
   d. Undefined

213. _____ refers to a major division on the geologic time scale; eras are divided into shorter units called periods.
   a. AASHTO Soil Classification System
   b. Era12
   c. Undefined
   d. Undefined

Chapter 13. Deserts and Wind Action

1. Any accumulation of material, by mechanical settling from water or air, chemical precipitation, evaporation from solution, etc is referred to as _____.
   a. Deposition13
   b. 1509 Istanbul earthquake
   c. Undefined
   d. Undefined

2. _____ is the displacement of solids (soil, mud, rock, and other particles) by the agents of wind, water, ice, movement in response to gravity, or living organisms.
   a. Thing
   b. Erosion13
   c. Undefined
   d. Undefined

3. A _____ is a landscape form or region that receives little precipitation - less than 250 mm (10 in) per year. It is a biome characterized by organisms adapted to sparse rainfall and rapid evaporation.
   a. Thing
   b. Desert13
   c. Undefined
   d. Undefined

4. A climate in which yearly precipitation is less than the potential loss of water by evaporation is a _____.
   a. Dry climate13
   b. 1509 Istanbul earthquake
   c. Undefined
   d. Undefined

5. Weather condition of an area including especially prevailing temperature and average daily/yearly rainfall over a long period of time is called _____.
   a. Climate13
   b. Thing
   c. Undefined
   d. Undefined

6. _____ refers to flood of very high discharge and short duration; sudden and local in extent.
   a. 1509 Istanbul earthquake
   b. Flash flood13
   c. Undefined
   d. Undefined

7. A mound of loose sand grains heaped up by the wind is a _____.
   a. 1509 Istanbul earthquake
   b. Sand dune13
   c. Undefined
   d. Undefined

8. _____ refers to a usually asymmetrical mound or ridge of sand that has been transported and deposited by wind. Dunes form in both arid and humid climates.
   a. 1509 Istanbul earthquake
   b. Dune13
   c. Undefined
   d. Undefined

9. _____ refers to any condensed water falling from the atmosphere to the surface of the earth. Common types include rain, snow, sleet, and hail.
   a. 1509 Istanbul earthquake
   b. Precipitation13
   c. Undefined
   d. Undefined

10. The _____ is that part of a planet's outer shell — including air, land, surface rocks and water — within which life occurs, and which biotic processes in turn alter or transform.
    a. Thing
    b. Biosphere13
    c. Undefined
    d. Undefined

11. An area with sparse vegetation owing to some physical or chemical property of the soil is referred to as _____.
   a. Thing
   b. Barren13
   c. Undefined
   d. Undefined

12. The situation in mass wasting that occurs when material free-falls or bounces down a cliff is called a _____.
   a. 1509 Istanbul earthquake
   b. Fall13
   c. Undefined
   d. Undefined

13. _____ refers to the process by which a rock or mineral is broken down into smaller fragments without altering its chemical makeup; weathering that affects only physical characteristics.
   a. Mechanical weathering13
   b. 1509 Istanbul earthquake
   c. Undefined
   d. Undefined

14. The process by which exposure to atmospheric agents, such as air or moisture, causes rocks and minerals to break down is called _____. This process takes place at or near the Earth's surface. _____ entails little or no movement of the material that it loosens from the rocks and minerals.
   a. Weathering13
   b. 1509 Istanbul earthquake
   c. Undefined
   d. Undefined

15. _____ is a term denoting the solid body of the Earth (i.e. the hydrosphere, lithosphere [including pedosphere] and in some definitions also the internal part of the Earth) and the atmosphere of the Earth.
   a. Geosphere13
   b. Thing
   c. Undefined
   d. Undefined

16. Any unconsolidated material at Earth's surface is _____.
   a. Debris13
   b. 1509 Istanbul earthquake
   c. Undefined
   d. Undefined

17. Earth's _____ is a layer of gases surrounding the planet Earth and retained by the Earth's gravity. It contains roughly 78% nitrogen and 21% oxygen, with trace amounts of other gases.
   a. Thing
   b. Atmosphere13
   c. Undefined
   d. Undefined

18. _____ in physical geography, describes the collective mass of water found on, under, and over the surface of a planet.
   a. Hydrosphere13
   b. Thing
   c. Undefined
   d. Undefined

19. Angular distance of a point on the earth's surface north or south of the equator, measured along a meridian, the equator being _____ 0°, the north pole _____ 90°N, and the south pole _____ 90°S.
   a. 1509 Istanbul earthquake
   b. Latitude13
   c. Undefined
   d. Undefined

20. _____ refers to water molecules in the gaseous state. Also is one state of the water cycle.

Chapter 13. Deserts and Wind Action

a. Water vapor13
b. Thing
c. Undefined
d. Undefined

21. _____ refers to water in the gaseous state.
   a. Vapor13
   b. 1509 Istanbul earthquake
   c. Undefined
   d. Undefined

22. _____ refers to the change of state of water from the liquid to vapor phase. Requires the addition of 80 calories per cubic centimeter.
   a. AASHTO Soil Classification System
   b. Evaporation13
   c. Undefined
   d. Undefined

23. The result of the process by which moist air on the windward side of a mountain rises and cools, causing precipitation and leaving the leeward side of the mountain dry is a _____.
   a. 1509 Istanbul earthquake
   b. Rain shadow effect13
   c. Undefined
   d. Undefined

24. _____ refers to a group of closely spaced mountains or parallel ridges.
   a. Mountain range13
   b. 1509 Istanbul earthquake
   c. Undefined
   d. Undefined

25. A _____ is a dry region on the surface of the Earth that is leeward or behind a mountain with respect to the prevailing wind direction. A _____ area is dry because, as moist air masses rise to top a mountain range or large mountain, the air cools and water vapor condenses as rain or snow, falling on the windward side or top of the mountain.
   a. Thing
   b. Rain shadow13
   c. Undefined
   d. Undefined

26. A large mass of rock projecting above surrounding terrain is called a _____.
   a. Mountain13
   b. 1509 Istanbul earthquake
   c. Undefined
   d. Undefined

27. Lacking any asymmetric accumulation of positive and negative charge. _____ molecules are generally insoluble in water.
   a. Nonpolar13
   b. Thing
   c. Undefined
   d. Undefined

28. A round or oval depression in the Earth's surface, containing the youngest section of rock in its lowest, central part is a _____.
   a. 1509 Istanbul earthquake
   b. Basin13
   c. Undefined
   d. Undefined

29. Stress that reduces the volume or length of a rock, as that produced by the convergence of plate margins is called _____.
   a. Compression13
   b. 1509 Istanbul earthquake
   c. Undefined
   d. Undefined

Chapter 13. Deserts and Wind Action

30. _____ refers to the change of state of water from the vapor to the liquid phase. Results in liberation of 80 calories per cubic centimeter.
    a. 1509 Istanbul earthquake
    b. Condensation13
    c. Undefined
    d. Undefined

31. An _____ is any more or less permanent or continuous, directed movement of ocean water that flows in one of the Earth's oceans.
    a. Ocean current13
    b. Thing
    c. Undefined
    d. Undefined

32. Low latitude areas characterized by high temperatures and high precipitation are referred to as _____. At high elevations, however, _____ mountains may be both cold and relatively dry.
    a. 1509 Istanbul earthquake
    b. Tropical13
    c. Undefined
    d. Undefined

33. _____ refers to the area of dry land that borders on a body of water.
    a. 1509 Istanbul earthquake
    b. Coast13
    c. Undefined
    d. Undefined

34. The bitterly cold, arid region centered at the south is referred to as the _____.
    a. Polar desert13
    b. 1509 Istanbul earthquake
    c. Undefined
    d. Undefined

35. Distinct crystals of ice are called _____. Commonly accumulates with a density of 50 - 200 kg·m, although wind-abraded and packed _____ may have a higher initial density.
    a. Snow13
    b. 1509 Istanbul earthquake
    c. Undefined
    d. Undefined

36. _____ refers to the set of physical features, such as mountains, valleys, and the shapes of landforms, that characterizes a given landscape.
    a. Topography13
    b. 1509 Istanbul earthquake
    c. Undefined
    d. Undefined

37. _____ refers to a body of water found on the Earth's surface and confined to a narrow topographic depression, down which it flows and transports rock particles, sediment, and dissolved particles. Rivers, creeks, brooks, and runs are all streams.
    a. 1509 Istanbul earthquake
    b. Stream13
    c. Undefined
    d. Undefined

38. Group of organisms of the same species occupying a certain area and sharing a common gene pool is referred to as _____.
    a. Population13
    b. Thing
    c. Undefined
    d. Undefined

39. _____ is the degradation of land in arid, semi arid and dry sub-humid areas resulting from various factors including climatic variations and human activities.

a. Desertification13 b. Thing
c. Undefined d. Undefined

40. _____ refers to a basic unit of the geologic time scale that is a subdivision of an era. Periods may be divided into smaller units called epochs.
    a. Period13 b. 1509 Istanbul earthquake
    c. Undefined d. Undefined

41. _____ refers to the top few meters of regolith, generally including some organic matter derived from plants.
    a. Soil13 b. 1509 Istanbul earthquake
    c. Undefined d. Undefined

42. The _____ is a landlocked endorheic sea in Central Asia; it lies between Kazakhstan in the north and Karakalpakstan, an autonomous region of Uzbekistan, in the south. Since the 1960s the _____ has been shrinking.
    a. Thing b. Aral Sea13
    c. Undefined d. Undefined

43. Any relatively sunken part of the Earth's surface, especially a low-lying area surrounded by higher ground is called a _____.
    a. Depression13 b. 1509 Istanbul earthquake
    c. Undefined d. Undefined

44. _____ refers to a biome, located in the centers of continents, that supports grasses; also called grassland.
    a. Prairie13 b. Thing
    c. Undefined d. Undefined

45. A major branch of a stream system is referred to as a _____.
    a. 1509 Istanbul earthquake b. River13
    c. Undefined d. Undefined

46. Water entering rivers, lakes, reservoirs, or the ocean from land surfaces is _____.
    a. Thing b. Runoff13
    c. Undefined d. Undefined

47. Temporary base level is referred to as _____.
    a. 1509 Istanbul earthquake b. Local base level13
    c. Undefined d. Undefined

48. The lowest level to which a stream can erode the channel through which it flows, generally equal to the prevailing global sea level is referred to as the _____.
    a. 1509 Istanbul earthquake b. Base level13
    c. Undefined d. Undefined

49. _____ is any particulate matter that can be transported by fluid flow and which eventually is deposited as a layer of solid particles on the bed or bottom of a body of water or other liquid.

a. Thing
b. Sediment13
c. Undefined
d. Undefined

50. A long, narrow depression, shaped and more or less filled by a stream is referred to as a _____.
a. 1509 Istanbul earthquake
b. Stream channel13
c. Undefined
d. Undefined

51. A flowage of water-saturated earth material possessing a high degree of fluidity during movement is _____.
a. Mudflow13
b. 1509 Istanbul earthquake
c. Undefined
d. Undefined

52. _____ refers to a feature on the surface of the planet Mars that very closely resembles certain types of stream channels on Earth.
a. 1509 Istanbul earthquake
b. Channel13
c. Undefined
d. Undefined

53. Rounded particles coarser than 2 mm in diameter are called _____.
a. 1509 Istanbul earthquake
b. Gravel13
c. Undefined
d. Undefined

54. A valley-deepening process caused by erosion of a stream bed is called _____.
a. 1509 Istanbul earthquake
b. Downcutting13
c. Undefined
d. Undefined

55. _____ refers to a desert valley that carries water only briefly after a rain.
a. Dry wash13
b. 1509 Istanbul earthquake
c. Undefined
d. Undefined

56. A small, deep, usually dry channel eroded by a short-lived or intermittent desert stream is an _____.
a. Arroyo13
b. AASHTO Soil Classification System
c. Undefined
d. Undefined

57. _____ refers to a clastic rock composed of particles more than 2 millimeters in diameter and marked by the roundness of its component grains and rock fragments.
a. 1509 Istanbul earthquake
b. Conglomerate13
c. Undefined
d. Undefined

58. _____ refers to a clastic rock composed of particles that range in diameter from 1/16 millimeter to 2 millimeters in diameter. Sandstones make up about 25% of all sedimentary rocks.
a. Sandstone13
b. 1509 Istanbul earthquake
c. Undefined
d. Undefined

59. The entire area between the tops of the slopes on both sides of a stream is a _____.
a. Valley13
b. 1509 Istanbul earthquake
c. Undefined
d. Undefined

Chapter 13. Deserts and Wind Action

60. A deeply gullied terrain in horizontally bedded rock in unvegetated arid or semiarid terrain is a _____.
    a. 1509 Istanbul earthquake
    b. Badland13
    c. Undefined
    d. Undefined

61. _____ refers to a sedimentary rock composed of detrital sediment particles less than 0.004 millimeters in diameter. _____ tends to be red, brown, black, or gray, and usually originate in relatively still waters.
    a. Shale13
    b. 1509 Istanbul earthquake
    c. Undefined
    d. Undefined

62. Aggregates of minerals or rock fragments are called _____.
    a. Rocks13
    b. 1509 Istanbul earthquake
    c. Undefined
    d. Undefined

63. _____ refers to a naturally formed aggregate of usually inorganic materials from within the Earth.
    a. 1509 Istanbul earthquake
    b. Rock13
    c. Undefined
    d. Undefined

64. _____ is a sedimentary rock composed largely of the mineral calcite (calcium carbonate: $CaCO_3$). _____ often contains variable amounts of silica in the form of chert or flint, as well as varying amounts of clay, silt and sand as disseminations, nodules, or layers within the rock.
    a. Limestone13
    b. Thing
    c. Undefined
    d. Undefined

65. _____ is the result of the transformation of a pre-existing rock type, the protolith, in a process called metamorphism, which means "change in form". The protolith is subjected to heat (greater than 150 degrees Celsius) and extreme pressure causing profound physical and/or chemical change.
    a. Thing
    b. Metamorphic rock13
    c. Undefined
    d. Undefined

66. _____ refers to the term from the Greek 'meta' and 'morph', commonly occurs to rocks which are subjected to increased heat and/or pressure. Also applies to the conversion of snow into glacial ice.
    a. Metamorphic13
    b. 1509 Istanbul earthquake
    c. Undefined
    d. Undefined

67. _____ refers to an outpouring of lava onto the land surface from a vent or fissure. Also, a solidified tongue like or sheet-like body formed by outpouring lava.
    a. 1509 Istanbul earthquake
    b. Lava flow13
    c. Undefined
    d. Undefined

68. _____ rocks are formed when molten rock (magma) cools and solidifies, with or without crystallization, either below the surface as intrusive (plutonic) rocks or on the surface as extrusive (volcanic) rocks. This magma can be derived from either the Earth's mantle or pre-existing rocks made molten by extreme temperature and pressure changes.
    a. Thing
    b. Igneous13
    c. Undefined
    d. Undefined

69. Magma that comes to the Earth's surface through a volcano or fissure is referred to as _____.

Chapter 13. Deserts and Wind Action

a. Lava13
b. 1509 Istanbul earthquake
c. Undefined
d. Undefined

70. Angular chunk of solid rock ejected during an eruption is referred to as a _____.
a. Block13
b. 1509 Istanbul earthquake
c. Undefined
d. Undefined

71. _____ refers to the process by which chemical reactions alter the chemical composition of rocks and minerals that are unstable at the Earth's surface and convert them into more stable substances; weathering that changes the chemical makeup of a rock or mineral.
a. 1509 Istanbul earthquake
b. Chemical weathering13
c. Undefined
d. Undefined

72. _____ refer to hydrous aluminum silicates that have a layered atomic structure. They are very fine grained and become plastic when wet. Most belong to one of three clay groups: kaolinite, illite, and smectite.
a. Clay minerals13
b. 1509 Istanbul earthquake
c. Undefined
d. Undefined

73. A hydrous aluminum-silicate that occurs as a platy grain of microscopic size with a sheet silicate structure is _____.
a. Clay mineral13
b. 1509 Istanbul earthquake
c. Undefined
d. Undefined

74. A naturally occurring, usually inorganic, solid consisting of either a single element or a compound, and having a definite chemical composition and a systematic internal arrangement of atoms is referred to as a _____.
a. Mineral13
b. 1509 Istanbul earthquake
c. Undefined
d. Undefined

75. _____ refers to the slowest form of mass movement, measured in millimeters or centimeters per year and occurring on virtually all slopes.
a. Creep13
b. 1509 Istanbul earthquake
c. Undefined
d. Undefined

76. An elevated area with relatively little internal relief is called a _____.
a. Plateau13
b. 1509 Istanbul earthquake
c. Undefined
d. Undefined

77. _____ is one of the three main rock groups and is formed in three main ways—by the deposition of the weathered remains of other rocks; by the deposition of the results of biogenic activity; and by precipitation from solution.
a. Event
b. Sedimentary rock13
c. Undefined
d. Undefined

78. The top of the ocean, where the water meets the atmosphere is called _____.
a. Sea level13
b. 1509 Istanbul earthquake
c. Undefined
d. Undefined

Chapter 13. Deserts and Wind Action

79. _____ refers to a small, conspicuous, isolated hill bounded by cliffs.
    a. Butte13
    b. 1509 Istanbul earthquake
    c. Undefined
    d. Undefined

80. A relatively small flat-topped hill or mountain is called a _____.
    a. Mesa13
    b. 1509 Istanbul earthquake
    c. Undefined
    d. Undefined

81. A fold in rock connecting two vertically offset, horizontal sections of sedimentary rocks is called the _____.
    a. Monocline13
    b. 1509 Istanbul earthquake
    c. Undefined
    d. Undefined

82. _____ refers to a bend that develops in an initially horizontal layer of rock, usually caused by plastic deformation. Folds occur most frequently in sedimentary rocks.
    a. 1509 Istanbul earthquake
    b. Fold13
    c. Undefined
    d. Undefined

83. A narrow ridge formed by the outcrop near-vertical sedimentary beds is called _____.
    a. Hogback13
    b. 1509 Istanbul earthquake
    c. Undefined
    d. Undefined

84. _____ refers to an asymmetric hill or ridge with a gentle slope on one side and a steep outcrop slope on the other.
    a. Cuesta13
    b. 1509 Istanbul earthquake
    c. Undefined
    d. Undefined

85. _____ refers to any physical, recognizable form or feature on the earth's surface, having a characteristic shape and range in composition, and produced by natural causes.
    a. 1509 Istanbul earthquake
    b. Landform13
    c. Undefined
    d. Undefined

86. Rocks formed by solidification of sediments formed and transported at the Earth's surface are referred to as _____.
    a. 1509 Istanbul earthquake
    b. Sedimentary rocks13
    c. Undefined
    d. Undefined

87. A high mountain peak that forms when the walls of three or more cirques intersect is called a _____.
    a. Horn13
    b. 1509 Istanbul earthquake
    c. Undefined
    d. Undefined

88. _____ refers to a crack or break in a rock. To break in random places instead of cleaving.
    a. Fracture13
    b. 1509 Istanbul earthquake
    c. Undefined
    d. Undefined

89. A fracture dividing a rock into two sections that have visibly moved relative to each other is a _____.

a. Fault13
b. 1509 Istanbul earthquake
c. Undefined
d. Undefined

90. A triangular deposit of sediment left by a stream that has lost velocity upon entering a broad, relatively flat valley is referred to as an _____.
   a. AASHTO Soil Classification System
   b. Alluvial fan13
   c. Undefined
   d. Undefined

91. _____ refers to pertaining to material or processes associated with transportation and or subaerial deposition by concentrated running water.
   a. Alluvial13
   b. AASHTO Soil Classification System
   c. Undefined
   d. Undefined

92. A shallow temporary lake on a flat valley floor in a dry region is referred to as a _____.
   a. Playa lake13
   b. 1509 Istanbul earthquake
   c. Undefined
   d. Undefined

93. A dry lake basin found in a desert is called a _____.
   a. Playa13
   b. 1509 Istanbul earthquake
   c. Undefined
   d. Undefined

94. A network of converging and diverging streams separated from each other by narrow strips of sand and gravel are referred to as a _____.
   a. Braided stream13
   b. 1509 Istanbul earthquake
   c. Undefined
   d. Undefined

95. _____ is a term used for ionic compounds composed of positively charged cations and negatively charged anions, so that the product is neutral and without a net charge.
   a. Salt13
   b. Thing
   c. Undefined
   d. Undefined

96. An apron of sediment along a mountain front created by the coalescence of alluvial fans is referred to as _____.
   a. Bajada13
   b. 1509 Istanbul earthquake
   c. Undefined
   d. Undefined

97. A broad surface at the base of a receding mountain is _____. The _____ develops when running water erodes most of the mass of the mountain.
   a. 1509 Istanbul earthquake
   b. Pediment13
   c. Undefined
   d. Undefined

98. _____ refers to all features created by the processes of deformation from minor fractures in bedrock to a major mountain chain.
   a. 1509 Istanbul earthquake
   b. Rock structure13
   c. Undefined
   d. Undefined

Chapter 13. Deserts and Wind Action

99. _____ refers to soil particles between the size of sand particles and clay particles, namely particles 0.002-0.2 mm in diameter.
   a. Silt13
   b. Thing
   c. Undefined
   d. Undefined

100. A chemical substance that resists changes in pH by accepting H^+ ions from or donating H^+ ions to solutions is called a _____.
   a. Buffer13
   b. Thing
   c. Undefined
   d. Undefined

101. _____ refers to levels within a soil profile that differ structurally and chemically. Generally divided into A, B, C, E, and 0 horizons.
   a. Thing
   b. Horizon13
   c. Undefined
   d. Undefined

102. _____ refers to extremely small fragments, usually of glass, that forms when escaping gases force a fine spray of magma from a volcano.
   a. Volcanic ash13
   b. 1509 Istanbul earthquake
   c. Undefined
   d. Undefined

103. Fine particles of pulverized rock blown from an explosion vent are called _____. Measuring less than 1/10 inch in diameter, _____ may be either solid or molten when first erupted.
   a. Ash13
   b. AASHTO Soil Classification System
   c. Undefined
   d. Undefined

104. _____ refers to the process by which solid, liquid, and gaseous materials are ejected into the earth's atmosphere and onto the earth's surface by volcanic activity. Eruptions range from the quiet overflow of liquid rock to the tremendously violent expulsion of pyroclastics.
   a. Eruption13
   b. AASHTO Soil Classification System
   c. Undefined
   d. Undefined

105. The solid structure created when lava, gases, and hot particles escape to the Earth's surface through vents is called a _____. Volcanoes are usually conical. A _____ is 'active' when it is erupting or has erupted recently. Volcanoes that have not erupted recently but are considered likely to erupt in the future are said to be 'dormant.' A _____ that has not erupted for a long time and is not expected to erupt in the future is 'extinct'.
   a. 1509 Istanbul earthquake
   b. Volcano13
   c. Undefined
   d. Undefined

106. The process of bouncing of grains along a surface by flowing air or water is referred to as _____.
   a. 1509 Istanbul earthquake
   b. Saltation13
   c. Undefined
   d. Undefined

107. _____ refers to a term loosely used for an igneous or metamorphic rock, as distinguished from a sedimentary rock. In mining, a rock that requires drilling and blasting for economical removal.

a. Hard rock13   b. 1509 Istanbul earthquake
c. Undefined   d. Undefined

108. A form of mechanical weathering that occurs when loose fragments or particles of rocks and minerals that are being transported, as by water or air, collide with each other or scrape the surfaces of stationary rocks is referred to as _____.
a. AASHTO Soil Classification System   b. Abrasion13
c. Undefined   d. Undefined

109. _____ refers to a stone that has been flattened and sharpened by wind abrasion. Ventifacts are commonly found strewn across a desert floor.
a. 1509 Istanbul earthquake   b. Ventifact13
c. Undefined   d. Undefined

110. A rock particle 2 to 64 mm in diameter is referred to as the _____.
a. Pebble13   b. 1509 Istanbul earthquake
c. Undefined   d. Undefined

111. Removal of fine particles by wind erosion is called _____.
a. Deflation13   b. 1509 Istanbul earthquake
c. Undefined   d. Undefined

112. _____ refers to the erosion of rock outcrops, boulders, and pebbles by abrasion caused by the impact of high-speed sand grains carried by the wind.
a. Sandblasting13   b. 1509 Istanbul earthquake
c. Undefined   d. Undefined

113. Mineral with the formula Si0 is referred to as _____.
a. Quartz13   b. 1509 Istanbul earthquake
c. Undefined   d. Undefined

114. A load of silt that is produced by the erosion of outwash and transported by wind is _____. Much _____ found in the Mississippi Valley, China, and Europe is believed to have been deposited during the Pleistocene Epoch.
a. Loess13   b. 1509 Istanbul earthquake
c. Undefined   d. Undefined

115. _____ refers to deposits of stratified sand, gravel, and silt that have been removed from a glacier by meltwater streams.
a. 1509 Istanbul earthquake   b. Glacial outwash13
c. Undefined   d. Undefined

116. The percentage of a soil, rock, or sediment's volume that is made up of pores is _____.
a. Porosity13   b. 1509 Istanbul earthquake
c. Undefined   d. Undefined

117. A load of sediment, consisting of sand and gravel that is deposited by meltwater in front of a glacier is called _____.

Chapter 13. Deserts and Wind Action

a. AASHTO Soil Classification System
c. Undefined
b. Outwash13
d. Undefined

118. The solid material that precipitates in the pore space of sediments, binding the grains together to form solid rock is referred to as _____.
   a. 1509 Istanbul earthquake
   c. Undefined
   b. Cement13
   d. Undefined

119. A movement within the Earth's crust or mantle, caused by the sudden rupture or repositioning of underground rocks as they release stress is an _____.
   a. Earthquake13
   c. Undefined
   b. AASHTO Soil Classification System
   d. Undefined

120. The first epoch of the Quaternary Period, beginning 2 to 3 million years ago and ending approximately 10,000 years ago is referred to as the _____.
   a. 1509 Istanbul earthquake
   c. Undefined
   b. Pleistocene epoch13
   d. Undefined

121. A geologic epoch, characterized by alternating glacial and interglacial stages, that ended about 10,000 years ago, that lasted for 2 million years is called the _____ epoch.
   a. Thing
   c. Undefined
   b. Pleistocene13
   d. Undefined

122. A unit of the geologic time scale that is a subdivision of a period is referred to as an _____.
   a. Epoch13
   c. Undefined
   b. AASHTO Soil Classification System
   d. Undefined

123. The nearly level plain that borders a stream and is subject to inundation under flood stage conditions unless protected artificially is called _____.
   a. Flood plain13
   c. Undefined
   b. 1509 Istanbul earthquake
   d. Undefined

124. _____ refers to finely ground rock material, usually associated with glaciers. Can be mixed with water and formed into loaves which, when baked for 45 minutes at 350 deg., are totally inedible.
   a. Rock flour13
   c. Undefined
   b. 1509 Istanbul earthquake
   d. Undefined

125. Of either earth or stone pebbles, generally covering a burial chamber or deposit is called _____.
   a. Mound13
   c. Undefined
   b. 1509 Istanbul earthquake
   d. Undefined

126. A measure of the effects of an earthquake at a particular place is called _____. _____ depends not only on the magnitude of the earthquake, but also on the distance from the epicenter and the local geology.
   a. Intensity13
   c. Undefined
   b. AASHTO Soil Classification System
   d. Undefined

Chapter 13. Deserts and Wind Action

127. One of several minerals containing one central carbon atom with strong covalent bonds to three oxygen atoms and typically having ionic bonds to one or more positive ions is _____.
    a. Carbonate13
    b. 1509 Istanbul earthquake
    c. Undefined
    d. Undefined

128. _____ refers to the process by which a given transport medium separates out certain particles, as on the basis of size, shape, or density.
    a. 1509 Istanbul earthquake
    b. Sorting13
    c. Undefined
    d. Undefined

129. The maximum angle at which a pile of unconsolidated material can remain stable is the _____.
    a. Angle of repose13
    b. AASHTO Soil Classification System
    c. Undefined
    d. Undefined

130. The steep leeward slope of a dune is called the _____.
    a. 1509 Istanbul earthquake
    b. Slip face13
    c. Undefined
    d. Undefined

131. _____ refers to the interval of time between volcanic eruptions.
    a. Repose13
    b. 1509 Istanbul earthquake
    c. Undefined
    d. Undefined

132. The distance that one face of a fault is displaced relative to the other is referred to as a _____.
    a. Slip13
    b. 1509 Istanbul earthquake
    c. Undefined
    d. Undefined

133. _____ refers to a closely packed layer of rock fragments concentrated in a layer along the Earth's surface by the deflation of finer particles.
    a. 1509 Istanbul earthquake
    b. Desert pavement13
    c. Undefined
    d. Undefined

134. The upper layer of water that is mixed by wind, waves, and currents is the _____.
    a. Surface layer13
    b. Thing
    c. Undefined
    d. Undefined

135. _____ refers to a wave with a flatter, rounded wave crest and trough. Swells are found away from the area where waves are generated by the wind.
    a. Swell13
    b. Thing
    c. Undefined
    d. Undefined

136. A thin, shiny red-brown or black layer, principally composed of iron manganese oxides, that coats the surfaces of many exposed desert rocks is a _____.
    a. Desert varnish13
    b. 1509 Istanbul earthquake
    c. Undefined
    d. Undefined

137. Age given in years or some other unit of time is the _____.

Chapter 13. Deserts and Wind Action

a. 1509 Istanbul earthquake
b. Numerical age13
c. Undefined
d. Undefined

138. _____ is a chemical element in the periodic table that has the symbol Mn and atomic number 25.
a. Thing
b. Manganese13
c. Undefined
d. Undefined

139. _____ refer to varieties of the same element that have different mass numbers; their nuclei contain the same number of protons but different numbers of neutrons.
a. AASHTO Soil Classification System
b. Isotopes13
c. Undefined
d. Undefined

140. An _____ is a form of an element whose nuclei have the same atomic number - the number of protons in the nucleus - but different mass numbers because they contain different numbers of neutrons.
a. Thing
b. Isotope13
c. Undefined
d. Undefined

141. _____ is a chemical element; it is a colorless, odorless, tasteless, non-toxic, and nearly inert monatomic that heads the noble gas series in the periodic table. Its atomic number is 2 and its boiling and melting points are the lowest among the elements. It exists only as a gas except in extreme conditions.
a. Helium13
b. Thing
c. Undefined
d. Undefined

142. One of several minerals containing negative oxygen ions bonded to one or more positive metallic ions are called _____.
a. Oxide13
b. AASHTO Soil Classification System
c. Undefined
d. Undefined

143. _____ is essential to all organisms, except for a few bacteria. It is mostly stably incorporated in the inside of metalloproteins, because in exposed or in free form it causes production of free radicals that are generally toxic to cells.
a. Thing
b. Iron13
c. Undefined
d. Undefined

144. _____ refers to an extremely durable, nonfoliated metamorphic rock derived from pure sandstone and consisting primarily of quartz.
a. Quartzite13
b. 1509 Istanbul earthquake
c. Undefined
d. Undefined

145. _____ refers to a tentative explanation of a given set of data that is expected to remain valid after future observation and experimentation.
a. Hypothesis13
b. 1509 Istanbul earthquake
c. Undefined
d. Undefined

146. _____ or capillarity is the ability of a narrow tube to draw a liquid upwards against the force of gravity. It occurs when the adhesive intermolecular forces between the liquid and a solid are stronger than the cohesive intermolecular forces within the liquid.

a. Thing
b. Capillary action13
c. Undefined
d. Undefined

147. Usually slow but effective process of weathering and erosion in which rocks are dissolved by water is a _____.
a. 1509 Istanbul earthquake
b. Solution13
c. Undefined
d. Undefined

148. A large mass of material or mixtures of material falling or sliding rapidly under the force of gravity is an _____. Avalanches often are classified by their content, such as snow, ice, soil, or rock avalanches. A mixture of these materials is a debris _____.
a. Avalanche13
b. AASHTO Soil Classification System
c. Undefined
d. Undefined

149. The mass movement of a single, intact mass of rock, soil, or unconsolidated material along a weak plane, such as a fault, fracture, or bedding plane is a _____. A _____ may involve as little as a minor displacement of soil or as much as the displacement of an entire mountainside.
a. 1509 Istanbul earthquake
b. Slide13
c. Undefined
d. Undefined

150. _____ refers to the structure in which relatively thin layers are inclined at an angle to the main bedding. Formed by currents of wind or water.
a. Cross-bedding13
b. 1509 Istanbul earthquake
c. Undefined
d. Undefined

151. _____ refers to the time period from 10,000 years ago to the present.
a. 1509 Istanbul earthquake
b. Holocene13
c. Undefined
d. Undefined

152. _____ occurs when living things move from one biome to another. In most cases organisms migrate to avoid local shortages of food, usually caused by winter. Animals may also migrate to a certain location to breed, as is the case with some fish.
a. Thing
b. Migration13
c. Undefined
d. Undefined

153. Small, low ridge of sand produced by the saltation of windblown sand is the _____.
a. Wind ripple13
b. 1509 Istanbul earthquake
c. Undefined
d. Undefined

154. A sedimentary structure consisting of a very small dune of sand or silt whose long dimension is at right angles to the current is a _____.
a. Ripple13
b. 1509 Istanbul earthquake
c. Undefined
d. Undefined

155. _____ refer to long ridges of sand oriented parallel to the prevailing wind; these dunes form where sand supplies are limited.

Chapter 13. Deserts and Wind Action

a. Longitudinal dunes13
b. 1509 Istanbul earthquake
c. Undefined
d. Undefined

156. _____ refers to one of a series of long, narrow dunes lying parallel both to each other and to the prevailing wind direction. Longitudinal dunes range from 60 meters to 100 kilometers in length and from 3 to 50 meters in height.
a. Longitudinal dune13
b. 1509 Istanbul earthquake
c. Undefined
d. Undefined

157. _____ refer to a series of long ridges oriented at right angles to the prevailing wind; these dunes form where vegetation is sparse and sand is very plentiful.
a. Transverse dunes13
b. 1509 Istanbul earthquake
c. Undefined
d. Undefined

158. One of a series of dunes having an especially steep slip face and a gentle windward slope and standing perpendicular to the prevailing wind direction and parallel to each other. Transverse dunes typically form in arid and semi-arid regions with plentiful sand, stable wind direction, and scarce vegetation. A _____ may be as much as 100 kilometers long, 200 meters high, and 3 kilometers wide.
a. Transverse dune13
b. 1509 Istanbul earthquake
c. Undefined
d. Undefined

159. _____ refers to a horseshoe-shaped dune having a concave windward slope and a convex leeward slope. Parabolic dunes tend to form along sandy ocean and lake shores. They may also develop from transverse dunes through deflation.
a. Parabolic dune13
b. 1509 Istanbul earthquake
c. Undefined
d. Undefined

160. _____ refers to a crescent-shaped dune with limbs downwind.
a. Barchan13
b. 1509 Istanbul earthquake
c. Undefined
d. Undefined

161. The scientific study of the Earth, its origins and evolution, the materials that make it up, and the processes that act on it is called _____.
a. 1509 Istanbul earthquake
b. Geology13
c. Undefined
d. Undefined

162. The force of attraction exerted by one body in the universe on another is _____. _____ is directly proportional to the product of the masses of the two attracted bodies. The force of attraction exerted by the Earth on bodies on or near its surface, tending to pull them toward the Earth's center.
a. 1509 Istanbul earthquake
b. Gravity13
c. Undefined
d. Undefined

163. _____ is an atmospheric gas comprized of one carbon and two oxygen atoms. A very widely known chemical compound, it is frequently called by its formula CO_2. In its solid state, it is commonly known as dry ice.
a. Carbon dioxide13
b. Thing
c. Undefined
d. Undefined

Chapter 13. Deserts and Wind Action

164. _____ is a chemical element in the periodic table that has the symbol C and atomic number 6. An abundant nonmetallic, tetravalent element, _____ has several allotropic forms.
   a. Thing
   b. Carbon13
   c. Undefined
   d. Undefined

165. The time between winter and summer is _____.
   a. Spring13
   b. 1509 Istanbul earthquake
   c. Undefined
   d. Undefined

166. A steep-sided, usually circular depression formed by either explosion or collapse at a volcanic vent is a _____.
   a. 1509 Istanbul earthquake
   b. Crater13
   c. Undefined
   d. Undefined

167. _____ refers to a streamlined, wind-sculpted ridge having the appearance of an inverted ship's hull that is oriented parallel to the prevailing wind.
   a. Yardang13
   b. 1509 Istanbul earthquake
   c. Undefined
   d. Undefined

168. _____ refers to a crescent-shaped dune that forms around a small patch of vegetation, lies perpendicular to the prevailing wind direction, and has a gentle, convex windward slope and a steep, concave leeward slope. Barchan dunes typically form in arid, inland deserts with stable wind direction and relatively little sand.
   a. 1509 Istanbul earthquake
   b. Barchan dune13
   c. Undefined
   d. Undefined

169. _____ refers to fragment of molten or semi-molten rock, 2 1/2 inches to many feet in diameter, which is blown out during an eruption. Because of their plastic condition, bombs are often modified in shape during their flight or upon impact.
   a. Bomb13
   b. 1509 Istanbul earthquake
   c. Undefined
   d. Undefined

170. _____ refers to an area with less than 25 cm of rain per year.
   a. Arid region13
   b. AASHTO Soil Classification System
   c. Undefined
   d. Undefined

171. A mineral or fuel deposit, known or not yet discovered, that may be or become available for human exploitation is called a _____.
   a. Resource13
   b. 1509 Istanbul earthquake
   c. Undefined
   d. Undefined

Chapter 14. Waves, Beaches, and Coasts

1. The movement of eroded particles by agents such as rivers, waves, glaciers, or wind is referred to as _____.
   a. 1509 Istanbul earthquake
   b. Transportation14
   c. Undefined
   d. Undefined

2. Any accumulation of material, by mechanical settling from water or air, chemical precipitation, evaporation from solution, etc is referred to as _____.
   a. Deposition14
   b. 1509 Istanbul earthquake
   c. Undefined
   d. Undefined

3. _____ is any particulate matter that can be transported by fluid flow and which eventually is deposited as a layer of solid particles on the bed or bottom of a body of water or other liquid.
   a. Thing
   b. Sediment14
   c. Undefined
   d. Undefined

4. _____ is the displacement of solids (soil, mud, rock, and other particles) by the agents of wind, water, ice, movement in response to gravity, or living organisms.
   a. Erosion14
   b. Thing
   c. Undefined
   d. Undefined

5. _____ in physical geography, describes the collective mass of water found on, under, and over the surface of a planet.
   a. Thing
   b. Hydrosphere14
   c. Undefined
   d. Undefined

6. _____ refers to the boundary between a body of water and dry land.
   a. 1509 Istanbul earthquake
   b. Shoreline14
   c. Undefined
   d. Undefined

7. _____ is a term denoting the solid body of the Earth (i.e. the hydrosphere, lithosphere [including pedosphere] and in some definitions also the internal part of the Earth) and the atmosphere of the Earth.
   a. Thing
   b. Geosphere14
   c. Undefined
   d. Undefined

8. Earth's _____ is a layer of gases surrounding the planet Earth and retained by the Earth's gravity. It contains roughly 78% nitrogen and 21% oxygen, with trace amounts of other gases.
   a. Thing
   b. Atmosphere14
   c. Undefined
   d. Undefined

9. Long, fast waves produced by earthquakes and other seismic disturbances of the sea floor is called _____.
   a. Thing
   b. Tsunami14
   c. Undefined
   d. Undefined

10. Ability to do work is referred to as _____. Most evident in glacial systems as radiant _____ from the sun and as latent _____ required to melt ice to water.
    a. Energy14
    b. AASHTO Soil Classification System
    c. Undefined
    d. Undefined

11. A major branch of a stream system is referred to as a _____.
   a. 1509 Istanbul earthquake
   b. River14
   c. Undefined
   d. Undefined

12. The direction or trend of a bedding plane or fault, as it intersects the horizontal is referred to as a _____.
   a. Strike14
   b. 1509 Istanbul earthquake
   c. Undefined
   d. Undefined

13. The situation in mass wasting that occurs when material free-falls or bounces down a cliff is called a _____.
   a. 1509 Istanbul earthquake
   b. Fall14
   c. Undefined
   d. Undefined

14. The periodic, rhythmic rise and fall of the sea surface caused by changes in gravitational forces external to the Earth is referred to as the _____.
   a. Tide14
   b. Thing
   c. Undefined
   d. Undefined

15. The point downstream where a river empties into another stream or water body is called _____.
   a. 1509 Istanbul earthquake
   b. Mouth14
   c. Undefined
   d. Undefined

16. _____ refers to a basic unit of the geologic time scale that is a subdivision of an era. Periods may be divided into smaller units called epochs.
   a. Period14
   b. 1509 Istanbul earthquake
   c. Undefined
   d. Undefined

17. The span of the sea surface over which the wind blows to form wind-driven waves is referred to as _____.
   a. Fetch14
   b. Thing
   c. Undefined
   d. Undefined

18. _____ refers to a wave with a flatter, rounded wave crest and trough. Swells are found away from the area where waves are generated by the wind .
   a. Swell14
   b. Thing
   c. Undefined
   d. Undefined

19. _____ refers to a collective term for breakers; also the wave activity in the area between the shoreline and the outer limit of breakers.
   a. Surf14
   b. 1509 Istanbul earthquake
   c. Undefined
   d. Undefined

20. The horizontal distance between wave crests is a _____.
   a. Wavelength14
   b. 1509 Istanbul earthquake
   c. Undefined
   d. Undefined

21. _____ refers to amplitude; the vertical distance between wave crest and trough.

Chapter 14. Waves, Beaches, and Coasts

a. 1509 Istanbul earthquake
b. Wave height14
c. Undefined
d. Undefined

22. The lowest part of a wave between successive wave crests is called _____.
a. Wave trough14
b. Thing
c. Undefined
d. Undefined

23. The highest part of a wave is referred to as the _____.
a. Thing
b. Wave crest14
c. Undefined
d. Undefined

24. _____ refers to the steep-walled, broad-floored shape considered diagnostic of former mountain glaciation. Often contrasted to the 'V' shape typical of mass wasting slopes feeding river systems.
a. Trough14
b. 1509 Istanbul earthquake
c. Undefined
d. Undefined

25. A movement within the Earth's crust or mantle, caused by the sudden rupture or repositioning of underground rocks as they release stress is an _____.
a. AASHTO Soil Classification System
b. Earthquake14
c. Undefined
d. Undefined

26. _____ refers to a volume of space in which a given electron occurs 90% of the time. It is the quantum state of the individual electrons in the electron cloud around a single atom.
a. Orbital14
b. Thing
c. Undefined
d. Undefined

27. A wave that has become so steep that the crest of the wave topples forward, moving faster than the main body of the wave is referred to as a _____.
a. 1509 Istanbul earthquake
b. Breaker14
c. Undefined
d. Undefined

28. The process by which a wave approaching the shore changes direction due to slowing of those parts of the wave that enter shallow water first, causing a sharp decrease in the angle at which the wave approaches until the wave is almost parallel to the coast is called _____.
a. 1509 Istanbul earthquake
b. Wave refraction14
c. Undefined
d. Undefined

29. The bending of waves on passing between media of different velocities is referred to as _____.
a. Refraction14
b. 1509 Istanbul earthquake
c. Undefined
d. Undefined

30. An ocean current that flows close and almost parallel to the shoreline and is caused by the rush of waves toward the shore is a _____.
a. 1509 Istanbul earthquake
b. Longshore current14
c. Undefined
d. Undefined

31. A strong, rapid, and brief current that flows out to sea, moving perpendicular to the shoreline is a _____.
   a. 1509 Istanbul earthquake
   b. Rip current14
   c. Undefined
   d. Undefined

32. Any relatively sunken part of the Earth's surface, especially a low-lying area surrounded by higher ground is called a _____.
   a. 1509 Istanbul earthquake
   b. Depression14
   c. Undefined
   d. Undefined

33. _____ refers to a feature on the surface of the planet Mars that very closely resembles certain types of stream channels on Earth.
   a. 1509 Istanbul earthquake
   b. Channel14
   c. Undefined
   d. Undefined

34. A pair of structures extending into the ocean at the entrance to a harbor or river that are built for the purpose of protecting against storm waves and sediment deposition are called _____.
   a. 1509 Istanbul earthquake
   b. Jetties14
   c. Undefined
   d. Undefined

35. _____ refers to the beginning or source area for a stream. Also called the headwaters.
   a. 1509 Istanbul earthquake
   b. Head14
   c. Undefined
   d. Undefined

36. A sedimentary structure consisting of a very small dune of sand or silt whose long dimension is at right angles to the current is a _____.
   a. 1509 Istanbul earthquake
   b. Ripple14
   c. Undefined
   d. Undefined

37. The portion of a foreshore that lies nearest to the sea and regularly receives the swash of breaking waves is the _____. The _____ is the steepest part of the foreshore.
   a. Beach face14
   b. 1509 Istanbul earthquake
   c. Undefined
   d. Undefined

38. _____ refers to a low, narrow layer or mound of sediment deposited on a backshore by storm waves.
   a. 1509 Istanbul earthquake
   b. Berm14
   c. Undefined
   d. Undefined

39. Rounded particles coarser than 2 mm in diameter are called _____.
   a. 1509 Istanbul earthquake
   b. Gravel14
   c. Undefined
   d. Undefined

40. A broad, gently sloping platform that may be exposed at low tide is referred to as the _____.
   a. Marine terrace14
   b. 1509 Istanbul earthquake
   c. Undefined
   d. Undefined

Chapter 14. Waves, Beaches, and Coasts

41. A flat, steplike surface that lines a stream above the floodplain, often paired one on each side of the stream, marking a former floodplain that existed at a higher level before regional uplift or an increase in discharge caused the stream to erode into it is called the _____.
 a. 1509 Istanbul earthquake
 b. Terrace14
 c. Undefined
 d. Undefined

42. The unstable, newly-formed front of a lava delta is a _____.
 a. 1509 Istanbul earthquake
 b. Bench14
 c. Undefined
 d. Undefined

43. _____ refers to a naturally formed aggregate of usually inorganic materials from within the Earth.
 a. 1509 Istanbul earthquake
 b. Rock14
 c. Undefined
 d. Undefined

44. _____ refers to the process by which chemical reactions alter the chemical composition of rocks and minerals that are unstable at the Earth's surface and convert them into more stable substances; weathering that changes the chemical makeup of a rock or mineral.
 a. 1509 Istanbul earthquake
 b. Chemical weathering14
 c. Undefined
 d. Undefined

45. The process by which exposure to atmospheric agents, such as air or moisture, causes rocks and minerals to break down is called _____. This process takes place at or near the Earth's surface. _____ entails little or no movement of the material that it loosens from the rocks and minerals.
 a. Weathering14
 b. 1509 Istanbul earthquake
 c. Undefined
 d. Undefined

46. Mineral with the formula SiO is referred to as _____.
 a. Quartz14
 b. 1509 Istanbul earthquake
 c. Undefined
 d. Undefined

47. One of several minerals containing one central carbon atom with strong covalent bonds to three oxygen atoms and typically having ionic bonds to one or more positive ions is _____.
 a. 1509 Istanbul earthquake
 b. Carbonate14
 c. Undefined
 d. Undefined

48. _____ is a chemical element in the periodic table that has the symbol Ti and atomic number 22. It is a light, strong, lustrous, corrosion-resistant (including resistance to sea water and chlorine) transition metal with a white-silvery-metallic color. _____ is used in strong light-weight alloys (most notably with iron and aluminium) and its most common compound, _____ dioxide, is used in white pigments.
 a. Thing
 b. Titanium14
 c. Undefined
 d. Undefined

49. Low latitude areas characterized by high temperatures and high precipitation are referred to as _____. At high elevations, however, _____ mountains may be both cold and relatively dry.

Chapter 14. Waves, Beaches, and Coasts

    a. 1509 Istanbul earthquake   b. Tropical14
    c. Undefined   d. Undefined

50. A naturally occurring, usually inorganic, solid consisting of either a single element or a compound, and having a definite chemical composition and a systematic internal arrangement of atoms is referred to as a _____.
    a. 1509 Istanbul earthquake   b. Mineral14
    c. Undefined   d. Undefined

51. _____ is a common gray to black volcanic rock. It is usually fine-grained due to rapid cooling of lava on the Earth's surface.
    a. Thing   b. Basalt14
    c. Undefined   d. Undefined

52. _____ refers to the area of dry land that borders on a body of water.
    a. 1509 Istanbul earthquake   b. Coast14
    c. Undefined   d. Undefined

53. Material is in _____ if it is adjusted to the physical and chemical conditions of its environment so that it does not change or alter with time.
    a. AASHTO Soil Classification System   b. Equilibrium14
    c. Undefined   d. Undefined

54. The process by which a current moves sediments along a surf zone is _____. _____ typically consists of sand, gravel, shell fragments, and pebbles.
    a. Longshore drift14   b. 1509 Istanbul earthquake
    c. Undefined   d. Undefined

55. _____ refers to a general term applied to all mineral material transported by a glacier and deposited directly by or from the ice, or by running water emanating from the glacier. Generally applies to Pleistocene glacial deposits.
    a. Drift14   b. 1509 Istanbul earthquake
    c. Undefined   d. Undefined

56. A spit that curves sharply at its coastal end is referred to as a _____.
    a. Hook14   b. 1509 Istanbul earthquake
    c. Undefined   d. Undefined

57. A narrow ridge of sand that stretches completely across the mouth of a bay is a _____.
    a. Baymouth bar14   b. 1509 Istanbul earthquake
    c. Undefined   d. Undefined

58. _____ refers to a narrow, fingerlike ridge of sand that extends from land into open water.
    a. 1509 Istanbul earthquake   b. Spit14
    c. Undefined   d. Undefined

Chapter 14. Waves, Beaches, and Coasts

59. The mass movement of a single, intact mass of rock, soil, or unconsolidated material along a weak plane, such as a fault, fracture, or bedding plane is a _____. A _____ may involve as little as a minor displacement of soil or as much as the displacement of an entire mountainside.
   a. 1509 Istanbul earthquake
   b. Slide14
   c. Undefined
   d. Undefined

60. A beach deposit of sand connecting the land to a rocky promontory is _____.
   a. Tombolo14
   b. 1509 Istanbul earthquake
   c. Undefined
   d. Undefined

61. _____ refers to the coming together of two lithospheric plates. _____ causes subduction when one or both plates are oceanic and mountain formation when both plates are continental.
   a. Convergence14
   b. 1509 Istanbul earthquake
   c. Undefined
   d. Undefined

62. A structure that juts out into a body of water perpendicular to the shoreline and is built to restore an eroding beach by intercepting longshore drift and trapping sand is referred to as a _____.
   a. Groin14
   b. 1509 Istanbul earthquake
   c. Undefined
   d. Undefined

63. _____ refers to a wall built seaward of a coast to intercept incoming waves and so protect a harbor or shore. Breakwaters are typically built parallel to the coast.
   a. 1509 Istanbul earthquake
   b. Breakwater14
   c. Undefined
   d. Undefined

64. _____ refers to a structure built along the bank of a stream channel or tidal outlet to direct the flow of a stream or tide and keep the sediment moving so that it cannot build up and fill the channel. Jetties are typically built in parallel pairs along both banks of the channel. Jetties that are built perpendicular to a coast tend to interrupt longshore drift and thus widen beaches.
   a. Jetty14
   b. 1509 Istanbul earthquake
   c. Undefined
   d. Undefined

65. _____ refers to a place in which water is stored, including the oceans, glaciers and polar ice, groundwater, lakes and rivers, the atmosphere, and the biosphere. A source or place of residence for elements in a chemical cycle or hydrologic cycle.
   a. 1509 Istanbul earthquake
   b. Reservoir14
   c. Undefined
   d. Undefined

66. A cliff that projects out from a coast into deep water is referred to as a _____.
   a. 1509 Istanbul earthquake
   b. Headland14
   c. Undefined
   d. Undefined

67. _____ is a sedimentary rock composed largely of the mineral calcite (calcium carbonate: $CaCO_3$). _____ often contains variable amounts of silica in the form of chert or flint, as well as varying amounts of clay, silt and sand as disseminations, nodules, or layers within the rock.

a. Thing
b. Limestone14
c. Undefined
d. Undefined

68. A pink-colored, felsic, plutonic rock that contains potassium and usually sodium feldspars, and has quartz content of about 10% is _____. _____ is commonly found on continents but virtually absent from the ocean basins.
   a. 1509 Istanbul earthquake
   b. Granite14
   c. Undefined
   d. Undefined

69. Aggregates of minerals or rock fragments are called _____.
   a. Rocks14
   b. 1509 Istanbul earthquake
   c. Undefined
   d. Undefined

70. The gradual straightening of an irregular shoreline by wave erosion of headlands and wave deposition in bays is referred to as _____.
   a. 1509 Istanbul earthquake
   b. Coastal straightening14
   c. Undefined
   d. Undefined

71. _____ is the geomorphic process by which soil, regolith, and rock move downslope under the force of gravity. Types of _____ include creep, slides, flows, topples, and falls, each with their own characteristic features, and take place over timescales from seconds to years.
   a. Thing
   b. Mass wasting14
   c. Undefined
   d. Undefined

72. Steep slope that retreats inland by mass wasting as wave erosion undercuts it is referred to as a _____.
   a. 1509 Istanbul earthquake
   b. Sea cliff14
   c. Undefined
   d. Undefined

73. The notches in the sides of a prominent coastal rocky headland eroded by crashing waves are a _____.
   a. 1509 Istanbul earthquake
   b. Sea cave14
   c. Undefined
   d. Undefined

74. _____ refers to a naturally formed opening beneath the surface of the Earth, generally formed by dissolution of carbonate bedrock. Caves may also form by erosion of coastal bedrock, partial melting of glaciers, or solidification of lava into hollow tubes.
   a. Cave14
   b. 1509 Istanbul earthquake
   c. Undefined
   d. Undefined

75. _____ refers to a downward and outward slide occurring along a concave slip plane. The material that breaks off in such a slide.
   a. 1509 Istanbul earthquake
   b. Slump14
   c. Undefined
   d. Undefined

76. Bridge of rock left above an opening eroded in a headland by waves is an _____.
   a. AASHTO Soil Classification System
   b. Arch14
   c. Undefined
   d. Undefined

Chapter 14. Waves, Beaches, and Coasts

77. A seaward-facing cliff along a steep shoreline formed by wave erosion at its base and mass wasting is called _____.
    a. 1509 Istanbul earthquake
    b. Wave-cut cliff14
    c. Undefined
    d. Undefined

78. A wall of stone, concrete, or other sturdy material, built along the shoreline to prevent erosion even by the strongest and highest of wave is a _____.
    a. 1509 Istanbul earthquake
    b. Seawall14
    c. Undefined
    d. Undefined

79. A coarse-grained, strongly foliated metamorphic rock that develops from phyllite and splits easily into flat, parallel slabs is _____.
    a. 1509 Istanbul earthquake
    b. Schist14
    c. Undefined
    d. Undefined

80. A pile of large, angular boulders built seaward of the shoreline to prevent erosion by waves or current is referred to as a _____.
    a. Riprap14
    b. 1509 Istanbul earthquake
    c. Undefined
    d. Undefined

81. The top of the ocean, where the water meets the atmosphere is called _____.
    a. 1509 Istanbul earthquake
    b. Sea level14
    c. Undefined
    d. Undefined

82. _____ refers to a bench or shelf along a shore at sea level, cut by wave erosion.
    a. 1509 Istanbul earthquake
    b. Wave-cut platform14
    c. Undefined
    d. Undefined

83. _____ refers to a landform produced by coastal erosion of a prominent headland. Sea arches form when sea caves are excavated so deeply by crashing waves that two caves eroding on opposite sides of the headland become joined. The overlying rocky roof is left as an arch.
    a. 1509 Istanbul earthquake
    b. Sea arch14
    c. Undefined
    d. Undefined

84. A small rock island that is an erosional remnant of a headland left behind as a wave eroded coast retreats inland is referred to as a _____.
    a. 1509 Istanbul earthquake
    b. Stack14
    c. Undefined
    d. Undefined

85. _____ refers to a crack or break in a rock. To break in random places instead of cleaving.
    a. Fracture14
    b. 1509 Istanbul earthquake
    c. Undefined
    d. Undefined

86. A long and narrow island that is built by waves along the coast is called _____.

Chapter 14. Waves, Beaches, and Coasts

a. Thing
b. Barrier island14
c. Undefined
d. Undefined

87. A geologic epoch, characterized by alternating glacial and interglacial stages, that ended about 10,000 years ago, that lasted for 2 million years is called the _____ epoch.
  a. Pleistocene14
  b. Thing
  c. Undefined
  d. Undefined

88. A moving body of ice that forms on land from the accumulation and compaction of snow, and that flows downslope or outward due to gravity and the pressure of its own weight is a _____.
  a. 1509 Istanbul earthquake
  b. Glacier14
  c. Undefined
  d. Undefined

89. A _____ is a body of comparatively shallow salt water separated from the deeper sea by a shallow or exposed sandbank, coral reef, or similar feature. Thus, the enclosed body of water behind a barrier reef or barrier islands or enclosed by an atoll reef is called a _____.
  a. Thing
  b. Lagoon14
  c. Undefined
  d. Undefined

90. The alternating horizontal movement of water associated with the rise and fall of the tide is _____.
  a. 1509 Istanbul earthquake
  b. Tidal current14
  c. Undefined
  d. Undefined

91. A deltalike feature created when a rapidly moving tidal current emerges from a narrow inlet and slows, depositing its load of sediment is referred to as a _____.
  a. Tidal delta14
  b. 1509 Istanbul earthquake
  c. Undefined
  d. Undefined

92. An alluvial fan having its apex at the mouth of a stream is a _____.
  a. Delta14
  b. 1509 Istanbul earthquake
  c. Undefined
  d. Undefined

93. A ridge-like accumulation that is being or was produced at the outer margin of an actively flowing glacier at any given time is referred to as the _____.
  a. End moraine14
  b. AASHTO Soil Classification System
  c. Undefined
  d. Undefined

94. _____ is the general term for debris of all sorts originally transported by glaciers or ice sheets that have since melted away. Till is another word used to describe the sediments left by glaciers.
  a. Moraine14
  b. Thing
  c. Undefined
  d. Undefined

95. _____ refers to a glacier of considerable thickness and more than 50,000 square kilometers in area, forming a continuous cover of snow and ice over a land surface, spreading outward in all directions and not confined by the underlying topography. Ice sheets are now confined to Polar Regions, but during the Pleistocene Epoch they covered large parts of North America and northern Europe.

Chapter 14. Waves, Beaches, and Coasts

a. Ice sheet14
b. AASHTO Soil Classification System
c. Undefined
d. Undefined

96. Any environmental change that adversely affects the lives and health of living things is referred to as _____.
    a. Pollution14
    b. Thing
    c. Undefined
    d. Undefined

97. An _____ is a semi-enclosed coastal body of water which has a free connection with the open sea and within which sea water mixes with fresh water. The key feature of an _____ is that it is a mixing place for sea water and a stream or river to supply fresh water.
    a. Thing
    b. Estuary14
    c. Undefined
    d. Undefined

98. Compacted and intergrown mass of crystalline ice with a density is _____.
    a. Glacial ice14
    b. 1509 Istanbul earthquake
    c. Undefined
    d. Undefined

99. A steep-sided inlet of the sea formed when a glacial trough was partially submerged is a _____.
    a. Fiord14
    b. 1509 Istanbul earthquake
    c. Undefined
    d. Undefined

100. Forces generated from within Earth that result in uplift, movement, or deformations of part of Earth's crust are called _____.
    a. 1509 Istanbul earthquake
    b. Tectonic forces14
    c. Undefined
    d. Undefined

101. A series of unmanned satellites orbiting at about 706 km above the surface of the earth is called _____. The satellites carry cameras similar to video cameras and take images or pictures showing features as small as 30 m or 80 m wide, depending on which camera is used.
    a. 1509 Istanbul earthquake
    b. Landsat14
    c. Undefined
    d. Undefined

102. The _____ is that part of a planet's outer shell — including air, land, surface rocks and water — within which life occurs, and which biotic processes in turn alter or transform.
    a. Biosphere14
    b. Thing
    c. Undefined
    d. Undefined

103. _____ refers to a ridge-like or mound-like structure, layered or massive, built by sedentary calcareous organisms; it is wave resistant and stands above the surrounding contemporaneously deposited sediment.
    a. 1509 Istanbul earthquake
    b. Reef14
    c. Undefined
    d. Undefined

104. A sediment formed from the accumulation of carbonate minerals precipitated organically or inorganically is a _____.

Chapter 14. Waves, Beaches, and Coasts

    a. 1509 Istanbul earthquake   b. Carbonate sediment14
    c. Undefined   d. Undefined

105. _____ are woody trees or shrubs that grow in coastal habitats or mangal (Hogarth, 1999), for which the term _____ swamp also would apply.
    a. Thing   b. Mangrove14
    c. Undefined   d. Undefined

106. _____ refers to soil type largely composed of partly decomposed organic material.
    a. Thing   b. Peat14
    c. Undefined   d. Undefined

107. The liquid portion of magma excluding the solid crystals is called _____.
    a. 1509 Istanbul earthquake   b. Melt14
    c. Undefined   d. Undefined

108. A slow but steady rise in Earth's surface temperature, caused by increasing concentrations of greenhouse gases in the atmosphere is referred to as _____.
    a. Global warming14   b. Thing
    c. Undefined   d. Undefined

109. _____ is an atmospheric gas comprized of one carbon and two oxygen atoms. A very widely known chemical compound, it is frequently called by its formula CO_2. In its solid state, it is commonly known as dry ice.
    a. Carbon dioxide14   b. Thing
    c. Undefined   d. Undefined

110. _____ is a chemical element in the periodic table that has the symbol C and atomic number 6. An abundant nonmetallic, tetravalent element, _____ has several allotropic forms.
    a. Thing   b. Carbon14
    c. Undefined   d. Undefined

111. A member of a group of easily combustible, organic sedimentary rocks composed mostly of plant remains and containing a high proportion of carbon is called _____.
    a. Coal14   b. 1509 Istanbul earthquake
    c. Undefined   d. Undefined

112. High sea level caused by the low pressure and high winds of hurricanes is a _____.
    a. 1509 Istanbul earthquake   b. Storm surge14
    c. Undefined   d. Undefined

113. _____ refers to a round or oval bulge on the Earth's surface, containing the oldest section of rock in its raised, central part.
    a. 1509 Istanbul earthquake   b. Dome14
    c. Undefined   d. Undefined

114. Angular chunk of solid rock ejected during an eruption is referred to as a _____.

Chapter 14. Waves, Beaches, and Coasts

a. 1509 Istanbul earthquake
b. Block14
c. Undefined
d. Undefined

115. A mineral or fuel deposit, known or not yet discovered, that may be or become available for human exploitation is called a _____.
   a. Resource14
   b. 1509 Istanbul earthquake
   c. Undefined
   d. Undefined

116. The scientific study of the Earth, its origins and evolution, the materials that make it up, and the processes that act on it is called _____.
   a. 1509 Istanbul earthquake
   b. Geology14
   c. Undefined
   d. Undefined

117. The entire area between the tops of the slopes on both sides of a stream is a _____.
   a. Valley14
   b. 1509 Istanbul earthquake
   c. Undefined
   d. Undefined

Chapter 15. Geologic Structures

1. The deposition of most water-laid sediment in horizontal or near-horizontal layers that are essentially parallel to Earth's surface is referred to as _____.
   a. AASHTO Soil Classification System
   b. Original horizontality15
   c. Undefined
   d. Undefined

2. The scientific study of the geological processes that deform the Earth's crust and create mountains is _____.
   a. Structural geology15
   b. 1509 Istanbul earthquake
   c. Undefined
   d. Undefined

3. The sequence in which events took place is _____.
   a. 1509 Istanbul earthquake
   b. Relative time15
   c. Undefined
   d. Undefined

4. _____ refers to a principle or law stating that within a sequence of undisturbed sedimentary rocks, the oldest layers are on the bottom, the youngest on the top.
   a. 1509 Istanbul earthquake
   b. Superposition15
   c. Undefined
   d. Undefined

5. The scientific study of the Earth, its origins and evolution, the materials that make it up, and the processes that act on it is called _____.
   a. Geology15
   b. 1509 Istanbul earthquake
   c. Undefined
   d. Undefined

6. A large mass of rock projecting above surrounding terrain is called a _____.
   a. 1509 Istanbul earthquake
   b. Mountain15
   c. Undefined
   d. Undefined

7. Aggregates of minerals or rock fragments are called _____.
   a. Rocks15
   b. 1509 Istanbul earthquake
   c. Undefined
   d. Undefined

8. _____ refers to a bend that develops in an initially horizontal layer of rock, usually caused by plastic deformation. Folds occur most frequently in sedimentary rocks.
   a. Fold15
   b. 1509 Istanbul earthquake
   c. Undefined
   d. Undefined

9. _____ refers to a naturally formed aggregate of usually inorganic materials from within the Earth.
   a. Rock15
   b. 1509 Istanbul earthquake
   c. Undefined
   d. Undefined

10. A movement within the Earth's crust or mantle, caused by the sudden rupture or repositioning of underground rocks as they release stress is an _____.
    a. AASHTO Soil Classification System
    b. Earthquake15
    c. Undefined
    d. Undefined

11. A fracture dividing a rock into two sections that have visibly moved relative to each other is a _____.

Chapter 15. Geologic Structures

a. 1509 Istanbul earthquake
b. Fault15
c. Undefined
d. Undefined

12. _____ refers to a long chain of mountain ranges.
a. Major mountain belt15
b. 1509 Istanbul earthquake
c. Undefined
d. Undefined

13. The processes by which crustal forces cause a rock formation to break and slip along a fault are called _____.
a. Faulting15
b. 1509 Istanbul earthquake
c. Undefined
d. Undefined

14. The processes by which crustal forces deform an area of crust so that layers of rock are pushed into folds are called _____.
a. 1509 Istanbul earthquake
b. Folding15
c. Undefined
d. Undefined

15. _____ refers to rigid parts of the Earth's crust and part of the Earth's upper mantle that moves and adjoins each other along zones of seismic activity.
a. 1509 Istanbul earthquake
b. Plate15
c. Undefined
d. Undefined

16. _____ refers to the study of the large-scale processes that collectively deform Earth's crust.
a. 1509 Istanbul earthquake
b. Tectonics15
c. Undefined
d. Undefined

17. A _____ is the outer layer of a planet, part of its lithosphere. Planetary _____ is generally composed of a less dense material than that of its deeper layers. The _____ of the Earth is composed mainly of basalt and granite.
a. Thing
b. Crust15
c. Undefined
d. Undefined

18. Forces generated from within Earth that result in uplift, movement, or deformations of part of Earth's crust are called _____.
a. Tectonic forces15
b. 1509 Istanbul earthquake
c. Undefined
d. Undefined

19. The force acting on a rock or another solid to deform it, measured in kilograms per square centimeter or pounds per square inch is _____.
a. 1509 Istanbul earthquake
b. Stress15
c. Undefined
d. Undefined

20. _____ refers to the change in the shape or volume of a rock that results from stress.
a. Strain15
b. 1509 Istanbul earthquake
c. Undefined
d. Undefined

21. _____ refers to a stress due to a force pushing together on a body.

a. 1509 Istanbul earthquake
b. Compressive stress15
c. Undefined
d. Undefined

22. The type of stress that tends to pull a body apart is _____.
    a. Tensional stress15
    b. 1509 Istanbul earthquake
    c. Undefined
    d. Undefined

23. _____ refers to stress due to forces that tend to cause movement or strain parallel to the direction of the forces.
    a. Shear stress15
    b. 1509 Istanbul earthquake
    c. Undefined
    d. Undefined

24. A numerical expression of the amount of energy released by an earthquake, determined by measuring earthquake waves on standardized recording instruments is called a _____. The number scale for magnitudes is logarithmic rather than arithmetic. Therefore, deflections on a seismograph for a _____ 5 earthquake, for example, are 10 times greater than those for a _____ 4 earthquake, 100 times greater than for a _____ 3 earthquake, and so on.
    a. Magnitude15
    b. 1509 Istanbul earthquake
    c. Undefined
    d. Undefined

25. Strain involving an increase in length is an _____. _____ can cause crustal thinning and faulting.
    a. Extension15
    b. AASHTO Soil Classification System
    c. Undefined
    d. Undefined

26. _____ refers to stress that causes two adjacent parts of a body to slide past one another.
    a. 1509 Istanbul earthquake
    b. Shear15
    c. Undefined
    d. Undefined

27. The motion of surfaces sliding past one another is called _____.
    a. 1509 Istanbul earthquake
    b. Shearing15
    c. Undefined
    d. Undefined

28. A material that undergoes little change under increasing force, until it breaks suddenly is a _____.
    a. Brittle material15
    b. 1509 Istanbul earthquake
    c. Undefined
    d. Undefined

29. _____ refers to a body in which strains are totally recoverable, as in a rubber band.
    a. Elastic15
    b. AASHTO Soil Classification System
    c. Undefined
    d. Undefined

30. _____ refers to capable of being molded and bent under stress.
    a. Ductile15
    b. 1509 Istanbul earthquake
    c. Undefined
    d. Undefined

31. _____ refers to capable of being molded into any form, which is retained.
    a. 1509 Istanbul earthquake
    b. Plastic15
    c. Undefined
    d. Undefined

Chapter 15. Geologic Structures

32. _____ refers to a material that undergoes smooth and continuous plastic deformation under increasing force and does not spring back to its original shape when the deforming force is released.
   a. 1509 Istanbul earthquake
   b. Ductile material15
   c. Undefined
   d. Undefined

33. _____ is the name given to changes in great masses of rock over a wide area, often within orogenic belts. The high temperatures and pressures in the depths of the Earth are the cause of the changes, and if the metamorphosed rocks are uplifted and exposed by erosion, they may occur over vast areas at the surface.
   a. Thing
   b. Regional metamorphism15
   c. Undefined
   d. Undefined

34. The process by which conditions within the Earth, below the zone of diagenesis, alter the mineral content, chemical composition, and structure of solid rock without melting it is called _____. Igneous, sedimentary, and metamorphic rocks may all undergo _____.
   a. 1509 Istanbul earthquake
   b. Metamorphism15
   c. Undefined
   d. Undefined

35. _____ refers to a crack or break in a rock. To break in random places instead of cleaving.
   a. Fracture15
   b. 1509 Istanbul earthquake
   c. Undefined
   d. Undefined

36. _____ is one of the three main rock groups and is formed in three main ways—by the deposition of the weathered remains of other rocks; by the deposition of the results of biogenic activity; and by precipitation from solution.
   a. Event
   b. Sedimentary rock15
   c. Undefined
   d. Undefined

37. An equal, all-sided pressure is called _____.
   a. Confining pressure15
   b. 1509 Istanbul earthquake
   c. Undefined
   d. Undefined

38. General term for the processes of folding, faulting, shearing, compression, or extension of rocks as the result of various natural forces is called _____.
   a. 1509 Istanbul earthquake
   b. Deformation15
   c. Undefined
   d. Undefined

39. _____ refers to general term referring to the rock underlying other unconsolidated material, i.e. soil.
   a. Bedrock15
   b. 1509 Istanbul earthquake
   c. Undefined
   d. Undefined

40. The _____ is the solid outermost shell of a rocky planet. On the Earth, the _____ includes the crust and the uppermost layer of the mantle (the upper mantle or lower _____) which is joined to the crust.
   a. Thing
   b. Lithosphere15
   c. Undefined
   d. Undefined

Chapter 15. Geologic Structures

41. The _____ meaning "new life" is the most recent of the three classic geological eras. It covers the 65.5 million years since the Cretaceous-Tertiary extinction event at the end of the Cretaceous that marked the demise of the last dinosaurs and the end of the Mesozoic Era. The _____ is ongoing.
   a. Thing
   b. Cenozoic Era15
   c. Undefined
   d. Undefined

42. _____ refers to the area of dry land that borders on a body of water.
   a. 1509 Istanbul earthquake
   b. Coast15
   c. Undefined
   d. Undefined

43. _____ refers to a major division on the geologic time scale; eras are divided into shorter units called periods.
   a. Era15
   b. AASHTO Soil Classification System
   c. Undefined
   d. Undefined

44. _____ is the displacement of solids (soil, mud, rock, and other particles) by the agents of wind, water, ice, movement in response to gravity, or living organisms.
   a. Erosion15
   b. Thing
   c. Undefined
   d. Undefined

45. _____ refers to a map representing the geology of a given area.
   a. Geologic map15
   b. 1509 Istanbul earthquake
   c. Undefined
   d. Undefined

46. _____ refers to the top few meters of regolith, generally including some organic matter derived from plants.
   a. 1509 Istanbul earthquake
   b. Soil15
   c. Undefined
   d. Undefined

47. The scientific law stating that sediments settling out from bodies of water are deposited horizontally or nearly horizontally in layers that lie parallel or nearly parallel to the Earth's surface is referred to as _____.
   a. Principle of original horizontality15
   b. 1509 Istanbul earthquake
   c. Undefined
   d. Undefined

48. Rocks formed by solidification of sediments formed and transported at the Earth's surface are referred to as _____.
   a. 1509 Istanbul earthquake
   b. Sedimentary rocks15
   c. Undefined
   d. Undefined

49. _____ refers to an outpouring of lava onto the land surface from a vent or fissure. Also, a solidified tongue like or sheet-like body formed by outpouring lava.
   a. 1509 Istanbul earthquake
   b. Lava flow15
   c. Undefined
   d. Undefined

50. _____ refers to volcanic ash that has fallen through the air from an eruption cloud. A deposit so formed is usually well sorted and layered.

Chapter 15. Geologic Structures

a. AASHTO Soil Classification System
c. Undefined
b. Ashfall15
d. Undefined

51. The direction or trend of a bedding plane or fault, as it intersects the horizontal is referred to as a _____.
a. Strike15
c. Undefined
b. 1509 Istanbul earthquake
d. Undefined

52. Parallel layers of sedimentary rock are called _____.
a. 1509 Istanbul earthquake
c. Undefined
b. Strata15
d. Undefined

53. Magma that comes to the Earth's surface through a volcano or fissure is referred to as _____.
a. Lava15
c. Undefined
b. 1509 Istanbul earthquake
d. Undefined

54. The angle formed by the inclined plane of a geological structure and the horizontal plane of the Earth's surface is referred to as a _____.
a. 1509 Istanbul earthquake
c. Undefined
b. Dip15
d. Undefined

55. A nearly flat surface separating two beds of sedimentary rock is a _____. Each _____ marks the end of one deposit and the beginning of another having different characteristics.
a. 1509 Istanbul earthquake
c. Undefined
b. Bedding plane15
d. Undefined

56. A vertical angle measured downward from the horizontal plane to an inclined plane is an _____.
a. AASHTO Soil Classification System
c. Undefined
b. Angle of dip15
d. Undefined

57. The division of sediment or sedimentary rock into parallel layers that can be distinguished from each other by such features as chemical composition and grain size is _____.
a. 1509 Istanbul earthquake
c. Undefined
b. Bedding15
d. Undefined

58. _____ refers to the compass direction in which the angle of dip is measured.
a. Direction of dip15
c. Undefined
b. 1509 Istanbul earthquake
d. Undefined

59. A representation of a portion of Earth in a vertical plane is a _____.
a. 1509 Istanbul earthquake
c. Undefined
b. Geologic cross section15
d. Undefined

60. Bridge of rock left above an opening eroded in a headland by waves is an _____.
a. AASHTO Soil Classification System
c. Undefined
b. Arch15
d. Undefined

Chapter 15. Geologic Structures

61. Cracking or rupturing of a body under stress is a _____.
   a. 1509 Istanbul earthquake
   b. Brittle strain15
   c. Undefined
   d. Undefined

62. _____ is the result of the transformation of a pre-existing rock type, the protolith, in a process called metamorphism, which means "change in form". The protolith is subjected to heat (greater than 150 degrees Celsius) and extreme pressure causing profound physical and/or chemical change.
   a. Metamorphic rock15
   b. Thing
   c. Undefined
   d. Undefined

63. _____ refers to the term from the Greek 'meta' and 'morph', commonly occurs to rocks which are subjected to increased heat and/or pressure. Also applies to the conversion of snow into glacial ice.
   a. Metamorphic15
   b. 1509 Istanbul earthquake
   c. Undefined
   d. Undefined

64. A naturally occurring, usually inorganic, solid consisting of either a single element or a compound, and having a definite chemical composition and a systematic internal arrangement of atoms is referred to as a _____.
   a. Mineral15
   b. 1509 Istanbul earthquake
   c. Undefined
   d. Undefined

65. _____ refers to huge slabs of rock that make up the Earth's crust. They can be continental or oceanic.
   a. Tectonic plate15
   b. Thing
   c. Undefined
   d. Undefined

66. _____ refers to line about which a fold appears to be hinged. Line of maximum curvature of a folded surface.
   a. 1509 Istanbul earthquake
   b. Hinge line15
   c. Undefined
   d. Undefined

67. A convex fold in a rock, the central part of which contains the oldest section of rock is referred to as the _____.
   a. Anticline15
   b. AASHTO Soil Classification System
   c. Undefined
   d. Undefined

68. A concave fold, the central part of which contains the youngest section of roc is called the _____.
   a. 1509 Istanbul earthquake
   b. Syncline15
   c. Undefined
   d. Undefined

69. Portion of a fold shared by an anticline and a syncline is referred to as a _____.
   a. Limb15
   b. 1509 Istanbul earthquake
   c. Undefined
   d. Undefined

70. A plane containing all of the hinge lines of a fold is called the _____.
   a. Axial plane15
   b. AASHTO Soil Classification System
   c. Undefined
   d. Undefined

71. An imaginary line that separates the drainage of two streams, often found along a ridge is referred to as the _____.

Chapter 15. Geologic Structures

a. Divide15
c. Undefined
b. 1509 Istanbul earthquake
d. Undefined

72. _____ refers to a fold in which the hinge line is not horizontal.
   a. 1509 Istanbul earthquake
   c. Undefined
   b. Plunging fold15
   d. Undefined

73. Angular chunk of solid rock ejected during an eruption is referred to as a _____.
   a. 1509 Istanbul earthquake
   c. Undefined
   b. Block15
   d. Undefined

74. The innermost layer of the Earth, consisting primarily of pure metals such as iron and nickel is the _____. The _____ is the densest layer of the Earth, and is divided into the outer _____, which is believed to be liquid, and the inner _____, which is believed to be solid.
   a. Core15
   c. Undefined
   b. 1509 Istanbul earthquake
   d. Undefined

75. A structure in which the beds dip toward a central point is a _____.
   a. 1509 Istanbul earthquake
   c. Undefined
   b. Structural basin15
   d. Undefined

76. _____ refers to a structure in which beds dip away from a central point.
   a. Structural dome15
   c. Undefined
   b. 1509 Istanbul earthquake
   d. Undefined

77. A round or oval depression in the Earth's surface, containing the youngest section of rock in its lowest, central part is a _____.
   a. Basin15
   c. Undefined
   b. 1509 Istanbul earthquake
   d. Undefined

78. _____ refers to a round or oval bulge on the Earth's surface, containing the oldest section of rock in its raised, central part.
   a. 1509 Istanbul earthquake
   c. Undefined
   b. Dome15
   d. Undefined

79. A body of rock identified by lithic characteristics and stratigraphic position and is mappable at the earth's surface or traceable in the subsurface is a _____.
   a. Formation15
   c. Undefined
   b. 1509 Istanbul earthquake
   d. Undefined

80. The relationship between distance on a map and the distance on the terrain being represented by that map is a _____.
   a. Scale15
   c. Undefined
   b. 1509 Istanbul earthquake
   d. Undefined

Chapter 15. Geologic Structures

81. The accumulation of precipitation into surface and underground areas, including lakes, rivers, and aquifers is a _____.
    a. Collection15
    b. 1509 Istanbul earthquake
    c. Undefined
    d. Undefined

82. A fold in which the limbs are parallel to one another is called an _____.
    a. AASHTO Soil Classification System
    b. Isoclinal fold15
    c. Undefined
    d. Undefined

83. Stress that slices rocks into parallel blocks that slide in opposite directions along their adjacent sides is called _____. _____ may be caused by transform motion.
    a. 1509 Istanbul earthquake
    b. Shearing stress15
    c. Undefined
    d. Undefined

84. A fold in which both limbs dip in the same direction is an _____.
    a. AASHTO Soil Classification System
    b. Overturned fold15
    c. Undefined
    d. Undefined

85. Any place where bedrock is visible on the surface of the Earth is referred to as _____.
    a. Outcrop15
    b. AASHTO Soil Classification System
    c. Undefined
    d. Undefined

86. A fold overturned to such an extent that the limbs are essentially horizontal is referred to as _____.
    a. 1509 Istanbul earthquake
    b. Recumbent fold15
    c. Undefined
    d. Undefined

87. _____ refers to a group of closely spaced mountains or parallel ridges.
    a. Mountain range15
    b. 1509 Istanbul earthquake
    c. Undefined
    d. Undefined

88. _____ refers to the coming together of two lithospheric plates. _____ causes subduction when one or both plates are oceanic and mountain formation when both plates are continental.
    a. Convergence15
    b. 1509 Istanbul earthquake
    c. Undefined
    d. Undefined

89. _____ refers to vertically oriented polygonal columns in a solid lava flow or shallow intrusion formed by contraction upon cooling. They are usually formed in basaltic lavas.
    a. Columnar jointing15
    b. 1509 Istanbul earthquake
    c. Undefined
    d. Undefined

90. Stress that stretches or extends rocks, so that they become thinner vertically and longer laterally is called _____. _____ may be caused by divergence or rifting.
    a. 1509 Istanbul earthquake
    b. Tension15
    c. Undefined
    d. Undefined

91. A feature found in caves that is formed when a stalactite and stalagmite join is referred to as a _____.

Chapter 15. Geologic Structures

a. Column15
b. 1509 Istanbul earthquake
c. Undefined
d. Undefined

92. The process by which exposure to atmospheric agents, such as air or moisture, causes rocks and minerals to break down is called _____. This process takes place at or near the Earth's surface. _____ entails little or no movement of the material that it loosens from the rocks and minerals.
a. Weathering15
b. 1509 Istanbul earthquake
c. Undefined
d. Undefined

93. A significant type of mechanical weathering that causes rocks to crack when overburden is removed is _____.
a. 1509 Istanbul earthquake
b. Pressure release15
c. Undefined
d. Undefined

94. Joints oriented in one direction approximately parallel to one another are called a _____.
a. 1509 Istanbul earthquake
b. Joint set15
c. Undefined
d. Undefined

95. The same as a mineral reserve except that it refers only to a metal-bearing deposit is referred to as _____.
a. Ore deposit15
b. AASHTO Soil Classification System
c. Undefined
d. Undefined

96. A mineral deposit that can be mined for a profit is called _____.
a. AASHTO Soil Classification System
b. Ore15
c. Undefined
d. Undefined

97. _____ refers to a place in which water is stored, including the oceans, glaciers and polar ice, groundwater, lakes and rivers, the atmosphere, and the biosphere. A source or place of residence for elements in a chemical cycle or hydrologic cycle.
a. 1509 Istanbul earthquake
b. Reservoir15
c. Undefined
d. Undefined

98. A high mountain peak that forms when the walls of three or more cirques intersect is called a _____.
a. 1509 Istanbul earthquake
b. Horn15
c. Undefined
d. Undefined

99. Differential stress that shortens a rock body is referred to as _____.
a. Compressional stress15
b. 1509 Istanbul earthquake
c. Undefined
d. Undefined

100. _____ refers to a fault in which two sections of rock have moved apart vertically, parallel to the dip of the fault plane.
a. Dip-slip fault15
b. 1509 Istanbul earthquake
c. Undefined
d. Undefined

101. _____ refers to a dip-slip fault marked by a generally steep dip along which the hanging wall has moved downward relative to the footwall.

a. 1509 Istanbul earthquake
b. Normal fault15
c. Undefined
d. Undefined

102. The distance that one face of a fault is displaced relative to the other is referred to as a _____.
   a. Slip15
   b. 1509 Istanbul earthquake
   c. Undefined
   d. Undefined

103. _____ refers to a fault in which two sections of rock have moved horizontally in opposite directions, parallel to the line of the fracture that divided them. Strike-slip faults are caused by shearing stress.
   a. Strike-slip fault15
   b. 1509 Istanbul earthquake
   c. Undefined
   d. Undefined

104. _____ refers to a fault with both strike-slip and dip-slip components.
   a. Oblique-slip fault15
   b. AASHTO Soil Classification System
   c. Undefined
   d. Undefined

105. _____ refers to a dip-slip fault marked by a hanging wall that has moved upward relative to the footwall. Reverse faults are often caused by the convergence of lithospheric plates.
   a. Reverse fault15
   b. 1509 Istanbul earthquake
   c. Undefined
   d. Undefined

106. _____ refers to the underlying surface of an inclined fault plane.
   a. Footwall15
   b. 1509 Istanbul earthquake
   c. Undefined
   d. Undefined

107. The overlying surface of an inclined fault plane is called a _____.
   a. Hanging wall15
   b. 1509 Istanbul earthquake
   c. Undefined
   d. Undefined

108. A range created by uplift along normal or vertical faults is called the _____.
   a. Fault-block mountain range15
   b. 1509 Istanbul earthquake
   c. Undefined
   d. Undefined

109. A mountain containing tall horsts interspersed with much lower grabens and bounded on at least one side by a high-angle normal fault is a _____.
   a. Fault-block mountain15
   b. 1509 Istanbul earthquake
   c. Undefined
   d. Undefined

110. A reverse fault marked by a dip of 45° or less is called _____.
   a. Thrust fault15
   b. 1509 Istanbul earthquake
   c. Undefined
   d. Undefined

111. _____ refers to extremely small fragments, usually of glass, that forms when escaping gases force a fine spray of magma from a volcano.

Chapter 15. Geologic Structures

a. Volcanic ash15	b. 1509 Istanbul earthquake
c. Undefined	d. Undefined

112. A block of rock that lies between two faults and has moved upward relative to the two adjacent fault blocks is referred to as a _____.
   a. Horst15
   b. 1509 Istanbul earthquake
   c. Undefined
   d. Undefined

113. Fine particles of pulverized rock blown from an explosion vent are called _____. Measuring less than 1/10 inch in diameter, _____ may be either solid or molten when first erupted.
   a. Ash15
   b. AASHTO Soil Classification System
   c. Undefined
   d. Undefined

114. Stress that reduces the volume or length of a rock, as that produced by the convergence of plate margins is called _____.
   a. Compression15
   b. 1509 Istanbul earthquake
   c. Undefined
   d. Undefined

115. _____ refers to a column or plug of rock salt that rises from depth because of its low density and pierces overlying sediments.
   a. 1509 Istanbul earthquake
   b. Salt dome15
   c. Undefined
   d. Undefined

116. _____ is a term used for ionic compounds composed of positively charged cations and negatively charged anions, so that the product is neutral and without a net charge.
   a. Salt15
   b. Thing
   c. Undefined
   d. Undefined

117. An evaporite composed of halite is referred to as _____.
   a. Rock salt15
   b. 1509 Istanbul earthquake
   c. Undefined
   d. Undefined

118. _____ refers to bodies of rock or magma that ascends within Earth's interior because they are less dense than the surrounding rock.
   a. 1509 Istanbul earthquake
   b. Diapir15
   c. Undefined
   d. Undefined

119. _____ is any particulate matter that can be transported by fluid flow and which eventually is deposited as a layer of solid particles on the bed or bottom of a body of water or other liquid.
   a. Sediment15
   b. Thing
   c. Undefined
   d. Undefined

120. _____ is the chemical element in the periodic table that has the symbol S and atomic number 16. It is an abundant, tasteless, odorless, multivalent non-metal. _____, in its native form, is a yellow crystaline solid. In nature, it can be found as the pure element or as sulfide and sulfate minerals.

Chapter 15. Geologic Structures

    a. Thing
    c. Undefined
    b. Sulfur15
    d. Undefined

121. _____ refers to a clastic rock composed of particles that range in diameter from 1/16 millimeter to 2 millimeters in diameter. Sandstones make up about 25% of all sedimentary rocks.
    a. 1509 Istanbul earthquake
    b. Sandstone15
    c. Undefined
    d. Undefined

122. A necessary part of an oil trap is a _____. The _____ is impermeable and hence keeps upwardly mobile oil and gas from escaping at the surface.
    a. 1509 Istanbul earthquake
    b. Cap rock15
    c. Undefined
    d. Undefined

123. An elevated area with relatively little internal relief is called a _____.
    a. Plateau15
    b. 1509 Istanbul earthquake
    c. Undefined
    d. Undefined

124. A climate in which yearly precipitation is less than the potential loss of water by evaporation is a _____.
    a. Dry climate15
    b. 1509 Istanbul earthquake
    c. Undefined
    d. Undefined

125. A moving body of ice that forms on land from the accumulation and compaction of snow, and that flows downslope or outward due to gravity and the pressure of its own weight is a _____.
    a. Glacier15
    b. 1509 Istanbul earthquake
    c. Undefined
    d. Undefined

126. Weather condition of an area including especially prevailing temperature and average daily/yearly rainfall over a long period of time is called _____.
    a. Thing
    b. Climate15
    c. Undefined
    d. Undefined

127. A liquid mixture of naturally occurring hydrocarbons is referred to as _____.
    a. 1509 Istanbul earthquake
    b. Crude oil15
    c. Undefined
    d. Undefined

128. _____ refers to a naturally formed opening beneath the surface of the Earth, generally formed by dissolution of carbonate bedrock. Caves may also form by erosion of coastal bedrock, partial melting of glaciers, or solidification of lava into hollow tubes.
    a. Cave15
    b. 1509 Istanbul earthquake
    c. Undefined
    d. Undefined

129. A rock in which hydrocarbons originate is referred to as a _____.
    a. 1509 Istanbul earthquake
    b. Source rock15
    c. Undefined
    d. Undefined

130. A gaseous mixture of naturally occurring hydrocarbons is _____.

Chapter 15. Geologic Structures

283

    a. 1509 Istanbul earthquake
    c. Undefined
    b. Natural gas15
    d. Undefined

131. _____ refers to a permeable rock containing oil or gas.
    a. Reservoir rock15
    c. Undefined
    b. 1509 Istanbul earthquake
    d. Undefined

132. _____ refers to an area underlain by one or more oil pools.
    a. Oil field15
    c. Undefined
    b. AASHTO Soil Classification System
    d. Undefined

133. _____ refers to any of a group of naturally occurring substances made up of hydrocarbons. These substances may be gaseous, liquid, or semi-solid.
    a. Petroleum15
    c. Undefined
    b. 1509 Istanbul earthquake
    d. Undefined

134. _____ occurs when living things move from one biome to another. In most cases organisms migrate to avoid local shortages of food, usually caused by winter. Animals may also migrate to a certain location to breed, as is the case with some fish.
    a. Thing
    c. Undefined
    b. Migration15
    d. Undefined

135. _____ is a chemical element; it is a colorless, odorless, tasteless, non-toxic, and nearly inert monatomic that heads the noble gas series in the periodic table. Its atomic number is 2 and its boiling and melting points are the lowest among the elements. It exists only as a gas except in extreme conditions.
    a. Helium15
    c. Undefined
    b. Thing
    d. Undefined

136. All processes that adds snow or ice to a glacier or to floating ice or snow cove are referred to as _____.
    a. AASHTO Soil Classification System
    c. Undefined
    b. Accumulation15
    d. Undefined

137. Ability to do work is referred to as _____. Most evident in glacial systems as radiant _____ from the sun and as latent _____ required to melt ice to water.
    a. Energy15
    c. Undefined
    b. AASHTO Soil Classification System
    d. Undefined

138. A geologic structure that allows for significant amounts of oil and gas to accumulate is called _____.
    a. Oil trap15
    c. Undefined
    b. AASHTO Soil Classification System
    d. Undefined

139. The _____ is an informal name for the eons of the geologic timescale that came before the current Phanerozoic eon. It spans from the formation of Earth around 4500 Ma (million years ago) to the evolution of abundant macroscopic hard-shelled fossils, which marked the beginning of the Cambrian.

Chapter 15. Geologic Structures

    a. Thing
    b. Precambrian15
    c. Undefined
    d. Undefined

140. The _____ period is one of the major divisions of the geologic timescale, reaching from the end of the Jurassic period, about 146 million years ago (Ma), to the beginning of the Paleocene epoch of the Tertiary period (65.5 Ma).
    a. Cretaceous15
    b. Thing
    c. Undefined
    d. Undefined

141. _____ refers to a strike-slip fault in which the block seen across the fault appears displaced to the right.
    a. 1509 Istanbul earthquake
    b. Right-lateral fault15
    c. Undefined
    d. Undefined

142. _____ refers to a body of water found on the Earth's surface and confined to a narrow topographic depression, down which it flows and transports rock particles, sediment, and dissolved particles. Rivers, creeks, brooks, and runs are all streams.
    a. Stream15
    b. 1509 Istanbul earthquake
    c. Undefined
    d. Undefined

143. A strike-slip fault in which the block seen across the fault appears displaced to the left is called a _____.
    a. 1509 Istanbul earthquake
    b. Left-lateral fault15
    c. Undefined
    d. Undefined

144. The entire area between the tops of the slopes on both sides of a stream is a _____.
    a. 1509 Istanbul earthquake
    b. Valley15
    c. Undefined
    d. Undefined

145. _____ refers to the water that lies beneath the ground surface, filling the cracks, crevices, and pore space of rocks.
    a. 1509 Istanbul earthquake
    b. Ground water15
    c. Undefined
    d. Undefined

146. A long, narrow depression, shaped and more or less filled by a stream is referred to as a _____.
    a. 1509 Istanbul earthquake
    b. Stream channel15
    c. Undefined
    d. Undefined

147. _____ refers to a feature on the surface of the planet Mars that very closely resembles certain types of stream channels on Earth.
    a. Channel15
    b. 1509 Istanbul earthquake
    c. Undefined
    d. Undefined

148. Scientists who study earthquake waves and what they tell us about the inside of the Earth are called a _____.
    a. 1509 Istanbul earthquake
    b. Seismologist15
    c. Undefined
    d. Undefined

149. _____ is a term used in geology, engineering and surveying to denote the motion of a surface (usually, the earth's surface) downwards relative to a datum such as sea-level.

Chapter 15. Geologic Structures

a. Thing
c. Undefined
b. Subsidence15
d. Undefined

150. The intermediate era of the Phanerozoic Eon, following the Paleozoic Era and preceding the Cenozoic Era, and marked by the dominance of marine and terrestrial reptiles, and the appearance of birds, mammals, and flowering plants is a _____.
a. Mesozoic Era15
c. Undefined
b. 1509 Istanbul earthquake
d. Undefined

151. The _____ is one of three geologic eras of the Phanerozoic eon. The division of time into eras dates back to Giovanni Arduino in the 18th century, although his original name for the era now called the _____ was "Secondary".
a. Thing
c. Undefined
b. Mesozoic15
d. Undefined

152. A plate boundary where the plates slip past each other as a the San Andreas Fault in California is a _____.
a. 1509 Istanbul earthquake
c. Undefined
b. Transform boundary15
d. Undefined

153. _____ refers to a tentative explanation of a given set of data that is expected to remain valid after future observation and experimentation.
a. Hypothesis15
c. Undefined
b. 1509 Istanbul earthquake
d. Undefined

154. _____ is a part of the theory of plate tectonics. _____ is the process by which continental drift occurs. This mechanism, which is a more accurate version of Alfred Wegener's original drift of continents that "plow" through the sea.
a. Thing
c. Undefined
b. Seafloor spreading15
d. Undefined

155. The mass movement of a single, intact mass of rock, soil, or unconsolidated material along a weak plane, such as a fault, fracture, or bedding plane is a _____. A _____ may involve as little as a minor displacement of soil or as much as the displacement of an entire mountainside.
a. 1509 Istanbul earthquake
c. Undefined
b. Slide15
d. Undefined

156. _____ refers to a crack in a glacier caused by rapid extension. Crevasses over 10 m deep would be healed by internal flow, but much deeper crevasses can be maintained by continued tension.
a. 1509 Istanbul earthquake
c. Undefined
b. Crevasse15
d. Undefined

Chapter 16. Earthquakes

1. A movement within the Earth's crust or mantle, caused by the sudden rupture or repositioning of underground rocks as they release stress is an _____.
   a. AASHTO Soil Classification System
   b. Earthquake16
   c. Undefined
   d. Undefined

2. A numerical expression of the amount of energy released by an earthquake, determined by measuring earthquake waves on standardized recording instruments is called a _____. The number scale for magnitudes is logarithmic rather than arithmetic. Therefore, deflections on a seismograph for a _____ 5 earthquake, for example, are 10 times greater than those for a _____ 4 earthquake, 100 times greater than for a _____ 3 earthquake, and so on.
   a. Magnitude16
   b. 1509 Istanbul earthquake
   c. Undefined
   d. Undefined

3. The point on the Earth's surface that is located directly above the focus of an earthquake is referred to as _____.
   a. Epicenter16
   b. AASHTO Soil Classification System
   c. Undefined
   d. Undefined

4. The direction or trend of a bedding plane or fault, as it intersects the horizontal is referred to as a _____.
   a. 1509 Istanbul earthquake
   b. Strike16
   c. Undefined
   d. Undefined

5. _____ refers to the steep cliff face that is formed by a slump.
   a. Scarp16
   b. 1509 Istanbul earthquake
   c. Undefined
   d. Undefined

6. A fracture dividing a rock into two sections that have visibly moved relative to each other is a _____.
   a. Fault16
   b. 1509 Istanbul earthquake
   c. Undefined
   d. Undefined

7. The _____ is that part of a planet's outer shell — including air, land, surface rocks and water — within which life occurs, and which biotic processes in turn alter or transform.
   a. Thing
   b. Biosphere16
   c. Undefined
   d. Undefined

8. A long, narrow depression, shaped and more or less filled by a stream is referred to as a _____.
   a. Stream channel16
   b. 1509 Istanbul earthquake
   c. Undefined
   d. Undefined

9. Water stored beneath the surface in open pore spaces and fractures in rock is called _____.
   a. Groundwater16
   b. 1509 Istanbul earthquake
   c. Undefined
   d. Undefined

10. _____ in physical geography, describes the collective mass of water found on, under, and over the surface of a planet.
    a. Hydrosphere16
    b. Thing
    c. Undefined
    d. Undefined

Chapter 16. Earthquakes

11. _____ refers to a feature on the surface of the planet Mars that very closely resembles certain types of stream channels on Earth.
    a. 1509 Istanbul earthquake
    b. Channel16
    c. Undefined
    d. Undefined

12. _____ refers to a body of water found on the Earth's surface and confined to a narrow topographic depression, down which it flows and transports rock particles, sediment, and dissolved particles. Rivers, creeks, brooks, and runs are all streams.
    a. 1509 Istanbul earthquake
    b. Stream16
    c. Undefined
    d. Undefined

13. The time between winter and summer is _____.
    a. 1509 Istanbul earthquake
    b. Spring16
    c. Undefined
    d. Undefined

14. Long, fast waves produced by earthquakes and other seismic disturbances of the sea floor is called _____.
    a. Tsunami16
    b. Thing
    c. Undefined
    d. Undefined

15. _____ refers to a naturally formed aggregate of usually inorganic materials from within the Earth.
    a. Rock16
    b. 1509 Istanbul earthquake
    c. Undefined
    d. Undefined

16. _____ refers to the top few meters of regolith, generally including some organic matter derived from plants.
    a. Soil16
    b. 1509 Istanbul earthquake
    c. Undefined
    d. Undefined

17. _____ is any particulate matter that can be transported by fluid flow and which eventually is deposited as a layer of solid particles on the bed or bottom of a body of water or other liquid.
    a. Thing
    b. Sediment16
    c. Undefined
    d. Undefined

18. Group of organisms of the same species occupying a certain area and sharing a common gene pool is referred to as _____.
    a. Population16
    b. Thing
    c. Undefined
    d. Undefined

19. _____ refers to low amplitude, continuous earthquake activity often associated with magma movement.
    a. 1509 Istanbul earthquake
    b. Tremor16
    c. Undefined
    d. Undefined

20. Angular chunk of solid rock ejected during an eruption is referred to as a _____.
    a. 1509 Istanbul earthquake
    b. Block16
    c. Undefined
    d. Undefined

21. The entire area between the tops of the slopes on both sides of a stream is a _____.

Chapter 16. Earthquakes

    a. Valley16
    c. Undefined
    b. 1509 Istanbul earthquake
    d. Undefined

22. _____ refers to rigid parts of the Earth's crust and part of the Earth's upper mantle that moves and adjoins each other along zones of seismic activity.
    a. Plate16
    b. 1509 Istanbul earthquake
    c. Undefined
    d. Undefined

23. A measure of the effects of an earthquake at a particular place is called _____. _____ depends not only on the magnitude of the earthquake, but also on the distance from the epicenter and the local geology.
    a. Intensity16
    b. AASHTO Soil Classification System
    c. Undefined
    d. Undefined

24. Ability to do work is referred to as _____. Most evident in glacial systems as radiant _____ from the sun and as latent _____ required to melt ice to water.
    a. Energy16
    b. AASHTO Soil Classification System
    c. Undefined
    d. Undefined

25. Aggregates of minerals or rock fragments are called _____.
    a. Rocks16
    b. 1509 Istanbul earthquake
    c. Undefined
    d. Undefined

26. One of a series of progressive disturbances that reverberate through the Earth to transmit the energy released from an earthquake is called a _____.
    a. 1509 Istanbul earthquake
    b. Seismic wave16
    c. Undefined
    d. Undefined

27. The mass movement of a single, intact mass of rock, soil, or unconsolidated material along a weak plane, such as a fault, fracture, or bedding plane is a _____. A _____ may involve as little as a minor displacement of soil or as much as the displacement of an entire mountainside.
    a. 1509 Istanbul earthquake
    b. Slide16
    c. Undefined
    d. Undefined

28. The sudden release of progressively stored strain in rocks results in movement along a fault is referred to as _____.
    a. Elastic rebound theory16
    b. AASHTO Soil Classification System
    c. Undefined
    d. Undefined

29. The sudden release of stored strain in rocks that results in movement along a fault is referred to as _____.
    a. Elastic rebound16
    b. AASHTO Soil Classification System
    c. Undefined
    d. Undefined

30. _____ refers to a body in which strains are totally recoverable, as in a rubber band.
    a. Elastic16
    b. AASHTO Soil Classification System
    c. Undefined
    d. Undefined

Chapter 16. Earthquakes

31. The force acting on a rock or another solid to deform it, measured in kilograms per square centimeter or pounds per square inch is _____.
    a. 1509 Istanbul earthquake
    b. Stress16
    c. Undefined
    d. Undefined

32. _____ refers to the change in the shape or volume of a rock that results from stress.
    a. Strain16
    b. 1509 Istanbul earthquake
    c. Undefined
    d. Undefined

33. Forces generated from within Earth that result in uplift, movement, or deformations of part of Earth's crust are called _____.
    a. Tectonic forces16
    b. 1509 Istanbul earthquake
    c. Undefined
    d. Undefined

34. _____ refers to a material that undergoes smooth and continuous plastic deformation under increasing force and does not spring back to its original shape when the deforming force is released.
    a. 1509 Istanbul earthquake
    b. Ductile material16
    c. Undefined
    d. Undefined

35. _____ refers to capable of being molded and bent under stress.
    a. Ductile16
    b. 1509 Istanbul earthquake
    c. Undefined
    d. Undefined

36. The processes by which crustal forces cause a rock formation to break and slip along a fault are called _____.
    a. Faulting16
    b. 1509 Istanbul earthquake
    c. Undefined
    d. Undefined

37. A reverse fault marked by a dip of 45° or less is called _____.
    a. 1509 Istanbul earthquake
    b. Thrust fault16
    c. Undefined
    d. Undefined

38. The subterranean cavity containing the gas-rich liquid magma, which feeds a volcano, is a _____.
    a. Magma chamber16
    b. 1509 Istanbul earthquake
    c. Undefined
    d. Undefined

39. _____ refers to the process by which solid, liquid, and gaseous materials are ejected into the earth's atmosphere and onto the earth's surface by volcanic activity. Eruptions range from the quiet overflow of liquid rock to the tremendously violent expulsion of pyroclastics.
    a. AASHTO Soil Classification System
    b. Eruption16
    c. Undefined
    d. Undefined

40. Molten rock that forms naturally within the Earth is _____. _____ may be either a liquid or a fluid mixture of liquid, crystals, and dissolved gases.
    a. Magma16
    b. 1509 Istanbul earthquake
    c. Undefined
    d. Undefined

Chapter 16. Earthquakes

41. The middle layer of the Earth, lying just below the crust and consisting of relatively dense rocks is called the _____. The _____ is divided into two sections, the upper _____ and the lower _____; the lower _____ has greater density than the upper _____.
    a. Mantle16
    b. 1509 Istanbul earthquake
    c. Undefined
    d. Undefined

42. A naturally occurring, usually inorganic, solid consisting of either a single element or a compound, and having a definite chemical composition and a systematic internal arrangement of atoms is referred to as a _____.
    a. Mineral16
    b. 1509 Istanbul earthquake
    c. Undefined
    d. Undefined

43. _____ refers to a crack or break in a rock. To break in random places instead of cleaving.
    a. 1509 Istanbul earthquake
    b. Fracture16
    c. Undefined
    d. Undefined

44. The relationship between distance on a map and the distance on the terrain being represented by that map is a _____.
    a. Scale16
    b. 1509 Istanbul earthquake
    c. Undefined
    d. Undefined

45. An igneous rock rich in magnesium that forms soils toxic to many plants is called _____. Soils derived from _____ are toxic to many plants due to their high mineral content, and the flora is generally very distinctive, with specialized, slow-growing species.
    a. Serpentine16
    b. Thing
    c. Undefined
    d. Undefined

46. A non-crystaline rock that results from very rapid cooling of magma is _____.
    a. Glass16
    b. 1509 Istanbul earthquake
    c. Undefined
    d. Undefined

47. The place on a buried fault where an earthquake occurs is the _____.
    a. 1509 Istanbul earthquake
    b. Hypocenter16
    c. Undefined
    d. Undefined

48. The initial point within the Earth that ruptures in an earthquake, directly below the epicenter is called the _____.
    a. Focus16
    b. 1509 Istanbul earthquake
    c. Undefined
    d. Undefined

49. A type of seismic wave that transmits energy from an earthquake's focus through the Earth's interior in all direction is the _____.
    a. Body wave16
    b. 1509 Istanbul earthquake
    c. Undefined
    d. Undefined

50. _____ refer to seismic waves that travel along the outer layer of Earth.

Chapter 16. Earthquakes

a. Surface waves16
b. 1509 Istanbul earthquake
c. Undefined
d. Undefined

51. One of a series of seismic waves that transmits energy from an earthquake's epicenter along the Earth's surface is called a _____.
   a. 1509 Istanbul earthquake
   b. Surface wave16
   c. Undefined
   d. Undefined

52. A steep slope or cliff formed directly by movement along a fault and representing the exposed surface of the fault before modification by erosion and weathering is a _____.
   a. 1509 Istanbul earthquake
   b. Fault scarp16
   c. Undefined
   d. Undefined

53. A compressional wave in which rock vibrates parallel to the direction of wave propagation is referred to as the _____.
   a. 1509 Istanbul earthquake
   b. P wave16
   c. Undefined
   d. Undefined

54. The motion of surfaces sliding past one another is called _____.
   a. 1509 Istanbul earthquake
   b. Shearing16
   c. Undefined
   d. Undefined

55. _____ refers to a body wave that causes the rocks along which it passes to move up and down perpendicular to the direction of its own movement.
   a. 1509 Istanbul earthquake
   b. S wave16
   c. Undefined
   d. Undefined

56. A seismic wave that involves oscillation perpendicular to the direction of propagation is called a _____.
   a. 1509 Istanbul earthquake
   b. Secondary wave16
   c. Undefined
   d. Undefined

57. _____ refers to a body wave that causes the compression of rocks when its energy acts upon them. When the P wave moves past a rock, the rock expands beyond its original volume, only to be compressed again by the next P wave. P waves are the fastest of all seismic waves.
   a. Primary wave16
   b. 1509 Istanbul earthquake
   c. Undefined
   d. Undefined

58. A type of surface seismic wave that causes the ground to move side to side in a horizontal plane perpendicular to the direction the wave is traveling is referred to as _____.
   a. Love waves16
   b. 1509 Istanbul earthquake
   c. Undefined
   d. Undefined

59. Types of surface seismic waves that behave like a rolling ocean wave and cause the ground to move in an elliptical path are referred to as _____.

a. Rayleigh waves16
c. Undefined
b. 1509 Istanbul earthquake
d. Undefined

60. An instrument that measures motion of the ground caused by earthquake waves is a _____.
   a. 1509 Istanbul earthquake
   b. Seismometer16
   c. Undefined
   d. Undefined

61. _____ refers to objects at rest tend to remain at rest, and objects in motion tend to stay in motion unless either is acted upon by an outside force.
   a. AASHTO Soil Classification System
   b. Inertia16
   c. Undefined
   d. Undefined

62. A machine for measuring the intensity of earthquakes by recording the seismic waves that they generate is referred to as _____.
   a. Seismograph16
   b. 1509 Istanbul earthquake
   c. Undefined
   d. Undefined

63. _____ refers to a visual record produced by a seismograph and showing the arrival times and magnitudes of various seismic waves.
   a. Seismogram16
   b. 1509 Istanbul earthquake
   c. Undefined
   d. Undefined

64. _____ refers to fragment of molten or semi-molten rock, 2 1/2 inches to many feet in diameter, which is blown out during an eruption. Because of their plastic condition, bombs are often modified in shape during their flight or upon impact.
   a. Bomb16
   b. 1509 Istanbul earthquake
   c. Undefined
   d. Undefined

65. A feature found in caves that is formed when a stalactite and stalagmite join is referred to as a _____.
   a. Column16
   b. 1509 Istanbul earthquake
   c. Undefined
   d. Undefined

66. A plot of seismic-wave arrival times against distance is the _____.
   a. 1509 Istanbul earthquake
   b. Travel-time curve16
   c. Undefined
   d. Undefined

67. Scientists who study earthquake waves and what they tell us about the inside of the Earth are called a _____.
   a. 1509 Istanbul earthquake
   b. Seismologist16
   c. Undefined
   d. Undefined

68. Distance between the focus and the epicenter of an earthquake is _____.
   a. 1509 Istanbul earthquake
   b. Depth of focus16
   c. Undefined
   d. Undefined

69. _____ refers to a secondary, or shear, body seismic wave that travels through the depth of the Earth. S-waves can only be transmitted by solids.

a. S-wave16
c. Undefined
b. 1509 Istanbul earthquake
d. Undefined

70. _____ refers to a 12-point scale developed to evaluate earthquake intensity based on the amount of damage to various structures.
   a. Modified mercalli intensity scale16
   b. 1509 Istanbul earthquake
   c. Undefined
   d. Undefined

71. _____ refers to a scale designed to measure the degree of intensity of earthquakes, ranging from I for the lowest intensity to XII for the highest. The classifications are based on human perceptions.
   a. Mercalli Intensity Scale16
   b. 1509 Istanbul earthquake
   c. Undefined
   d. Undefined

72. _____ refers to an earthquake rating scale based upon subjective reports of human reactions to ground shaking and upon the damage caused by an earthquake.
   a. AASHTO Soil Classification System
   b. Intensity scale16
   c. Undefined
   d. Undefined

73. _____ refers to a descriptive term applied to igneous rocks that are transitional between basic and acidic with silica between 54% and 65%.
   a. Intermediate16
   b. AASHTO Soil Classification System
   c. Undefined
   d. Undefined

74. A small rock island that is an erosional remnant of a headland left behind as a wave eroded coast retreats inland is referred to as a _____.
   a. Stack16
   b. 1509 Istanbul earthquake
   c. Undefined
   d. Undefined

75. The situation in mass wasting that occurs when material free-falls or bounces down a cliff is called a _____.
   a. 1509 Istanbul earthquake
   b. Fall16
   c. Undefined
   d. Undefined

76. A major branch of a stream system is referred to as a _____.
   a. 1509 Istanbul earthquake
   b. River16
   c. Undefined
   d. Undefined

77. An alluvial fan having its apex at the mouth of a stream is a _____.
   a. Delta16
   b. 1509 Istanbul earthquake
   c. Undefined
   d. Undefined

78. A logarithmic scale that measures the amount of energy released during an earthquake on the basis of the amplitude of the highest peak recorded on a seismogram is a _____. Each unit increase in the _____ represents a 10-fold increase in the amplitude recorded on the seismogram and a 30-fold increase in energy released by the earthquake. Theoretically the _____ has no upper limit, but the yield point of the Earth's rocks imposes an effective limit between 9.0 and 9.5.

Chapter 16. Earthquakes

    a. Richter scale16
    b. 1509 Istanbul earthquake
    c. Undefined
    d. Undefined

79. _____ refers to a numerical means of measuring an earthquake's total energy release. It is calculated by measuring the total length of fault rupture and then factoring in the depth of rupture, total slip along the rupture, and the strength of the faulted rocks.
    a. Seismic moment16
    b. 1509 Istanbul earthquake
    c. Undefined
    d. Undefined

80. _____ refers to a more precise measure of earthquake magnitude than the Richter scale that is derived from the amount of displacement that occurs along a fault zone.
    a. 1509 Istanbul earthquake
    b. Moment magnitude16
    c. Undefined
    d. Undefined

81. The intensity of shaking and ground disruption in an earthquake that can be expected over the long term at some specified location, expressed in the form of a _____ map.
    a. Seismic hazard16
    b. 1509 Istanbul earthquake
    c. Undefined
    d. Undefined

82. A large mass of rock projecting above surrounding terrain is called a _____.
    a. 1509 Istanbul earthquake
    b. Mountain16
    c. Undefined
    d. Undefined

83. The earthquake damage that can be expected over the long term for a specified region, such as a county or state, usually measured in terms of average dollar loss per year is a _____.
    a. Seismic risk16
    b. 1509 Istanbul earthquake
    c. Undefined
    d. Undefined

84. Any unconsolidated material at Earth's surface is _____.
    a. 1509 Istanbul earthquake
    b. Debris16
    c. Undefined
    d. Undefined

85. Standards for the design and construction of new buildings that specify the level of shaking a structure must be able to withstand in an earthquake, based on the maximum intensity expected from the seismic hazard are called the _____.
    a. Building code16
    b. 1509 Istanbul earthquake
    c. Undefined
    d. Undefined

86. _____ refers to a term loosely used for an igneous or metamorphic rock, as distinguished from a sedimentary rock. In mining, a rock that requires drilling and blasting for economical removal.
    a. Hard rock16
    b. 1509 Istanbul earthquake
    c. Undefined
    d. Undefined

87. _____ is a term used in geology, engineering and surveying to denote the motion of a surface (usually, the earth's surface) downwards relative to a datum such as sea-level.

Chapter 16. Earthquakes

a. Subsidence16   b. Thing
c. Undefined   d. Undefined

88. _____ refers to the conversion of moderately cohesive, unconsolidated sediment into a fluid, water-saturated mass.
   a. Liquefaction16   b. 1509 Istanbul earthquake
   c. Undefined   d. Undefined

89. _____ refers to general term referring to the rock underlying other unconsolidated material, i.e. soil.
   a. Bedrock16   b. 1509 Istanbul earthquake
   c. Undefined   d. Undefined

90. A fine-grained, foliated metamorphic rock that develops from shale and tends to break into thin, flat sheets is called _____.
   a. 1509 Istanbul earthquake   b. Slate16
   c. Undefined   d. Undefined

91. _____ refers to a basic unit of the geologic time scale that is a subdivision of an era. Periods may be divided into smaller units called epochs.
   a. 1509 Istanbul earthquake   b. Period16
   c. Undefined   d. Undefined

92. _____ refers to a ground tremor caused by the repositioning of rocks after an earthquake. Aftershocks may continue to occur for as long as two years after the initial earthquake. The intensity of an earthquake's aftershocks decreases over time.
   a. Aftershock16   b. AASHTO Soil Classification System
   c. Undefined   d. Undefined

93. Stress that reduces the volume or length of a rock, as that produced by the convergence of plate margins is called _____.
   a. Compression16   b. 1509 Istanbul earthquake
   c. Undefined   d. Undefined

94. _____ refer to small earthquakes that often precede a major earthquake.
   a. 1509 Istanbul earthquake   b. Foreshocks16
   c. Undefined   d. Undefined

95. _____ refers to a minor, barely detectable earthquake, generally preceding a full-scale earthquake with approximately the same focus. Major quakes may follow a cluster of foreshocks by as little as a few seconds or as much as several weeks.
   a. 1509 Istanbul earthquake   b. Foreshock16
   c. Undefined   d. Undefined

96. The periodic, rhythmic rise and fall of the sea surface caused by changes in gravitational forces external to the Earth is referred to as the _____.

Chapter 16. Earthquakes

   a. Tide16
   c. Undefined
   b. Thing
   d. Undefined

97. _____ refers to amplitude; the vertical distance between wave crest and trough.
   a. 1509 Istanbul earthquake
   c. Undefined
   b. Wave height16
   d. Undefined

98. The horizontal distance between wave crests is a _____.
   a. Wavelength16
   c. Undefined
   b. 1509 Istanbul earthquake
   d. Undefined

99. The vertical column of seawater that extends from the surface to the bottom is called _____.
   a. Thing
   c. Undefined
   b. Water column16
   d. Undefined

100. The _____ is the lowest layer in an ocean, existing below the thermocline. The _____ is not well mixed, consists of horizontal layers of equal density, and is often as cold as -1 to 4 degrees Celsius. Ninety percent of the total volume of Earth's oceans is found in the _____.
   a. Deep ocean16
   c. Undefined
   b. Thing
   d. Undefined

101. The top of the ocean, where the water meets the atmosphere is called _____.
   a. 1509 Istanbul earthquake
   c. Undefined
   b. Sea level16
   d. Undefined

102. _____ refers to the set of physical features, such as mountains, valleys, and the shapes of landforms, that characterizes a given landscape.
   a. 1509 Istanbul earthquake
   c. Undefined
   b. Topography16
   d. Undefined

103. _____ refers to the area of dry land that borders on a body of water.
   a. Coast16
   c. Undefined
   b. 1509 Istanbul earthquake
   d. Undefined

104. Major belt around the edge of the Pacific Ocean on which most composite volcanoes are located and where many earthquakes occur is called _____.
   a. Circum-pacific belt16
   c. Undefined
   b. 1509 Istanbul earthquake
   d. Undefined

105. A plate boundary at which plates approach each other is referred to as a _____.
   a. 1509 Istanbul earthquake
   c. Undefined
   b. Convergent boundary16
   d. Undefined

106. A plate boundary at which the plates are moving apart as a result of spreading is referred to as _____.

Chapter 16. Earthquakes

a. 1509 Istanbul earthquake
c. Undefined
b. Divergent boundary16
d. Undefined

107. A plate boundary where the plates slip past each other as a the San Andreas Fault in California is a _____.
a. Transform boundary16
b. 1509 Istanbul earthquake
c. Undefined
d. Undefined

108. _____ refers to the study of the global-scale movements of Earth's crust that have resulted in.
a. Plate tectonics16
b. Thing
c. Undefined
d. Undefined

109. _____ refers to the study of the large-scale processes that collectively deform Earth's crust.
a. Tectonics16
b. 1509 Istanbul earthquake
c. Undefined
d. Undefined

110. The zone of convergence of two tectonic plates, one of which usually overrides the other is referred to as the _____.
a. Subduction zone16
b. 1509 Istanbul earthquake
c. Undefined
d. Undefined

111. The downward movement of a plate into the mantle that occurs in trenches, which are also known as _____ zones.
a. Thing
b. Subduction16
c. Undefined
d. Undefined

112. _____ refers to a chain of volcanic islands generally located a few hundred kilometers from a trench where there is active subduction of one oceanic plate beneath another.
a. 1509 Istanbul earthquake
b. Volcanic island arc16
c. Undefined
d. Undefined

113. Deep steep-sided depression in the ocean floor caused by the subduction of oceanic crust beneath either other oceanic crust or continental crust is an _____.
a. Oceanic trench16
b. AASHTO Soil Classification System
c. Undefined
d. Undefined

114. A zone in the upper mantle, usually beneath an oceanic trench, where a cool, brittle plate, being subducted back into the mantle, gives rise to deep earthquakes is the _____.
a. Benioff zone16
b. 1509 Istanbul earthquake
c. Undefined
d. Undefined

115. An elongated depression in the seafloor produced by bending of oceanic crust during subduction is a _____.
a. 1509 Istanbul earthquake
b. Trench16
c. Undefined
d. Undefined

116. The angle formed by the inclined plane of a geological structure and the horizontal plane of the Earth's surface is referred to as a _____.

Chapter 16. Earthquakes

   a. Dip16
   c. Undefined
   b. 1509 Istanbul earthquake
   d. Undefined

117. _____ refers to a giant mountain range that lies under the ocean and extends around the world.
   a. Mid-oceanic ridge16
   c. Undefined
   b. 1509 Istanbul earthquake
   d. Undefined

118. _____ refers to a group of closely spaced mountains or parallel ridges.
   a. 1509 Istanbul earthquake
   c. Undefined
   b. Mountain range16
   d. Undefined

119. The topographically highest hillslope position of a hillslope profile and exhibiting a nearly level surface is referred to as the _____.
   a. Summit16
   c. Undefined
   b. 1509 Istanbul earthquake
   d. Undefined

120. The relationship between humans and their geological environment is called _____.
   a. AASHTO Soil Classification System
   c. Undefined
   b. Environmental geology16
   d. Undefined

121. The scientific study of the Earth, its origins and evolution, the materials that make it up, and the processes that act on it is called _____.
   a. Geology16
   c. Undefined
   b. 1509 Istanbul earthquake
   d. Undefined

122. _____ refers to capable of being molded into any form, which is retained.
   a. 1509 Istanbul earthquake
   c. Undefined
   b. Plastic16
   d. Undefined

123. _____ refers to a vertical conduit through the Earth's crust below a volcano, through which magmatic materials have passed. Commonly filled with volcanic breccia and fragments of older rock.
   a. Pipe16
   c. Undefined
   b. 1509 Istanbul earthquake
   d. Undefined

124. _____ is a chemical element in the periodic table that has the symbol C and atomic number 6. An abundant nonmetallic, tetravalent element, _____ has several allotropic forms.
   a. Thing
   c. Undefined
   b. Carbon16
   d. Undefined

125. Usually slow but effective process of weathering and erosion in which rocks are dissolved by water is a _____.
   a. 1509 Istanbul earthquake
   c. Undefined
   b. Solution16
   d. Undefined

126. _____ refers to a flat thinnish dressed stone.

Chapter 16. Earthquakes

a. 1509 Istanbul earthquake
b. Slab16
c. Undefined
d. Undefined

127. A _____ is a valley created by the formation of a rift. They are produced by tensional tectonic forces which occur at divergent plate boundaries.
 a. Rift valley16
 b. Thing
 c. Undefined
 d. Undefined

128. _____ refers to a long, narrow trough bounded by normal faults. It represents a region where divergence is taking place.
 a. Rift16
 b. 1509 Istanbul earthquake
 c. Undefined
 d. Undefined

129. Strain involving an increase in length is an _____. _____ can cause crustal thinning and faulting.
 a. Extension16
 b. AASHTO Soil Classification System
 c. Undefined
 d. Undefined

130. _____ refers to a dip-slip fault marked by a generally steep dip along which the hanging wall has moved downward relative to the footwall.
 a. 1509 Istanbul earthquake
 b. Normal fault16
 c. Undefined
 d. Undefined

131. The distance that one face of a fault is displaced relative to the other is referred to as a _____.
 a. Slip16
 b. 1509 Istanbul earthquake
 c. Undefined
 d. Undefined

132. A round or oval depression in the Earth's surface, containing the youngest section of rock in its lowest, central part is a _____.
 a. 1509 Istanbul earthquake
 b. Basin16
 c. Undefined
 d. Undefined

133. _____ refers to the area where two continental plates have joined together through continental collision. Suture zones are marked by extremely high mountain ranges, such as the Himalayas and the Alps.
 a. 1509 Istanbul earthquake
 b. Suture zone16
 c. Undefined
 d. Undefined

134. A _____ is the outer layer of a planet, part of its lithosphere. Planetary _____ is generally composed of a less dense material than that of its deeper layers. The _____ of the Earth is composed mainly of basalt and granite.
 a. Thing
 b. Crust16
 c. Undefined
 d. Undefined

135. _____ refers to a map representing the geology of a given area.
 a. 1509 Istanbul earthquake
 b. Geologic map16
 c. Undefined
 d. Undefined

Chapter 16. Earthquakes

136. The _____ is the solid outermost shell of a rocky planet. On the Earth, the _____ includes the crust and the uppermost layer of the mantle (the upper mantle or lower _____) which is joined to the crust.
   a. Lithosphere16
   b. Thing
   c. Undefined
   d. Undefined

137. Stress that stretches or extends rocks, so that they become thinner vertically and longer laterally is called _____. _____ may be caused by divergence or rifting.
   a. Tension16
   b. 1509 Istanbul earthquake
   c. Undefined
   d. Undefined

138. _____ refers to the coming together of two lithospheric plates. _____ causes subduction when one or both plates are oceanic and mountain formation when both plates are continental.
   a. Convergence16
   b. 1509 Istanbul earthquake
   c. Undefined
   d. Undefined

139. Observable phenomena that occur before an earthquake and indicate that an event is soon to occur are referred to as _____.
   a. 1509 Istanbul earthquake
   b. Precursors16
   c. Undefined
   d. Undefined

140. The property, possessed by certain materials, to attract or repel similar materials is _____. _____ is associated with moving electricity.
   a. 1509 Istanbul earthquake
   b. Magnetism16
   c. Undefined
   d. Undefined

141. The percentage of a soil, rock, or sediment's volume that is made up of pores is _____.
   a. 1509 Istanbul earthquake
   b. Porosity16
   c. Undefined
   d. Undefined

142. _____ refers to the spontaneous decay of certain unstable atomic nuclei.
   a. Radioactive decay16
   b. 1509 Istanbul earthquake
   c. Undefined
   d. Undefined

143. A term used to describe the property of releasing energy or particles from an unstable atom is called _____.
   a. Radioactive16
   b. Thing
   c. Undefined
   d. Undefined

144. When refined, _____ is a silvery white, weakly radioactive metal, which is slightly softer than steel. It is malleable, ductile, and slightly paramagnetic. _____ metal has very high density, 65% more dense than lead, but slightly less dense than gold. When finely divided, it can react with cold water; in air, _____ metal becomes coated with _____ oxide.
   a. Uranium16
   b. Thing
   c. Undefined
   d. Undefined

Chapter 16. Earthquakes

145. A chemical _____, often called simply _____, is a chemical substance that cannot be divided or changed into other chemical substances by any ordinary chemical technique. An _____ is a class of substances that contain the same number of protons in all its atoms.
    a. Element16
    b. Thing
    c. Undefined
    d. Undefined

146. _____ refers to a radioactive gas that is formed by the disintegration of radium, _____ is one of the heaviest gases and is considered to be a health hazard.
    a. Radon16
    b. Thing
    c. Undefined
    d. Undefined

147. _____ refers to a natural spring marked by the intermittent escape of hot water and steam.
    a. 1509 Istanbul earthquake
    b. Geyser16
    c. Undefined
    d. Undefined

148. _____ refers to the altitude, or vertical distance, above or below sea level.
    a. AASHTO Soil Classification System
    b. Elevation16
    c. Undefined
    d. Undefined

149. _____ is the geomorphic process by which soil, regolith, and rock move downslope under the force of gravity. Types of _____ include creep, slides, flows, topples, and falls, each with their own characteristic features, and take place over timescales from seconds to years.
    a. Mass wasting16
    b. Thing
    c. Undefined
    d. Undefined

150. _____ refers to the process of emplacement of magma in pre-existing rock. Also, the term refers to igneous rock mass so formed within the surrounding rock.
    a. Intrusion16
    b. AASHTO Soil Classification System
    c. Undefined
    d. Undefined

151. _____ refers to pertaining to magma.
    a. 1509 Istanbul earthquake
    b. Magmatic16
    c. Undefined
    d. Undefined

152. _____ refers to the return period of an event, such as a flood or earthquake, of a given magnitude. For flooding, it is the average interval of time within which a given flood will be equaled or exceeded by the annual maximum discharge.
    a. Recurrence interval16
    b. 1509 Istanbul earthquake
    c. Undefined
    d. Undefined

153. Age given in years or some other unit of time is the _____.
    a. 1509 Istanbul earthquake
    b. Numerical age16
    c. Undefined
    d. Undefined

154. _____ refers to extremely small fragments, usually of glass, that forms when escaping gases force a fine spray of magma from a volcano.

Chapter 16. Earthquakes

    a. 1509 Istanbul earthquake
    b. Volcanic ash16
    c. Undefined
    d. Undefined

155. Fine particles of pulverized rock blown from an explosion vent are called _____. Measuring less than 1/10 inch in diameter, _____ may be either solid or molten when first erupted.
    a. Ash16
    b. AASHTO Soil Classification System
    c. Undefined
    d. Undefined

156. _____ refers to a locked fault segment that has not experienced seismic activity for a long time. Because stress tends to accumulate in seismic gaps, they often become the sites of major earthquakes.
    a. Seismic gap16
    b. 1509 Istanbul earthquake
    c. Undefined
    d. Undefined

157. _____ refers to the slowest form of mass movement, measured in millimeters or centimeters per year and occurring on virtually all slopes.
    a. 1509 Istanbul earthquake
    b. Creep16
    c. Undefined
    d. Undefined

158. _____ refers to a strike-slip fault in which the block seen across the fault appears displaced to the right.
    a. 1509 Istanbul earthquake
    b. Right-lateral fault16
    c. Undefined
    d. Undefined

159. A region of considerable extent where the combination of deposition and subsidence has formed thick accumulations of sediment and sedimentary rock is called _____.
    a. 1509 Istanbul earthquake
    b. Sedimentary basin16
    c. Undefined
    d. Undefined

160. A body of rock identified by lithic characteristics and stratigraphic position and is mappable at the earth's surface or traceable in the subsurface is a _____.
    a. Formation16
    b. 1509 Istanbul earthquake
    c. Undefined
    d. Undefined

Chapter 17. Earth`s Interior and Geophysical Properties

1. Earth's crust that includes both the continents and the continental shelves is the _____.
   a. Continental crust17
   b. 1509 Istanbul earthquake
   c. Undefined
   d. Undefined

2. The _____ is the solid outermost shell of a rocky planet. On the Earth, the _____ includes the crust and the uppermost layer of the mantle (the upper mantle or lower _____) which is joined to the crust.
   a. Lithosphere17
   b. Thing
   c. Undefined
   d. Undefined

3. _____ is a common gray to black volcanic rock. It is usually fine-grained due to rapid cooling of lava on the Earth's surface.
   a. Thing
   b. Basalt17
   c. Undefined
   d. Undefined

4. The middle layer of the Earth, lying just below the crust and consisting of relatively dense rocks is called the _____. The _____ is divided into two sections, the upper _____ and the lower _____; the lower _____ has greater density than the upper _____.
   a. 1509 Istanbul earthquake
   b. Mantle17
   c. Undefined
   d. Undefined

5. Aggregates of minerals or rock fragments are called _____.
   a. 1509 Istanbul earthquake
   b. Rocks17
   c. Undefined
   d. Undefined

6. A _____ is the outer layer of a planet, part of its lithosphere. Planetary _____ is generally composed of a less dense material than that of its deeper layers. The _____ of the Earth is composed mainly of basalt and granite.
   a. Thing
   b. Crust17
   c. Undefined
   d. Undefined

7. _____ refers to a vertical conduit through the Earth's crust below a volcano, through which magmatic materials have passed. Commonly filled with volcanic breccia and fragments of older rock.
   a. Pipe17
   b. 1509 Istanbul earthquake
   c. Undefined
   d. Undefined

8. _____ refers to a naturally formed aggregate of usually inorganic materials from within the Earth.
   a. 1509 Istanbul earthquake
   b. Rock17
   c. Undefined
   d. Undefined

9. Any portion of a meteoroid that survives its traverse through Earth's atmosphere and strikes the surface is referred to as a _____.
   a. 1509 Istanbul earthquake
   b. Meteorite17
   c. Undefined
   d. Undefined

10. The innermost layer of the Earth, consisting primarily of pure metals such as iron and nickel is the _____. The _____ is the densest layer of the Earth, and is divided into the outer _____, which is believed to be liquid, and the inner _____, which is believed to be solid.

a. Core17
b. 1509 Istanbul earthquake
c. Undefined
d. Undefined

11. The branch of geology that studies the physics of the Earth, using the physical principles underlying such phenomena as seismic waves, heat flow, gravity, and magnetism to investigate planetary properties is called _____.
   a. Geophysics17
   b. 1509 Istanbul earthquake
   c. Undefined
   d. Undefined

12. _____ refers to the study of the global-scale movements of Earth's crust that have resulted in.
   a. Thing
   b. Plate tectonics17
   c. Undefined
   d. Undefined

13. The _____ is the region of the Earth between 100-200 km below the surface that is the weak or "soft" zone in the upper mantle. It lies just below the lithosphere, which is involved in plate movements and isostatic adjustments. In spite of its heat, pressures keep it plastic, and it has a relatively low density.
   a. Thing
   b. Asthenosphere17
   c. Undefined
   d. Undefined

14. _____ refers to the study of the large-scale processes that collectively deform Earth's crust.
   a. Tectonics17
   b. 1509 Istanbul earthquake
   c. Undefined
   d. Undefined

15. _____ refers to capable of being molded into any form, which is retained.
   a. 1509 Istanbul earthquake
   b. Plastic17
   c. Undefined
   d. Undefined

16. _____ refers to capable of being molded and bent under stress.
   a. Ductile17
   b. 1509 Istanbul earthquake
   c. Undefined
   d. Undefined

17. _____ refers to rigid parts of the Earth's crust and part of the Earth's upper mantle that moves and adjoins each other along zones of seismic activity.
   a. 1509 Istanbul earthquake
   b. Plate17
   c. Undefined
   d. Undefined

18. _____ refers to a boundary in which two plates move together, resulting in oceanic lithosphere being thrust beneath an overriding plate, eventually to be reabsorbed into the mantle. It can also involve the collision of two continental plates to create a mountain system.
   a. Convergent plate boundary17
   b. 1509 Istanbul earthquake
   c. Undefined
   d. Undefined

19. _____ refers to the process of emplacement of magma in pre-existing rock. Also, the term refers to igneous rock mass so formed within the surrounding rock.
   a. Intrusion17
   b. AASHTO Soil Classification System
   c. Undefined
   d. Undefined

Chapter 17. Earth's Interior and Geophysical Properties

20. _____ is the displacement of solids (soil, mud, rock, and other particles) by the agents of wind, water, ice, movement in response to gravity, or living organisms.
    a. Erosion17
    b. Thing
    c. Undefined
    d. Undefined

21. The scientific study of the Earth, its origins and evolution, the materials that make it up, and the processes that act on it is called _____.
    a. 1509 Istanbul earthquake
    b. Geology17
    c. Undefined
    d. Undefined

22. The region within which the magnetism of a given substance or particle affects other substances is referred to as _____.
    a. Magnetic field17
    b. 1509 Istanbul earthquake
    c. Undefined
    d. Undefined

23. One of a series of progressive disturbances that reverberate through the Earth to transmit the energy released from an earthquake is called a _____.
    a. 1509 Istanbul earthquake
    b. Seismic wave17
    c. Undefined
    d. Undefined

24. The force of attraction exerted by one body in the universe on another is _____. _____ is directly proportional to the product of the masses of the two attracted bodies. The force of attraction exerted by the Earth on bodies on or near its surface, tending to pull them toward the Earth's center.
    a. 1509 Istanbul earthquake
    b. Gravity17
    c. Undefined
    d. Undefined

25. A movement within the Earth's crust or mantle, caused by the sudden rupture or repositioning of underground rocks as they release stress is an _____.
    a. Earthquake17
    b. AASHTO Soil Classification System
    c. Undefined
    d. Undefined

26. _____ refers to fragment of molten or semi-molten rock, 2 1/2 inches to many feet in diameter, which is blown out during an eruption. Because of their plastic condition, bombs are often modified in shape during their flight or upon impact.
    a. 1509 Istanbul earthquake
    b. Bomb17
    c. Undefined
    d. Undefined

27. The return of part of the energy of seismic waves to Earth's surface after the waves bounce off a rock boundary is referred to as _____.
    a. Seismic reflection17
    b. 1509 Istanbul earthquake
    c. Undefined
    d. Undefined

28. Ability to do work is referred to as _____. Most evident in glacial systems as radiant _____ from the sun and as latent _____ required to melt ice to water.
    a. Energy17
    b. AASHTO Soil Classification System
    c. Undefined
    d. Undefined

29. _____ refers to a visual record produced by a seismograph and showing the arrival times and magnitudes of various seismic waves.
   a. 1509 Istanbul earthquake
   b. Seismogram17
   c. Undefined
   d. Undefined

30. A machine for measuring the intensity of earthquakes by recording the seismic waves that they generate is referred to as _____.
   a. 1509 Istanbul earthquake
   b. Seismograph17
   c. Undefined
   d. Undefined

31. _____ refers to the bending of seismic waves as they pass from one material to another.
   a. Seismic refraction17
   b. 1509 Istanbul earthquake
   c. Undefined
   d. Undefined

32. The bending of waves on passing between media of different velocities is referred to as _____.
   a. Refraction17
   b. 1509 Istanbul earthquake
   c. Undefined
   d. Undefined

33. The direction or trend of a bedding plane or fault, as it intersects the horizontal is referred to as a _____.
   a. 1509 Istanbul earthquake
   b. Strike17
   c. Undefined
   d. Undefined

34. Rocks formed by solidification of sediments formed and transported at the Earth's surface are referred to as _____.
   a. Sedimentary rocks17
   b. 1509 Istanbul earthquake
   c. Undefined
   d. Undefined

35. _____ is the result of the transformation of a pre-existing rock type, the protolith, in a process called metamorphism, which means "change in form". The protolith is subjected to heat (greater than 150 degrees Celsius) and extreme pressure causing profound physical and/or chemical change.
   a. Metamorphic rock17
   b. Thing
   c. Undefined
   d. Undefined

36. _____ is one of the three main rock groups and is formed in three main ways—by the deposition of the weathered remains of other rocks; by the deposition of the results of biogenic activity; and by precipitation from solution.
   a. Sedimentary rock17
   b. Event
   c. Undefined
   d. Undefined

37. _____ refers to the term from the Greek 'meta' and 'morph', commonly occurs to rocks which are subjected to increased heat and/or pressure. Also applies to the conversion of snow into glacial ice.
   a. 1509 Istanbul earthquake
   b. Metamorphic17
   c. Undefined
   d. Undefined

38. _____ rocks are formed when molten rock (magma) cools and solidifies, with or without crystallization, either below the surface as intrusive (plutonic) rocks or on the surface as extrusive (volcanic) rocks. This magma can be derived from either the Earth's mantle or pre-existing rocks made molten by extreme temperature and pressure changes.

a. Igneous17
b. Thing
c. Undefined
d. Undefined

39. A pink-colored, felsic, plutonic rock that contains potassium and usually sodium feldspars, and has quartz content of about 10% is _____. _____ is commonly found on continents but virtually absent from the ocean basins.
   a. Granite17
   b. 1509 Istanbul earthquake
   c. Undefined
   d. Undefined

40. _____ refers to a coarse-grained, foliated metamorphic rock marked by bands of light-colored minerals such as quartz and feldspar that alternate with bands of dark-colored minerals. This alternation develops through metamorphic differentiation.
   a. 1509 Istanbul earthquake
   b. Gneiss17
   c. Undefined
   d. Undefined

41. A region of considerable extent where the combination of deposition and subsidence has formed thick accumulations of sediment and sedimentary rock is called _____.
   a. Sedimentary basin17
   b. 1509 Istanbul earthquake
   c. Undefined
   d. Undefined

42. A round or oval depression in the Earth's surface, containing the youngest section of rock in its lowest, central part is a _____.
   a. 1509 Istanbul earthquake
   b. Basin17
   c. Undefined
   d. Undefined

43. The undifferentiated rocks that underlie the rocks of interest in an area are referred to as _____.
   a. 1509 Istanbul earthquake
   b. Basement17
   c. Undefined
   d. Undefined

44. The _____ is an informal name for the eons of the geologic timescale that came before the current Phanerozoic eon. It spans from the formation of Earth around 4500 Ma (million years ago) to the evolution of abundant macroscopic hard-shelled fossils, which marked the beginning of the Cambrian.
   a. Thing
   b. Precambrian17
   c. Undefined
   d. Undefined

45. Aluminium is the chemical element in the periodic table that has the symbol Al and atomic number 13. It is a silvery and ductile member of the poor metal group of chemical elements. Aluminium is found primarily as the ore bauxite and is remarkable for its resistance to corrosion (due to the phenomenon of passivation) and its light weight. Aluminium is used in many industries to make millions of different products and is very important to the world economy.
   a. Thing
   b. Aluminum17
   c. Undefined
   d. Undefined

46. An extrusive igneous rock is referred to as _____.
   a. 1509 Istanbul earthquake
   b. Volcanic rock17
   c. Undefined
   d. Undefined

47. _____ refers to a crack or break in a rock. To break in random places instead of cleaving.

Chapter 17. Earth`s Interior and Geophysical Properties

    a. 1509 Istanbul earthquake
    c. Undefined
    b. Fracture17
    d. Undefined

48. A gaseous mixture of naturally occurring hydrocarbons is _____.
    a. 1509 Istanbul earthquake
    b. Natural gas17
    c. Undefined
    d. Undefined

49. _____ is a chemical element in the periodic table that has the symbol H and atomic number 1. At standard temperature and pressure it is a colorless, odorless, nonmetallic, univalent, tasteless, highly flammable diatomic gas.
    a. Hydrogen17
    b. Thing
    c. Undefined
    d. Undefined

50. _____ is a chemical element; it is a colorless, odorless, tasteless, non-toxic, and nearly inert monatomic that heads the noble gas series in the periodic table. Its atomic number is 2 and its boiling and melting points are the lowest among the elements. It exists only as a gas except in extreme conditions.
    a. Thing
    b. Helium17
    c. Undefined
    d. Undefined

51. A mineral deposit that can be mined for a profit is called _____.
    a. AASHTO Soil Classification System
    b. Ore17
    c. Undefined
    d. Undefined

52. _____ is a chemical element in the periodic table that has the symbol Cu (L.: Cuprum) and atomic number 29. It is a ductile metal with excellent electrical conductivity, and finds extensive use as a building material, as an electrical conductor, and as a component of various alloys.
    a. Thing
    b. Copper17
    c. Undefined
    d. Undefined

53. _____ is a metallic chemical element in the periodic table that has the symbol Ni and atomic number 28. Notable characteristicsNickel is a silvery white metal that takes on a high polish. It belongs to the iron group, and is hard, malleable, and ductile. It occurs combined with sulfur in millerite, with arsenic in the mineral niccolite, and with arsenic and sulfur in _____ glance.
    a. Thing
    b. Nickel17
    c. Undefined
    d. Undefined

54. _____ is a chemical element in the periodic table that has the symbol Au and atomic number 79. A soft, shiny, yellow, dense, malleable, ductile (trivalent and univalent) transition metal, _____ does not react with most chemicals but is attacked by chlorine, fluorine and aqua regia.
    a. Thing
    b. Gold17
    c. Undefined
    d. Undefined

55. A body of rock identified by lithic characteristics and stratigraphic position and is mappable at the earth's surface or traceable in the subsurface is a _____.
    a. 1509 Istanbul earthquake
    b. Formation17
    c. Undefined
    d. Undefined

Chapter 17. Earth's Interior and Geophysical Properties

56. A naturally occurring, usually inorganic, solid consisting of either a single element or a compound, and having a definite chemical composition and a systematic internal arrangement of atoms is referred to as a _____.
    a. Mineral17
    b. 1509 Istanbul earthquake
    c. Undefined
    d. Undefined

57. The point on the Earth's surface that is located directly above the focus of an earthquake is referred to as _____.
    a. AASHTO Soil Classification System
    b. Epicenter17
    c. Undefined
    d. Undefined

58. The initial point within the Earth that ruptures in an earthquake, directly below the epicenter is called the _____.
    a. 1509 Istanbul earthquake
    b. Focus17
    c. Undefined
    d. Undefined

59. _____ refers to earth's crust, which is formed at mid-oceanic ridges, typically 5 to 10 kilometers thick with a density of 3.0 grams per centimeter cubed.
    a. AASHTO Soil Classification System
    b. Oceanic crust17
    c. Undefined
    d. Undefined

60. A compressional wave in which rock vibrates parallel to the direction of wave propagation is referred to as the _____.
    a. P wave17
    b. 1509 Istanbul earthquake
    c. Undefined
    d. Undefined

61. An intrusive rock formed inside the Earth is referred to as a _____.
    a. Plutonic rock17
    b. 1509 Istanbul earthquake
    c. Undefined
    d. Undefined

62. Describing a substance in which the atoms are arranged in a regular, repeating, orderly pattern is called _____.
    a. 1509 Istanbul earthquake
    b. Crystalline17
    c. Undefined
    d. Undefined

63. _____ refers to igneous rocks formed beneath the surface of the Earth; typically with large crystals due to the slowness of cooling.
    a. 1509 Istanbul earthquake
    b. Plutonic17
    c. Undefined
    d. Undefined

64. A coarse-grained, strongly foliated metamorphic rock that develops from phyllite and splits easily into flat, parallel slabs is _____.
    a. Schist17
    b. 1509 Istanbul earthquake
    c. Undefined
    d. Undefined

65. _____ is the chemical element in the periodic table that has the symbol Mg and atomic number 12 and an atomic mass of 24.31.
    a. Thing
    b. Magnesium17
    c. Undefined
    d. Undefined

66. _____ is the chemical element in the periodic table that has the symbol Si and atomic number 14. It is the second most abundant element in the Earth's crust, making up 25.7% of it by weight.
   a. Silicon17
   b. Thing
   c. Undefined
   d. Undefined

67. _____ refers to a term used to describe the amount of light-colored feldspar and silica minerals in an igneous rock.
   a. 1509 Istanbul earthquake
   b. Felsic17
   c. Undefined
   d. Undefined

68. _____ refers to a term used to describe the amount of dark-colored iron and magnesium minerals in an igneous rock.
   a. Mafic17
   b. 1509 Istanbul earthquake
   c. Undefined
   d. Undefined

69. _____ is essential to all organisms, except for a few bacteria. It is mostly stably incorporated in the inside of metalloproteins, because in exposed or in free form it causes production of free radicals that are generally toxic to cells.
   a. Thing
   b. Iron17
   c. Undefined
   d. Undefined

70. A primary, or compression, body seismic wave that travels through the depth of the earth is called a _____.
   a. P-wave17
   b. 1509 Istanbul earthquake
   c. Undefined
   d. Undefined

71. _____ refers to the upper portion of the mantle extending from the Moho to a depth of 400km.
   a. AASHTO Soil Classification System
   b. Upper mantle17
   c. Undefined
   d. Undefined

72. The subterranean cavity containing the gas-rich liquid magma, which feeds a volcano, is a _____.
   a. Magma chamber17
   b. 1509 Istanbul earthquake
   c. Undefined
   d. Undefined

73. Molten rock that forms naturally within the Earth is _____. _____ may be either a liquid or a fluid mixture of liquid, crystals, and dissolved gases.
   a. Magma17
   b. 1509 Istanbul earthquake
   c. Undefined
   d. Undefined

74. Rock composed entirely or almost entirely of ferromagnesian minerals is referred to as _____.
   a. Ultramafic rock17
   b. AASHTO Soil Classification System
   c. Undefined
   d. Undefined

75. _____ refers to a tentative explanation of a given set of data that is expected to remain valid after future observation and experimentation.
   a. 1509 Istanbul earthquake
   b. Hypothesis17
   c. Undefined
   d. Undefined

Chapter 17. Earth`s Interior and Geophysical Properties

76. _____ refers to igneous rocks made mostly of the mafic minerals hypersthene, augite, and/or olivine.
    a. Ultramafic17
    b. AASHTO Soil Classification System
    c. Undefined
    d. Undefined

77. An igneous rock composed primarily of the iron-magnesium silicate olivine and having a silica content of less than 40% is _____.
    a. 1509 Istanbul earthquake
    b. Peridotite17
    c. Undefined
    d. Undefined

78. Iron/magnesium bearing mineral, such as augite, hornblende, olivine, or biotite is a _____.
    a. Ferromagnesian mineral17
    b. 1509 Istanbul earthquake
    c. Undefined
    d. Undefined

79. _____ refers to minerals or rocks that are rich in iron and magnesium, such as olivine and pyroxene.
    a. 1509 Istanbul earthquake
    b. Ferromagnesian17
    c. Undefined
    d. Undefined

80. A _____ is formed when molten rock (magma) cools and solidifies, with or without crystallization, either below the surface as intrusive (plutonic) rocks or on the surface as extrusive (volcanic) rocks. This magma can be derived from either the Earth's mantle or pre-existing rocks made molten by extreme temperature and pressure changes.
    a. Thing
    b. Igneous rock17
    c. Undefined
    d. Undefined

81. A ferromagnesian mineral is _____.
    a. Olivine17
    b. AASHTO Soil Classification System
    c. Undefined
    d. Undefined

82. An area within the Earth's upper mantle in which both P waves and S waves travel at markedly slower velocities than in the outermost part of the upper mantle is the _____. The _____ occurs in the range between 100 and 350 kilometers of depth.
    a. 1509 Istanbul earthquake
    b. Low-velocity zone17
    c. Undefined
    d. Undefined

83. _____ is a solid in which the constituent atoms, molecules, or ions are packed in a regularly ordered, repeating pattern extending in all three spatial dimensions.
    a. Thing
    b. Crystal17
    c. Undefined
    d. Undefined

84. _____ refers to a body wave that causes the rocks along which it passes to move up and down perpendicular to the direction of its own movement.
    a. 1509 Istanbul earthquake
    b. S wave17
    c. Undefined
    d. Undefined

85. The process whereby a computer first synthesizes data on the velocities of seismic waves from thousands of recent earthquakes to make a series of images depicting successive planes within the Earth, and then uses these images to construct a three-dimensional representation of the Earth's interior is referred to as _____.

Chapter 17. Earth's Interior and Geophysical Properties

a. Seismic tomography17
b. 1509 Istanbul earthquake
c. Undefined
d. Undefined

86. An area in the upper mantle, ranging from 100 to 200 kilometers in width, from which magma rises in a plume to form volcanoes. A _____ may endure for 10 million years or more.
a. 1509 Istanbul earthquake
b. Hot spot17
c. Undefined
d. Undefined

87. _____ refers to a giant mountain range that lies under the ocean and extends around the world.
a. Mid-oceanic ridge17
b. 1509 Istanbul earthquake
c. Undefined
d. Undefined

88. The region that extends from 103° to 143° from the epicenter of an earthquake and is marked by the absence of P waves is the _____. The _____ is due to the refraction of seismic waves in the liquid outer core.
a. P-wave shadow zone17
b. 1509 Istanbul earthquake
c. Undefined
d. Undefined

89. The zone between 105 and 140 degrees distance from an earthquake epicenter, which direct waves do not penetrate because of refraction by Earth's core, is the _____.
a. Shadow zone17
b. 1509 Istanbul earthquake
c. Undefined
d. Undefined

90. The boundary between the crust and underlying mantle, about 2890 km below the surface, where we encounter the most extreme change in properties found anywhere in Earth's interior is referred to as _____.
a. Core-mantle boundary17
b. 1509 Istanbul earthquake
c. Undefined
d. Undefined

91. _____ refers to the lower and largest portion of the mantle extending from a depth of 670km to 2900km. It composes approximately 50% of the mass of the planet.
a. 1509 Istanbul earthquake
b. Lower mantle17
c. Undefined
d. Undefined

92. _____ refers to a flat thinnish dressed stone.
a. 1509 Istanbul earthquake
b. Slab17
c. Undefined
d. Undefined

93. _____ refers to a mass of hotter-than-normal mantle material that ascends toward the surface, where it may lead to igneous activity. These plumes of solid yet mobile material may originate as deep as the core-mantle boundary.
a. Mantle plume17
b. 1509 Istanbul earthquake
c. Undefined
d. Undefined

94. _____ is the transfer of heat by currents within a fluid. It may arise from temperature differences either within the fluid or between the fluid and its boundary, other sources of density variations (such as variable salinity), or from the application of an external motive force.

Chapter 17. Earth's Interior and Geophysical Properties

a. Convection17   b. Event
c. Undefined   d. Undefined

95. The region within an arc of 154° directly opposite an earthquake's epicenter that is marked by the absence of S waves is the _____. The _____ is due to the fact that S waves cannot penetrate the liquid outer core.
  a. 1509 Istanbul earthquake
  b. S-wave shadow zone17
  c. Undefined
  d. Undefined

96. _____ refers to a secondary, or shear, body seismic wave that travels through the depth of the Earth. S-waves can only be transmitted by solids.
  a. S-wave17
  b. 1509 Istanbul earthquake
  c. Undefined
  d. Undefined

97. A chemical _____, often called simply _____, is a chemical substance that cannot be divided or changed into other chemical substances by any ordinary chemical technique. An _____ is a class of substances that contain the same number of protons in all its atoms.
  a. Thing
  b. Element17
  c. Undefined
  d. Undefined

98. _____ is the chemical element in the periodic table that has the symbol S and atomic number 16. It is an abundant, tasteless, odorless, multivalent non-metal. _____, in its native form, is a yellow crystaline solid. In nature, it can be found as the pure element or as sulfide and sulfate minerals.
  a. Sulfur17
  b. Thing
  c. Undefined
  d. Undefined

99. _____ is a chemical element in the periodic table. It has the symbol O and atomic number 8. _____ is the second most common element on Earth, composing around 46% of the mass of Earth's crust and 28% of the mass of Earth as a whole, and is the third most common element in the universe.
  a. Oxygen17
  b. Thing
  c. Undefined
  d. Undefined

100. Earth's _____ is a layer of gases surrounding the planet Earth and retained by the Earth's gravity. It contains roughly 78% nitrogen and 21% oxygen, with trace amounts of other gases.
  a. Thing
  b. Atmosphere17
  c. Undefined
  d. Undefined

101. _____ refers to the luminous phenomenon observed when a meteoroid enters Earth's atmosphere and burns up; popularly called a 'shooting star'.
  a. Meteor17
  b. 1509 Istanbul earthquake
  c. Undefined
  d. Undefined

102. _____ refers to one of the three main categories of meteorites. Such meteorites are composed largely of silicate minerals with inclusions of other minerals.
  a. 1509 Istanbul earthquake
  b. Stony meteorite17
  c. Undefined
  d. Undefined

103. _____ refers to one of the three main categories of meteorites. This group is composed largely of iron with varying amounts of nickel. Most meteorite finds are irons.
- a. Iron meteorite17
- b. AASHTO Soil Classification System
- c. Undefined
- d. Undefined

104. _____ refers to one of the three main categories of meteorites. This group, as the name implies, is a mixture of iron and silicate minerals.
- a. Stony-iron meteorite17
- b. 1509 Istanbul earthquake
- c. Undefined
- d. Undefined

105. Any one of numerous minerals that have the silicon-oxygen tetrahedron as their basic structure is called _____.
- a. 1509 Istanbul earthquake
- b. Silicate mineral17
- c. Undefined
- d. Undefined

106. One of several rock-forming minerals that contain silicon, oxygen, and usually one or more other common elements is _____.
- a. Silicate17
- b. 1509 Istanbul earthquake
- c. Undefined
- d. Undefined

107. A metal that is manufactured by combining two or more molten metals is called _____. An _____ is always harder than its component metals. Bronze is an _____ of copper and tin.
- a. Alloy17
- b. AASHTO Soil Classification System
- c. Undefined
- d. Undefined

108. _____ refer to small nuggets of rocky material that exist in certain meteorites. These droplets of matter are believed to have condensed from our solar system's original nebula about five billion years ago. Their primary element is iron.
- a. 1509 Istanbul earthquake
- b. Chondrules17
- c. Undefined
- d. Undefined

109. Round silicate grain within some stony meteorites is referred to as _____.
- a. 1509 Istanbul earthquake
- b. Chondrule17
- c. Undefined
- d. Undefined

110. A type of primitive stoney meteorite containing chondrules, quenched droplets of early condensates from the solar nebula is called _____.
- a. 1509 Istanbul earthquake
- b. Chondrite17
- c. Undefined
- d. Undefined

111. A chemical compound composed only of the elements carbon and hydrogen is called _____.
- a. Hydrocarbon17
- b. Thing
- c. Undefined
- d. Undefined

112. An _____ is any molecule that contains both amino and carboxylic acid functional groups. They are the basic structural building units of proteins. They form short polymer chains called peptides or polypeptides which in turn form structures called proteins.

Chapter 17. Earth's Interior and Geophysical Properties

    a. Thing   b. Amino acid17
    c. Undefined   d. Undefined

113. An igneous rock rich in magnesium that forms soils toxic to many plants is called _____. Soils derived from _____ are toxic to many plants due to their high mineral content, and the flora is generally very distinctive, with specialized, slow-growing species.
    a. Thing   b. Serpentine17
    c. Undefined   d. Undefined

114. An electrically neutral substance that consists of two or more elements combined in specific, constant proportions is a _____. A _____ typically has physical characteristics different from those of its constituent elements.
    a. Compound17   b. 1509 Istanbul earthquake
    c. Undefined   d. Undefined

115. _____ is a chemical element in the periodic table that has the symbol C and atomic number 6. An abundant nonmetallic, tetravalent element, _____ has several allotropic forms.
    a. Thing   b. Carbon17
    c. Undefined   d. Undefined

116. An _____ is a water-soluble, sour-tasting chemical compound that when dissolved in water, gives a solution with a pH of less than 7.
    a. Acid17   b. Thing
    c. Undefined   d. Undefined

117. An _____ is any member of a large class of chemical compounds whose molecules contain carbon, with the exception of carbides, carbonates, carbon oxides and gases containing carbon.
    a. Thing   b. Organic compound17
    c. Undefined   d. Undefined

118. A steep-sided, usually circular depression formed by either explosion or collapse at a volcanic vent is a _____.
    a. Crater17   b. 1509 Istanbul earthquake
    c. Undefined   d. Undefined

119. Stony meteorite containing chondrules and composed mostly of serpentine and large quantities of organic materials is _____.
    a. Carbonaceous chondrite17   b. 1509 Istanbul earthquake
    c. Undefined   d. Undefined

120. Rocks that crystallize from molten material at the surface of the earth or within the earth are called _____.
    a. AASHTO Soil Classification System   b. Igneous rocks17
    c. Undefined   d. Undefined

121. A clastic rock composed of particles more than 2 millimeters in diameter and marked by the angularity of its component grains and rock fragments is called _____.

Chapter 17. Earth's Interior and Geophysical Properties

a. Breccia17
b. 1509 Istanbul earthquake
c. Undefined
d. Undefined

122. Any small, solid particle that has an orbit in the solar system is a _____.
a. Meteoroid17
b. 1509 Istanbul earthquake
c. Undefined
d. Undefined

123. Determining the age of a rock or mineral through its radioactive elements and decay products is referred to as _____.
a. Isotopic dating17
b. AASHTO Soil Classification System
c. Undefined
d. Undefined

124. _____ refers to the seismic discontinuity located in the upper mantle just beneath the asthenosphere and characterized by a marked increase in the velocity of seismic waves.
a. Transition zone17
b. 1509 Istanbul earthquake
c. Undefined
d. Undefined

125. The outer portion of the core of the earth, which is composed of liquid iron-nickel metal is called the _____.
a. AASHTO Soil Classification System
b. Outer core17
c. Undefined
d. Undefined

126. _____ is any particulate matter that can be transported by fluid flow and which eventually is deposited as a layer of solid particles on the bed or bottom of a body of water or other liquid.
a. Thing
b. Sediment17
c. Undefined
d. Undefined

127. An _____ is a form of an element whose nuclei have the same atomic number - the number of protons in the nucleus - but different mass numbers because they contain different numbers of neutrons.
a. Thing
b. Isotope17
c. Undefined
d. Undefined

128. Angular chunk of solid rock ejected during an eruption is referred to as a _____.
a. Block17
b. 1509 Istanbul earthquake
c. Undefined
d. Undefined

129. A feature found in caves that is formed when a stalactite and stalagmite join is referred to as a _____.
a. Column17
b. 1509 Istanbul earthquake
c. Undefined
d. Undefined

130. A large mass of rock projecting above surrounding terrain is called a _____.
a. 1509 Istanbul earthquake
b. Mountain17
c. Undefined
d. Undefined

131. The rise of Earth's crust after the removal of glacial ice is referred to as _____.

a. Crustal rebound17
b. 1509 Istanbul earthquake
c. Undefined
d. Undefined

132. A fluid's resistance to flow is called _____. _____ increases as temperatures decreases.
a. Viscosity17
b. 1509 Istanbul earthquake
c. Undefined
d. Undefined

133. A moving body of ice that forms on land from the accumulation and compaction of snow, and that flows downslope or outward due to gravity and the pressure of its own weight is a _____.
a. Glacier17
b. 1509 Istanbul earthquake
c. Undefined
d. Undefined

134. The liquid portion of magma excluding the solid crystals is called _____.
a. Melt17
b. 1509 Istanbul earthquake
c. Undefined
d. Undefined

135. A type of glacial movement that occurs within the glacier, below a depth of approximately 50 meters, in which the ice is not fractured, is referred to as _____.
a. 1509 Istanbul earthquake
b. Plastic flow17
c. Undefined
d. Undefined

136. Concept of vertical movement of sections of Earth's crust to achieve balance or equilibrium is referred to as _____.
a. AASHTO Soil Classification System
b. Isostatic adjustment17
c. Undefined
d. Undefined

137. An unconfined glacier that covers much or all of a continent is referred to as _____.
a. Continental ice sheet17
b. 1509 Istanbul earthquake
c. Undefined
d. Undefined

138. The first epoch of the Quaternary Period, beginning 2 to 3 million years ago and ending approximately 10,000 years ago is referred to as the _____.
a. Pleistocene epoch17
b. 1509 Istanbul earthquake
c. Undefined
d. Undefined

139. A geologic epoch, characterized by alternating glacial and interglacial stages, that ended about 10,000 years ago, that lasted for 2 million years is called the _____ epoch.
a. Pleistocene17
b. Thing
c. Undefined
d. Undefined

140. _____ refers to a glacier of considerable thickness and more than 50,000 square kilometers in area, forming a continuous cover of snow and ice over a land surface, spreading outward in all directions and not confined by the underlying topography. Ice sheets are now confined to Polar Regions, but during the Pleistocene Epoch they covered large parts of North America and northern Europe.

Chapter 17. Earth's Interior and Geophysical Properties

a. AASHTO Soil Classification System
b. Ice sheet17
c. Undefined
d. Undefined

141. A unit of the geologic time scale that is a subdivision of a period is referred to as an _____.
a. Epoch17
b. AASHTO Soil Classification System
c. Undefined
d. Undefined

142. _____ refers to the period of Earth's history from about 2 million years ago to the present; also, the rocks and deposits of that age.
a. Quaternary17
b. 1509 Istanbul earthquake
c. Undefined
d. Undefined

143. _____ refers to a group of closely spaced mountains or parallel ridges.
a. 1509 Istanbul earthquake
b. Mountain range17
c. Undefined
d. Undefined

144. The zone of convergence of two tectonic plates, one of which usually overrides the other is referred to as the _____.
a. Subduction zone17
b. 1509 Istanbul earthquake
c. Undefined
d. Undefined

145. The downward movement of a plate into the mantle that occurs in trenches, which are also known as _____ zones.
a. Thing
b. Subduction17
c. Undefined
d. Undefined

146. _____ refers both to animals and plants, of having a resemblance in structure, due to descent from a common progenitor with subsequent modification.
a. Thing
b. Homogeneous17
c. Undefined
d. Undefined

147. An instrument that measures the gravitational attraction between Earth and a mass within the instrument is referred to as _____.
a. Gravity meter17
b. 1509 Istanbul earthquake
c. Undefined
d. Undefined

148. The time between winter and summer is _____.
a. Spring17
b. 1509 Istanbul earthquake
c. Undefined
d. Undefined

149. A hole or opening, as at the bed of a glacier is a _____. When the rate of deformation into a space behind an obstacle is less the rate of movement past the obstacle, a _____ will form.
a. Cavity17
b. 1509 Istanbul earthquake
c. Undefined
d. Undefined

Chapter 17. Earth's Interior and Geophysical Properties

150. _____ refers to a naturally formed opening beneath the surface of the Earth, generally formed by dissolution of carbonate bedrock. Caves may also form by erosion of coastal bedrock, partial melting of glaciers, or solidification of lava into hollow tubes.
    a. Cave17
    b. 1509 Istanbul earthquake
    c. Undefined
    d. Undefined

151. The same as a mineral reserve except that it refers only to a metal-bearing deposit is referred to as _____.
    a. AASHTO Soil Classification System
    b. Ore deposit17
    c. Undefined
    d. Undefined

152. Material is in _____ if it is adjusted to the physical and chemical conditions of its environment so that it does not change or alter with time.
    a. AASHTO Soil Classification System
    b. Equilibrium17
    c. Undefined
    d. Undefined

153. Forces generated from within Earth that result in uplift, movement, or deformations of part of Earth's crust are called _____.
    a. 1509 Istanbul earthquake
    b. Tectonic forces17
    c. Undefined
    d. Undefined

154. The top of the ocean, where the water meets the atmosphere is called _____.
    a. 1509 Istanbul earthquake
    b. Sea level17
    c. Undefined
    d. Undefined

155. _____ refers to the altitude, or vertical distance, above or below sea level.
    a. AASHTO Soil Classification System
    b. Elevation17
    c. Undefined
    d. Undefined

156. A greater than normal gravitational attraction is referred to as a _____.
    a. Positive gravity anomaly17
    b. 1509 Istanbul earthquake
    c. Undefined
    d. Undefined

157. The difference between an actual measurement of gravity at a given location and the measurement predicted by theoretical calculation is called _____.
    a. 1509 Istanbul earthquake
    b. Gravity anomaly17
    c. Undefined
    d. Undefined

158. A deviation from the average or expected value is an _____. In paleomagnetism, a 'positive' _____ is a stronger-than-average magnetic field at the earth's surface.
    a. Anomaly17
    b. AASHTO Soil Classification System
    c. Undefined
    d. Undefined

159. _____ refers to less than normal gravitational attraction.
    a. Negative gravity anomaly17
    b. 1509 Istanbul earthquake
    c. Undefined
    d. Undefined

Chapter 17. Earth's Interior and Geophysical Properties

160. Uplift of the crust of the earth that results from unloading such as results from the melting of ice sheets is an _____.
   a. AASHTO Soil Classification System
   b. Isostatic rebound17
   c. Undefined
   d. Undefined

161. An area where the strength of the magnetic field is greatest and where the magnetic lines of force appear to leave or enter Earth is called the _____.
   a. 1509 Istanbul earthquake
   b. Magnetic pole17
   c. Undefined
   d. Undefined

162. The property, possessed by certain materials, to attract or repel similar materials is _____. _____ is associated with moving electricity.
   a. 1509 Istanbul earthquake
   b. Magnetism17
   c. Undefined
   d. Undefined

163. The process by which the Earth's magnetic north pole and its magnetic south pole reverse their positions over time is referred to as _____.
   a. 1509 Istanbul earthquake
   b. Magnetic reversal17
   c. Undefined
   d. Undefined

164. The magnetic positive or negative character of a magnetic pole is called _____.
   a. Polarity17
   b. 1509 Istanbul earthquake
   c. Undefined
   d. Undefined

165. _____ refers to a magnetic field the same as that which presently exists.
   a. Normal polarity17
   b. 1509 Istanbul earthquake
   c. Undefined
   d. Undefined

166. _____ is a ferrimagnetic mineral form of iron(II,III) oxide, with chemical formula Fe_3O_4, one of several iron oxides and a member of the spinel group.
   a. Thing
   b. Magnetite17
   c. Undefined
   d. Undefined

167. _____ refers to an outpouring of lava onto the land surface from a vent or fissure. Also, a solidified tongue like or sheet-like body formed by outpouring lava.
   a. 1509 Istanbul earthquake
   b. Lava flow17
   c. Undefined
   d. Undefined

168. More or less straight row of standing stone is called an _____.
   a. AASHTO Soil Classification System
   b. Alignment17
   c. Undefined
   d. Undefined

169. An _____ is the smallest possible particle of a chemical element that retains its chemical properties.
   a. Thing
   b. Atom17
   c. Undefined
   d. Undefined

Chapter 17. Earth's Interior and Geophysical Properties

170. Magma that comes to the Earth's surface through a volcano or fissure is referred to as _____.
    a. Lava17
    b. 1509 Istanbul earthquake
    c. Undefined
    d. Undefined

171. The temperature above which a material loses its magnetization is called the _____.
    a. Curie point17
    b. 1509 Istanbul earthquake
    c. Undefined
    d. Undefined

172. _____ refers to the record of the changing direction of Earth's magnetic field as stored in lava flows. Used to accurately date extremely ancient events.
    a. Thing
    b. Paleomagnetism17
    c. Undefined
    d. Undefined

173. _____ refers to a basic unit of the geologic time scale that is a subdivision of an era. Periods may be divided into smaller units called epochs.
    a. Period17
    b. 1509 Istanbul earthquake
    c. Undefined
    d. Undefined

174. _____ refers to wind or water currents promoted by the fact that warming causes expansion, decreases density, and thus causes the warmer air or water to rise. Conversely, the cooler air or water sinks.
    a. Thing
    b. Convection currents17
    c. Undefined
    d. Undefined

175. _____ refers to one of thousands of small planetlike bodies, ranging in size from a few hundred kilometers to less than one kilometer across. Most asteroids' orbits lie between those of Mars and Jupiter.
    a. AASHTO Soil Classification System
    b. Asteroid17
    c. Undefined
    d. Undefined

176. _____ refers to an object which circles the sun in a non-circular orbit. Commonly made up of a large mass of rock debris and ice.
    a. Comet17
    b. 1509 Istanbul earthquake
    c. Undefined
    d. Undefined

177. A design carved or chipped out on the slabs of Breton tombs is a _____. It is a highly version of an antropomorphic figure.
    a. 1509 Istanbul earthquake
    b. Shield17
    c. Undefined
    d. Undefined

178. Bright streaks that appear to radiate from certain craters on the lunar surface are _____. The _____ consist of fine debris ejected from the primary crater.
    a. 1509 Istanbul earthquake
    b. Rays17
    c. Undefined
    d. Undefined

179. In biology and ecology, _____ is the ceasing of existence of a species or group of taxa. The moment of _____ is generally considered to be the death of the last individual of that species. The death of all members of a species is _____.

a. Thing
b. Extinction17
c. Undefined
d. Undefined

180. The intermediate era of the Phanerozoic Eon, following the Paleozoic Era and preceding the Cenozoic Era, and marked by the dominance of marine and terrestrial reptiles, and the appearance of birds, mammals, and flowering plants is a _____.
a. Mesozoic Era17
b. 1509 Istanbul earthquake
c. Undefined
d. Undefined

181. The _____ is one of three geologic eras of the Phanerozoic eon. The division of time into eras dates back to Giovanni Arduino in the 18th century, although his original name for the era now called the _____ was "Secondary".
a. Thing
b. Mesozoic17
c. Undefined
d. Undefined

182. The relationship between distance on a map and the distance on the terrain being represented by that map is a _____.
a. 1509 Istanbul earthquake
b. Scale17
c. Undefined
d. Undefined

183. _____ refers to a major division on the geologic time scale; eras are divided into shorter units called periods.
a. Era17
b. AASHTO Soil Classification System
c. Undefined
d. Undefined

184. _____ refers to a magnetic field opposite to that which presently exists.
a. 1509 Istanbul earthquake
b. Reverse polarity17
c. Undefined
d. Undefined

185. A sensitive instrument used to measure the intensity of Earth's magnetic field at various points is referred to as a _____.
a. Magnetometer17
b. 1509 Istanbul earthquake
c. Undefined
d. Undefined

186. The innermost portion of the core, which is composed, of solid iron-nickel metal is the _____.
a. AASHTO Soil Classification System
b. Inner core17
c. Undefined
d. Undefined

187. Gravity is called the _____.
a. Driving force17
b. 1509 Istanbul earthquake
c. Undefined
d. Undefined

188. The mechanism that sustains Earth's magnetic field, essentially driven by convection in the outer core is called _____.
a. 1509 Istanbul earthquake
b. Geodynamo17
c. Undefined
d. Undefined

189. Scientists who study earthquake waves and what they tell us about the inside of the Earth are called a _____.

a. 1509 Istanbul earthquake
b. Seismologist17
c. Undefined
d. Undefined

190. A mineral or fuel deposit, known or not yet discovered, that may be or become available for human exploitation is called a _____.
   a. 1509 Istanbul earthquake
   b. Resource17
   c. Undefined
   d. Undefined

191. _____ refers to magnetic bands in the sea floor that run parallel to the mid-ocean ridge .
   a. Thing
   b. Magnetic anomalies17
   c. Undefined
   d. Undefined

192. _____ refers to greater than average strength of the Earth's magnetic field.
   a. 1509 Istanbul earthquake
   b. Positive magnetic anomaly17
   c. Undefined
   d. Undefined

193. A deviation from the average strength of Earth's magnetic field is a _____.
   a. 1509 Istanbul earthquake
   b. Magnetic anomaly17
   c. Undefined
   d. Undefined

194. _____ is a sedimentary rock composed largely of the mineral calcite (calcium carbonate: $CaCO_3$). _____ often contains variable amounts of silica in the form of chert or flint, as well as varying amounts of clay, silt and sand as disseminations, nodules, or layers within the rock.
   a. Thing
   b. Limestone17
   c. Undefined
   d. Undefined

195. Usually slow but effective process of weathering and erosion in which rocks are dissolved by water is a _____.
   a. 1509 Istanbul earthquake
   b. Solution17
   c. Undefined
   d. Undefined

196. _____ refers to any of a group of dark, dense, phaneritic, intrusive rocks that are the plutonic equivalent to basalt.
   a. 1509 Istanbul earthquake
   b. Gabbro17
   c. Undefined
   d. Undefined

197. _____ refers to a discordant pluton that is substantially wider than it is thick. Dikes are often steeply inclined or nearly vertical.
   a. Dike17
   b. 1509 Istanbul earthquake
   c. Undefined
   d. Undefined

198. Less than average strength of Earth's magnetic field is _____.
   a. Negative magnetic anomaly17
   b. 1509 Istanbul earthquake
   c. Undefined
   d. Undefined

199. _____ refers to a block of rock that lies between two faults and has moved downward to form a depression between the two adjacent fault blocks.

Chapter 17. Earth`s Interior and Geophysical Properties

    a. Graben17
    b. 1509 Istanbul earthquake
    c. Undefined
    d. Undefined

200. A section of rock separated from other rock by one or more faults is referred to as _____.
    a. Fault block17
    b. 1509 Istanbul earthquake
    c. Undefined
    d. Undefined

201. A fracture dividing a rock into two sections that have visibly moved relative to each other is a _____.
    a. Fault17
    b. 1509 Istanbul earthquake
    c. Undefined
    d. Undefined

202. _____ refers to the gradual increase in temperature with depth in the crust. The average is 30°C per kilometer in the upper crust.
    a. 1509 Istanbul earthquake
    b. Geothermal gradient17
    c. Undefined
    d. Undefined

203. _____ is the naturally hot interior of Earth. The heat is maintained by naturally occurring nuclear reactions in Earth's interior.
    a. Thing
    b. Geothermal17
    c. Undefined
    d. Undefined

204. The vertical drop in a stream's elevation over a given horizontal distance, expressed as an angle is referred to as a _____.
    a. 1509 Istanbul earthquake
    b. Gradient17
    c. Undefined
    d. Undefined

205. Gradual loss of heat from Earth's interior out into space is called _____.
    a. 1509 Istanbul earthquake
    b. Heat flow17
    c. Undefined
    d. Undefined

206. When refined, _____ is a silvery white, weakly radioactive metal, which is slightly softer than steel. It is malleable, ductile, and slightly paramagnetic. _____ metal has very high density, 65% more dense than lead, but slightly less dense than gold. When finely divided, it can react with cold water; in air, _____ metal becomes coated with _____ oxide.
    a. Thing
    b. Uranium17
    c. Undefined
    d. Undefined

207. A term used to describe the property of releasing energy or particles from an unstable atom is called _____.
    a. Thing
    b. Radioactive17
    c. Undefined
    d. Undefined

208. _____ refer to varieties of the same element that have different mass numbers; their nuclei contain the same number of protons but different numbers of neutrons.
    a. Isotopes17
    b. AASHTO Soil Classification System
    c. Undefined
    d. Undefined

Chapter 17. Earth's Interior and Geophysical Properties

209. _____ refers to the spontaneous decay of certain unstable atomic nuclei.
 a. 1509 Istanbul earthquake
 b. Radioactive decay17
 c. Undefined
 d. Undefined

210. _____ refers to the boundary between the crust and the mantle, at a depth of 5 to 45 km, marked by an abrupt increase in P-wave velocity to more than 8 km/s.
 a. 1509 Istanbul earthquake
 b. Mohorovicic discontinuity17
 c. Undefined
 d. Undefined

211. _____ refers to a sudden change with depth in one or more of the physical properties of the material making up Earth's interior. The boundary between two dissimilar materials in Earth's interior as determined by the behavior of seismic waves.
 a. Discontinuity17
 b. 1509 Istanbul earthquake
 c. Undefined
 d. Undefined

212. The equilibrium maintained between the gravity tending to depress and the buoyancy tending to raise a given segment of the lithosphere as it floats above the asthenosphere is called _____.
 a. Isostasy17
 b. AASHTO Soil Classification System
 c. Undefined
 d. Undefined

213. Compacted and intergrown mass of crystalline ice with a density is _____.
 a. Glacial ice17
 b. 1509 Istanbul earthquake
 c. Undefined
 d. Undefined

214. _____ is a term used in geology, engineering and surveying to denote the motion of a surface (usually, the earth's surface) downwards relative to a datum such as sea-level.
 a. Subsidence17
 b. Thing
 c. Undefined
 d. Undefined

215. _____ refers to a place in which water is stored, including the oceans, glaciers and polar ice, groundwater, lakes and rivers, the atmosphere, and the biosphere. A source or place of residence for elements in a chemical cycle or hydrologic cycle.
 a. 1509 Istanbul earthquake
 b. Reservoir17
 c. Undefined
 d. Undefined

Chapter 18. The Sea Floor

1. _____ in physical geography, describes the collective mass of water found on, under, and over the surface of a planet.
   a. Thing
   b. Hydrosphere18
   c. Undefined
   d. Undefined

2. _____ state that earth is made up of four basic systems: the lithosphere, the hydrosphere, the atmosphere, and the biosphere. These systems interact to produce most of the geological processes that occur on Earth. An event involving one of these systems may affect some or all of the others.
   a. AASHTO Soil Classification System
   b. Earth systems18
   c. Undefined
   d. Undefined

3. All the parts of our planet and all their interactions, taken together is an _____.
   a. Earth system18
   b. AASHTO Soil Classification System
   c. Undefined
   d. Undefined

4. _____ is a term denoting the solid body of the Earth (i.e. the hydrosphere, lithosphere [including pedosphere] and in some definitions also the internal part of the Earth) and the atmosphere of the Earth.
   a. Geosphere18
   b. Thing
   c. Undefined
   d. Undefined

5. The _____ is that part of a planet's outer shell — including air, land, surface rocks and water — within which life occurs, and which biotic processes in turn alter or transform.
   a. Thing
   b. Biosphere18
   c. Undefined
   d. Undefined

6. A type of coral reef that develops at some distance from the coast creating a lagoon between itself and the coast is called a _____.
   a. Thing
   b. Barrier reef18
   c. Undefined
   d. Undefined

7. _____ refers to a ridge-like or mound-like structure, layered or massive, built by sedentary calcareous organisms; it is wave resistant and stands above the surrounding contemporaneously deposited sediment.
   a. Reef18
   b. 1509 Istanbul earthquake
   c. Undefined
   d. Undefined

8. The _____ is the lowest layer in an ocean, existing below the thermocline. The _____ is not well mixed, consists of horizontal layers of equal density, and is often as cold as -1 to 4 degrees Celsius. Ninety percent of the total volume of Earth's oceans is found in the _____.
   a. Deep ocean18
   b. Thing
   c. Undefined
   d. Undefined

9. _____ refers to elongated rises on the ocean floor where basalt periodically erupts, forming new oceanic crust; similar to continental rift zones.
   a. Mid-oceanic ridges18
   b. 1509 Istanbul earthquake
   c. Undefined
   d. Undefined

10. _____ refers to a giant mountain range that lies under the ocean and extends around the world.

Chapter 18. The Sea Floor

a. Mid-oceanic ridge18
b. 1509 Istanbul earthquake
c. Undefined
d. Undefined

11. _____ refers to the study of the global-scale movements of Earth's crust that have resulted in.
   a. Plate tectonics18
   b. Thing
   c. Undefined
   d. Undefined

12. Deep steep-sided depression in the ocean floor caused by the subduction of oceanic crust beneath either other oceanic crust or continental crust is an _____.
   a. Oceanic trench18
   b. AASHTO Soil Classification System
   c. Undefined
   d. Undefined

13. Linear zone of irregular topography on the deep-ocean floor that follows transform faults and their inactive extensions is called the _____.
   a. Fracture zone18
   b. 1509 Istanbul earthquake
   c. Undefined
   d. Undefined

14. _____ refers to the study of the large-scale processes that collectively deform Earth's crust.
   a. Tectonics18
   b. 1509 Istanbul earthquake
   c. Undefined
   d. Undefined

15. _____ refers to a crack or break in a rock. To break in random places instead of cleaving.
   a. Fracture18
   b. 1509 Istanbul earthquake
   c. Undefined
   d. Undefined

16. An elongated depression in the seafloor produced by bending of oceanic crust during subduction is a _____.
   a. Trench18
   b. 1509 Istanbul earthquake
   c. Undefined
   d. Undefined

17. Aggregates of minerals or rock fragments are called _____.
   a. Rocks18
   b. 1509 Istanbul earthquake
   c. Undefined
   d. Undefined

18. _____ refers to rigid parts of the Earth's crust and part of the Earth's upper mantle that moves and adjoins each other along zones of seismic activity.
   a. Plate18
   b. 1509 Istanbul earthquake
   c. Undefined
   d. Undefined

19. _____ refers to a naturally formed aggregate of usually inorganic materials from within the Earth.
   a. Rock18
   b. 1509 Istanbul earthquake
   c. Undefined
   d. Undefined

20. _____ refers to the mechanism by which the earth is believed to have formed from a small nucleus by additions of solid bodies, such as meteorites, asteroids, or planetesimals. Also used in plate tectonics to indicate the addition of terranes to a continent.

Chapter 18. The Sea Floor

a. Accretion18
b. AASHTO Soil Classification System
c. Undefined
d. Undefined

21. _____ refers to the spontaneous decay of certain unstable atomic nuclei.
a. Radioactive decay18
b. 1509 Istanbul earthquake
c. Undefined
d. Undefined

22. A term used to describe the property of releasing energy or particles from an unstable atom is called _____.
a. Radioactive18
b. Thing
c. Undefined
d. Undefined

23. The diagenetic process by which the volume or thickness of sediment is reduced due to pressure from overlying layers of sediment is called _____.
a. Compaction18
b. 1509 Istanbul earthquake
c. Undefined
d. Undefined

24. When refined, _____ is a silvery white, weakly radioactive metal, which is slightly softer than steel. It is malleable, ductile, and slightly paramagnetic. _____ metal has very high density, 65% more dense than lead, but slightly less dense than gold. When finely divided, it can react with cold water; in air, _____ metal becomes coated with _____ oxide.
a. Thing
b. Uranium18
c. Undefined
d. Undefined

25. A chemical _____, often called simply _____, is a chemical substance that cannot be divided or changed into other chemical substances by any ordinary chemical technique. An _____ is a class of substances that contain the same number of protons in all its atoms.
a. Thing
b. Element18
c. Undefined
d. Undefined

26. The innermost layer of the Earth, consisting primarily of pure metals such as iron and nickel is the _____. The _____ is the densest layer of the Earth, and is divided into the outer _____, which is believed to be liquid, and the inner _____, which is believed to be solid.
a. Core18
b. 1509 Istanbul earthquake
c. Undefined
d. Undefined

27. _____ is essential to all organisms, except for a few bacteria. It is mostly stably incorporated in the inside of metalloproteins, because in exposed or in free form it causes production of free radicals that are generally toxic to cells.
a. Thing
b. Iron18
c. Undefined
d. Undefined

28. _____ refers to water molecules in the gaseous state. Also is one state of the water cycle.
a. Thing
b. Water vapor18
c. Undefined
d. Undefined

29. _____ refers to water in the gaseous state.

Chapter 18. The Sea Floor

  a. 1509 Istanbul earthquake
  b. Vapor18
  c. Undefined
  d. Undefined

30. Magma that comes to the Earth's surface through a volcano or fissure is referred to as _____.
  a. Lava18
  b. 1509 Istanbul earthquake
  c. Undefined
  d. Undefined

31. _____ refers to the change of state of water from the vapor to the liquid phase. Results in liberation of 80 calories per cubic centimeter.
  a. Condensation18
  b. 1509 Istanbul earthquake
  c. Undefined
  d. Undefined

32. _____ refers to the process by which solid, liquid, and gaseous materials are ejected into the earth's atmosphere and onto the earth's surface by volcanic activity. Eruptions range from the quiet overflow of liquid rock to the tremendously violent expulsion of pyroclastics.
  a. AASHTO Soil Classification System
  b. Eruption18
  c. Undefined
  d. Undefined

33. _____ is a common gray to black volcanic rock. It is usually fine-grained due to rapid cooling of lava on the Earth's surface.
  a. Basalt18
  b. Thing
  c. Undefined
  d. Undefined

34. _____ refers to the process by which chemical reactions alter the chemical composition of rocks and minerals that are unstable at the Earth's surface and convert them into more stable substances; weathering that changes the chemical makeup of a rock or mineral.
  a. 1509 Istanbul earthquake
  b. Chemical weathering18
  c. Undefined
  d. Undefined

35. The process by which exposure to atmospheric agents, such as air or moisture, causes rocks and minerals to break down is called _____. This process takes place at or near the Earth's surface. _____ entails little or no movement of the material that it loosens from the rocks and minerals.
  a. Weathering18
  b. 1509 Istanbul earthquake
  c. Undefined
  d. Undefined

36. _____ is the chemical element in the periodic table that has the symbol Mg and atomic number 12 and an atomic mass of 24.31.
  a. Magnesium18
  b. Thing
  c. Undefined
  d. Undefined

37. _____ is the chemical element with atomic number 17 and symbol Cl. It is a halogen, found in the periodic table in group 17. As _____ gas, it is greenish yellow, is two and one half times as heavy as air, has an intensely disagreeable suffocating odor, and is exceedingly poisonous. In its liquid and solid form it is a powerful oxidizing, bleaching, and disinfecting agent.

Chapter 18. The Sea Floor

a. Thing
b. Chlorine18
c. Undefined
d. Undefined

38. A naturally occurring, usually inorganic, solid consisting of either a single element or a compound, and having a definite chemical composition and a systematic internal arrangement of atoms is referred to as a _____.
a. 1509 Istanbul earthquake
b. Mineral18
c. Undefined
d. Undefined

39. _____ is the chemical element in the periodic table that has the symbol Ca and atomic number 20. _____ is a soft grey alkaline earth metal that is used as a reducing agent in the extraction of thorium, zirconium and uranium. _____ is also the fifth most abundant element in the Earth's crust.
a. Calcium18
b. Thing
c. Undefined
d. Undefined

40. _____ is the chemical element in the periodic table that has the symbol Na (Natrium in Latin) and atomic number 11. _____ is a soft, waxy, silvery reactive metal belonging to the alkali metals that is abundant in natural compounds (especially halite). It is highly reactive.
a. Thing
b. Sodium18
c. Undefined
d. Undefined

41. A body of rock identified by lithic characteristics and stratigraphic position and is mappable at the earth's surface or traceable in the subsurface is a _____.
a. 1509 Istanbul earthquake
b. Formation18
c. Undefined
d. Undefined

42. _____ refers to an object which circles the sun in a non-circular orbit. Commonly made up of a large mass of rock debris and ice.
a. Comet18
b. 1509 Istanbul earthquake
c. Undefined
d. Undefined

43. _____ refers to the set of physical features, such as mountains, valleys, and the shapes of landforms, that characterizes a given landscape.
a. Topography18
b. 1509 Istanbul earthquake
c. Undefined
d. Undefined

44. _____ is any particulate matter that can be transported by fluid flow and which eventually is deposited as a layer of solid particles on the bed or bottom of a body of water or other liquid.
a. Sediment18
b. Thing
c. Undefined
d. Undefined

45. _____ refers to a vertical conduit through the Earth's crust below a volcano, through which magmatic materials have passed. Commonly filled with volcanic breccia and fragments of older rock.
a. Pipe18
b. 1509 Istanbul earthquake
c. Undefined
d. Undefined

Chapter 18. The Sea Floor

46. The scientific study of the Earth, its origins and evolution, the materials that make it up, and the processes that act on it is called _____.
    - a. 1509 Istanbul earthquake
    - b. Geology18
    - c. Undefined
    - d. Undefined

47. A _____ is a type of hydrothermal vent found on the ocean floor. Generally hundreds of meters wide, they are formed when superheated water from below the Earth's crust comes through the ocean floor.
    - a. Thing
    - b. Black smoker18
    - c. Undefined
    - d. Undefined

48. An instrument used to determine the depth of water by measuring the time interval between emission of a sound signal and the return of its echo from the bottom is called _____.
    - a. Echo sounder18
    - b. AASHTO Soil Classification System
    - c. Undefined
    - d. Undefined

49. _____ is a chemical element in the periodic table that has the symbol Mn and atomic number 25.
    - a. Manganese18
    - b. Thing
    - c. Undefined
    - d. Undefined

50. The return of part of the energy of seismic waves to Earth's surface after the waves bounce off a rock boundary is referred to as _____.
    - a. 1509 Istanbul earthquake
    - b. Seismic reflection18
    - c. Undefined
    - d. Undefined

51. A measure of the effects of an earthquake at a particular place is called _____. _____ depends not only on the magnitude of the earthquake, but also on the distance from the epicenter and the local geology.
    - a. AASHTO Soil Classification System
    - b. Intensity18
    - c. Undefined
    - d. Undefined

52. The solid structure created when lava, gases, and hot particles escape to the Earth's surface through vents is called a _____. Volcanoes are usually conical. A _____ is 'active' when it is erupting or has erupted recently. Volcanoes that have not erupted recently but are considered likely to erupt in the future are said to be 'dormant.' A _____ that has not erupted for a long time and is not expected to erupt in the future is 'extinct'.
    - a. 1509 Istanbul earthquake
    - b. Volcano18
    - c. Undefined
    - d. Undefined

53. The periodic, rhythmic rise and fall of the sea surface caused by changes in gravitational forces external to the Earth is referred to as the _____.
    - a. Thing
    - b. Tide18
    - c. Undefined
    - d. Undefined

54. A movement within the Earth's crust or mantle, caused by the sudden rupture or repositioning of underground rocks as they release stress is an _____.
    - a. AASHTO Soil Classification System
    - b. Earthquake18
    - c. Undefined
    - d. Undefined

55. _____ refers to a dip-slip fault marked by a generally steep dip along which the hanging wall has moved downward relative to the footwall.
- a. 1509 Istanbul earthquake
- b. Normal fault18
- c. Undefined
- d. Undefined

56. A fracture dividing a rock into two sections that have visibly moved relative to each other is a _____.
- a. Fault18
- b. 1509 Istanbul earthquake
- c. Undefined
- d. Undefined

57. The situation in mass wasting that occurs when material free-falls or bounces down a cliff is called a _____.
- a. Fall18
- b. 1509 Istanbul earthquake
- c. Undefined
- d. Undefined

58. _____ refer to the earthquake generated waves that travel along the outer layer of Earth and are responsible for most of the surface damage. L waves have longer periods than other seismic waves.
- a. Long waves18
- b. 1509 Istanbul earthquake
- c. Undefined
- d. Undefined

59. A _____ is the outer layer of a planet, part of its lithosphere. Planetary _____ is generally composed of a less dense material than that of its deeper layers. The _____ of the Earth is composed mainly of basalt and granite.
- a. Thing
- b. Crust18
- c. Undefined
- d. Undefined

60. The force acting on a rock or another solid to deform it, measured in kilograms per square centimeter or pounds per square inch is _____.
- a. 1509 Istanbul earthquake
- b. Stress18
- c. Undefined
- d. Undefined

61. _____ is a means of electricity generation achieved by capturing the energy contained in moving water mass due to tides.
- a. Thing
- b. Tidal energy18
- c. Undefined
- d. Undefined

62. An instrument that measures motion of the ground caused by earthquake waves is a _____.
- a. 1509 Istanbul earthquake
- b. Seismometer18
- c. Undefined
- d. Undefined

63. Ability to do work is referred to as _____. Most evident in glacial systems as radiant _____ from the sun and as latent _____ required to melt ice to water.
- a. Energy18
- b. AASHTO Soil Classification System
- c. Undefined
- d. Undefined

64. _____ refers to a basic unit of the geologic time scale that is a subdivision of an era. Periods may be divided into smaller units called epochs.

Chapter 18. The Sea Floor

a. 1509 Istanbul earthquake
c. Undefined
b. Period18
d. Undefined

65. An instrument that measures and records the subbottom structure of the sea floor is a _____.
   a. Seismic profiler18
   c. Undefined
   b. 1509 Istanbul earthquake
   d. Undefined

66. A nearly flat surface separating two beds of sedimentary rock is a _____. Each _____ marks the end of one deposit and the beginning of another having different characteristics.
   a. 1509 Istanbul earthquake
   c. Undefined
   b. Bedding plane18
   d. Undefined

67. The division of sediment or sedimentary rock into parallel layers that can be distinguished from each other by such features as chemical composition and grain size is _____.
   a. Bedding18
   c. Undefined
   b. 1509 Istanbul earthquake
   d. Undefined

68. _____ refers to a bend that develops in an initially horizontal layer of rock, usually caused by plastic deformation. Folds occur most frequently in sedimentary rocks.
   a. 1509 Istanbul earthquake
   c. Undefined
   b. Fold18
   d. Undefined

69. _____ refers to the bending of seismic waves as they pass from one material to another.
   a. 1509 Istanbul earthquake
   c. Undefined
   b. Seismic refraction18
   d. Undefined

70. The bending of waves on passing between media of different velocities is referred to as _____.
   a. 1509 Istanbul earthquake
   c. Undefined
   b. Refraction18
   d. Undefined

71. The force of attraction exerted by one body in the universe on another is _____. _____ is directly proportional to the product of the masses of the two attracted bodies. The force of attraction exerted by the Earth on bodies on or near its surface, tending to pull them toward the Earth's center.
   a. 1509 Istanbul earthquake
   c. Undefined
   b. Gravity18
   d. Undefined

72. A sensitive instrument used to measure the intensity of Earth's magnetic field at various points is referred to as a _____.
   a. Magnetometer18
   c. Undefined
   b. 1509 Istanbul earthquake
   d. Undefined

73. _____ refers to the zone of transition from a continent to the adjacent ocean basin. It generally includes a continental shelf, continental slope, and continental rise.
   a. Continental margin18
   c. Undefined
   b. Thing
   d. Undefined

74. _____ the part of the continental margin that lies between the continental shelf and the bottom of the ocean. Sunlight does not penetrate this area, and mostly it is home to scavengers. It is characterized by a relatively steep slope of 3° to 6°.
- a. Thing
- b. Continental slope18
- c. Undefined
- d. Undefined

75. The shallow part of the seafloor immediately adjacent to a continent is called the _____.
- a. Continental shelf18
- b. Thing
- c. Undefined
- d. Undefined

76. The gently sloping area at the base of the continental slope is called the _____.
- a. Continental rise18
- b. Thing
- c. Undefined
- d. Undefined

77. _____ refers to the area of dry land that borders on a body of water.
- a. 1509 Istanbul earthquake
- b. Coast18
- c. Undefined
- d. Undefined

78. _____ is a flat or very gently sloping area of the deep ocean basin floor. They are among the Earth's flattest and smoothest regions and the least explored. They cover approximately 40% of the ocean floor and reach depths between 2,200 and 5,500 m). They generally lie between the foot of a continental rise and a mid-oceanic ridge.
- a. Thing
- b. Abyssal plain18
- c. Undefined
- d. Undefined

79. A margin consisting of a continental shelf, a continental slope, and an oceanic trench is referred to as _____.
- a. Active continental margin18
- b. AASHTO Soil Classification System
- c. Undefined
- d. Undefined

80. _____ refers to a continental margin characterized by volcanic activity and frequent earthquakes and associated with subduction or transform faulting.
- a. AASHTO Soil Classification System
- b. Active margin18
- c. Undefined
- d. Undefined

81. A _____ is a mountain rising from the seafloor that does not reach to the surface of the ocean. They are often found in groupings or submerged archipelagos.
- a. Thing
- b. Seamount18
- c. Undefined
- d. Undefined

82. A _____ is a steep-sided valley on the seafloor of the continental slope. Submarine canyons are generally found as extensions to large rivers, and have been found to extend 1km below sea level, and extend for hundreds of kilometers.
- a. Submarine canyon18
- b. Thing
- c. Undefined
- d. Undefined

83. Submarine ridge with which no earthquakes are associated is referred to as the _____.

Chapter 18. The Sea Floor

    a. AASHTO Soil Classification System   b. Aseismic ridge18
    c. Undefined   d. Undefined

84. _____ refers to an artificial steepening of slope angles on a topographic profile caused by using a vertical scale that differs from the horizontal scale.
    a. 1509 Istanbul earthquake   b. Vertical exaggeration18
    c. Undefined   d. Undefined

85. _____ is a chemical element in the periodic table that has the symbol Pb and atomic number 82. A soft, heavy, toxic and malleable poor metal, _____ is bluish white when freshly cut but tarnishes to dull gray when exposed to air. _____ is used in building construction, _____-acid batteries, bullets and shot, and is part of solder, pewter, and fusible alloys.
    a. Lead18   b. Thing
    c. Undefined   d. Undefined

86. A _____ is a fissure in a planet's surface from which geothermally heated water issues. Hydrothermal vents are commonly found in places that are also volcanically active, where hot magma is relatively near the planet's surface.
    a. Thing   b. Hydrothermal vent18
    c. Undefined   d. Undefined

87. The stress exerted by the fluids that fill the voids between particles of rock or soil is referred to as _____.
    a. Pore pressure18   b. 1509 Istanbul earthquake
    c. Undefined   d. Undefined

88. An opening in the Earth's surface through which lava, gases, and hot particles are expelled is a _____. Also called volcanic _____ and volcano.
    a. Vent18   b. 1509 Istanbul earthquake
    c. Undefined   d. Undefined

89. _____ refers to a continental margin that is located at the 'trailing edge' of a continent and as a result shows little geological activity.
    a. Passive continental margin18   b. Thing
    c. Undefined   d. Undefined

90. The entire area between the tops of the slopes on both sides of a stream is a _____.
    a. Valley18   b. 1509 Istanbul earthquake
    c. Undefined   d. Undefined

91. A mineral or fuel deposit, known or not yet discovered, that may be or become available for human exploitation is called a _____.
    a. 1509 Istanbul earthquake   b. Resource18
    c. Undefined   d. Undefined

92. The process of determining that two or more geographically distant rocks or rock strata originated in the same time period is referred to as _____.

Chapter 18. The Sea Floor

a. Correlation18
c. Undefined

b. 1509 Istanbul earthquake
d. Undefined

93. The relationship between distance on a map and the distance on the terrain being represented by that map is a _____.

a. Scale18
c. Undefined

b. 1509 Istanbul earthquake
d. Undefined

94. The top of the ocean, where the water meets the atmosphere is called _____.

a. 1509 Istanbul earthquake
c. Undefined

b. Sea level18
d. Undefined

95. An extremely slow moving, thick sheet of ice that covers a large part of a continent is a _____.

a. Continental glacier18
c. Undefined

b. 1509 Istanbul earthquake
d. Undefined

96. The first epoch of the Quaternary Period, beginning 2 to 3 million years ago and ending approximately 10,000 years ago is referred to as the _____.

a. Pleistocene epoch18
c. Undefined

b. 1509 Istanbul earthquake
d. Undefined

97. A geologic epoch, characterized by alternating glacial and interglacial stages, that ended about 10,000 years ago, that lasted for 2 million years is called the _____ epoch.

a. Thing
c. Undefined

b. Pleistocene18
d. Undefined

98. A moving body of ice that forms on land from the accumulation and compaction of snow, and that flows downslope or outward due to gravity and the pressure of its own weight is a _____.

a. 1509 Istanbul earthquake
c. Undefined

b. Glacier18
d. Undefined

99. A unit of the geologic time scale that is a subdivision of a period is referred to as an _____.

a. AASHTO Soil Classification System
c. Undefined

b. Epoch18
d. Undefined

100. _____ refers to a clastic rock composed of particles that range in diameter from 1/16 millimeter to 2 millimeters in diameter. Sandstones make up about 25% of all sedimentary rocks.

a. Sandstone18
c. Undefined

b. 1509 Istanbul earthquake
d. Undefined

101. _____ is a sedimentary rock composed largely of the mineral calcite (calcium carbonate: $CaCO_3$). _____ often contains variable amounts of silica in the form of chert or flint, as well as varying amounts of clay, silt and sand as disseminations, nodules, or layers within the rock.

a. Thing
c. Undefined

b. Limestone18
d. Undefined

Chapter 18. The Sea Floor

102. _____ refers to a sedimentary rock composed of detrital sediment particles less than 0.004 millimeters in diameter. _____ tends to be red, brown, black, or gray, and usually originate in relatively still waters.
    a. Shale18
    b. 1509 Istanbul earthquake
    c. Undefined
    d. Undefined

103. Earth's crust that includes both the continents and the continental shelves is the _____.
    a. 1509 Istanbul earthquake
    b. Continental crust18
    c. Undefined
    d. Undefined

104. _____ refers to earth's crust, which is formed at mid-oceanic ridges, typically 5 to 10 kilometers thick with a density of 3.0 grams per centimeter cubed.
    a. AASHTO Soil Classification System
    b. Oceanic crust18
    c. Undefined
    d. Undefined

105. The excavation of earth material from the bottom of a body of water by a floating barge or raft equipped to scoop up, discharge by conveyors, and process or transport materials is called _____.
    a. Dredging18
    b. 1509 Istanbul earthquake
    c. Undefined
    d. Undefined

106. _____ refers to the beginning or source area for a stream. Also called the headwaters.
    a. Head18
    b. 1509 Istanbul earthquake
    c. Undefined
    d. Undefined

107. Great fan-shaped deposit of sediment on the deep-sea floor at the base of many submarine canyons is an _____.
    a. Abyssal fan18
    b. AASHTO Soil Classification System
    c. Undefined
    d. Undefined

108. The process by which a current moves sediments along a surf zone is _____. _____ typically consists of sand, gravel, shell fragments, and pebbles.
    a. Longshore drift18
    b. 1509 Istanbul earthquake
    c. Undefined
    d. Undefined

109. _____ is the displacement of solids (soil, mud, rock, and other particles) by the agents of wind, water, ice, movement in response to gravity, or living organisms.
    a. Erosion18
    b. Thing
    c. Undefined
    d. Undefined

110. _____ refers to a general term applied to all mineral material transported by a glacier and deposited directly by or from the ice, or by running water emanating from the glacier. Generally applies to Pleistocene glacial deposits.
    a. 1509 Istanbul earthquake
    b. Drift18
    c. Undefined
    d. Undefined

111. A _____, often called an ice age, is a geological phenomenon in which massive ice sheets form in the Arctic and Antarctic and advance toward the equator.

a. Glaciation18
b. Thing
c. Undefined
d. Undefined

112. Strain involving an increase in length is an _____. _____ can cause crustal thinning and faulting.
   a. AASHTO Soil Classification System
   b. Extension18
   c. Undefined
   d. Undefined

113. A major branch of a stream system is referred to as a _____.
   a. 1509 Istanbul earthquake
   b. River18
   c. Undefined
   d. Undefined

114. _____ refers to a downslope movement of dense, sediment-laden water created when sand and mud on the continental shelf and slope are dislodged and thrown into suspension.
   a. Turbidity current18
   b. 1509 Istanbul earthquake
   c. Undefined
   d. Undefined

115. _____ refers to a feature on the surface of the planet Mars that very closely resembles certain types of stream channels on Earth.
   a. Channel18
   b. 1509 Istanbul earthquake
   c. Undefined
   d. Undefined

116. The point on the Earth's surface that is located directly above the focus of an earthquake is referred to as _____.
   a. Epicenter18
   b. AASHTO Soil Classification System
   c. Undefined
   d. Undefined

117. A continental margin far from a plate margin, with no volcanoes and few earthquakes is a _____.
   a. 1509 Istanbul earthquake
   b. Passive margin18
   c. Undefined
   d. Undefined

118. A large mass of rock projecting above surrounding terrain is called a _____.
   a. 1509 Istanbul earthquake
   b. Mountain18
   c. Undefined
   d. Undefined

119. A bottom current that flows parallel to the slopes of the continental margin is referred to as a _____.
   a. Contour current18
   b. 1509 Istanbul earthquake
   c. Undefined
   d. Undefined

120. Any accumulation of material, by mechanical settling from water or air, chemical precipitation, evaporation from solution, etc is referred to as _____.
   a. 1509 Istanbul earthquake
   b. Deposition18
   c. Undefined
   d. Undefined

121. A line that connects points of equal elevation on a topographic map is called a _____.
   a. 1509 Istanbul earthquake
   b. Contour18
   c. Undefined
   d. Undefined

122. _____ refers to soil particles between the size of sand particles and clay particles, namely particles 0.002-0.2 mm in diameter.
   a. Thing
   b. Silt18
   c. Undefined
   d. Undefined

123. A preserved remnant or impression of an organism that lived in the past is referred to as _____.
   a. Fossil18
   b. Thing
   c. Undefined
   d. Undefined

124. _____ refers to a bed formed by the deposition of sediment in relatively still water, marked by the presence of particles that vary in size, density, and shape. The particles settle in a gradual slope with the coarsest particles at the bottom and the finest at the top.
   a. 1509 Istanbul earthquake
   b. Graded bed18
   c. Undefined
   d. Undefined

125. _____ refers to the mapping of rocks lying along and beneath the ocean floor by recording the reflections and refractions of seismic waves.
   a. 1509 Istanbul earthquake
   b. Seismic profiling18
   c. Undefined
   d. Undefined

126. The undifferentiated rocks that underlie the rocks of interest in an area are referred to as _____.
   a. 1509 Istanbul earthquake
   b. Basement18
   c. Undefined
   d. Undefined

127. A bed that formed horizontal or nearly horizontal layers at the time of deposition, in which the coarsest particles are concentrated at the bottom and grade gradually upward into fine silt is _____.
   a. Graded bedding18
   b. 1509 Istanbul earthquake
   c. Undefined
   d. Undefined

128. _____ refers to the portion of seafloor that lies between the continental margin and the oceanic ridge system. This region comprises almost 30 percent of Earth's surface.
   a. 1509 Istanbul earthquake
   b. Deep-ocean basin18
   c. Undefined
   d. Undefined

129. A round or oval depression in the Earth's surface, containing the youngest section of rock in its lowest, central part is a _____.
   a. 1509 Istanbul earthquake
   b. Basin18
   c. Undefined
   d. Undefined

130. Any relatively sunken part of the Earth's surface, especially a low-lying area surrounded by higher ground is called a _____.
   a. Depression18
   b. 1509 Istanbul earthquake
   c. Undefined
   d. Undefined

131. The vertical difference between the summit of a mountain and the adjacent valley or plain is referred to as a _____.

Chapter 18. The Sea Floor

a. 1509 Istanbul earthquake
b. Relief18
c. Undefined
d. Undefined

132. A zone in the upper mantle, usually beneath an oceanic trench, where a cool, brittle plate, being subducted back into the mantle, gives rise to deep earthquakes is the _____.
 a. Benioff zone18
 b. 1509 Istanbul earthquake
 c. Undefined
 d. Undefined

133. The angle formed by the inclined plane of a geological structure and the horizontal plane of the Earth's surface is referred to as a _____.
 a. Dip18
 b. 1509 Istanbul earthquake
 c. Undefined
 d. Undefined

134. An igneous rock formed from lava that has flowed out onto the Earth's surface, characterized by rapid solidification and grains that are so small as to be barely visible to the naked eye are referred to as _____.
 a. Extrusive rock18
 b. AASHTO Soil Classification System
 c. Undefined
 d. Undefined

135. _____ refers to a descriptive term applied to igneous rocks that are transitional between basic and acidic with silica between 54% and 65%.
 a. AASHTO Soil Classification System
 b. Intermediate18
 c. Undefined
 d. Undefined

136. _____ refers to the dark, aphanitic, extrusive rock that has a silica content of about 60% and is the second most abundant volcanic rock. Andesites are found in large quantities in the Andes Mountains.
 a. AASHTO Soil Classification System
 b. Andesite18
 c. Undefined
 d. Undefined

137. Gradual loss of heat from Earth's interior out into space is called _____.
 a. 1509 Istanbul earthquake
 b. Heat flow18
 c. Undefined
 d. Undefined

138. The middle layer of the Earth, lying just below the crust and consisting of relatively dense rocks is called the _____. The _____ is divided into two sections, the upper _____ and the lower _____; the lower _____ has greater density than the upper _____.
 a. 1509 Istanbul earthquake
 b. Mantle18
 c. Undefined
 d. Undefined

139. _____ refers to a group of closely spaced mountains or parallel ridges.
 a. 1509 Istanbul earthquake
 b. Mountain range18
 c. Undefined
 d. Undefined

140. A _____ is a valley created by the formation of a rift. They are produced by tensional tectonic forces which occur at divergent plate boundaries.

Chapter 18. The Sea Floor

a. Rift valley18
b. Thing
c. Undefined
d. Undefined

141. _____ refers to a long, narrow trough bounded by normal faults. It represents a region where divergence is taking place.
a. 1509 Istanbul earthquake
b. Rift18
c. Undefined
d. Undefined

142. _____ refers to drop out of a saturated solution as crystals. The crystals that drop out of a saturated solution.
a. 1509 Istanbul earthquake
b. Precipitate18
c. Undefined
d. Undefined

143. A spring in which the water is 6-9°C warmer than the mean annual air temperature of its locality is called _____.
a. Hot spring18
b. 1509 Istanbul earthquake
c. Undefined
d. Undefined

144. Usually slow but effective process of weathering and erosion in which rocks are dissolved by water is a _____.
a. 1509 Istanbul earthquake
b. Solution18
c. Undefined
d. Undefined

145. One of the minerals that is abundant in the hot water that seeps through hydrothermal vents is _____.
a. Sulfide18
b. Thing
c. Undefined
d. Undefined

146. The time between winter and summer is _____.
a. 1509 Istanbul earthquake
b. Spring18
c. Undefined
d. Undefined

147. Of either earth or stone pebbles, generally covering a burial chamber or deposit is called _____.
a. Mound18
b. 1509 Istanbul earthquake
c. Undefined
d. Undefined

148. An area in the upper mantle, ranging from 100 to 200 kilometers in width, from which magma rises in a plume to form volcanoes. A _____ may endure for 10 million years or more.
a. Hot spot18
b. 1509 Istanbul earthquake
c. Undefined
d. Undefined

149. _____ refers to the tearing apart of a plate to form a depression in the Earth's crust and often eventually separating the plate into two or more smaller plates.
a. Rifting18
b. 1509 Istanbul earthquake
c. Undefined
d. Undefined

150. Molten rock that forms naturally within the Earth is _____. _____ may be either a liquid or a fluid mixture of liquid, crystals, and dissolved gases.

a. 1509 Istanbul earthquake
b. Magma18
c. Undefined
d. Undefined

151. The gas that is produced in anoxic sediments is referred to as _____.
a. Hydrogen sulfide18
b. Thing
c. Undefined
d. Undefined

152. _____ is a chemical element in the periodic table that has the symbol H and atomic number 1. At standard temperature and pressure it is a colorless, odorless, nonmetallic, univalent, tasteless, highly flammable diatomic gas.
a. Thing
b. Hydrogen18
c. Undefined
d. Undefined

153. _____ refers to any condensed water falling from the atmosphere to the surface of the earth. Common types include rain, snow, sleet, and hail.
a. Precipitation18
b. 1509 Istanbul earthquake
c. Undefined
d. Undefined

154. In biology, _____ is the process by which novel traits arise in populations and are passed on from generation to generation. Its action over large stretches of time explains the origin of new species and ultimately the vast diversity of the biological world.
a. Concept
b. Evolution18
c. Undefined
d. Undefined

155. _____ refers to the altitude, or vertical distance, above or below sea level.
a. Elevation18
b. AASHTO Soil Classification System
c. Undefined
d. Undefined

156. Angular distance of a point on the earth's surface north or south of the equator, measured along a meridian, the equator being _____ 0°, the north pole _____ 90°N, and the south pole _____ 90°S.
a. 1509 Istanbul earthquake
b. Latitude18
c. Undefined
d. Undefined

157. The topographically highest hillslope position of a hillslope profile and exhibiting a nearly level surface is referred to as the _____.
a. 1509 Istanbul earthquake
b. Summit18
c. Undefined
d. Undefined

158. A _____ is a flat topped seamount. Guyots show evidence of having been above the surface with gradual subsidence through stages from fringed reefed mountain, coral atoll, and finally a flat topped submerged mountain.
a. Guyot18
b. Thing
c. Undefined
d. Undefined

159. _____ is a term used in geology, engineering and surveying to denote the motion of a surface (usually, the earth's surface) downwards relative to a datum such as sea-level.

Chapter 18. The Sea Floor

    a. Thing
    b. Subsidence18
    c. Undefined
    d. Undefined

160. _____ refers to a sediment, sedimentary rock, or soil type which is formed from or contains a high proportion of calcium carbonate in the form of calcite or aragonite. It is also used to refer to relatively alkaline soil.
    a. Calcareous18
    b. Thing
    c. Undefined
    d. Undefined

161. A _____ extends directly out from a shoreline, and more or less following the trend of the shore.
    a. Fringing reef18
    b. Thing
    c. Undefined
    d. Undefined

162. An _____ is a type of low, coral island found in tropical oceans and consisting of a coral-algal reef surrounding a central depression. The depression may be part of the emergent island, but more typically is a part of the sea (that is, a lagoon), or very rarely is an enclosed body of fresh, brackish, or highly saline water.
    a. Thing
    b. Atoll18
    c. Undefined
    d. Undefined

163. A _____ is a body of comparatively shallow salt water separated from the deeper sea by a shallow or exposed sandbank, coral reef, or similar feature. Thus, the enclosed body of water behind a barrier reef or barrier islands or enclosed by an atoll reef is called a _____.
    a. Lagoon18
    b. Thing
    c. Undefined
    d. Undefined

164. A volcano constructed by the ejection of debris and lava flows from a central point, forming a more or less symmetrical volcano is called a _____.
    a. Central volcano18
    b. 1509 Istanbul earthquake
    c. Undefined
    d. Undefined

165. _____ was a British naturalist who achieved lasting fame as originator of the theory of evolution through natural selection.
    a. Charles Darwin18
    b. Person
    c. Undefined
    d. Undefined

166. _____ refers to the boundary between a body of water and dry land.
    a. 1509 Istanbul earthquake
    b. Shoreline18
    c. Undefined
    d. Undefined

167. One of several minerals containing one central carbon atom with strong covalent bonds to three oxygen atoms and typically having ionic bonds to one or more positive ions is _____.
    a. 1509 Istanbul earthquake
    b. Carbonate18
    c. Undefined
    d. Undefined

168. A wave that has become so steep that the crest of the wave topples forward, moving faster than the main body of the wave is referred to as a _____.

a. Breaker18
b. 1509 Istanbul earthquake
c. Undefined
d. Undefined

169. _____ refers to a volcano that is not presently erupting and is not likely to do so for a very long time in the future.
   a. Extinct volcano18
   b. AASHTO Soil Classification System
   c. Undefined
   d. Undefined

170. _____ refers to a body of water found on the Earth's surface and confined to a narrow topographic depression, down which it flows and transports rock particles, sediment, and dissolved particles. Rivers, creeks, brooks, and runs are all streams.
   a. 1509 Istanbul earthquake
   b. Stream18
   c. Undefined
   d. Undefined

171. _____ refers to a tentative explanation of a given set of data that is expected to remain valid after future observation and experimentation.
   a. Hypothesis18
   b. 1509 Istanbul earthquake
   c. Undefined
   d. Undefined

172. Seafloor sediments derived from terrestrial weathering and erosion is _____.
   a. 1509 Istanbul earthquake
   b. Terrigenous sediment18
   c. Undefined
   d. Undefined

173. Sediment made up of fine-grained clay and the skeletons of microscopic organisms that settle slowly down through the ocean water is referred to as _____.
   a. Pelagic sediment18
   b. 1509 Istanbul earthquake
   c. Undefined
   d. Undefined

174. A negatively charged particle that orbits rapidly around the nucleus of an atom is referred to as an _____.
   a. Electron18
   b. AASHTO Soil Classification System
   c. Undefined
   d. Undefined

175. A group of tiny single-celled organisms that live in surface waters and whose secretions and calcite shells account for most of the oceans carbonate sediments is called _____.
   a. 1509 Istanbul earthquake
   b. Foraminifera18
   c. Undefined
   d. Undefined

176. _____ refers to extremely small fragments, usually of glass, that forms when escaping gases force a fine spray of magma from a volcano.
   a. Volcanic ash18
   b. 1509 Istanbul earthquake
   c. Undefined
   d. Undefined

177. Fine particles of pulverized rock blown from an explosion vent are called _____. Measuring less than 1/10 inch in diameter, _____ may be either solid or molten when first erupted.
   a. Ash18
   b. AASHTO Soil Classification System
   c. Undefined
   d. Undefined

Chapter 18. The Sea Floor

178. Includes all bodies of water, lakes, rivers, ponds, and so on that are on the surface of the earth, in contrast to groundwater, which lies below the surface is _____.
 a. Surface water18
 b. Thing
 c. Undefined
 d. Undefined

179. All processes that adds snow or ice to a glacier or to floating ice or snow cove are referred to as _____.
 a. AASHTO Soil Classification System
 b. Accumulation18
 c. Undefined
 d. Undefined

180. A distinctive rock sequence found in many mountain ranges on continents is _____.
 a. AASHTO Soil Classification System
 b. Ophiolite18
 c. Undefined
 d. Undefined

181. Rock composed entirely or almost entirely of ferromagnesian minerals is referred to as _____.
 a. AASHTO Soil Classification System
 b. Ultramafic rock18
 c. Undefined
 d. Undefined

182. A section of rock separated from other rock by one or more faults is referred to as _____.
 a. 1509 Istanbul earthquake
 b. Fault block18
 c. Undefined
 d. Undefined

183. _____ refers to igneous rocks made mostly of the mafic minerals hypersthene, augite, and/or olivine.
 a. AASHTO Soil Classification System
 b. Ultramafic18
 c. Undefined
 d. Undefined

184. _____ refers to any of a group of dark, dense, phaneritic, intrusive rocks that are the plutonic equivalent to basalt.
 a. 1509 Istanbul earthquake
 b. Gabbro18
 c. Undefined
 d. Undefined

185. Angular chunk of solid rock ejected during an eruption is referred to as a _____.
 a. Block18
 b. 1509 Istanbul earthquake
 c. Undefined
 d. Undefined

186. _____ refers to the process of emplacement of magma in pre-existing rock. Also, the term refers to igneous rock mass so formed within the surrounding rock.
 a. AASHTO Soil Classification System
 b. Intrusion18
 c. Undefined
 d. Undefined

187. A member of a group of sedimentary rocks that consist primarily of microscopic silica crystals is _____. _____ may be either organic or inorganic, but the most common forms are inorganic.
 a. Chert18
 b. 1509 Istanbul earthquake
 c. Undefined
 d. Undefined

188. _____ refers to a discordant pluton that is substantially wider than it is thick. Dikes are often steeply inclined or nearly vertical.

Chapter 18. The Sea Floor

a. 1509 Istanbul earthquake
c. Undefined
b. Dike18
d. Undefined

189. _____ refers to a concordant pluton that is substantially wider than it is thick. Sills form within a few kilometers of the Earth's surface.
   a. 1509 Istanbul earthquake
   c. Undefined
   b. Sill18
   d. Undefined

190. The processes by which crustal forces cause a rock formation to break and slip along a fault are called _____.
   a. Faulting18
   c. Undefined
   b. 1509 Istanbul earthquake
   d. Undefined

191. _____ is one of the three main rock groups and is formed in three main ways—by the deposition of the weathered remains of other rocks; by the deposition of the results of biogenic activity; and by precipitation from solution.
   a. Event
   c. Undefined
   b. Sedimentary rock18
   d. Undefined

192. A gaseous mixture of naturally occurring hydrocarbons is _____.
   a. 1509 Istanbul earthquake
   c. Undefined
   b. Natural gas18
   d. Undefined

193. A chemical or biochemical sedimentary rock composed of calcium phosphate precipitated from phosphaterich seawater and formed diagenetically by the interaction between muddy or carbonate sediments and the phosphate-rich water is _____.
   a. Phosphorite18
   c. Undefined
   b. 1509 Istanbul earthquake
   d. Undefined

194. Rounded particles coarser than 2 mm in diameter are called _____.
   a. 1509 Istanbul earthquake
   c. Undefined
   b. Gravel18
   d. Undefined

195. _____ is a chemical element in the periodic table that has the symbol Au and atomic number 79. A soft, shiny, yellow, dense, malleable, ductile (trivalent and univalent) transition metal, _____ does not react with most chemicals but is attacked by chlorine, fluorine and aqua regia.
   a. Gold18
   c. Undefined
   b. Thing
   d. Undefined

196. A type of hydrogenous sediment scattered on the ocean floor, consisting mainly of manganese and iron and usually containing small amounts of copper, nickel, and cobalt are _____.
   a. Manganese nodules18
   c. Undefined
   b. 1509 Istanbul earthquake
   d. Undefined

197. _____ is a rock concretion on the sea bottom formed of concentric layers of iron and manganese hydroxides around a core. They are one of the slowest of all geological phenomena – in the order of a centimeter over several million years.

Chapter 18. The Sea Floor

a. Manganese nodule18
b. Thing
c. Undefined
d. Undefined

198. _____ is a chemical element in the periodic table that has the symbol Co and atomic number 27. _____ is a hard ferromagnetic silver-white element.
   a. Cobalt18
   b. Thing
   c. Undefined
   d. Undefined

199. _____ is a chemical element in the periodic table that has the symbol Cu (L.: Cuprum) and atomic number 29. It is a ductile metal with excellent electrical conductivity, and finds extensive use as a building material, as an electrical conductor, and as a component of various alloys.
   a. Copper18
   b. Thing
   c. Undefined
   d. Undefined

200. _____ is a metallic chemical element in the periodic table that has the symbol Ni and atomic number 28. Notable characteristicsNickel is a silvery white metal that takes on a high polish. It belongs to the iron group, and is hard, malleable, and ductile. It occurs combined with sulfur in millerite, with arsenic in the mineral niccolite, and with arsenic and sulfur in _____ glance.
   a. Nickel18
   b. Thing
   c. Undefined
   d. Undefined

201. _____ is a chemical element with the symbol Ag. A soft white lustrous transition metal, it has the highest electrical and thermal conductivity of any metal and occurs in minerals and in free form.
   a. Thing
   b. Silver18
   c. Undefined
   d. Undefined

202. _____ is a chemical element in the periodic table that has the symbol Zn and atomic number 30.
   a. Thing
   b. Zinc18
   c. Undefined
   d. Undefined

203. _____ is a term used for ionic compounds composed of positively charged cations and negatively charged anions, so that the product is neutral and without a net charge.
   a. Salt18
   b. Thing
   c. Undefined
   d. Undefined

204. The process by which conditions within the Earth, below the zone of diagenesis, alter the mineral content, chemical composition, and structure of solid rock without melting it is called _____. Igneous, sedimentary, and metamorphic rocks may all undergo _____.
   a. 1509 Istanbul earthquake
   b. Metamorphism18
   c. Undefined
   d. Undefined

205. An igneous rock composed primarily of the iron-magnesium silicate olivine and having a silica content of less than 40% is _____.
   a. Peridotite18
   b. 1509 Istanbul earthquake
   c. Undefined
   d. Undefined

206. An igneous rock rich in magnesium that forms soils toxic to many plants is called _____. Soils derived from _____ are toxic to many plants due to their high mineral content, and the flora is generally very distinctive, with specialized, slow-growing species.
   a. Serpentine18
   b. Thing
   c. Undefined
   d. Undefined

207. _____ refers to the boundary between the crust and the mantle, at a depth of 5 to 45 km, marked by an abrupt increase in P-wave velocity to more than 8 km/s.
   a. Mohorovicic discontinuity18
   b. 1509 Istanbul earthquake
   c. Undefined
   d. Undefined

208. _____ refers to a sudden change with depth in one or more of the physical properties of the material making up Earth's interior. The boundary between two dissimilar materials in Earth's interior as determined by the behavior of seismic waves.
   a. Discontinuity18
   b. 1509 Istanbul earthquake
   c. Undefined
   d. Undefined

209. Determining the age of a rock or mineral through its radioactive elements and decay products is referred to as _____.
   a. AASHTO Soil Classification System
   b. Isotopic dating18
   c. Undefined
   d. Undefined

210. The _____ meaning "new life" is the most recent of the three classic geological eras. It covers the 65.5 million years since the Cretaceous-Tertiary extinction event at the end of the Cretaceous that marked the demise of the last dinosaurs and the end of the Mesozoic Era. The _____ is ongoing.
   a. Cenozoic Era18
   b. Thing
   c. Undefined
   d. Undefined

211. The _____ is one of three geologic eras of the Phanerozoic eon. The division of time into eras dates back to Giovanni Arduino in the 18th century, although his original name for the era now called the _____ was "Secondary".
   a. Mesozoic18
   b. Thing
   c. Undefined
   d. Undefined

212. _____ refers to a major division on the geologic time scale; eras are divided into shorter units called periods.
   a. AASHTO Soil Classification System
   b. Era18
   c. Undefined
   d. Undefined

213. _____ refers to the earliest era of the Phanerozoic Eon, marked by the presence of marine invertebrates, fish, amphibians, insects, and land plants.
   a. 1509 Istanbul earthquake
   b. Paleozoic era18
   c. Undefined
   d. Undefined

214. The _____ is an informal name for the eons of the geologic timescale that came before the current Phanerozoic eon. It spans from the formation of Earth around 4500 Ma (million years ago) to the evolution of abundant macroscopic hard-shelled fossils, which marked the beginning of the Cambrian.

a. Thing
b. Precambrian18
c. Undefined
d. Undefined

215. The _____ Era is a major division of the geologic timescale, one of four geologic eras. The division of time into eras, the largest division of geologic time, dates back to Giovanni Arduino in the 18th century, although his original name for the era now called the _____ was "Primitive".
a. Paleozoic18
b. Thing
c. Undefined
d. Undefined

216. The set of geological processes that result in the expulsion of lava, pyroclastics, and gases at the Earth's surface is referred to as _____.
a. 1509 Istanbul earthquake
b. Volcanism18
c. Undefined
d. Undefined

217. The circulation of water through hot volcanic rocks and magmas, producing hot springs and geysers on the surface is called _____.
a. 1509 Istanbul earthquake
b. Hydrothermal activity18
c. Undefined
d. Undefined

Chapter 19. Plate Tectonics

1. _____ refers to the study of the global-scale movements of Earth's crust that have resulted in.
   a. Thing
   b. Plate tectonics19
   c. Undefined
   d. Undefined

2. _____ refers to a tentative explanation of a given set of data that is expected to remain valid after future observation and experimentation.
   a. 1509 Istanbul earthquake
   b. Hypothesis19
   c. Undefined
   d. Undefined

3. _____ refers to the study of the large-scale processes that collectively deform Earth's crust.
   a. Tectonics19
   b. 1509 Istanbul earthquake
   c. Undefined
   d. Undefined

4. _____ refers to rigid parts of the Earth's crust and part of the Earth's upper mantle that moves and adjoins each other along zones of seismic activity.
   a. 1509 Istanbul earthquake
   b. Plate19
   c. Undefined
   d. Undefined

5. A large mass of rock projecting above surrounding terrain is called a _____.
   a. Mountain19
   b. 1509 Istanbul earthquake
   c. Undefined
   d. Undefined

6. A fracture dividing a rock into two sections that have visibly moved relative to each other is a _____.
   a. 1509 Istanbul earthquake
   b. Fault19
   c. Undefined
   d. Undefined

7. _____ refers to a bend that develops in an initially horizontal layer of rock, usually caused by plastic deformation. Folds occur most frequently in sedimentary rocks.
   a. 1509 Istanbul earthquake
   b. Fold19
   c. Undefined
   d. Undefined

8. _____ refers to movement of continents with respect to one another over the earth's surface.
   a. Thing
   b. Continental drift19
   c. Undefined
   d. Undefined

9. The middle layer of the Earth, lying just below the crust and consisting of relatively dense rocks is called the _____. The _____ is divided into two sections, the upper _____ and the lower _____; the lower _____ has greater density than the upper _____.
   a. 1509 Istanbul earthquake
   b. Mantle19
   c. Undefined
   d. Undefined

10. _____ refers to a general term applied to all mineral material transported by a glacier and deposited directly by or from the ice, or by running water emanating from the glacier. Generally applies to Pleistocene glacial deposits.
    a. Drift19
    b. 1509 Istanbul earthquake
    c. Undefined
    d. Undefined

Chapter 19. Plate Tectonics

11. A _____ is the outer layer of a planet, part of its lithosphere. Planetary _____ is generally composed of a less dense material than that of its deeper layers. The _____ of the Earth is composed mainly of basalt and granite.
    a. Thing
    b. Crust19
    c. Undefined
    d. Undefined

12. _____ is a part of the theory of plate tectonics. _____ is the process by which continental drift occurs. This mechanism, which is a more accurate version of Alfred Wegener's original drift of continents that "plow" through the sea.
    a. Seafloor spreading19
    b. Thing
    c. Undefined
    d. Undefined

13. _____ refers to a giant mountain range that lies under the ocean and extends around the world.
    a. 1509 Istanbul earthquake
    b. Mid-oceanic ridge19
    c. Undefined
    d. Undefined

14. Deep steep-sided depression in the ocean floor caused by the subduction of oceanic crust beneath either other oceanic crust or continental crust is an _____.
    a. AASHTO Soil Classification System
    b. Oceanic trench19
    c. Undefined
    d. Undefined

15. _____ refers to levels within a soil profile that differ structurally and chemically. Generally divided into A, B, C, E, and 0 horizons.
    a. Horizon19
    b. Thing
    c. Undefined
    d. Undefined

16. An elongated depression in the seafloor produced by bending of oceanic crust during subduction is a _____.
    a. Trench19
    b. 1509 Istanbul earthquake
    c. Undefined
    d. Undefined

17. A plate boundary at which the plates are moving apart as a result of spreading is referred to as _____.
    a. Divergent boundary19
    b. 1509 Istanbul earthquake
    c. Undefined
    d. Undefined

18. Vesicular ejecta that are the product of basaltic magma are called _____.
    a. Scotia19
    b. 1509 Istanbul earthquake
    c. Undefined
    d. Undefined

19. The zone of convergence of two tectonic plates, one of which usually overrides the other is referred to as the _____.
    a. Subduction zone19
    b. 1509 Istanbul earthquake
    c. Undefined
    d. Undefined

20. The downward movement of a plate into the mantle that occurs in trenches, which are also known as _____ zones.
    a. Thing
    b. Subduction19
    c. Undefined
    d. Undefined

21. The _____ is a geologic period that extends from about 299.0 Ma to 248.0 Ma. It is the last period of the Palaeozoic Era. As with most older geologic periods, the strata that define the _____ are well identified, but the exact date of the period's start is uncertain by a few million years.
   a. Permian19
   b. Thing
   c. Undefined
   d. Undefined

22. _____ refers to the proposed supercontinent that 200 million years ago began to break apart and form the present landmasses.
   a. Pangaea19
   b. 1509 Istanbul earthquake
   c. Undefined
   d. Undefined

23. A preserved remnant or impression of an organism that lived in the past is referred to as _____.
   a. Thing
   b. Fossil19
   c. Undefined
   d. Undefined

24. Aggregates of minerals or rock fragments are called _____.
   a. Rocks19
   b. 1509 Istanbul earthquake
   c. Undefined
   d. Undefined

25. _____ refers to a naturally formed aggregate of usually inorganic materials from within the Earth.
   a. 1509 Istanbul earthquake
   b. Rock19
   c. Undefined
   d. Undefined

26. _____ is the name given to the supercontinent that existed during the Paleozoic and Mesozoic eras, before the process of plate tectonics separated each of the component continents into their current configuration.
   a. Thing
   b. Pangea19
   c. Undefined
   d. Undefined

27. The southern portion of Pangaea consisting of South America, Africa, Australia, India, and Antarctica is a _____.
   a. Gondwanaland19
   b. 1509 Istanbul earthquake
   c. Undefined
   d. Undefined

28. A _____, often called an ice age, is a geological phenomenon in which massive ice sheets form in the Arctic and Antarctic and advance toward the equator.
   a. Glaciation19
   b. Thing
   c. Undefined
   d. Undefined

29. The _____ Era is a major division of the geologic timescale, one of four geologic eras. The division of time into eras, the largest division of geologic time, dates back to Giovanni Arduino in the 18th century, although his original name for the era now called the _____ was "Primitive".
   a. Paleozoic19
   b. Thing
   c. Undefined
   d. Undefined

30. _____ was a supercontinent that broke off from the Pangaean supercontinent in the late Mesozoic era. It included most of the landmasses which make up today's continents of the northern hemisphere.

Chapter 19. Plate Tectonics

    a. Thing
    b. Laurasia19
    c. Undefined
    d. Undefined

31. Weather condition of an area including especially prevailing temperature and average daily/yearly rainfall over a long period of time is called _____.
    a. Thing
    b. Climate19
    c. Undefined
    d. Undefined

32. Drift that is deposited directly from glacial ice and therefore not sorted is _____.
    a. Glacial till19
    b. 1509 Istanbul earthquake
    c. Undefined
    d. Undefined

33. _____ refer to multiple scratches or minute lines, generally parallel but occasionally cross-cutting, inscribed on a rock surface by a geologic agent. Common indicators of direction of glacier flow.
    a. Striations19
    b. 1509 Istanbul earthquake
    c. Undefined
    d. Undefined

34. One of a group of usually parallel scratches engraved in bedrock by a glacier or other geological agent is _____.
    a. 1509 Istanbul earthquake
    b. Striation19
    c. Undefined
    d. Undefined

35. Dominantly unsorted and unstratified drift, generally unconsolidated deposited directly by and underneath a glacier without subsequent reworking by meltwater, and consisting of a hetergeneous mixture of clay, silt, sand, gravel, stones, and boulders is called _____.
    a. Till19
    b. 1509 Istanbul earthquake
    c. Undefined
    d. Undefined

36. A _____ is a type of biotic reef that develops in tropical waters by the growth of coralline algae, hermatypic corals, and other marine organisms.
    a. Thing
    b. Coral reef19
    c. Undefined
    d. Undefined

37. _____ refers to a ridge-like or mound-like structure, layered or massive, built by sedentary calcareous organisms; it is wave resistant and stands above the surrounding contemporaneously deposited sediment.
    a. 1509 Istanbul earthquake
    b. Reef19
    c. Undefined
    d. Undefined

38. _____ refers to a clastic rock composed of particles that range in diameter from 1/16 millimeter to 2 millimeters in diameter. Sandstones make up about 25% of all sedimentary rocks.
    a. 1509 Istanbul earthquake
    b. Sandstone19
    c. Undefined
    d. Undefined

39. Angular distance of a point on the earth's surface north or south of the equator, measured along a meridian, the equator being _____ 0°, the north pole _____ 90°N, and the south pole _____ 90°S.

a. 1509 Istanbul earthquake
c. Undefined
b. Latitude19
d. Undefined

40. A _____ is a landscape form or region that receives little precipitation - less than 250 mm (10 in) per year. It is a biome characterized by organisms adapted to sparse rainfall and rapid evaporation.
   a. Desert19
   c. Undefined
   b. Thing
   d. Undefined

41. Rocks formed by solidification of sediments formed and transported at the Earth's surface are referred to as _____.
   a. 1509 Istanbul earthquake
   c. Undefined
   b. Sedimentary rocks19
   d. Undefined

42. _____ is one of the three main rock groups and is formed in three main ways—by the deposition of the weathered remains of other rocks; by the deposition of the results of biogenic activity; and by precipitation from solution.
   a. Event
   c. Undefined
   b. Sedimentary rock19
   d. Undefined

43. _____ refers to a basic unit of the geologic time scale that is a subdivision of an era. Periods may be divided into smaller units called epochs.
   a. 1509 Istanbul earthquake
   c. Undefined
   b. Period19
   d. Undefined

44. The _____ is a geologic period that extends from about 245 to 202 Ma (million years ago). As the first period of the Mesozoic Era, the _____ follows the Permian and is followed by the Jurassic.
   a. Triassic19
   c. Undefined
   b. Thing
   d. Undefined

45. A major division of geology that examines the materials of Earth and seeks to understand the processes and forces acting beneath and upon Earth's surface is referred to as _____.
   a. Physical geology19
   c. Undefined
   b. 1509 Istanbul earthquake
   d. Undefined

46. The _____ period is one of the major divisions of the geologic timescale, reaching from the end of the Jurassic period, about 146 million years ago (Ma), to the beginning of the Paleocene epoch of the Tertiary period (65.5 Ma).
   a. Cretaceous19
   c. Undefined
   b. Thing
   d. Undefined

47. The scientific study of the Earth, its origins and evolution, the materials that make it up, and the processes that act on it is called _____.
   a. 1509 Istanbul earthquake
   c. Undefined
   b. Geology19
   d. Undefined

48. An apparent movement of the Earth's poles is called _____.

Chapter 19. Plate Tectonics

a. 1509 Istanbul earthquake
c. Undefined
b. Polar wandering19
d. Undefined

49. _____ refers to the set of physical features, such as mountains, valleys, and the shapes of landforms, that characterizes a given landscape.
a. Topography19
c. Undefined
b. 1509 Istanbul earthquake
d. Undefined

50. _____ refers to a group of closely spaced mountains or parallel ridges.
a. 1509 Istanbul earthquake
c. Undefined
b. Mountain range19
d. Undefined

51. _____ refers to earth's crust, which is formed at mid-oceanic ridges, typically 5 to 10 kilometers thick with a density of 3.0 grams per centimeter cubed.
a. Oceanic crust19
c. Undefined
b. AASHTO Soil Classification System
d. Undefined

52. The periodic, rhythmic rise and fall of the sea surface caused by changes in gravitational forces external to the Earth is referred to as the _____.
a. Thing
c. Undefined
b. Tide19
d. Undefined

53. _____ refers to the record of the changing direction of Earth's magnetic field as stored in lava flows. Used to accurately date extremely ancient events.
a. Thing
c. Undefined
b. Paleomagnetism19
d. Undefined

54. _____ refers to the height of floodwaters in feet or meters above an established datum plane.
a. Stage19
c. Undefined
b. 1509 Istanbul earthquake
d. Undefined

55. The property, possessed by certain materials, to attract or repel similar materials is _____. _____ is associated with moving electricity.
a. Magnetism19
c. Undefined
b. 1509 Istanbul earthquake
d. Undefined

56. An area where the strength of the magnetic field is greatest and where the magnetic lines of force appear to leave or enter Earth is called the _____.
a. Magnetic pole19
c. Undefined
b. 1509 Istanbul earthquake
d. Undefined

57. The region within which the magnetism of a given substance or particle affects other substances is referred to as _____.
a. Magnetic field19
c. Undefined
b. 1509 Istanbul earthquake
d. Undefined

Chapter 19. Plate Tectonics

58. The temperature above which a material loses its magnetization is called the _____.
    a. Curie point19
    b. 1509 Istanbul earthquake
    c. Undefined
    d. Undefined

59. _____ is a ferrimagnetic mineral form of iron(II,III) oxide, with chemical formula Fe_3O_4, one of several iron oxides and a member of the spinel group.
    a. Magnetite19
    b. Thing
    c. Undefined
    d. Undefined

60. _____ refers to an outpouring of lava onto the land surface from a vent or fissure. Also, a solidified tongue like or sheet-like body formed by outpouring lava.
    a. 1509 Istanbul earthquake
    b. Lava flow19
    c. Undefined
    d. Undefined

61. Magma that comes to the Earth's surface through a volcano or fissure is referred to as _____.
    a. Lava19
    b. 1509 Istanbul earthquake
    c. Undefined
    d. Undefined

62. _____ refers to a sedimentary rock composed of detrital sediment particles less than 0.004 millimeters in diameter. _____ tends to be red, brown, black, or gray, and usually originate in relatively still waters.
    a. 1509 Istanbul earthquake
    b. Shale19
    c. Undefined
    d. Undefined

63. _____ is essential to all organisms, except for a few bacteria. It is mostly stably incorporated in the inside of metalloproteins, because in exposed or in free form it causes production of free radicals that are generally toxic to cells.
    a. Thing
    b. Iron19
    c. Undefined
    d. Undefined

64. More or less straight row of standing stone is called an _____.
    a. Alignment19
    b. AASHTO Soil Classification System
    c. Undefined
    d. Undefined

65. A naturally occurring, usually inorganic, solid consisting of either a single element or a compound, and having a definite chemical composition and a systematic internal arrangement of atoms is referred to as a _____.
    a. 1509 Istanbul earthquake
    b. Mineral19
    c. Undefined
    d. Undefined

66. The angle formed by the inclined plane of a geological structure and the horizontal plane of the Earth's surface is referred to as a _____.
    a. 1509 Istanbul earthquake
    b. Dip19
    c. Undefined
    d. Undefined

67. _____ the part of the continental margin that lies between the continental shelf and the bottom of the ocean. Sunlight does not penetrate this area, and mostly it is home to scavengers. It is characterized by a relatively steep slope of 3° to 6°.

Chapter 19. Plate Tectonics

    a. Thing
    b. Continental slope19
    c. Undefined
    d. Undefined

68. _____ refers to the boundary between a body of water and dry land.
    a. 1509 Istanbul earthquake
    b. Shoreline19
    c. Undefined
    d. Undefined

69. A moving body of ice that forms on land from the accumulation and compaction of snow, and that flows downslope or outward due to gravity and the pressure of its own weight is a _____.
    a. 1509 Istanbul earthquake
    b. Glacier19
    c. Undefined
    d. Undefined

70. An extremely slow moving, thick sheet of ice that covers a large part of a continent is a _____.
    a. 1509 Istanbul earthquake
    b. Continental glacier19
    c. Undefined
    d. Undefined

71. _____ refers to the earliest era of the Phanerozoic Eon, marked by the presence of marine invertebrates, fish, amphibians, insects, and land plants.
    a. Paleozoic era19
    b. 1509 Istanbul earthquake
    c. Undefined
    d. Undefined

72. _____ refers to a major division on the geologic time scale; eras are divided into shorter units called periods.
    a. Era19
    b. AASHTO Soil Classification System
    c. Undefined
    d. Undefined

73. The _____ is an informal name for the eons of the geologic timescale that came before the current Phanerozoic eon. It spans from the formation of Earth around 4500 Ma (million years ago) to the evolution of abundant macroscopic hard-shelled fossils, which marked the beginning of the Cambrian.
    a. Precambrian19
    b. Thing
    c. Undefined
    d. Undefined

74. _____ is the transfer of heat by currents within a fluid. It may arise from temperature differences either within the fluid or between the fluid and its boundary, other sources of density variations (such as variable salinity), or from the application of an external motive force.
    a. Event
    b. Convection19
    c. Undefined
    d. Undefined

75. _____ refers to capable of being molded and bent under stress.
    a. 1509 Istanbul earthquake
    b. Ductile19
    c. Undefined
    d. Undefined

76. The crest of the mid-oceanic ridge, where sea floor is moving away in opposite directions on either side is referred to as the _____.
    a. Spreading axis19
    b. 1509 Istanbul earthquake
    c. Undefined
    d. Undefined

77. The set of geological processes that result in the expulsion of lava, pyroclastics, and gases at the Earth's surface is referred to as _____.
   a. 1509 Istanbul earthquake
   b. Volcanism19
   c. Undefined
   d. Undefined

78. Gradual loss of heat from Earth's interior out into space is called _____.
   a. 1509 Istanbul earthquake
   b. Heat flow19
   c. Undefined
   d. Undefined

79. A zone in the upper mantle, usually beneath an oceanic trench, where a cool, brittle plate, being subducted back into the mantle, gives rise to deep earthquakes is the _____.
   a. 1509 Istanbul earthquake
   b. Benioff zone19
   c. Undefined
   d. Undefined

80. A _____ is a valley created by the formation of a rift. They are produced by tensional tectonic forces which occur at divergent plate boundaries.
   a. Thing
   b. Rift valley19
   c. Undefined
   d. Undefined

81. A movement within the Earth's crust or mantle, caused by the sudden rupture or repositioning of underground rocks as they release stress is an _____.
   a. AASHTO Soil Classification System
   b. Earthquake19
   c. Undefined
   d. Undefined

82. The process by which two lithospheric plates separated by rifting move farther apart, with soft mantle rock rising between them and forming new oceanic lithospheres is called _____.
   a. Divergence19
   b. 1509 Istanbul earthquake
   c. Undefined
   d. Undefined

83. The entire area between the tops of the slopes on both sides of a stream is a _____.
   a. 1509 Istanbul earthquake
   b. Valley19
   c. Undefined
   d. Undefined

84. Molten rock that forms naturally within the Earth is _____. _____ may be either a liquid or a fluid mixture of liquid, crystals, and dissolved gases.
   a. 1509 Istanbul earthquake
   b. Magma19
   c. Undefined
   d. Undefined

85. _____ refers to a long, narrow trough bounded by normal faults. It represents a region where divergence is taking place.
   a. Rift19
   b. 1509 Istanbul earthquake
   c. Undefined
   d. Undefined

86. The incomplete melting of a rock composed of minerals with differing melting points is called _____ When _____ occurs, the minerals with higher melting points remain solid while the minerals whose melting points have been reached turn to magma.

Chapter 19. Plate Tectonics

a. 1509 Istanbul earthquake
b. Partial melting19
c. Undefined
d. Undefined

87. _____ refers to the process by which solid, liquid, and gaseous materials are ejected into the earth's atmosphere and onto the earth's surface by volcanic activity. Eruptions range from the quiet overflow of liquid rock to the tremendously violent expulsion of pyroclastics.
a. AASHTO Soil Classification System
b. Eruption19
c. Undefined
d. Undefined

88. _____ is a common gray to black volcanic rock. It is usually fine-grained due to rapid cooling of lava on the Earth's surface.
a. Thing
b. Basalt19
c. Undefined
d. Undefined

89. Material is in _____ if it is adjusted to the physical and chemical conditions of its environment so that it does not change or alter with time.
a. AASHTO Soil Classification System
b. Equilibrium19
c. Undefined
d. Undefined

90. The force of attraction exerted by one body in the universe on another is _____. _____ is directly proportional to the product of the masses of the two attracted bodies. The force of attraction exerted by the Earth on bodies on or near its surface, tending to pull them toward the Earth's center.
a. Gravity19
b. 1509 Istanbul earthquake
c. Undefined
d. Undefined

91. Sediment made up of fine-grained clay and the skeletons of microscopic organisms that settle slowly down through the ocean water is referred to as _____.
a. Pelagic sediment19
b. 1509 Istanbul earthquake
c. Undefined
d. Undefined

92. _____ is any particulate matter that can be transported by fluid flow and which eventually is deposited as a layer of solid particles on the bed or bottom of a body of water or other liquid.
a. Thing
b. Sediment19
c. Undefined
d. Undefined

93. The _____ is the solid outermost shell of a rocky planet. On the Earth, the _____ includes the crust and the uppermost layer of the mantle (the upper mantle or lower _____) which is joined to the crust.
a. Thing
b. Lithosphere19
c. Undefined
d. Undefined

94. The _____ is the region of the Earth between 100-200 km below the surface that is the weak or "soft" zone in the upper mantle. It lies just below the lithosphere, which is involved in plate movements and isostatic adjustments. In spite of its heat, pressures keep it plastic, and it has a relatively low density.
a. Asthenosphere19
b. Thing
c. Undefined
d. Undefined

Chapter 19. Plate Tectonics

95. _____ refers to the ratio of the weight of a particular volume of a given substance to the weight of an equal volume of pure water.
   a. 1509 Istanbul earthquake
   b. Specific gravity19
   c. Undefined
   d. Undefined

96. _____ refers to a boundary in which two plates move apart, resulting in upwelling of material from the mantle to create new seafloor.
   a. Divergent plate boundary19
   b. 1509 Istanbul earthquake
   c. Undefined
   d. Undefined

97. _____ refers to a boundary in which two plates move together, resulting in oceanic lithosphere being thrust beneath an overriding plate, eventually to be reabsorbed into the mantle. It can also involve the collision of two continental plates to create a mountain system.
   a. 1509 Istanbul earthquake
   b. Convergent plate boundary19
   c. Undefined
   d. Undefined

98. _____ refers to a boundary between two plates that are sliding past each other.
   a. Transform plate boundary19
   b. 1509 Istanbul earthquake
   c. Undefined
   d. Undefined

99. _____ refers to magnetic bands in the sea floor that run parallel to the mid-ocean ridge .
   a. Magnetic anomalies19
   b. Thing
   c. Undefined
   d. Undefined

100. A sensitive instrument used to measure the intensity of Earth's magnetic field at various points is referred to as a _____.
   a. 1509 Istanbul earthquake
   b. Magnetometer19
   c. Undefined
   d. Undefined

101. The process by which the Earth's magnetic north pole and its magnetic south pole reverse their positions over time is referred to as _____.
   a. Magnetic reversal19
   b. 1509 Istanbul earthquake
   c. Undefined
   d. Undefined

102. The process of determining that two or more geographically distant rocks or rock strata originated in the same time period is referred to as _____.
   a. 1509 Istanbul earthquake
   b. Correlation19
   c. Undefined
   d. Undefined

103. _____ refers to a discordant pluton that is substantially wider than it is thick. Dikes are often steeply inclined or nearly vertical.
   a. Dike19
   b. 1509 Istanbul earthquake
   c. Undefined
   d. Undefined

104. Strain involving an increase in length is an _____. _____ can cause crustal thinning and faulting.

Chapter 19. Plate Tectonics

a. AASHTO Soil Classification System
b. Extension19
c. Undefined
d. Undefined

105. _____ refers to a crack or break in a rock. To break in random places instead of cleaving.
a. 1509 Istanbul earthquake
b. Fracture19
c. Undefined
d. Undefined

106. _____ refers to greater than average strength of the Earth's magnetic field.
a. 1509 Istanbul earthquake
b. Positive magnetic anomaly19
c. Undefined
d. Undefined

107. A deviation from the average strength of Earth's magnetic field is a _____.
a. 1509 Istanbul earthquake
b. Magnetic anomaly19
c. Undefined
d. Undefined

108. A deviation from the average or expected value is an _____. In paleomagnetism, a 'positive' _____ is a stronger-than-average magnetic field at the earth's surface.
a. AASHTO Soil Classification System
b. Anomaly19
c. Undefined
d. Undefined

109. Less than average strength of Earth's magnetic field is _____.
a. 1509 Istanbul earthquake
b. Negative magnetic anomaly19
c. Undefined
d. Undefined

110. A _____ is formed when molten rock (magma) cools and solidifies, with or without crystallization, either below the surface as intrusive (plutonic) rocks or on the surface as extrusive (volcanic) rocks. This magma can be derived from either the Earth's mantle or pre-existing rocks made molten by extreme temperature and pressure changes.
a. Thing
b. Igneous rock19
c. Undefined
d. Undefined

111. _____ rocks are formed when molten rock (magma) cools and solidifies, with or without crystallization, either below the surface as intrusive (plutonic) rocks or on the surface as extrusive (volcanic) rocks. This magma can be derived from either the Earth's mantle or pre-existing rocks made molten by extreme temperature and pressure changes.
a. Thing
b. Igneous19
c. Undefined
d. Undefined

112. The innermost layer of the Earth, consisting primarily of pure metals such as iron and nickel is the _____. The _____ is the densest layer of the Earth, and is divided into the outer _____, which is believed to be liquid, and the inner _____, which is believed to be solid.
a. Core19
b. 1509 Istanbul earthquake
c. Undefined
d. Undefined

113. _____ refer to plate boundaries with mostly horizontal movement that connect spreading centers to each other or to subduction zones.

a. Transform faults19   b. 1509 Istanbul earthquake
c. Undefined   d. Undefined

114. A _____ is a geological fault that is a special case of strike-slip faulting which terminates abruptly, at both ends, at a major transverse geological feature. Transform faults comprise one of the three types of plate boundaries in plate tectonics.
a. Transform fault19   b. Thing
c. Undefined   d. Undefined

115. Linear zone of irregular topography on the deep-ocean floor that follows transform faults and their inactive extensions is called the _____.
a. Fracture zone19   b. 1509 Istanbul earthquake
c. Undefined   d. Undefined

116. The direction or trend of a bedding plane or fault, as it intersects the horizontal is referred to as a _____.
a. 1509 Istanbul earthquake   b. Strike19
c. Undefined   d. Undefined

117. _____ refers to the tearing apart of a plate to form a depression in the Earth's crust and often eventually separating the plate into two or more smaller plates.
a. 1509 Istanbul earthquake   b. Rifting19
c. Undefined   d. Undefined

118. Earth's crust that includes both the continents and the continental shelves is the _____.
a. Continental crust19   b. 1509 Istanbul earthquake
c. Undefined   d. Undefined

119. Upward movement of deep, nutrient-rich water along coasts is referred to as _____.
a. Upwelling19   b. Thing
c. Undefined   d. Undefined

120. _____ refers to a dip-slip fault marked by a generally steep dip along which the hanging wall has moved downward relative to the footwall.
a. Normal fault19   b. 1509 Istanbul earthquake
c. Undefined   d. Undefined

121. _____ refers to a block of rock that lies between two faults and has moved downward to form a depression between the two adjacent fault blocks.
a. Graben19   b. 1509 Istanbul earthquake
c. Undefined   d. Undefined

122. A section of rock separated from other rock by one or more faults is referred to as _____.
a. 1509 Istanbul earthquake   b. Fault block19
c. Undefined   d. Undefined

Chapter 19. Plate Tectonics

123. A round or oval depression in the Earth's surface, containing the youngest section of rock in its lowest, central part is a _____.
 a. 1509 Istanbul earthquake
 b. Basin19
 c. Undefined
 d. Undefined

124. Angular chunk of solid rock ejected during an eruption is referred to as a _____.
 a. Block19
 b. 1509 Istanbul earthquake
 c. Undefined
 d. Undefined

125. The shallow part of the seafloor immediately adjacent to a continent is called the _____.
 a. Thing
 b. Continental shelf19
 c. Undefined
 d. Undefined

126. The processes by which crustal forces cause a rock formation to break and slip along a fault are called _____.
 a. Faulting19
 b. 1509 Istanbul earthquake
 c. Undefined
 d. Undefined

127. A major branch of a stream system is referred to as a _____.
 a. River19
 b. 1509 Istanbul earthquake
 c. Undefined
 d. Undefined

128. An evaporite composed of halite is referred to as _____.
 a. 1509 Istanbul earthquake
 b. Rock salt19
 c. Undefined
 d. Undefined

129. _____ is a term used for ionic compounds composed of positively charged cations and negatively charged anions, so that the product is neutral and without a net charge.
 a. Salt19
 b. Thing
 c. Undefined
 d. Undefined

130. _____ refers to any condensed water falling from the atmosphere to the surface of the earth. Common types include rain, snow, sleet, and hail.
 a. 1509 Istanbul earthquake
 b. Precipitation19
 c. Undefined
 d. Undefined

131. _____ is the displacement of solids (soil, mud, rock, and other particles) by the agents of wind, water, ice, movement in response to gravity, or living organisms.
 a. Erosion19
 b. Thing
 c. Undefined
 d. Undefined

132. _____ is a term used in geology, engineering and surveying to denote the motion of a surface (usually, the earth's surface) downwards relative to a datum such as sea-level.
 a. Thing
 b. Subsidence19
 c. Undefined
 d. Undefined

133. _____ refers to a continental margin that is located at the 'trailing edge' of a continent and as a result shows little geological activity.
   a. Thing
   b. Passive continental margin19
   c. Undefined
   d. Undefined

134. _____ refers to the zone of transition from a continent to the adjacent ocean basin. It generally includes a continental shelf, continental slope, and continental rise.
   a. Thing
   b. Continental margin19
   c. Undefined
   d. Undefined

135. _____ refers to a downslope movement of dense, sediment-laden water created when sand and mud on the continental shelf and slope are dislodged and thrown into suspension.
   a. 1509 Istanbul earthquake
   b. Turbidity current19
   c. Undefined
   d. Undefined

136. The gently sloping area at the base of the continental slope is called the _____.
   a. Thing
   b. Continental rise19
   c. Undefined
   d. Undefined

137. Lava extruded beneath water characterized by pillow-type shapes is called _____.
   a. Pillow lava19
   b. 1509 Istanbul earthquake
   c. Undefined
   d. Undefined

138. The mass movement of a single, intact mass of rock, soil, or unconsolidated material along a weak plane, such as a fault, fracture, or bedding plane is a _____. A _____ may involve as little as a minor displacement of soil or as much as the displacement of an entire mountainside.
   a. Slide19
   b. 1509 Istanbul earthquake
   c. Undefined
   d. Undefined

139. _____ refers to a chain of volcanic islands generally located a few hundred kilometers from a trench where there is active subduction of one oceanic plate beneath another.
   a. Volcanic island arc19
   b. 1509 Istanbul earthquake
   c. Undefined
   d. Undefined

140. _____ refers to the coming together of two lithospheric plates. _____ causes subduction when one or both plates are oceanic and mountain formation when both plates are continental.
   a. 1509 Istanbul earthquake
   b. Convergence19
   c. Undefined
   d. Undefined

141. A depression landward of a volcanic arc in a subduction zone, which is lined with trapped sediment from the volcanic arc and the plate interior is a _____.
   a. Backarc basin19
   b. 1509 Istanbul earthquake
   c. Undefined
   d. Undefined

142. The _____ refers to those areas of oceans to which little or no light penetrates.

Chapter 19. Plate Tectonics

a. Thing
b. Deep sea19
c. Undefined
d. Undefined

143. An intrusive rock, as distinguished from the preexisting country rock that surrounds it is called _____.
 a. Pluton19
 b. 1509 Istanbul earthquake
 c. Undefined
 d. Undefined

144. Submarine ridge with which no earthquakes are associated is referred to as the _____.
 a. Aseismic ridge19
 b. AASHTO Soil Classification System
 c. Undefined
 d. Undefined

145. A mass of sediment and oceanic lithosphere that is transferred from a subducting plate to the less dense, overriding plate with which it converges is an _____.
 a. Accretionary wedge19
 b. AASHTO Soil Classification System
 c. Undefined
 d. Undefined

146. A depression in the sea floor located between an accretionary wedge and a volcanic arc in a subduction zone, and lined with trapped sediment is a _____.
 a. Forearc basin19
 b. 1509 Istanbul earthquake
 c. Undefined
 d. Undefined

147. A chain of volcanoes fueled by magma that rises from an underlying subducting plate is called a _____.
 a. Volcanic arc19
 b. 1509 Istanbul earthquake
 c. Undefined
 d. Undefined

148. _____ refers to line about which a fold appears to be hinged. Line of maximum curvature of a folded surface.
 a. Hinge line19
 b. 1509 Istanbul earthquake
 c. Undefined
 d. Undefined

149. The situation in mass wasting that occurs when material free-falls or bounces down a cliff is called a _____.
 a. Fall19
 b. 1509 Istanbul earthquake
 c. Undefined
 d. Undefined

150. A margin consisting of a continental shelf, a continental slope, and an oceanic trench is referred to as _____.
 a. AASHTO Soil Classification System
 b. Active continental margin19
 c. Undefined
 d. Undefined

151. _____ refers to a line of batholiths or volcanoes. Generally the line, as seen from above, is curved.
 a. Magmatic arc19
 b. 1509 Istanbul earthquake
 c. Undefined
 d. Undefined

152. _____ refers to pertaining to magma.
 a. Magmatic19
 b. 1509 Istanbul earthquake
 c. Undefined
 d. Undefined

Chapter 19. Plate Tectonics

153. _____ is the name given to changes in great masses of rock over a wide area, often within orogenic belts. The high temperatures and pressures in the depths of the Earth are the cause of the changes, and if the metamorphosed rocks are uplifted and exposed by erosion, they may occur over vast areas at the surface.
- a. Thing
- b. Regional metamorphism19
- c. Undefined
- d. Undefined

154. The process by which conditions within the Earth, below the zone of diagenesis, alter the mineral content, chemical composition, and structure of solid rock without melting it is called _____. Igneous, sedimentary, and metamorphic rocks may all undergo _____.
- a. 1509 Istanbul earthquake
- b. Metamorphism19
- c. Undefined
- d. Undefined

155. A reverse fault marked by a dip of 45° or less is called _____.
- a. 1509 Istanbul earthquake
- b. Thrust fault19
- c. Undefined
- d. Undefined

156. The segment of the Earth's continents that have remained tectonically stable and relatively earthquake-free for a vast period of time is a _____. The _____ is composed of the continental shield and the surrounding continental platform.
- a. Craton19
- b. 1509 Istanbul earthquake
- c. Undefined
- d. Undefined

157. A region of considerable extent where the combination of deposition and subsidence has formed thick accumulations of sediment and sedimentary rock is called _____.
- a. Sedimentary basin19
- b. 1509 Istanbul earthquake
- c. Undefined
- d. Undefined

158. A sediment-filled basin on a continent, landward of a magmatic arc, and caused indirectly by ocean-continent convergence is a _____.
- a. 1509 Istanbul earthquake
- b. Foreland basin19
- c. Undefined
- d. Undefined

159. The top of the ocean, where the water meets the atmosphere is called _____.
- a. 1509 Istanbul earthquake
- b. Sea level19
- c. Undefined
- d. Undefined

160. The intermediate era of the Phanerozoic Eon, following the Paleozoic Era and preceding the Cenozoic Era, and marked by the dominance of marine and terrestrial reptiles, and the appearance of birds, mammals, and flowering plants is a _____.
- a. Mesozoic Era19
- b. 1509 Istanbul earthquake
- c. Undefined
- d. Undefined

161. The _____ is one of three geologic eras of the Phanerozoic eon. The division of time into eras dates back to Giovanni Arduino in the 18th century, although his original name for the era now called the _____ was "Secondary".

Chapter 19. Plate Tectonics

    a. Mesozoic19
    c. Undefined
    b. Thing
    d. Undefined

162. _____ occurs when living things move from one biome to another. In most cases organisms migrate to avoid local shortages of food, usually caused by winter. Animals may also migrate to a certain location to breed, as is the case with some fish.
    a. Thing
    c. Undefined
    b. Migration19
    d. Undefined

163. _____ refers to the area where two continental plates have joined together through continental collision. Suture zones are marked by extremely high mountain ranges, such as the Himalayas and the Alps.
    a. Suture zone19
    c. Undefined
    b. 1509 Istanbul earthquake
    d. Undefined

164. _____ refers to the altitude, or vertical distance, above or below sea level.
    a. Elevation19
    c. Undefined
    b. AASHTO Soil Classification System
    d. Undefined

165. The process by which the overriding plate in a subduction zone becomes stretched to the point of rifting, so that magma can then rise into the gap created by the rift is called _____. _____ typically occurs when the subducting plate sinks more rapidly than the overriding plate moves forward.
    a. Backarc spreading19
    c. Undefined
    b. 1509 Istanbul earthquake
    d. Undefined

166. _____ refers to elongated rises on the ocean floor where basalt periodically erupts, forming new oceanic crust; similar to continental rift zones.
    a. 1509 Istanbul earthquake
    c. Undefined
    b. Mid-oceanic ridges19
    d. Undefined

167. A body of mantle rock, hotter than its surroundings, that ascends because it is less dense than the surrounding rock is referred to as _____.
    a. Mantle diapir19
    c. Undefined
    b. 1509 Istanbul earthquake
    d. Undefined

168. _____ refers to bodies of rock or magma that ascends within Earth's interior because they are less dense than the surrounding rock.
    a. Diapir19
    c. Undefined
    b. 1509 Istanbul earthquake
    d. Undefined

169. _____ refers to the cycle of movement in the asthenosphere that causes the plates of the lithosphere to move. Heated material in the asthenosphere becomes less dense and rises toward the solid lithosphere, through which it cannot rise further. It therefore begins to move horizontally, dragging the lithosphere along with it and pushing forward the cooler, denser material in its path. The cooler material eventually sinks down lower into the mantle, becoming heated there and rising up again, continuing the cycle.

a. 1509 Istanbul earthquake
b. Convection cell19
c. Undefined
d. Undefined

170. A plate boundary where the plates slip past each other as a the San Andreas Fault in California is a _____.
   a. Transform boundary19
   b. 1509 Istanbul earthquake
   c. Undefined
   d. Undefined

171. _____ refers to a ground tremor caused by the repositioning of rocks after an earthquake. Aftershocks may continue to occur for as long as two years after the initial earthquake. The intensity of an earthquake's aftershocks decreases over time.
   a. AASHTO Soil Classification System
   b. Aftershock19
   c. Undefined
   d. Undefined

172. Major belt around the edge of the Pacific Ocean on which most composite volcanoes are located and where many earthquakes occur is called _____.
   a. 1509 Istanbul earthquake
   b. Circum-pacific belt19
   c. Undefined
   d. Undefined

173. _____ is a sedimentary rock composed largely of the mineral calcite (calcium carbonate: $CaCO_3$). _____ often contains variable amounts of silica in the form of chert or flint, as well as varying amounts of clay, silt and sand as disseminations, nodules, or layers within the rock.
   a. Thing
   b. Limestone19
   c. Undefined
   d. Undefined

174. An _____ is a volcanic event that is distinguished by its duration or style.
   a. Episode19
   b. AASHTO Soil Classification System
   c. Undefined
   d. Undefined

175. Portion of a fold shared by an anticline and a syncline is referred to as a _____.
   a. Limb19
   b. 1509 Istanbul earthquake
   c. Undefined
   d. Undefined

176. _____ refers to a descriptive term applied to igneous rocks that are transitional between basic and acidic with silica between 54% and 65%.
   a. Intermediate19
   b. AASHTO Soil Classification System
   c. Undefined
   d. Undefined

177. _____ refers to the process of emplacement of magma in pre-existing rock. Also, the term refers to igneous rock mass so formed within the surrounding rock.
   a. Intrusion19
   b. AASHTO Soil Classification System
   c. Undefined
   d. Undefined

178. The boundary between the crust and underlying mantle, about 2890 km below the surface, where we encounter the most extreme change in properties found anywhere in Earth's interior is referred to as _____.

Chapter 19. Plate Tectonics

    a. 1509 Istanbul earthquake
    b. Core-mantle boundary19
    c. Undefined
    d. Undefined

179. The process whereby a computer first synthesizes data on the velocities of seismic waves from thousands of recent earthquakes to make a series of images depicting successive planes within the Earth, and then uses these images to construct a three-dimensional representation of the Earth's interior is referred to as _____.
    a. Seismic tomography19
    b. 1509 Istanbul earthquake
    c. Undefined
    d. Undefined

180. One of a series of progressive disturbances that reverberate through the Earth to transmit the energy released from an earthquake is called a _____.
    a. 1509 Istanbul earthquake
    b. Seismic wave19
    c. Undefined
    d. Undefined

181. _____ refers to a mass of hotter-than-normal mantle material that ascends toward the surface, where it may lead to igneous activity. These plumes of solid yet mobile material may originate as deep as the core-mantle boundary.
    a. 1509 Istanbul earthquake
    b. Mantle plume19
    c. Undefined
    d. Undefined

182. A mechanism that contributes to plate motion in which cool, dense oceanic crust sinks into the mantle and 'pulls' the trailing lithosphere along is called _____.
    a. Slab-pull19
    b. 1509 Istanbul earthquake
    c. Undefined
    d. Undefined

183. _____ refers to a flat thinnish dressed stone.
    a. Slab19
    b. 1509 Istanbul earthquake
    c. Undefined
    d. Undefined

184. An area in the upper mantle, ranging from 100 to 200 kilometers in width, from which magma rises in a plume to form volcanoes. A _____ may endure for 10 million years or more.
    a. Hot spot19
    b. 1509 Istanbul earthquake
    c. Undefined
    d. Undefined

185. A feature found in caves that is formed when a stalactite and stalagmite join is referred to as a _____.
    a. 1509 Istanbul earthquake
    b. Column19
    c. Undefined
    d. Undefined

186. _____ refers to the beginning or source area for a stream. Also called the headwaters.
    a. 1509 Istanbul earthquake
    b. Head19
    c. Undefined
    d. Undefined

187. Flows of basaltic lava that issue from numerous cracks or fissures and commonly cover extensive areas to thicknesses of hundreds of meters are called _____.
    a. 1509 Istanbul earthquake
    b. Flood basalts19
    c. Undefined
    d. Undefined

Chapter 19. Plate Tectonics

188. An immense basaltic lava plateau extending many kilometers in flat, layered flows originating from fissure eruptions is called a _____.
   a. Flood basalt19
   b. 1509 Istanbul earthquake
   c. Undefined
   d. Undefined

189. _____ refers to a round or oval bulge on the Earth's surface, containing the oldest section of rock in its raised, central part.
   a. Dome19
   b. 1509 Istanbul earthquake
   c. Undefined
   d. Undefined

190. _____ refers to an inactive, sediment-filled rift that forms above a mantle plume. The rift becomes inactive as two other rifts widen to form an ocean.
   a. Failed rift19
   b. 1509 Istanbul earthquake
   c. Undefined
   d. Undefined

191. A _____ is a flat topped seamount. Guyots show evidence of having been above the surface with gradual subsidence through stages from fringed reefed mountain, coral atoll, and finally a flat topped submerged mountain.
   a. Guyot19
   b. Thing
   c. Undefined
   d. Undefined

192. A _____ is a mountain rising from the seafloor that does not reach to the surface of the ocean. They are often found in groupings or submerged archipelagos.
   a. Seamount19
   b. Thing
   c. Undefined
   d. Undefined

193. _____ refers to a volcano that is erupting. Also, a volcano that is not presently erupting, but that has erupted within historical time and is considered likely to do so in the future.
   a. AASHTO Soil Classification System
   b. Active volcano19
   c. Undefined
   d. Undefined

194. The solid structure created when lava, gases, and hot particles escape to the Earth's surface through vents is called a _____. Volcanoes are usually conical. A _____ is 'active' when it is erupting or has erupted recently. Volcanoes that have not erupted recently but are considered likely to erupt in the future are said to be 'dormant.' A _____ that has not erupted for a long time and is not expected to erupt in the future is 'extinct'.
   a. Volcano19
   b. 1509 Istanbul earthquake
   c. Undefined
   d. Undefined

195. The same as a mineral reserve except that it refers only to a metal-bearing deposit is referred to as _____.
   a. Ore deposit19
   b. AASHTO Soil Classification System
   c. Undefined
   d. Undefined

196. A mineral deposit that can be mined for a profit is called _____.
   a. AASHTO Soil Classification System
   b. Ore19
   c. Undefined
   d. Undefined

197. A spring in which the water is 6-9°C warmer than the mean annual air temperature of its locality is called _____.

Chapter 19. Plate Tectonics

a. 1509 Istanbul earthquake
b. Hot spring19
c. Undefined
d. Undefined

198. _____ is a chemical element in the periodic table that has the symbol Mn and atomic number 25.
a. Manganese19
b. Thing
c. Undefined
d. Undefined

199. _____ is a chemical element in the periodic table that has the symbol Cu (L.: Cuprum) and atomic number 29. It is a ductile metal with excellent electrical conductivity, and finds extensive use as a building material, as an electrical conductor, and as a component of various alloys.
a. Copper19
b. Thing
c. Undefined
d. Undefined

200. _____ is a chemical element with the symbol Ag. A soft white lustrous transition metal, it has the highest electrical and thermal conductivity of any metal and occurs in minerals and in free form.
a. Silver19
b. Thing
c. Undefined
d. Undefined

201. The time between winter and summer is _____.
a. 1509 Istanbul earthquake
b. Spring19
c. Undefined
d. Undefined

202. _____ is a chemical element in the periodic table that has the symbol Au and atomic number 79. A soft, shiny, yellow, dense, malleable, ductile (trivalent and univalent) transition metal, _____ does not react with most chemicals but is attacked by chlorine, fluorine and aqua regia.
a. Thing
b. Gold19
c. Undefined
d. Undefined

203. _____ is a chemical element in the periodic table that has the symbol Zn and atomic number 30.
a. Thing
b. Zinc19
c. Undefined
d. Undefined

204. One of the minerals that is abundant in the hot water that seeps through hydrothermal vents is _____.
a. Sulfide19
b. Thing
c. Undefined
d. Undefined

205. Of either earth or stone pebbles, generally covering a burial chamber or deposit is called _____.
a. Mound19
b. 1509 Istanbul earthquake
c. Undefined
d. Undefined

206. The part of an ore, usually metallic, that is economically desirable is called _____.
a. AASHTO Soil Classification System
b. Ore mineral19
c. Undefined
d. Undefined

207. Usually slow but effective process of weathering and erosion in which rocks are dissolved by water is a _____.

a. Solution19
b. 1509 Istanbul earthquake
c. Undefined
d. Undefined

208. Any relatively sunken part of the Earth's surface, especially a low-lying area surrounded by higher ground is called a _____.
a. 1509 Istanbul earthquake
b. Depression19
c. Undefined
d. Undefined

209. Power generated by using the heat energy of the earth is called _____.
a. Geothermal power19
b. 1509 Istanbul earthquake
c. Undefined
d. Undefined

210. _____ is the naturally hot interior of Earth. The heat is maintained by naturally occurring nuclear reactions in Earth's interior.
a. Geothermal19
b. Thing
c. Undefined
d. Undefined

211. A distinctive rock sequence found in many mountain ranges on continents is _____.
a. AASHTO Soil Classification System
b. Ophiolite19
c. Undefined
d. Undefined

212. Rock composed entirely or almost entirely of ferromagnesian minerals is referred to as _____.
a. AASHTO Soil Classification System
b. Ultramafic rock19
c. Undefined
d. Undefined

213. _____ refers to igneous rocks made mostly of the mafic minerals hypersthene, augite, and/or olivine.
a. AASHTO Soil Classification System
b. Ultramafic19
c. Undefined
d. Undefined

214. _____ is a chemical element in the periodic table that has the symbol Pb and atomic number 82. A soft, heavy, toxic and malleable poor metal, _____ is bluish white when freshly cut but tarnishes to dull gray when exposed to air. _____ is used in building construction, _____-acid batteries, bullets and shot, and is part of solder, pewter, and fusible alloys.
a. Thing
b. Lead19
c. Undefined
d. Undefined

215. An unusually large deposit of sulfide minerals is called a _____.
a. Massive sulfide deposit19
b. 1509 Istanbul earthquake
c. Undefined
d. Undefined

216. A complex of old Precambrian metamorphic and plutonic rocks exposed over a large area is a _____.
a. Precambrian shield19
b. 1509 Istanbul earthquake
c. Undefined
d. Undefined

217. An extrusive igneous rock is referred to as _____.

Chapter 19. Plate Tectonics

a. Volcanic rock19
b. 1509 Istanbul earthquake
c. Undefined
d. Undefined

218. An igneous pluton that is not tabular in shape is _____.
a. 1509 Istanbul earthquake
b. Massive19
c. Undefined
d. Undefined

219. A design carved or chipped out on the slabs of Breton tombs is a _____. It is a highly version of an antropomorphic figure.
a. 1509 Istanbul earthquake
b. Shield19
c. Undefined
d. Undefined

220. _____ refers to the upper portion of the mantle extending from the Moho to a depth of 400km.
a. AASHTO Soil Classification System
b. Upper mantle19
c. Undefined
d. Undefined

221. A copper deposit, usually of low grade, in which the copper-bearing minerals occur in disseminated grains and/or in veinlets through a large volume of rock, is called _____.
a. Porphyry copper19
b. 1509 Istanbul earthquake
c. Undefined
d. Undefined

222. _____ is a chemical element that has the symbol W (L. wolframium) and atomic number 74. A very hard, heavy, steel-gray to white transition metal, _____ is found in several ores including wolframite and scheelite and is remarkable for its robust physical properties, especially the fact that it has a higher melting point than any other non-alloy in existence.
a. Tungsten19
b. Thing
c. Undefined
d. Undefined

223. An igneous rock with a porphyritic texture is referred to as _____.
a. Porphyry19
b. 1509 Istanbul earthquake
c. Undefined
d. Undefined

224. Rocks that crystallize from molten material at the surface of the earth or within the earth are called _____.
a. Igneous rocks19
b. AASHTO Soil Classification System
c. Undefined
d. Undefined

225. A hole or opening, as at the bed of a glacier is a _____. When the rate of deformation into a space behind an obstacle is less the rate of movement past the obstacle, a _____ will form.
a. Cavity19
b. 1509 Istanbul earthquake
c. Undefined
d. Undefined

226. _____ refers to the hot, watery solution that escapes from a mass of magma during the latter stages of crystallization. Such solutions may alter the surrounding country rock and are frequently the source of significant ore deposits.
a. Hydrothermal solution19
b. 1509 Istanbul earthquake
c. Undefined
d. Undefined

227. Any accumulation of material, by mechanical settling from water or air, chemical precipitation, evaporation from solution, etc is referred to as _____.
   a. Deposition19
   b. 1509 Istanbul earthquake
   c. Undefined
   d. Undefined

228. In biology, _____ is the process by which novel traits arise in populations and are passed on from generation to generation. Its action over large stretches of time explains the origin of new species and ultimately the vast diversity of the biological world.
   a. Evolution19
   b. Concept
   c. Undefined
   d. Undefined

229. _____ refers to wind or water currents promoted by the fact that warming causes expansion, decreases density, and thus causes the warmer air or water to rise. Conversely, the cooler air or water sinks.
   a. Convection currents19
   b. Thing
   c. Undefined
   d. Undefined

230. The convergence of two continental plates, resulting in the formation of mountain ranges is called _____.
   a. Continental collision19
   b. 1509 Istanbul earthquake
   c. Undefined
   d. Undefined

231. A _____ or mid-oceanic ridge is an underwater mountain range, formed by plate tectonics. This uplifting of the ocean floor occurs when convection currents beneath the ocean bed force magma up where two tectonic plates meet at a divergent boundary.
   a. Thing
   b. Mid-ocean ridge19
   c. Undefined
   d. Undefined

Chapter 20. Mountain Belts and the Continental Crust

1. Describing a mineral that will not react with or convert to a new mineral or substance, given enough time is referred to as _____.
   - a. Stable20
   - b. 1509 Istanbul earthquake
   - c. Undefined
   - d. Undefined

2. The process by which conditions within the Earth, below the zone of diagenesis, alter the mineral content, chemical composition, and structure of solid rock without melting it is called _____. Igneous, sedimentary, and metamorphic rocks may all undergo _____.
   - a. Metamorphism20
   - b. 1509 Istanbul earthquake
   - c. Undefined
   - d. Undefined

3. The set of geological processes that result in the expulsion of lava, pyroclastics, and gases at the Earth's surface is referred to as _____.
   - a. 1509 Istanbul earthquake
   - b. Volcanism20
   - c. Undefined
   - d. Undefined

4. _____ refers to the height of floodwaters in feet or meters above an established datum plane.
   - a. Stage20
   - b. 1509 Istanbul earthquake
   - c. Undefined
   - d. Undefined

5. Aggregates of minerals or rock fragments are called _____.
   - a. Rocks20
   - b. 1509 Istanbul earthquake
   - c. Undefined
   - d. Undefined

6. _____ refers to a naturally formed aggregate of usually inorganic materials from within the Earth.
   - a. 1509 Istanbul earthquake
   - b. Rock20
   - c. Undefined
   - d. Undefined

7. A large mass of rock projecting above surrounding terrain is called a _____.
   - a. Mountain20
   - b. 1509 Istanbul earthquake
   - c. Undefined
   - d. Undefined

8. _____ refers to rigid parts of the Earth's crust and part of the Earth's upper mantle that moves and adjoins each other along zones of seismic activity.
   - a. 1509 Istanbul earthquake
   - b. Plate20
   - c. Undefined
   - d. Undefined

9. _____ state that earth is made up of four basic systems: the lithosphere, the hydrosphere, the atmosphere, and the biosphere. These systems interact to produce most of the geological processes that occur on Earth. An event involving one of these systems may affect some or all of the others.
   - a. Earth systems20
   - b. AASHTO Soil Classification System
   - c. Undefined
   - d. Undefined

10. All the parts of our planet and all their interactions, taken together is an _____.
    - a. AASHTO Soil Classification System
    - b. Earth system20
    - c. Undefined
    - d. Undefined

11. _____ is a term denoting the solid body of the Earth (i.e. the hydrosphere, lithosphere [including pedosphere] and in some definitions also the internal part of the Earth) and the atmosphere of the Earth.
   a. Thing
   b. Geosphere20
   c. Undefined
   d. Undefined

12. _____ in physical geography, describes the collective mass of water found on, under, and over the surface of a planet.
   a. Thing
   b. Hydrosphere20
   c. Undefined
   d. Undefined

13. _____ is the displacement of solids (soil, mud, rock, and other particles) by the agents of wind, water, ice, movement in response to gravity, or living organisms.
   a. Thing
   b. Erosion20
   c. Undefined
   d. Undefined

14. A moving body of ice that forms on land from the accumulation and compaction of snow, and that flows downslope or outward due to gravity and the pressure of its own weight is a _____.
   a. Glacier20
   b. 1509 Istanbul earthquake
   c. Undefined
   d. Undefined

15. _____ refers to drop out of a saturated solution as crystals. The crystals that drop out of a saturated solution.
   a. Precipitate20
   b. 1509 Istanbul earthquake
   c. Undefined
   d. Undefined

16. Earth's _____ is a layer of gases surrounding the planet Earth and retained by the Earth's gravity. It contains roughly 78% nitrogen and 21% oxygen, with trace amounts of other gases.
   a. Atmosphere20
   b. Thing
   c. Undefined
   d. Undefined

17. _____ refers to the altitude, or vertical distance, above or below sea level.
   a. Elevation20
   b. AASHTO Soil Classification System
   c. Undefined
   d. Undefined

18. Distinct crystals of ice are called _____. Commonly accumulates with a density of 50 - 200 kg·m, although wind-abraded and packed _____ may have a higher initial density.
   a. Snow20
   b. 1509 Istanbul earthquake
   c. Undefined
   d. Undefined

19. _____ refers to general term referring to the rock underlying other unconsolidated material, i.e. soil.
   a. 1509 Istanbul earthquake
   b. Bedrock20
   c. Undefined
   d. Undefined

20. The _____ is the solid outermost shell of a rocky planet. On the Earth, the _____ includes the crust and the uppermost layer of the mantle (the upper mantle or lower _____) which is joined to the crust.

Chapter 20. Mountain Belts and the Continental Crust

a. Lithosphere20
b. Thing
c. Undefined
d. Undefined

21. Preexisting rocks that have been altered by heat, pressure, or chemically active fluids are _____.
a. Metamorphic rocks20
b. 1509 Istanbul earthquake
c. Undefined
d. Undefined

22. _____ is the result of the transformation of a pre-existing rock type, the protolith, in a process called metamorphism, which means "change in form". The protolith is subjected to heat (greater than 150 degrees Celsius) and extreme pressure causing profound physical and/or chemical change.
a. Thing
b. Metamorphic rock20
c. Undefined
d. Undefined

23. _____ refers to a group of closely spaced mountains or parallel ridges.
a. 1509 Istanbul earthquake
b. Mountain range20
c. Undefined
d. Undefined

24. _____ refers to the term from the Greek 'meta' and 'morph', commonly occurs to rocks which are subjected to increased heat and/or pressure. Also applies to the conversion of snow into glacial ice.
a. Metamorphic20
b. 1509 Istanbul earthquake
c. Undefined
d. Undefined

25. _____ rocks are formed when molten rock (magma) cools and solidifies, with or without crystallization, either below the surface as intrusive (plutonic) rocks or on the surface as extrusive (volcanic) rocks. This magma can be derived from either the Earth's mantle or pre-existing rocks made molten by extreme temperature and pressure changes.
a. Igneous20
b. Thing
c. Undefined
d. Undefined

26. The initial point within the Earth that ruptures in an earthquake, directly below the epicenter is called the _____.
a. Focus20
b. 1509 Istanbul earthquake
c. Undefined
d. Undefined

27. _____ refers to a long chain of mountain ranges.
a. Major mountain belt20
b. 1509 Istanbul earthquake
c. Undefined
d. Undefined

28. Concept of vertical movement of sections of Earth's crust to achieve balance or equilibrium is referred to as _____.
a. AASHTO Soil Classification System
b. Isostatic adjustment20
c. Undefined
d. Undefined

29. Earth's crust that includes both the continents and the continental shelves is the _____.
a. 1509 Istanbul earthquake
b. Continental crust20
c. Undefined
d. Undefined

30. The middle layer of the Earth, lying just below the crust and consisting of relatively dense rocks is called the _____. The _____ is divided into two sections, the upper _____ and the lower _____; the lower _____ has greater density than the upper _____.
   a. Mantle20
   b. 1509 Istanbul earthquake
   c. Undefined
   d. Undefined

31. A _____ is the outer layer of a planet, part of its lithosphere. Planetary _____ is generally composed of a less dense material than that of its deeper layers. The _____ of the Earth is composed mainly of basalt and granite.
   a. Thing
   b. Crust20
   c. Undefined
   d. Undefined

32. _____ refers to the area of dry land that borders on a body of water.
   a. Coast20
   b. 1509 Istanbul earthquake
   c. Undefined
   d. Undefined

33. The segment of the Earth's continents that have remained tectonically stable and relatively earthquake-free for a vast period of time is a _____. The _____ is composed of the continental shield and the surrounding continental platform.
   a. Craton20
   b. 1509 Istanbul earthquake
   c. Undefined
   d. Undefined

34. An elongated depression in the seafloor produced by bending of oceanic crust during subduction is a _____.
   a. Trench20
   b. 1509 Istanbul earthquake
   c. Undefined
   d. Undefined

35. A design carved or chipped out on the slabs of Breton tombs is a _____. It is a highly version of an antropomorphic figure.
   a. Shield20
   b. 1509 Istanbul earthquake
   c. Undefined
   d. Undefined

36. The top of the ocean, where the water meets the atmosphere is called _____.
   a. Sea level20
   b. 1509 Istanbul earthquake
   c. Undefined
   d. Undefined

37. An _____ is a volcanic event that is distinguished by its duration or style.
   a. Episode20
   b. AASHTO Soil Classification System
   c. Undefined
   d. Undefined

38. A preserved remnant or impression of an organism that lived in the past is referred to as _____.
   a. Fossil20
   b. Thing
   c. Undefined
   d. Undefined

39. The _____ is an informal name for the eons of the geologic timescale that came before the current Phanerozoic eon. It spans from the formation of Earth around 4500 Ma (million years ago) to the evolution of abundant macroscopic hard-shelled fossils, which marked the beginning of the Cambrian.

a. Precambrian20 b. Thing
c. Undefined d. Undefined

40. The undifferentiated rocks that underlie the rocks of interest in an area are referred to as _____.
a. Basement20 b. 1509 Istanbul earthquake
c. Undefined d. Undefined

41. _____ is one of the three main rock groups and is formed in three main ways—by the deposition of the weathered remains of other rocks; by the deposition of the results of biogenic activity; and by precipitation from solution.
a. Event b. Sedimentary rock20
c. Undefined d. Undefined

42. The _____ Era is a major division of the geologic timescale, one of four geologic eras. The division of time into eras, the largest division of geologic time, dates back to Giovanni Arduino in the 18th century, although his original name for the era now called the _____ was "Primitive".
a. Paleozoic20 b. Thing
c. Undefined d. Undefined

43. _____ refers to a basic unit of the geologic time scale that is a subdivision of an era. Periods may be divided into smaller units called epochs.
a. 1509 Istanbul earthquake b. Period20
c. Undefined d. Undefined

44. A pink-colored, felsic, plutonic rock that contains potassium and usually sodium feldspars, and has quartz content of about 10% is _____. _____ is commonly found on continents but virtually absent from the ocean basins.
a. 1509 Istanbul earthquake b. Granite20
c. Undefined d. Undefined

45. _____ refers to a coarse-grained, foliated metamorphic rock marked by bands of light-colored minerals such as quartz and feldspar that alternate with bands of dark-colored minerals. This alternation develops through metamorphic differentiation.
a. 1509 Istanbul earthquake b. Gneiss20
c. Undefined d. Undefined

46. _____ refers to a round or oval bulge on the Earth's surface, containing the oldest section of rock in its raised, central part.
a. Dome20 b. 1509 Istanbul earthquake
c. Undefined d. Undefined

47. An extrusive igneous rock is referred to as _____.
a. Volcanic rock20 b. 1509 Istanbul earthquake
c. Undefined d. Undefined

48. Rocks formed by solidification of sediments formed and transported at the Earth's surface are referred to as _____.

a. 1509 Istanbul earthquake
b. Sedimentary rocks20
c. Undefined
d. Undefined

49. _____ is any particulate matter that can be transported by fluid flow and which eventually is deposited as a layer of solid particles on the bed or bottom of a body of water or other liquid.
   a. Sediment20
   b. Thing
   c. Undefined
   d. Undefined

50. General term for the processes of folding, faulting, shearing, compression, or extension of rocks as the result of various natural forces is called _____.
   a. Deformation20
   b. 1509 Istanbul earthquake
   c. Undefined
   d. Undefined

51. A fracture dividing a rock into two sections that have visibly moved relative to each other is a _____.
   a. Fault20
   b. 1509 Istanbul earthquake
   c. Undefined
   d. Undefined

52. A round or oval depression in the Earth's surface, containing the youngest section of rock in its lowest, central part is a _____.
   a. Basin20
   b. 1509 Istanbul earthquake
   c. Undefined
   d. Undefined

53. _____ refers to a bend that develops in an initially horizontal layer of rock, usually caused by plastic deformation. Folds occur most frequently in sedimentary rocks.
   a. Fold20
   b. 1509 Istanbul earthquake
   c. Undefined
   d. Undefined

54. _____ refers to a rugged region of the lunar surface representing an early period in lunar history when intense meteorite bombardment formed craters.
   a. 1509 Istanbul earthquake
   b. Highland20
   c. Undefined
   d. Undefined

55. _____ refers to a clastic rock composed of particles that range in diameter from 1/16 millimeter to 2 millimeters in diameter. Sandstones make up about 25% of all sedimentary rocks.
   a. 1509 Istanbul earthquake
   b. Sandstone20
   c. Undefined
   d. Undefined

56. _____ is a sedimentary rock composed largely of the mineral calcite (calcium carbonate: $CaCO_3$). _____ often contains variable amounts of silica in the form of chert or flint, as well as varying amounts of clay, silt and sand as disseminations, nodules, or layers within the rock.
   a. Limestone20
   b. Thing
   c. Undefined
   d. Undefined

57. _____ refers to a sedimentary rock composed of detrital sediment particles less than 0.004 millimeters in diameter. _____ tends to be red, brown, black, or gray, and usually originate in relatively still waters.

a. 1509 Istanbul earthquake b. Shale20
c. Undefined d. Undefined

58. The processes by which crustal forces cause a rock formation to break and slip along a fault are called _____.
a. Faulting20 b. 1509 Istanbul earthquake
c. Undefined d. Undefined

59. The processes by which crustal forces deform an area of crust so that layers of rock are pushed into folds are called _____.
a. 1509 Istanbul earthquake b. Folding20
c. Undefined d. Undefined

60. A fold overturned to such an extent that the limbs are essentially horizontal is referred to as _____.
a. Recumbent fold20 b. 1509 Istanbul earthquake
c. Undefined d. Undefined

61. _____ refers to a line of batholiths or volcanoes. Generally the line, as seen from above, is curved.
a. 1509 Istanbul earthquake b. Magmatic arc20
c. Undefined d. Undefined

62. _____ refers to pertaining to magma.
a. Magmatic20 b. 1509 Istanbul earthquake
c. Undefined d. Undefined

63. Rock composed entirely or almost entirely of ferromagnesian minerals is referred to as _____.
a. Ultramafic rock20 b. AASHTO Soil Classification System
c. Undefined d. Undefined

64. _____ refers to igneous rocks made mostly of the mafic minerals hypersthene, augite, and/or olivine.
a. Ultramafic20 b. AASHTO Soil Classification System
c. Undefined d. Undefined

65. An igneous rock rich in magnesium that forms soils toxic to many plants is called _____. Soils derived from _____ are toxic to many plants due to their high mineral content, and the flora is generally very distinctive, with specialized, slow-growing species.
a. Serpentine20 b. Thing
c. Undefined d. Undefined

66. A naturally occurring, usually inorganic, solid consisting of either a single element or a compound, and having a definite chemical composition and a systematic internal arrangement of atoms is referred to as a _____.
a. 1509 Istanbul earthquake b. Mineral20
c. Undefined d. Undefined

67. _____ is the chemical element in the periodic table that has the symbol Mg and atomic number 12 and an atomic mass of 24.31.

Chapter 20. Mountain Belts and the Continental Crust

    a. Magnesium20
    b. Thing
    c. Undefined
    d. Undefined

68. One of several rock-forming minerals that contain silicon, oxygen, and usually one or more other common elements is _____.
    a. 1509 Istanbul earthquake
    b. Silicate20
    c. Undefined
    d. Undefined

69. The layering within metamorphic rocks is called _____ and it occurs when a strong compressive force is applied from one direction to a recrystallizing rock. This causes the platy or elongated crystals of minerals, such as mica and chlorite, to grow with their long axes perpendicular to the direction of the force.
    a. Foliation20
    b. Thing
    c. Undefined
    d. Undefined

70. _____ refers to the top few meters of regolith, generally including some organic matter derived from plants.
    a. 1509 Istanbul earthquake
    b. Soil20
    c. Undefined
    d. Undefined

71. The scientific study of the Earth, its origins and evolution, the materials that make it up, and the processes that act on it is called _____.
    a. 1509 Istanbul earthquake
    b. Geology20
    c. Undefined
    d. Undefined

72. The mass movement of a single, intact mass of rock, soil, or unconsolidated material along a weak plane, such as a fault, fracture, or bedding plane is a _____. A _____ may involve as little as a minor displacement of soil or as much as the displacement of an entire mountainside.
    a. 1509 Istanbul earthquake
    b. Slide20
    c. Undefined
    d. Undefined

73. The relationship between distance on a map and the distance on the terrain being represented by that map is a _____.
    a. Scale20
    b. 1509 Istanbul earthquake
    c. Undefined
    d. Undefined

74. _____ refers to a dip-slip fault marked by a hanging wall that has moved upward relative to the footwall. Reverse faults are often caused by the convergence of lithospheric plates.
    a. 1509 Istanbul earthquake
    b. Reverse fault20
    c. Undefined
    d. Undefined

75. _____ refers to a portion of a major mountain belt characterized by large thrust faults, stacked one upon another. Layered rock between the faults was folded when faulting was taking place.
    a. 1509 Istanbul earthquake
    b. Fold and thrust belt20
    c. Undefined
    d. Undefined

76. Major fault in a mountain belt above which rocks have been intensely folded and faulted is referred to as _____.

a. 1509 Istanbul earthquake
c. Undefined
b. Detachment fault20
d. Undefined

77. A reverse fault marked by a dip of 45° or less is called _____.
   a. Thrust fault20
   c. Undefined
   b. 1509 Istanbul earthquake
   d. Undefined

78. The force acting on a rock or another solid to deform it, measured in kilograms per square centimeter or pounds per square inch is _____.
   a. 1509 Istanbul earthquake
   c. Undefined
   b. Stress20
   d. Undefined

79. The incomplete melting of a rock composed of minerals with differing melting points is called _____ When _____ occurs, the minerals with higher melting points remain solid while the minerals whose melting points have been reached turn to magma.
   a. Partial melting20
   c. Undefined
   b. 1509 Istanbul earthquake
   d. Undefined

80. _____ refers to a rock that incorporates both metamorphic and igneous materials.
   a. Migmatite20
   c. Undefined
   b. 1509 Istanbul earthquake
   d. Undefined

81. _____ refers to bodies of rock or magma that ascends within Earth's interior because they are less dense than the surrounding rock.
   a. Diapir20
   c. Undefined
   b. 1509 Istanbul earthquake
   d. Undefined

82. Molten rock that forms naturally within the Earth is _____. _____ may be either a liquid or a fluid mixture of liquid, crystals, and dissolved gases.
   a. 1509 Istanbul earthquake
   c. Undefined
   b. Magma20
   d. Undefined

83. Strain involving an increase in length is an _____. _____ can cause crustal thinning and faulting.
   a. AASHTO Soil Classification System
   c. Undefined
   b. Extension20
   d. Undefined

84. _____ refers to earth's crust, which is formed at mid-oceanic ridges, typically 5 to 10 kilometers thick with a density of 3.0 grams per centimeter cubed.
   a. Oceanic crust20
   c. Undefined
   b. AASHTO Soil Classification System
   d. Undefined

85. A movement within the Earth's crust or mantle, caused by the sudden rupture or repositioning of underground rocks as they release stress is an _____.
   a. Earthquake20
   c. Undefined
   b. AASHTO Soil Classification System
   d. Undefined

Chapter 20. Mountain Belts and the Continental Crust

86. In biology, _____ is the process by which novel traits arise in populations and are passed on from generation to generation. Its action over large stretches of time explains the origin of new species and ultimately the vast diversity of the biological world.
   a. Evolution20
   b. Concept
   c. Undefined
   d. Undefined

87. Stage in the evolution of major mountain belts characterized by the accumulation of great thicknesses of sedimentary or volcanic rocks is called the _____.
   a. AASHTO Soil Classification System
   b. Accumulation stage20
   c. Undefined
   d. Undefined

88. All processes that adds snow or ice to a glacier or to floating ice or snow cove are referred to as _____.
   a. Accumulation20
   b. AASHTO Soil Classification System
   c. Undefined
   d. Undefined

89. _____ refers to a chain of volcanic islands generally located a few hundred kilometers from a trench where there is active subduction of one oceanic plate beneath another.
   a. 1509 Istanbul earthquake
   b. Volcanic island arc20
   c. Undefined
   d. Undefined

90. A sandstone in which more than 90% of the grains are quartz is the _____.
   a. 1509 Istanbul earthquake
   b. Quartz sandstone20
   c. Undefined
   d. Undefined

91. A continental margin far from a plate margin, with no volcanoes and few earthquakes is a _____.
   a. 1509 Istanbul earthquake
   b. Passive margin20
   c. Undefined
   d. Undefined

92. Mineral with the formula SiO is referred to as _____.
   a. 1509 Istanbul earthquake
   b. Quartz20
   c. Undefined
   d. Undefined

93. _____ refers to a continental margin that is located at the 'trailing edge' of a continent and as a result shows little geological activity.
   a. Passive continental margin20
   b. Thing
   c. Undefined
   d. Undefined

94. _____ refers to the zone of transition from a continent to the adjacent ocean basin. It generally includes a continental shelf, continental slope, and continental rise.
   a. Continental margin20
   b. Thing
   c. Undefined
   d. Undefined

95. _____ refers to a boundary in which two plates move together, resulting in oceanic lithosphere being thrust beneath an overriding plate, eventually to be reabsorbed into the mantle. It can also involve the collision of two continental plates to create a mountain system.

Chapter 20. Mountain Belts and the Continental Crust

a. 1509 Istanbul earthquake
b. Convergent plate boundary20
c. Undefined
d. Undefined

96. A plate boundary at which plates approach each other is referred to as a _____.
a. Convergent boundary20
b. 1509 Istanbul earthquake
c. Undefined
d. Undefined

97. Being or pertaining to rock fragments formed in a volcanic eruption is referred to as _____.
a. 1509 Istanbul earthquake
b. Pyroclastic20
c. Undefined
d. Undefined

98. Sandstone composed of poorly sorted angular clasts is referred to as the _____.
a. Graywacke20
b. 1509 Istanbul earthquake
c. Undefined
d. Undefined

99. _____ refers to the solid matter in which a fossil or crystal is embedded.
a. 1509 Istanbul earthquake
b. Matrix20
c. Undefined
d. Undefined

100. An episode of mountain building is called _____.
a. AASHTO Soil Classification System
b. Orogeny20
c. Undefined
d. Undefined

101. _____ is the name given to changes in great masses of rock over a wide area, often within orogenic belts. The high temperatures and pressures in the depths of the Earth are the cause of the changes, and if the metamorphosed rocks are uplifted and exposed by erosion, they may occur over vast areas at the surface.
a. Thing
b. Regional metamorphism20
c. Undefined
d. Undefined

102. A coarse-grained, strongly foliated metamorphic rock that develops from phyllite and splits easily into flat, parallel slabs is _____.
a. Schist20
b. 1509 Istanbul earthquake
c. Undefined
d. Undefined

103. _____ refers to the upper portion of the mantle extending from the Moho to a depth of 400km.
a. AASHTO Soil Classification System
b. Upper mantle20
c. Undefined
d. Undefined

104. A mass of sediment and oceanic lithosphere that is transferred from a subducting plate to the less dense, overriding plate with which it converges is an _____.
a. AASHTO Soil Classification System
b. Accretionary wedge20
c. Undefined
d. Undefined

105. The zone of convergence of two tectonic plates, one of which usually overrides the other is referred to as the _____.

Chapter 20. Mountain Belts and the Continental Crust

    a. Subduction zone20
    c. Undefined
    b. 1509 Istanbul earthquake
    d. Undefined

106. The downward movement of a plate into the mantle that occurs in trenches, which are also known as _____ zones.
   a. Thing
   b. Subduction20
   c. Undefined
   d. Undefined

107. The motion of surfaces sliding past one another is called _____.
   a. 1509 Istanbul earthquake
   b. Shearing20
   c. Undefined
   d. Undefined

108. _____ refers to the coming together of two lithospheric plates. _____ causes subduction when one or both plates are oceanic and mountain formation when both plates are continental.
   a. 1509 Istanbul earthquake
   b. Convergence20
   c. Undefined
   d. Undefined

109. The force of attraction exerted by one body in the universe on another is _____. _____ is directly proportional to the product of the masses of the two attracted bodies. The force of attraction exerted by the Earth on bodies on or near its surface, tending to pull them toward the Earth's center.
   a. 1509 Istanbul earthquake
   b. Gravity20
   c. Undefined
   d. Undefined

110. _____ refers to a crack or break in a rock. To break in random places instead of cleaving.
   a. Fracture20
   b. 1509 Istanbul earthquake
   c. Undefined
   d. Undefined

111. _____ refers to capable of being molded into any form, which is retained.
   a. Plastic20
   b. 1509 Istanbul earthquake
   c. Undefined
   d. Undefined

112. _____ refers to capable of being molded and bent under stress.
   a. 1509 Istanbul earthquake
   b. Ductile20
   c. Undefined
   d. Undefined

113. The _____ period is the second of the six (seven in North America) periods of the Paleozoic era. It follows the Cambrian period and is followed by the Silurian period.
   a. Ordovician20
   b. Thing
   c. Undefined
   d. Undefined

114. The _____ is a major division of the geologic timescale that begins about 542 Ma (million years ago) at the end of the Proterozoic eon and ended about 488.3 Ma with the beginning of the Ordovician period (ICS, 2004).
   a. Cambrian20
   b. Thing
   c. Undefined
   d. Undefined

115. During the _____ Period the first fish evolved legs and started to walk on land as amphibians, and the first arthropods like insects and spiders also started to colonize terrestrial habitats.
  a. Thing
  b. Devonian20
  c. Undefined
  d. Undefined

116. The _____ is a geologic period that extends from about 245 to 202 Ma (million years ago). As the first period of the Mesozoic Era, the _____ follows the Permian and is followed by the Jurassic.
  a. Thing
  b. Triassic20
  c. Undefined
  d. Undefined

117. _____ refers to the tearing apart of a plate to form a depression in the Earth's crust and often eventually separating the plate into two or more smaller plates.
  a. 1509 Istanbul earthquake
  b. Rifting20
  c. Undefined
  d. Undefined

118. The _____ is a geologic period that extends from about 299.0 Ma to 248.0 Ma. It is the last period of the Palaeozoic Era. As with most older geologic periods, the strata that define the _____ are well identified, but the exact date of the period's start is uncertain by a few million years.
  a. Permian20
  b. Thing
  c. Undefined
  d. Undefined

119. _____ refers to a particular region or locale.
  a. 1509 Istanbul earthquake
  b. Terrane20
  c. Undefined
  d. Undefined

120. _____ refers to the proposed supercontinent that 200 million years ago began to break apart and form the present landmasses.
  a. Pangaea20
  b. 1509 Istanbul earthquake
  c. Undefined
  d. Undefined

121. An elevated area with relatively little internal relief is called a _____.
  a. 1509 Istanbul earthquake
  b. Plateau20
  c. Undefined
  d. Undefined

122. _____ refers to a dip-slip fault marked by a generally steep dip along which the hanging wall has moved downward relative to the footwall.
  a. 1509 Istanbul earthquake
  b. Normal fault20
  c. Undefined
  d. Undefined

123. The process by which two lithospheric plates separated by rifting move farther apart, with soft mantle rock rising between them and forming new oceanic lithospheres is called _____.
  a. 1509 Istanbul earthquake
  b. Divergence20
  c. Undefined
  d. Undefined

124. _____ is a part of the theory of plate tectonics. _____ is the process by which continental drift occurs. This mechanism, which is a more accurate version of Alfred Wegener's original drift of continents that "plow" through the sea.

Chapter 20. Mountain Belts and the Continental Crust

a. Seafloor spreading20
b. Thing
c. Undefined
d. Undefined

125. The intermediate era of the Phanerozoic Eon, following the Paleozoic Era and preceding the Cenozoic Era, and marked by the dominance of marine and terrestrial reptiles, and the appearance of birds, mammals, and flowering plants is a _____.

a. Mesozoic Era20
b. 1509 Istanbul earthquake
c. Undefined
d. Undefined

126. _____ refers to the area where two continental plates have joined together through continental collision. Suture zones are marked by extremely high mountain ranges, such as the Himalayas and the Alps.

a. 1509 Istanbul earthquake
b. Suture zone20
c. Undefined
d. Undefined

127. The _____ is one of three geologic eras of the Phanerozoic eon. The division of time into eras dates back to Giovanni Arduino in the 18th century, although his original name for the era now called the _____ was "Secondary".

a. Thing
b. Mesozoic20
c. Undefined
d. Undefined

128. _____ refers to a major division on the geologic time scale; eras are divided into shorter units called periods.

a. Era20
b. AASHTO Soil Classification System
c. Undefined
d. Undefined

129. A plate boundary at which the plates are moving apart as a result of spreading is referred to as _____.

a. Divergent boundary20
b. 1509 Istanbul earthquake
c. Undefined
d. Undefined

130. The cycle of splitting of a continent, opening of an ocean basin, followed by closing of the basin and collision of the continents is the _____.

a. Wilson cycle20
b. 1509 Istanbul earthquake
c. Undefined
d. Undefined

131. _____ refers to a tentative explanation of a given set of data that is expected to remain valid after future observation and experimentation.

a. 1509 Istanbul earthquake
b. Hypothesis20
c. Undefined
d. Undefined

132. Rocks that crystallize from molten material at the surface of the earth or within the earth are called _____.

a. AASHTO Soil Classification System
b. Igneous rocks20
c. Undefined
d. Undefined

133. A _____ is formed when molten rock (magma) cools and solidifies, with or without crystallization, either below the surface as intrusive (plutonic) rocks or on the surface as extrusive (volcanic) rocks. This magma can be derived from either the Earth's mantle or pre-existing rocks made molten by extreme temperature and pressure changes.

Chapter 20. Mountain Belts and the Continental Crust

a. Thing
b. Igneous rock20
c. Undefined
d. Undefined

134. _____ refers to a change in relation to base level, often caused by regional uplift, which causes the forces of erosion to intensify.
   a. Rejuvenation20
   b. 1509 Istanbul earthquake
   c. Undefined
   d. Undefined

135. _____ refers to a stress due to a force pushing together on a body.
   a. Compressive stress20
   b. 1509 Istanbul earthquake
   c. Undefined
   d. Undefined

136. Material is in _____ if it is adjusted to the physical and chemical conditions of its environment so that it does not change or alter with time.
   a. Equilibrium20
   b. AASHTO Soil Classification System
   c. Undefined
   d. Undefined

137. _____ refers to igneous rocks formed beneath the surface of the Earth; typically with large crystals due to the slowness of cooling.
   a. 1509 Istanbul earthquake
   b. Plutonic20
   c. Undefined
   d. Undefined

138. The equilibrium maintained between the gravity tending to depress and the buoyancy tending to raise a given segment of the lithosphere as it floats above the asthenosphere is called _____.
   a. AASHTO Soil Classification System
   b. Isostasy20
   c. Undefined
   d. Undefined

139. A range created by uplift along normal or vertical faults is called the _____.
   a. 1509 Istanbul earthquake
   b. Fault-block mountain range20
   c. Undefined
   d. Undefined

140. A mountain containing tall horsts interspersed with much lower grabens and bounded on at least one side by a high-angle normal fault is a _____.
   a. 1509 Istanbul earthquake
   b. Fault-block mountain20
   c. Undefined
   d. Undefined

141. Angular chunk of solid rock ejected during an eruption is referred to as a _____.
   a. 1509 Istanbul earthquake
   b. Block20
   c. Undefined
   d. Undefined

142. _____ refers to the study of the large-scale processes that collectively deform Earth's crust.
   a. 1509 Istanbul earthquake
   b. Tectonics20
   c. Undefined
   d. Undefined

143. Weather condition of an area including especially prevailing temperature and average daily/yearly rainfall over a long period of time is called _____.

a. Thing
b. Climate20
c. Undefined
d. Undefined

144. The process by which exposure to atmospheric agents, such as air or moisture, causes rocks and minerals to break down is called _____. This process takes place at or near the Earth's surface. _____ entails little or no movement of the material that it loosens from the rocks and minerals.
   a. 1509 Istanbul earthquake
   b. Weathering20
   c. Undefined
   d. Undefined

145. _____ refers to any condensed water falling from the atmosphere to the surface of the earth. Common types include rain, snow, sleet, and hail.
   a. 1509 Istanbul earthquake
   b. Precipitation20
   c. Undefined
   d. Undefined

146. A _____, often called an ice age, is a geological phenomenon in which massive ice sheets form in the Arctic and Antarctic and advance toward the equator.
   a. Thing
   b. Glaciation20
   c. Undefined
   d. Undefined

147. _____ refers to a body of water found on the Earth's surface and confined to a narrow topographic depression, down which it flows and transports rock particles, sediment, and dissolved particles. Rivers, creeks, brooks, and runs are all streams.
   a. 1509 Istanbul earthquake
   b. Stream20
   c. Undefined
   d. Undefined

148. A _____ is a dry region on the surface of the Earth that is leeward or behind a mountain with respect to the prevailing wind direction. A _____ area is dry because, as moist air masses rise to top a mountain range or large mountain, the air cools and water vapor condenses as rain or snow, falling on the windward side or top of the mountain.
   a. Thing
   b. Rain shadow20
   c. Undefined
   d. Undefined

149. A major branch of a stream system is referred to as a _____.
   a. 1509 Istanbul earthquake
   b. River20
   c. Undefined
   d. Undefined

150. A mineral or fuel deposit, known or not yet discovered, that may be or become available for human exploitation is called a _____.
   a. Resource20
   b. 1509 Istanbul earthquake
   c. Undefined
   d. Undefined

151. _____ refers to the change in the shape or volume of a rock that results from stress.
   a. 1509 Istanbul earthquake
   b. Strain20
   c. Undefined
   d. Undefined

152. A section of rock separated from other rock by one or more faults is referred to as _____.

Chapter 20. Mountain Belts and the Continental Crust

    a. Fault block20
    c. Undefined
    b. 1509 Istanbul earthquake
    d. Undefined

153. _____ refers to the process by which solid, liquid, and gaseous materials are ejected into the earth's atmosphere and onto the earth's surface by volcanic activity. Eruptions range from the quiet overflow of liquid rock to the tremendously violent expulsion of pyroclastics.
    a. AASHTO Soil Classification System
    c. Undefined
    b. Eruption20
    d. Undefined

154. The detachment of part of the mantle portion of the lithosphere beneath a mountain belt is called _____.
    a. Lithospheric delamination20
    c. Undefined
    b. 1509 Istanbul earthquake
    d. Undefined

155. The _____ is the region of the Earth between 100-200 km below the surface that is the weak or "soft" zone in the upper mantle. It lies just below the lithosphere, which is involved in plate movements and isostatic adjustments. In spite of its heat, pressures keep it plastic, and it has a relatively low density.
    a. Thing
    c. Undefined
    b. Asthenosphere20
    d. Undefined

156. _____ refers to the process of emplacement of magma in pre-existing rock. Also, the term refers to igneous rock mass so formed within the surrounding rock.
    a. Intrusion20
    c. Undefined
    b. AASHTO Soil Classification System
    d. Undefined

157. An intrusive rock, as distinguished from the preexisting country rock that surrounds it is called _____.
    a. 1509 Istanbul earthquake
    c. Undefined
    b. Pluton20
    d. Undefined

158. _____ refers to any of a group of felsic igneous rocks that are the extrusive equivalents of granite.
    a. Rhyolite20
    c. Undefined
    b. 1509 Istanbul earthquake
    d. Undefined

159. An elongated mountain belt arrayed around a continental craton and formed by a later episode of compressive deformation is an _____.
    a. AASHTO Soil Classification System
    c. Undefined
    b. Orogen20
    d. Undefined

160. _____ refers to the earliest era of the Phanerozoic Eon, marked by the presence of marine invertebrates, fish, amphibians, insects, and land plants.
    a. Paleozoic era20
    c. Undefined
    b. 1509 Istanbul earthquake
    d. Undefined

161. The _____ meaning "new life" is the most recent of the three classic geological eras. It covers the 65.5 million years since the Cretaceous-Tertiary extinction event at the end of the Cretaceous that marked the demise of the last dinosaurs and the end of the Mesozoic Era. The _____ is ongoing.

a. Thing
b. Cenozoic Era20
c. Undefined
d. Undefined

162. A fault-bounded body of rock - sometimes thousands of square kilometers in area - that originated elsewhere geographically and has then moved, perhaps long distances, by plate motion is referred to as _____.
   a. Displaced terrane20
   b. 1509 Istanbul earthquake
   c. Undefined
   d. Undefined

163. _____ refers to terrane that did not form at its present site on a continent.
   a. Accreted terrane20
   b. AASHTO Soil Classification System
   c. Undefined
   d. Undefined

164. Fault-bounded bodies of rock that have been transported some distance from their place of origin and that are unrelated to adjacent rock bodies or terranes are referred to as _____.
   a. AASHTO Soil Classification System
   b. Exotic terranes20
   c. Undefined
   d. Undefined

165. A piece of continental crust of exotic or different origin than the main mass is called the _____.
   a. Exotic terrane20
   b. AASHTO Soil Classification System
   c. Undefined
   d. Undefined

166. Various different species of fossils in a rock are referred to as _____.
   a. Fossil assemblage20
   b. 1509 Istanbul earthquake
   c. Undefined
   d. Undefined

167. A terrane that may not have formed at its present site is a _____.
   a. Suspect terrane20
   b. 1509 Istanbul earthquake
   c. Undefined
   d. Undefined

168. _____ refers to a general term applied to all mineral material transported by a glacier and deposited directly by or from the ice, or by running water emanating from the glacier. Generally applies to Pleistocene glacial deposits.
   a. 1509 Istanbul earthquake
   b. Drift20
   c. Undefined
   d. Undefined

169. _____ refers to the study of the global-scale movements of Earth's crust that have resulted in.
   a. Plate tectonics20
   b. Thing
   c. Undefined
   d. Undefined

170. A complex of old Precambrian metamorphic and plutonic rocks exposed over a large area is a _____.
   a. Precambrian shield20
   b. 1509 Istanbul earthquake
   c. Undefined
   d. Undefined

171. An intrusive rock formed inside the Earth is referred to as a _____.
   a. 1509 Istanbul earthquake
   b. Plutonic rock20
   c. Undefined
   d. Undefined

Chapter 21. Geologic Resources

1. Rocks that crystallize from molten material at the surface of the earth or within the earth are called _____.
   a. Igneous rocks21
   b. AASHTO Soil Classification System
   c. Undefined
   d. Undefined

2. A _____ is formed when molten rock (magma) cools and solidifies, with or without crystallization, either below the surface as intrusive (plutonic) rocks or on the surface as extrusive (volcanic) rocks. This magma can be derived from either the Earth's mantle or pre-existing rocks made molten by extreme temperature and pressure changes.
   a. Thing
   b. Igneous rock21
   c. Undefined
   d. Undefined

3. The same as a mineral reserve except that it refers only to a metal-bearing deposit is referred to as _____.
   a. Ore deposit21
   b. AASHTO Soil Classification System
   c. Undefined
   d. Undefined

4. _____ refers to the change of state of water from the liquid to vapor phase. Requires the addition of 80 calories per cubic centimeter.
   a. AASHTO Soil Classification System
   b. Evaporation21
   c. Undefined
   d. Undefined

5. Dense, viscous petroleum that flows slowly or not at all are referred to as _____.
   a. Heavy crude21
   b. 1509 Istanbul earthquake
   c. Undefined
   d. Undefined

6. _____ is a chemical element in the periodic table. It has the symbol K (L. kalium) and atomic number 19. _____ is a soft silvery-white metallic alkali metal that occurs naturally bound to other elements in seawater and many minerals.
   a. Potassium21
   b. Thing
   c. Undefined
   d. Undefined

7. A brown or black clastic source rock containing kerogen is called _____.
   a. AASHTO Soil Classification System
   b. Oil shale21
   c. Undefined
   d. Undefined

8. Inorganic chemical sediment that precipitates when the salty water in which it had dissolved evaporates is called _____.
   a. Evaporite21
   b. AASHTO Soil Classification System
   c. Undefined
   d. Undefined

9. Aluminium is the chemical element in the periodic table that has the symbol Al and atomic number 13. It is a silvery and ductile member of the poor metal group of chemical elements. Aluminium is found primarily as the ore bauxite and is remarkable for its resistance to corrosion (due to the phenomenon of passivation) and its light weight. Aluminium is used in many industries to make millions of different products and is very important to the world economy.
   a. Thing
   b. Aluminum21
   c. Undefined
   d. Undefined

10. A mixture of unconsolidated sand and clay that contains semi-solid bitumen is called _____.

a. Oil sand21
c. Undefined
b. AASHTO Soil Classification System
d. Undefined

11. A mineral or fuel deposit, known or not yet discovered, that may be or become available for human exploitation is called a _____.
   a. 1509 Istanbul earthquake
   c. Undefined
   b. Resource21
   d. Undefined

12. The discovered deposits of a geologic material that are economically and legally feasible to recover under present circumstances are referred to as _____.
   a. Reserves21
   c. Undefined
   b. 1509 Istanbul earthquake
   d. Undefined

13. A known resource that can be exploited for profit with available technology under existing political and economic conditions is called the _____.
   a. Reserve21
   c. Undefined
   b. 1509 Istanbul earthquake
   d. Undefined

14. When refined, _____ is a silvery white, weakly radioactive metal, which is slightly softer than steel. It is malleable, ductile, and slightly paramagnetic. _____ metal has very high density, 65% more dense than lead, but slightly less dense than gold. When finely divided, it can react with cold water; in air, _____ metal becomes coated with _____ oxide.
   a. Uranium21
   c. Undefined
   b. Thing
   d. Undefined

15. A naturally occurring, usually inorganic, solid consisting of either a single element or a compound, and having a definite chemical composition and a systematic internal arrangement of atoms is referred to as a _____.
   a. 1509 Istanbul earthquake
   c. Undefined
   b. Mineral21
   d. Undefined

16. _____ rocks are formed when molten rock (magma) cools and solidifies, with or without crystallization, either below the surface as intrusive (plutonic) rocks or on the surface as extrusive (volcanic) rocks. This magma can be derived from either the Earth's mantle or pre-existing rocks made molten by extreme temperature and pressure changes.
   a. Igneous21
   c. Undefined
   b. Thing
   d. Undefined

17. _____ is a chemical element in the periodic table that has the symbol Cu (L.: Cuprum) and atomic number 29. It is a ductile metal with excellent electrical conductivity, and finds extensive use as a building material, as an electrical conductor, and as a component of various alloys.
   a. Thing
   c. Undefined
   b. Copper21
   d. Undefined

18. Ability to do work is referred to as _____. Most evident in glacial systems as radiant _____ from the sun and as latent _____ required to melt ice to water.

Chapter 21. Geologic Resources

    a. AASHTO Soil Classification System   b. Energy21
    c. Undefined   d. Undefined

19. _____ is a chemical element with the symbol Ag. A soft white lustrous transition metal, it has the highest electrical and thermal conductivity of any metal and occurs in minerals and in free form.
    a. Thing   b. Silver21
    c. Undefined   d. Undefined

20. _____ refers to a sedimentary rock composed of detrital sediment particles less than 0.004 millimeters in diameter. _____ tends to be red, brown, black, or gray, and usually originate in relatively still waters.
    a. Shale21   b. 1509 Istanbul earthquake
    c. Undefined   d. Undefined

21. Aggregates of minerals or rock fragments are called _____.
    a. Rocks21   b. 1509 Istanbul earthquake
    c. Undefined   d. Undefined

22. A member of a group of easily combustible, organic sedimentary rocks composed mostly of plant remains and containing a high proportion of carbon is called _____.
    a. 1509 Istanbul earthquake   b. Coal21
    c. Undefined   d. Undefined

23. _____ is a chemical element in the periodic table that has the symbol Au and atomic number 79. A soft, shiny, yellow, dense, malleable, ductile (trivalent and univalent) transition metal, _____ does not react with most chemicals but is attacked by chlorine, fluorine and aqua regia.
    a. Thing   b. Gold21
    c. Undefined   d. Undefined

24. _____ is a chemical element in the periodic table that has the symbol Pb and atomic number 82. A soft, heavy, toxic and malleable poor metal, _____ is bluish white when freshly cut but tarnishes to dull gray when exposed to air. _____ is used in building construction, _____-acid batteries, bullets and shot, and is part of solder, pewter, and fusible alloys.
    a. Thing   b. Lead21
    c. Undefined   d. Undefined

25. _____ is essential to all organisms, except for a few bacteria. It is mostly stably incorporated in the inside of metalloproteins, because in exposed or in free form it causes production of free radicals that are generally toxic to cells.
    a. Iron21   b. Thing
    c. Undefined   d. Undefined

26. _____ is a chemical element in the periodic table that has the symbol Zn and atomic number 30.
    a. Zinc21   b. Thing
    c. Undefined   d. Undefined

27. _____ refers to a naturally formed aggregate of usually inorganic materials from within the Earth.

a. 1509 Istanbul earthquake b. Rock21
c. Undefined d. Undefined

28. A mineral deposit that can be mined for a profit is called _____.
a. AASHTO Soil Classification System b. Ore21
c. Undefined d. Undefined

29. _____ is a term used for ionic compounds composed of positively charged cations and negatively charged anions, so that the product is neutral and without a net charge.
a. Thing b. Salt21
c. Undefined d. Undefined

30. _____ refer to valuable materials of geologic origin that can be extracted from Earth.
a. Geologic resources21 b. 1509 Istanbul earthquake
c. Undefined d. Undefined

31. _____ state that earth is made up of four basic systems: the lithosphere, the hydrosphere, the atmosphere, and the biosphere. These systems interact to produce most of the geological processes that occur on Earth. An event involving one of these systems may affect some or all of the others.
a. Earth systems21 b. AASHTO Soil Classification System
c. Undefined d. Undefined

32. All the parts of our planet and all their interactions, taken together is an _____.
a. Earth system21 b. AASHTO Soil Classification System
c. Undefined d. Undefined

33. _____ in physical geography, describes the collective mass of water found on, under, and over the surface of a planet.
a. Hydrosphere21 b. Thing
c. Undefined d. Undefined

34. _____ refers to any of a group of naturally occurring substances made up of hydrocarbons. These substances may be gaseous, liquid, or semi-solid.
a. Petroleum21 b. 1509 Istanbul earthquake
c. Undefined d. Undefined

35. Earth's _____ is a layer of gases surrounding the planet Earth and retained by the Earth's gravity. It contains roughly 78% nitrogen and 21% oxygen, with trace amounts of other gases.
a. Atmosphere21 b. Thing
c. Undefined d. Undefined

36. _____ is a term denoting the solid body of the Earth (i.e. the hydrosphere, lithosphere [including pedosphere] and in some definitions also the internal part of the Earth) and the atmosphere of the Earth.
a. Thing b. Geosphere21
c. Undefined d. Undefined

Chapter 21. Geologic Resources

37. _____ refers to a process leading to chemical changes in matter; involves the making and/or breaking of chemical bonds.
   a. Thing
   b. Chemical reaction21
   c. Undefined
   d. Undefined

38. Any one of numerous minerals that have the silicon-oxygen tetrahedron as their basic structure is called _____.
   a. 1509 Istanbul earthquake
   b. Silicate mineral21
   c. Undefined
   d. Undefined

39. One of several rock-forming minerals that contain silicon, oxygen, and usually one or more other common elements is _____.
   a. Silicate21
   b. 1509 Istanbul earthquake
   c. Undefined
   d. Undefined

40. One of several minerals containing negative oxygen ions bonded to one or more positive metallic ions are called _____.
   a. AASHTO Soil Classification System
   b. Oxide21
   c. Undefined
   d. Undefined

41. The _____ is that part of a planet's outer shell — including air, land, surface rocks and water — within which life occurs, and which biotic processes in turn alter or transform.
   a. Biosphere21
   b. Thing
   c. Undefined
   d. Undefined

42. _____ is a chemical element in the periodic table that has the symbol Mn and atomic number 25.
   a. Thing
   b. Manganese21
   c. Undefined
   d. Undefined

43. _____ is a chemical element in the periodic table that has the symbol Cr and atomic number 24. _____ (0) is unstable in oxygen, immediately producing a thin oxide layer that is impermeable to oxygen and protects the metal below.
   a. Thing
   b. Chromium21
   c. Undefined
   d. Undefined

44. _____ is a chemical element in the periodic table that has the symbol Pt and atomic number 78. A heavy, malleable, ductile, precious, grey-white transition metal, _____ is resistant to corrosion and occurs in some nickel and copper ores along with some native deposits.
   a. Platinum21
   b. Thing
   c. Undefined
   d. Undefined

45. _____ is a metallic chemical element in the periodic table that has the symbol Ni and atomic number 28. Notable characteristicsNickel is a silvery white metal that takes on a high polish. It belongs to the iron group, and is hard, malleable, and ductile. It occurs combined with sulfur in millerite, with arsenic in the mineral niccolite, and with arsenic and sulfur in _____ glance.
   a. Thing
   b. Nickel21
   c. Undefined
   d. Undefined

46. Mineral with the formula SiO is referred to as _____.
   a. Quartz21
   b. 1509 Istanbul earthquake
   c. Undefined
   d. Undefined

47. A non-crystaline rock that results from very rapid cooling of magma is _____.
   a. 1509 Istanbul earthquake
   b. Glass21
   c. Undefined
   d. Undefined

48. _____ is a chemical element in the periodic table that has the symbol Sn and atomic number 50. This silvery, malleable poor metal that is not easily oxidized in air and resists corrosion, is found in many alloys and is used to coat other metals to prevent corrosion. _____ is obtained chiefly from the mineral cassiterite, where it occurs as an oxide.
   a. Thing
   b. Tin21
   c. Undefined
   d. Undefined

49. _____ refers to capable of being molded into any form, which is retained.
   a. 1509 Istanbul earthquake
   b. Plastic21
   c. Undefined
   d. Undefined

50. _____ is the chemical element in the periodic table that has the symbol Si and atomic number 14. It is the second most abundant element in the Earth's crust, making up 25.7% of it by weight.
   a. Silicon21
   b. Thing
   c. Undefined
   d. Undefined

51. _____ is a chemical element in the periodic table that has the symbol Hg and atomic number 80. A heavy, silvery, transition metal, _____ is one of five elements that are liquid at or near standard room temperature (the others are the metals caesium, francium, and gallium, and the nonmetal bromine).
   a. Thing
   b. Mercury21
   c. Undefined
   d. Undefined

52. Group of organisms of the same species occupying a certain area and sharing a common gene pool is referred to as _____.
   a. Thing
   b. Population21
   c. Undefined
   d. Undefined

53. _____ refers to solidified lava that fills the conduit of a volcano. It is usually more resistant to erosion than the material making up the surrounding cone, and may remain standing as a solitary pinnacle when the rest of the original structure has eroded away.
   a. 1509 Istanbul earthquake
   b. Plug21
   c. Undefined
   d. Undefined

54. A gaseous mixture of naturally occurring hydrocarbons is _____.
   a. 1509 Istanbul earthquake
   b. Natural gas21
   c. Undefined
   d. Undefined

55. _____ is the naturally hot interior of Earth. The heat is maintained by naturally occurring nuclear reactions in Earth's interior.

Chapter 21. Geologic Resources

    a. Thing
    b. Geothermal21
    c. Undefined
    d. Undefined

56. _____ is a sedimentary rock composed largely of the mineral calcite (calcium carbonate: $CaCO_3$). _____ often contains variable amounts of silica in the form of chert or flint, as well as varying amounts of clay, silt and sand as disseminations, nodules, or layers within the rock.
    a. Thing
    b. Limestone21
    c. Undefined
    d. Undefined

57. The solid material that precipitates in the pore space of sediments, binding the grains together to form solid rock is referred to as _____.
    a. 1509 Istanbul earthquake
    b. Cement21
    c. Undefined
    d. Undefined

58. Rounded particles coarser than 2 mm in diameter are called _____.
    a. 1509 Istanbul earthquake
    b. Gravel21
    c. Undefined
    d. Undefined

59. _____ is the chemical element in the periodic table that has the symbol S and atomic number 16. It is an abundant, tasteless, odorless, multivalent non-metal. _____, in its native form, is a yellow crystaline solid. In nature, it can be found as the pure element or as sulfide and sulfate minerals.
    a. Thing
    b. Sulfur21
    c. Undefined
    d. Undefined

60. _____ refers to the water that lies beneath the ground surface, filling the cracks, crevices, and pore space of rocks.
    a. Ground water21
    b. 1509 Istanbul earthquake
    c. Undefined
    d. Undefined

61. _____ refer to the valuable minerals of an area that are presently legally recoverable or that may be so in the future; includes both the known ore bodies and the potential ores of a region.
    a. Mineral resources21
    b. 1509 Istanbul earthquake
    c. Undefined
    d. Undefined

62. All discovered and undiscovered deposits of a useful mineral that can be extracted now or at some time in the future are called _____.
    a. 1509 Istanbul earthquake
    b. Mineral resource21
    c. Undefined
    d. Undefined

63. Describing a substance in which the atoms are arranged in a regular, repeating, orderly pattern is called _____.
    a. 1509 Istanbul earthquake
    b. Crystalline21
    c. Undefined
    d. Undefined

64. A _____ is a natural resource (such as a mineral, plant, etc,) that is used too quickly by something to be replenished, or that cannot be replenished at all. Examples are rain forests, fossil fuels, such as oil, natural gas, etc.

a. Thing
b. Nonrenewable resource21
c. Undefined
d. Undefined

65. The movement of eroded particles by agents such as rivers, waves, glaciers, or wind is referred to as _____.
a. Transportation21
b. 1509 Istanbul earthquake
c. Undefined
d. Undefined

66. A liquid mixture of naturally occurring hydrocarbons is referred to as _____.
a. 1509 Istanbul earthquake
b. Crude oil21
c. Undefined
d. Undefined

67. An electrically neutral substance that consists of two or more elements combined in specific, constant proportions is a _____. A _____ typically has physical characteristics different from those of its constituent elements.
a. 1509 Istanbul earthquake
b. Compound21
c. Undefined
d. Undefined

68. _____ is a chemical element in the periodic table that has the symbol H and atomic number 1. At standard temperature and pressure it is a colorless, odorless, nonmetallic, univalent, tasteless, highly flammable diatomic gas.
a. Hydrogen21
b. Thing
c. Undefined
d. Undefined

69. _____ is a chemical element in the periodic table that has the symbol C and atomic number 6. An abundant nonmetallic, tetravalent element, _____ has several allotropic forms.
a. Carbon21
b. Thing
c. Undefined
d. Undefined

70. A chemical compound composed only of the elements carbon and hydrogen is called _____.
a. Thing
b. Hydrocarbon21
c. Undefined
d. Undefined

71. All processes that adds snow or ice to a glacier or to floating ice or snow cove are referred to as _____.
a. Accumulation21
b. AASHTO Soil Classification System
c. Undefined
d. Undefined

72. A rock in which hydrocarbons originate is referred to as a _____.
a. 1509 Istanbul earthquake
b. Source rock21
c. Undefined
d. Undefined

73. _____ refers to a clastic rock composed of particles that range in diameter from 1/16 millimeter to 2 millimeters in diameter. Sandstones make up about 25% of all sedimentary rocks.
a. Sandstone21
b. 1509 Istanbul earthquake
c. Undefined
d. Undefined

74. _____ refers to a bend that develops in an initially horizontal layer of rock, usually caused by plastic deformation. Folds occur most frequently in sedimentary rocks.

a. 1509 Istanbul earthquake
b. Fold21
c. Undefined
d. Undefined

75. _____ refers to a permeable rock containing oil or gas.
   a. Reservoir rock21
   b. 1509 Istanbul earthquake
   c. Undefined
   d. Undefined

76. _____ refers to a place in which water is stored, including the oceans, glaciers and polar ice, groundwater, lakes and rivers, the atmosphere, and the biosphere. A source or place of residence for elements in a chemical cycle or hydrologic cycle.
   a. 1509 Istanbul earthquake
   b. Reservoir21
   c. Undefined
   d. Undefined

77. Any unconsolidated material at Earth's surface is _____.
   a. Debris21
   b. 1509 Istanbul earthquake
   c. Undefined
   d. Undefined

78. The innermost layer of the Earth, consisting primarily of pure metals such as iron and nickel is the _____. The _____ is the densest layer of the Earth, and is divided into the outer _____, which is believed to be liquid, and the inner _____, which is believed to be solid.
   a. 1509 Istanbul earthquake
   b. Core21
   c. Undefined
   d. Undefined

79. _____ refers to a ridge-like or mound-like structure, layered or massive, built by sedentary calcareous organisms; it is wave resistant and stands above the surrounding contemporaneously deposited sediment.
   a. 1509 Istanbul earthquake
   b. Reef21
   c. Undefined
   d. Undefined

80. _____ refers to an area underlain by one or more oil pools.
   a. Oil field21
   b. AASHTO Soil Classification System
   c. Undefined
   d. Undefined

81. A reverse fault marked by a dip of 45° or less is called _____.
   a. Thrust fault21
   b. 1509 Istanbul earthquake
   c. Undefined
   d. Undefined

82. Stress that reduces the volume or length of a rock, as that produced by the convergence of plate margins is called _____.
   a. Compression21
   b. 1509 Istanbul earthquake
   c. Undefined
   d. Undefined

83. A fracture dividing a rock into two sections that have visibly moved relative to each other is a _____.
   a. Fault21
   b. 1509 Istanbul earthquake
   c. Undefined
   d. Undefined

84. A large mass of rock projecting above surrounding terrain is called a _____.

Chapter 21. Geologic Resources

    a. 1509 Istanbul earthquake
    b. Mountain21
    c. Undefined
    d. Undefined

85. An accumulation of oil that results from a change in the character of the reservoir rock, rather than from structural deformation is referred to as a _____.
    a. Stratigraphic trap21
    b. 1509 Istanbul earthquake
    c. Undefined
    d. Undefined

86. The study of rock strata, especially of their distribution, deposition, and age is called _____.
    a. 1509 Istanbul earthquake
    b. Stratigraphic21
    c. Undefined
    d. Undefined

87. The processes by which crustal forces cause a rock formation to break and slip along a fault are called _____.
    a. 1509 Istanbul earthquake
    b. Faulting21
    c. Undefined
    d. Undefined

88. The processes by which crustal forces deform an area of crust so that layers of rock are pushed into folds are called _____.
    a. 1509 Istanbul earthquake
    b. Folding21
    c. Undefined
    d. Undefined

89. _____ refers to a vertical conduit through the Earth's crust below a volcano, through which magmatic materials have passed. Commonly filled with volcanic breccia and fragments of older rock.
    a. 1509 Istanbul earthquake
    b. Pipe21
    c. Undefined
    d. Undefined

90. A _____ is a liquid that dissolves a solid, liquid, or gaseous solute, resulting in a solution. The most common _____ in everyday life is water.
    a. Solvent21
    b. Thing
    c. Undefined
    d. Undefined

91. Includes all bodies of water, lakes, rivers, ponds, and so on that are on the surface of the earth, in contrast to groundwater, which lies below the surface is _____.
    a. Surface water21
    b. Thing
    c. Undefined
    d. Undefined

92. _____ refers to a general term applied to all mineral material transported by a glacier and deposited directly by or from the ice, or by running water emanating from the glacier. Generally applies to Pleistocene glacial deposits.
    a. Drift21
    b. 1509 Istanbul earthquake
    c. Undefined
    d. Undefined

93. The liquid portion of magma excluding the solid crystals is called _____.
    a. 1509 Istanbul earthquake
    b. Melt21
    c. Undefined
    d. Undefined

94. _____ is a term used in geology, engineering and surveying to denote the motion of a surface (usually, the earth's surface) downwards relative to a datum such as sea-level.
   a. Thing
   b. Subsidence21
   c. Undefined
   d. Undefined

95. _____ refers to a discordant pluton that is substantially wider than it is thick. Dikes are often steeply inclined or nearly vertical.
   a. Dike21
   b. 1509 Istanbul earthquake
   c. Undefined
   d. Undefined

96. _____ refers to a sand body that is large enough to hold a commercial reserve of asphalt or other thick oil. It is usually surface excavated to remove the thick hydrocarbons.
   a. 1509 Istanbul earthquake
   b. Tar sand21
   c. Undefined
   d. Undefined

97. A fluid's resistance to flow is called _____. _____ increases as temperatures decreases.
   a. Viscosity21
   b. 1509 Istanbul earthquake
   c. Undefined
   d. Undefined

98. _____ is a chemical element in the periodic table that has the symbol V and atomic number 23. A rare, soft and ductile element, _____ is found combined in certain minerals and is used mainly to produce certain alloys. It is one of the 26 elements commonly found in living things.
   a. Thing
   b. Vanadium21
   c. Undefined
   d. Undefined

99. A body of rock identified by lithic characteristics and stratigraphic position and is mappable at the earth's surface or traceable in the subsurface is a _____.
   a. 1509 Istanbul earthquake
   b. Formation21
   c. Undefined
   d. Undefined

100. A major branch of a stream system is referred to as a _____.
   a. 1509 Istanbul earthquake
   b. River21
   c. Undefined
   d. Undefined

101. The scientific study of the Earth, its origins and evolution, the materials that make it up, and the processes that act on it is called _____.
   a. Geology21
   b. 1509 Istanbul earthquake
   c. Undefined
   d. Undefined

102. _____ is a solid in which the constituent atoms, molecules, or ions are packed in a regularly ordered, repeating pattern extending in all three spatial dimensions.
   a. Crystal21
   b. Thing
   c. Undefined
   d. Undefined

103. _____ is any particulate matter that can be transported by fluid flow and which eventually is deposited as a layer of solid particles on the bed or bottom of a body of water or other liquid.

| a. Thing | b. Sediment21 |
| c. Undefined | d. Undefined |

104. Describing a mineral that will not react with or convert to a new mineral or substance, given enough time is referred to as _____.

| a. Stable21 | b. 1509 Istanbul earthquake |
| c. Undefined | d. Undefined |

105. A slow but steady rise in Earth's surface temperature, caused by increasing concentrations of greenhouse gases in the atmosphere is referred to as _____.

| a. Thing | b. Global warming21 |
| c. Undefined | d. Undefined |

106. _____ is an atmospheric gas comprized of one carbon and two oxygen atoms. A very widely known chemical compound, it is frequently called by its formula CO_2. In its solid state, it is commonly known as dry ice.

| a. Thing | b. Carbon dioxide21 |
| c. Undefined | d. Undefined |

107. _____ refers to a gas, such as carbon dioxide or methane, that traps sunlight energy in a planet's atmosphere as heat; a gas that participates in the greenhouse effect.

| a. Greenhouse gas21 | b. Thing |
| c. Undefined | d. Undefined |

108. A preserved remnant or impression of an organism that lived in the past is referred to as _____.

| a. Thing | b. Fossil21 |
| c. Undefined | d. Undefined |

109. The relationship between distance on a map and the distance on the terrain being represented by that map is a _____.

| a. 1509 Istanbul earthquake | b. Scale21 |
| c. Undefined | d. Undefined |

110. Restoration of the land to usable condition after mining has ceased is _____.

| a. Reclamation21 | b. 1509 Istanbul earthquake |
| c. Undefined | d. Undefined |

111. _____ in referring to sedinent grains, loose, separate, or unattached to one another.

| a. AASHTO Soil Classification System | b. Unconsolidated21 |
| c. Undefined | d. Undefined |

112. The diagenetic process by which the volume or thickness of sediment is reduced due to pressure from overlying layers of sediment is called _____.

| a. 1509 Istanbul earthquake | b. Compaction21 |
| c. Undefined | d. Undefined |

113. _____ refers to a soft, brownish coal that develops from peat through bacterial action, is rich in kerogen, and has a carbon content of 70%, which makes it a more efficient heating fuel than peat.
  a. 1509 Istanbul earthquake
  b. Lignite21
  c. Undefined
  d. Undefined

114. _____ refers to the height of floodwaters in feet or meters above an established datum plane.
  a. 1509 Istanbul earthquake
  b. Stage21
  c. Undefined
  d. Undefined

115. _____ refers to soil type largely composed of partly decomposed organic material.
  a. Peat21
  b. Thing
  c. Undefined
  d. Undefined

116. A shiny black coal that develops from deeply buried lignite through heat and pressure, and that has a carbon content of 80% to 93%, which makes it a more efficient heating fuel than lignite is _____.
  a. Bituminous coal21
  b. 1509 Istanbul earthquake
  c. Undefined
  d. Undefined

117. _____ is the result of the transformation of a pre-existing rock type, the protolith, in a process called metamorphism, which means "change in form". The protolith is subjected to heat (greater than 150 degrees Celsius) and extreme pressure causing profound physical and/or chemical change.
  a. Thing
  b. Metamorphic rock21
  c. Undefined
  d. Undefined

118. _____ refers to the term from the Greek 'meta' and 'morph', commonly occurs to rocks which are subjected to increased heat and/or pressure. Also applies to the conversion of snow into glacial ice.
  a. 1509 Istanbul earthquake
  b. Metamorphic21
  c. Undefined
  d. Undefined

119. A hard, jet-black coal that develops from lignite and bituminous coal through metamorphism, has a carbon content of 92% to 98%, and contains little or no gas is called _____. _____ burns with an extremely hot, blue flame and very little smoke, but it is difficult to ignite and both difficult and dangerous to mine.
  a. Anthracite21
  b. AASHTO Soil Classification System
  c. Undefined
  d. Undefined

120. _____ refers to a mine in which the valuable material is exposed at the surface by removing a strip of overburden.
  a. 1509 Istanbul earthquake
  b. Strip mine21
  c. Undefined
  d. Undefined

121. _____ refers to the upper part of a sedimentary deposit. Its weight causes compaction of the lower part.
  a. Overburden21
  b. AASHTO Soil Classification System
  c. Undefined
  d. Undefined

122. An elongated depression in the seafloor produced by bending of oceanic crust during subduction is a _____.

Chapter 21. Geologic Resources

a. Trench21
b. 1509 Istanbul earthquake
c. Undefined
d. Undefined

123. The _____ is a geologic period that extends from about 299.0 Ma to 248.0 Ma. It is the last period of the Palaeozoic Era. As with most older geologic periods, the strata that define the _____ are well identified, but the exact date of the period's start is uncertain by a few million years.
a. Permian21
b. Thing
c. Undefined
d. Undefined

124. The _____ Era is a major division of the geologic timescale, one of four geologic eras. The division of time into eras, the largest division of geologic time, dates back to Giovanni Arduino in the 18th century, although his original name for the era now called the _____ was "Primitive".
a. Thing
b. Paleozoic21
c. Undefined
d. Undefined

125. An episode of mountain building is called _____.
a. AASHTO Soil Classification System
b. Orogeny21
c. Undefined
d. Undefined

126. Surficial mining, in which the resource is exposed by removing the overburden is called _____.
a. 1509 Istanbul earthquake
b. Strip-mining21
c. Undefined
d. Undefined

127. Strain involving an increase in length is an _____. _____ can cause crustal thinning and faulting.
a. AASHTO Soil Classification System
b. Extension21
c. Undefined
d. Undefined

128. A round or oval depression in the Earth's surface, containing the youngest section of rock in its lowest, central part is a _____.
a. 1509 Istanbul earthquake
b. Basin21
c. Undefined
d. Undefined

129. _____ refers to a coal's carbon content depending upon its degree of metamorphism.
a. 1509 Istanbul earthquake
b. Rank21
c. Undefined
d. Undefined

130. _____ refers to a body of water found on the Earth's surface and confined to a narrow topographic depression, down which it flows and transports rock particles, sediment, and dissolved particles. Rivers, creeks, brooks, and runs are all streams.
a. 1509 Istanbul earthquake
b. Stream21
c. Undefined
d. Undefined

131. _____ is the uppermost layer of soil, usually the top 15-20 cm. It has the highest concentration of organic matter and microorganisms, and is where most of the Earth's biological soil activity occurs.

Chapter 21. Geologic Resources

    a. Thing
    c. Undefined
    b. Topsoil21
    d. Undefined

132. An area with sparse vegetation owing to some physical or chemical property of the soil is referred to as _____.
    a. Barren21
    b. Thing
    c. Undefined
    d. Undefined

133. Fine particles of pulverized rock blown from an explosion vent are called _____. Measuring less than 1/10 inch in diameter, _____ may be either solid or molten when first erupted.
    a. AASHTO Soil Classification System
    b. Ash21
    c. Undefined
    d. Undefined

134. Rocks formed by solidification of sediments formed and transported at the Earth's surface are referred to as _____.
    a. Sedimentary rocks21
    b. 1509 Istanbul earthquake
    c. Undefined
    d. Undefined

135. A vein filled with minerals that contain large amounts of chemically bound water and are known to crystallize from hot-water solutions is called _____.
    a. 1509 Istanbul earthquake
    b. Hydrothermal vein21
    c. Undefined
    d. Undefined

136. _____ is one of the three main rock groups and is formed in three main ways—by the deposition of the weathered remains of other rocks; by the deposition of the results of biogenic activity; and by precipitation from solution.
    a. Sedimentary rock21
    b. Event
    c. Undefined
    d. Undefined

137. A sheetlike deposit of minerals precipitated in fractures or joints that are foreign to the host rock is called a _____.
    a. Vein21
    b. 1509 Istanbul earthquake
    c. Undefined
    d. Undefined

138. _____ refers to drop out of a saturated solution as crystals. The crystals that drop out of a saturated solution.
    a. 1509 Istanbul earthquake
    b. Precipitate21
    c. Undefined
    d. Undefined

139. A material that forms as the organic matter of buried wood is either filled in or replaced by inorganic silica carried in by ground water is called _____.
    a. 1509 Istanbul earthquake
    b. Petrified wood21
    c. Undefined
    d. Undefined

140. _____ refers to a feature on the surface of the planet Mars that very closely resembles certain types of stream channels on Earth.
    a. 1509 Istanbul earthquake
    b. Channel21
    c. Undefined
    d. Undefined

Chapter 21. Geologic Resources

141. A chemical or biochemical sedimentary rock composed of calcium phosphate precipitated from phosphaterich seawater and formed diagenetically by the interaction between muddy or carbonate sediments and the phosphate-rich water is _____.
   a. Phosphorite21
   b. 1509 Istanbul earthquake
   c. Undefined
   d. Undefined

142. During the _____ Period the first fish evolved legs and started to walk on land as amphibians, and the first arthropods like insects and spiders also started to colonize terrestrial habitats.
   a. Thing
   b. Devonian21
   c. Undefined
   d. Undefined

143. The presence of contaminants in the air in concentrations that overcome the normal dispersive ability of the air and that interfere directly or indirectly with human health, safety, or comfort or with the full use and enjoyment of property is referred to as _____.
   a. Air pollution21
   b. Thing
   c. Undefined
   d. Undefined

144. _____ refer to coal, oil, natural gas, and all other solid or liquid hydrocarbon fuels.
   a. 1509 Istanbul earthquake
   b. Fossil fuels21
   c. Undefined
   d. Undefined

145. _____ refers to an energy deposit formed from the remains of extinct organisms.
   a. Thing
   b. Fossil fuel21
   c. Undefined
   d. Undefined

146. Any environmental change that adversely affects the lives and health of living things is referred to as _____.
   a. Thing
   b. Pollution21
   c. Undefined
   d. Undefined

147. A nuclear reactor that manufactures more fissionable isotopes than it consumes is a _____. Breeder reactors use the widely available, nonfissionable uranium isotope U-238, together with small amounts of fissionable U-235, to produce a fissionable isotope of plutonium.
   a. Breeder reactor21
   b. 1509 Istanbul earthquake
   c. Undefined
   d. Undefined

148. _____ refers to a self-sustaining nuclear reaction that occurs when atomic nuclei undergo fission. Free neutrons are released that split other nuclei, causing more fissions and the release of more neutrons, which split other nuclei, and so on.
   a. 1509 Istanbul earthquake
   b. Chain reaction21
   c. Undefined
   d. Undefined

149. _____ refers to a timeline based on a stratigraphic succession that provides a chronological record of the history of a region. The entire span of time since the Earth formed.
   a. Geologic time21
   b. 1509 Istanbul earthquake
   c. Undefined
   d. Undefined

Chapter 21. Geologic Resources

150. _____ is a radioactive, metallic, chemical element. It has the symbol Pu and the atomic number 94. It is the element used in most modern nuclear weapons. The most important isotope of _____ is ^{239}Pu, with a half-life of 24,110 years. It can be made from natural uranium and is fissile.
   a. Plutonium21
   b. Thing
   c. Undefined
   d. Undefined

151. A particle that is found in the nucleus of an atom, has a mass approximately equal to that of a proton, and has no electric charge is referred to as a _____.
   a. 1509 Istanbul earthquake
   b. Neutron21
   c. Undefined
   d. Undefined

152. Electricity generated by falling water that is used to drive turbines is called _____.
   a. 1509 Istanbul earthquake
   b. Hydroelectric power21
   c. Undefined
   d. Undefined

153. Power generated by using the heat energy of the earth is called _____.
   a. Geothermal power21
   b. 1509 Istanbul earthquake
   c. Undefined
   d. Undefined

154. A spring in which the water is 6-9°C warmer than the mean annual air temperature of its locality is called _____.
   a. 1509 Istanbul earthquake
   b. Hot spring21
   c. Undefined
   d. Undefined

155. The time between winter and summer is _____.
   a. 1509 Istanbul earthquake
   b. Spring21
   c. Undefined
   d. Undefined

156. Energy derived from the Sun, including energy from solar generating systems, hydroelectric systems, and wind power is called _____.
   a. Solar energy21
   b. 1509 Istanbul earthquake
   c. Undefined
   d. Undefined

157. An _____ is any more or less permanent or continuous, directed movement of ocean water that flows in one of the Earth's oceans.
   a. Thing
   b. Ocean current21
   c. Undefined
   d. Undefined

158. _____ is a means of electricity generation achieved by capturing the energy contained in moving water mass due to tides.
   a. Thing
   b. Tidal power21
   c. Undefined
   d. Undefined

159. A _____ is any natural resource that is depleted at a rate slower than the rate at which it regenerates.
   a. Renewable resource21
   b. Thing
   c. Undefined
   d. Undefined

Chapter 21. Geologic Resources

160. As yet undiscovered mineral deposits and also known mineral deposits for which recovery is not yet economically feasible is called _____.
   a. 1509 Istanbul earthquake
   b. Potential ore21
   c. Undefined
   d. Undefined

161. _____ refers to a type of iron oxide that has a brick-red color when powdered.
   a. Hematite21
   b. 1509 Istanbul earthquake
   c. Undefined
   d. Undefined

162. _____ refers to a type of iron oxide that is yellowish-brown when powdered.
   a. 1509 Istanbul earthquake
   b. Limonite21
   c. Undefined
   d. Undefined

163. The part of an ore, usually metallic, that is economically desirable is called _____.
   a. AASHTO Soil Classification System
   b. Ore mineral21
   c. Undefined
   d. Undefined

164. _____ refers to the process of emplacement of magma in pre-existing rock. Also, the term refers to igneous rock mass so formed within the surrounding rock.
   a. AASHTO Soil Classification System
   b. Intrusion21
   c. Undefined
   d. Undefined

165. The _____ is an informal name for the eons of the geologic timescale that came before the current Phanerozoic eon. It spans from the formation of Earth around 4500 Ma (million years ago) to the evolution of abundant macroscopic hard-shelled fossils, which marked the beginning of the Cambrian.
   a. Thing
   b. Precambrian21
   c. Undefined
   d. Undefined

166. _____ refers to a concordant pluton that is substantially wider than it is thick. Sills form within a few kilometers of the Earth's surface.
   a. 1509 Istanbul earthquake
   b. Sill21
   c. Undefined
   d. Undefined

167. _____ refers to the formation and growth of a crystalline solid from a liquid or gas.
   a. Crystallization21
   b. 1509 Istanbul earthquake
   c. Undefined
   d. Undefined

168. _____ refers to any rock that was older than and intruded by an igneous body.
   a. 1509 Istanbul earthquake
   b. Country rock21
   c. Undefined
   d. Undefined

169. An intrusive rock, as distinguished from the preexisting country rock that surrounds it is called _____.
   a. Pluton21
   b. 1509 Istanbul earthquake
   c. Undefined
   d. Undefined

Chapter 21. Geologic Resources

170. Molten rock that forms naturally within the Earth is _____. _____ may be either a liquid or a fluid mixture of liquid, crystals, and dissolved gases.
a. 1509 Istanbul earthquake
b. Magma21
c. Undefined
d. Undefined

171. An _____ is the smallest possible particle of a chemical element that retains its chemical properties.
a. Thing
b. Atom21
c. Undefined
d. Undefined

172. One of the minerals that is abundant in the hot water that seeps through hydrothermal vents is _____.
a. Sulfide21
b. Thing
c. Undefined
d. Undefined

173. _____ is the transfer of heat by currents within a fluid. It may arise from temperature differences either within the fluid or between the fluid and its boundary, other sources of density variations (such as variable salinity), or from the application of an external motive force.
a. Event
b. Convection21
c. Undefined
d. Undefined

174. _____ refers to the hot, watery solution that escapes from a mass of magma during the latter stages of crystallization. Such solutions may alter the surrounding country rock and are frequently the source of significant ore deposits.
a. 1509 Istanbul earthquake
b. Hydrothermal solution21
c. Undefined
d. Undefined

175. Usually slow but effective process of weathering and erosion in which rocks are dissolved by water is a _____.
a. 1509 Istanbul earthquake
b. Solution21
c. Undefined
d. Undefined

176. _____ refers to igneous rocks formed beneath the surface of the Earth; typically with large crystals due to the slowness of cooling.
a. Plutonic21
b. 1509 Istanbul earthquake
c. Undefined
d. Undefined

177. _____ refers to a crack or break in a rock. To break in random places instead of cleaving.
a. 1509 Istanbul earthquake
b. Fracture21
c. Undefined
d. Undefined

178. _____ is a chemical element that has the symbol W (L. wolframium) and atomic number 74. A very hard, heavy, steel-gray to white transition metal, _____ is found in several ores including wolframite and scheelite and is remarkable for its robust physical properties, especially the fact that it has a higher melting point than any other non-alloy in existence.
a. Tungsten21
b. Thing
c. Undefined
d. Undefined

179. _____ refers to pertaining to magma.

a. 1509 Istanbul earthquake
c. Undefined
b. Magmatic21
d. Undefined

180. _____ is the name given to the changes that take place when magma is injected into the surrounding solid rock (country rock). The changes that occur are greatest wherever the magma comes into contact with the rock because the temperatures are highest at this boundary and decrease with distance from it.
   a. Thing
   b. Contact metamorphism21
   c. Undefined
   d. Undefined

181. The process by which conditions within the Earth, below the zone of diagenesis, alter the mineral content, chemical composition, and structure of solid rock without melting it is called _____. Igneous, sedimentary, and metamorphic rocks may all undergo _____.
   a. 1509 Istanbul earthquake
   b. Metamorphism21
   c. Undefined
   d. Undefined

182. A crystallized rock, typically porphyritic, having hairline fractures that contain copper and other metals is called _____.
   a. Porphyry copper deposit21
   b. 1509 Istanbul earthquake
   c. Undefined
   d. Undefined

183. A copper deposit, usually of low grade, in which the copper-bearing minerals occur in disseminated grains and/or in veinlets through a large volume of rock, is called _____.
   a. Porphyry copper21
   b. 1509 Istanbul earthquake
   c. Undefined
   d. Undefined

184. An igneous rock with a porphyritic texture is referred to as _____.
   a. 1509 Istanbul earthquake
   b. Porphyry21
   c. Undefined
   d. Undefined

185. A pink-colored, felsic, plutonic rock that contains potassium and usually sodium feldspars, and has quartz content of about 10% is _____. _____ is commonly found on continents but virtually absent from the ocean basins.
   a. 1509 Istanbul earthquake
   b. Granite21
   c. Undefined
   d. Undefined

186. An intrusive rock formed inside the Earth is referred to as a _____.
   a. 1509 Istanbul earthquake
   b. Plutonic rock21
   c. Undefined
   d. Undefined

187. A coarse-grained igneous rock with exceptionally large crystals, formed from a magma that contains a high proportion of water is referred to as _____.
   a. Pegmatite21
   b. 1509 Istanbul earthquake
   c. Undefined
   d. Undefined

188. _____ refers to any condensed water falling from the atmosphere to the surface of the earth. Common types include rain, snow, sleet, and hail.

a. 1509 Istanbul earthquake
c. Undefined
b. Precipitation21
d. Undefined

189. A member of a group of sedimentary rocks that consist primarily of microscopic silica crystals is _____. _____ may be either organic or inorganic, but the most common forms are inorganic.
   a. 1509 Istanbul earthquake
   b. Chert21
   c. Undefined
   d. Undefined

190. The process by which exposure to atmospheric agents, such as air or moisture, causes rocks and minerals to break down is called _____. This process takes place at or near the Earth's surface. _____ entails little or no movement of the material that it loosens from the rocks and minerals.
   a. Weathering21
   b. 1509 Istanbul earthquake
   c. Undefined
   d. Undefined

191. Water entering rivers, lakes, reservoirs, or the ocean from land surfaces is _____.
   a. Thing
   b. Runoff21
   c. Undefined
   d. Undefined

192. _____ is a chemical element in the periodic table that has the symbol Ti and atomic number 22. It is a light, strong, lustrous, corrosion-resistant (including resistance to sea water and chlorine) transition metal with a white-silvery-metallic color. _____ is used in strong light-weight alloys (most notably with iron and aluminium) and its most common compound, _____ dioxide, is used in white pigments.
   a. Titanium21
   b. Thing
   c. Undefined
   d. Undefined

193. A rock particle 2 to 64 mm in diameter is referred to as the _____.
   a. 1509 Istanbul earthquake
   b. Pebble21
   c. Undefined
   d. Undefined

194. _____ refers to a deposit formed when heavy minerals are mechanically concentrated by currents, most commonly streams and waves. Placers are sources of gold, tin, platinum, diamonds, and other valuable minerals.
   a. 1509 Istanbul earthquake
   b. Placer21
   c. Undefined
   d. Undefined

195. Mine in which ore is exposed at the surface in a large excavation is referred to as the _____.
   a. Open-pit mine21
   b. AASHTO Soil Classification System
   c. Undefined
   d. Undefined

196. Surface mines in which valuable mineral grains are extracted from stream bar or beach deposits are referred to as a _____.
   a. 1509 Istanbul earthquake
   b. Placer mine21
   c. Undefined
   d. Undefined

197. An _____ is a water-soluble, sour-tasting chemical compound that when dissolved in water, gives a solution with a pH of less than 7.

a. Thing
b. Acid21
c. Undefined
d. Undefined

198. _____ refers to the major constituent of acid precipitation. Formed as a result of sulfur dioxide emissions reacting with water vapor in the atmosphere.
   a. Thing
   b. Sulfuric acid21
   c. Undefined
   d. Undefined

199. _____ is a chemical element in the periodic table. It has the symbol O and atomic number 8. _____ is the second most common element on Earth, composing around 46% of the mass of Earth's crust and 28% of the mass of Earth as a whole, and is the third most common element in the universe.
   a. Oxygen21
   b. Thing
   c. Undefined
   d. Undefined

200. A _____ is an environment "at the interface between truly terrestrial ecosystems...and truly aquatic systems...making them different from each yet highly dependent on both."
   a. Wetland21
   b. Thing
   c. Undefined
   d. Undefined

201. _____ is a ferrimagnetic mineral form of iron(II,III) oxide, with chemical formula Fe_3O_4, one of several iron oxides and a member of the spinel group.
   a. Thing
   b. Magnetite21
   c. Undefined
   d. Undefined

202. A metal that is manufactured by combining two or more molten metals is called _____. An _____ is always harder than its component metals. Bronze is an _____ of copper and tin.
   a. Alloy21
   b. AASHTO Soil Classification System
   c. Undefined
   d. Undefined

203. A thin, sheetlike igneous intrusion into a crevice is referred to as a _____.
   a. 1509 Istanbul earthquake
   b. Vein deposit21
   c. Undefined
   d. Undefined

204. _____ refers to a small, conspicuous, isolated hill bounded by cliffs.
   a. 1509 Istanbul earthquake
   b. Butte21
   c. Undefined
   d. Undefined

205. Low latitude areas characterized by high temperatures and high precipitation are referred to as _____. At high elevations, however, _____ mountains may be both cold and relatively dry.
   a. Tropical21
   b. 1509 Istanbul earthquake
   c. Undefined
   d. Undefined

206. _____ refers to the principal ore of aluminum.
   a. 1509 Istanbul earthquake
   b. Bauxite21
   c. Undefined
   d. Undefined

Chapter 21. Geologic Resources

207. _____ refers to mining from open excavations, most commonly for low-grade copper and iron deposits, and coal.
   a. Open-pit mining21
   b. AASHTO Soil Classification System
   c. Undefined
   d. Undefined

208. A chemical _____, often called simply _____, is a chemical substance that cannot be divided or changed into other chemical substances by any ordinary chemical technique. An _____ is a class of substances that contain the same number of protons in all its atoms.
   a. Thing
   b. Element21
   c. Undefined
   d. Undefined

209. A deposit of heavy or durable minerals, such as gold or diamonds, typically found where the flow of water abruptly slows is called a _____.
   a. 1509 Istanbul earthquake
   b. Placer deposit21
   c. Undefined
   d. Undefined

210. A main mineralized unit that may not be economically valuable in itself but to which workable deposits are related is the _____. An ore deposit from which a placer is derived; the mother rock of a placer.
   a. 1509 Istanbul earthquake
   b. Mother Lode21
   c. Undefined
   d. Undefined

211. A mineral deposit consisting of a zone of veins in consolidated rock, as opposed to a placer deposit is called _____.
   a. 1509 Istanbul earthquake
   b. Lode21
   c. Undefined
   d. Undefined

212. _____ is a chemical element in the periodic table. Its symbol is Mo and its atomic number 42. _____ is a transition metal. The pure metal is silvery white in color and very hard, and has one of the highest melting points of all pure elements.
   a. Thing
   b. Molybdenum21
   c. Undefined
   d. Undefined

213. _____ is a chemical element in the periodic table that has the symbol Co and atomic number 27. _____ is a hard ferromagnetic silver-white element.
   a. Cobalt21
   b. Thing
   c. Undefined
   d. Undefined

214. _____ refers to rigid parts of the Earth's crust and part of the Earth's upper mantle that moves and adjoins each other along zones of seismic activity.
   a. Plate21
   b. 1509 Istanbul earthquake
   c. Undefined
   d. Undefined

215. Angular chunk of solid rock ejected during an eruption is referred to as a _____.
   a. 1509 Istanbul earthquake
   b. Block21
   c. Undefined
   d. Undefined

Chapter 21. Geologic Resources

216. _____ refers to deposits of stratified sand, gravel, and silt that have been removed from a glacier by meltwater streams.
   a. 1509 Istanbul earthquake
   b. Glacial outwash21
   c. Undefined
   d. Undefined

217. A mound of loose sand grains heaped up by the wind is a _____.
   a. Sand dune21
   b. 1509 Istanbul earthquake
   c. Undefined
   d. Undefined

218. A load of sediment, consisting of sand and gravel that is deposited by meltwater in front of a glacier is called _____.
   a. AASHTO Soil Classification System
   b. Outwash21
   c. Undefined
   d. Undefined

219. _____ refers to a usually asymmetrical mound or ridge of sand that has been transported and deposited by wind. Dunes form in both arid and humid climates.
   a. 1509 Istanbul earthquake
   b. Dune21
   c. Undefined
   d. Undefined

220. A pyroclastic cone composed primarily of cinders is referred to as the _____.
   a. Cinder cone21
   b. 1509 Istanbul earthquake
   c. Undefined
   d. Undefined

221. _____ refers to pyroclast approximately the size of a sand grain. Sometimes defined as between 4 and 32 millimeters in diameter.
   a. 1509 Istanbul earthquake
   b. Cinder21
   c. Undefined
   d. Undefined

222. _____ refers to the top few meters of regolith, generally including some organic matter derived from plants.
   a. Soil21
   b. 1509 Istanbul earthquake
   c. Undefined
   d. Undefined

223. A _____ is a polyatomic ion or radical consisting of one phosphorus atom and four oxygen. In the ionic form, it carries a -3 formal charge, and is denoted PO_4^{3-}.
   a. Phosphate21
   b. Thing
   c. Undefined
   d. Undefined

224. _____ refers to a salt of nitric acid; a compound containing the radical NO_3; biologically, the final form of nitrogen from the oxidation of organic nitrogen compounds.
   a. Nitrate21
   b. Thing
   c. Undefined
   d. Undefined

225. An evaporite composed of halite is referred to as _____.
   a. 1509 Istanbul earthquake
   b. Rock salt21
   c. Undefined
   d. Undefined

Chapter 21. Geologic Resources

226. _____ refers to a column or plug of rock salt that rises from depth because of its low density and pierces overlying sediments.
   a. Salt dome21
   b. 1509 Istanbul earthquake
   c. Undefined
   d. Undefined

227. _____ refers to a round or oval bulge on the Earth's surface, containing the oldest section of rock in its raised, central part.
   a. Dome21
   b. 1509 Istanbul earthquake
   c. Undefined
   d. Undefined

228. _____ refers to levels within a soil profile that differ structurally and chemically. Generally divided into A, B, C, E, and 0 horizons.
   a. Horizon21
   b. Thing
   c. Undefined
   d. Undefined

229. A necessary part of an oil trap is a _____. The _____ is impermeable and hence keeps upwardly mobile oil and gas from escaping at the surface.
   a. 1509 Istanbul earthquake
   b. Cap rock21
   c. Undefined
   d. Undefined

230. The degree of resistance of a given mineral to scratching, indicating the strength of the bonds that hold the mineral's atoms together is called _____. The _____ of a mineral is measured by rubbing it with substances of known _____.
   a. Hardness21
   b. 1509 Istanbul earthquake
   c. Undefined
   d. Undefined

231. An igneous rock rich in magnesium that forms soils toxic to many plants is called _____. Soils derived from _____ are toxic to many plants due to their high mineral content, and the flora is generally very distinctive, with specialized, slow-growing species.
   a. Thing
   b. Serpentine21
   c. Undefined
   d. Undefined

232. _____ refers to the ratio of the weight of a particular volume of a given substance to the weight of an equal volume of pure water.
   a. Specific gravity21
   b. 1509 Istanbul earthquake
   c. Undefined
   d. Undefined

233. The force of attraction exerted by one body in the universe on another is _____. _____ is directly proportional to the product of the masses of the two attracted bodies. The force of attraction exerted by the Earth on bodies on or near its surface, tending to pull them toward the Earth's center.
   a. Gravity21
   b. 1509 Istanbul earthquake
   c. Undefined
   d. Undefined

234. _____ is a chemical element in the periodic table that has the symbol B and atomic number 5. A trivalent metalloid element, _____ occurs abundantly in the ore borax.

a. Boron21
b. Thing
c. Undefined
d. Undefined

235. _____, or diatomaceous earth, is a siliceous sedimentary rock formed from the accumulations of diatoms or other nanoplankton.
   a. Diatomite21
   b. 1509 Istanbul earthquake
   c. Undefined
   d. Undefined

236. A type of hydrogenous sediment scattered on the ocean floor, consisting mainly of manganese and iron and usually containing small amounts of copper, nickel, and cobalt are _____.
   a. 1509 Istanbul earthquake
   b. Manganese nodules21
   c. Undefined
   d. Undefined

237. _____ is a rock concretion on the sea bottom formed of concentric layers of iron and manganese hydroxides around a core. They are one of the slowest of all geological phenomena – in the order of a centimeter over several million years.
   a. Manganese nodule21
   b. Thing
   c. Undefined
   d. Undefined

238. The _____ refers to those areas of oceans to which little or no light penetrates.
   a. Thing
   b. Deep sea21
   c. Undefined
   d. Undefined

239. A convex fold in a rock, the central part of which contains the oldest section of rock is referred to as the _____.
   a. AASHTO Soil Classification System
   b. Anticline21
   c. Undefined
   d. Undefined

240. Any economic mineral deposit in which the desired mineral occurs as scattered particles in the rock but in sufficient quantity to make the deposit an ore is referred to as _____.
   a. 1509 Istanbul earthquake
   b. Disseminated deposit21
   c. Undefined
   d. Undefined

241. The zone of convergence of two tectonic plates, one of which usually overrides the other is referred to as the _____.
   a. Subduction zone21
   b. 1509 Istanbul earthquake
   c. Undefined
   d. Undefined

242. The downward movement of a plate into the mantle that occurs in trenches, which are also known as _____ zones.
   a. Thing
   b. Subduction21
   c. Undefined
   d. Undefined

Chapter 22. The Earth's Companions

1. The warming of the atmosphere caused by COD CH4, and other gases that absorb infrared radiation and slow its escape from Earth's surface is called _____.
   - a. Thing
   - b. Greenhouse effect22
   - c. Undefined
   - d. Undefined

2. Earth's _____ is a layer of gases surrounding the planet Earth and retained by the Earth's gravity. It contains roughly 78% nitrogen and 21% oxygen, with trace amounts of other gases.
   - a. Thing
   - b. Atmosphere22
   - c. Undefined
   - d. Undefined

3. A body of rock identified by lithic characteristics and stratigraphic position and is mappable at the earth's surface or traceable in the subsurface is a _____.
   - a. Formation22
   - b. 1509 Istanbul earthquake
   - c. Undefined
   - d. Undefined

4. _____ is a chemical element in the periodic table that has the symbol Hg and atomic number 80. A heavy, silvery, transition metal, _____ is one of five elements that are liquid at or near standard room temperature (the others are the metals caesium, francium, and gallium, and the nonmetal bromine).
   - a. Mercury22
   - b. Thing
   - c. Undefined
   - d. Undefined

5. A large volume of interstellar gas and dust is referred to as _____.
   - a. 1509 Istanbul earthquake
   - b. Nebula22
   - c. Undefined
   - d. Undefined

6. _____ refers to the height of floodwaters in feet or meters above an established datum plane.
   - a. 1509 Istanbul earthquake
   - b. Stage22
   - c. Undefined
   - d. Undefined

7. A _____ is the outer layer of a planet, part of its lithosphere. Planetary _____ is generally composed of a less dense material than that of its deeper layers. The _____ of the Earth is composed mainly of basalt and granite.
   - a. Crust22
   - b. Thing
   - c. Undefined
   - d. Undefined

8. _____ refers to one of thousands of small planetlike bodies, ranging in size from a few hundred kilometers to less than one kilometer across. Most asteroids' orbits lie between those of Mars and Jupiter.
   - a. AASHTO Soil Classification System
   - b. Asteroid22
   - c. Undefined
   - d. Undefined

9. _____ refers to the luminous phenomenon observed when a meteoroid enters Earth's atmosphere and burns up; popularly called a 'shooting star'.
   - a. Meteor22
   - b. 1509 Istanbul earthquake
   - c. Undefined
   - d. Undefined

10. _____ refers to an object which circles the sun in a non-circular orbit. Commonly made up of a large mass of rock debris and ice.

a. 1509 Istanbul earthquake
c. Undefined
b. Comet22
d. Undefined

11. An igneous pluton that is not tabular in shape is _____.
   a. Massive22
   b. 1509 Istanbul earthquake
   c. Undefined
   d. Undefined

12. _____ is a metallic chemical element in the periodic table that has the symbol Ni and atomic number 28. Notable characteristicsNickel is a silvery white metal that takes on a high polish. It belongs to the iron group, and is hard, malleable, and ductile. It occurs combined with sulfur in millerite, with arsenic in the mineral niccolite, and with arsenic and sulfur in _____ glance.
   a. Thing
   b. Nickel22
   c. Undefined
   d. Undefined

13. The force of attraction exerted by one body in the universe on another is _____. _____ is directly proportional to the product of the masses of the two attracted bodies. The force of attraction exerted by the Earth on bodies on or near its surface, tending to pull them toward the Earth's center.
   a. 1509 Istanbul earthquake
   b. Gravity22
   c. Undefined
   d. Undefined

14. _____ is a chemical element in the periodic table that has the symbol H and atomic number 1. At standard temperature and pressure it is a colorless, odorless, nonmetallic, univalent, tasteless, highly flammable diatomic gas.
   a. Thing
   b. Hydrogen22
   c. Undefined
   d. Undefined

15. _____ is a chemical element; it is a colorless, odorless, tasteless, non-toxic, and nearly inert monatomic that heads the noble gas series in the periodic table. Its atomic number is 2 and its boiling and melting points are the lowest among the elements. It exists only as a gas except in extreme conditions.
   a. Thing
   b. Helium22
   c. Undefined
   d. Undefined

16. An _____ is the smallest possible particle of a chemical element that retains its chemical properties.
   a. Thing
   b. Atom22
   c. Undefined
   d. Undefined

17. The innermost layer of the Earth, consisting primarily of pure metals such as iron and nickel is the _____. The _____ is the densest layer of the Earth, and is divided into the outer _____, which is believed to be liquid, and the inner _____, which is believed to be solid.
   a. 1509 Istanbul earthquake
   b. Core22
   c. Undefined
   d. Undefined

18. Ability to do work is referred to as _____. Most evident in glacial systems as radiant _____ from the sun and as latent _____ required to melt ice to water.
   a. Energy22
   b. AASHTO Soil Classification System
   c. Undefined
   d. Undefined

19. _____ refers to a volume of space in which a given electron occurs 90% of the time. It is the quantum state of the individual electrons in the electron cloud around a single atom.
   a. Orbital22
   b. Thing
   c. Undefined
   d. Undefined

20. _____ refers to a naturally formed aggregate of usually inorganic materials from within the Earth.
   a. 1509 Istanbul earthquake
   b. Rock22
   c. Undefined
   d. Undefined

21. An electrically neutral substance that consists of two or more elements combined in specific, constant proportions is a _____. A _____ typically has physical characteristics different from those of its constituent elements.
   a. 1509 Istanbul earthquake
   b. Compound22
   c. Undefined
   d. Undefined

22. _____ is a compound of nitrogen and hydrogen with the formula NH_3. At standard temperature and pressure _____ is a gas. It is toxic and corrosive to some materials, and has a characteristic pungent odor.
   a. Ammonia22
   b. Thing
   c. Undefined
   d. Undefined

23. One of several rock-forming minerals that contain silicon, oxygen, and usually one or more other common elements is _____.
   a. 1509 Istanbul earthquake
   b. Silicate22
   c. Undefined
   d. Undefined

24. _____ refers to one of the Earthlike planets: Mercury, Venus, Earth, and Mars. These planets have similar densities.
   a. 1509 Istanbul earthquake
   b. Terrestrial planet22
   c. Undefined
   d. Undefined

25. The relationship between distance on a map and the distance on the terrain being represented by that map is a _____.
   a. 1509 Istanbul earthquake
   b. Scale22
   c. Undefined
   d. Undefined

26. _____ refers to a tentative explanation of a given set of data that is expected to remain valid after future observation and experimentation.
   a. Hypothesis22
   b. 1509 Istanbul earthquake
   c. Undefined
   d. Undefined

27. A chemical _____, often called simply _____, is a chemical substance that cannot be divided or changed into other chemical substances by any ordinary chemical technique. An _____ is a class of substances that contain the same number of protons in all its atoms.
   a. Element22
   b. Thing
   c. Undefined
   d. Undefined

Chapter 22. The Earth's Companions

28. _____ is a chemical element in the periodic table that has the symbol C and atomic number 6. An abundant nonmetallic, tetravalent element, _____ has several allotropic forms.
   a. Thing
   b. Carbon22
   c. Undefined
   d. Undefined

29. _____ is essential to all organisms, except for a few bacteria. It is mostly stably incorporated in the inside of metalloproteins, because in exposed or in free form it causes production of free radicals that are generally toxic to cells.
   a. Thing
   b. Iron22
   c. Undefined
   d. Undefined

30. _____ refers to the smallest possible unit of a substance that has the properties of that substance.
   a. Molecule22
   b. 1509 Istanbul earthquake
   c. Undefined
   d. Undefined

31. _____ refers to the change of state of water from the vapor to the liquid phase. Results in liberation of 80 calories per cubic centimeter.
   a. Condensation22
   b. 1509 Istanbul earthquake
   c. Undefined
   d. Undefined

32. _____ refers to a place in which water is stored, including the oceans, glaciers and polar ice, groundwater, lakes and rivers, the atmosphere, and the biosphere. A source or place of residence for elements in a chemical cycle or hydrologic cycle.
   a. Reservoir22
   b. 1509 Istanbul earthquake
   c. Undefined
   d. Undefined

33. The situation in mass wasting that occurs when material free-falls or bounces down a cliff is called a _____.
   a. Fall22
   b. 1509 Istanbul earthquake
   c. Undefined
   d. Undefined

34. A large mass of rock projecting above surrounding terrain is called a _____.
   a. Mountain22
   b. 1509 Istanbul earthquake
   c. Undefined
   d. Undefined

35. A term used to describe the property of releasing energy or particles from an unstable atom is called _____.
   a. Thing
   b. Radioactive22
   c. Undefined
   d. Undefined

36. The middle layer of the Earth, lying just below the crust and consisting of relatively dense rocks is called the _____. The _____ is divided into two sections, the upper _____ and the lower _____; the lower _____ has greater density than the upper _____.
   a. 1509 Istanbul earthquake
   b. Mantle22
   c. Undefined
   d. Undefined

37. Any unconsolidated material at Earth's surface is _____.

Chapter 22. The Earth`s Companions

a. 1509 Istanbul earthquake
b. Debris22
c. Undefined
d. Undefined

38. A steep-sided, usually circular depression formed by either explosion or collapse at a volcanic vent is a _____.
a. 1509 Istanbul earthquake
b. Crater22
c. Undefined
d. Undefined

39. _____ refers to the process by which solid, liquid, and gaseous materials are ejected into the earth's atmosphere and onto the earth's surface by volcanic activity. Eruptions range from the quiet overflow of liquid rock to the tremendously violent expulsion of pyroclastics.
a. Eruption22
b. AASHTO Soil Classification System
c. Undefined
d. Undefined

40. _____ refers to rigid parts of the Earth's crust and part of the Earth's upper mantle that moves and adjoins each other along zones of seismic activity.
a. Plate22
b. 1509 Istanbul earthquake
c. Undefined
d. Undefined

41. The smooth areas on our moon's surface that were incorrectly thought to be seas are referred to as _____.
a. 1509 Istanbul earthquake
b. Maria22
c. Undefined
d. Undefined

42. An area with sparse vegetation owing to some physical or chemical property of the soil is referred to as _____.
a. Barren22
b. Thing
c. Undefined
d. Undefined

43. _____ refers to a rugged region of the lunar surface representing an early period in lunar history when intense meteorite bombardment formed craters.
a. Highland22
b. 1509 Istanbul earthquake
c. Undefined
d. Undefined

44. _____ is the chemical element in the periodic table that has the symbol Mg and atomic number 12 and an atomic mass of 24.31.
a. Magnesium22
b. Thing
c. Undefined
d. Undefined

45. _____ is a chemical element in the periodic table that has the symbol Ti and atomic number 22. It is a light, strong, lustrous, corrosion-resistant (including resistance to sea water and chlorine) transition metal with a white-silvery-metallic color. _____ is used in strong light-weight alloys (most notably with iron and aluminium) and its most common compound, _____ dioxide, is used in white pigments.
a. Titanium22
b. Thing
c. Undefined
d. Undefined

46. _____ is a common gray to black volcanic rock. It is usually fine-grained due to rapid cooling of lava on the Earth's surface.

a. Basalt22
b. Thing
c. Undefined
d. Undefined

47. Magma that comes to the Earth's surface through a volcano or fissure is referred to as _____.
   a. Lava22
   b. 1509 Istanbul earthquake
   c. Undefined
   d. Undefined

48. A crystalline rock composed almost entirely of calcium-rich plagioclase feldspar is referred to as the _____.
   a. AASHTO Soil Classification System
   b. Anorthosite22
   c. Undefined
   d. Undefined

49. Aluminium is the chemical element in the periodic table that has the symbol Al and atomic number 13. It is a silvery and ductile member of the poor metal group of chemical elements. Aluminium is found primarily as the ore bauxite and is remarkable for its resistance to corrosion (due to the phenomenon of passivation) and its light weight. Aluminium is used in many industries to make millions of different products and is very important to the world economy.
   a. Aluminum22
   b. Thing
   c. Undefined
   d. Undefined

50. _____ is the chemical element in the periodic table that has the symbol Ca and atomic number 20. _____ is a soft grey alkaline earth metal that is used as a reducing agent in the extraction of thorium, zirconium and uranium. _____ is also the fifth most abundant element in the Earth's crust.
   a. Calcium22
   b. Thing
   c. Undefined
   d. Undefined

51. Bright streaks that appear to radiate from certain craters on the lunar surface are _____. The _____ consist of fine debris ejected from the primary crater.
   a. Rays22
   b. 1509 Istanbul earthquake
   c. Undefined
   d. Undefined

52. A general term for the higher ground of a region, in contrast with valley, plain, or other lower lying adjacent land is called _____.
   a. AASHTO Soil Classification System
   b. Upland22
   c. Undefined
   d. Undefined

53. Aggregates of minerals or rock fragments are called _____.
   a. 1509 Istanbul earthquake
   b. Rocks22
   c. Undefined
   d. Undefined

54. _____ refers to the study of the global-scale movements of Earth's crust that have resulted in.
   a. Plate tectonics22
   b. Thing
   c. Undefined
   d. Undefined

55. _____ refers to the study of the large-scale processes that collectively deform Earth's crust.
   a. 1509 Istanbul earthquake
   b. Tectonics22
   c. Undefined
   d. Undefined

56. _____ is the displacement of solids (soil, mud, rock, and other particles) by the agents of wind, water, ice, movement in response to gravity, or living organisms.
   a. Thing
   b. Erosion22
   c. Undefined
   d. Undefined

57. _____ refers to a group of closely spaced mountains or parallel ridges.
   a. 1509 Istanbul earthquake
   b. Mountain range22
   c. Undefined
   d. Undefined

58. _____ refers to any physical, recognizable form or feature on the earth's surface, having a characteristic shape and range in composition, and produced by natural causes.
   a. 1509 Istanbul earthquake
   b. Landform22
   c. Undefined
   d. Undefined

59. _____ refers to wind or water currents promoted by the fact that warming causes expansion, decreases density, and thus causes the warmer air or water to rise. Conversely, the cooler air or water sinks.
   a. Thing
   b. Convection currents22
   c. Undefined
   d. Undefined

60. _____ is the transfer of heat by currents within a fluid. It may arise from temperature differences either within the fluid or between the fluid and its boundary, other sources of density variations (such as variable salinity), or from the application of an external motive force.
   a. Convection22
   b. Event
   c. Undefined
   d. Undefined

61. One of a series of progressive disturbances that reverberate through the Earth to transmit the energy released from an earthquake is called a _____.
   a. Seismic wave22
   b. 1509 Istanbul earthquake
   c. Undefined
   d. Undefined

62. The upper layer of water that is mixed by wind, waves, and currents is the _____ .
   a. Surface layer22
   b. Thing
   c. Undefined
   d. Undefined

63. The layer of rock and mineral fragments that nearly everywhere covers Earth's land surface is referred to as _____.
   a. Regolith22
   b. 1509 Istanbul earthquake
   c. Undefined
   d. Undefined

64. The _____ is the solid outermost shell of a rocky planet. On the Earth, the _____ includes the crust and the uppermost layer of the mantle (the upper mantle or lower _____) which is joined to the crust.
   a. Thing
   b. Lithosphere22
   c. Undefined
   d. Undefined

65. Angular sedimentary particles coarser than 2 mm in diameter are referred to as _____.

a. 1509 Istanbul earthquake
b. Rubble22
c. Undefined
d. Undefined

66. _____ refers to the steep cliff face that is formed by a slump.
   a. 1509 Istanbul earthquake
   b. Scarp22
   c. Undefined
   d. Undefined

67. _____ refers to a basic unit of the geologic time scale that is a subdivision of an era. Periods may be divided into smaller units called epochs.
   a. Period22
   b. 1509 Istanbul earthquake
   c. Undefined
   d. Undefined

68. _____ is an atmospheric gas comprized of one carbon and two oxygen atoms. A very widely known chemical compound, it is frequently called by its formula CO_2. In its solid state, it is commonly known as dry ice.
   a. Carbon dioxide22
   b. Thing
   c. Undefined
   d. Undefined

69. _____ is a chemical element in the periodic table. It has the symbol O and atomic number 8. _____ is the second most common element on Earth, composing around 46% of the mass of Earth's crust and 28% of the mass of Earth as a whole, and is the third most common element in the universe.
   a. Oxygen22
   b. Thing
   c. Undefined
   d. Undefined

70. Gradual loss of heat from Earth's interior out into space is called _____.
   a. 1509 Istanbul earthquake
   b. Heat flow22
   c. Undefined
   d. Undefined

71. Molten rock that forms naturally within the Earth is _____. _____ may be either a liquid or a fluid mixture of liquid, crystals, and dissolved gases.
   a. Magma22
   b. 1509 Istanbul earthquake
   c. Undefined
   d. Undefined

72. The liquid portion of magma excluding the solid crystals is called _____.
   a. Melt22
   b. 1509 Istanbul earthquake
   c. Undefined
   d. Undefined

73. _____ is a solid in which the constituent atoms, molecules, or ions are packed in a regularly ordered, repeating pattern extending in all three spatial dimensions.
   a. Thing
   b. Crystal22
   c. Undefined
   d. Undefined

74. A _____ is a landscape form or region that receives little precipitation - less than 250 mm (10 in) per year. It is a biome characterized by organisms adapted to sparse rainfall and rapid evaporation.
   a. Desert22
   b. Thing
   c. Undefined
   d. Undefined

75. _____ refers to a usually asymmetrical mound or ridge of sand that has been transported and deposited by wind. Dunes form in both arid and humid climates.
   a. Dune22
   b. 1509 Istanbul earthquake
   c. Undefined
   d. Undefined

76. The _____ is the lowest layer in an ocean, existing below the thermocline. The _____ is not well mixed, consists of horizontal layers of equal density, and is often as cold as -1 to 4 degrees Celsius.
   a. Thing
   b. Deep layer22
   c. Undefined
   d. Undefined

77. The topographically highest hillslope position of a hillslope profile and exhibiting a nearly level surface is referred to as the _____.
   a. Summit22
   b. 1509 Istanbul earthquake
   c. Undefined
   d. Undefined

78. The solid structure created when lava, gases, and hot particles escape to the Earth's surface through vents is called a _____. Volcanoes are usually conical. A _____ is 'active' when it is erupting or has erupted recently. Volcanoes that have not erupted recently but are considered likely to erupt in the future are said to be 'dormant.' A _____ that has not erupted for a long time and is not expected to erupt in the future is 'extinct'.
   a. 1509 Istanbul earthquake
   b. Volcano22
   c. Undefined
   d. Undefined

79. _____ refers to a feature on the surface of the planet Mars that very closely resembles certain types of stream channels on Earth.
   a. Channel22
   b. 1509 Istanbul earthquake
   c. Undefined
   d. Undefined

80. A flat, steplike surface that lines a stream above the floodplain, often paired one on each side of the stream, marking a former floodplain that existed at a higher level before regional uplift or an increase in discharge caused the stream to erode into it is called the _____.
   a. Terrace22
   b. 1509 Istanbul earthquake
   c. Undefined
   d. Undefined

81. A round or oval depression in the Earth's surface, containing the youngest section of rock in its lowest, central part is a _____.
   a. 1509 Istanbul earthquake
   b. Basin22
   c. Undefined
   d. Undefined

82. _____ refers to a general term applied to all mineral material transported by a glacier and deposited directly by or from the ice, or by running water emanating from the glacier. Generally applies to Pleistocene glacial deposits.
   a. 1509 Istanbul earthquake
   b. Drift22
   c. Undefined
   d. Undefined

83. Weather condition of an area including especially prevailing temperature and average daily/yearly rainfall over a long period of time is called _____.

a. Thing
b. Climate22
c. Undefined
d. Undefined

84. _____ refers to the top few meters of regolith, generally including some organic matter derived from plants.
   a. Soil22
   b. 1509 Istanbul earthquake
   c. Undefined
   d. Undefined

85. _____ refers to the process by which chemical reactions alter the chemical composition of rocks and minerals that are unstable at the Earth's surface and convert them into more stable substances; weathering that changes the chemical makeup of a rock or mineral.
   a. 1509 Istanbul earthquake
   b. Chemical weathering22
   c. Undefined
   d. Undefined

86. The process by which exposure to atmospheric agents, such as air or moisture, causes rocks and minerals to break down is called _____. This process takes place at or near the Earth's surface. _____ entails little or no movement of the material that it loosens from the rocks and minerals.
   a. 1509 Istanbul earthquake
   b. Weathering22
   c. Undefined
   d. Undefined

87. A preserved remnant or impression of an organism that lived in the past is referred to as _____.
   a. Fossil22
   b. Thing
   c. Undefined
   d. Undefined

88. _____ refers to a process leading to chemical changes in matter; involves the making and/or breaking of chemical bonds.
   a. Chemical reaction22
   b. Thing
   c. Undefined
   d. Undefined

89. _____ is a chemical element in the periodic table that has the symbol Pb and atomic number 82. A soft, heavy, toxic and malleable poor metal, _____ is bluish white when freshly cut but tarnishes to dull gray when exposed to air. _____ is used in building construction, _____-acid batteries, bullets and shot, and is part of solder, pewter, and fusible alloys.
   a. Thing
   b. Lead22
   c. Undefined
   d. Undefined

90. One of several minerals containing one central carbon atom with strong covalent bonds to three oxygen atoms and typically having ionic bonds to one or more positive ions is _____.
   a. 1509 Istanbul earthquake
   b. Carbonate22
   c. Undefined
   d. Undefined

91. _____ is any particulate matter that can be transported by fluid flow and which eventually is deposited as a layer of solid particles on the bed or bottom of a body of water or other liquid.
   a. Thing
   b. Sediment22
   c. Undefined
   d. Undefined

92. _____ refer to coal, oil, natural gas, and all other solid or liquid hydrocarbon fuels.

Chapter 22. The Earth`s Companions

a. Fossil fuels22
c. Undefined

b. 1509 Istanbul earthquake
d. Undefined

93. _____ refers to an energy deposit formed from the remains of extinct organisms.
a. Thing
c. Undefined

b. Fossil fuel22
d. Undefined

94. A sedimentary rock formed from the accumulation of carbonate minerals precipitated organically or inorganically is _____.
a. Carbonate rock22
c. Undefined

b. 1509 Istanbul earthquake
d. Undefined

95. A high mountain pass that forms when part of an arête erodes is referred to as a _____.
a. Col22
c. Undefined

b. 1509 Istanbul earthquake
d. Undefined

96. _____ is the chemical element in the periodic table that has the symbol Si and atomic number 14. It is the second most abundant element in the Earth's crust, making up 25.7% of it by weight.
a. Silicon22
c. Undefined

b. Thing
d. Undefined

97. The deflection of large bodies of water or air to the right in the Northern Hemisphere and to the left in the Southern Hemisphere is referred to as the _____.
a. Coriolis effect22
c. Undefined

b. Thing
d. Undefined

98. _____ refers to a body of water found on the Earth's surface and confined to a narrow topographic depression, down which it flows and transports rock particles, sediment, and dissolved particles. Rivers, creeks, brooks, and runs are all streams.
a. Stream22
c. Undefined

b. 1509 Istanbul earthquake
d. Undefined

99. Low latitude areas characterized by high temperatures and high precipitation are referred to as _____. At high elevations, however, _____ mountains may be both cold and relatively dry.
a. Tropical22
c. Undefined

b. 1509 Istanbul earthquake
d. Undefined

100. The region within which the magnetism of a given substance or particle affects other substances is referred to as _____.
a. 1509 Istanbul earthquake
c. Undefined

b. Magnetic field22
d. Undefined

101. _____ is the chemical element in the periodic table that has the symbol S and atomic number 16. It is an abundant, tasteless, odorless, multivalent non-metal. _____, in its native form, is a yellow crystaline solid. In nature, it can be found as the pure element or as sulfide and sulfate minerals.

a. Sulfur22 b. Thing
c. Undefined d. Undefined

102. _____ refers to the spontaneous decay of certain unstable atomic nuclei.
a. 1509 Istanbul earthquake b. Radioactive decay22
c. Undefined d. Undefined

103. A chemical compound composed only of the elements carbon and hydrogen is called _____.
a. Thing b. Hydrocarbon22
c. Undefined d. Undefined

104. _____ is a physical or chemical phenomenon or a process in which atoms, molecules, or ions enter some bulk phase - gas, liquid or solid material. In nutrition, amino acids are broken down through digestion, which begins in the stomach.
a. Thing b. Absorption22
c. Undefined d. Undefined

105. A major branch of a stream system is referred to as a _____.
a. 1509 Istanbul earthquake b. River22
c. Undefined d. Undefined

106. Any portion of a meteoroid that survives its traverse through Earth's atmosphere and strikes the surface is referred to as a _____.
a. 1509 Istanbul earthquake b. Meteorite22
c. Undefined d. Undefined

107. _____ refers to the color of a mineral in its powdered form. This color is usually determined by rubbing the mineral against an unglazed porcelain slab and observing the mark made by it on the slab.
a. 1509 Istanbul earthquake b. Streak22
c. Undefined d. Undefined

108. Any small, solid particle that has an orbit in the solar system is a _____.
a. Meteoroid22 b. 1509 Istanbul earthquake
c. Undefined d. Undefined

109. _____ refers to one of the three main categories of meteorites. Such meteorites are composed largely of silicate minerals with inclusions of other minerals.
a. 1509 Istanbul earthquake b. Stony meteorite22
c. Undefined d. Undefined

110. _____ refer to small nuggets of rocky material that exist in certain meteorites. These droplets of matter are believed to have condensed from our solar system's original nebula about five billion years ago. Their primary element is iron.
a. 1509 Istanbul earthquake b. Chondrules22
c. Undefined d. Undefined

111. Round silicate grain within some stony meteorites is referred to as _____.
   a. Chondrule22
   b. 1509 Istanbul earthquake
   c. Undefined
   d. Undefined

112. Stony meteorite containing chondrules and composed mostly of serpentine and large quantities of organic materials is _____.
   a. Carbonaceous chondrite22
   b. 1509 Istanbul earthquake
   c. Undefined
   d. Undefined

113. A type of primitive stoney meteorite containing chondrules, quenched droplets of early condensates from the solar nebula is called _____.
   a. 1509 Istanbul earthquake
   b. Chondrite22
   c. Undefined
   d. Undefined

114. A member of a group of easily combustible, organic sedimentary rocks composed mostly of plant remains and containing a high proportion of carbon is called _____.
   a. 1509 Istanbul earthquake
   b. Coal22
   c. Undefined
   d. Undefined

115. Any environmental change that adversely affects the lives and health of living things is referred to as _____.
   a. Thing
   b. Pollution22
   c. Undefined
   d. Undefined

116. The fuzzy, gaseous component of a comet's head is a _____.
   a. Coma22
   b. 1509 Istanbul earthquake
   c. Undefined
   d. Undefined

117. _____ refers to the central part of an atom, containing most of the atom's mass and having a positive charge due to the presence of protons.
   a. Nucleus22
   b. 1509 Istanbul earthquake
   c. Undefined
   d. Undefined

118. Angular chunk of solid rock ejected during an eruption is referred to as a _____.
   a. Block22
   b. 1509 Istanbul earthquake
   c. Undefined
   d. Undefined

119. A spherical accumulation of water in the crystalline form is referred to as a _____.
   a. 1509 Istanbul earthquake
   b. Snowball22
   c. Undefined
   d. Undefined

120. Block of glacier-derived ice floating in water is called an _____.
   a. Iceberg22
   b. AASHTO Soil Classification System
   c. Undefined
   d. Undefined

121. _____ refers to energy that is actually doing work; the energy of a mass of matter that is moving. Moving matter performs work by transferring its motion to other matter, such as leg muscles pushing bicycle pedals.

a. Kinetic energy22   b. Thing
c. Undefined   d. Undefined

122. _____ refers to fragment of molten or semi-molten rock, 2 1/2 inches to many feet in diameter, which is blown out during an eruption. Because of their plastic condition, bombs are often modified in shape during their flight or upon impact.
a. Bomb22   b. 1509 Istanbul earthquake
c. Undefined   d. Undefined

123. The _____ period is one of the major divisions of the geologic timescale, reaching from the end of the Jurassic period, about 146 million years ago (Ma), to the beginning of the Paleocene epoch of the Tertiary period (65.5 Ma).
a. Thing   b. Cretaceous22
c. Undefined   d. Undefined

124. _____ refers to abrupt disappearance of a large fraction of a biota, thought to be caused by such environmental catastrophes as meteor impacts; significant mass extinctions occurred at the end of the Permian and Cretaceous periods.
a. Thing   b. Mass extinction22
c. Undefined   d. Undefined

125. In biology and ecology, _____ is the ceasing of existence of a species or group of taxa. The moment of _____ is generally considered to be the death of the last individual of that species. The death of all members of a species is _____.
a. Extinction22   b. Thing
c. Undefined   d. Undefined

126. The top of the ocean, where the water meets the atmosphere is called _____.
a. Sea level22   b. 1509 Istanbul earthquake
c. Undefined   d. Undefined

127. The scientific study of the Earth, its origins and evolution, the materials that make it up, and the processes that act on it is called _____.
a. 1509 Istanbul earthquake   b. Geology22
c. Undefined   d. Undefined

ANSWER KEY

Chapter 1
1. a	2. b	3. b	4. a	5. b	6. b	7. a	8. b	9. a	10. b
11. b	12. b	13. a	14. b	15. a	16. a	17. a	18. a	19. a	20. a
21. a	22. b	23. b	24. b	25. a	26. a	27. a	28. b	29. a	30. b
31. a	32. a	33. b	34. b	35. b	36. b	37. a	38. a	39. a	40. b
41. a	42. b	43. a	44. b	45. b	46. a	47. b	48. b	49. a	50. a
51. b	52. b	53. a	54. a	55. b	56. b	57. b	58. a	59. a	60. b
61. a	62. b	63. b	64. b	65. b	66. a	67. a	68. a	69. b	70. a
71. a	72. a	73. b	74. b	75. b	76. a	77. a	78. a	79. a	80. b

Chapter 2
1. b	2. a	3. b	4. a	5. a	6. a	7. b	8. b	9. b	10. b
11. a	12. a	13. a	14. a	15. a	16. b	17. b	18. b	19. a	20. b
21. b	22. a	23. a	24. b	25. a	26. a	27. b	28. b	29. b	30. b
31. a	32. a	33. b	34. b	35. b	36. a	37. b	38. a	39. a	40. b
41. a	42. b	43. a	44. a	45. b	46. a	47. b	48. b	49. b	50. a
51. a	52. b	53. b	54. a	55. b	56. a	57. b	58. a	59. a	60. a
61. b	62. a	63. a	64. a	65. a	66. a	67. a	68. a	69. a	70. a
71. b	72. b	73. b	74. a	75. b	76. b	77. b	78. a	79. a	80. b
81. a	82. a	83. a	84. a	85. a	86. b	87. a	88. a	89. a	90. a
91. a	92. a	93. b	94. b	95. b	96. a	97. a	98. a	99. a	100. b
101. b	102. a	103. a	104. a	105. a	106. a	107. b	108. a	109. b	110. a
111. a	112. b	113. a	114. b	115. b	116. b	117. b	118. a	119. b	120. a
121. a	122. b	123. b	124. a	125. b	126. a	127. a	128. a	129. a	130. a
131. a	132. a	133. b	134. b	135. a	136. a	137. a	138. b	139. b	140. b
141. a	142. a	143. a	144. a	145. b					

Chapter 3
1. b	2. b	3. a	4. a	5. a	6. b	7. b	8. a	9. a	10. b
11. a	12. b	13. b	14. a	15. a	16. b	17. a	18. b	19. b	20. b
21. a	22. b	23. a	24. a	25. b	26. a	27. a	28. a	29. b	30. b
31. b	32. b	33. b	34. a	35. a	36. a	37. b	38. a	39. a	40. b
41. b	42. b	43. b	44. b	45. b	46. b	47. b	48. a	49. b	50. a
51. a	52. b	53. b	54. a	55. a	56. a	57. b	58. b	59. a	60. a
61. b	62. a	63. b	64. a	65. a	66. a	67. b	68. b	69. a	70. b
71. b	72. b	73. b	74. a	75. a	76. a	77. b	78. a	79. a	80. a
81. a	82. a	83. b	84. a	85. a	86. b	87. b	88. a	89. b	90. b
91. a	92. b	93. b	94. b	95. b	96. b	97. a	98. b	99. a	100. a
101. a	102. a	103. b	104. b	105. a	106. b	107. a	108. a	109. a	110. a
111. b	112. b	113. b	114. b	115. b	116. b	117. b	118. a	119. a	120. a
121. b	122. a	123. b	124. a	125. b	126. b	127. a	128. b	129. b	130. b
131. b	132. a	133. a	134. b	135. a	136. b	137. a	138. a		

Chapter 4

1. a	2. b	3. b	4. b	5. b	6. a	7. b	8. b	9. a	10. a
11. a	12. b	13. a	14. b	15. b	16. b	17. a	18. b	19. b	20. a
21. a	22. b	23. b	24. b	25. b	26. a	27. a	28. a	29. a	30. a
31. a	32. b	33. b	34. b	35. b	36. b	37. a	38. a	39. b	40. b
41. a	42. b	43. a	44. a	45. a	46. a	47. a	48. a	49. a	50. b
51. a	52. a	53. b	54. a	55. b	56. b	57. a	58. a	59. a	60. a
61. a	62. a	63. a	64. a	65. a	66. a	67. a	68. b	69. a	70. b
71. a	72. b	73. a	74. a	75. b	76. b	77. b	78. a	79. a	80. b
81. a	82. b	83. b	84. b	85. a	86. a	87. b	88. a	89. a	90. a
91. b	92. b	93. a	94. a	95. a	96. b	97. b	98. a	99. a	100. b
101. b	102. b	103. b	104. b	105. b	106. b	107. a	108. a	109. b	110. a
111. b	112. b	113. a	114. b	115. a	116. b	117. a	118. a	119. b	120. b
121. b	122. b	123. a	124. a	125. a	126. a	127. a	128. b	129. b	130. b
131. b	132. a	133. b	134. b	135. a	136. b	137. a	138. a	139. a	140. b
141. b	142. b	143. b	144. a	145. b	146. b	147. a	148. a	149. a	150. a
151. b	152. a	153. b	154. a	155. a	156. a	157. a	158. b	159. b	160. b
161. b	162. a	163. a	164. b	165. b	166. a	167. a	168. b	169. a	170. a
171. a	172. b	173. b	174. b	175. a	176. b	177. b	178. b	179. a	180. a
181. a	182. a	183. b	184. a	185. b	186. a	187. b	188. b	189. a	190. a

Chapter 5

1. a	2. a	3. a	4. a	5. b	6. b	7. b	8. a	9. b	10. b
11. b	12. a	13. a	14. a	15. a	16. b	17. a	18. a	19. a	20. a
21. b	22. b	23. b	24. a	25. a	26. b	27. a	28. b	29. a	30. a
31. b	32. a	33. b	34. b	35. b	36. a	37. b	38. b	39. b	40. a
41. a	42. b	43. b	44. b	45. b	46. b	47. b	48. b	49. a	50. a
51. b	52. a	53. b	54. b	55. b	56. b	57. a	58. b	59. b	60. b
61. b	62. a	63. a	64. a	65. a	66. b	67. a	68. b	69. a	70. b
71. b	72. a	73. a	74. a	75. b	76. b	77. a	78. a	79. a	80. b
81. b	82. a	83. a	84. b	85. a	86. b	87. a	88. b	89. b	90. b
91. a	92. a	93. b	94. b	95. b	96. a	97. b	98. a	99. a	100. b
101. a	102. a	103. a	104. a	105. b	106. b	107. b	108. a	109. a	110. a
111. b	112. a	113. b	114. a	115. a	116. b	117. b	118. a	119. b	120. a
121. b	122. b	123. b	124. a	125. b	126. a	127. a	128. b	129. b	130. a
131. b	132. a	133. b	134. b	135. a	136. a	137. a	138. a	139. b	140. b
141. a	142. b	143. b	144. b	145. b	146. a	147. a	148. b	149. b	150. b
151. a	152. a	153. b	154. b	155. b	156. b	157. a	158. a	159. b	160. a
161. a	162. b	163. a	164. b	165. b	166. a	167. b	168. a	169. a	170. b
171. a	172. a	173. b	174. b	175. b	176. a				

ANSWER KEY

Chapter 6

1. a	2. b	3. b	4. b	5. a	6. a	7. b	8. b	9. a	10. a
11. a	12. a	13. a	14. a	15. a	16. a	17. b	18. a	19. a	20. a
21. b	22. a	23. a	24. a	25. b	26. b	27. a	28. b	29. b	30. a
31. a	32. a	33. a	34. a	35. b	36. b	37. b	38. b	39. a	40. a
41. a	42. a	43. b	44. a	45. b	46. a	47. a	48. b	49. b	50. a
51. a	52. a	53. a	54. a	55. a	56. b	57. b	58. b	59. a	60. a
61. a	62. a	63. b	64. a	65. b	66. a	67. a	68. b	69. a	70. a
71. b	72. a	73. b	74. a	75. a	76. b	77. a	78. a	79. a	80. a
81. b	82. b	83. a	84. b	85. a	86. a	87. b	88. b	89. a	90. a
91. a	92. a	93. a	94. b	95. b	96. b	97. b	98. b	99. a	100. b
101. b	102. b	103. b	104. a	105. b	106. a	107. b	108. a	109. a	110. a
111. b	112. b	113. b	114. b	115. b	116. b	117. a	118. a	119. a	120. b
121. b	122. a	123. b	124. a	125. b	126. b	127. a	128. b	129. a	130. b
131. b	132. a	133. b	134. a	135. b	136. a	137. a	138. b	139. b	140. b
141. a	142. a	143. a	144. b	145. a	146. b	147. a	148. b	149. b	150. b
151. b	152. b	153. a	154. a	155. a	156. a	157. b	158. b	159. b	160. a
161. b	162. a	163. b	164. b	165. b	166. a	167. b	168. a	169. a	170. a
171. b	172. b	173. a	174. a	175. b	176. b	177. b	178. b	179. a	180. b
181. a	182. a	183. a	184. b	185. a	186. a	187. b	188. b	189. b	190. a
191. a	192. a	193. b	194. a	195. a	196. b	197. a	198. b	199. a	200. b
201. a	202. b	203. b	204. b	205. b	206. b	207. b			

Chapter 7

1. b	2. a	3. a	4. b	5. b	6. b	7. a	8. b	9. b	10. b
11. a	12. a	13. a	14. b	15. b	16. b	17. a	18. a	19. a	20. a
21. b	22. a	23. b	24. b	25. b	26. a	27. a	28. a	29. a	30. a
31. a	32. a	33. a	34. a	35. a	36. b	37. b	38. a	39. a	40. a
41. b	42. a	43. b	44. a	45. b	46. b	47. a	48. a	49. a	50. b
51. a	52. b	53. b	54. b	55. a	56. a	57. a	58. b	59. b	60. b
61. a	62. b	63. b	64. a	65. b	66. b	67. a	68. a	69. a	70. a
71. b	72. a	73. a	74. b	75. a	76. b	77. b	78. a	79. b	80. a
81. b	82. a	83. b	84. a	85. b	86. b	87. b	88. a	89. b	90. b
91. b	92. a	93. a	94. b	95. b	96. a	97. b	98. a	99. b	100. b
101. b	102. b	103. b	104. a	105. a	106. a	107. a	108. b	109. a	110. a
111. a	112. b	113. b	114. b	115. b	116. a	117. b	118. b	119. a	120. a
121. a	122. b	123. b	124. a	125. a	126. a	127. a	128. a	129. b	130. a
131. b	132. b	133. a	134. b	135. a	136. b	137. a	138. b	139. a	140. b
141. a	142. a	143. b	144. b	145. a	146. a	147. b	148. b	149. b	150. b
151. a	152. a	153. a	154. a	155. a	156. a	157. b	158. a	159. a	160. a
161. a	162. a	163. a	164. b	165. b	166. a	167. b	168. b	169. a	170. a

Chapter 8

1. b	2. b	3. a	4. b	5. a	6. a	7. b	8. a	9. a	10. a
11. a	12. a	13. a	14. b	15. a	16. a	17. b	18. b	19. a	20. a
21. b	22. b	23. b	24. a	25. a	26. a	27. a	28. b	29. a	30. b
31. a	32. b	33. a	34. a	35. a	36. b	37. b	38. b	39. b	40. b
41. a	42. b	43. b	44. b	45. b	46. a	47. b	48. b	49. b	50. a
51. a	52. a	53. b	54. b	55. b	56. a	57. a	58. b	59. b	60. b
61. a	62. a	63. b	64. b	65. a	66. b	67. a	68. a	69. a	70. a
71. a	72. b	73. a	74. b	75. a	76. b	77. a	78. a	79. a	80. a
81. a	82. a	83. a	84. b	85. b	86. a	87. a	88. b	89. a	90. b
91. b	92. b	93. b	94. b	95. b	96. a	97. b	98. b	99. b	100. a
101. a	102. b	103. a	104. b	105. a	106. b	107. b	108. b	109. b	110. b
111. a	112. a	113. a	114. b	115. a	116. a	117. a	118. b	119. b	120. a
121. b	122. b	123. a	124. b	125. b	126. b	127. a	128. b	129. b	130. a
131. a	132. a	133. b	134. b	135. a	136. a	137. b	138. b	139. a	140. b
141. a	142. a	143. b	144. a	145. b	146. b	147. a	148. b	149. b	150. b
151. a	152. a	153. b	154. b	155. a	156. b	157. b	158. b	159. b	160. b

Chapter 9

1. b	2. b	3. b	4. a	5. a	6. b	7. b	8. a	9. b	10. a
11. a	12. b	13. b	14. b	15. b	16. a	17. a	18. b	19. a	20. a
21. a	22. a	23. b	24. b	25. b	26. a	27. a	28. a	29. b	30. b
31. a	32. a	33. b	34. a	35. a	36. a	37. b	38. a	39. b	40. b
41. a	42. b	43. a	44. a	45. a	46. b	47. a	48. a	49. b	50. b
51. b	52. b	53. a	54. b	55. b	56. b	57. b	58. b	59. b	60. b
61. a	62. a	63. b	64. a	65. b	66. a	67. a	68. a	69. a	70. a
71. a	72. b	73. b	74. b	75. a	76. a	77. a	78. b	79. b	80. a
81. b	82. b	83. a	84. a	85. a	86. a	87. b	88. b	89. b	90. b
91. a	92. b	93. b	94. a	95. b	96. b	97. b	98. b	99. b	100. a
101. a	102. b	103. b	104. b	105. a					

ANSWER KEY

Chapter 10

1. b	2. a	3. b	4. b	5. a	6. a	7. b	8. b	9. a	10. a
11. b	12. a	13. a	14. b	15. a	16. a	17. a	18. a	19. b	20. a
21. b	22. b	23. a	24. b	25. b	26. a	27. b	28. a	29. a	30. b
31. a	32. b	33. a	34. b	35. a	36. b	37. a	38. b	39. a	40. b
41. b	42. b	43. a	44. b	45. b	46. b	47. b	48. b	49. a	50. b
51. a	52. b	53. b	54. b	55. b	56. a	57. b	58. a	59. b	60. b
61. a	62. a	63. a	64. b	65. a	66. a	67. a	68. a	69. b	70. b
71. a	72. b	73. a	74. a	75. b	76. b	77. b	78. a	79. a	80. b
81. a	82. a	83. a	84. b	85. b	86. b	87. b	88. a	89. b	90. b
91. a	92. a	93. a	94. a	95. b	96. a	97. b	98. b	99. a	100. a
101. b	102. b	103. a	104. a	105. a	106. b	107. b	108. a	109. a	110. a
111. b	112. b	113. b	114. a	115. a	116. a	117. a	118. b	119. b	120. a
121. b	122. b	123. b	124. a	125. a	126. a	127. b	128. a	129. a	130. a
131. a	132. b	133. b	134. a	135. a	136. a	137. a	138. b	139. a	140. b
141. a	142. b	143. a	144. b	145. a	146. a	147. b	148. b	149. b	150. a
151. a	152. b	153. a	154. b	155. a	156. b	157. a	158. b	159. a	160. a
161. b	162. b	163. a	164. a	165. a	166. b	167. b	168. a	169. b	170. a
171. b	172. b	173. a	174. b	175. a	176. b	177. b	178. b	179. a	180. b
181. b	182. a	183. b	184. a	185. a	186. a				

Chapter 11

1. a	2. b	3. a	4. a	5. a	6. a	7. a	8. a	9. b	10. b
11. a	12. a	13. b	14. a	15. b	16. b	17. b	18. a	19. b	20. a
21. b	22. b	23. a	24. b	25. b	26. b	27. a	28. b	29. a	30. a
31. b	32. a	33. a	34. b	35. b	36. a	37. a	38. b	39. a	40. b
41. a	42. b	43. b	44. a	45. b	46. b	47. a	48. b	49. a	50. a
51. b	52. b	53. a	54. b	55. b	56. a	57. a	58. b	59. b	60. a
61. b	62. b	63. a	64. a	65. a	66. b	67. a	68. b	69. a	70. b
71. b	72. a	73. a	74. b	75. b	76. a	77. b	78. a	79. a	80. a
81. a	82. b	83. a	84. b	85. b	86. b	87. a	88. b	89. b	90. b
91. b	92. b	93. b	94. a	95. a	96. b	97. a	98. b	99. a	100. b
101. b	102. a	103. b	104. a	105. b	106. a	107. b	108. b	109. b	110. a
111. a	112. a	113. b	114. b	115. b	116. b	117. b	118. a	119. b	120. b
121. b	122. b	123. b	124. b	125. a	126. a	127. b	128. b	129. a	130. a
131. a	132. b	133. b	134. b	135. a	136. a	137. a	138. a	139. b	140. a
141. b	142. a	143. b	144. b	145. b	146. a	147. b	148. b	149. b	150. b
151. a	152. a	153. b	154. a	155. b	156. a	157. a	158. b	159. b	160. a
161. b	162. a	163. b	164. a	165. b	166. b	167. a			

Chapter 12

1. b	2. a	3. b	4. b	5. a	6. a	7. a	8. a	9. b	10. b
11. a	12. b	13. b	14. b	15. a	16. b	17. b	18. b	19. a	20. b
21. b	22. b	23. b	24. b	25. b	26. a	27. a	28. b	29. b	30. a
31. a	32. a	33. a	34. a	35. b	36. a	37. a	38. b	39. b	40. a
41. a	42. b	43. a	44. b	45. b	46. a	47. b	48. a	49. a	50. a
51. b	52. a	53. a	54. a	55. b	56. b	57. b	58. a	59. a	60. a
61. a	62. a	63. a	64. a	65. b	66. b	67. b	68. b	69. b	70. b
71. b	72. a	73. b	74. a	75. b	76. b	77. b	78. a	79. a	80. b
81. a	82. b	83. b	84. a	85. a	86. b	87. b	88. b	89. b	90. b
91. b	92. b	93. a	94. b	95. b	96. b	97. a	98. a	99. b	100. b
101. b	102. b	103. b	104. b	105. a	106. b	107. b	108. a	109. a	110. a
111. a	112. a	113. b	114. a	115. b	116. b	117. b	118. a	119. a	120. a
121. a	122. b	123. a	124. b	125. b	126. a	127. a	128. a	129. a	130. a
131. b	132. a	133. a	134. a	135. a	136. b	137. b	138. a	139. a	140. a
141. a	142. a	143. a	144. b	145. a	146. a	147. b	148. b	149. b	150. b
151. a	152. b	153. b	154. a	155. a	156. b	157. b	158. a	159. a	160. a
161. b	162. b	163. a	164. a	165. b	166. a	167. b	168. b	169. a	170. a
171. a	172. a	173. a	174. a	175. a	176. b	177. a	178. a	179. a	180. b
181. a	182. a	183. b	184. b	185. b	186. a	187. b	188. b	189. a	190. b
191. a	192. a	193. a	194. a	195. a	196. b	197. a	198. b	199. a	200. a
201. a	202. b	203. b	204. a	205. b	206. b	207. a	208. a	209. b	210. b
211. b	212. a	213. b							

Chapter 13

1. a	2. b	3. b	4. a	5. a	6. b	7. b	8. b	9. b	10. b
11. b	12. b	13. a	14. a	15. a	16. a	17. b	18. a	19. b	20. a
21. a	22. b	23. b	24. a	25. b	26. a	27. a	28. b	29. a	30. b
31. a	32. b	33. b	34. a	35. a	36. a	37. b	38. a	39. a	40. a
41. a	42. b	43. a	44. a	45. b	46. b	47. b	48. b	49. b	50. b
51. a	52. b	53. b	54. b	55. a	56. a	57. b	58. a	59. a	60. b
61. a	62. a	63. b	64. a	65. b	66. a	67. b	68. b	69. a	70. a
71. b	72. a	73. a	74. a	75. a	76. a	77. b	78. a	79. a	80. a
81. a	82. b	83. a	84. a	85. b	86. b	87. a	88. a	89. a	90. b
91. a	92. a	93. a	94. a	95. a	96. a	97. b	98. b	99. a	100. a
101. b	102. a	103. a	104. a	105. b	106. b	107. a	108. b	109. b	110. a
111. a	112. a	113. a	114. a	115. b	116. a	117. b	118. b	119. a	120. b
121. b	122. a	123. a	124. a	125. a	126. a	127. a	128. b	129. a	130. b
131. a	132. a	133. b	134. a	135. a	136. a	137. b	138. b	139. b	140. a
141. a	142. a	143. b	144. a	145. a	146. b	147. b	148. a	149. b	150. a
151. b	152. a	153. a	154. a	155. a	156. a	157. a	158. a	159. a	160. a
161. b	162. b	163. a	164. b	165. a	166. b	167. a	168. b	169. a	170. a
171. a									

ANSWER KEY

Chapter 14

1. b	2. a	3. b	4. a	5. b	6. b	7. b	8. b	9. b	10. a
11. b	12. a	13. b	14. a	15. b	16. a	17. a	18. a	19. a	20. a
21. b	22. a	23. b	24. a	25. b	26. a	27. b	28. b	29. a	30. b
31. b	32. b	33. b	34. b	35. b	36. b	37. a	38. b	39. b	40. a
41. b	42. b	43. b	44. b	45. a	46. a	47. b	48. b	49. b	50. b
51. b	52. b	53. b	54. a	55. a	56. a	57. a	58. b	59. b	60. a
61. a	62. a	63. b	64. a	65. b	66. b	67. b	68. b	69. a	70. b
71. b	72. b	73. b	74. a	75. b	76. b	77. b	78. b	79. b	80. a
81. b	82. b	83. b	84. b	85. a	86. b	87. a	88. b	89. b	90. b
91. a	92. a	93. a	94. a	95. a	96. a	97. b	98. a	99. a	100. b
101. b	102. a	103. b	104. b	105. b	106. b	107. b	108. a	109. a	110. b
111. a	112. b	113. b	114. b	115. a	116. b	117. a			

Chapter 15

1. b	2. a	3. b	4. b	5. a	6. b	7. a	8. a	9. a	10. b
11. b	12. a	13. a	14. b	15. b	16. b	17. b	18. a	19. b	20. a
21. b	22. a	23. a	24. a	25. a	26. b	27. b	28. a	29. a	30. a
31. b	32. b	33. b	34. b	35. a	36. b	37. a	38. b	39. a	40. b
41. b	42. b	43. a	44. a	45. a	46. b	47. a	48. b	49. b	50. b
51. a	52. b	53. a	54. b	55. b	56. b	57. b	58. a	59. b	60. b
61. b	62. a	63. a	64. a	65. a	66. b	67. a	68. b	69. a	70. a
71. a	72. b	73. b	74. a	75. b	76. a	77. a	78. b	79. a	80. a
81. a	82. b	83. b	84. b	85. a	86. b	87. a	88. a	89. a	90. b
91. a	92. a	93. b	94. b	95. a	96. b	97. b	98. b	99. a	100. a
101. b	102. a	103. a	104. a	105. a	106. a	107. a	108. a	109. a	110. a
111. a	112. a	113. a	114. a	115. b	116. a	117. a	118. b	119. a	120. b
121. b	122. b	123. a	124. a	125. a	126. b	127. b	128. a	129. b	130. b
131. a	132. a	133. a	134. b	135. a	136. b	137. a	138. a	139. b	140. a
141. b	142. a	143. b	144. b	145. b	146. b	147. a	148. b	149. b	150. a
151. b	152. b	153. a	154. b	155. b	156. b				

Chapter 16

1. b	2. a	3. a	4. b	5. a	6. a	7. b	8. a	9. a	10. a
11. b	12. b	13. b	14. a	15. a	16. a	17. b	18. a	19. b	20. b
21. a	22. a	23. a	24. a	25. a	26. b	27. b	28. a	29. a	30. a
31. b	32. a	33. a	34. b	35. a	36. a	37. b	38. a	39. b	40. a
41. a	42. a	43. b	44. a	45. a	46. a	47. b	48. a	49. a	50. a
51. b	52. b	53. b	54. b	55. b	56. b	57. a	58. a	59. a	60. b
61. b	62. a	63. a	64. a	65. a	66. b	67. b	68. b	69. a	70. a
71. a	72. b	73. a	74. a	75. b	76. b	77. a	78. a	79. a	80. b
81. a	82. b	83. a	84. b	85. a	86. a	87. a	88. a	89. a	90. b
91. b	92. a	93. a	94. b	95. b	96. a	97. b	98. a	99. b	100. a
101. b	102. b	103. a	104. a	105. b	106. b	107. a	108. a	109. a	110. b
111. b	112. b	113. a	114. a	115. b	116. a	117. a	118. b	119. a	120. b
121. a	122. b	123. a	124. b	125. b	126. b	127. a	128. a	129. a	130. b
131. a	132. b	133. b	134. b	135. b	136. a	137. a	138. a	139. b	140. b
141. b	142. a	143. a	144. a	145. a	146. a	147. b	148. b	149. a	150. a
151. b	152. a	153. b	154. b	155. a	156. a	157. b	158. b	159. b	160. a

Chapter 17

1. a	2. a	3. b	4. b	5. b	6. b	7. a	8. b	9. b	10. a
11. a	12. b	13. b	14. a	15. b	16. a	17. b	18. a	19. a	20. a
21. b	22. a	23. b	24. b	25. a	26. b	27. a	28. a	29. b	30. b
31. a	32. a	33. b	34. a	35. a	36. a	37. b	38. a	39. a	40. b
41. a	42. b	43. b	44. b	45. b	46. b	47. b	48. b	49. a	50. b
51. b	52. b	53. b	54. b	55. b	56. a	57. b	58. b	59. b	60. a
61. a	62. b	63. b	64. a	65. b	66. a	67. b	68. a	69. b	70. a
71. b	72. a	73. a	74. a	75. b	76. a	77. b	78. a	79. b	80. b
81. a	82. b	83. b	84. b	85. a	86. b	87. a	88. a	89. a	90. a
91. b	92. b	93. a	94. a	95. b	96. a	97. b	98. a	99. a	100. b
101. a	102. b	103. a	104. a	105. b	106. a	107. a	108. b	109. b	110. b
111. a	112. b	113. b	114. a	115. b	116. a	117. b	118. a	119. a	120. b
121. a	122. a	123. a	124. a	125. b	126. b	127. b	128. a	129. a	130. b
131. a	132. a	133. a	134. a	135. b	136. b	137. a	138. a	139. a	140. b
141. a	142. a	143. b	144. a	145. b	146. b	147. a	148. a	149. a	150. a
151. b	152. b	153. b	154. b	155. b	156. a	157. b	158. a	159. a	160. b
161. b	162. b	163. b	164. a	165. a	166. b	167. b	168. b	169. b	170. a
171. a	172. b	173. a	174. b	175. b	176. a	177. b	178. b	179. b	180. a
181. b	182. b	183. a	184. b	185. a	186. b	187. b	188. b	189. b	190. b
191. b	192. b	193. b	194. b	195. b	196. b	197. a	198. a	199. a	200. a
201. a	202. b	203. b	204. b	205. b	206. b	207. b	208. a	209. b	210. b
211. a	212. a	213. a	214. a	215. b					

ANSWER KEY

Chapter 18

1. b	2. b	3. a	4. a	5. b	6. b	7. a	8. a	9. a	10. a
11. a	12. a	13. a	14. a	15. a	16. a	17. a	18. a	19. a	20. a
21. a	22. a	23. a	24. b	25. b	26. a	27. b	28. b	29. b	30. a
31. a	32. b	33. a	34. b	35. a	36. a	37. b	38. b	39. a	40. b
41. b	42. a	43. a	44. a	45. a	46. b	47. b	48. a	49. a	50. b
51. b	52. b	53. b	54. b	55. b	56. a	57. a	58. a	59. b	60. b
61. b	62. b	63. a	64. b	65. a	66. b	67. a	68. b	69. b	70. b
71. b	72. a	73. a	74. b	75. a	76. a	77. b	78. b	79. a	80. b
81. b	82. a	83. b	84. b	85. a	86. b	87. a	88. a	89. a	90. a
91. b	92. a	93. a	94. b	95. a	96. a	97. b	98. b	99. b	100. a
101. b	102. a	103. b	104. b	105. a	106. a	107. a	108. a	109. a	110. b
111. a	112. b	113. b	114. a	115. a	116. a	117. b	118. b	119. a	120. b
121. b	122. a	123. a	124. b	125. b	126. b	127. a	128. b	129. b	130. a
131. b	132. a	133. a	134. a	135. b	136. b	137. b	138. b	139. b	140. a
141. b	142. b	143. a	144. b	145. a	146. b	147. a	148. a	149. a	150. b
151. a	152. b	153. a	154. b	155. a	156. b	157. b	158. a	159. b	160. a
161. a	162. b	163. a	164. a	165. a	166. b	167. b	168. a	169. a	170. b
171. a	172. b	173. a	174. a	175. b	176. a	177. a	178. a	179. b	180. b
181. b	182. b	183. b	184. b	185. a	186. b	187. a	188. b	189. b	190. a
191. b	192. b	193. a	194. b	195. a	196. a	197. a	198. a	199. a	200. a
201. b	202. b	203. a	204. b	205. a	206. a	207. a	208. a	209. b	210. a
211. a	212. b	213. b	214. b	215. a	216. b	217. b			

Chapter 19

1. b	2. b	3. a	4. b	5. a	6. b	7. b	8. b	9. b	10. a
11. b	12. a	13. b	14. b	15. a	16. a	17. a	18. a	19. a	20. b
21. a	22. a	23. b	24. a	25. b	26. b	27. a	28. a	29. a	30. b
31. b	32. a	33. a	34. b	35. a	36. b	37. b	38. b	39. b	40. a
41. b	42. b	43. b	44. a	45. a	46. a	47. b	48. b	49. a	50. b
51. a	52. b	53. b	54. a	55. a	56. a	57. a	58. a	59. a	60. b
61. a	62. b	63. b	64. a	65. b	66. b	67. b	68. b	69. b	70. b
71. a	72. a	73. a	74. b	75. b	76. a	77. b	78. b	79. b	80. b
81. b	82. a	83. b	84. b	85. a	86. b	87. b	88. b	89. b	90. a
91. a	92. b	93. b	94. a	95. b	96. a	97. b	98. a	99. a	100. b
101. a	102. b	103. a	104. b	105. b	106. b	107. b	108. b	109. b	110. b
111. b	112. a	113. a	114. a	115. a	116. b	117. b	118. a	119. a	120. a
121. a	122. b	123. b	124. a	125. b	126. a	127. a	128. b	129. a	130. b
131. a	132. b	133. b	134. b	135. b	136. b	137. a	138. a	139. a	140. b
141. a	142. b	143. a	144. a	145. a	146. a	147. a	148. a	149. a	150. b
151. a	152. a	153. b	154. b	155. b	156. a	157. a	158. a	159. b	160. a
161. a	162. b	163. a	164. a	165. a	166. b	167. a	168. a	169. b	170. a
171. b	172. b	173. b	174. a	175. a	176. a	177. a	178. b	179. a	180. b
181. b	182. a	183. a	184. a	185. b	186. b	187. b	188. a	189. a	190. a
191. a	192. a	193. b	194. a	195. a	196. b	197. b	198. a	199. a	200. a
201. b	202. b	203. b	204. a	205. a	206. b	207. a	208. b	209. a	210. a
211. b	212. b	213. b	214. b	215. a	216. a	217. a	218. b	219. b	220. b
221. a	222. a	223. a	224. a	225. a	226. a	227. a	228. a	229. a	230. a
231. b									

Chapter 20

1. a	2. a	3. b	4. a	5. a	6. b	7. a	8. b	9. a	10. b
11. b	12. b	13. b	14. a	15. a	16. a	17. a	18. a	19. b	20. a
21. a	22. b	23. b	24. a	25. a	26. a	27. a	28. b	29. b	30. a
31. b	32. a	33. a	34. a	35. a	36. a	37. a	38. a	39. a	40. a
41. b	42. a	43. b	44. b	45. b	46. a	47. a	48. b	49. a	50. a
51. a	52. a	53. a	54. b	55. b	56. a	57. b	58. a	59. b	60. a
61. b	62. a	63. a	64. a	65. a	66. b	67. a	68. b	69. a	70. b
71. b	72. b	73. a	74. b	75. b	76. b	77. a	78. b	79. a	80. a
81. a	82. b	83. b	84. a	85. a	86. a	87. b	88. a	89. b	90. b
91. b	92. b	93. a	94. a	95. b	96. a	97. b	98. a	99. b	100. b
101. b	102. a	103. b	104. b	105. a	106. b	107. b	108. b	109. b	110. a
111. a	112. b	113. a	114. a	115. b	116. b	117. b	118. a	119. b	120. a
121. b	122. b	123. b	124. a	125. a	126. b	127. b	128. a	129. a	130. a
131. b	132. b	133. b	134. a	135. a	136. a	137. b	138. b	139. b	140. b
141. b	142. b	143. b	144. b	145. b	146. b	147. b	148. b	149. b	150. a
151. b	152. a	153. b	154. b	155. b	156. a	157. b	158. a	159. b	160. a
161. b	162. a	163. a	164. b	165. a	166. a	167. a	168. b	169. a	170. a
171. b									

ANSWER KEY

Chapter 21

1. a	2. b	3. a	4. b	5. a	6. a	7. b	8. a	9. b	10. a
11. b	12. a	13. a	14. a	15. b	16. a	17. b	18. b	19. b	20. a
21. a	22. b	23. b	24. b	25. a	26. a	27. b	28. b	29. b	30. a
31. a	32. a	33. a	34. a	35. a	36. b	37. b	38. b	39. a	40. b
41. a	42. b	43. b	44. a	45. b	46. a	47. b	48. b	49. b	50. a
51. b	52. b	53. b	54. b	55. b	56. b	57. b	58. b	59. b	60. a
61. a	62. b	63. b	64. b	65. a	66. b	67. b	68. a	69. a	70. b
71. a	72. b	73. a	74. b	75. a	76. b	77. a	78. b	79. b	80. a
81. a	82. a	83. a	84. b	85. a	86. b	87. b	88. b	89. b	90. a
91. a	92. a	93. b	94. b	95. a	96. b	97. a	98. b	99. b	100. b
101. a	102. a	103. b	104. a	105. b	106. b	107. a	108. b	109. b	110. a
111. b	112. b	113. b	114. b	115. a	116. a	117. b	118. b	119. a	120. b
121. a	122. a	123. a	124. b	125. b	126. b	127. b	128. b	129. b	130. b
131. b	132. a	133. b	134. a	135. b	136. a	137. a	138. b	139. b	140. b
141. a	142. b	143. a	144. b	145. b	146. b	147. a	148. b	149. a	150. a
151. b	152. b	153. a	154. b	155. b	156. a	157. b	158. b	159. a	160. b
161. a	162. b	163. b	164. b	165. b	166. b	167. a	168. b	169. a	170. b
171. b	172. a	173. b	174. b	175. b	176. a	177. b	178. a	179. b	180. b
181. b	182. a	183. a	184. b	185. b	186. b	187. b	188. b	189. b	190. a
191. b	192. a	193. b	194. b	195. a	196. b	197. b	198. b	199. a	200. a
201. b	202. a	203. b	204. b	205. a	206. b	207. a	208. b	209. b	210. b
211. b	212. b	213. a	214. a	215. b	216. b	217. a	218. b	219. b	220. a
221. b	222. a	223. a	224. a	225. b	226. a	227. a	228. a	229. b	230. a
231. b	232. a	233. a	234. a	235. a	236. b	237. a	238. b	239. b	240. b
241. a	242. b								

Chapter 22

1. b	2. b	3. a	4. a	5. b	6. b	7. a	8. b	9. a	10. b
11. a	12. b	13. b	14. b	15. b	16. b	17. b	18. a	19. a	20. b
21. b	22. a	23. b	24. b	25. b	26. a	27. a	28. b	29. b	30. a
31. a	32. a	33. a	34. a	35. b	36. b	37. b	38. b	39. a	40. a
41. b	42. a	43. a	44. a	45. a	46. a	47. a	48. b	49. a	50. a
51. a	52. b	53. b	54. a	55. b	56. a	57. b	58. b	59. b	60. a
61. a	62. a	63. a	64. b	65. b	66. b	67. a	68. a	69. a	70. b
71. a	72. a	73. b	74. a	75. a	76. b	77. a	78. b	79. a	80. a
81. b	82. b	83. b	84. a	85. b	86. b	87. a	88. a	89. b	90. a
91. b	92. a	93. a	94. a	95. a	96. a	97. a	98. a	99. a	100. b
101. a	102. b	103. b	104. b	105. b	106. b	107. b	108. a	109. b	110. b
111. a	112. a	113. b	114. b	115. b	116. a	117. a	118. a	119. b	120. a
121. a	122. a	123. b	124. b	125. a	126. a	127. b			

www.ingramcontent.com/pod-product-compliance
Lightning Source LLC
Chambersburg PA
CBHW081755300426
44116CB00014B/2124